OXFORD MONOGR
INTERNATIONA

FORMALISM AND THE SOURCES OF INTERNATIONAL LAW

OXFORD MONOGRAPHS IN INTERNATIONAL LAW

The aim of this series is to publish important and original pieces of research on all aspects of international law. Topics that are given particular prominence are those which, while of interest to the academic lawyer, also have important bearing on issues which touch the actual conduct of international relations. Nonetheless, the series is wide in scope and includes monographs on the history and philosophical foundations of international law.

RECENT TITLES IN THE SERIES

The International Minimum Standard and Fair and Equitable Treatment
Martins Paparinskis

Disobeying the Security Council
Countermeasures against Wrongful Sanctions
Antonios Tzanakopoulos

The Margin of Appreciation in International Human Rights Law: Deference and Proportionality
Andrew Legg

Individual Criminal Responsibility in International Law
Elies van Sliedregt

Extraterritorial Application of Human Rights Treaties: Law, Principles, and Policy
Marko Milanovic

Maritime Security and the Law of the Sea
Natalie Klein

Extraterritorial Use of Force against Non-State Actors
Noam Lubell

State Responsibility for International Terrorism
Kimberley N. Trapp

Formalism and the Sources of International Law

A Theory of the Ascertainment of Legal Rules

JEAN D'ASPREMONT

OXFORD
UNIVERSITY PRESS

OXFORD
UNIVERSITY PRESS

Great Clarendon Street, Oxford, OX2 6DP
United Kingdom

Oxford University Press is a department of the University of Oxford. It furthers the University's objective of excellence in research, scholarship, and education by publishing worldwide. Oxford is a registered trade mark of Oxford University Press in the UK and in certain other countries

First Edition published in 2011
First published in paperback 2013

Impression: 1

British Library Cataloguing in Publication Data
Data available

Library of Congress Cataloguing in Publication Data
Data available

ISBN 978–0–19–969631–4 (Hbk.)
ISBN 978–0–19–968226–3 (Pbk.)

Printed in Great Britain
on acid-free paper by
CPI Group (UK) Ltd., Croydon CR0 4YY

General Editors' Preface

Every generation of international law scholars grapples with the fundamentals of the subject, and it can be said without much exaggeration that no question is more fundamental and central to the understanding of international law than the question of its sources. How international law is made, how it is distinguished from non-law, and how international legal rules form into a legal system are matters that have engaged the imagination and intellectual curiosity of scholars for centuries. Dr d'Aspremont has revisited these questions, and in his stimulating study has provided a thorough examination of the role formalism can play in the ascertainment of the rules of international law and in their distinction from non-law. It is a rewarding study not only for those interested in the sources of international law but for all interested in the theoretical foundations of the subject in general.

AVL, DS, ST
Oxford, April 2011

Acknowledgements

This book is yet another typical illustration of a Socratic thought-forming process. Indeed, the argument developed here is not only the outcome of a personal inquiry into the theory of the ascertainment of international legal rules started a long time ago. It has also been nurtured over the years by numerous discussions, debates, and exchanges with colleagues and friends. I can only mention here some of those who have been the most instrumental in moulding the thoughts spelled out in the following pages. May all the others who, wittingly or unwittingly, have contributed to my reflections be thanked as well. Mentioning those to whom I am the most indebted allows me to simultaneously sketch out the history of this work.

Even though I had already broached the topic in one of my very first publications a dozen years ago, without realizing that it would occupy me for so long, my thinking about the theory of the ascertainment of international legal rules properly began as early as 2005 during a one-year Global Research Fellowship at NYU School of Law, for which I am very grateful to Joseph Weiler. It is on that occasion that some of my colleagues and fellow senior researchers—Frank Haldemann probably being the most influential of them in this respect—triggered my interest in the theory of international law and especially in that of the sources of international law. Although my reflections continued in the following years, it is especially in 2009, 2010, and 2011 that the manuscript of this book took shape and became a reality, thanks to a generous grant from the *Netherlands Organisation for Scientific Research* (NWO), which allowed me to be relieved of teaching and programme-management. As a result of this significant public financial support, this book was written with the full awareness of the fact that public grants are made possible by compulsory levies upon tax-payers. I hope that the contribution to the international legal scholarship attempted by this book will—albeit only modestly—offset part of my debt to Dutch tax-payers.

During these years, the argument made here has been presented to a wide variety of different audiences all over the world. I regret the greenhouse gas emissions entailed by this intense travelling and I hope that scholars of the 21st century will some day be able to dramatically rein in the—often overlooked—environmental harm of their scientific activities. I am nonetheless very thankful to all those colleagues who have invited me to present my thoughts or convened these scholarly meetings and provided me with useful comments. I am thinking in particular of Nicholas Tsagourias, Amaya Ubeda, Fleur Johns, Ben Saul, Tan Hsien-Li Teresa, Simon Chesterman, Rémi Bachand, René Provost, Matthias Goldmann, Armin von Bogdandy, Ghassan Faramand, Pierre Charpentier, and Jean-Philippe Kot. I am also very thankful for all of those who have listened to the argument during these meetings and whose anonymous reactions and comments have proved highly helpful. A research stay at the Australian National University (ANU) in March 2010 has allowed me to make great headways in the manuscript. The guidance of Sarah Heathcote, who kindly invited me, and those of Hilary Charlesworth, Matthew Zagor, Katherine Young, and Wayne Morgan were extremely useful. The comments received from my colleagues at the Amsterdam Center for International Law (ACIL) on the occasion of a luncheon meeting helped me further sharpen my thoughts. A stay at the Max Planck Institute for Comparative Public Law and International Law in July 2010 offered me the possibility to confront my conception of the rationale of formalism with that of the formalism that inspired the research project on the international exercise of public authority. The debates with the numerous students who I have had the privilege to lecture over the last years in Amsterdam, Louvain-la-Neuve, Leiden, The Hague, Bujumbura, or Kinshasa have been extremely conducive to the developments of my thoughts as well.

Although the argument was nurtured by the abovementioned exchanges, its conception and writing inevitably remained an individual cerebral effort and a solitary exercise. This is why the flattering confidence that André Nollkaemper granted me and the stimulating environment of the ACIL, where he allowed me to carry out my research, also played a crucial role. In the same vein, I cannot help mentioning the invaluable and impressive collection of rare classics of international law that Alain Brouillet kindly put at my disposal.

Finally, I am very grateful to all those that have commented upon (parts of) the manuscript: Frank Haldemann, Armin von Bogdandy, Matthias Goldmann, Nicholas Tsagourias, Nagy Boldizsár, Jörg Kammerhofer, Gleider Hernández, Janne Nijman, Grietje Baars, Sahib Singh, Dov Jacobs, Marco Aurélio de Almeida Alves, Séverine Helbert, and Chie Kojima. I am also thankful to Fanny Schaus, who helped me prepare the bibliography, Lauren Macleod, who formatted the footnotes and, above all, Julia Ward, who meticulously reviewed several versions of the manuscript. John Louth and Merel Alstein's confidence and advice during the writing and review processes together with the insightful reviewers' remarks have been essential and I wish to thank them warmly as well.

Preface to the Paperback Edition

Since its publication in October 2011, *Formalism and the Sources of International Law* (hereafter FSIL) has fueled significant debate. Some of these exchanges are published in a series of appendixes to this paperback edition. Those new materials usefully shed light on other facets of the argument of FSIL. The paperback edition also comes with a new introduction.

The publication of these new materials, including reactions by the author of FSIL, does certainly not aim to further vindicate the main thesis of FSIL or rebut the—sharp—criticisms formulated so far. The author of FSIL fundamentally believes that, once a thesis is floated within a given epistemic community, it is of little avail to try to keep full ownership of (and control over) it. Ideas, once aired, fall into the public domain and accede to an autonomous existence. The new materials included in this edition are thus also meant to show which autonomous path the argument made in FSIL has gone down since its airing.

Acknowleding the autonomous life (and the incontrolable character) of the ideas defended in FSIL does not boil down to a denial of their author's belief in their paradigm-determining character. Indeed, the new materials which have been included in the paperback edition are all premised on the conviction that FSIL touches on debates which are symptomatic of the unprecedented paradigm crisis currently at play in the epistemic community of international law. Indeed, in its author's eyes, the questions discussed in FSIL are not, in Thomas Kuhn's terms, mere anomalies that research and thinking about international law will resolve as a matter of their daily puzzle-solving business. They rather constitute questions determinative of the very paradigm by virtue of which the system of knowledge about international law is defined and operates. This is why, whatever turns the debate about FSIL may take, it is hoped that this new paperback edition will further buoy international legal scholars' realization that contemporary paradigmatic debates about international law are no longer between traditional schools of thoughts or pre-defined methodological packages. They are between formal and non-formal techniques of cognition.

JdA
Manchester, 15 January 2013

Summary Contents

Detailed Contents

List of Abbreviations

CLS	Critical Legal Studies
GAL	Global Administrative Law
ICJ	International Court of Justice
ICJ Statute	Statute of the International Court of Justice
ICRC	International Committee of the Red Cross
ICTY	International Criminal Tribunal for the former Yugoslavia
ILC	International Law Commission
ILDC	International Law in Domestic Courts
ILP	International Legal Process
NAIL	New Approaches to International Law
PCIJ	Permanent Court of International Justice
TRN	Transnational Regulatory Networks
TWAIL	Third World Approaches to International Law
Vienna Convention	Vienna Convention on the Law of Treaties

Journals

Am. J. Comp. L.	American Journal of Comparative Law
AJIL	American Journal of International Law
Am. J. Legal Hist.	American Journal of Legal History
Am. Rev. Int'l Arb.	American Review of International Arbitration
ASIL Proceedings	American Society of International Law Proceedings
Am. U. J. Int'l L. & Pol'y	American University Journal of International Law and Policy
ARV	Archiv des Völkerrechts
Asian YBIL	Asian Yearbook of International Law
Aust. YBIL	Australian Yearbook of International Law
Austl. J. Leg. Phil.	Australian Journal of Legal Philosophy
BYBIL	British Year Book of International Law
Calif. L. Rev.	California Law Review
Cal. W. Int'l L. J.	California Western International Law Journal
Cal. W. L. Rev.	California Western Law Review

CJILJ	Canadian Journal of Law and Jurisprudence
Canadian YBIL	Canadian Yearbook of International Law
Cardozo L. Rev.	Cardozo Law Review
RCADI	Collected Courses
———	College Law Review
Colo. J. Int'l Envtl. L. & Pol'y	Colorado Journal of Environmental Law & Policy
Colum. J. Transnat'l L.	Columbia Journal of Transnational Law
Colum. L. Rev.	Columbia Law Review
Connecticut J. Int'l L.	Connecticut Journal of International Law
Cornell. L. Rev.	Cornell Law Review
Denv.J. Int'l L. & Pol'y	Denver Journal of International Law and Policy
EJIL	European Journal of International Law
FYBIL	Finnish Yearbook of International Law
Ga. J. Int'l & Comp. L.	Georgia Journal of International and Comparative Law
Ga. L. Rev.	Georgia Law Review
Geo. L. J.	Georgetown Law Journal
Geo. Wash. L. Rev.	George Washington Law Review
German YBIL	German Yearbook of International Law
———	Global Jurist
HJLR	Hague Journal on the Rule of Law
———	Hague Yearbook of International Law
Harv. Int'l L. J.	Harvard International Law Journal
Harv. L. Rev.	Harvard Law Review
Harvard JIL	Harvard Journal of International Law
Hastings L. J.	Hastings Law Journal
Houston L. Rev.	Houston Law Review
Ind. J. Global Legal Studies	Indiana Journal of Global Legal Studies
Indian J. Int'l L.	Indian Journal of International Law
ICON	International Journal of Constitutional Law
———	International Legal Theory
IOLR	International Organizations Law Review
Iowa L. Rev.	Iowa Law Review
Israel L. Rev.	Israel Law Review

———	Israel Yearbook on Human Rights
———	Journal of Conflict Resolution
JLS	Journal of Legal Studies
LCP	Law and Contemporary Problems
———	Law and Philosophy
LQR	Law Quarterly Review
———	Legal Theory
LJIL	Leiden Journal of International Law
Maine L. Rev.	Maine Law Review
Mich. L. Rev.	Michigan Law Review
Minn. L. Rev.	Minnesota Law Review
Miss. L. J.	Mississippi Law Journal
NILR	Netherlands International Law Review
NYIL	Netherlands Yearbook of International Law
NYU JILP	New York University Journal of International Law & Politics
NYULR	New York University Law Review
New Eng. L Rev.	New England Law Review
NoFo	No Foundations
Nord. J. Int'l L.	Nordic Journal of International Law
Northwest. U. L. Rev.	Northwestern University Law Review
Osgoode Hall L. J.	Osgoode Hall Law Journal
OJLS	Oxford Journal of Legal Studies
———	Philosophical Investigations
———	Revue Belge de Droit International
RDILC	Revue de droit international et legislation comparée
———	Revue générale de droit international public
———	Revue québécoise de droit international
San Diego L. Rev.	San Diego Law Review
Stan. L. Rev.	Stanford Law Review
Syracuse J. Int'l L. & Com.	Syracuse Journal of International Law and Commerce
Syracuse L. Rev.	Syracuse Law Review
Tex. L. Rev.	Texas Law Review
———	Theoretical Inquiries in Law

Transnat'l L. & Contemp. Probs.	Transnational Law and Contemporary Problems
U.T.L.J.	University of Toronto Law Journal
———	Valaparaiso University Law Review
Va. J. Int'l L.	Virginia Journal of International Law
Va. L. Rev.	Virginia Law Review
Vand. L. Rev.	Vanderbilt Law Review
Wisconsin Int'l L. J.	Wisconsin International Law Journal
Wm & Mary L. Rev.	William and Mary Law Review
Yale J. Int'l L.	Yale Journal of International Law
Yale L. J.	Yale Law Journal

Introduction to the Paperback Edition

Prolegomena: A paradox

At the origin of the inquiry found in this book lies a paradox. This paradox can be spelled out as follows. Nothing has been more ontologically threatening for international law—and for the professional community organized around it—than the rampant contemporary post-ontological mindset of the international legal scholarship. The (self-proclaimed) post-ontological era—and the correlative broadening of the substantive agenda of research that has accompanied it—have aggravated the impoverishment of our state of reflection about the theory of sources. Indeed, having become too busy reflecting on legitimacy, accountability, participation, transparency or newly obsessed by epistemological and sociological introspection, international lawyers—and especially international legal scholars—have come to severely neglect the thinking about the most elementary tool of cognition of their object of study: the theory of sources. Said differently, the post-ontological era of international law has witnessed a move away from (theoretical reflections about) the theory of sources. This move away from the theory of sources has led international legal scholars to demote the theory of sources to a debate of secondary importance—let alone an unnecessary constraining straightjacket—and, as a result, output, effect, impact of norms or even compliance have been elevated in a central defining characteristic of international law. The reasons thereof have not always been a dogmatic repulsion towards the theory of sources. The agenda behind such a move (this is what I have called the 'politics of deformalization') includes the perceived need to expand or reform international law, the urge to buoy its legitimacy or the accountability of its main power-wielding actors, a religious attachment to pluralism, or the necessity to allow greater argumentative creativity—to name only a few. Interestingly, such a growing disinterest for the theory of sources has also been witnessed in international case-law where judges seem to take less and less pains to explain how (and according to which indicators) they identify and ascertain the rules they apply.

The agenda behind the theory of sources

In contrast to such a postontological conceptual nonchalance, this book makes a plea for preserving the central cognitive role of the theory of sources—albeit in a reformed configuration. The reasons for advocating the preservation of a theory of sources are multifold. First, the book, in a functionally agnostic fashion, submits that, whatever function is assigned to it—whether freedom-restricting, behavior-conducting, progress-enhancing, society-structuring, hopes-conveying or simply intellect-stimulating—international law needs to be formally ascertained and cognized to a reasonable extent. The book also takes the centrality of the theory of sources as a precondition for the critique of international law. Indeed, it argues that a (reformed) theory of sources also makes possible the critique of law—and thus its reform. Eventually, the books argues that a theory of sources is an indispensible condition for the existence of a common vocabulary without which there cannot be any interpretative community of international law. All-in-all, the book takes the view that, short of a theory of sources able to provide sufficient ascertaining indicators, international law is at best a platform for discursive practices and the profession organized around it a cacophonic debating henhouse.

Cognitive biases assumed

As the foregoing sufficiently indicates, the book is premised on a strong conceptual and methodological bias which its author critically and transparently assumes. Making a plea for the preservation of the central role of the theory of sources is certainly not neutral and manifests a particular choice for a particular take on law. It is not denied that the source theory is accordingly a particular 'value fact'[1] which boils down to a choice for a certain cognitive approach—in the form of a set of formal law-ascertaining indicators—in order to make sense of law and of its practices. It must be emphasized that such a choice is made in full acceptance of the conceptual, theoretical, explanatory or descriptive virtues of alternative approaches to law and cognition which the book does not seek to invalidate. In the same vein, it is acknowledged that approaching international law from the standpoint of its sources corresponds to a formal conception of law zeroed in on law as a product. Those approaches to international law which focuses on the product rather than the processes are often said to be static. One of the ambitions of the book is to show that product-based approaches to international law ought not necessarily to be condemned to be static. According to the argument made in the book, theories of sources, if grounded in the social practice of law-applying authorities can change—and can be changed. This is the so-called social thesis which provides dynamism of a (n)—otherwise entirely static—product-centered conception of law.

Current deficiencies in sources theory

In the specific context of international law, the book argues that the social practices of law-applying authorities have long ceased to reflect the practices which the ancestral article 38 of the ICJ Statute was meant to reflect. This is why, approaching the sources of international from the standpoint of article 38 no longer makes much sense as it does not reflect the current consensus among its main important law-applying authorities. Instead, such a theory of sources ought to radically depart from the static pedigree-determining blueprints found in the mainstream literature and be

[1] M. Greenberg, "How Facts Make Law" Legal Theory, Vol. 10, pp. 157–198, 2004.

shaped as a dynamic model of rule-ascertainment grounded in an ever-evolving social practice. On top of advocating a move away from article 38—and especially the abandonment of the law-ascertaining role of State intent for the identification of treaties and unilateral promises—or that of those associated doctrines conveying the illusion of formalism in the delimitation of customary international law—the book also calls for a more pluralistic conception of law-applying authorities which ought not be restricted to domestic and international courts and tribunals. New actors have come to produce social practice determinative of the ascertainment indicators contained in the theory of sources of international law.

New forms of exercises of international public authority

While critically re-evaluating the theory of source of international law, the book simultaneously acknowledges that much international normative activity nowadays takes place outside the ambit of traditional international law and that only a limited part of the exercise of public authority at the international level results in the creation of international legal rules. In that sense, it concurs with the idea that the mainstream theory of sources falls short of capturing most exercises of public authority at the international level. Yet, at the same time, the book challenges the urge of international lawyers to apprehend these normative phenomena through their own cognitive instruments with a view to necessarily including them in their scope of expertise and elevate them in legal materials. In that sense, the book calls for some critical self-reflection as to the gluttony of international lawyers which systematically—and almost obsessively—seek to label law every phenomenon they want to apprehend and on which they claim exclusive ownership. At the same time, the book makes the argument that if we were to (decide to) design law-ascertaining yardsticks allowing the capture of such untraditional exercises of public authority as international law, the theory of sources that would allow such capture ought to be dynamic and formal in nature, that is that it ought to rest on formal indicators grounded in social practice.

Questions left unanswered

As was expressed (and sometimes regretted) in some of the reactions published in the new appendix, this book only aims at offering a theoretical framework for a greater awareness of (and self-reflection about) the responsibility of those potentially engaged in the (reflection about the) production of communitarian semantics that shape the theory of sources. The book is also meant to give observers—and especially legal scholars—a better grasp of the dynamics at play in the formation and evolutions of the cognitive languages of the interpretative community of international law. In that sense, this work has never been meant to provide an absolute theory or puzzle-solving paradigm. As a result, there are many—even foundational—questions that this book inevitably leaves unanswered. One of them pertains to the modes of cognition of the consistency of the social practice that is necessary for the existence of law-ascertainment criterial. Indeed, such a practice is not an objectively observable fact. The book does not discuss how to cognize such practice. An equally important question left unanswered is the determination of the actors whose practice can qualify as generating communitarian semantics. This is a issue whose importance should not be underestimated for altering our understanding of law-applying authority (and thus our definition of those who produce social practice) necessarily impact the semantics that inform law-ascertainment criteria. Although this book does not venture to answer these two fundamental questions, the book should be seen as an invitation to further inquire an debate these questions with full awareness of their policy dimensions.

Formalism, reductionism and ecumenism

I feel it necessary to conclude this new introduction with a twofold caveat. First, I must repeat once again that the plea for a—dynamic and reformed—conception of sources grounded in social practice of law-applying authorities—broadly construed—should certainly not be conflated with a naïve objectivist defense of formalism in legal argumentation. The idea of argumentative truth and immanent intelligibility of legal arguments has long been refuted (provided it has ever been advocated[2]) and the book is obviously not meant to rehabilitate this type of formalism. After all, we are all Legal Realists[3]. In that sense, the approach to formalism vindicated by the book is reductionist, for it is solely limited to the use of a few formal ascertaining indicators. A second caveat pertains to the coexistence of the "value fact" at the heart of this book, i.e. the choice for a source-based approach to law, with other approaches to international law. The social thesis in which the dynamic conception of the sources of international law defended in the book is grounded has some doctrinal reconciliatory virtues, for it helps reconcile some allegedly antonymic trends in international legal scholarship while acknowledging the added value of the descriptive, analytical and the specific critiques of other approaches to international law. In that sense, there is some ecumenism in the argument made in this book, for, even if international law is also a product in need of occasional snapshots, it is also (constructed as) a much more complex phenomenon that calls for complementary cognitive tools.

[2] Brian Z. Tamanaha, *Beyond the Formalist-Realist Divide: The Role of Politics in Judging*, Princeton University Press, 2009.

[3] Michael Steven Green, Legal Realism as Theory of Law, William & Mary Law Review, Vol. 46, pp. 1915–2000, 2005.

1

Introduction

1.1 Setting the Stage: The Retreat from Formal Law-Ascertainment

Law is a process in that it is both the product and the source of a flux of various dynamics which static formal concepts inevitably fail to capture. Once the object of much controversy, this assertion is nowadays uncontested. Yet, law is not only a process. Law also constitutes a set of *rules* which, at times and for multiple purposes, need to be ascertained. While not excluding the dynamic character of the whole phenomenon of law, this study primarily approaches international law as a set of rules.

The ascertainment of international legal rules had, until recently, remained a central concern of the international legal scholarship which has long elevated the elaboration of criteria for the identification of law—through a theory of the sources—into one of its paramount tasks.[1] However, the quest for a consensus on the criteria necessary for the identification of international legal rules no longer occupies a prominent position on the contemporary agenda of international legal scholars. Indeed, international legal scholars are becoming much less sensitive to the necessity of rigorously distinguishing law from non-law. Normativity has been correlatively construed as a *continuum*[2] and the identification of law has grown into 'a matter of "more or less"'.[3] This growing acceptance of the idea of a penumbra between law and non-law has provoked a move away from questions of law-ascertainment, increasingly perceived as irrelevant. A correlative greater feeling of liberty has followed, paving the way for the use of a wide variety of looser law-identification criteria.

[1] This has been particularly the case in European continental traditions of international law. See e.g. P.-M. Dupuy, 'Cours général de droit international public' (2002) 297 RCADI 9–490, 205) or P. Reuter, 'Principes de droit international public' (1961) 103 RCADI 425–655, 459.

[2] For some famous support to the idea of normative continuum, see R. Baxter, 'International Law in "Her Infinite Variety"' (1980) 29 ICLQ 549, 563; O. Schachter, 'The Twilight Existence of Non-binding International Agreements' (1977) 71 AJIL 296; A. Boyle, 'Some Reflections on the Relationship of Treaties and Soft Law' (1999) 48 ICLQ 901, 913; C. Chinkin, 'The Challenge of Soft Law: Development and Change in International Law' (1989) 38 ICLQ 850, 866. A. Pellet, 'Complementarity of International Treaty Law, Customary Law and Non-Contractual Law-Making' in R. Wolfrum and V. Röben (eds), *Developments of International Law in Treaty Making* (Springer, Berlin, 2005) 409, 415.

[3] The expression is from M. Koskenniemi, *From Apology to Utopia: The Structure of International Legal Argument*, (CUP, Cambridge, 2005) 393.

The retreat from the question of ascertainment has been dramatically accentuated by the undeniable finding that much of the international normative activity takes place outside the remit of traditional international law, and that only a limited part of the exercise of public authority at the international level nowadays materializes itself in the creation of norms which can be considered international legal rules according to a classical understanding of international law. Indeed, international norm-making has undergone an intricate and multi-fold pluralization. First, normative authority at the international level is no longer exercised by a closed circle of high-ranking officials acting on behalf of States, but has instead turned into an aggregation of complex procedures involving non-State actors.[4] As a result, public authority is now exercised at the international level in a growing number of informal ways which are estranged from the classical international law-making processes.[5] Second, traditional international law-making processes themselves have endured a process of pluralization, which has manifested itself in a diversification of the types of instruments through which norms are produced at the international level. Eventually, the effects of these pluralized exercises of public authority have gradually ceased to be confined to their sphere of origin, for law has grown more post-national and the international and domestic spheres have become more entangled.[6] This complex pluralization of norm- and law-making processes at the international level has, in turn, fractured the *substance* of the norms produced, including that of international legal rules. In that sense, the pluralization of international norm- and law-making processes has been accompanied by a diversification of international legal norms themselves.

These manifestations of normativity outside the remit of international law are not entirely new but they have grown extremely diverse, fragmented, and of an unprecedented degree. Whether they are perceived as the reflection of a healthy pluralism or a daunting fragmentation,[7] these various forms of pluralization of international

[4] This has sometimes been called 'verticalization'. See J. Klabbers, 'Setting the Scene', 14, in J. Klabbers, A. Peters, and G. Ulfstein (eds), The *Constitutionalization of International Law* (OUP, Oxford, 2009). On the role of non-State actors more specifically, see J. d'Aspremont (ed), *Participants in the International Legal System—Multiple Perspectives on Non-State Actors in International Law* (Routledge, London, 2011).

[5] See M. Goldmann, 'Inside Relative Normativity: From Sources to Standard Instruments for the Exercise of International Public Authority' (2008) 9 *German Law Journal* (2008) 1865 and A. von Bogdandy, P. Dann, and M. Goldmann, 'Developing the Publicness of Public International Law: Towards a Legal Framework for Global Governance Activities' (2008) 9 *German Law Journal* (2008) 1375.

[6] N. Krisch, *Beyond Constitutionalism—The Pluralist Structure of Postnational Law* (OUP, Oxford, 2010), 6–11.

[7] On the discourses about the pluralization of the substance of law see M. Koskenniemi, 'The Fate of Public International Law: Between Technique and Politics' (2007) 70 MLR 1–30; See also M. Koskenniemi, *From Apology to Utopia: The Structure of International Legal Argument* (CUP, Cambridge, 2005) 392–4. M. Prost,'All Shouting the Same Slogans: International Law's Unities and the Politics of Fragmentation' (2006) 17 FYBIL 131–59 or M. Prost, *The Concept of Unity in Public International Law*, Hart Monographs in Transnational and International Law (Hart, Oxford, 2011) (forthcoming); see also A.-C. Martineau, 'The Rhetoric of Fragmentation: Fear and Faith in International Law' (2009) 22 LJIL 1–28.

norm- and law-making processes have further cast into doubt the relevance of traditional international law-ascertainment. Indeed, confronted with such a pluralized normative activity at the international level, international lawyers have endured a greater inability to capture these developments through classical concepts, which has further enticed them to take some freedom with law-ascertainment with a view to more easily engaging with the multiplication of these pluralized forms of norm-making.[8] In this context, the idea that formal law-ascertainment has grown inappropriate to capture contemporary international norms has become even more prevalent.[9]

This overall liberalization of the ascertainment of international legal rules has resulted in contemporary scholarly debates in the field of international law turning more cacophonic. Indeed, scholars often talk past each other.[10] The impression is nowadays rife that the international legal scholarship has become a cluster of different scholarly communities, each using different criteria for the ascertainment of international legal rules. For a long time, such a cacophony had been averted by virtue of a systematic use of commonly shared formal law-ascertainment criteria. Despite occasionally resting on artificial constructions,[11] this use of formal criteria for the identification of international legal rules allowed international lawyers to reach a reasonable consensus as to how to distinguish between law and non-law. Generations of international lawyers were trained[12] to identify international legal rules by virtue of the formal source from which they emanate, a blueprint that has

[8] One of the first studies on Transnational Regulatory Networks (TRNs), see Anne-Marie Slaughter, *A New World Order* (Princeton UP, Princeton, 2004); see also the project on Global Administrative Law. See B. Kingsbury, N. Krisch, and R. Steward, 'The Emergence of Global Administrative Law' (2005) 68 LCP 15–61, 29; C. Harlow, 'Global Administrative Law: The Quest for Principles and Values' (2006) 17 EJIL 197–214; see also B. Kingsbury, 'The Concept of Law in Global Administrative Law' (2009) 20(1) EJIL 23–57. See also the project of the Max Planck Institute for Comparative Public Law and International Law on the international exercise of public authority. See M. Goldmann, 'Inside Relative Normativity: From Sources to Standards Instruments for the Exercise of International Public Authority' (2008) 9 *German Law Journal* 1865 and A. von Bogdandy, P. Dann, and M. Goldmann, 'Developing the Publicness of Public International Law: Towards a Legal Framework for Global Governance Activities' (2008) 9 *German Law Journal* 1375. Some of the projects are discussed below.

[9] B. Kingsbury and M. Donaldson, 'From Bilateralism to Publicness in International Law', *From Bilateralism to Community Interest: Essays in Honour of Judge Bruno Simma* (OUP, Oxford, 2011) (forthcoming) 79, 89; N. Krisch, *Beyond Constitutionalism—The Pluralist Structure of Postnational Law* (OUP, Oxford, 2010) 12; J. Brunnée and S.J. Toope, *Legitimacy and Legality in International Law. An Interactional Account* (CUP, Cambridge, 2010) 46; F. Megret, 'International Law as Law', in J. Crawford and M. Koskenniemi (eds), *Cambridge Companion to International Law* (CUP, Cambridge, 2011) (forthcoming), available at <http://papers.ssrn.com/sol3/papers.cfm?abstract_id=1672824>, 20.

[10] I already made this point in J. d'Aspremont, 'Softness in International Law: A Rejoinder to Tony D'Amato' (2009) 20 EJIL 911–17.

[11] The most obvious of them—although not always perceivable as such thanks to the formal veils under which it has been shrewdly shrouded—being customary international law. Cfr *infra* 7.1 and 7.2.1.

[12] On the training of international lawyers, see generally the remarks of A. Orford, 'Embodying Internationalism: the Making of International Lawyers' (1998) 19 Aust. YBIL 1. See more generally, M. Foucault, *L'archéologie du savoir* (Paris, Gallimard, 1969).

continuously been perpetuated until recently. The prominence of formal law-ascertainment in the international legal scholarship has, however, come to an end as a result of the abovementioned move away from formal identification of law.[13]

Obviously not all lawyers and scholars have turned a blind eye to law-identification. Yet, among those that still deem it necessary to take pains to identify international legal rules, other blueprints of law-ascertainment have been preferred to the traditional formal yardsticks widely in use until recently. For instance, a growing number of scholars and lawyers, drawing on a disconnect between the international rules identified by formal law-ascertainment mechanisms and commands actually relied upon by actors, have decided to revamp their law-ascertaining criteria by shifting from source-based to effect- (or impact-)based[14] approaches, thereby bypassing completely any formal identification of law. Because they require enhanced legitimacy of law to ensure compliance, these effect- (or impact-)based law-ascertainment blueprints have further lured them away from the question of law-ascertainment. The international legal scholarship has also experienced a revival of process-based conceptions of law-identification which have similarly accentuated the current deformalization of the identification of international legal rules.[15] These

[13] J. Klabbers, 'Constitutionalism and the Making of International Law' (2008) 5 NoFo 84, 89. Such a finding was already made by Virally: M. Virally, 'A Propos de la "Lex Ferenda"', in Daniel Bardonnet (ed), *Mélanges Reuter: le droit international: unité et diversité,* (Paris, Pedone, 1981) 519–33, 521. Albeit for different reasons which are explored later, this finding has also been made by scholars affiliated to deconstructivism and critical legal studies. See e.g. M. Koskenniemi, *From Apology to Utopia* (CUP, NY, 2005), 393.

[14] For a few examples, see J. Alvarez, *International Organizations as Law-makers* (OUP, Oxford, 2005); For J. Brunnée and S.J. Toope, international law ought to be defined by the sense of obligation among its addressees, which indirectly grounds law-ascertainment in the impact of rules on their addressees. See J. Brunnée and S.J. Toope, *Legitimacy and Legality in International Law. An Interactional Account* (CUP, Cambridge, 2010) 7 ('The distinctiveness of law lies not in form or in enforcement but in the creation and effects of legal obligation'). Their interactional account of international law is further examined below. Cfr *infra* 5.1. A similar use of non-formal law-identification criteria can be found in the studies about non-State actors. See e.g. A. Peters, L. Koechlin, T. Förster, and G. Fenner Zinkernagel, 'Non-State actors as standard setters: framing the issue in an interdisciplinary fashion', in A. Peters, et al. (eds), *Non-State Actors as Standard Setters,* (CUP, Cambridge, 2009) 1–32. These effect-based approaches must be distinguished from the subtle conception defended by F. Kratochwil based on the *principled rule-application* of a norm which refers to the explicitness and contextual variation in the reasoning process and the application of rules in 'like' situations in the future: *Rules Norms and Decisions: On the Conditions of Practical and Legal Reasoning in International Relations and Domestic Affairs* (CUP, Cambridge, 1989) 206–8. See also F. Kratochwil, 'Legal Theory and International Law', in D. Armstrong (ed), *Routledge Handbook of International Law* (Routledge, London, 2009) 58. Likewise, effects-based conceptions must be distinguished from the conceptions based on expectations and the relative normativity of the Heidelberg project on the international exercise of public authority. See in this respect the very interesting work of M. Goldmann, 'Inside Relative Normativity: From Sources to Standards Instruments for the Exercise of International Public Authority' (2008) 9 *German Law Journal* 1865 and A. von Bogdandy, P. Dann, and M. Goldmann, 'Developing the Publicness of Public International Law: Towards a Legal Framework for Global Governance Activities' (2008) 9 *German Law Journal* 1375. While adhering to a non-formal law-identification criteria, these authors have tried to formalize it. Some of these examples are discussed in chapter 5 below.

[15] See e.g. R. Higgins, *Problems and Process: International Law and How We Use It* (OUP, Oxford, 1995) 8–10. The work of the New Haven Law School is further discussed below at 4.2.3. For another illustration of the contemporary tendency towards process-based law-identification, see P. S. Berman,

various types of deformalization of law-ascertainment in the theory of the sources of international law have, in turn, aggravated the scholarly cacophony generated by the abovementioned move away from questions of law-ascertainment witnessed in the international legal scholarship.

1.2 The Argument: Rejuvenating Formalism in the Theory of the Sources of International Law

It is against the backdrop of this sweeping retreat away from formal international law-ascertainment, that this book not only calls for the preservation of the distinction between law and non-law, but makes a plea for some elementary formalism in the theory of the ascertainment of international legal rules. While *not* being construed as a tool to delineate the whole phenomenon of law—and especially the flux of dynamics at the origin of the creation of legal rules, the content thereof, or the sense of obligation therein[16]—or a theory to describe the operation of international law, formalism is solely championed here for its virtues in terms of distinguishing law from non-law and ascertaining international legal rules.

Nowadays, advocating formalism in the theory of the sources of international law may certainly sound idiosyncratic. The contradictions of formalism have long been unearthed and formalism has unanimously grown to be the culprit of many of the ailments of international law. This book does not seek to obfuscate the undeniable limits of formalism in legal argumentation or to rebut these criticisms. Indeed, the formalism that is discussed here is alien to the classical formalist theory of immanent intelligibility and adjudicative neutrality which have particularly been the target of realist and, later, the powerful postmodern critiques. The book rather makes the case for a preservation of formalism in the theory of the sources of international law for the sake of the ascertainment of international legal rules and the necessity to draw a line between law and non-law.

Preserving the centrality of formalism in the theory of the sources of international law, however, requires more than mere repetition of the old formal templates. The rejuvenation attempted here first necessitates that the illusions of formalism that accompany the ascertainment of customary international law, or that of certain international legal acts, be dispelled. Revealing the mirage of formalism that lies behind some of the existing sources of international law does not amount to a call for an abolition of such modes of creation of international law. It simply aims at raising awareness of the cost and contradictions of the non-formal law-ascertainment that lies behind sources like customary international law. By the same token, revitalizing formalism at the level of the ascertainment of international rules also necessitates that

'A Pluralist Approach to International Law' (2007) 32 Yale J. Int'l L. 301. For a hybrid law-ascertainment approach based on both effect and processes, see H.G. Cohen, 'Finding International Law: Rethinking the Doctrine of Sources' (2007) 93 Iowa L. Rev. 65.

[16] This is further explained in the following chapter. Cfr *infra* 2.1.1.

some paradigms of the postmodern[17] critique of formalism be taken into account. It simultaneously calls upon us to move away from the current intent-based identification of international legal acts found in the mainstream theory of the sources of international law. In sum, the rejuvenation of formalism in the ascertainment of international legal rules undertaken in this book involves both the abandonment of the fallacious formal trappings of some of the existing sources of international law—like customary international law—while requiring that the theoretical foundations of formalism in the ascertainment of international legal acts, like treaties, be revisited.

The foregoing shows that the revitalization of formalism in the theory of the sources of international law attempted in the following chapters cannot be construed as yet another objection against the already much-discussed phenomenon of 'relative normativity'.[18] Indeed, relative normativity, as was constructed by international legal scholars,[19] includes a wide array of different departures from a legal system made of strictly horizontal and bilateral rules: the establishment of hierarchies of norms (*jus cogens*), the generalization of obligations *omnium*, or the universalization of the interest States may have in the application of legal obligation contracted by others (*obligations erga omnes*). It is true that the abovementioned deformalization ongoing in the theory of the sources of international law inextricably reinforces some dimensions of the phenomenon of relative normativity. However, relative normativity being a much wider phenomenon, the rejuvenation of formalism in the ascertainment of international legal rules advocated in this book does not seek to do away with the other manifestations of relative normativity, and in particular the universalization of legal interests in the application of norms (*obligations erga omnes*) or that of hierarchies (*jus cogens*). The rationales of the preservation of formalism in international law-ascertainment spelled out below will further underpin the differences between the argument made here and the traditional objections against relative normativity.[20]

[17] Postmodernism is used here in a generic sense to describe some of the new approaches to international law, including those approaches affiliated with critical legal studies and structuralism. See *infra* 4.1.4 and 4.2.4. The concept thus not refers to the second generation of critical legal scholars as it is sometimes the case in the literature. See D. Kennedy, 'A Rotation in Contemporary Legal Scholarship' (2011) 12 *German Law Journal* 338, especially 356–61. On the concept of postmodernism in general, see D. Patterson, 'Postmodernism', in D. Patterson (ed), *A Companion to Philosophy of Law and Legal Theory* (Blackwell, Oxford, 1999) 375, 375.

[18] The most famous broadside against normative relativity has been initiated by Prosper Weil. See P. Weil, 'Towards Relative Normativity in International Law' (1983) 77 AJIL 413 (translated from 'Vers une normativité relative en droit international?' (1982) 86 *Revue générale de droit international public* 5–47). For a criticism of Weil's argument, see U. Fastenrath, 'Relative Normativity in International Law' (1993) 4 EJIL 305–40; J. Tasioulas, 'In Defence of Relative Normativity: Communitarian Values and The Nicaragua Case' (1996) 16 Oxford J. Leg. Stud. 85; D. Shelton, 'International Law and 'Relative Normativity'' in Malcolm D. Evans (ed) *International Law* (OUP, Oxford, 2006) 159–85; R.A. Falk, 'To What Extent are International Law and International Lawyers Ideologically Neutral? in A. Cassese and J.H.H. Weiler (eds), *Change and Stability in International Law-Making* (De Gruyter, Berlin, 1988) 137. For a counter-reaction to these criticisms, see J. Beckett, 'Behind Relative Normativity: Rules and Process as Prerequisites of Law' (2001) 12 EJIL 627–50.

[19] See P. Weil, 'Towards Relative Normativity in International Law' (1983) 77 AJIL 413.

[20] Cfr *infra* 2.2.

The argument made here is structured as follows. After these introductory considerations, I start, in chapter 2, by explaining how I construe formalism for the sake of the argument made here and mention a few of the rationales of formalism at the level of law-ascertainment. In chapter 3, I briefly outline how formalism outpaced natural law theory and became the dominant model of understanding of law-identification in both general theory of law and in the theory of the sources of international law. Such an overview of the rise of formalism in general legal theory and in the theory of the sources of international law should contribute to the elucidation of some of its political foundations, as well as some of its limits. Chapter 4 then discusses the various criticisms of formalism that have been formulated in the context of general legal theory and depicts how these criticisms subsequently trickled down into the theory of the sources of international law. It is only once the criticisms levelled against formalism have been duly explained that I expound, in chapter 5, on the various manifestations of the deformalization of law-ascertainment in the theory of the sources of international law and their multi-fold agenda. After explaining in chapter 6 what I perceive as the most insightful lessons that can be learned from the critiques of formalism, I engage in chapters 7 and 8 in an attempt to revisit formalism in the theory of the sources of international law and ground it in the social practice of international law-applying authorities. This will require that some of the illusions of formalism that pervade the mainstream theory of the sources of international law are dispelled, and will call for a reconstruction of our concept of law-applying authority whose practice is conducive to the meaning of formal law-ascertainment indicators. Chapter 9 concludes this study with some of the possible insights which can be gained from the theory of international law-ascertainment presented here for the new forms of exercise of public authority outside the traditional channels of international law-making.

1.3 Preliminary Caveats About the Argument Made in this Book

Before I begin this inquiry, my ambition for this book must be clearly elucidated. In the following paragraphs, I do not shy away from relying on general legal theory. In particular, the so-called source and social theses devised in general legal theory have been the linchpins of my argument. Yet, this book is not intended to be a contribution to the general theory of law. Even though general legal theorists may identify here some postures which correspond with those pervading the debates in general law theory,[21] the defence of formalism at the level of international law-ascertainment undertaken here is probably too restricted to the sources of international law to be germane to general legal theory. This is why, while making mention of some important debates in general legal theory and in the philosophy of law, the call for the preservation (and rejuvenation) of formalism in international legal scholarship

[21] In particular, the argument made here can be seen as being the reflection of a so-called 'post-realist' posture. See D. Kennedy, 'A Rotation in Contemporary Legal Scholarship' (2011) 12 *German Law Journal* 338, 346–50.

that is made in this book is primarily addressed to international lawyers. Yet, it cannot be ignored that its grappling with some debates which have unfolded in general legal theory or political philosophy may occasionally be of interest beyond international legal circles.

It is to appeal to a wide readership of international lawyers—who arguably often resist any inquiry into the ontology of the ascertainment of international legal rules—that I have tried to formulate my argument in simple terms. Indeed, I strongly believe that obscurity of language is frequently used to camouflage unachieved or half-baked thoughts. By using a simple vocabulary, I hope to clearly lay bare all the underpinnings of the different parts of my argument and the conceptual tools on which it rests with a view to making them accessible and useful to many international lawyers and not only those that are well-versed in theoretical debates about sources. In doing so, I hope to simultaneously facilitate the continuation of the discussion about formalism in the theory of the sources of international law which this book certainly does not seek to exhaust.

It should be similarly emphasized that, although law-ascertainment inevitably bears upon how one construes law as a whole,[22] the theory of ascertainment defended here does not seek to put forward a new general theory of international law. The theory undertaken here is far more modest than that.[23] It zeroes in only on the ontology of law-ascertainment and does not make any hubristic argument about the ontology of international law as a whole. It will, for instance, be shown that a defence of formal law-ascertainment cannot be conflated with a plea for international legal positivism although the latter has usually abided by formal identification of rules.[24]

Even though the argument here is constructed for a wide readership of international lawyers, its significant theoretical dimension and its focus on the deformalization at play in the international legal scholarship may at times seem arcane to those who are actually engaged in the *practice of international law*. To such practitioners, aside from some inevitable ambiguities in interpretation and ostensible conflicts of rules, a few borderline cases where law cannot be distinguished from non-law, or the inevitable tendency of advocates and counsel to use non-formal law-identification criteria to unearth rules supporting their argument, international law may seem to work properly and an invitation for a return to greater formalism be a purely academic whim. It is true that, by contrast to the determination of the content of law, the ascertainment of international legal rules is not a continuous and recurring controversy in practice.[25] In that sense, this work may look overly introspective to practitioners since it discusses international legal scholarship more than international law itself. Yet, I believe that the kinship between the international legal scholarship and international practice—whether by virtue of legal education or professional

[22] For a more radical affirmation of this point, see J. Beckett, 'Countering Uncertainty and Ending Up/Down Arguments: Prolegomena to a Response to NAIL' (2005) 16 EJIL 213, especially 217.

[23] This is, in my view, one of the main differences between Hart and Kelsen. See *infra* 3.1.3.

[24] Cfr *infra* 2.1.2.

[25] In the same vein, see M. Prost, *Unitas multiplex—Les unités du droit international et la politique de la fragmentation* (McGill University, Montreal, 2008) 160, available at <http://digitool.library.mcgill.ca/>.

interchanges—is too important for these contemporary debates to be entirely ignored by practitioners. Because of the continuous exchanges between practice and scholarship, the possibility that the current deformalization of law-ascertainment in the theory of the sources of international law will eventually trickle down into the practice of international law cannot be excluded. The greater unease and hesitations of international tribunals that are examined in chapter 7 seem to underpin that probability. Likewise, it should not be ignored that, too often, States themselves either nurture or take advantage of the uncertainty inherent in the use of non-formal law-ascertainment criteria with a view to preserving their freedom of action.[26] This is particularly true as far as customary international law is concerned. Indeed, while the practice of international law-making indicates a great awareness by States of the thin line between law and non-law,[27] States can also seek to benefit from the absence of clear formal custom-identification standards and engage in ascertainment-avoidance strategies. The non-formal character of custom-identification criteria discussed in chapter 7 will illustrate that point. Hence, the argument made here, even though it is not meant to offer any pragmatic theory that could help lawyers solve most practical issues and describe the whole phenomenon of law,[28] can help them decipher contemporary practice as well as provide some modest guidance to those international actors actively engaged in international law-ascertainment.

As the structure of the argument and the nomenclatures on which it builds show, this book is undoubtedly informed by a European continental approach to international law.[29] I certainly do not seek to conceal this epistemic bias. On the contrary, it is important to unveil it at the preliminary stage, for I believe that it is precisely what enables the book to provide a refreshing and innovative take on the sources of international law by, on the one hand, making use of concepts and taxonomies with which the dominant universal legal scholarship is not always familiar and, on the other hand, examining the question of sources of international law from the angle—unexplored in continental traditions of international law—of

[26] In the same vein, see G.M. Danilenko, *Law-Making in the International Community* (Dordrecht, Martinus Nijhoff, 1993) 19. See also M. Reisman, 'Soft Law and Law Jobs' (2011) 2 *Journal of International Dispute Settlement* 25, 26.

[27] See e.g. the conscious choice of a majority of States during the negotiating process about a new framework to tackle global-warming in the second half of 2009, whereby States decided that any agreement they could reach would take the form of a political agreement and not an international legal act. See H. Cooper and B. Knowlton, 'Leaders delay action on climate agreement', International Herald Tribune, 16 November 2009, 1. See the similar opinion expressed by D. Shelton, 'Soft Law' in D. Armstrong (ed), *Handbook of International Law*, (Routledge, London, 2009) 68, 78 or K. Raustiala, 'Form and Substance in International Agreements' (2005) 99 AJIL 581, 587. See also A. Aust, who argues that such clear awareness is reflected in the terminology of agreements: A. Aust, *Modern Treaty Law and Practice* (2nd edn, CUP, Cambridge, 2007) 33; C. Lipson, 'Why are some international agreements informal' (1991) 45 *International Organization* 495.

[28] For a similar acknowledgement that formalism, while being necessary, should not be thought as a problem-solving theory, see G.P. Fletcher, 'Law as a Discourse' (1991–1992) 13 Cardozo L. Rev. 1631, 1634. For further insights on the conception of formalism that is espoused here, see *infra* 2.1.

[29] On some of the main differences between the areas of interests of continental, US, and Third World international legal scholarships, see M. Koskenniemi, 'International Legal Theory and Doctrine', *Max Planck Encyclopedia of Public International Law*, available at <http://www.mpepil.com>, para. 28.

formal law-ascertainment. Although I have a distinctive jurisprudential point of view, this feature allows a wide spectrum of international lawyers across all traditions of international law to find in this study useful tools to refresh their understanding of the sources of international law.

Another preliminary caveat must be formulated about the reductionism inherent in the—non-historical—mapping undertaken in some of the following chapters. Needless to say, such mapping will sometimes come at the cost of some inevitable overgeneralization, for scholarly thinking rarely fits into one box or stands at one end of a given spectrum. In other words, a legal scholar's conception of international law rarely has all the trappings of one precise school of thought and often borrows from several traditions. Any description of international legal scholarship based on a taxonomy of schools of thought would inevitably be overgeneralizing.[30] A broad brush and an overall mapping based on trends, movements, and schools are, however, indispensable tools to deconstruct and reconstruct formalism at the level of law-ascertainment in a manner which remains intelligible to a large number of international legal scholars, even those who are not used to the sometimes obscure and intimidating jargon of legal theorists.[31]

Finally, it should be emphasized at this introductory stage that, although the following chapters zero in on the problems of ascertainment of rules originating in traditional international law-making processes, they do not turn a blind eye to the new forms of norm-making at the international level. Although not falling within the scope of the inquiry undertaken here, these new forms of norm-making at the international level ought to be borne in mind, for they shed light on the more limited role nowadays played by traditional international law in global governance. This more limited role of international law and the unprecedented multiplication of modes of norm-making is what has prodded many scholars to turn their attention away from the former in order to research the latter. This is well-illustrated by the research projects on governmental networks, Global Administrative Law (GAL), or the international exercise of public authority.[32] While acknowledging that the use of a non-formal yardstick is indispensable if one wants to capture these new forms of norm-making, the following paragraphs occasionally reflect upon the non-formal criteria used by the authors affiliated to these various research projects to identify the

[30] To borrow a metaphor from D. Kennedy, such mapping is inevitably reminiscent of the all-embracing descriptions of religious groups by secular commentators. See D. Kennedy, 'When Renewal Repeats: Thinking Against the Box' (1999–2000) 32 NYU JILP 335, 374.

[31] It is interesting to note that the criticism of overgeneralization has also been levelled against the international legal scholarship affiliated with critical legal studies and deconstructivism, which has also carried a mapping of the different traditions of international law. See e.g. P.-M. Dupuy, 'Some Reflections on Contemporary International Law and the Appeal to the Universal Values: A Response to Martti Koskenniemi' (2005) 16 EJIL 131–8.

[32] See *supra* note 8. It should be noted, however, that GAL has not entirely excluded traditional law-making processes, as it has, for instance, attempted to include international institutional law. See e.g. B. Kingsbury and L. Casini, 'Global Administrative Law Dimensions of International Organizations Law' (2009) 6 IOLR (2009) 319–58.

product of these alternative norm-making processes. Yet, the present study does not in any way engage with them nor question their move away from formalism, for it simply does not grapple with the same international norm-production processes.[33] They nonetheless constitute insightful theoretical frameworks which will not be ignored throughout the following chapters.

[33] I have engaged in one dimension of this phenomenon elsewhere, see J. d'Aspremont (ed), *Participants in the International Legal System—Multiple Perspectives on Non-State Actors in International Law* (London, Routledge, 2011).

2

The Concept and the Rationale of Formalism in International Law

2.1 Formalism and its Multiple Meanings

2.1.1 The concept of formalism espoused in this book: formalism as a theory of law-ascertainment based on social practice

Formalism is construed here as a particular conception of law-ascertainment. In general, ascertaining legal rules is a complex operation which cannot be improvised, for law-ascertainment presupposes that legal scholars and experts, as well as law-applying officials, first agree on a few basic standards allowing them to identify the law that they study or apply. In that sense, law-ascertainment necessitates an *a priori* standardization of law-identification criteria. Such standardization can be formal, non-formal, or hybrid. Formalism as law-ascertainment contrasts with the use of non-formal or hybrid law-ascertaining criteria in that it refers to the use of formal yardsticks to distinguish law from non-law. According to a formal conception of law-identification, any norm that meets such predefined formal standards is a rule of law. This formal standardization will materialize itself in predefined formal indicators. These predefined indicators can be linguistic or material. This means that formal ascertainment of legal rules does not automatically necessitate the existence of a written instrument where the rule concerned is enshrined. Indeed, linguistic indicators—that is, the use of a given predefined language—can be oral and do not necessarily need to be translated in writing. Likewise, material indicators—that is, the use of a more or less deliberate given procedure—can be exclusive of any written document. While recognizing the possibility of formal ascertainment of legal rules through the use of non-written indicators, this book nonetheless seeks to demonstrate that written linguistic indicators should play the predominant role in the ascertainment of international legal rules if formalism is to achieve any of the rationales described below. In making this argument, this book simultaneously attempts to show that those rules of international law which are ascertained short of any written instrument suffer from significant problems of normativity. Examples will be provided in chapter 7.

The understanding of formalism espoused here thus requires an inquiry into whether a norm purporting to be law meets the formal standards associated with such a predefined pedigree. This is why formalism in the theory of law-ascertainment is often referred to in the literature as the *source thesis*: the term 'source', in this context, referring more generally to the origin and the making of the norm. The so-called source thesis provides that law is ascertained by its pedigree defined in formal terms and that, as a result, identifying the law boils down to a formal pedigree test.[1] Because the pedigree is defined in formal terms, the source thesis entails formal law-ascertainment. The source thesis is often contrasted with models of law-ascertainment based on substantive criteria. Although the argument made in this book backs away from an overly orthodox conception of the source thesis, the concept of the source thesis is, therefore, used in the following chapters to refer to formal ascertainment of legal rules. Because it happens that in some legal systems the standardized formal pedigree of rules takes the form of rules or principles, formal law-ascertainment is sometimes also conceptualized as a *rule-approach* to law,[2] which contrasts with effect- (or impact-)based or process-based definitions of law.[3]

It is of the utmost importance to point out that ascertainment of rules and evidence of rules are two distinct intellectual operations. The former is aimed at identifying *in abstracto* what a rule is, whereas the latter arises when a law-addressee or a law-applying authority respectively invokes or applies such a rule *in concreto*. Yet, law-ascertainment and evidence of law are closely intertwined. Indeed, evidence of law entails that the law-ascertainment criteria of the rule concerned be verified *in concreto*.[4] Evidence of law thus requires that the authority or the individual applying or invoking the rule demonstrates the actual existence of indicators by virtue of which the rule can be said to have been created—whether they relate to the source, the law-making procedure, the content, or the effect of the rule. This does not mean, however, that if the ascertainment of a rule has been made formal, the evidence of that rule will necessarily be formal. In fact, it may well be that the formal criterion by virtue of which a rule is identified is evidenced through a non-formal evidentiary process. Evidentiary processes can be informal. It is, for instance, conceivable that the existence of a written legal agreement be demonstrated by virtue of the subsequent behaviour of the relevant contracting parties.[5] The contrary is also true. A rule whose ascertainment is non-formal can well be evidenced through a formal evidentiary process. This is well-illustrated by the scholarly attempts—which

[1] On the source thesis, see generally J. Raz, 'Legal Positivism and the Sources of Law', in J. Raz, *The Authority of Law: Essays on Law and Morality* (Clarendon, Oxford, 1983) 37–52.

[2] M. Koskenniemi, *From Apology to Utopia: The Structure of International Legal Argument* (CUP, Cambridge, 2005) 189; N. Purvis, 'Critical Legal Studies in Public International Law' (1991) 32 Harvard JIL 81, 84.

[3] See *infra* 5.1.

[4] On the evidentiary processes before international courts, see generally H. Ruiz Fabri and J.-M. Sorel (eds), *La preuve devant les jurisdictions internationales* (Pedone, Paris, 2007); see also A. Riddell and B. Plant, *Evidence before the International Court of Justice* (British Institute of International and Comparative Law, London, 1999); P. Kinsch, 'On the Uncertainties surrounding the Standard of Proof in Proceedings before International Courts and Tribunals', in G. Venturini and S. Bariatti (eds), *Individual rights and international justice—Liber Fausto Pocar* (Giuffrè, Milan, 2009) 427–42.

[5] See the analysis of the case-law of the ICJ on the ascertainment of international agreements, *infra* 7.2.3 and 7.2.4.

are described below[6]—to formalize custom-evidence in the theory of the sources of international law.[7]

As is envisaged here, formalism is thus restricted to a method of ascertainment of *international legal rules*. The ascertaining virtues of formalism, as envisaged here, do not extend to the certification of the *subjects* and *participants* of the international legal system. Indeed, there is no formal certification of the existence of subjects and actors of international law.[8] Probably with the exception of international organizations,[9] it seems that this can hardly be otherwise.[10] The plea for formalism made here does not bear upon the identification of the subjects and participants in the international legal system.[11] The idea that formalism and the certification of the subjects of international law are unrelated is also underpinned by the fact that, even though international law can significantly impact the creation and the form of new subjects,[12] there are no positive rules on the certification of the new subjects that can be formally ascertained. Hence, the concept of formalism espoused in this book must be restricted to the use of formal yardsticks for the ascertainment of international legal rules while bearing no consequences for the identification of the subjects and participants of the international legal system.

Likewise, it should be made clear once again that formalism is not envisaged here as a means to describe and delineate the whole phenomenon of law,[13] and in particular, to determine the content of international legal rules[14] or to explain the

[6] Cfr *infra* 7.1 and 7.2.1.

[7] For a similar distinction between the ascertainment of customary international rules and the evidence of customary international rules, see P. Daillier, M. Forteau, and A. Pellet, *Droit international public* (8th edn, LGDJ, Paris, 2009) 364.

[8] See e.g. J. d'Aspremont, 'Non-State Actors in International Law: Oscillating Between Concepts and Dynamics' in J. d'Aspremont (ed), *Participants in the International Legal System—Multiple Perspectives on Non-State Actors in International Law* (Routledge, London, 2011) 1. See also J. d'Aspremont, 'Regulating Statehood: The Kosovo Status Settlement' (2007) 20(3) LJIL 649–68.

[9] On the question of definition, identification and conceptualization of international organizations, see the illuminating article of C. Brölmann, 'A Flat Earth? International Organizations in the System of International Law', in *International Organizations, Series: Library of Essays in International Law* (Ashgate, Farnham, 2006) 183–206; from the same author, see *The Institutional Veil in Public International Law—International Organisations and the Law of Treaties* (Hart, Oxford, 2007) 11–22.

[10] It has even been argued that with respect to questions of personality, continuity, and identity, formalism should be resisted. See especially M. Craven, *The Decolonization of International Law* (OUP, Oxford, 2007) 216–31.

[11] For contemporary developments and some diverging perspectives on the role and status of the various participants in the international legal system, irrespective of their being a subject of international law, see J. d'Aspremont (ed), *Participants in the International Legal System—Multiple Perspectives on Non-State Actors in International Law* (Routledge, London, 2011).

[12] See generally G. Abi-Saab, 'Cours général de droit international public' (1987) 207 RCADI 9–463, 68; See also, M. Kohen, 'Introduction', in M. G. Kohen (ed), *Secession. International Law Perspectives* (CUP, Cambridge, 2006) 4, 6, and 19–20.

[13] See *contra* J. Beckett, 'Countering Uncertainty and Ending Up/Down Arguments: Prolegomena to a Response to NAIL' (2005) 16 EJIL 213–38, 217 (who argues that we must chose a general theory of law first before being able to engage in the ascertainment of legal rules).

[14] For a more ambitious attempt to describe the 'complete phenomenon of law' with the help of formalism, see M. Bos, *A Methodology of International Law* (T.M.C. Asser Instituut, Amsterdam/NY/Oxford, 1984) 2.

sense of obligation therein.[15] While it helps us to draw a line between law and non-law, formalism falls short of providing any indication as to the substantive content of international legal rules once they have been ascertained.[16] Indeed, even if formally ascertained as such, rules must still be interpreted.[17] It is true that, if a criterion like the intent of the parties is elevated into a law-ascertainment indicator and if that intent is supposed to be inferred from the instrument, interpretation of the content of the instrument will be necessary to unearth the intent and thus to ascertain law.[18] This, however, is a consequence of the use of a non-formal law-identification criteria like intent. It is a question which I will revert to later.[19] As such, law-ascertainment and interpretation of the content of rules remain two distinct operations and this is why formalism, as is envisaged here, is unable to describe the entire phenomenon of law and falls short of providing an indication as to the substantive content of international legal rules.

Although the concept of formalism employed here is alien to the determination of the content of international legal rules and is restricted to their ascertainment, it is important to note that the formal identification of rules through a standard pedigree does not entirely stifle indeterminacy at the level of law-ascertainment. On the contrary, formalism inevitably brings about some indeterminacy. Indeed, because of the indeterminacy of the language with which the standard pedigree of the rules is defined, formalism as a set of standardized criteria of law-identification inevitably fails to produce an autonomous and self-contained linguistic convention for the sake of law-identification. As will be explained in chapter 3,[20] proponents of the source thesis have, however, devised several conceptual strategies to overcome the non-self-sufficiency of the source thesis and rein in, as far as possible, the inevitable indeterminacy of the formal standards of law-ascertainment. In this regard, this book adopts a particular understanding of formal law-ascertainment *derived from social practice.* Such a particular conception of the ontology of formal law-ascertainment has been designated in the literature as the *social thesis.* The archetype social thesis purports to supplement the classical source-based criteria of identification of international legal rules (the source thesis), with a view to endowing it with some limited autonomy, by inferring the meaning of the standard pedigree of rules from the practice of law-applying authorities.[21] While the social thesis does not completely eliminate

[15] This is a traditional criticism levelled against formalism which is said to fail to explain how law generates a sense of obligation. See e.g. J. Brunnée and S.J. Toope, *Legitimacy and Legality in International Law. An Interactional Account* (CUP, Cambridge, 2010) especially 46–52.

[16] See J. Beckett, 'Behind Relative Normativity: Rules and Process as Prerequisites of Law', (2001) 12 EJIL 627–50. See also J. Beckett, 'Countering Uncertainty and Ending Up/Down Arguments: Prolegomena to a Response to NAIL' (2005) 16 EJIL 213, 217.

[17] On the illusion of formalism behind the principles of interpretation of international law, see *infra* 7.1.

[18] O. Corten, *Méthodologie du droit international public* (Editions de l'Université de Bruxelles, Brussels, 2009) 213–14.

[19] Cfr *infra* 7.2.3.

[20] See *infra* 3.1.3 and 3.1.4.

[21] It has also been referred to as the 'exclusive internal point of view'. See G.P. Fletcher, 'Law as a Discourse' (1992) 13 Cardozo L. Rev. 1631, 1634.

indeterminacy or provide autonomy from the source thesis, it still constitutes, as will be developed in chapter 8, a useful framework within which the indeterminacy of formal standards of law-ascertainment can be domesticated without falling into naïve objectivism. In that sense, and thanks to its definitional advantages, the social thesis remains one of the central tenets of the rejuvenation of formalism envisaged here. This is true even if the peculiarities of international law—and the unique configuration of its law-making processes—have always impeded a mechanical and full transposition of the social thesis into the theory of the sources of international law.

The idea that a legal system must rest on some elementary formal standardization of law-identification criteria originating in social practice is not new. This is the well-known conception embraced by Herbert Hart in the *Concept of Law*. While acknowledging the abiding indeterminacy of law, Hart construed law as rooted in *social conventions*, allowing it to be constructed without raising the question of the validity of the ultimate rule from which the system as a whole is derived.[22] As will be argued in chapter 8,[23] such a construction, if transposed into international law, allows us—at least for the sake of the ascertainment of international legal rules—to leave aside the question of the validity of the international legal system as a whole.[24] While Hart's theory can prove significantly helpful in sharpening formalism in the context of international law, I argue that Hart's insights are insufficient to rejuvenate formalism in international law. In fact, it is well-known that Hart not only demoted international law to a very primitive set of rules which lacks a systemic character but also failed to elucidate the political foundations of his formal understanding of law. This is why Hart's theory—although instrumental in the revitalization of formalism in the context of international law attempted here—is, as such, insufficient to explain the foundations of formalism in international law and convincingly refute the current trend of deformalization of law-ascertainment. The same is true with the work of his followers. Although the argument of this book also borrows from the approaches of Joseph Raz, Jules Coleman, and Will Waluchow,[25] none of them has offered a modernization of Hart's formalism that fits the specificities of the sources of international law. As far as the ascertainment of international legal rules is

[22] H.L.A. Hart, *The Concept of Law* (2nd edn, OUP, Oxford, 1997) 108–9. For a recent re-appraisal of Hart's relevance in international legal scholarship, see J. d'Aspremont, 'Hart et le Positivisme Postmoderne' (2009) 113 *Revue générale de droit international public* 635–54.

[23] See *infra* 8.3.

[24] Fragmentary—and sometimes diverging—transpositions of Hart's *Concept of law* in international law have already been undertaken, especially with respect to customary international law. See the work G.H.J. Van Hoof, *Rethinking the Sources of International Law* (Kluwer Law, The Hague, 1983); G.M. Danilenko, *Law-Making in the International Community* (Martinus Nijhoff, Dordrecht, 1993) 16; G.M. Danilenko, 'The Theory of International Customary International Law' (1998) 31 German YBIL 9–47. H. Meijers, 'How is International Law Made?—The Stage of Growth of International Law and the Use of Its Customary Rules' (1979) 9 NYIL 3; R.M. Walden, 'Customary International Law: A Jurisprudential Analysis' (1978) 13 Israel L. Rev. 86–102. See also the general course of P.-M. Dupuy, 'L'unité de l'ordre juridique international—Cours général de droit international public' (2002) 297 RCADI9–490. Although her theory has some natural law overtones, see also S. Besson, 'Theorizing the Sources of International Law', in S. Besson and J. Tasioulas (eds), *The Philosophy of International Law* (OUP, Oxford, 2010) 163, 180–5.

[25] See *infra* 3.1.4.

concerned, a more relevant adjustment of Hart's thesis is probably found in the endeavours of Brian Tamanaha,[26] as well as William Twining,[27] to refresh Hart's theory in order to accommodate a wider range of contemporary phenomena. In particular, they advocate a broader conception of law-applying authorities at the origin of the social practice in which formal law-ascertainment is grounded in order to embrace a wide range of social actors.[28] As explained in chapter 3, these accounts provide insights for the application of Hart's social thesis in the theory of the sources of international law.

Some similarities probably exist between the promotion of formalism advocated here and some of the Hart-based *constructivist* accounts of international law, according to which international rules are seen as prescriptive statements that require a formal approach.[29] However, contrary to these particular constructivist understandings of the normative character of international law, the argument made here and developed in chapters 7 and 8 does not elevate formalism into a constitutive element of rules.

As will be shown in chapter 8, some very relevant insights for the theory of ascertainment are found in the *philosophy of language*. Consequently, elucidating some of the roots of formalism inevitably requires some *detours* through philosophy: the arguments developed here will accordingly allude to the work of some of the philosophers who have grappled with these questions.[30] The argument made here, as chapter 8 will demonstrate, has been particularly nurtured by the insights offered by philosophers like Ludwig Wittgenstein who, themselves, influenced Hart and his followers.[31] However, the occasional references to their philosophical work should by no means be interpreted as an endeavour to borrow authority from their

[26] See B. Tamanaha, *A General Jurisprudence of Law and Society* (OUP, Oxford, 2001); see also B. Tamanaha, 'The Contemporary Relevance of Legal Positivism', St John's University School of Law, Legal Studies Research Paper Series, Paper #07-0065 (January 2007).

[27] Twining acknowledges that he has himself been very widely influenced by Tamanaha. See W. Twining, *General Jurisprudence: Understanding Law from a Global Perspective* (CUP, Cambridge, 2009) 94–5.

[28] See eg. B. Tamanaha, *A General Jurisprudence of Law and Society* (OUP, Oxford, 2001) 142.

[29] See N. Onuf, *World of Our Making: Rules and Rules in Social Theory and International Relations* (University of South Carolina Press, South Carolina, 1989); N. Onuf, 'The Constitution of International Society' (1994) 5 EJIL 1, 6; N. Onuf, 'Do Rules Say What They Do? From Ordinary Language to International Law' (1985) 26 Harvard JIL 385. On the defence by constructivists of some of the main theses of positivism, see B. Kingsbury, 'The International Legal Order', IILJ Paper Series, 19. For a criticism of constructivism, see J.H.H. Weiler, 'The Geology of International Law—Governance, Democracy and Legitimacy' (2004) 64 ZaöRV 547, 560.

[30] Constructivists like Nicholas Onuf also borrow from the philosophy of language, in particular the work of John Searle, eg. J. Searle, *Speech Acts* (CUP, Cambridge, 1969)and J. Searle, *Expression and Meaning* (CUP, Cambridge, 1979), with a view to devising a taxonomy of international rules. See N. Onuf, 'Do Rules Say What They Do? From Ordinary Language to International Law' (1985) 26 Harvard JIL 385.

[31] The influence of Wittgenstein on Hart has nonetheless been the object of diverging opinions. See e.g. the debate on the extent of the influence of Wittgenstein and Austin on Hart's concept of law between Timothy Endicott and Nicos Stavropoulos, 'Hart's Semantics', in J. Coleman (ed), *Hart's Postscript: Essays on the Postscript to 'The Concept of Law'* (OUP, Oxford, 2001) 41 and 59 respectively. The influence of Wittgenstein on Hart has also been qualified by N. Lacey, *A Life of H.L.A. Hart: The Nightmare and the Noble Dream* (OUP, Oxford, 2004) 218.

'ch international legal scholars rarely grasp completely. By the same rences should not be seen as an attempt to directly and naïvely of the abovementioned philosophers into international law. Their mplex and subtle to provide ready-made solutions for a peculiar ...ternational law. Moreover, if the identification of international legal ...es hinges on some formal standards rooted in social practice, as is advocated here, it does not need to 'borrow' anything from other social sciences to ensure its internal coherence. References to the work of Wittgenstein are simply and modestly aimed at helping international legal scholars and international lawyers to disentangle some of the theoretical uncertainties that beset the use of formalism in international law.

Finally, it should be made clear that, as formalism refers here to the use of formal indicators to ascertain international legal rules, the concept of deformalization that is also used throughout this book means the move a way from formal law-ascertainment and the resort to non-formal law-ascertainment criteria. The meaning of deformalization in this book thus departs from the use of that concept to refer to norm-making by informal non-territorial networks.[32]

2.1.2 Other conceptions of formalism

In the theory of the sources of international law, formalism has been understood in various manners, and not only as formal law-ascertainment. It is fair to say that a large part of the scholarly debate about formalism—and about the school of international law advocating the resort to formal law-ascertainment criteria—has been riddled by mutual misunderstandings and diverging conceptions. Proponents and opponents of formalism have been using incompatible notions, with the latter's criticisms of the former ending up 'knocking down a straw man'.[33] While this book stands by an understanding of formalism as a theory of law-ascertainment and does not seek to address alternative conceptions of formalism, such alternative conceptions ought, nevertheless, to be mentioned to avert any misunderstanding of the argument made here.

Formalism as a theory of adjudicative neutrality and immanent intelligibility of legal arguments

Formalism is often construed by legal scholarship as a theory of adjudicative neutrality and immanent intelligibility of legal arguments. This is probably how formalism is most commonly understood.[34] According to this construction, formalism is meant

[32] M. Koskenniemi, 'Constitutionalism as a Mindset: Reflections on Kantian Themes about International Law and Globalization' (2007) 8 *Theoretical Inquiries in Law* (2007) 13.

[33] The expression is from M.H. Kramer, *In Defense of Legal Positivism: Law Without Trimmings* (OUP, Oxford, 2007) 49 (when discussing the critique of positivism as a whole); see F. Shauer, 'Positivism as Pariah', in R.P. George (ed) *The Autonomy of Law: Essays of Legal Positivism* (OUP, Oxford, 1996) 31–56.

[34] See e.g. C.C. Goetsch, 'The Future of Legal Formalism' (1980) 24 Am. J. Legal Hist. 221. See also E.J. Weinrib, 'Legal Formalism', in D. Patterson (ed), *A Companion to Philosophy of Law and Legal Theory* (Blackwell Publishers Ltd, Oxford, 1999) 332–42. See also the remarks of O. Corten, *Méthodologie du droit international public* (Editions de l'Université de Bruxelles, Brussels, 2009) 57.

to provide predictability in the behaviour of law-applying authorities while simultaneously endowing judicial decisions with a greater legitimacy and authority.[35] In that sense, formalism is the antithesis of radical rule-scepticism and legal realism, which construe law-application as totally indeterminate, and equate law with law-application.[36] Formalism in legal argumentation minimizes choice in law-application and maximizes predictability. Such conceptualization of formalism has often gone hand-in-hand with portrayals of the international legal order as a system.[37] This type of formalism has, in the history of most legal systems, been subject to oscillations, with periods of dominance of formal legal argumentation succeeded by dramatic movements towards deformalization of legal argumentation.[38]

Much of the criticism of formalism in the legal scholarship has been directed at such an understanding of formalism reminiscent of a Kantian conception of universal reason. This is particularly true with respect to the realist objections against the 'abuse of logic',[39] the 'abuse of deduction',[40] and the 'mechanical jurisprudence'[41] that are supposedly brought about by formalism.[42] All these critiques are premised on the idea that formalism is first and foremost a theory of adjudication[43] and constitutes some form of dispute-management technique which allows for the identification of the specific rules meant to settle legal disputes.[44] Although its theory

[35] See E.J. Weinrib, 'Legal Formalism: On the Immanent Rationality of Law' (May 1988) 97(6) Yale L. J. 949–1016; S.V. Scott, 'International Law as Ideology: Theorizing the Relationship between International Law and International Politics' (1994) 5 EJIL 313–25, especially 322. See also the remarks of Koskenniemi, 'What is International Law For?' in M. Evans (ed), *International Law* (2nd edn, OUP, 2006) 57, 69.

[36] Such a binary understanding of formalism is found in the *Concept of Law*. Hart construes formalism and rule-scepticism as the 'Scylla and Charybdis of justice theory' and rejects both of them. See *The Concept of Law* (2nd edn, OUP, Oxford, 1997) 124–54. See also the remarks of Judge Ad Hoc Sur in his separate opinion appended to the Order of 28 May 2009 in ICJ, *Questions relating to the Obligation to Prosecute or Extradite (Belgium v. Senegal)*, Rec. 2009, available at <http://www.icj-cij.org>.

[37] See the remarks of A.-C. Martineau, 'The Rhetoric of Fragmentation: Fear and Faith in International Law' (2009) 22 LJIL 1–28, 7–8. It should be made clear that in some strands of the legal scholarship no distinction is made between a legal order and a legal system. On this point, see J. d'Aspremont, 'Hart et le positivisme postmoderne' (2009) 113 *Revue générale de droit international public* 635–54.

[38] This has been insightfully described by D. Kennedy, 'When Renewal Repeats: Thinking Against the Box' (2000) 32 NYU JILP 335–500, 335. It is interesting to note that such a finding had already been made by Hart. See Hart, *The Concept of Law* (2nd edn, OUP, Oxford, 1997) 130.

[39] A.J. Sebok, 'Misunderstanding Positivism' (1995) 93 Mich. L. Rev. 2054, 2093.

[40] D. Kennedy, *The Rise and Fall of Classical Legal Thoughts* (re-edited in 2006, Beard Books, Washington DC) at xviii.

[41] This is the famous expression of Roscoe Pound, 'Mechanical Jurisprudence' (1908) 8 Colum. L. Rev. 605.

[42] See also the criticisms of R.H. Pildes, 'Conflicts Between American and European Views: The Dark Side of Legalism' (2003–2004) 44 Va. J. Int'l L. 145.

[43] On the realist criticisms of formalism as a theory of legal reasoning in adjudication, see generally A.J. Sebok, 'Misunderstanding Positivism' (1995) 93 Mich. L. Rev. 2054 especially 2071. See also *infra* 4.1.2.

[44] This understanding permeates the critique of positivism by B. Kingsbury 'The International Legal Order', NYU Law School Public Law & Legal Theory Research Paper No. 01–04 (2003); Institute for International Law and Justice (IILJ) History and Theory of International Law Series, Working Paper No. 2003/1.

about making social choices also includes a law-ascertainment dimension, the process-based approach of the New Haven School primarily construes formalism as a theory of adjudication and legal argumentation for the promotion of reform.[45] Many scholars affiliated with critical legal studies also understand formalism from the vantage point of legal argumentation.[46] Some legal positivists have also castigated that form of formalism which they have perceived as nothing more than a 'noble dream'.[47]

It is interesting to note that these—in my view very cogent—objections against formal legal argumentation have failed to universally undermine the fidelity of international lawyers to that type of formalism. In particular, old-style legal positivism,[48] whose adherents have been among the strongest advocates of the resort to formalism in law-ascertainment, has continued to enjoy significant support in the European[49] and Asian[50] traditions of international law. American international legal scholars have long distanced themselves from formal legal argumentation, at least since the objections formulated by realists, liberals, and scholars of policy-oriented jurisprudence.[51]

Whatever the reasons for preserving or repudiating formalism in legal argumentation may be, it is absolutely fundamental to make clear that this book does not discuss formalism from the perspective of legal argumentation and

[45] See e.g. R. Higgins, 'Policy Considerations and the International Judicial Process' (1968) 17 ICLQ 58; M. Reisman, 'The View from the New Haven School of International Law' (1992) 86 ASIL Proceedings 118; L. Chen, 'Perspectives from the New Haven School' (1993) 87 ASIL Proceedings 407, 408.

[46] See e.g. D. Kennedy, 'The Disciplines of International Law and Policy' (1999) 12 LJIL 84; D. Kennedy, 'When Renewal Repeats: Thinking Against the Box' (2000) 32 NYU JILP 335. M. Koskenniemi, *The Gentle Civilizer of Nations: The Rise and Fall of International Law 1870–1960* (CUP, Cambridge, 2002) 502. M. Koskenniemi, *From Apology to Utopia: The Structure of International Legal Argument* (CUP, Cambridge, 2005) 306. N. Purvis, 'Critical Legal Studies in Public International Law' (1991) 32 Harvard JIL 81–127, 81; T. Skouteris, 'Fin de NAIL: New Approaches to International Law and its Impact on Contemporary International Legal Scholarship' (1997) 10 LJIL 415; T. Skouteris, *The Notion of Progress in International Law Discourse* (LEI Universiteit, Leiden, 2008), chapter 3, later published as *The Notion of Progress in International Law Discourse* (T.M.C. Asser, The Hague, 2010). For a similar interpretation of formalism from the vantage point of critical legal studies, see I. Scobbie, 'Towards the Elimination of International Law: Some Radical Scepticism about Sceptical Radicalism' (1990) 61 BYBIL 339–62, 345.

[47] H.L.A. Hart, 'American Jurisprudence through English Eyes: The Nightmare and the Noble Dream' (1976–1977) 11 Ga. L. Rev. 969, especially 978–89.

[48] For an attempt to move away from this old-style of legal positivism in the international legal scholarship, see J. d'Aspremont and J. Kammerhofer (eds), *International Legal Positivism in a Postmodern World* (CUP, Cambridge, 2012) (forthcoming).

[49] For some critical views on that sort of positivism in the European tradition of international law, see E. Jouannet, 'French and American Perspectives on International Law: Legal Cultures and International Law' (2006) 58 Maine L. Rev. 292.

[50] For an outline of some strands of the Asian legal scholarship, see J. d'Aspremont, 'International Law in Asia: the Limits to the Constitutionalist and Liberal Doctrines' (2008) 13 Asian YBIL 89–111.

[51] See generally A.J. Sebok, 'Misunderstanding Positivism' (1995) 93 Mich. L. Rev. 2054–132. See also M. Tushnet, 'Critical Legal Studies: A Political History' (1991) 100 Yale L. J. 1515–44. Some of these schools of thought are analyzed *infra* 4.2.

adjudication.[52] This does not mean, however, that formal law-ascertainment is immune from the problems with which formal legal argumentation and legal adjudication are saddled, in particular those arising in connection with the inevitable indeterminacy of formal standards.[53] Indeed, the ascertainment of international legal rules can also be subject to legal argumentation and legal adjudication. As the following chapters will make clear, the conception of formal law-ascertainment that is discussed here does not, however, aim to stifle the indeterminacy as well as the contradictions necessarily afflicting legal argumentation, including legal argumentation about law-ascertainment. This book only zeroes in on the theory of ascertainment itself—and not on legal argumentation about law-ascertainment. Yet, this does not mean that the rejuvenation of the theory of ascertainment put forward here does not help to temper some of the indeterminacy and contradictions inherent in legal argumentation about the identification of international legal rules, as the following paragraphs will demonstrate.

Formalism, voluntarism, and State-centricism

In the literature, commentators often equate formalism with a law-ascertainment mechanism that is exclusively based on State's consent.[54] So construed, formalism has been lampooned for assuring the continued authority of the State.[55] The international legal scholarship of the 19th century is often portrayed as promoting such a conception of formalism, which ultimately became an acclamation of State sovereignty. The early 1927 decision of the Permanent Court of International Justice

[52] For a similar distinction, see J. Beckett, 'Behind Relative Normativity: Rules and Process as Prerequisites of Law' (2001) 12 EJIL 627–50, especially 629; J. Beckett, 'Countering Uncertainty and Ending Up/Down Arguments: Prolegomena to a Response to NAIL' (2005) 16 EJIL 213, 217.

[53] It is sometimes contended that interpretation is solely a constitutive element of legal practice and argumentation but not a constitutive element of the identification of law, for interpretation necessarily takes place within a pre-established framework. Hence, interpretation is only a secondary or parasitic operation. In that sense, interpretation 'repairs the fabric of understanding' and 'enables practice to go on'. It is only a therapeutic activity. See D. Patterson, 'Wittgenstein and Constitutional Theory' (1993–1994) 72 Tex. L. Rev. 1837; D. Patterson, 'Wittgenstein on Understanding and Interpretation' (2006) 29 *Philosophical Investigations* 129–39; D. Patterson, 'Interpretation of Law' (2005) 42 San Diego L. Rev. 685. The argument made here does not go as far as claiming that law-ascertainment can be entirely severed from interpretation. However, it is argued that law-ascertainment can grow more autononous from the interpretation of the content of law.

[54] This perception permeates very different strands of contemporary legal scholarship. See e.g. A. Carty, 'Conservative and Progressive Visions in French International Legal Doctrine' (2005) 16 EJIL 525–37; D. Kennedy, 'The Sources of International Law' (1987) 2 Am. U. J. Int'l L. & Pol'y 1, 20. D. Kennedy, 'When Renewal Repeats: Thinking Against the Box' (2000) 32 NYU JILP 335, 355, 366. J. Brunnée and S.J. Toope, 'An Interactional Theory of International Legal Obligation', *University of Toronto Legal Studies Research Series*, No. 08–16, July 2008, 31–3, available at <http://ssrn.com/abstract=1162882>; On this association, see the remarks of O. Elias and C.L. Lim., *The Paradox of Consensualism in International Law* (Kluwer Law International, The Hague, 1998) especially 193 or the remarks by O. Corten, *Méthodologie du droit international public* (Editions de l'Université de Bruxelles, Brussels, 2009) 53–4 and 58.

[55] A. Carty, 'Conservative and Progressive Visions in French International Legal Doctrine' (2005) 16 EJIL 525–37.

in the famous *Lotus case*[56] is often—mistakenly in my view—interpreted as the culmination of this association of formalism with voluntarism,[57] allowing it to survive in 20th and 21st century legal scholarship.[58]

There is no doubt that, if conflated with voluntarism, formalism remains inextricably plagued by contradictions and fails to offer a satisfying theory to explain the binding character of international law.[59] It certainly is not the place, however, to discuss the contradictions of formalism construed as a theory about the foundation of the binding nature of law. Indeed, this book backs away from such a conception of formalism. According to the argument made here, voluntarism is primarily an approach to the authority and legitimacy of international law, which is a different question to the ascertainment of rules.[60] This book—although not ignoring the impact of formal law-ascertainment on the authority and legitimacy of international law—does not seek to explain why international law is binding or why subjects abide

[56] The *Lotus* case, PCIJ, Ser. A, No. 10, 1927.

[57] For some early criticisms, see J.-L. Bierly 'The "Lotus" Case' (1928) 44 LQR 154; C. de Visscher, 'Justice et médiation internationales' (1928) 9 RDILC 33, 77–8; J. Verzijl, 'L'affaire du "Lotus" devant la Cour permanente de Justice internationale' (1928) 9 RDILC 1. For some famous contentions that contemporary international law has allegedly moved away from the principle established in the *Lotus* case, see the declaration of Judge Bedjaoui and the opinion of Judge Shahabuddeen appended to the Advisory Opinion on the *Legality of the Threat or Use of Nuclear Weapons*, ICJ Rep. (1996) 268. and 394–6. More recently, see the declaration of Judge Simma appended to the Advisory Opinion on the *Accordance with International Law of the Unilateral Declaration of Independence in Respect of Kosovo*, 22 July 2010, 1–3, available at <http://www.icj-cij.org>. However, the *Lotus* case could equally be interpreted as the start of a new era where a previous unbridled freedom comes to be checked by international law and can thus be interpreted as being a more progressive decision than what is usually argued. On this point, see the comments of O. Spiermann, *International legal argument in the Permanent Court of International Justice, The Rise of the International Judiciary* (CUP, Cambridge, 2005) 248–63. See also O. Spiermann, 'A Permanent Court of International Justice' (2003) 72 Nord. J. Int'l. L. 399, 410–12 (citing M. Huber at the Institut de Droit international, in (1931) 36 *Annuaire de l'Institut de Droit international* 79); see also A. Pellet, 'Lotus que de sottises on profère en ton nom!: remarques sur le concept de souveraineté dans la jurisprudence de la Cour mondiale', in Edwige Belliard (ed), *Mélanges en l'honneur de Jean-Pierre Puissochet: l'État souverain dans le monde d'aujourd'hui* (Pedone, Paris, 2008) 215–30. On other misinterpretations of the CPIJ decision in the *Lotus* case, see J. d'Aspremont, 'Unilateral v. Multilateral Exercises of Universal Criminal Jurisdiction' (2010) 43 Israel L. Rev. 301–29.

[58] For criticism of voluntarism, see generally G. Fitzmaurice, *The General Principles of International Law* (1957-II) 92 RCADI 1–227, 36; A. Pellet, 'The Normative Dilemma: Will and Consent in International Law-Making' (1988–1989) 12 Aust. YBIL 22, 26.

[59] See e.g. M. Koskenniemi, *From Apology to Utopia: The Structure of International Legal Argument* (CUP, Cambridge, 2005) 303–87. A. Carty, 'Conservative and Progressive Visions in French International Legal Doctrine' (2005) 16 EJIL 525–37, especially 534.

[60] Using the distinction between the question of the *sources* of law and the question of the *foundations* of law, R. Kolb makes the same argument. See R. Kolb, *Réflexions de philosophie du droit international. Problèmes fondamentaux du droit international public: Théorie et Philosophie du droit international* (Bruylant, Brussels, 2003) 51; See also S. Besson, 'Theorizing the Sources of International Law', in S. Besson and J. Tasioulas (eds), *The Philosophy of International Law* (OUP, Oxford, 2010) 163, 166. To S. Besson, however, consent is insufficient to ensure the authority and legitimacy of international legal rules, see S. Besson, ibid, 166 and 175. In the same vein, see N. Krisch, *Beyond Constitutionalism—The Pluralist Structure of Postnational Law* (OUP, Oxford, 2010) 3. See *contra* D. Lefkowitz, 'The Sources of International Law: Some Philosophical Reflections', in S. Besson and J. Tasioulas (eds), ibid, 187, 192–94.

by its rules. This book is thus premised on the idea that formalism and voluntarism cannot be inherently associated.[61]

This being said, because this book revisits the theory of the sources of international law, it inevitably looks at the creation of international law from a primarily State-centric perspective. This is due to the fact that mainstream conceptions of the sources of international law remain largely informed by State's consent. Yet, the current State-centric character of mainstream theory of the sources of international law does not entail that, as a matter of principle, formalism in law-ascertainment must necessarily be assimilated with State's intent,[62] like those found in the work of pre-modern international legal scholars and classicists.[63] It will be shown in the following chapters that formalism does not mean that law exclusively emanates from the State, as formalism is indifferent as to the actual *material source*[64] of law. Indeed, formal law-ascertainment criteria can well lead to the identification of certain norms as legal rules despite the fact that they do not originate in the will of States. For instance, in the pluralized contemporary international legal system, it would be entirely conceivable for law to emanate from non-State entities, while its identification remains conducted upon the basis of formal criteria.[65] While formalism—as it is construed here—does not bestow a law-ascertainment role on State's consent, the reverse is certainly true too. Consent alone does not automatically involve the use of any formal law-ascertaining criterion.[66] For instance, when they are construed as being a

[61] The conflation between formalism and consensualism has long been rejected by normativist approaches to international law, as is illustrated by H. Kelsen. On the conception of formalism, see *infra* 3.1.3. In the same vein, see also S. Besson, 'Theorizing the Sources of International Law', in S. Besson and J. Tasioulas (eds), ibid, 163, 166.

[62] For similar criticisms of the association of the source doctrine and consensualism, see G.J.H. Van Hoof, *Rethinking the Sources of International Law* (Kluwer Law, The Hague, 1983) 289. See also M. Payandeh, 'The Concept of International Law in the Jurisprudence of H.L.A. Hart' (2010) 21 EJIL 967, 970–1.

[63] Cfr *infra* 3.2.1.

[64] On the distinction between material and formal sources, see generally L. Oppenheim, *International Law*, vol. 1 (8th edn, Longmans, London, 1955) 24. See the remarks of P.E. Corbett, 'The Consent of States and the Sources of the Law of Nations' (1925) 5 BYBIL 20–30; C. Rousseau, *Principes généraux du droit international public*, tome 1 (Paris, Pedone, 1944) 106–8; G. Fitzmaurice, 'Some Problems Regarding the Formal Sources of International Law', in *Symbolae Verzijl* (Martinus Nijhoff, The Hague, 1958) 153. G. Abi-Saab, 'Les sources du droit international. Essai de déconstruction', in *Le Droit international dans un monde en mutation: liber amicorum en hommage au Professeur Eduardo Jimenez de Arechaga* (Fundación de Cultura Universitaria, Montevideo, 1994)30; See also the controversial account of this distinction made by G. Scelle, 'Essai sur les sources formelles du droit international', in *Recueil sur les sources en l'honneur de Francois Gény* vol. III (Paris, Sirey, 1935) 400–30. P. Dailler and A. Pellet, *Droit international Public* (6th edn, LGDJ, Paris, 1999) 111–12; A. Pellet, 'Article 38', in A. Zimmermann, C. Tomuschat, and K. Oellers-Frahm (eds), *The Statute of the International Court of Justice* (OUP, Oxford, 2002) 677, 714–16.

[65] On this aspect of the pluralization of international law and the role of non-State actors, see J. d'Aspremont (ed), *Participants in the International Legal System—Multiple Perspectives on Non-State Actors in International Law* (Routledge, London, 2011).

[66] For a criticism of this portrayal of the 19th century and its use as progress narrative tool, see D. Kennedy, 'International Law and Nineteenth Century: History of an Illusion' (1996) 65 Nord. J. Int'l L. 385.

manifestation of implicit State's consent,[67] customary rules are not ascertained by virtue of formal criteria.[68]

The need to distinguish between formalism and State's consent explains why the conception of formalism advocated in this book does not prejudge the identity of the actors from whom the law emanates. The argument made in this book is thus not averse to the theoretical possibility of international legal rules made by non-State entities. It must again be repeated that formalism as law-ascertainment is simply indifferent regarding the *material source of law*. It is only concerned about how law is identified, no matter who or what may have been the primary norm-making force.

Formalism and formal law-making processes

Formal law-ascertainment is sometimes associated with the existence of a formal procedure through which a rule is made.[69] According to this view, a rule can only have a proper existence in the legal system concerned—and hence yield any effect therein—if the procedural forms prescribed by that system for a rule to be a legal rule have been respected.[70] Yet, it will be shown in the following chapters that, as far as formal ascertainment of international legal rules is concerned, such a conception of formalism is too restrictive and cannot be generalized in the theory of the sources of international law. International legal rules are—and should be able to be—identified by virtue of formal criteria even though their making has not been subject to a formal procedure. This is well-illustrated by the flourishing practice of agreements in simplified forms which are discussed below.[71] It will nonetheless be shown that material and procedural aspects of law-making procedures can sometimes provide useful indicators supplementing formal law-identification yardsticks.[72]

[67] Anzilotti, *Scritti di diritto internazionale pubblico* (Cedam, Padova, 1956–7) 1, 38. See also H. Triepel, *Völkerrecht und Landesrecht* (Scientia Verlag, Aalen, 1899) 95. G.I. Tunkin, *The Theory of International Law* (Harvard UP, Cambridge, 1974) 124. C. Chaumont, 'Cours général de droit international public' (1970) 129 RCADI 333, 440. For an attempt to modernize the consensual conception of customary international law, see A. Orakhelashvili, *The Interpretation of Acts and Rules in Public International Law* (OUP, Oxford, 2008) 70–107.

[68] On the ascertainment of customary rules, see *infra* 7.1 and 7.2.1.

[69] J. Salmon (ed), *Dictionnaire de droit international public* (Bruylant, Brussels, 2001) 516.

[70] A variant of this understanding of formalism provides that the jurisdiction of international judicial bodies is made strictly dependent on the fulfilment of a formal procedure. International courts have usually backed away from this type of formalism. See PCIJ, *The Mavrommatis Palestine Concessions, Greece vs. Britain*, judgment of 30 August 1924, Ser. A., No. 2, 1924, 34 ('The Court, whose jurisdiction is international, is not bound to attach to matters of form the same degree of importance which they might possess in municipal law. Even, therefore, if the application were premature because the Treaty of Lausanne had not yet been ratified, this circumstance would now be covered by the subsequent deposit of the necessary ratifications'). In the same vein, see *Application of the Convention on the Prevention and Punishment of the Crime of Genocide (Bosnia and Herzegovina v. Serbia and Montenegro)*, Judgment on the preliminary objections, of 11 July 1996, ICJ Rep. (1966) para. 26. More recently, see the Joint Declaration of Judges Al-Khasawneh, Simma, Bennouna, Cançado Trindade, and Yusuf appended to the case concerning Ahmadou Sadio Diallo *(Republic of Guinea v. Democratic Republic of the Congo)*, 30 November 2010, available at <http://www.icj-cij.org/docket/index.php?p1=3&p2=3&k=7a&case=103&code=gc&p3=4>.

[71] Cfr *infra* 7.1.

[72] Cfr *infra* 7.2.4 and 7.3.1.

Formalism as a general descriptive theory of international law

Formalism is often associated—mostly by its critics—with a general descriptive theory of international law. In that sense, it is thought to provide a (commonly inadequate) approach to delineate the whole phenomenon of law, and make sense of how international law is made and why it is complied with.[73] In the following chapters, I do not construe formalism as a tool to describe how law is made or and how law generates a sense of obligation. International law is a complex phenomenon that can certainly not be reduced to formal ascertainment mechanisms. In particular, there is little doubt that formal law-ascertainment does not suffice to describe the intricate phenomenon of the making of international law. Likewise, although—as I will subsequently explain—formal law-ascertainment is an indispensable condition for the authority of international law,[74] formal law-ascertainment does not, in itself, suffice to generate a sense of obligation.[75] There is much more that is needed for a rule that has been ascertained by virtue of formal indicators to generate a sense of obligation among its addressees. Formalism is more modestly construed here as a theory to distinguish between law and non-law by virtue of formal indicators, irrespective of the 'shared understandings'[76] which have generated the rule concerned and whether or not they actually generate compliance.

Formalism and legal positivism

Formalism is also often conflated with legal positivism.[77] This is not utterly accidental, since legal positivists have not only commonly defended formalism in legal argumentation,[78] but have also usually been the most fervent supporters of formalism in the ascertainment of legal rules.[79] Indeed, legal positivist theorists have

[73] J. Brunnée and S.J. Toope, *Legitimacy and Legality in International Law. An Interactional Account* (CUP, Cambridge, 2010) 46–52.

[74] Cfr *infra* 2.2.

[75] In that sense, I concur with Brunnée and Toope, that formalism offers only limited guidance in analysing how (the sense of) obligation is created in international law. See J. Brunnée and S.J. Toope, *Legitimacy and Legality in International Law. An Interactional Account* (CUP, Cambridge, 2010) 34 and 46.

[76] On the concept of 'shared understanding' in the international society, see J. Brunnée and S.J. Toope, ibid, 56–87.

[77] See for instance, G.J.H. Van Hoof, *Rethinking the sources of international law* (Kluwer Law, The Hague, 1983) 283 (positivism being labelled an 'analytical approach' to the sources of international law); J. Salmon (ed), *Dictionnaire de droit international public* (Bruylant, Brussels, 2001) 516; to some extent, the same association is made by J. Beckett, 'Behind Relative Normativity: Rules and Process as Prerequisites of Law' (2001) 12 EJIL 627–50. See also J. Brunnée and S.J. Toope, 'International Law and Constructivism: Elements of an International Theory of International Law' (2000) 39 Colum. J. Transnat'l L. 19, 22 or J. Brunnée and S.J. Toope, *Legitimacy and Legality in International Law. An Interactional Account* (CUP, Cambridge, 2010) 46.

[78] See *contra* H.L.A. Hart, 'American Jurisprudence through English Eyes: The Nightmare and the Noble Dream' (1976–1977) 11 Ga. L. Rev. 969, especially 978–89. See also the account of the work of J. Bentham *infra* 3.1.2.

[79] In international legal scholarship, see e.g. A. Orakhelashvili, *The Interpretation of Acts and Rules in Public International Law* (OUP, Oxford, 2008) 51–60. See also the examples *infra* 3.2.

adhered to a strict formal law-ascertaining blueprint, i.e. the so-called *source thesis.* As was explained above, the source thesis provides that law is determined by its source and that, as a result, identifying the law boils down to a pedigree test.[80]

Although legal positivists have traditionally promoted the use of formalism for law-ascertainment purposes,[81] formalism is but one of the many tenets of legal positivism.[82] Accordingly, they ought to be distinguished.[83] In defending formal law-identification, this book falls short of supporting legal positivism as a whole.

Besides the fact that formalism constitutes only one of the aspects of legal positivism, there is another reason why the defence of formalism attempted in this book must be severed from the debate about legal positivism. The debate about legal positivism in general legal theory or in the international legal scholarship manifests so many different, if not conflicting, meanings of positivism—even among legal positivists themselves[84]—that the debate about legal positivism has proved almost unfathomable and unintelligible.[85] Likewise, positivism has often been faulted for positions which were, to a very large extent, straw men,[86] thereby further clouding scholarly discussions about the exact tenets of legal positivism. The criticisms of legal positivism thus cannot be transposed to formalism.[87] Because of the extreme

[80] On the concept of the source thesis, cfr *supra* 2.1.1.

[81] See the account made by G.P. Fletcher, *Basic Concepts of Legal Thought* (OUP, Oxford, 1996) 37–8.

[82] On the difference between formalism and legal positivism, see A.J. Sebok, 'Misunderstanding Positivism' (1995) 93 Mich. L. Rev. 2054–132.

[83] M. Koskenniemi concurs with this idea. See M. Koskenniemi, *From Apology to Utopia: The Structure of International Legal Argument* (CUP, Cambridge, 2005) 191; see also B. Simma and A. Paulus, 'The Responsibility of Individuals for Human Rights Abuses in Internal Conflicts: A Positivist View' (1999) 93 AJIL 302, 307.

[84] Compare e.g. the five meanings of positivism by Hart in 'Positivism and the Separation of Law and Morals' (1958) 71(4) Harv. L. Rev. 593–629 with the three meanings of positivism of N. Bobbio in *Essais de théorie du droit* (Bruylant/LGDJ, Paris, 1998) 24. See the understanding of positivism of L. Oppenheim, 'The Science of International Law: Its Task and Method' (1908) 2 AJIL 313, especially 326 and 333. See also the definition of positivism provided by N. Onuf, 'Global Law-Making and Legal Thought', in N. Onuf (ed), *Law-Making in the Global Community* (Carolina Academic Press, Durham, 1982) 1–13. See the various meanings of positivism referred to in J. Salmon (ed), *Dictionnaire de droit international public* (Bruylant, Brussels, 2001) 852–4.

[85] W. Twining, *General Jurisprudence: Understanding Law from a Global Perspective* (CUP, Cambridge, 2009) 25; G. Pino, 'The Place of Legal Positivism in Contemporary Constitutional States' (1999) 18 *Law and Philosophy* 513–36; See also F. Chevrette and H. Cyr, 'De Quel Positivisme Parlez-vous?', in L. Rolland and P. Noreau (eds), *Mélanges Andrée Lajoie* (Themis, Montreal, 2008) 33–60; See also M. Koskenniemi, *From Apology to Utopia: The Structure of International Legal Argument* (CUP, Cambridge, 2005) 131, note 258.

[86] For such an example of a criticism of positivism, see H. Morgenthau, 'Positivism, Functionalism and International Law' (1940) 34 AJIL 260, especially 261–3.

[87] Legal positivism has been the object of systematic condemnation in American jurisprudence. See e.g. J. Boyle, 'Ideals and Things: International Legal Scholarship and the Prison-house of Language' (1985) 26 Harv. Int'l L. J. 327. Concerning the debate about positivism, see the remarks of N. Onuf, 'Global Law-Making and Legal Thought', in N. Onuf (ed), *Law-Making in the Global Community* (Carolina Academic Press, Durham, 1982) 1, 5. On the negative implication of the use of the term 'positivism' in the literature, see G. Gaja, 'Positivism and Dualism in Dionisio Anzilotti' (1992) 3 EJIL 123. For some exceptions in American international legal scholarship, see A. Somek, 'Kelsen Lives' (2007) 18 EJIL 409–51.

difficulty of reaching any consensus on the meaning of positivism, this book does not engage with the current debates about the relevance of legal positivism.[88] Instead, I explore the ontology of formalism in law-ascertainment irrespective of the school of thought that had earlier championed it. For this reason, the promotion of formalism attempted in this book should not be construed as an endeavour to revive legal positivism as a whole in the international legal scholarship. Only if positivism is reduced to the source and social theses can the following chapters be perceived as making a plea for a refreshed positivist take on international law.[89]

The 'culture of formalism'

Martti Koskenniemi's plea for a 'culture of formalism' is well-known.[90] This aspect of his work—which is not devoid of irony—has singled him out among scholars affiliated with critical legal studies and deconstructivism because such a plea has been perceived as an endeavour to soften some of the effect of deconstruction.[91] It is not necessary to describe here the infinite variety of strands in the scholarship affiliated to deconstructivism and critical legal studies. A brief account of such doctrines will be provided when I describe how deconstructivism and critical legal studies impacted on the theory of the sources of international law in chapter 4.[92] Yet, it is important at this stage to emphasize that the formalism in the theory of the sources of international law advocated in this book can certainly not be conflated with the culture of formalism famously put forward by Koskenniemi, although both ideas share some common characteristics.

It must be acknowledged that Koskenniemi's culture of formalism is not easy to fathom. Indeed, in his published work, he has always remained rather terse and concise when it comes to the specifics of that notion. I must thus resist the temptation of (mis)reading his words so as to make them fit into the argument

[88] A direct attempt to engage with the debate about the relevance of international legal positivism is carried out in J. d'Aspremont and J. Kammerhofer (eds), *International Legal Positivism in a Postmodern World* (CUP, Cambridge, 2012) (forthcoming).

[89] I have espoused such a restricted conception of legal positivism elsewhere. See J. d'Aspremont, 'Hart et le positivisme postmoderne' (2009) 113 *Revue générale de droit international public* 635–54; see also J. d'Aspremont, 'Non-state actors from the perspective of legal positivism', in J. d'Aspremont (ed), *Participants in the International Legal System—Multiple Perspectives on Non-State Actors in International Law* (London, Routledge, 2011) 23.

[90] See the famous plea of M. Koskenniemi for a culture of formalism. See M. Koskenniemi, *The Gentle Civilizer of Nations: The Rise and Fall of International Law 1870–1960* (CUP, Cambridge, 2002) 502–9. M. Koskenniemi, 'What is International Law For?', in M. Evans (ed), *International Law* (2nd edn, OUP, Oxford, 57) 69–70. See also C. Schmitt, 'Hans Morgenthau and the Image of Law in International Relations', in M. Byers (ed), *The Role of Law in International Politics: Essays in International Relations and International Law* (OUP, Oxford, 2000) 17, 32–3.

[91] He has been categorized as a mild 'crit' for attempting to domesticate deconstruction. On the distinctive aspects of the critical legal project of Martti Koskenniemi, see e.g. J.A. Beckett, '"Rebel Without a Cause" Martti Koskenniemi and the Critical Legal Project' (2006) 7 *German Law Review* 1045, 1065. Such attempts to domesticate deconstruction have long been the object of criticisms in general legal theory. See e.g. P. Schlag, '"Le Hors de Texte, C'est Moi"—The Politics of Form and the Domestication of Deconstruction' (1990) 11 Cardozo L. Rev. 1631.

[92] See *infra* 4.2.4.

defended in this book. Nonetheless, from Koskenniemi's own work and the interpretations thereof,[93] this culture of formalism can be understood as a 'culture of resistance to power, a social practice of accountability, openness, and equality whose status cannot be reduced to the political positions of any one of the parties whose claims are treated within it'.[94] In particular, this culture of formalism, while still premised on the idea of an impossibility of the universal, represents the possibility of universal legal argumentation as it avoids the dangers of imperialism by remaining empty, while seeking to preserve the possibility for alternative voices to be heard and make claims about the deficiencies of the law. In that sense, it is opposed to the formalism in legal argumentation[95] and must be construed as a 'regulative ideal'[96] or a necessary unattainable 'horizon'.[97] According to Koskenniemi, this culture of formalism necessarily accompanies the 'critique' of law, for it is what protects the critique from being hijacked by those who previously instrumentalized the law in order to conceal their political goals while preserving the possibility of a universal debate. This is why the culture of formalism is a cornerstone of Koskenniemi's project, as it invites international lawyers, once they have laid bare the subjectivity of their claim, to focus on the universality of all legal claims.

Koskenniemi's culture of formalism—like the formalism discussed here—is not a tool that dictates the outcome of legal reasoning or provides a ready-made solution for political questions to which the law is applied. It rather is a practice or a communicative culture which aspires to the universality of legal arguments for the sake of equality and openness. Only those legal claims which could also be held against ourselves would be valid. The culture of formalism is thus an 'interpretative safeguard'.[98] Surely, this type of practice does not materialize itself in any kind of indicator—like the formalism put forward in this book. Although the conception of formalism discussed in this book and the abovementioned culture of formalism are thus very distinct, it is my firm belief, as is further explained in chapters 4, 6, and 7, that Koskenniemi's culture of formalism does not collide with the use of formal indicators in the sources of international law. Indeed, the use of such formal indicators does not prevent the debate about—and the critique of—law and

[93] Among others, see E. Jouannet, 'Présentation critique', in M. Koskenniemi, *La Politique du Droit International* (Paris, Pedone, 2007) 32–3. See also Ignacio de la Rasilla del Moral, 'Martti Koskenniemi and The Spirit of the Beehive in International Law' (2010) 10 *Global Jurist*; J. von Bernstorff, 'Sisyphus was an international lawyer. On M. Koskenniemi's "From Apologia to Utopia" and the place of law in international politics' (2006) 7 *German Law Journal* 1015, 1029–31; J.A. Beckett, '"Rebel Without a Cause" Martti Koskenniemi and the Critical Legal Project' (2006) 7 *German Law Review* 1045; See also the book review of M. Koskenniemi, *The Gentle Civilizer of Nations: The Rise and Fall of International Law 1870–1960* by Nicholas Tsagourias (2003) 16 LJIL 397, 398–9.

[94] M. Koskenniemi, *The Gentle Civilizer of Nations: The Rise and Fall of International Law 1870–1960* (CUP, Cambridge, 2002) 500.

[95] Cfr *supra* 2.1.2.

[96] M. Koskenniemi, 'What is International Law For?', in M. Evans (ed), *International Law*, (2nd edn, OUP, Oxford, 2006) 57, 70.

[97] M. Koskenniemi, *The Gentle Civilizer of Nations: The Rise and Fall of International Law 1870–1960* (CUP, Cambridge, 2002) 508.

[98] J. Beckett, '"Rebel Without a Cause?" Martti Koskenniemi and the Critical Legal Project' (2006) 7 *German Law Review* 1045, 1070.

allow alternative voices to be heard. In facts, the formalism advocated here equally aspires—although via a radically different path—to making of international legal claims through a common platform. If understood along the lines suggested in this book, formalism in the theory of the sources of international law simply allows these debates to take place by ensuring that they are conducted on the basis of a shared—albeit formal—vocabulary. It is thus instrumental in the existence of an open political debate about law and, ultimately, power. Because the conception of formalism discussed in this book and Koskenniemi's culture of formalism are, in my view, not, as a matter of principle, incompatible, the latter occasionally provides relevant insights for the argument made in the following chapters.

2.2 Rationale of Formalism in the Theory of the Sources of International Law

As explained above, international legal scholars have been increasingly inclined to move away from formal law-ascertainment.[99] In so doing, they have espoused approaches that either bypass the question of the ascertainment of legal rules or ground it in effect- (or impact-)based or process-based theories.[100]

While coming to terms with the limits of formalism, this book advocates the preservation of some elementary formalism for the reasons which are spelled out here. These various underpinnings of formal law-ascertainment constitute—what I call—*the politics of formalism*. The main argument for defending and modernizing formalism in law-ascertainment lies in its contribution to the normative character of international law, i.e. the ability of international law to provide identifiable commands to its addressees. In that sense, it will be argued that preserving the normative character of international law is not a self-justifying purpose because preserving normativity helps bolster the authority, legitimacy, and efficacy of international law. Equally important are the consequences of formal law-ascertainment in terms of the ability of the international legal scholarship to generate a meaningful debate. Formalism in law-ascertainment simultaneously contributes to the preservation of the possibility of a critique of international legal rules. It also is contended that formalism can be instrumental in reinforcing the rule of law in the international legal system. Formal law-ascertainment may eventually be sought to serve additional purposes which will be briefly mentioned.

The necessity of preserving the normative character and authority of international law

Even though various virtues can be attributed to formalism in law-ascertainment, I advocate some elementary formal law-ascertainment in international law as *a necessary condition to preserve the normative character of international law*, in that uncertainty regarding the existence of international legal rules prevents them from

[99] Cfr *supra* 1.1. [100] Cfr *supra* 1.1 and *infra* 5.1.

providing for meaningful commands.[101] Indeed, in the absence of these elementary formal standards of identification, I submit that actors are not able to anticipate—and thus adapt to—the effects (or lack thereof) produced by the rule in question. Likewise, short of any formal law-ascertainment criteria, law-applying authorities will be at pains to evidence the applicable law to the cases submitted to them, which in turn will further diminish the ability of actors to anticipate the effects (or lack thereof) of the rule concerned. As a result, the rule that cannot be clearly ascertained will fall short of generating any change in the behaviour of its addressees.[102] This is why it is argued here that the impossibility of drawing a distinction between law and non-law would irremediably strip international legal rules of their normative character.

While this book is premised on the—rather simple—idea that international law needs to rest on a minimum consensus over some elementary formal standardization in order for international legal rules to remain *normative,* I must emphasize that I do not mean to elevate normativity to a constitutive element of international law. Normativity is certainly not a distinctive feature of law. Normativity is found in other social systems and law does not have the monopoly of normativity. In that sense, the argument made here departs from those positivist[103] as well as constructivist[104] accounts that understand the normative sufficiency of rules as a constitutive element of their legal character. In the view adopted here, the normative character of international legal rules is not a necessary condition for them to be legal rules. If the normative character of international law is not a constitutive element of law as is argued here, one may wonder why this book holds the preservation of the normative

[101] In the same vein, see H.L.A. Hart, *The Concept of Law* (2nd edn, OUP, Oxford, 1997) 124. Hart borrows from J.L. Austin the speech-act theory and the claims of the latter regarding the performative function of language, a notion that can be understood in Hart's view by recognizing that 'given a background of rules or conventions which provide that if a person says certain words then certain other rules shall be brought into operation, this determines the function, or in a broad sense, the meaning of the words in question'. See H.L.A. Hart, 'Jhering's Heaven of Concepts and Modern Analytical Jurisprudence', reproduced in *Hart's Collected Essays in Jurisprudence and Philosophy* (Clarendon, Oxford, 1983) 265, 274–6.

[102] J. Hathaway, 'American Defender of Democratic Legitimacy' (2000) 11 EJIL 121, 128–9. Although he embraces a relative normativity, M. Goldmann also pleads for some formalization in the identification of alternative instruments of law with a view to preserving its normative character. See 'Inside Relative Normativity: From Sources to Standard Instruments for the Exercise of International Public Authority' (2008) 9 *German Law Journal* 1865, 1879 ('The operator with an internal perspective cannot wait until the instrument causes certain effects, is being complied with or not, before he or she makes a judgment about its legal quality that will allow him or her to determine the conditions for its validity and legality....Only by way of formal criteria the operator within a legal system may anticipate the legal quality of the instrument he or she intends to adopt and apply the legal regime provided by international institutional law for instruments of this kind. Formal criteria would enable the identification and classification of an instrument before its "normative ripples"').

[103] Interestingly, this is also what H.L.A. Hart seems to imply. See *The Concept of Law* (2nd edn, OUP, Oxford, 1997) 124. This is what I defended elsewhere as well. See J. d'Aspremont, 'Les dispositions non-normatives des actes juridiques conventionnels' (2003) 36 *Revue Belge de Droit International* 492.

[104] N. Onuf, 'Do Rules Say What They Do? From Ordinary Language to International Law' (1985) 26 Harvard JIL 385.

character of international legal rules in such a high importance. I thus need to explain why, in my view, the normativity of international law ought to be safeguarded.

First, I contend that preserving the normativity is not only of doctrinal importance[105] as it fundamentally bears upon the ability of international law to fulfil most of the functions assigned to it.[106] Indeed, many of the functions that can be assigned to international law—and, irrespective of my distinctive jurisprudential point of view, I do not want to prejudge many of them here[107]—presuppose that international law retains sufficient meaning to be capable of instructing the actors subjected to it. Second, I am of the opinion that normativity ought to be supported if international law is to retain some *authority*.[108] The authority of law can, itself, be divided into two different sub-questions, namely that of compliance with international law by its addressees,[109] and that of the authority of international lawyers

[105] For an account of the necessity of preserving law-ascertainment for reasons pertaining to the preservation of international law as a proper field of study, see F. Kratochwil, *Rules Norms and Decisions: On the Conditions of Practical and Legal Reasoning in International Relations and Domestic Affairs* (CUP, Cambridge, 1989) 205.

[106] D. Lefkowitz, 'The Sources of International Law: Some Philosophical Reflections', in S. Besson and J. Tasioulas (eds), *The Philosophy of International Law* (OUP, Oxford, 2010) 187, 195. For a review of some of the most important functions that international law can play, see D.M. Johnston, 'Functionalism in the Theory of International Law' (1988) 26 Canadian YBIL 3, especially 25.

[107] In that sense my argument also departs from that of Prosper Weil (see P. Weil, 'Towards Relative Normativity in International Law' (1983) 77 AJIL 413, especially 420–1) and bears some limited resemblance to that of M. Koskenniemi (M. Koskenniemi, 'What is International Law For?', in M. Evans (ed) *International Law* (2nd edn, OUP, Oxford, 2006) 57, 57. For a rebuttal of the idea that Koskenniemi expresses a total disinterest for the question of the functions of international law, see J. Beckett, 'Countering Uncertainty and Ending Up/Down Arguments: Prolegomena to a Response to NAIL' (2005) 16 EJIL 213.

[108] In the same sense, G.M. Danilenko, *Law-Making in the International Community* (Martinus Nijhoff, Dordrecht, 1993) 21. Although he phrased it in terms of effectiveness, A. Orakhelashvili seems to be of the same opinion. See A. Orakhelashvili, *The Interpretation of Acts and Rules in Public International Law* (OUP, Oxford, 2008) 51. S. Besson is more reserved as to the impact of sources of international law on the authority of international legal rules—a debate she phrases in terms of 'normativity'. She, however, recognizes that validity—a debate she phrases in terms of 'legality'—is an important part of the legitimacy of international law. See S. Besson, 'Theorizing the Sources of International Law', in S. Besson and J. Tasioulas (eds), *The Philosophy of International Law* (OUP, Oxford, 2010) 163, 174 and 180. Although contending that formal law-identification is insufficient to ensure the authority of international law, J. Brunnée and S.J. Toope argue that the distinction between law and non-law is fundamental to preserve it. See J. Brunnée and S.J. Toope, *Legitimacy and Legality in International Law. An Interactional Account* (CUP, Cambridge, 2010) 46.

[109] For a survey of the recent developments in the study of compliance in both international relations and international law scholarship, see K. Raustiala and A.-M. Slaughter, 'International Law, International Relations and Compliance', in W. Carlnaes, T. Risse, and B. Simmons (eds), *The Handbook of International Relations* (Sage Publications, London, 2002) 538–58. For an insightful account of various compliance theories, see A.T. Guzman, 'A Compliance-Based Theory of International Law' (2002) 90 Calif. L. Rev. 1823. From the same author see A.T. Guzman, *How International Law Works: A Rationale Choice Theory* (OUP, Oxford, 2008) and the comments of N. Petersen, 'How Rational is International Law' (2010) 20 EJIL 1247–62. See also the recent empirical contribution of M. Scharf on the contemporary theories of compliance, 'International Law in Crisis: A Qualitative Empirical Contribution to the Compliance Debate' (2009) 31 Cardozo L. Rev. 45.

within norm-making processes and political establishments.[110] Formalism in legal argumentation—albeit the object of severe criticisms—is often seen as fostering these two facets of the authority of international law by backing away from naturalistic underpinnings of the authority of law.[111] It is not coincidental in this regard that classical Kantian formalism was aimed at toning down natural law with a view to enhancing the authority of law.[112]

Yet, what is true with respect to formalism in legal argumentation also applies to formalism in law-ascertainment. Indeed, it seems hard to deny that, if international law cannot be normative because of the difficulty in ascertaining its rules, the authority of international law can be gravely enfeebled.[113] It is precisely one of the reasons why constitutionalist theories of international law—which are examined below[114]—have been supportive of formalism in law-ascertainment.[115] It can thus be reasonably argued that, because it contributes to shoring up the normative character of international law, formal law-ascertainment helps bolster its authority.[116] This does not mean, however, that formal law-ascertainment, in itself, suffices to generate a sense of obligation.

[110] On the question of the authority of law, see generally, V.A. Wellman, 'Authority of Law', in D. Patterson (ed), *A Companion to Philosophy of Law and Legal Theory* (Blackwell Publishers Ltd, Oxford, 1999) 573–82.

[111] D. Kennedy, 'A New Stream of International Legal Scholarship' (1988) 7 Wisconsin Int'l L. J. 29. See also J. Brunnée and S.J. Toope, 'International Law and Constructivism: Elements of an International Theory of International Law' (2000) 39 Colum. J. Transnat'l L. 19. In different terms, this also seems to be expressed by S.V. Scott, 'International Law as Ideology: Theorizing the Relationship between International Law and International Politics' (1994) 5 EJIL 313–25; M. Koskenniemi, 'What is International Law For?', in M. Evans (ed) *International Law* (2nd edn, OUP, Oxford, 2006) 57, 69. N. Purvis, 'Critical Legal Studies in Public International Law' (1991) 32 Harvard JIL 81, 109; D. Shelton, *Commitment and Compliance, The Role of Non-Binding Norms in the International Legal System* (OUP, Oxford, 2000); see also T. Skouteris, *The Notion of Progress in International Law Discourse* (LEI Universiteit, Leiden, 2008) 134, later published as *The Notion of Progress in International Law Discourse* (T.M.C. Asser, The Hague, 2010).

[112] See the remarks of M. Koskenniemi, 'Formalism, Fragmentation, Freedom' (2007) 4 NoFo 7–9. See also the remarks of G. Fletcher, 'Why Kant' (1987) 87 Colum. L. Rev. 421. On Kant and International Law, see generally A. Perreau-Saussine, 'Immanuel Kant on International Law', in S. Besson and J. Tasioulas (eds), *The Philosophy of International Law* (OUP, Oxford, 2010) 53–75. See also P. Capps and J. Rivers, 'Kant's Concept of International Law' (2010) 16 *Legal Theory* 229.

[113] C. Tomuschat, 'International law: ensuring the survival of mankind on the eve of a new century: general course on public international law' (1999) 281 RCADI 9–438, 26–9; This also seems to be indicated by K. Raustiala, 'Form and Substance in International Agreements' (2005) 99 AJIL 581.

[114] Cfr *infra* 3.2.3.

[115] See e.g. A. Peters, 'Global Constitutionalism Revisited' (2005) 11 *International Legal Theory* 39, 49; J. Klabbers, 'Constitutionalism Lite' (2004) 1 IOLR 31, 47; Although he analyses this question through the prism of positivism, this also is the opinion of A. Orakhelashvili, *The Interpretation of Acts and Rules in Public International Law* (OUP, Oxford, 2008) 53.

[116] The normative character of international law being one of Thomas Franck's four parameters for the legitimacy of law and hence a factor contributing to a better compliance with international legal rules, formalism in the theory of the sources of international law could be seen as parameter of the legitimacy of international law. See generally T.M. Franck, *The Power of Legitimacy Among Nations* (OUP, Oxford, 1990). T.M. Franck, 'Fairness in the International Legal and Institutional System' (1993) 240-III RCADI 13, chapter 2; T.M. Franck, *Fairness in International Law and Institutions* (OUP, Oxford, 1995) chapter 2. On the relationship between legitimacy and compliance, see J.H.H. Weiler, 'The Geology of International Law—Governance, Democracy and Legitimacy' (2004) 64 ZaöRV 547; see also S. Besson, 'Theorizing

The question of the authority of law, whilst providing a fascinating research agenda[117] by virtue of the permanent crisis of authority of international law,[118] lies outside the ambit of the inquiry undertaken here. As a result, this work does not prejudge the seminal theories that have been devised in connection with the authority of international law, like, for instance, Franck's fairness theory of law,[119] Bodansky's legitimacy theory,[120] Brunnée and Toope's interactional account,[121] Onuf's[122] or Kratochwil's[123] constructivist accounts of the authority of law, Posner's sceptical account of legalism,[124] or the relevance of the methods used to capture the impact of law on decision-making processes that were devised by the scholars of the International Legal Process (ILP), who have inquired into the role of law in affecting the course of international affairs.[125] The same is true with respect to modern natural law theory, which is not necessarily incompatible with a formalist understanding of law-identification as will be further explained below.[126]

the Sources of International Law', in S. Besson and J. Tasioulas (eds), *The Philosophy of International Law* (OUP, Oxford, 2010) 163, 173–78.

[117] See e.g. B. Kingsbury, 'The International Legal Order' in P. Cane and M. Tushnet (eds), *Oxford Handbook of Legal Studies* (OUP, Oxford, 2003) 271–97; D. Shelton, *Commitment and Compliance, The Role of Non-Binding Norms in the International Legal System* (OUP, Oxford, 2000); M. Koskenniemi, 'What is International Law For?', in M. Evans (ed), *International Law* (2nd edn, OUP, Oxford, 2006) 57, 69; T. Skouteris, *The Notion of Progress in International Law Discourse* (LEI Universiteit, Leiden, 2008) chapter 3, later published as *The Notion of Progress in International Law Discourse* (T.M.C. Asser, The Hague, 2010); S.V. Scott, 'International Law as Ideology: Theorizing the Relationship between International Law and International Politics' (1994) 5 EJIL 313–25. See more generally J. Finnis, 'On the Incoherence of Legal Positivism,' in M. Patterson (ed), *Philosophy of Law and Legal Theory: An Anthology* (Blackwell, Oxford, 2004) 134, 142.

[118] On the permanent character of the authority crisis of international law, see generally A. Orford, 'The Destiny of International Law' (2004) 17 LJIL 442.

[119] T.M. Franck, *Fairness in International Law and Institutions* (OUP, Oxford, 1995); T.M. Franck, *The Power of Legitimacy Among Nations* (OUP, Oxford, 1990); T. Franck, 'The Legitimacy of the International Legal System' (1998) 82 AJIL 751.

[120] D. Bodansky, 'The Legitimacy of International Governance: A Coming Challenge for International Environmental Law?' (1999) 93 AJIL 596.

[121] See J. Brunnée and S.J. Toope, *Legitimacy and Legality in International Law. An Interactional Account* (CUP, Cambridge, 2010).

[122] N. Onuf 'Do Rules Say What They Do? From Ordinary Language to International Law' (1985) 26 Harv. Int'l L. J. 385, 397–402.

[123] F. Kratochwil, *Rules Norms and Decisions: On the Conditions of Practical and Legal Reasoning in International Relations and Domestic Affairs* (CUP, Cambridge, 1989) 124.

[124] E. Posner, *The Perils of Global Legalism* (University of Chicago Press, Chicago, 2009).

[125] A. Chayes, T. Ehrlich, and A.F. Lowenfeld, *International Legal Process* (Little Brown & Co., Boston, 1968). See M. Ellen O'Connell, 'New International Legal Process' (1999) 93 AJIL 334. See also H.H. Koh, 'Why Do Nations Obey International Law?' (1999) 106 Yale J. Int'l L. 2599 and H.H. Koh, 'Bringing International Law Home' (1998) 35 Houston L. Rev. 623. For an attempt to use Koh's theory for law-ascertainment purposes, see H.G. Cohen, 'Finding International Law: Rethinking the Doctrine of Sources' (2007) 93 Iowa L. Rev. 65. See more generally the presentation by M.E. O'Connell, Legal Process School, *Max Planck Encyclopedia of Public International Law*, available at <http://www.mpepil.com>.

[126] See e.g. the discussion *infra* 4.1.1. about Fuller's criteria for the inner morality of law which do not contradict formal law-ascertaining criteria, for their objective is not to ascertain law but simply to ascertain its authority.

The significance of scholarly debates about international law

As I have explained elsewhere, it seems that contemporary scholarly debates in the field of international law have grown more cacophonic, for scholars often talk past each other.[127] Indeed, I believe that international legal scholars have lost sense of the elementary standards that make it possible to distinguish between law and non-law. It is as if the international legal scholarship had turned into a cluster of different scholarly communities, each of them using different criteria for the ascertainment of international legal rules. Such a growing cacophony can be traced back to the lack of consensus over how to identify international legal rules. I argue that formalism not only preserves the normative character of law but also helps international legal scholars share a common language as to what constitutes law, thereby preventing the international legal scholarship from becoming completely meaningless. In other words, I believe that the use of formal standards to ascertain international legal rules, although it does not do away with the inevitable indeterminacy of rules, helps to preserve the significance of scholarly debates about international law and prevent them from becoming a henhouse or a Tower of Babel.

It is true that other disciplines have also manifested a similar cacophony in the ascertainment of their objects of study. They classically have tried to offset it by resorting to specific methodologies whereby each academic work takes pains to systematically and continuously (re)define its vocabulary. It is defended here that such a methodological posture, however, does little to alleviate the absence of consensus on the criteria to identify the subject-matter of one's discipline. Even if international legal scholars were to clearly and systematically spell out how they ascertain international legal rules in each of their academic pieces, this would not automatically allow their studies to connect with one another, for each of them would still continue to resort to different law-ascertainment criteria and, hence, grapple with radically different kinds of materials or phenomena. In the light of the foregoing, formalism in law-ascertainment can thus also be justified by the need to preserve the significance of the debates within international legal scholarship.[128]

The possibility of a critique of international legal rules

Besides preserving the environment where a critique of law can take place, it is argued here that formal law-ascertainment of international legal rules is also a necessary condition for the critique itself. Even though it does little to determinate the whole phenomenon of law—and especially the content of legal rules—and only partake in the identification of legal rules, formalism in law-ascertainment allows the possibility of a critique of law in the

[127] I already made this point in J. d'Aspremont, 'Softness in International Law: A Rejoinder to Tony D'Amato' (2009) 20 EJIL 911–17. See also J. d'Aspremont, 'La doctrine du droit international face à la tentation d'une juridicisation sans limites' (2008) 112 *Revue générale de droit international public* 849–66.

[128] Compare with the analytical conceptualism as methodology advocated by M. Bos which seeks to address the same concern but through other means. See M. Bos, *A Methodology of International Law* (T.M.C. Asser Instituut, Amsterdam/NY/Oxford, 1984) especially 1–35.

first place. Indeed, any critique of law—whether moral, economic, political, etc—presupposes that international rules be preliminarily ascertained. Formal ascertainment of international legal rules allows norms to be evaluated. Short of any ascertainment, there simply is no critique possible for lack of object.[129] It should nonetheless be made clear that, while being a necessary condition for the critique of law, formalism does not, however, provide for the yardstick or the standard of evaluation of that critique. The standard of evaluation is entirely relative, for it stems from the critique concerned and not from law-ascertainment criteria.

The formal identification of law not only preserves the possibility of a critique but also helps safeguard the usefulness of our evaluations of the current state of the law. Indeed, the deformalization of law-ascertainment witnessed in the contemporary theory of the sources of international law, because it can obfuscate the actual absence of legal rules or their insufficient development, dims the—sometimes acute—necessity of lobbying for the adoption of new rules or the change of the existing ones.[130] Such a deformalization simultaneously gives the impression that legal reform may be achieved in law faculties and tribunals and not in parliaments, governing bodies of international organizations, and international intergovernmental law-making fora. This is why it is contended here that formalism in law-identification allows a more effective channelling and use of our evaluations and criticisms of the current state of international law.

The international rule of law

Another weighty reason why formalism in law-ascertainment can be promoted lies in the sustainability of the rule of law in the legal system concerned.[131] In this sense, formalism can be construed as the indispensable condition for ensuring that the framework within which rules are ascertained through formal procedure lives up to the rule of law.[132] Indeed, for law to be a substitute to unbridled arbitrary power, clear law-ascertaining criteria are needed.[133] By the same token, it does not seem

[129] W. Twining, *General Jurisprudence: Understanding Law from a Global Perspective*, (CUP, Cambridge, 2009) 27; J.S. Boyle, 'Positivism, Natural Law and Disestablishment: Some Questions Raised by MacCormick's Moralistic Amoralism' (1985–1986) 20 *Valaparaiso University Law Review* 55; A. Buchanan, *Justice, Legitimacy and Self-Determination. Moral Foundations for International Law* (OUP, Oxford, 2007) 21.

[130] In the same vein, see W.M. Reisman, 'The Cult of Custom in the Late 20th Century' (1987) 17 Cal. W. Int'l L. J. 133, 136.

[131] On the Rule of Law in international law, see generally Société Française pour le Droit International, *L'Etat de droit en droit international: Colloque de Bruxelles* (Paris, Pedone, 2007). On the various meanings of the rule of law in the context of international law, see A. Nollkaemper, 'The Internationalized Rule of Law' (2009) 1 HJLR 74–8.

[132] This point is irrespective of who is entitled to the rule of law. See the argument of J. Waldron, according to whom States are not entitled to the rule of law. J. Waldron, 'Are Sovereigns Entitled to the Benefit of the International Rule of Law?', *NYU Public Law and Legal Theory Research Paper Series*, 09–01 (2009) 2. See the reaction of A. Somek, 'Defective Law', *University of Iowa Legal Studies Research Paper* No. 10–33 (2010) 5.

[133] N. Onuf, 'The Constitution of International Society' (1995) 5 EJIL 1–19, especially 13; F. Schauer, 'Formalism' (1998) 97 Yale L. J. 509; A.L. Paulus, 'International Law After Postmodernism' (2001) 14 LJIL 748; B. Cheng, 'On the Nature and Sources of International Law', in B. Cheng (ed),

unreasonable to claim that the impossibility of ascertaining legal rules with sufficient certainty permits a high degree of subjectivity in the identification of the applicable law,[134] thereby allowing addressees of rules to more easily manipulate the rules.[135]

This is the argument also made by *constitutionalist* legal scholars,[136] whose theory will be examined in chapter 3.[137] International legal constitutionalist approaches are premised on the necessity of some elementary formal standards to ascertain the law. According to that view, short of formal law-ascertaining standards, no system can sustain the rule of law. Even though in the following chapters I depart from some of the tenets of the constitutionalist readings of international law,[138] it seems to me undisputable that the rule of law can hardly be realized without some elementary law-ascertaining standards. The ascertainment-avoidance strategies in which some States deliberately engage to preserve their freedom of action[139]—and which allow some glaring manipulations of international legal rules—are particularly obvious in the case of customary international law which, as will be demonstrated in chapter 7, is identified by virtue of non-formal criteria.

Other potential grounds for preserving formal law-ascertainment

The question of the viability of legal systems has always been a central concern of legal theory. For instance, it has been contended that a legal system whose rules are systematically left unenforced would probably grow unviable.[140] This issue has also

International Law: Teaching and Practice (Stevens, London, 1982) 203, 206; D. Lefkowitz, 'The Sources of International Law: Some Philosophical Reflections', in S. Besson and J. Tasioulas (eds), *The Philosophy of International Law* (OUP, Oxford, 2010) 187, 195; See also the introductory remarks of H. Charlesworth, 'Human Rights and the Rule of Law After Conflict', in P. Cane (ed), *The Hart-Fuller Debate Fifty Years On* (Hart, Oxford, 2010) 43, 44.

[134] See generally J. Raz, 'The Rule of Law and its Virtue, in J. Raz (ed), *The Authority of Law—Essays on Law and Morality* (Clarendon, Oxford, 1979) 210, 215–16.

[135] In the same vein, see G.M. Danilenko, *Law-Making in the International Community*, (Martinus Nijhoff, Dordrecht, 1993) 16–17. See also J. Hathaway, 'American Defender of Democratic Legitimacy' (2000) 11 EJIL 121, 128–29.

[136] C. Tomuschat, 'General Course on Public International Law' 26–9. On this aspect of constitutionalism, see the remarks of J. Klabbers, 'Constitutionalism and the Making of International Law' (2008) 5 NoFo 84, 85 and 103.

[137] See *infra* 3.2.3.

[138] I have already expressed some disagreement with the constitutionalist understanding of international law in J. d'Aspremont, 'The Foundations of the International Legal Order' (2007) 18 FYBIL 219–55; J. d'Aspremont and Fr. Dopagne, 'Two Constitutionalisms in Europe: Pursuing an Articulation of the European and International Legal Orders' (2009) 68 ZaÖRV 939–78; J. d'Aspremont, 'International Law in Asia: the Limits to the Western Constitutionalist and Liberal Doctrines' (2008) 13 Asian YBIL 89–111.

[139] See the account made by C. Lipson of the practice of deformalization and practice and the benefits thereof. C. Lipson, 'Why are some international agreements informal' (1991) 45 *International Organization* 495, especially 501.

[140] A. D'Amato, 'What "Counts" as Law?' in N.G. Onuf (ed), *Law-Making in the Global Community* (Carolina Academic Press, Durham, 1982), 83, 85–6. See B. Tamanaha's assumption that a legal system may exist despite the fact that an overwhelming majority of those subjected to the rules live in general disregard of the vast bulk of them. B. Tamanaha, *A General Jurisprudence of Law and Society* (OUP, Oxford, 2001) 142–8. According to Tamanaha, the requirement of general obedience does not correspond to social reality.

been discussed in connection with immoral rules,[141] especially since Hart's famous reference to the *minimum content of natural law*, which—in my view—was the object of much misunderstanding.[142] Likewise, the argument has been made in the literature that, short of any elementary law-ascertainment yardsticks, a legal system would prove unviable. This last aspect is certainly worthy of mention here. Indeed, it could be argued that formalism at the level of law-ascertainment contributes to the viability of the international legal system.[143] This contention is certainly not unreasonable, for it cannot be totally excluded that a legal system lacking any clear law-identification standards, on top of failing to generate meaningful indications to those subjected to it, could be beset by insufficiencies affecting its viability. The argument made here, while not ignoring this point, does however not necessitate that this possible rationale of formalism be further discussed.

Formal law-ascertainment is sometimes also promoted as allowing the realization of the *formal unity of international law*.[144] This conception of the unity of international law has been subject to various and diverging conceptualizations.[145] It is true that, if international legal rules are identified on the basis of a unified standardized pedigree, they can be seen as belonging to a single set of rules. Such a set of rules can be construed as an order or a system, this distinction—more common in the French and German scholarship—referring to the question whether international law is not a 'random collection of such norms' and whether there are 'meaningful relationships between them'.[146] The argument made here is irrespective of the contribution of formal law-ascertainment to the systemic unity of international law although there seems to be little doubt that the former is conducive to the latter.

[141] In the same sense, see A. D'Amato, ibid, 84.

[142] See *The Concept of Law* (2nd edn, OUP, Oxford, 1997) 193–200 and (1958) 71 Harv. L. Rev. 593, 622–3. The reference to the minimum concept of natural law has often been the object of misunderstanding. It has, for instance, been conflated with a criterion of law-ascertainment. For an illustration of a misuse of Hart's minimum content of natural law as requiring some morality in law to be obligatory, see K.E. Himma, 'Hart and Austin Together Again for the First Time: Coercive Enforcement and Theory of Legal Obligation', available at SSRN: <http://ssrn.com/abstract=727465>. For additional critical remarks, cfr *infra* 3.1.3 and 4.1.1.

[143] This argument has been made by C. Tomuschat, 'International law: ensuring the survival of mankind on the eve of a new century: general course on public international law' (1999) 281 RCADI 9–438, 26–9; G. Abi-Saab, 'Cours général de droit international public' (1987–III) 207 RCADI 9–463, 35. See also R. Jennings, 'The Identification of International Law' in B. Cheng (ed), *International Law: Teaching and Practice* (Stevens, London, 1982) 3, 3.

[144] See generally P.-M. Dupuy, 'L'unité de l'ordre juridique international: cours général de droit international public (2002) 297 RCADI 9–490.

[145] For a survey of the various conceptions of the formal unity of international law, see Mario Prost, *Unitas multiplex—Les unités du droit international et la politique de la fragmentatiebom*, McGill University, Montreal, 2008, 165, available at <http://digitool.library.mcgill.ca/>.

[146] See the conclusion of the Report of the ILC Study Group of the International Law Commission, 18 July 2006, A/CN.4/L.702, para. 14, 7. See also the seminal article of Jean Combacau, 'Le droit international : bric-à-brac ou système?' (1986) 31 *Archives de philosophie du droit* 85–105.

3

The Emergence of Formal Law-Ascertainment in the Theory of the Sources of International Law

Because theoretical debates about the roots of formalism in law-ascertainment first arose in general legal theory before trickling down into the theory of the sources of international law, a brief reminder of how formalism has been discussed in the former is necessary (3.1) before I turn to the analysis of formalism in the latter (3.2).

3.1 The Emergence of Formal Law-Ascertainment in General Legal Theory: A Sketch

3.1.1 Introduction

It is a bad habit of the contemporary international legal scholarship, at least in some parts of the world,[1] to be excessively preoccupied with ruminating on the thoughts of others, especially those of old classical political theorists. These authorities are employed by these scholars to provide convincing foundations and evidence in support of their arguments and conclusions.[2] Whilst it may be a necessity in contemporary jurisprudence to systematically situate any debate by reference to existing scholarship,[3] this peculiar tendency of international legal scholars to seek the support of old masters can be construed as reflecting a certain unease and insecurity held by some authors. Recalling the thoughts of others may also be instrumental in structuring one's own thoughts, while simultaneously satisfying one's vanity by conveying the impression of a wide knowledge of the theoretical background of the question studied. In the present chapter, I shall resist this

[1] For some similar criticisms of current academic writing, see R. Jennings, 'International Reform and Progressive Development', in G. Hafner et al. (eds), *Liber Amicorum Professor Seidle-Hohenveldern—in honour of his 80th birthday* (Kluwer Law International, The Hague, 1998) 325, 336 or F. Rossel, 'Goodbye Law Reviews' (1936–1937) 23 Va. L. Rev. 38, 42.

[2] It is interesting to note that Descartes and Hobbes themselves rarely refer to the thoughts of their predecessors.

[3] W. Twining, 'Implications of "Globalisation" for Law as a Discipline'in A. Halpin and V. Roeben, *Theorising the Global Legal Order* (Hart, Oxford, 2009) 39, 44.

temptation and, accordingly, I shall not indulge in a comprehensive review of the main positivist theorists, who have advocated a conception of law based on formalism. I, nonetheless, deem it necessary here to expound upon how formal law-ascertainment emerged in general legal theory.

Being exclusively intended to shed some light on the origins of formal law-ascertainment, this chapter will remain concise. As a result, it will, at times, be impressionistic and inevitably suffer from a lack of comprehensiveness and a few unavoidable overgeneralizations. In the same vein, my interpretation of the authors mentioned in the following paragraphs constitutes only one of a few readings possible. Ultimately, it should be stressed that the rundown undertaken below can only be selective and inescapably focused on a small number of theorists whose contribution to the systematization of formal law-ascertainment is deemed fundamental. Yet, this overview, despite its shortcomings, will suffice to elucidate some of the foundations of formal law-ascertainment in general theory before, in subsequent chapters, testing their applicability in international law.

Traces of formalism in the theory of law-ascertainment can be found in ancient legal systems.[4] It was, however, with the emergence of positivist legal theory that formal law-ascertainment became the object of systematization. Indeed, legal positivist theorists, as was explained earlier,[5] have strictly abided by a blueprint of formal law-ascertainment: the so-called *source thesis*. It is, indeed, unfortunate that the formal law-ascertainment that accompanies the adoption of the source thesis has often been the object of some misinterpretation. For instance, because of their adherence to the source thesis, legal positivists have been accused of providing a theoretical underpinning for conservatism, inaction, and even authoritarianism.[6] It will be shown below that such an understanding of the formal law-ascertainment embraced by legal positivists is ill-founded. The source thesis that has been embraced by most legal positivists is precisely aimed at elaborating a framework for law to be critiqued and reformed. By drawing a clear distinction between describing, explaining, and interpreting law, the source thesis, corroborated by the separation between law and morality which has been called the 'separation thesis'—although not providing the yardstick of appraisal itself—allows for moral criticisms of law and recommendation of changes.[7] It comes as no surprise, therefore, that mainstream

[4] E.g. formal law-ascertainment was already present in Roman law. See the remarks of N. Onuf, 'Global Law-Making and Legal Thought', in N. Onuf (ed), *Law-Making in the Global Community* (Carolina Academic Press, Durham, 1982) 1, 9.

[5] Cfr *supra* 2.1.2.

[6] See e.g. W. Friedmann, *The Changing Structure of International Law* (Stevens, London, 1964) 77; G. P. Fletcher, *Basic Concepts of Legal Thought* (OUP, Oxford, 1996) 38; see also the foreword of E. Jouannet in O. Corten, *Le discours du droit international: pour un positivisme critique* (Pedone, Paris, 2009) 31.

[7] W. Twining, *General Jurisprudence: Understanding Law from a Global Perspective* (CUP, Cambridge, 2009) 27; J.S. Boyle, 'Positivism, Natural Law and Disestablishment: Some Questions Raised by MacCormick's Moralistic Amoralism' (1985–1986) 20 *Valaparaiso University Law Review* 55; *contra* A. D'Amato, 'What "Counts" as Law?' in N.G. Onuf (ed), *Law-Making in the Global Community* (Carolina Academic Press, Durham, 1982) 83, 90; L. Oppenheim, 'The Science of International Law: Its Task and Method' (1908) 2 AJIL 313, 318.

positivist thinkers like Austin, Bentham, Hart, MacCormick, and Kelsen have all proven to be progressive law reformers.[8]

Even though the source thesis—and hence the model of formal law-ascertainment with which it comes—has always remained one of the trademarks of legal positivism,[9] it would be incorrect to exclusively associate the source thesis with legal positivism. Interestingly enough, natural law theorists, despite endorsing a theory of substantive validity, have also embraced the source thesis, i.e. the idea that the identification of law requires a pedigree test. It could even be argued that natural law theorists were the very first scholars to formulate the source thesis.[10] Indeed, by advocating a bipartite classification of law, based on the distinction between natural and positive law, Aquinas—who coined the term 'positive law'—and later Hugo Grotius—who allegedly excised theology from the *jus gentium* of Vitoria and Gentili by construing international law by reference to both its source and its content[11]—although they still abided by a substantive conception of validity, also resorted to a pedigree test to identify law.[12] The positive law of natural law theorists also required some formal reasoning for the sake of its identification. It can thus be contended that legal positivism and natural law theory have in common the espousal of the source thesis at the heart of formal law-ascertainment.[13] Indeed, this is probably one of the reasons why some of the most prominent natural law theorists—like Grotius—have sometimes been simultaneously reputed as the forefathers of legal positivism[14] and vice-versa.[15]

The common denominator that exists between natural law theorists and legal positivists, however, should not be exaggerated. Because natural law theorists still ground law in some metaphysical sources—be it God, Morality, or Reason—and construe law-identification as a deductive process, formalism is but incidental to natural law theory. In contrast, for early legal positivists, formalism was the central paradigm in law-ascertainment. This chapter, accordingly, leaves aside the incidental

[8] This is highlighted by F. Schauer, 'Postivism as Pariah', in R.P. George (ed), *The Autonomy of Law: Essays of Legal Positivism* (OUP, Oxford, 1996) 31, 37. On these authors, see *infra* 3.1.2 and 3.1.3.

[9] See, however, the few qualifications put forward by J. Coleman, 'Authority and Reason', in R.P. George (ed), *The Autonomy of Law: Essays of Legal Positivism* (OUP, Oxford, 1996) 287, 306.

[10] On natural law theories, see generally B. Bix, 'Natural Law Theory', in D. Patterson (ed), *A Companion to Philosophy of Law and Legal Theory* (Blackwell, 1999) 223–40.

[11] On the influence of Spanish late scholasticism on Grotius, see W.G. Grewe, *The Epochs of International Law* (De Gruyter, 2000) 187.

[12] J. Finnis. 'The Truth in Legal Positivism', in R.P. George (ed.) *The Autonomy of Law: Essays of Legal Positivism* (OUP, Oxford, 1996) 195, 199; see also J. Finnis, 'On the Incoherence of Legal Positivism', in D. Patterson (ed), *A Companion to Philosophy of Law and Legal Theory* (Blackwell, Oxford, 1999) 134, 136–9; see also A. D'Amato, 'What "Counts" as Law?' in N.G. Onuf (ed), *Law-Making in the Global Community* (Carolina Academic Press, Durham, 1982) 83, 88.

[13] B. Bix, 'Natural Law Theory', in D. Patterson (eds), *A Companion to Philosophy of Law and Legal Theory* (Blackwell, Oxford, 1999) 223, 230.

[14] On the contribution of Grotius, see generally *International Law and the Grotian Heritage* (T.M.C. Asser Instituut, The Hague, 1985).

[15] On the idea that Hobbes is a natural law theorist, see J. Finnis, 'On the Incoherence of Legal Positivism', in D. Patterson (ed), *An Anthology of Philosophy of Law and Legal Theory* (Blackwell, Oxford, 2003) 134, 135.

source thesis found in some natural law stances and exclusively zeroes in on the development of the source thesis among positivist theorists, with a view to evaluating the manner in which this has fostered formal law-ascertainment. Natural law theory will be more carefully examined in the next chapter, which pays attention to the objections of natural law theorists to formal law-ascertainment as the ultimate and exclusive law-identification criterion.[16]

While the uses of formalism by legal positivist and natural law theorists must be carefully distinguished, nuances must also be made among legal positivists themselves, for their understandings of the source thesis have not always been identical. Indeed, early positivist thinkers, like Hobbes, Bentham, and Austin, have claimed that law is grounded in the command of an authority. In doing so, they have rooted the source thesis in a theory of authority. As a result, formal law-ascertainment has been construed as the consequence of the necessity to identify the authority at the origin of legal rules. Subsequent positivist thinkers, like Hart and Raz, backed away from such a 'reductionist'[17] conception of the source thesis by reversing the articulation between law and authority. The law-making powers of the authority are, according to them, determined by rules which have an autonomous existence and are not derived from authority. Because they have reversed the law-authority model, these positivist thinkers have been forced to supplement the source thesis by what they called the 'social thesis' (also referred to as the 'conventionality thesis'), i.e. the idea that rules, instead of being grounded in authority, are derived from social conventions.

Because of these radically different understandings of the source thesis among positivist theorists themselves, this chapter will draw a distinction between the earlier theorists who abided by a restrictive conception of the source thesis (3.1.2) and those later theorists like Hart (3.1.3) and his followers (3.1.4) who supplemented the source thesis with the so-called 'social thesis'. It will be shown in chapters 7 and 8 that the departure by Hart and his followers from a theory of authority and the grounding of law in social conventions—although these authors have been rather contemptuous towards international law—provide a crucial underpinning to the theory of ascertainment of international legal rules.

3.1.2 Formal law-ascertainment and the restrictive source thesis: Hobbes, Bentham, and Austin

As was alluded to above, some of the first serious conceptualizations of positive law were found in Aristotelian philosophy, especially in the work of Thomas Aquinas. However, the Aristotelian and Scholastic theorists, despite resorting to a form of the source thesis, still construed metaphysical truth derived from God as a necessary constitutive element of legality. It was René Descartes who first made possible a criticism of the Scholastic conception of law by putting forward a dualistic

[16] Cfr *infra* 4.1.1.

[17] The expression is from J. Raz, *The Authority of Law: Essays on Law and Morality* (Clarendon, Oxford, 1983) 53.

understanding of the Being. Indeed, through his separation of nature and human beings, Descartes destroyed the foundation of the Unitarian Aristotelian and Scholastic conceptions of the world,[18] thereby forcing legal scholars to trace the origin of law to a source other than God or nature. Descartes thus paved the way for early legal positivism—according to which law is grounded in the will of the individual—as well as post-Thomist natural law theory—for which law originates in reason.[19] It is upon the ruins of Aristotelian and Scholastic Unitarian philosophy that legal positivism emerged as a counter-reaction to this (neo-)Scholastic legal theory, according to which moral truth is a necessary condition of legality. It is against this backdrop that Thomas Hobbes can be seen as the ancestor of legal positivism.[20]

At this stage it is necessary to stress that the positivist theory of law, like that of Hobbes, which arose in reaction to earlier Aristotelian and Thomist conceptions, is essentially different from the sociological positivist philosophy which rested in the conviction that social life could be analyzed and reformed through the careful use of the mathematical techniques of measurement and analysis and which purported to give science the possibility to be construed as a consistent and coherent doctrinal body.[21] This sociological positivist theory—which later was closely associated with August Comte[22] (who probably offered one of the first systematizations of epistemological philosophy) and Emile Durkheim[23]—was not concerned with the identification of normative rules. Its aim was solely to ensure the possibility of knowledge by basing science on the observation of constants (scientific laws). Values and ideals were simply some of the constants that science was supposed to accommodate. The foregoing does not mean that legal positivism emerged in total isolation from hard sciences. Indeed, Hobbes, who can be considered the first real legal positivist theorist, applied the scientific methods of Galileo. This is precisely what led him to reject the scholastic proposition that law stems from God or nature. Instead, he argued that law is solely based on the will of individuals endowed with authority. Likewise Jeremy Bentham proved amenable to sociological positivism[24] but took pains not to conflate epistemological positivism and legal positivism.

[18] Some have even argued that this could also be traced back to Althusius. See M. Villey, *La formation de la pensée juridique moderne* (Quadridge/PUF, Paris, 2003) 523.

[19] M. Villey, ibid, 507.

[20] In the same vein, see W.G. Grewe, *The Epochs of International Law* (De Gruyter, Berlin, 2000) 349.

[21] On the relationships between epistemological positivism and legal positivism, see G.P. Fletcher, *Basic Concepts of Legal Thought* (OUP, Oxford, 1996) 32–3; See also F. Chevrette and H. Cyr, 'De Quel Positivisme Parlez-vous?', in L. Rolland and P. Noreau (eds), *Mélanges Andrée Lajoie* (Themis, Montreal, 2008) 33–60, especially 39–44. See also V.M. Waline, 'Positivisme philosophique, juridique et sociologique', in *Mélanges Carré de Malberg* (Sirey, Paris, 1933) 519–34.

[22] See A. Comte, *Discours sur l'esprit positif* (Vrin, Paris, 2003). Compare the criticism of Comte's account of positivism by J.S. Mill, *Auguste Comte and Positivism* (Trübner, London, 1865) (first published in the Westminster Review in 1865).

[23] See generally S. Lukes, *Emile Durkheim: His Life and Work, a Historical and Critical Study* (Stanford UP, Palo Alto, 1985).

[24] J. Bentham, *An Introduction to the Principles of Morals and Legislation* (Kessinger, Whitefish, 2005 edition, first published 1781, London) xiii.

In the same way as legal positivism should not be confused with epistemological positivism, it should not be conflated with logical positivism either. Logical positivism flourished much later, in the inter-war period of the 20th century. It sought to rethink empiricism by means of interpretation of the recent advances made at that time in the physical and formal sciences. The philosophers of that school espoused a radically anti-metaphysical stance and adopted empiricist criteria of meaning. They elaborated a model of 'verifiability' of statements by combining empiricism and analytic truth, incorporating mathematical and logico-linguistic constructs and deductions in epistemology. Its breeding place was the so-called *Vienna Circle*. Logical positivism is nonetheless not entirely disconnected from English legal positivism, for Ludwig Wittgenstein's exchanges with the Vienna Circle eventually enticed him to write the *Tractatus Logico-Philosophicus*[25] which proved influential to Hart.[26] I revert to Wittgenstein's theory in chapter 8, when I analyze his possible contribution to the rejuvenation of the social foundations of formal law-ascertainment in the theory of the sources of international law.[27] The argument made here—although it is informed by Wittgenstein's work which is, itself, not without some connection to logical positivism—remains alien from the debates of sociological and logical positivism.

As was indicated earlier, legal positivism is inextricably associated with Thomas Hobbes, who can reasonably be considered the progenitor of legal positivism. It is probably in his *Dialogue between a Philosopher and a student of the common law of England* that Hobbes has offered the most astute description of his positivist understanding of law. In this work, Hobbes ridicules a lawyer who believes that law is reason, with a view to proving his argument that law is the promulgated command of the Sovereign.[28] In making the argument that it is the King who makes the law and not lawyers, it is interesting to note that Hobbes demotes formalism—which he construes as adjudicatory neutrality and a theory of legal argumentation and not as a theory of law-ascertainment[29]—to a form of art which he does not seem to take seriously.[30] Hobbes appears to resent both formalism and lawyers alike.

Because of his disdain of formalism as a theory of legal argumentation together with his denial of the possibility of a legal order among States, one may be tempted to see Hobbes as nothing more than the precursor of the 20th century realists in the field of international relations, rather than the forefather of formal

[25] L. Wittgenstein, *Tractatus Logico-Philosophicus* (1st edn, Routledge & Kegan Paul, London, 1922).

[26] See e.g. Hart, 'Jhering's Heaven of Concepts and Modern Analytical Jurisprudence', reproduced In *Hart's collected Essays in Jurisprudence and Philosophy* (Clarendon, Oxford, 1983) 265, 271. The influence of Wittgenstein on Hart has been the object of diverging opinions. See generally N. Stavropoulos, 'Hart's Semantics', in J. Coleman (ed), *Hart's Postscript: Essays on the Postscript to 'The Concept of Law'* (OUP, Oxford, 2001) 59, 86. The influence of Wittgenstein on Hart has been qualified by N. Lacey, *A Life of H.L.A. Hart: The Nightmare and the Noble Dream* (OUP, Oxford, 2004) 218.

[27] Cfr *infra* 8.2.

[28] See J. Cropsey (ed), T. Hobbes, *A Dialogue Between A Philosopher and a Student of the Common Laws of England* (Chicago UP, Chicago, 1997).

[29] On this distinction, cfr *supra* 2.1.

[30] T. Hobbes and J. Cropsey (ed), *A Dialogue Between A Philosopher and a Student of the Common Laws of England* (Chicago UP, Chicago, 1997) 17.

law-ascertainment. This ambiguity is probably one of the few reasons why the proposition that Hobbes paved the way for legal positivism is often contested.[31] This being said, Hobbes' attack is solely directed at formalism as a theory of legal argumentation. Likewise, his denial of a possibility of an international law leaves his espousal of formalism unaffected.[32] Hobbes still embraces the proposition that (domestic) law is identified through its pedigree. Indeed, Hobbes likens law to a language, comparing legal validity to linguistic meaning, and as such is not so averse to formal law-ascertainment, for he grounds law on some linguistic conventions which are the product of a deliberate enactment.[33] In that sense, Hobbes is probably better portrayed as foreshadowing the positivist theorists who floated the social thesis.[34] It is true, however, that the deliberate enactment of linguistic conventions in Hobbes' theory is the exclusive product of the will of the Sovereign and remains alien to any collective enactment as posited by the social thesis. Despite this, Hobbes clearly ushered in the rise of formal law-ascertainment as the central tenet of the positivist conception of law.

Because of the ambiguities in Hobbes' theory and his general dislike of formal legal argumentation, Jeremy Bentham can more convincingly be considered the *real* forefather of formal law-ascertainment. Like Hobbes, Bentham abided by a command-based source thesis but refined Hobbes' source thesis by streamlining the formal language of law.[35] Bentham's account of formal law-ascertainment is probably scattered in his complete works—from which some important parts have been irremediably lost. Moreover, his oft-cited *Introduction to the Principles of Morals and Legislation* usually disappoints any reader, especially legal scholars, in the quest for some elegant picture of positive law. Having been envisaged as a mere introduction to his principles of utilitarian morals,[36] which had been first developed in his earlier work *A Fragment on Government*,[37] and their application to the concept of law,

[31] For a criticism of the idea that Hobbes has been the precursor of legal positivism, see S. Coyle, 'Thomas Hobbes and the Intellectual Origins of Legal Positivism' (2003) 16 CJILJ 243–70; see also D. Dyzenhaus, 'Hobbes and the Legitimacy of Law' (2001) 20 *Law and Philosophy* 461–98.

[32] On the contrast between the foundations of legal positivism found in Hobbes' theories and his finding that only the law of nature prevails in inter-State relations, see W.G. Grewe, *The Epochs of International Law* (De Gruyter, Berlin, 2000) 350–1.

[33] See E. Curley (ed), *Hobbes, Leviathan* (Hackett, Indianapolis, 1994) 175 and the interpretation of J.B. Murphy, *Philosophy of positive law: foundations of jurisprudence* (Yale UP, Yale, 2005) 118–19.

[34] Cfr *infra* chapter 8.

[35] While Bentham espouses Hobbes' source thesis, he dismisses Hobbes' social contract theory and hails Humes for having, before him, shown its weaknesses. See J. Bentham, *A Fragment on Government* (Cambridge Texts on the History of Political Thought, CUP, Cambridge, 1988) 51.

[36] It is interesting to note that, in *A Fragment on Government*, Bentham credits Hume for showing that 'the foundations of all virtue are laid in utility' (at 51). For Hart, the principle of utility was also endorsed by Beccaria and Helvetius before being more systematized by Bentham: H.L.A. Hart, *Essays on Bentham: Studies in Jurisprudence and Political Theory* (Clarendon, Oxford, 1982) 48. According to Julien Cazala, the idea that balance between pain and pleasure is the foundation of human action is already found in Epicurus and Lucretius (see J. Cazala, 'Jeremy Bentham et le droit international' (2005) 109 *Revue générale de droit international public* 363, 365. See the more comprehensive study of the origin of utilitarianism by Mohammed El-Shakankiri, *La philosophie juridique de Jeremy Bentham* (LGDJ, Paris, 1970).

[37] J. Bentham, *A Fragment on Government, Cambridge Texts on the History of Political Thought* (CUP, Cambridge, 1988).

Introduction boils down to a hastily cobbled hotchpotch of ideas ending abruptly—even after the 1789 addition—at the peak of its argument on positive law. Despite their weaknesses, however, these writings still provide a very clear idea of Bentham's perceived necessity to conceive law as based on a set of linguistic nomenclatures. Indeed, Bentham recognized the indeterminacy of language.[38] To rein in that indeterminacy, law must be defined, he argues, on the basis of consistent and immediately identifiable forms.[39]

This attempt by Bentham to devise a set of formal conventions was entirely inspired by his utilitarian philosophy.[40] It was premised on the idea that language is indeterminate and has so often been used as an instrument of mystification and oppression to deceive men—which, interestingly, was not without deconstructivist overtones.[41] Although the possession of language elevated man above the beast, language is, according to Bentham, a source of both confusion and deception which had been exploited consciously and unconsciously by reactionary and revolutionary alike.[42] The indeterminacy of the language of law in Bentham's theory is the direct consequence of his dismissal of the Aristotelian idea that words have meanings of their own and also a probable manifestation of Hume's influence on his ideas.[43] His ambition was to facilitate criticism of law and, in turn, enable law reform—the famous argument of 'quietism'.[44] It is in that sense that formal law-ascertainment boils down to a requirement of a utilitarian philosophy of morals.

Bentham is naturally of special importance to international lawyers, having been the one who coined the term 'international law'.[45] Bentham's theory also holds

[38] J. Bentham, *An Introduction to the Principles of Morals and Legislation* (Kessinger, Whitefish, 2005 edn, first published 1781, London) 332–3: 'uncertainty is of the very essence of every particle of law so denominated'.

[39] J. Bentham, ibid, 330–6.

[40] For a criticism of the utilitarian goals of the formalism of Bentham, see J. Raz, *The Authority of Law: Essays on Law and Morality* (Clarendon, Oxford, 1983) 166–7. For another kind of criticism, see B. Williams, *Utilitarianism: For and Against* (CUP, Cambridge, 1973).

[41] See the parallel drawn between some aspects of deconstructivism and Bentham's theory by I. Scobbie, 'Towards the Elimination of International Law: Some Radical Scepticism about Sceptical Radicalism' (1990) 61 BYBIL 339–62, 345–6.

[42] J. Bentham, *An Introduction to the Principles of Morals and Legislation* (Kessinger, Whitefish, 2005) 332–3. On this particular point of Bentham's theory, see the remarks of Hart: H.L.A. Hart, *Essays on Bentham: Studies in Jurisprudence and Political Theory* (Clarendon, Oxford, 1982) 9.

[43] A. Quinton, 'Hume', in R. Monk and F. Raphael (eds), *The Great Philosophers* (Phoenix Publishing, London, 2001) 215, 263.

[44] This is the famous argument of 'quietism' which Bentham ascribed to natural law theories which, according to him, preclude moral criticism of law. Only the source thesis—and its correlative separation of law and morality—allows for moral criticism of law. This argument was extensively discussed and entirely espoused by Hart in his debate with Fuller: H.L.A. Hart, 'Positivism and the Separation of Law and Morals' (1958) 71(4) Harv. L. Rev. 593–629, 598. The argument was also made by Kelsen. See H. Kelsen, 'Law, State and Justice in the Pure Theory of Law' (1948) 57 Yale L. J. 337–90, 383–4. For a criticism of the idea that the source thesis allows for moral criticism of law, see L. Murphy, 'Better to See Law This Way' (2008) 83 NYULR 1098 or L. Murphy, 'Concepts of Law' (2005) 30 Austl. J. Leg. Phil. 1.

[45] J. Bentham, *An Introduction to the Principles of Morals and Legislation* (Kessinger, Whitefish, 2005) 326: In a footnote, he stated: 'The word *international* it must be acknowledged, is a new one; though, it is hoped, sufficiently analogous and intelligible. It is calculated to express in a more significant way, the branch of the law which goes commonly under the name of the *law of nations*: an appellation so

greater appeal to international lawyers than more advanced source thesis conceptions, for he construes the power of the Sovereign as originating in something else other than law.[46] While, for Hobbes, the power of the law-making Sovereign is based upon a contract with the people, Bentham sees the power of the Sovereign as partly natural, partly man-made. However, it is argued here that there is a more fundamental reason why Bentham's theory is so important to international lawyers. International lawyers should remember Bentham as the one who established the theoretical foundations of formalism in law, whether or not they share the utilitarian philosophy or morals underlying it.[47] Bentham, while he shared Hobbes' loathing of lawyers, believed in the need for formalism. He came to terms with the indeterminacy of the language of law and, accordingly, called for a consensus on some elementary formal yardsticks for the identification of law. Indeed, for Bentham, the indeterminacy of law does not correspond with any natural phenomenon; it is a human artefact. Because it is made by man, the indeterminacy of the language of law can thus only be unmade by man.[48] Bentham saw legal theory as being all about defining legal terminology.[49]

Be that as it may, one can hardly dispute that Bentham's conception of formal law-ascertainment still remains very elementary. Bentham, even if he advocated the existence of a consensus on some formal standards, did not offer much of a solution to this indeterminacy apart from his own views on how the language of law should be shaped. The formalism in law-ascertainment advocated by Bentham, like that of Hobbes, falls short of proposing a real social thesis, for law is not grounded in social conventions. For Bentham, the formal nomenclatures which he called for ought to be devised by legal experts and theorists. Bestowing the devise of such formal nomenclatures upon legal scholars lacks sound theoretical underpinnings in Bentham's theory, because legal formal law-ascertainment remains somewhat secondary in his theory. While usefully pointing to the necessity of formalism to identify legal rules, Bentham did little to disentangle its social foundations. This

uncharacteristic that, were it not for the force of custom, it would seem rather to refer to international jurisprudence. The chancellor D'Aguesseau has already made, I find, a similar remark: he says, that what is commonly called *droit* des *gens*, ought rather to be termed *droit* entre *les gens*'. The adjective 'public' was adjoined to the expression international law by Etienne Dumont in his 1802 translation of Bentham's seminal work and amounted to a direct reference to the authors of international law as well as the subjects whose relations it regulates. On the contribution of Etienne Dumont to the refinement and clarification of Bentham's theory, see D. Lieberman, 'From Bentham to Benthamism' (1985) 28 *The Historical Journal* 199–224, 201. See also E. Nys, 'The Codification of International Law' (1911) 5 AJIL 871–900, especially 872, 876.

[46] See the comments of Hart in H.L.A. Hart, *Essays on Bentham: Studies in Jurisprudence and Political Theory* (Clarendon, Oxford, 1982) 221.

[47] For a Kantian critique of utilitarianism, see J. Rawls, who argues that utilitarianism is inconsistent with the principles of justice as fairness: J. Rawls, *A Theory of Justice* (Revised edn, Harvard UP, USA, 1999). On the relevance of Rawls' theory in international law, see A. D'Amato, 'International Law and Rawls' Theory of Justice' (1975) 5 Denv. J. Int'l L. & Pol'y 525.

[48] See H.L.A. Hart, *Essays on Bentham: Studies in Jurisprudence and Political Theory* (Clarendon, Oxford, 1982) 26.

[49] J. Bentham, *An Introduction to the Principles of Morals and Legislation* (Kessinger, Whitefish, 2005) 325.

probably corresponds with the general feeling that Bentham remains a theorist who triggered new fundamental questions without providing convincing answers to these questions.[50]

Nor were such answers provided by his followers. The most famous of them, John Austin, despite being extensively influenced by Bentham, failed to devise a refined theory of formalism or put formal law-ascertainment at the centre of his concept of law. His difficulty in writing and general insecurity partly explained why he ultimately did not refine the theory of Bentham, to whom he was so much indebted.

Austin never concealed Bentham's influence, and in particular that his adherence to the source thesis was very much inspired by the principle of utility.[51] He also shared Bentham's criticisms of Hobbes and the idea of the social contract.[52] Austin strictly followed the command-based source thesis of his predecessors, for he describes positive law by reference to a pedigree and not to its content. Positive law is made by a 'sovereign person, or a sovereign body of person' and is addressed 'to a member or members of the independent political society wherein that person or body is sovereign or supreme.'[53]

While Austin's command-based source thesis is—subject to a few exceptions[54]—not fundamentally different from that of Bentham or that of Hobbes,[55] Austin is especially remembered for expounding, not only upon the concept of supremacy and its connection with the concept of sanction, but also upon the so-called 'separation thesis'. In his *The Province of Jurisprudence Determined,* Austin explains that 'no *positive* law is *legally* unjust' because law, being positive owing to its pedigree (the source thesis), might have any kind of content be it morally good or morally bad (the separation thesis).[56]

Austin's source thesis has been much criticized for many different reasons, even among those who abide by the source thesis. For instance, his theory has been deemed inapplicable in pluralistic societies where political power is diffuse.[57] Likewise, Austin has been reproved for resorting to a language which later fuelled the

[50] H.L.A. Hart, *Essays on Bentham: Studies in Jurisprudence and Political Theory* (Clarendon, Oxford, 1982) 4.

[51] See J. Austin, *The Province of Jurisprudence Determined and The Uses of the Study of Jurisprudence* (Hackett, Indianapolis, first published 1832, reprinted 1998) Lecture VI, 294. On Austin, see generally A. Truyol Y Serra, 'John Austin et la philosophie du droit' (1970) *Archives de philosophie du droit* 151–63.

[52] J. Austin, ibid, 328.

[53] J. Austin, ibid, 193.

[54] The main difference between Austin and Bentham lies in the possibility of legal limitations to the sovereign. Bentham is amenable to that possibility, whilst Austin rejects it completely. Indeed, for Austin, 'supreme power limited by positive law is a flat contradiction in terms': see e.g. J. Austin, ibid, 255. Bentham also accepts that some commands would still be law even if supported only by moral and religious sanctions or those only accompanied by an offer of reward. This led Hart to find Bentham's theory more subtle than Austin's. See Hart, *Essays on Bentham: Studies in Jurisprudence and Political Theory* (Clarendon, Oxford, 1982) 108–9.

[55] His definitions of law, sovereign and political society are very similar to those of Bentham and Hobbes. See the introduction by Hart in J. Austin, ibid, p. xvi.

[56] J. Austin, ibid, 261.

[57] See R. Dworkin, 'The Model of Rules', in D. Patterson (ed), *An Anthology of Philosophy of Law and Legal Theory* (Blackwell, Oxford, 203) 46, 49.

ill-founded accusation that positivism is a doctrine at the service of authoritarian regimes.[58] Austin has also been very much criticized by international lawyers for the step back in the conceptualization of international law associated with his theory. Indeed, contrary to Bentham, Austin saw international law as merely a set of moral principles, for they were not backed by sanction.[59]

Despite these criticisms, and even though Austin's theory is not as subtle as that of Bentham, his work must be mentioned here because he extricated the source thesis (and thus formal law-ascertainment) from the political and philosophical discussions in which they were embedded in the writings of Hobbes and Bentham. In doing so, he gave the source thesis the autonomy that it lacked thus far. That means that he—somewhat inadvertently—elevated formal law-ascertainment into a central tenet of the theory of law. Interestingly, however, it is in the counter-reaction ignited by the radical character of his command-based source thesis that his most important legacy is probably found. Indeed, Hart took great pains to rebut Austin's command-based source thesis. And it is in dismissing Austin that Hart set off a revolution in legal theory and completely reversed the articulation between law and authority. As a result, formal law-ascertainment, which in the work of Hobbes, Bentham, and Austin had only been secondary, became the very linchpin of the concept of law.

3.1.3 The emergence of the social thesis: from Kelsen to Hart

In the works of Hobbes and Austin, formal law-ascertainment had remained a secondary and incidental element of the law-identification process. Bentham came very close to elevating formal law-ascertainment to the cornerstone of his concept of law but failed—at least in the writings which have reached us and which have not been irremediably lost—to adequately explain why. It was not until the next generation of legal positivists undertook a refinement of the source thesis that formal standardization became central to their concept of law.

The transformation of formal law-ascertainment into a central keystone of the source thesis was first brilliantly realized by Hans Kelsen. Yet, it should be made clear that Kelsen's ambitions exceeded law-ascertainment, for he sought to build a whole

[58] 'Political or civil liberty has been erected into an idol, and extolled with extravagant praises by doting and fanatical worshippers. But political or civil liberty is not more worthy of eulogy than political or legal restraint. Political or civil liberty, like political or legal restraint, may be generally useful, or generally pernicious; and it is not as being liberty, but as conducing to the general good, that political or civil liberty is an object deserving applause': J. Austin, *The Province of Jurisprudence Determined and The Uses of the Study of Jurisprudence* (Hackett, Indianapolis, first published 1832, reprinted 1998) Lecture VI, 269.

[59] 'International law, or the law obtaining between nations, regards the conduct of sovereigns considered as related to one another... And hence it inevitably follows, that the law obtaining between nations is not positive law: for every positive law is set by a given sovereign to a person or persons in a state of subjection to its author. As I have already intimated, the law obtaining between nations is law (improperly so-called) set by general opinion. The duties which it imposes are enforced by moral sanctions: by fear on the part of nations, or by fear on the part of sovereigns, of provoking general hostility, and incurring its probable evils, in case they shall violate maxims generally received and respected': J. Austin, ibid, 201. See also Austin's criticisms of De Martens, who had considered international law as positive law: J. Austin, ibid, 215.

theory of law.[60] Kelsen's contribution to the theory of ascertainment is nonetheless fundamental and ought to be briefly discussed here.[61]

Like his predecessors, Kelsen supported the separation thesis—i.e. the idea that the identification of law is solely based on its source and is alien to its moral value[62]—as a necessary consequence of the source thesis. He even pushed the argument further by inferring from the separation thesis an unprecedented restrictive understanding of the missions of legal scholarship. Indeed, he argued that, while law itself cannot be 'pure' because it is the product of a political activity, legal scholarship can only be a pure theory—and allow for critiques of law[63]—if it zeroes in on the description of law and strips away from the objects of its investigation anything that is not law. The Pure Theory of Law thus eliminates moral judgments from any legal science properly so-called.[64]

Kelsen's theory has captivated international lawyers, for Kelsen devoted much work to the study of international law which, contrary to Austin, he considered a legal system. For the sake of our study, what is of greater importance is the revolution brought about by Kelsen's theory in placing formal law-ascertainment at the centre of his concept of law. Indeed, Kelsen adroitly brought formal law-ascertainment into the centre of the picture, for the validity of law cannot be conceived without the Grundnorm. In this sense, one can only determine what law is on the basis of such a Grundnorm. Because law is identified in accordance with the rules about how law is made, or in other words because law regulates its own creation, a formal test becomes necessary to identify the law. Law is law because it can be certified that it has been created in accordance with the rules regulating the creation of law. As a result, *the*

[60] H. Kelsen, *General Theory of Law and State* (Harvard UP, Cambridge, 1945) 175–7.

[61] I owe some of the aspects of the following understanding of Kelsen's theory to very interesting exchanges with Jörg Kammerhofer. All approximations remain mine.

[62] On Kelsen's separation' thesis, see J. von Bernstorff and T. Dunlap, *The Public International Law Theory of Hans Kelsen—Believing in Universal Law* (CUP, Cambridge, 2010) 250–5.

[63] Kelsen's argument that the source thesis allows for criticism of law is similar to that of Bentham. See H. Kelsen, 'Law, State and Justice in the Pure Theory of Law' (1948) 57 Yale L. J. 377, 383–4: 'The real effect of the terminological identification of law and justice is an illicit justification of any positive law'.

[64] The implicit agenda behind some aspects of Kelsen's Pure Theory has been the object of much discussion. See, for instance, B. Simma, according to whom Kelsen was intent on countering Hegel which had been translated into legal theory by Jellinek and thus aimed at strengthening the idea of an international rule of law: B. Simma, 'The Contribution of Alfred Verdross to the Theory of International Law' (1995) 6 EJIL 33–54, 41. Some similar arguments are made by F. Rigaux, who argues that Kelsen opposed not only Hegel but also Triepel's dualism: F. Rigaux, 'Hans Kelsen on International Law' (1998) 9(2) EJIL 325–43, 326. See the criticism of Hegel by Kelsen, 'Les rapports de système entre le droit interne et le droit international public' (1926-IV) 14 RCADI 227–331, 324. The Kantian dimension of Kelsen's agenda and his ambition to devise a theory of law directed at the pacification of inter-State relations have also attracted much attention. See D. Zolo, 'Hans Kelsen: International Peace through International Law' (1998) 9(2) EJIL 306–24. See also C. Leben, *Hans Kelsen, Ecrits français de droit international* (PUF, Paris, 2001) introduction, 19; C. Leben, *Controverses sur la Théorie Pure du Droit* (Panthéon-Assas, Paris, 2005) 11. See also J. Nijman, *The Concept of International Legal Personality: An Enquiry Into the History and Theory of International Law* (T.M.C. Asser, The Hague, 2004) 176–77; D. Dyzenhaus, *Legality and Legitimacy: Carl Schmitt, Hans Kelsen, and Hermann Heller in Weimar* (Clarendon, Oxford, 1997) 157–8, cited by F. Haldemann, 'Gustav Radbruch vs. Hans Kelsen: A Debate on Nazi Law' (2005) 18(2) *Ratio Juris* 174.

existence of law becomes a question of validity, validity being the specific form of existence of rules.[65] In that sense, it can be said that Kelsen gave consistency to the idea that validity and the existence of rules about rules are two sides of the same coin. On the one hand, a rule needs to be validated according to the law-ascertaining rules in order to exist. On the other hand, law cannot exist without law-ascertaining rules. In my view, transforming the law-identification process into a formal pedigree test is probably Kelsen's most important contribution to the theory of ascertainment. Indeed, Hart and his followers followed Kelsen's approach in this respect. As a result of Kelsen's work, identifying law became a strictly formal test based on its conformity with the law-ascertaining rules of the system.

As was said above, Kelsen aimed at providing a general theory of law and did not limit it to ascertainment. It is thus not necessary here to further discuss the other main tenets of Kelsen's theory, i.e. the hypothetical Grundnorm or the equation between the law and the State[66] which are inherent in his attempt to keep 'Is' and 'Ought' categorically apart. Yet, a few words must still be said about the foundation of the Grundnorm as it inevitably bears upon the foundations of formal law-ascertainment discussed here. As is well-known, Kelsen grounded the ultimate regulation of law's creation in the Grundnorm. Although the argument can be made that he has subsequently changed his mind on this point[67] and came close to construing the Grundnorm as a fiction,[68] Kelsen argued that this ultimate law-ascertaining rule is hypothetical—a position which is not devoid of Kantian overtones.[69] This position was much criticized in the literature.[70] Here is not the place to discuss this aspect of Kelsen's theory. It suffices to say that Hart and his followers departed from this aspect of Kelsen's theory. In particular, Hart completely skirted the problem of the foundation of the Grundnorm by grounding the ultimate rule on which the system is based on social facts.[71] In doing so, it did not follow Kelsen's claim that any normative system necessarily rests on a Grundnorm, even a hypothetical one. However, contrary to Kelsen's *Pure Theory of Law*, Hart's *Concept of Law* did not seek, in my view, to offer a general theory of law.[72] His 'Rule of Recognition' is not

[65] On the extent of this conceptual revolution, see N. Bobbio, 'Kelsen et les sources du droit' in *Essais de théorie du droit* (Bruylant/LGDJ, Paris, 1998) 235.

[66] On Kelsen's conception of law as a coercive order, see H. Kelsen, 'Theorie du droit international public' (1953–III) 84 RCADI 1–203, 28. On this particular aspect of Kelsen's theory, see J. Kammerhofer, 'Kelsen—Which Kelsen?' (2009) 22 LJIL 225, 227–33, 236–40.

[67] See Paulson's controversial contention that Kelsen eventually reverted to classical voluntary positivism: S. Paulson, 'Toward Periodization of the Pure Theory of Law', in Letizia, Gianformaggio (eds), *Hans Kelsen's Legal Theory: A diachronic Point of View* (Giappichelli, Turin, 1990) 11.

[68] I owe this point to interesting exchanges with Séverine Helbert.

[69] On the neo-Kantian character of the Grundnorm, see S. Paulson, 'The Neo-Kantian Dimension of Kelsen's Pure Theory of Law' (1992) 12 OJLS 311. See also J. Kammerhofer, *Uncertainty in International Law: A Kelsenian Perspective* (Routledge, London, 2010) 250–3.

[70] For an attempt to rebut this criticism of Kelsen, see J. Kammerhofer, ibid, 197.

[71] For Sebok, Hart should be praised for working out the deficiencies of early positivist theories: A. Sebok, 'Misunderstanding Positivism' (1995) 93 Mich. L. Rev. 2054–132, 2061.

[72] According to Jason Beckett, one cannot, however, estrange law-ascertainment from a general theory of law. See J. Beckett, 'Countering Uncertainty and Ending Up/Down Arguments: Prolegomena to a Response to NAIL' (2005) 16 EJIL 213, 217.

meant to constitute a logical necessity of normative system.[73] Likewise, Hart did not centre his *Concept of Law* on the necessity to abide by the distinction between 'Is' and 'Ought', the objection formulated by Kelsenian scholars against Hart's social thesis.[74] Yet, despite its more modest ambit, Hart's *Concept of Law* remains, in my view, the most germane contribution to the theory of law-ascertainment in international law. The following paragraphs zero in on the main tenets of Hart's theory of ascertainment.

Hart refined the source thesis by backing away from the command-based concept of law of his predecessors. He followed Kelsen in putting the legal system (instead of the law-making Sovereign) at the centre of his concept of law and subjecting the identification of law to law-ascertaining rules.[75] In doing so, he reinforced the reversal of the dichotomy between law and authority undertaken by Kelsen. However, he stopped short of making these law-ascertaining rules depend on a hypothetical ultimate norm. While strictly abiding by the proposition that the identification of law requires a formal test on the basis of law-ascertaining rules, Hart replaced the hypothetical rule of Kelsen by a social fact, i.e. the practice of law-applying authorities. This *tour de force* has been called the *social thesis* (or the *conventionality thesis*).[76] It is argued here that grounding the ultimate law-ascertaining rule in a social practice constitutes Hart's most important contribution to the theory of law as well as the theory of the sources of international law.[77] The following paragraphs are aimed at explaining the most important aspects of Hart's social thesis.

Hart's theory—as well as his life[78]—are well-known to most legal scholars and it would be of no avail here to repeat or summarize his general concept of law. Moreover, international lawyers, in particular, are very familiar with Hart's concept of law thanks to his systematization of the distinction—previously devised by Jhering[79]—between primary and secondary rules which helped them delineate some of the most important mechanisms on which the international legal system rests.[80] It is thus not necessary to revert here to this dichotomy. Nor is it necessary to

[73] In the same vein, see J. Kammerhofer, *Uncertainty in International Law: A Kelsenian Perspective* (Routledge, London, 2010) 228.

[74] J. Kammerhofer, ibid, pp. 224–30.

[75] On this abiding conceptual question, see S. Shapiro, 'On Hart's Way Out', in J. Coleman (ed), *Hart's Postscript: Essays on the Postscript to 'The Concept of Law'* (OUP, Oxford, 2001) 149, 152–3.

[76] According to Raz, of all these theses, the social thesis is the most fundamental. It is also the one that gave its name to 'positivism' which indicates that the law is 'posited', i.e. that law is made by the activities of human beings: J. Raz, *The Authority of Law: Essays on Law and Morality* (Clarendon, Oxford, 1983) 38.

[77] This is what I have argued elsewhere. See J. d'Aspremont, 'Hart et le positivisme postmoderne' (2009–3) *Revue générale de droit international public* 635–54.

[78] See N. Lacey, *A Life of H.L.A. Hart: The Nightmare and the Noble Dream* (OUP, Oxford, 2004).

[79] The distinction is often traced back to Jhering. For criticism of this distinction, see N. Bobbio, 'Nouvelles réflexions sur les normes primaires et secondaires', in N. Bobbio, *Essais de théorie du droit* (Bruylant/LGDJ, Paris, 1998) 159.

[80] See, for example, the second report on State Responsibility by Roberto Ago, Doc a/CN.4/233, (20 April 1970) *Annuaire de la Commission du droit international*, 1970, vol. II, 178–9, paras 7–11. On the importance of this distinction in the law of State Responsibility and for an attempt at elaborating a taxonomy of primary obligations, see J. Combacau and D. Alland, 'Primary and Secondary Rules in the Law of State Responsibility: Categorizing International Obligations' (1985) NYIL 82–109.

expound here upon the *soft* or *inclusive positivism* endorsed by Hart at the end of his life and according to which nothing prevents rules of recognition to refer to moral criteria to identify the law (the so-called 'incorporation thesis'). This—modest—concession to natural lawyers that morality can be a law-ascertaining criterion has nourished an enormous amount of literature[81] and has even been challenged by some of Hart's followers.[82] This aspect of Hart's theory will only be briefly examined in the next chapter together with the criticisms of formal law-ascertainment.[83] For the sake of the argument made here, I only need to provide a snapshot of some of the most fundamental aspects of Hart's social thesis, for they can help international lawyers to further grasp the foundations of formalism which Hart's predecessors had begun to disentangle.

A preliminary terminological remark must be formulated to avoid any misunderstanding. Hart did not cast his adherence to the source and social theses under the term *formalism*. To him, formalism had a totally different meaning, for it was construed as a theory of adjudicative neutrality and immanent intelligibility of legal arguments, which is probably the dominant understanding of formalism in general legal theory.[84] In that sense, Hart interpreted formalism as a—mistaken—approach aimed at minimizing uncertainty in law-application and maximizing legal certainty and predictability. In Hart's view, formalism was thus the anti-thesis of rule-scepticism or legal realism, which construe law-application as totally indeterminate and which equate law with law-application. Hart uncompromisingly rejected formalism as a theory of adjudicative neutrality and immanent intelligibility of legal arguments, construing it as just as misleading and inaccurate as rule-scepticism. In his view, formalism and rule-scepticism are the 'Scylla and Charybdis of justice theory'.[85] This is why Hart's insightful elaboration of the social and source theses are not to be conflated with Hart's rejection of formalism, a term which he uses to describe a flawed theory of adjudicative neutrality and immanent intelligibility of legal arguments.

To a very large extent, Hart remains an heir of the abovementioned positivist and utilitarian theorists.[86] Bentham's influence on Hart is probably the most

[81] See, for instance, the contributions compiled in the book edited by J. Coleman, *Hart's Postscript: Essays on the Postscript to the Concept of Law* (OUP, Oxford, 2001). See also M. Kramer, *In Defense of Legal Positivism: Law Without Trimmings* (OUP, Oxford, 1999) 199; R.B. Kar, 'Hart's Response to Exclusive Legal Positivism', Loyola Law School, Legal Studies Paper No. 2007–10, February 2007.

[82] J. Raz and S. Shapiro opposed Hart's inclusive legal positivism. See e.g. S. Shapiro, 'On Hart's Way Out' in J. Coleman (ed), *Hart's Postscript: Essays on the Postscript to the Concept of Law* (OUP, Oxford, 2001) 149, 191. W.J. Waluchow and J. Coleman sided with Hart by pursuing his inclusive legal positivist approach. See W.J. Waluchow, *Inclusive Legal Positivism* (Clarendon, Oxford, 1994) especially 80–164; J. Coleman 'Incorporationism, Conventionality and the Practical Difference Thesis' in J. Coleman (ed), *Hart's Postscript: Essays on the Postscript to the Concept of Law* (OUP, Oxford, 2001) 99. See MacCormick's attempt to reconcile exclusive and inclusive legal positivism in MacCormick, *Institutions of Law* (OUP, Oxford, 2009) 263–79.

[83] Cfr *infra* 4.1.1.

[84] On the different meanings of formalism, see *supra* 2.1.

[85] H.L.A. Hart, *The Concept of Law* (2nd edn, OUP, Oxford, 1997) 124–54.

[86] Although Hart's approach is analytical and not historical, the influence of Weber cannot be denied either. The influence of Weber on Hart is reported by N. Lacey, *A Life of H.L.A. Hart: The Nightmare and*

obvious[87] although the influence of others, including Kelsen, cannot be denied.[88] Accordingly, it is no surprise that utilitarian philosophy permeates his conception of formal law-ascertainment, although he sometimes takes distance from it, especially in his work on criminal responsibility and punishment.[89] Like his predecessors, Hart also contends that the problem of immoral laws is not a problem of validity but a problem of obedience and it is, accordingly, up to each individual to make a judgment about the law's moral claim to obedience.[90] While following the utilitarian line of reasoning of his predecessors, Hart, however, clearly rejected their proposition that law is based on a command backed by coercion or sanction. Even if he agrees that law is an expression of will, coercion no longer constitutes a central feature of any legal system, for it is conceivable that a legal system does not need coercive sanctions.[91]

In Hart's view, following Kelsen and contrary to Hobbes, Bentham, and Austin, the legal system precedes the law-making authority. It follows that law is inevitably the result of a law-making process defined by law itself. It is thus the system that ascertains law and not the authority. To identify law, therefore, one needs to look at the law-ascertaining rules (what he calls 'rules of recognition'). Again, as in Kelsen's theory, these law-ascertaining rules must themselves be ascertained as rules of the legal system. There is, however, one important distinction between the theories of Kelsen and Hart on the nature of these law-ascertaining rules from which all secondary rules are derived. While Kelsen sees all secondary rules as having been ultimately validated as rules of the system by a hypothetical Grundnorm, Hart construes the ultimate rule of recognition from which all secondary rules are derived as being grounded in the social practice of the law-applying authorities, who must feel an internal sense of obligation to obey the rules that is quite separate from the threats or rewards they associate with compliance (the so-called internal point of view). In that sense, law exists when there is a community of officials who perceive

the Noble Dream (OUP, Oxford, 2004) 230. It is interesting to note that Hart himself generally dismissed the notion that legal positivism is the logical product of the emergence of a highly organized society as advocated by Weber. For criticism of the non-historical approach of Hart, see N. Lacey, 'Philosophy, Political Morality, and History: Explaining the Enduring Resonance of the Hart-Fuller Debate' (2008) 83 NYULR 1059; D. Dyzenhaus, 'The Grudge Informer Case Revisited' (2008) 89 NYULR 1000.

[87] A clear example is H.L.A. Hart, 'Positivism and the Separation of Law and Morals' (1958) 71(4) Harv. L. Rev. 593–629, 595–97.

[88] According to N. Bobbio, Hart revived Bentham's theories with some subtle Kelsenian transplants: N. Bobbio *Essais de théorie du droit* (Bruylant/LGDJ, Paris, 1998) 56.

[89] See the remarks of N. Lacey in *A Life of H.L.A. Hart: The Nightmare and the Noble Dream* (OUP, Oxford, 2004) 281 and W. Twining in *General Jurisprudence: Understanding Law from a Global Perspective* (CUP, Cambridge, 2009) 149.

[90] This question was the focal point of his famous debate with Fuller in the Harvard Law Review. See in particular H.L.A. Hart, 'Positivism and the Separation of Law and Morals' (1958) 71(4) Harv. L. Rev. 593–629, 618–20. See also H.L.A. Hart, *The Concept of Law* (2nd edn, OUP, Oxford, 1997) 212 (where he criticises Radbruch on that point). This debate has been characterized by Fuller as boiling down to 'who should do the dirty work': L. Fuller, 'Positivism and Fidelity to Law—A Reply to Professor Hart' (1958) 71(4) Harv. L. Rev. 630–72, 649. On this debate, see the symposium in NYU Law Review and especially David Dyzenhaus, 'The Grudge Informer Case Revisited' (2008) 89 NYULR 1000.

[91] H.L.A. Hart, *The Concept of Law* (2nd edn, OUP, Oxford, 1997) 36–8 and 216–20.

the law as having a distinctive authority and when a sufficient number of citizens conform to the primary rules, regardless of their reasons for conforming. For Hart, the reasons why officials abide by the rule of recognition does not matter, so long as they engage in the sort of conduct that bespeaks commitment or supportiveness, which sustains the functioning of the legal system. As a result, the ultimate rule of recognition from which all the rules of the system are derived is neither valid nor invalid. It simply exists (or does not exist) as a matter of social fact.[92]

As will be explained below, this social thesis was rejected by Dworkin who argues, among other things, that rules of recognition must be accepted not only by officials but also by citizens. For Hart, it is implausible that most members of the public in a complex society will grasp and accept the criteria of recognition.[93] This does not mean that obedience by the public is of no relevance at all for Hart. Indeed, Hart acknowledges that (the display of) obedience by the people to the primary rules—irrespective of their motives for abiding by the primary rules—is an important element for the viability of the system as a whole, but he claims that the existence of the legal system itself does not hinge on the obedience of the people.[94]

As the foregoing shows, the so-called *internal point of view* is what allows Hart to ground the law-ascertaining rules in social conventions. It is thus the central tenet of his social thesis.[95] It means that law-applying officials uphold the rules not simply as commonly accepted standards but as common standards for themselves and others. The internal point of view—which was probably not invented by Hart[96]—is another major difference between Kelsen and Hart. Even though both Hart and Kelsen placed validity at the centre of their understandings of law, the test of validity in Kelsen's theory remains carried out from an external point of view, for the Grundnorm, being hypothetical, is not grounded in the system itself but outside it. For Hart, testing validity—and thus the existence of rules—can only be done from an internal perspective, because the law-ascertaining criteria necessarily originate in a practice within the legal system.[97]

Hart's understanding of formal law-ascertainment is essential to the argument made in this book. Indeed, the internal social practice on which Hart's concept of law rests is what makes the emergence of a language of law possible despite law's inevitable indeterminacy. Hart acknowledges that law, because its commands are

[92] See in particular, H.L.A. Hart, ibid, pp. 116–17.

[93] H.L.A. Hart, ibid, pp. 59–60 and 110–11.

[94] On Hart's famous distinction between efficacy and effectiveness of law, see G. Postema, 'Rethinking the Efficacy of Law', in M. Kramer, et al. (eds), *The Legacy of H.L.A. Hart: Legal, Political and Moral Philosophy* (OUP, Oxford, 2008) 45, 47.

[95] For further discussion on the internal point of view see MacCormick, cited in J. Finnis, 'On Hart's Ways: Law as Reason and as Fact', in M. Kramer, et al. (eds), ibid, 3, 12. For criticisms of the internal perspective, see 3–25. See also R.B. Kar, who argued that Hart's theory must be refined by adding the reference to the second-person standpoint in order to reconcile Hart, Shapiro, and Dworkin: R.B. Kar, 'Hart's Response to Exclusive Legal Positivism' (2007) 95 Geo. L. J. 393, and Loyola-LA Legal Studies Paper No. 2007–10.

[96] See U. Scarpelli, *Qu'est-ce que le positivisme juridique* (Bruylant/LGDJ, Paris, 1996) 38.

[97] This is the interpreation of U. Scarpelli, ibid, pp. 35–45.

conveyed through words, is fundamentally indeterminate.[98] So too are the rules of recognition.[99] Hart, in that sense, follows Bentham, for he rejects any Aristotelian proposition of the existence of an inner meaning of words, including for the standardization of rules of recognition. For Hart, the meaning of words is thus not already given but is found in the internal social practice. He contends that, to know the meaning of words, we must look at concepts when they are at work. Social practice thus provides the meaning of the words upon which the language of law is based. This manifestation of the social thesis has been called the *semantic thesis.*[100] Rules are thus ascertained by a practice conceived in terms of convergent behaviours and agreements in judgments among law-applying authorities.[101]

Because Hart believes that the meaning of law, and especially the meaning of the rule of recognition, must be inferred from the social conventions among the law-applying authorities, Hart's social thesis is probably the most elaborated doctrine in support of formal law-ascertainment. Formal law-ascertainment, which is necessary to ascertain what the law is and what it means, is grounded in the social practice of law-making officials. By grounding law in social practice, Hart makes the argument that law can be a meaningful normative language only if lawyers and law-applying authorities share the same law-ascertaining criteria. If they disagree about the criteria for the identification of law, they are effectively speaking different languages, which in turn deprives law of is normative character.

It is important to note once again that Hart does not claim that his social thesis completely eliminates the indeterminacy of law. Social practice, itself, is beset by ambiguities and will not always substantiate the meaning of rules. However, for Hart, what is required is not that law be fully determinate; Hart's social thesis accommodates some unavoidable uncertainty. According to Hart, a legal system simply needs sufficiently clear formal law-ascertainment standards. The internal social practice usually provides such elementary yardsticks to make law normative.[102]

It is no secret that Hart's social thesis—and the proposition that the meaning of words, and hence the meaning of rules, must be acquired by looking at how words are ordinarily used—is derived from the philosophy of language, and especially that of Wittgenstein.[103] Even though the real benefit of Hart's forays into Wittgenstein's

[98] It has been argued that Hart only restricted indeterminacy to problems of vagueness and ignored problems of ambiguity. On this point as well as the work of Michael Thaler on the distinction between vagueness (denotation) and ambiguity (connotation), see J. Kammerhofer, *Uncertainty in International Law: A Kelsenian Perspective* (Routledge, London, 2010) 118.

[99] H.L.A. Hart, *The Concept of Law* (2nd edn, OUP, Oxford, 1997) 144–50.

[100] J. Raz, *The Authority of Law: Essays on Law and Morality* (Clarendon, Oxford, 1983) 37.

[101] H.L.A. Hart, 'Jhering's Heaven of Concepts and Modern Analytical Jurisprudence', reproduced in H.L.A. Hart, *Essays in Jurisprudence and Philosophy* (Clarendon, Oxford, 1983) 265, 277.

[102] '[Dworkin's] criticism of soft positivism seems to . . . exaggerate both the degree of certainty which a consistent positivist must attribute to a body of legal standards and the uncertainty that will result if the criteria of legal validity include conformity with specific moral principles or values . . . .[T]he exclusion of all uncertainty at whatever costs in other values is not a goal which I have ever envisaged for the rule of recognition': H.L.A. Hart, *The Concept of Law* (2nd edn, OUP, Oxford, 1997) 251.

[103] See e.g. H.L.A. Hart, 'Jhering's Heaven of Concepts and Modern Analytical Jurisprudence', reproduced in H.L.A. Hart, *Essays in Jurisprudence and Philosophy*, (Clarendon, Oxford, 1983) 265,

philosophies should probably not be exaggerated,[104] Hart has usefully borrowed from the explanations of the origins of linguistic conventions provided by the philosophers of language. The argument made in this book will, to a large extent, follow the line of Hart's social thesis and, hence, draw upon the philosophy of language. It will be proven that Hart, despite his disappointing and unconvincing portrayal of international law as a very primitive set of rules, still provides most of the key elements to revisit the ontology of formal law-ascertainment in contemporary international law.

While Hart's social thesis is decisive in understanding the foundations of formal law-ascertainment, one must acknowledge that Hart's theory suffers from some weaknesses that prevent it from constituting a self-sufficient and unassailable justification of formal law-ascertainment. In particular, Hart failed to elaborate on the amount and the type of practice which is necessary for it to crystallize into a social law-ascertaining convention.[105] He did not explain how social conventions work and form themselves, including the extent to which the social position of law-applying authority determines social practice.[106] Likewise, devised on the model of domestic law, Hart's picture does not capture all the contemporary complexities of other legal systems.[107] Most significantly Hart did not identify the political foundations of his model of formal law-ascertainment. He made a very subtle and convincing plea for formal law-ascertainment but failed to spell out why such a blueprint should be preferred to any other. It is as if Hart did not deem it necessary to defend the external cogency of his understanding of formal law-ascertainment. It can be extrapolated from this that Hart probably thought that the utilitarian philosophy provided sufficient explanation as to the desirability of that conceptualization.[108] However, given the disrepute of utilitarianism among some theorists,[109] and especially in Kantian theory,[110] more was needed to convincingly buttress his social thesis.

271. On Wittgenstein's influence on Hart, see generally N. Stavropoulos, 'Hart's Semantics', in J. Coleman (ed), *Hart's Postscript: Essays on the Postscript to 'The Concept of Law'* (OUP, Oxford, 2001) 59, 86. The influence of Wittgenstein on Hart has been qualified by N. Lacey, *A Life of H.L.A. Hart: The Nightmare and the Noble Dream* (OUP, Oxford, 2004) 218–21.

[104] According to J. Raz, very little seems to have been gained in all of Hart's forays into the philosophy of language: J. Raz, 'The Nature and Theory of Law' in J. Coleman (ed), *Hart's Postscript: Essays on the Postscript to 'The Concept of Law'* (OUP, Oxford, 2001) 1, 6. Endicott has gone even further by claiming that there is no semantic theory in Hart's work and that it is incorrect to think that Hart relied on Wittgenstein. See T. Endicott, 'Herbert Hart and the Semantic Sting' in J. Coleman (ed), ibid, 41.

[105] Such a criticism was made by J. Raz, *The Authority of Law: Essays on Law and Morality* (Clarendon, Oxford, 1983) 92 as well as by N. Stavropoulos in J. Coleman (ed), ibid, 72.

[106] The same can be said of most of Hart's followers. See A. Somek, 'The Spirit of Legal Positivism' (2011) 12 *German Law Journal* 729, 742–743.

[107] W. Twining, *General Jurisprudence: Understanding Law from a Global Perspective*, (CUP, Cambridge, 2009) 12.

[108] In his 1957 Harvard Law Review article, Hart simply referred to utilitarian theories of ethics developed by utilitarians like Bentham.

[109] For a criticism of utilitarianism in law, see P. Soper, 'Law's Normative Claims', in R.P. George (ed), *The Autonomy of Law: Essays of Legal Positivism* (OUP, Oxford, 1996) 215, 215.

[110] The most modern Kantian critique of utilitarianism has been devised by J. Rawls, who argues that utilitarianism is inconsistent with the principles of justice as fairness. See W. Twining, *General Jurisprudence: Understanding Law from a Global Perspective* (CUP, Cambridge, 2009) 155.

3.1.4 Formal law-ascertainment after Hart

Advocates of formal law-ascertainment after Hart have not brought about any radical deviations from Hart's conception of law-ascertainment. Hart's followers have mostly been concerned with explaining, purifying, or qualifying Hart's theory. Yet, they certainly introduced welcome refinements and brought Hart's concept of law to a higher level of subtlety. It would be of no use to comprehensively report all their additions to and refinements of Hart's concept of law. Many of them are only of significance if applied in domestic legal systems and it would not make much sense to mechanically transpose them into the international legal system. Accordingly, only the insights formulated by Hart's followers that prove instrumental in the revitalization of formal law-ascertainment in the theory of the sources of international law are mentioned here.

Joseph Raz is probably the most-discussed advocate of formal law-ascertainment after Hart. It is well-known that, while spending a great deal of time explaining and sharpening Hart's theory, Raz backed away from Hart's inclusive positivism.[111] He also tried to substantiate the social thesis because he perceived the claim that the identification of law is a matter of social fact as still leaving open the question of whether or not those social facts on which rules of recognition are based do or do not endow it with moral merit.[112] The latter raises the question—unanswered by Hart—of the authority of law, which proved a central theme of Raz's theory and which led him to elaborate on the substantive features that a legal system must possess to have moral authority.[113] In doing so, Raz probably provides a conception of the legal system which is more elaborate and subtle than that of Hart.[114]

Although that does not bring about a radical change in the understanding of law-ascertainment, Raz's conception of the legal system departs from that of Hart because he argues that there are other types of laws than primary norms—what he calls duty-imposing laws—and secondary norms—which Raz construes as power-conferring laws, citing in particular what he calls laws instituting rights, categorizing

[111] Raz's exclusive legal positivism is well-explained in J. Raz, 'Legal Positivism and the Sources of Law', in *The Authority of Law: Essays on Law and Morality* (Clarendon, Oxford, 1983) 37–52. See remarks on Raz's exclusive positivism by M. Kramer *In Defense of Legal Positivism: Law Without Trimmings* (OUP, Oxford, 1999) 197–8. See the criticisms of Raz's exclusive legal positivism by K.E. Himma, 'The Instantiation Thesis and Raz's Critique of Inclusive Positivism' (Jan 2001) 20(1) *Law and Philosophy* 61–79; K.E. Himma, 'Bringing Hart and Raz to the Table: Coleman's compatibility thesis' (2001) 21 OJLS 609–27. See also the criticisms by J. Coleman, 'Authority and Reason', in R.P. George (ed), *The Autonomy of Law: Essays of Legal Positivism* (OUP, Oxford, 1996), 287, 288.

[112] J. Raz, *Practical Reason and Norms* (OUP, Oxford, 1975) 162 and J. Raz, 'Legal Validity' in J. Raz *The Authority of Law: Essays on Law and Morality* (Clarendon, Oxford, 1983) 146–62.

[113] See generally, J. Raz, *The Authority of Law: Essays on Law and Morality* (Clarendon, Oxford, 1983). On Raz's theory of the authority of law, see generally, T. May, 'On Raz and the Obligations to Obey Law' (1997) 16 *Law and Philosophy* 19–36.

[114] On the institutional character of a legal system, see J. Raz, ibid, 88. On the institutional positivism developed by Hart, see S. Coyle, 'Hart, Raz and the Concept of a Legal System' (2002) 21 *Law and Philosophy* 275–304.

rules, or rules of scopes.[115] Raz also contends that laws of the system belong to the system not because of this rule of recognition but because they are all recognized by the primary organs.[116] Raz attempts to address the issue caused by Hart's absence of standards by which to determine who administers the secondary rules, i.e. who qualifies as legal officials, which allegedly makes it impossible to distinguish law from non-institutionalized forms of normative order. Raz, accordingly, elaborates on the three features which characterize legal systems: comprehensiveness, supremacy over other institutionalized normative systems, and openness.[117] These features are well-known and have been intensively discussed in the literature. Their relevance to the theory of the sources of international law, however, is not certain. More interestingly for our purposes, Raz saw Hart's social thesis as the 'strong social thesis', because he interpreted Hart as having claimed that the existence and content of every law is fully determined by social sources.[118] This interpretation is not without importance, as I will illustrate below.[119] Beyond this, Raz's institutional conception of law proves too restricted to domestic legal systems and, in my view, it would be superfluous to dwell upon it here.

The same can be said about Neil MacCormick, who remained, despite calling himself a 'post-positivist'[120], a follower of Hart's conception of law.[121] Although he proffered the opinion that Hart's theory leaves 'much unfinished business',[122] MacCormick did not radically flesh out Hart's social thesis. His interests lay elsewhere, especially in the institutional dimensions of law. In that sense, MacCormick's understanding of law—although it rests on a rejection of Raz's exclusive legal positivism[123]—bears some resemblance to Raz's work, for MacCormick contends that the law speaks through institutional agencies and that these agencies speak with authority.[124] It is interesting to note that MacCormick distanced himself from Hart's social thesis when he adopted Martin Krygier's criticism[125] of its 'internal point of view', for the latter fails to distinguish between rules and habits.[126]

[115] J. Raz, *The Concept of a Legal System* (2nd edn, OUP, Oxford, 1980) 224.

[116] J. Raz, *The Authority of Law: Essays on Law and Morality* (Clarendon, Oxford, 1983) 200.

[117] J. Raz, ibid, p. 121. For a criticism of these three elements, see B. Tamanaha, *A General Jurisprudence of Law and Society* (OUP, Oxford, 2001) 139–41.

[118] J. Raz, ibid, p. 46. See also J. Raz, 'The Institutional Nature of Law' in J. Raz, ibid, 103.

[119] Cfr *infra* chapter 8.

[120] On this point see K. Pretroski, 'Is Post-Positivism Possible' (2011) 12 *German Law Journal* 663; H. M. De Jong and W.W. Werner, 'Continuity and Change in Legal Positivism (1998) 17 *Law & Philosophy* 233, 249. See *contra* T. Bustamante, 'Comment on Petroski—On MacCormick's Post-Positivism' (2011) 12 *German Law Journal* 693.

[121] N. MacCormick, *Institutions of Law: An Essay in Legal Theory* (OUP, Oxford, 2008) 278–9.

[122] N. MacCormick, 'The Concept of Law and the Concept of Law' in R.P. George (ed), *The Autonomy of Law: Essays of Legal Positivism* (OUP, Oxford, 1996) 163, 191.

[123] N. MacCormick, *Institutions of Law. An Essay in Legal Theory* (OUP, Oxford, 2008) 263–77.

[124] N. MacCormick, 'The Concept of Law and the Concept of Law' in R.P. George (ed), *The Autonomy of Law: Essays of Legal Positivism* (OUP, Oxford, 1996) 163, 170. For MacCormick, 'The rule of recognition presupposes the existence of judges. But if the rule of recognition is necessary to validate the rule of adjudication, we are in a logically vicious circle': N. MacCormick, 'The Concept of Law and the Concept of Law' in R.P. George (ed), ibid, 179.

[125] M. Krygier, 'The Concept of Law and Social Theory' (1982) 2 OJLS 2.

[126] N. MacCormick, *Institutions of Law: An Essay in Legal Theory* (OUP, Oxford, 2008) 62.

MacCormick's recent work also reflects a departure from Hart's source thesis, for the former provides a definition of law based on the perspective of the rule-user, rather than the rule-maker. His shift to norm-using from norm-giving constitutes the key of his institutional theory of law which aims at providing a more intelligible account of elaborate bodies of norms.[127] Interestingly, the move away from the source thesis in MacCormick's works is, nonetheless, accompanied by an attempt to formalize effect- (or impact-)based ascertainment models.[128] The attempts to formalize effect- (or impact-)based conceptions of law-ascertainment will be discussed below.[129]

Jules Coleman—who is probably Hart's most loyal disciple—undertook to reconcile Hart with some of his critics.[130] In doing so, he tried to refine Hart's inclusive positivism[131] and elaborate on the social thesis—in particular expounding upon the idea that law is an inter-subjective practice wherein participants coordinate their behaviour through the use of a grammar[132]—while at the same time rejecting Hart's justification for the separation between law and morality.[133]

Hart's concept of law, and law-ascertainment, is also perpetuated by Brian Tamanaha[134] and William Twining,[135] although in slightly different manners. These two authors have also attempted to revitalize and refine Hart's source and social theses.[136] Their contribution is quite essential and noteworthy, for they have

[127] N. MacCormick, ibid, 245.

[128] N. MacCormick, ibid, 39–60.

[129] Cfr *infra* 5.1.

[130] J. Coleman, 'Negative and Positive Positivism', reproduced in D. Patterson, *An Anthology of Philosophy of Law and Legal* Theory (Blackwell, Oxford, 2003) 116.

[131] Coleman deems his 'incorporationist' thesis as lying somewhere between the exclusive legal positivism of Raz and the interpretivism of Dworkin. See J. Coleman, 'Authority and Reason', in R.P. George (ed), *The Autonomy of Law: Essays of Legal Positivism* (OUP, Oxford, 1996) 287, 288. One of Coleman's strongest arguments in favour of inclusive legal positivism is his idea that the rules of recognition, being directed at officials and not at citizens, are rules of validation and not rules of identification. Such a finding leads Coleman to reject exclusive legal positivism, for nothing precludes rules of validation from prescribing that some moral principles are law—which is not conceivable in the case of rules of identification. See J. Coleman, 'Authority and Reason', in R.P. George (ed), ibid, 292.

[132] J. Coleman, *The Practice of Principle* (OUP, Oxford, 2001) 99. On this aspect of Coleman's work, see A. Somek, 'The Spirit of Legal Positivism' (2011) 12 *German Law Journal* 729.

[133] The separability thesis is the claim that there is at least one conceivable form of recognition (and therefore one possible legal system) that does not specify truth as a moral principle among the truth conditions for any proposition of law. Consequently, a particular rule of recognition may specify truth as a moral principle as a truth condition for some or all propositions of law without violating the separability thesis, since it does not follow from the fact that, in one community, in order to be law a norm must be a principle of morality: being a true principle of morality is a necessary condition of legality in all possible legal systems: J. Coleman, 'Negative and Positive Positivism', reproduced in D. Patterson, *An Anthology of Philosophy of Law and Legal* Theory (Blackwell, Oxford, 2003) 118. See also the remarks by J. von Bernstorff and T. Dunlap, *The Public International Law Theory of Hans Kelsen—Believing in Universal Law* (CUP, Cambridge, 2010) 250–5.

[134] See B. Tamanaha, *A General Jurisprudence of Law and Society* (OUP, Oxford, 2001); B. Tamanaha, 'The Contemporary Relevance of Legal Positivism', St John's University School of Law, Legal Studies Research Paper Series, Paper #07-0065, January 2007.

[135] Twining acknowledges that he has himself been very widely influenced by Tamanaha. See W. Twining in *General Jurisprudence: Understanding Law from a Global Perspective* (CUP, Cambridge, 2009) 94–5.

[136] B. Tamanaha, *A General Jurisprudence of Law and Society* (OUP, Oxford, 2001) 167.

pruned Hart's theory of some debilitating and hidden limitations, in particular the elements that necessarily exclude actors other than State officials from the source thesis and which were only applicable to State law and Western domestic societies.[137] In doing so, they have tried to amend Hart's source thesis to accommodate a wider range of contemporary phenomena, most notably non-State law.

In particular, Brian Tamanaha, in his famous *General Jurisprudence of Law and Society*,[138] defends a reconstruction of some of the main postulates of legal positivism under what he calls 'socio-legal positivism'.[139] While his socio-legal positivism still abides by the necessity of law-ascertaining criteria, he faults Hart's theory for failing to establish in precise terms who administers the secondary rules, i.e. who qualifies as a legal official, which, as a result, allegedly makes it impossible to distinguish law from non-institutionalized forms of normative order.[140] It raised a 'chicken and egg' problem in that Hart's understanding of law seems to presuppose the anteriority of secondary rules identifying legal officials who thereafter generate the rules of recognition.[141] The refinement advocated by Tamanaha boils down to considering that a 'legal official' is 'whomever, as a matter of social practice, members of the group (including legal officials themselves) identify and treat as "legal officials"'.[142] The social practice on which the rule of recognition is based must, accordingly, not be restricted to strictly-defined law-applying officials but must include a wide variety of social actors.[143] Tamanaha's socio-legal positivism thus conditions the existence of a legal system on the production and reproduction of secondary rules by broadly defined legal actors and, correlatively, enlarges the social thesis. Tamanaha is also critical of Hart's concept of acceptance of the secondary rules by legal officials. To him, some agreement in the social practices of legal officials suffices, irrespective of their attitudes towards the secondary rules of recognition and whether or not they accept them.[144] As will be shown below, these various insights will have a particular echo in the revitalization of formal law-ascertainment that is undertaken here.[145]

Mention must also be made of Dennis Patterson. Like Raz, MacCormick, and Coleman, Dennis Patterson also followed Hart's social thesis. Patterson focused particularly on the influence of Wittgenstein's philosophy of language on the social thesis and, on that occasion, offered one of the clearest accounts of the social thesis and of its foundations.[146] Patterson's clarifications on one of the most fundamental aspects of Hart's (and hence Wittgenstein's) theory have constituted a welcome contribution to the legal theory and have been conducive to the dissemination of a better understanding of formalism at the level of law-ascertainment.[147]

[137] See B. Tamanaha, ibid, 133, 150. [138] B. Tamanaha, ibid.
[139] B. Tamanaha, ibid, chapter 6, 132. [140] B. Tamanaha, ibid, p. 139.
[141] B. Tamanaha, ibid, 141. [142] B. Tamanaha, ibid, 142.
[143] B. Tamanaha, ibid, 159–66. [144] B. Tamanaha, ibid, 153–4. [145] Cfr *infra* chapter 8.
[146] D. Patterson, 'Wittgenstein and Constitutional Theory' (1993–1994) 72 Tex. L. Rev. 1837; D. Patterson, 'Wittgenstein on Understanding and Interpretation' (2006) 29 *Philosophical Investigations* 129–39; D. Patterson, 'Interpretation of Law' (2005) 42 San Diego L. Rev. 685.
[147] D. Patterson has also relied on Wittgenstein's communitarian semantics to defend objectivism in legal argumentation, see D. Patterson, 'Normativity and Objectivity in Law' (2001) 43 Wm. & Mary L.

Outside Anglo-Saxon circles and especially in continental Europe, Hart has also continued to wield considerable influence and his theory has been subject to refinements as well. The European scholar who spent the greatest deal of time explaining and promoting Hart's theses was most likely Norberto Bobbio. Bobbio, like Hart, conditioned the existence of law on the existence of law-ascertaining criteria which are conceivable without a legal system.[148] It is true that Bobbio did not much dwell upon the social thesis and the idea that the meaning of words stems from a social practice. However, he did help demonstrate that the source thesis should not be construed as an ideology from which is classically derived a moral duty to obey law,[149] or as a set of sub-theories pertaining to interpretation, jurisdiction, completeness of the legal order, role of interpreters, etc. Furthermore, he also pointed to an understanding of the source thesis as a method with which to approach law and construct legal arguments.[150] In stressing that the source thesis is a method, Bobbio convincingly shows that the positivist approaches, based on the source thesis, are only some of the many different manners in which the indeterminacy of law can be domesticated. Bobbio did not deny that choosing to apprehend law on the basis of the source thesis is not a neutral choice: it is a political decision about how one approaches law.

Because Bobbio saw the source thesis as being only one approach among others, he, more so than Hart, felt the need to explain why such an understanding of the source thesis should be preferred. Bobbio's writing about the justification of the source thesis is more explicit than that of Hart. Like Hart, Bobbio defended the adoption of the source thesis to allow a distinction between law-identification and law-evaluation,[151] but Bobbio also made it very clear that the source thesis is a method that enables law to be a language. As such, it is a tool which has no other definite political purpose other than to allow the lawmaker to modify the judgment of its addressees. Like Hart, Bobbio—although he explained it more convincingly—thus shared the ambition to preserve the normative character of law, i.e. its ability to stipulate directives and, hence, to influence the behaviour of its addressees.[152] In construing law as a language used by the lawmaker to modify the behaviour of those subjected to it, Bobbio usefully showed that, as a method, the source thesis

Rev. 325. It has been explained in chapter 2 that the argument made here is irrespective of formalism in legal argumentation. See *infra* 2.1.2.

[148] N. Bobbio *Essais de théorie du droit* (Bruylant/LGDJ, Paris, 1998) 12.

[149] This aspect of positivism is probably one that has been the most subject to criticism. For an example of that aspect of positivism, see B. Kingsbury, 'Legal Positivism as Normative Politics: International Society, Balance of Power and Lassa Oppenheim's Positive International Law' (2002) 13(2) EJIL 401–37.

[150] N. Bobbio, *Essais de théorie du droit* (Bruylant/LGDJ, Paris, 1998) 23–53. See also N. Bobbio and D. Zolo, 'Hans Kelsen, the Theory of Law and the International Legal System: A Talk' (1998) 9 EJIL 355–67, 359–60. A similar understanding of positivism as a method can be found in M. Kramer, *In Defense of Legal Positivism: Law Without Trimmings* (OUP, Oxford, 1999) 182.

[151] N. Bobbio, *Essais de théorie du droit* (Bruylant/LGDJ, Paris, 1998) 38.

[152] N. Bobbio, ibid, pp. 39–53. Similar criticisms against positivism as an ideology have been raised by Uberto Scarpelli, *Qu'est-ce que le positivisme juridique* (Bruylant/LGDJ, Paris, 1996) 1.

entails that rules are necessarily prescriptive and not descriptive. They are not value-judgements. They are commands which aim at modifying the behaviour of those subjected to them. From the vantage point of the legal system, they can neither be right nor wrong. As a result, in Bobbio's view, legal scholarship should only be about the study of this language and the clarification of the meaning of its commands.[153]

As can be inferred from the foregoing, Hart's legacy is inestimable. In particular, his supplementation of the source thesis (i.e. the idea that law is identified through its pedigree) with a social thesis (i.e. the idea that the meaning of law-ascertaining criteria is found in a social practice) has proved fundamental in understanding formal law-ascertainment. The above brief outline of the work of some of his followers shows that general legal theory remains deeply influenced by Hart's findings. The refinements that have been floated by some such followers have proved very insightful and inform the rejuvenation of formalism in international law undertaken here. It is now the aim of the next section to gauge the extent to which, and how, the debates about formal law-ascertainment have infused the theory of the sources of international law.

3.2 Formal Law-Ascertainment in the Theory of the Sources of International Law

It is not difficult to understand how the source and social theses, although devised in the context of domestic law, can potentially provide sound foundations for formal law-ascertainment in international law. Applied to international law, the source thesis provides that a rule is an international legal rule if it can be identified as such on the basis of the law-ascertainment criteria prescribed by the international legal system. The social thesis, in turn, postulates that law-ascertaining criteria are the result of a social practice of those applying and making international law. This section will show that, while formal law-ascertainment for the sake of law-identification has been gradually embraced in mainstream international legal scholarship, very few scholars have actually ventured into exploring the ontology of the source thesis in the particular context of international law. The following paragraphs will more specifically depict how formal law-ascertainment emerged as the mainstream law-identification process in international legal scholarship without being buttressed by strong theoretical justifications. A distinction is drawn between modern and classical theory of the sources of international law on the one hand (3.2.1) and the theory of the 20th and 21st centuries on the other (3.2.2). A word must also be said about a specific strand of the contemporary international legal scholarship. Indeed, the second half of the 20th century has experienced the consolidation of constitutionalist approaches to international law. Nowadays, this theory thrives and enjoys a great deal of support among international legal scholars. Because constitutionalist theory still adheres to the source thesis—albeit for different reasons than simply for

[153] N. Bobbio, *Essais de théorie du droit* (Bruylant/LGDJ, Paris, 1998) 2–3.

law-identification, this specific understanding of law will be examined in a separate section (3.2.3).

3.2.1 Modern and classical theories of sources of international law

Although international law existed—in various forms—long before scholastic theory[154] and it has been proven that treaties were concluded before the emergence of a systematized concept of international law,[155] international law as a complete system of rules first emerged as a product of scholastic thought.[156] It is commonly argued that it was Grotius who decisively contributed to the severance of the theory of international law from its scholastic theological origins and envisaged the existence of voluntary law.[157] According to this reading, the consensual dimension of Grotius' theory allowed it to provide a theoretical explanatory framework for the settlement of the Thirty Years' War and the Peace of Westphalia.[158] Grotius, however, remained attached to a natural law tradition by adopting a hybrid conception of international law, whereby the validity of voluntary law still remained subject to substantive criteria provided by natural law.

It took another century and a half before the theory of the sources of international law could move away from models of substantive validity.[159] Indeed, the premodern theory of international law remained dominated by naturalist scholars in the tradition of Hugo Grotius—exemplified by Samuel Pufendorf[160] and subsequently by Christian von Wolff, who borrowed from Aristotelian theory.[161] Even though, among these naturalist scholars, very few denied the existence of a separate body of voluntary law and all proved instrumental in the subsequent emergence of an

[154] D.J. Bederman, *International Law in Antiquity* (CUP, Cambridge, 2001). On ancient international law, see also D.J. Bederman, 'International Law in the Ancient World' in D. Armstrong (ed), *Routledge Handbook of International Law* (Routledge, London, 2009) 115–25.

[155] P. Allott, 'The Concept of International Law' (1999) 10 EJIL 31, 42.

[156] F. de Vitoria, *Political Writings*, A. Pagden and J. Lawrance (eds) (CUP, Cambridge, 1991); A. Gentili, *On the Law of War* (Clarendon, Oxford, 1933). On Gentili, see generally B. Kingsbury and B. Straumann (eds), *The Roman Foundations of the Law of Nations* (OUP, 2011).

[157] On the contribution of Grotius, see generally Asser Instituut, *International Law and the Grotian Heritage* (T.M.C. Asser Instituut, The Hague, 1985). See also E. Jouannet, *Emer de Vattel et l'émergence doctrinale du droit international classique* (Pedone, Paris, 1998) 350. For a different reading of Grotius and some support for the idea that Grotius simply continued the Spanish scholasticism, see W.G. Grewe, *The Epochs of International Law* (De Gruyter, Berlin, 2000) 192–93.

[158] See M.W. Janis, 'Sovereignty and International Law, Hobbes and Grotius', in R.St J. Macdonald (eds), *Essays in Honour of Wang Tieya* (Martinus Nijhoff, The Hague, 1993) 391–400, 399.

[159] An interesting account of this severance from natural law theories is provided by 'Les origines de la notion autonome du droit des gens', in F.M. van Asbect et al., *Symbolae Verzijl: présentées au professeur J.H.W. Verzijl à l'occasion de son LXX-ième anniversaire* (Martinus Nijhoff, The Hague, 1958) 177–89.

[160] S. Pufendorf, *On the Law of Nature and of Nations* (Clarendon, Oxford, 1934, originally 1672). See the comments by E. Jouannet, *Emer de Vattel et l'émergence doctrinale du droit international classique* (Pedone, Paris, 1998) 361.

[161] For an English translation of one part of Wolff's work, see C. Wolff, *Law of Nations Treated According to A Scientific Method* (Clarendon, Oxford, 1934).

autonomisation of international law from natural law,[162] they however continued to infer voluntary law from natural law.[163]

The 1758 work of Emmerich de Vattel,[164] while being inevitably influenced by the conceptions of his predecessors,[165] constituted a significant move away from the dualism of pre-modern scholars. Vattel produced the first systematic international law treatise of the modern kind, conceived as a handbook for lawyers and statesmen. This Polish diplomat of Swiss origin, who translated the work of von Wolff and enriched political and diplomatic practice, transformed von Wolff's philosophical system into the language of diplomatic practice.[166] Vattel elevated voluntary law to the central kingship of international law, only resorting incidentally to natural law when appropriate. In a manner very reminiscent of Hobbes,[167] he completely purged international law of Christian morality and stripped the work of his predecessors of any utopian paradigm, for he relied on State practice. Vattel did not, however, deny the existence of divine natural law but refrained from generalizing its application and re-modelled it so as to reflect the practice of inter-State relations. In Vattel's view, the role of natural law is confined to the freedom—derived from natural law—of States to do anything that dovetails with their self-interests.[168]

In 1785, Georg Friedrich de Martens departed more radically from natural law tradition than Vattel[169] and ignited a tradition of international law based on its systematic presentation in treaty and custom.[170] However, like Vattel, he failed to formalize law-ascertainment. This being said, Martens' work bolstered Vattel's move away from substantive validity and contributed to the durable entrenchment of voluntarism in the theory of the sources of international law.

It is not the place to discuss the consistency and the objectivity of the legal arguments upon which the systematizations of these scholars were based.[171] For

[162] For the remarkable account of the diverging interpretations which have been made of their contribution to the autonomisation of international law, see E. Jouannet, *Emer de Vattel et l'émergence doctrinale du droit international classique* (Pedone, Paris, 1998) 343.

[163] See N. Onuf, 'Civitas Maxima: Wolff, Vattel and the Fate of Republicanism' (1994) 88 AJIL 280.

[164] E. de Vattel, *The Law of Nations* (Carnegie Institution of Washington, Washington DC, 1916, first published 1758). See the work of E. Jouannet, *Emer de Vattel et l'émergence doctrinale du droit international classique* (Pedone, Paris, 1998). See also the remarks by N. Onuf, ibid, 283.

[165] On the continuity between Wolff and Vattel, see E. Jouannet, ibid, pp. 403–8.

[166] Explained by Stefan Oeter, 'The German Influence on Public International Law', in Société Française pour le Droit International, *Droit International et diversité juridique, Journée franco-allemande* (Pedone, Paris, 2008) 33–4.

[167] This resemblance is also highlighted by E. Jouannet, *Emer de Vattel et l'émergence doctrinale du droit international classique* (Pedone, Paris, 1998) 423. On Hobbes, cfr *supra* 3.1.2.

[168] E. de Vattel, *The Law of Nations* (Carnegie Institution of Washington, Washington DC, 1916).

[169] G.F. De Martens, *Primae lineae iuris gentium Europaearum practici in usum auditorum adumbratae* (Johann Christian Dieterich, Göttingen, 1785). On Georg Friedrich von Martens, see generally M. Koskenniemi, 'Into Positivism: Georg Friedrich von Martens (1756–1821)' (2008) 15 *Constellations* 189–207.

[170] On the changes in the scholarship following Martens, see E. Keene, 'The Age of Grotius', in D. Armstrong, *Routledge Handbook of International Law* (Routledge, London, 2009) 126, 129.

[171] See W. Grewe, *The Epochs of International Law* (De Gruyter, Berlin, 2000); N. Onuf, 'Civitas Maxima: Wolff, Vattel and the Fate of Republicanism' (1994) 88 AJIL 280; M. Koskenniemi, *The Gentle Civilizer of Nations: The Rise and Fall of International Law 1870–1960* (CUP, Cambridge, 2002);

the purposes of the argument made here, it is only required to stress that, while in von Wolff's understanding law-identification, despite a preliminary autonomisation, remains predominantly dependant upon substantive validity, in Vattel's and Martens' systems, by contrast, law-ascertainment boils down to identifying the will of States. Notwithstanding the apologetic overtones of such a voluntarist conception of international law, this surely is a major step away from substantive validity. It is not yet the embrace of formal law-ascertainment, however. Indeed, their theory still lacks a source thesis since identification of the law is completely dependant on the subjective will of States, which is not captured in formal terms. Formalism, as it is understood here, was thus absent from Vattel's theory.

Despite the impact of Vattel's and Martens' voluntarism on legal scholarship, it must be pointed out that von Wolff's dualism did not completely vanish as a result and references to reason or natural law continued to infuse the conceptions of international law in the first part of the 19th century.[172] Nevertheless, under the influence of Vattel and Martens, natural law and reason became demoted to a secondary parameter. This is well-illustrated by the famous treatises of Henry Wheaton[173] and Robert Phillimore[174] who, although they grounded law in reason, natural law, or the will of God, still identified law through State's consent as reflected in practice. The same can also be said of Theodore Woolsey.[175]

It is fair to contend that, subject to a few exceptions,[176] the great majority of 19th century international legal scholars—at least according to the image of that period that we have inherited[177]—strove to rein in the speculative character of natural law approaches by gradually coming to adhere to a fully-fledged voluntary conception of law—which required some law-ascertainment indicators. Yet, despite the 19th century having been classically portrayed as formal,[178] the theory of the sources of international law designed at that time fell short of any formal law-ascertainment mechanism, for the capture of that will through formal standards remained unfathomable. In other words, legal scholars of the 19th century elevated the will of the State to the only 'objective validator'[179] of international law, but failed to carve formal criteria with which to capture it.

A. Nussbaum, *A Concise History of the Law of Nations* (Revised edn, MacMillan, NY, 1954). For a discussion about the tensions between the utopian and apologist aspects of these classicists' theories, see M. Koskenniemi, *From Apology to Utopia* (CUP, Cambridge, 2005) 108–22.

[172] See the account of the remnants of natural law theories in the 19th century scholarship made by C. Rousseau, *Principes généraux du droit international public*, tome 1 (Pedone, Paris, 1944) 24–5. See also W.G. Grewe, *The Epochs of International Law* (De Gruyter, Berlin, 2000) 501–12.

[173] H. Wheaton, *Elements of International Law* (1836).

[174] R. Phillimore, *Commentaries upon International Law*, 4 vols, (AG Benning, London, 1854–61).

[175] T.D. Woolsey, *Introduction to the Study of International Law* (4th edn, Scribner, Armstrong & Co, New York, 1877).

[176] See e.g. J. Lorimer, *Principes de Droit International* (C. Muquardt, Brussels 1884) 19–29.

[177] See generally, D. Kennedy, 'International Law and the Nineteenth Century: History of an Illusion' (1996) 65 Nord. J. Int'l. L. 385.

[178] See D. Kennedy, ibid, 416.

[179] This expression comes from A. D'Amato, 'What "Counts" as Law?' in N.G. Onuf (ed), *Law-Making in the Global Community* (Carolina Academic Press, Durham, 1982) 83, 98.

It is precisely because law-ascertainment fell short of any formal mechanisms to capture the will of the State, while simultaneously failing to provide any formal standards with which to identify those States—initially understood as the Christian nations[180]—that are entitled to engage in legal relations with one another, that the 19th century theory of the sources of international law has, retrospectively, been seen by some contemporary scholars as culturally biased as well as dominantly apologetic.[181] This is probably true. I do not, however, need to discuss that here. What is of relevance is how 20th century scholars handled this absence of formal law-ascertainment mechanisms. Indeed, since the scholars of the 19th century failed to carve formal indicators for the identification of international legal rules, the task of formalizing international law-ascertainment was left to their successors.

3.2.2 International law in the 20th and 21st centuries

Like in general legal theory, formalism as a law-ascertainment model emerged in the theory of the sources of international law in reaction to doctrines that were deemed too amenable to natural law. Although 19th century scholars backed away from natural law approaches, as has been explained in the previous section, they still recognized a moderate duality of law and the existence of some 'objective principles'. The scholars of the 20th century, while recognizing that natural law had 'supplied one of the necessary crutches with whose help mankind walked out of the institutions of the Middle Ages',[182] resolutely retreated from such dualism and endorsed a rule-approach or source-based approach of law-identification.[183]

In their great majority, 20th century scholars did not shed the idea of their predecessors that international law rests on the consent of States. Subject to a few exceptions,[184] they agreed that natural law does not constitute a source of law *per se,*

[180] G. van der Molen, 'The Present Crisis in the Law of Nations', in *Symbolae Verzijl* (Martinus Nijhoff, The Hague, 1958) 238–54; J.H.W. Verzijl, 'Western European Influence on the Foundations of International Law' (1955) 1 *International Relations* 137–46. On this question, see also the account of the various tendencies of the legal scholarship of that time by M. Koskenniemi, *The Gentle Civilizer of Nations: The Rise and Fall of International Law 1870–1960* (CUP, Cambridge, 2002) 98–178.

[181] M. Koskeniemi, *From Apology to Utopia* (Cambridge, New York, 2005) 108–22. See also the criticism by D. Kennedy, 'The Sources of International Law' (1987) 2 Am. U. J. Int'l L. & Pol'y 1.

[182] L. Oppenheim, 'The Science of International Law: Its Task and Method' (1908) 2 AJIL 313, 329.

[183] D. Anzilotti, 'Il diritto internazionale nei giudizi interni' (1905), reprinted in *Scritti di diritto internazionale pubblico* (Cedam, Padova, 1956–7) 318; T.J. Lawrence, *The Principles of International Law* (7th edn, MacMillan, London, 1923) 1–14; L. Oppenheim, 'The Science of International Law: Its Task and Method' (1908) 2 AJIL 313 and L. Oppenheim, *International Law: A Treatise* (1st edn, 1905 & 1906), especially 92; G. Schwarzenberger, *International Law* (3d edn, Stevens, London, 1957);P. Guggenheim, 'What is positive international law?', in G. Lipsky, *Law and Politics in the World Community, Essays on Hans Kelsen's Pure Theory and Related Problems of International Law* (University of California Press, Berkeley, 1953) 15–30. For an overview of that period, see W.G. Grewe, *The Epochs of International Law* (De Gruyter, Berlin, 2000) 601–5.

[184] See e.g. L. Le Fur, 'Philosophie du droit international' (1921) XXVIII *Revue générale de droit international public* 565–603 or L. Le Fur, 'La théorie du droit naturel depuis le XVIIème siècle et la doctrine moderne' (1927-III) 18 RCADI 259–442. For an understanding of natural law as a formal source of law, see G. Fitzmaurice, 'Some Problems Regarding the Formal Sources of International Law', in *Symbolae Verzijl* (Martinus Nijhoff, The Hague, 1958) 161–8.

although the content of rules may reflect some principles of morality.[185] The consensus on the idea that the will of the State is the most obvious *material source* of law[186] thus remained unchallenged.[187] The main difference between 19th century and 20th century international legal scholars lies in the fact that the latter tried to devise formal law-ascertaining criteria with which to capture State consent.[188] This is precisely how 20th century scholars ended up grounding the identification of international legal rules in a theory of allegedly formal sources[189]—a construction which continues to enjoy a strong support among 21st century scholars.[190] In their view, international legal rules stem from the will of States expressed through one of the formal sources of international law. The systemic character of the theory of the sources which they elaborated proved instrumental in their vision of international law as constituting a system.[191]

[185] C. Rousseau, *Principes généraux du droit international public*, tome 1 (Pedone, Paris, 1944) 32–3; J. Basdevant, 'Règles générales du droit de la paix' (1936-IV) 58 RCADI 477–8. See also A. D'Amato, 'What "Counts" as Law?' in N.G. Onuf (ed), *Law-Making in the Global Community* (Carolina Academic Press, Durham, 1982) 83, 90. This came to be reflected in the case-law as well. See the statement of the ICJ in the *Southwest Africa* case: 'a court of law can take account of moral principles only in so far as these are given sufficient expression in legal form', Second Phase, ICJ Rep. (1966) para. 49 (18 July 1966). This idea was not fundamentally challenged in the early 21st century. See P.-M. Dupuy, 'L'unité de l'ordre juridique international: cours général de droit international public' (2002) 297 RCADI 9, 31–2 and 200–2. See J. Verhoeven, 'Considérations sur ce qui est commun' (2008) 334 RCADI 15–434, 110; A. Orakhelashvili, *The Interpretation of Acts and Rules in Public International Law* (OUP, Oxford, 2008) 51; A. Orakhelashvili, 'Natural Law and Justice', *Max Planck Encyclopedia of Public International Law*, available at <http://www.mpepil.com>, para. 33. See, however, the natural law overtones found in some constitutionalist approaches, *infra* 3.2.3.

[186] On the distinction between material and formal sources, see generally L. Oppenheim, *International Law*, vol. 1 (8th edn, London, 1955) 24. See the remarks of P.E. Corbett, 'The Consent of States and the Sources of the Law of Nations' (1925) 5 BYBIL 20–30; C. Rousseau, *Principes généraux du droit international public*, tome 1 (Pedone, Paris, 1944) 106–8; G. Fitzmaurice, 'Some Problems Regarding the Formal Sources of International Law', in *Symbolae Verzijl* (Martinus Nijhoff, The Hague, 1958) 153. G. Abi-Saab, 'Les sources du droit international. Essai de déconstruction', in *Le Droit international dans un monde en mutation: liber amicorum en hommage au Professeur Eduardo Jimenez de Arechaga* (Fundación de Cultura Universitaria, Montevideo, 1994) 29–49, 30; See also the controversial account of this distinction made by G. Scelle, 'Essai sur les sources formelles du droit international', in *Recueil sur les sources en l'honneur de Francois Gény* vol. III (Sirey, Paris, 1935) 400–30; P. Dailler and A. Pellet, *Droit international public* (6th edn, LGDJ, Paris, 1999) 111–12.

[187] One of the first most complete expressions of this formal consensual understanding of international law, has been offered by D. Anzilotti, *Corso di diritto internazionale* (Athenaeum, Roma, 1923) 27. For a more recent manifestation of the voluntary nature of international law, see P. Weil, 'Vers une normativité relative en droit international' (1982) 87 *Revue générale de droit international public* 5. For a judicial expression of that idea, see PCIJ, *Lotus*, PCIJ Publications, Series A, No.10, 18.

[188] See the refinement of the theory of consent by Elias and Lim, *The Paradox of Consensualism in International Law* (Kluwer, The Hague, 1998).

[189] See generally A. Pellet, 'Cours Général: Le droit international entre souveraineté et communauté internationale' (2007) 2 *Anuário Brasileiro de Direito Internacional* 12–74, especially 15, 19, and 31. See also G. Buzzini, 'La Théorie des sources face au droit international général' (2002) 106 *Revue générale de droit international public* 581, especially 584–90.

[190] See e.g. A. Orakhelashvili, *The Interpretation of Acts and Rules in Public International Law* (OUP, Oxford, 2008) 51–60.

[191] Likewise, it cannot be excluded that the practice of law-applying authorities will itself yield contradictions. That does not bar that practice from providing a meaning to law-ascertainment criteria.

Needless to say, such predominance of the source thesis did not remain entirely unchallenged. In the 20th century, some serious contestations of formal law-identification in the United States and, to a more limited extent, in Europe, consolidated. Some of these critiques are examined in further detail below.[192] The most severe rejection of formalism in law-ascertainment was famously spearheaded by the New Haven School which, drawing on the earlier critique by legal realists, advocated a process-based identification of international law leading to an abandonment of the distinction between law and non-law.[193] It also gained ground in liberal American scholarship, which was embodied at that time by the dominant Colombia Law School.[194] Such a critique was taken seriously enough to generate the need to engage in some tentative reconciliation between the source thesis and process-based approaches.[195] Although it is true that American scholars of international law have not been averse to process-based approaches such as that of the New Haven School—and the less formal approach of the liberal Columbia School of International Law,[196] especially in the aftermath of the Second World War[197]—not all American scholars backed away from a rule-based understanding of international law.[198] The process-based models of international law-ascertainment probably contributed to the realization by many (American or non-American) scholars that law-making is a continuing social process.[199] It did not, however, lure most of them away from formal law-ascertainment. Indeed, this American contestation of formalism did not

See, among others, A.-C. Martineau, 'The Rhetoric of Fragmentation: Fear and Faith in International Law' (2009) 22 LJIL 1–28, 7–8.

[192] See *infra* 4.2.

[193] See *infra* 4.2.3.

[194] See e.g. O. Schachter, 'Towards a Theory of International Obligation' (1967–1968) 8 Va. J. Int'l L. 300; O. Schachter, 'International Law in Theory and Practice' (1982–V) 178 RCADI 1–395, 60–74. For some comments on the deformalization advocated by the Colombia School of International Law, see D. Kennedy, 'When Renewal Repeats: Thinking Against the Box' (2000) 32 NYU JILP 335, 380.

[195] This attempt to reconcile the New Haven School with the classical source thesis proved very one-sided in favour of formalism. For instance, G. Abi-Saab, who was not entirely insensitive to process-based approaches, defended formal law-identification. G. Abi-Saab, 'Cours général de droit international public' (1987–VIII) 207 RCADI 9–464, 39: '(L)e "droit en mouvement" est un processus en tant que tel. Car c'est un processus "encadré", "structuré", "cadencé" et "téléologique". Ce sont ces qualificatifs qui font sa juridicité. Sans eux, peut-être y a-t-il processus; mais pas de droit'. Such a synthesis was already advocated by C.W. Jenks, *The Common Law of Mankind* (Stevens, London, 1955) and by G.J.H. Van Hoof, *Rethinking the Sources of International Law* (Kluwer, Deventer, 1983) 44. See also B. Cheng, 'Epilogue: On the Nature and Sources of International Law', in B. Cheng (eds), *International Law: Teaching and Practice* (Stevens, London, 1982) 203, 204–9.

[196] D. Kennedy, 'The Disciplines of International Law and Policy' (1999) 12 LJIL 19.

[197] D. Kennedy, 'A New Stream of International Legal Scholarship' (1988) 7 Wisconsin Int'l L. J. 4.

[198] D. Kennedy, 'The Disciplines of International Law and Policy'(1999) 12 LJIL 9–133 at 27–8; See also D. Kennedy, 'A New Stream of International Legal Scholarship' (1988) 7 Wisconsin Int'l L. J. 1, 3. The New Haven Law School process-based conception has probably prodded some American scholars to completely skirt the question of law-definition by engaging in theories of authority of law. See e.g. T. Franck, 'Fairness in the international legal and institutional system: general course on public international law' (1993–III) 240 RCADI 1–498, 23.

[199] B. Cheng, 'On the Nature and Sources of International Law', in B. Cheng (eds), *International Law: Teaching and Practice* (Stevens, London, 1982) 203, 204; See also A. Pellet, 'The Normative Dilemma: Will and Consent in International Law-Making' (1988–1989) 12 Aust. YBIL 22. For another embracing

provoke a challenge to the global dominance of formalism in the international legal scholarship of the 20th century.[200] As a result, it is not unreasonable to contend that, in their great majority, international legal scholars—despite their diverging conceptions of the theory of the sources—have all used formal law-ascertainment criteria throughout the 20th century. It is only in the last decades of the 20th century and in the 21st century that the dominance of formal law-ascertainment has come to experience a significant erosion. This erosion is further discussed below.[201]

The idea that international legal rules are identified by virtue of their source was thus solidly entrenched in the legal scholarship throughout the 20th century. Even during the storm caused by articles 53 and 64 of the Vienna Convention on the Law of Treaties in the second half of the 20th century and the acceptance of substantive constraints on the treaty-making powers of States (and subsequently international organizations) brought about by the concept of *jus cogens*,[202] international legal scholars continued to show almost unflinching adherence to formal law-identification.[203] In the sense described above, law-ascertainment in the 20th century theory of the sources of international law thus remained firmly and continuously governed by the source thesis. This centrality of the source thesis in the 20th century conception of international law came with a unanimous rejection of the Austinian sanction-based understanding of law.[204]

It should be made clear, however, that the general adherence to the source thesis by 20th century international legal scholars did not mean that they entirely excluded perspectives that embraced aspects other than pure legal forms[205]—as is illustrated

of process-based conception of international law, see also D.M. Johnston, 'Functionalism in the Theory of International Law' (1988) 26 Canadian YBIL 3.

200 On the non-amenability of British legal scholars towards process-based approaches to law, see R. Higgins, 'Policy Considerations and the International Judicial Process' (1968) 17 ICLQ 58.

201 Cfr *infra* 5.1 and 5.2.

202 On some classical attempts to catalog norms of *jus cogens*, see R. Ago, 'Droit des traités à la lumière de la Convention de Vienne' (1971) 132 RCADI 297–331, 324. A. Verdross and B. Simma, *Universelles Völkerrecht* (3rd edn, Duncker & Humblot, Berlin, 1984) 265–6. Whiteman, 'Jus Cogens in International Law with a Projected List' (1977) 7 Ga. J. Int'l. & Comp. L. 609; For criticisms of these classifications, see A. D'Amato, 'It's a Bird, It's a Plane, It's Jus Cogens' (1990) 6 Connecticut J. Int'l L. 1. See also the criticisms of E.J. Criddle and E. Fox-Decent, 'A Fiduciary Theory of Jus Cogens (2009) 34 YJIL 331. On the various foundations of *jus cogens*, see R. Kolb, *Théorie du ius cogens international: essai de relecture du concept* (PUF, Paris, 2001); see also the remarks of Robert P. Barnidge 'Questioning the Legitimacy of Jus Cogens in the Global Legal Order' (2008) 38 *Israel Yearbook on Human Rights* 199.

203 On the severance of *jus cogens* from natural law, see A. Orakhelashvili, 'Natural Law and Justice', *Max Planck Encyclopedia of Public International Law*, available at <http://www.mpepil.com> para. 34.

204 For a famous rejection of the Austinian conception of law, see ICJ, *South West African* case, ICJ Rep. (1966) 46.

205 L. Henkin, *How Nations Behave* (Columbia UP, New York, 1979); L. Henkin, 'International Law: Politics, Values and Functions: General Course on Public International Law' (1989) 216 RCADI 9, 62 *et seq*. O. Schachter, ' Non Conventional Concerted Acts', in M. Bedjaoui (ed), *International Law: Achievements and Prospects* (Martinus Nijhoff, The Hague, 1991) 265–9. This is also highlighted by M. Koskenniemi, *From Apology to Utopia* (Cambridge UP, Cambridge, 2005) 191, who takes the example of G. Schwarzenberger, *Power and Politics* (3rd edn, Stevens, London, 1964); G. Schwarzenberger, *The Inductive Approach to International Law* (Stevens, London, 1965); See also P. Guggenheim, 'What is positive international law?', in G. Lipsky, *Law and Politics in the World Community, Essays on Hans Kelsen's Pure Theory and Related Problems of International Law* (University of California Press, Berkeley, 1953).

by the growing interest in transnational law[206] in the second half of the 20th century, the occasional revivals of natural law theory,[207] or the recognition that extra-legal parameters may prove decisive in international adjudication.[208] They also remained, for definitional necessities, amenable to the 'publicness'[209] of international law and the idea that international law is also identified through the subjects whose relations it regulates.[210] Likewise, 20th century scholars came to terms with the drawbacks of a rule-approach to international law,[211] although that did not suffice to justify an abandonment of formal law-ascertainment.

The centrality of the source thesis in law-ascertainment in the 20th century scholarship mostly materialized in the so-called *theory of the sources* of international law, which I will examine in chapter 7. Yet, notwithstanding the widespread adherence to the source thesis, it is important to note that the terminology of 'source' was not unanimously considered adequate to describe how international legal rules are identified. In particular and among other reasons, it has been contended that the concept of source does not adequately reflect the process through which international rules are made,[212] does not apply to the source of secondary rules of international law,[213] is not fitting for customary international law[214]—which has remained non-formal even in the contemporary

Cfr. J. Verhoeven, 'Considérations sur ce qui est commun: Cours général de droit international public' (2008) 334 RCADI 15–434, 109.

[206] 'I shall use, instead of "international law", the term "transnational law" to include all law which regulates actions or events that transcend national frontiers. Both public and private international law are included, as are other rules which do not wholly fit such standard categories': P. Jessup, *Transnational Law* (Yale UP, Connecticut, 1956) 156. For a contemporary account of the concept of transnational law, see C. Scott, '"Transnational Law" as Proto-Concept: Three Conceptions' (2009) 10 *German Law Journal* 877.

[207] See J. von Bernstorff and T. Dunlap, *The Public International Law Theory of Hans Kelsen—Believing in Universal Law* (CUP, Cambridge, 2010) 253.

[208] See P. Guggenheim, 'What is positive international law?', in G. Lipsky, *Law and Politics in the World Community, Essays on Hans Kelsen's Pure Theory and Related Problems of International Law* (University of California Press, Berkeley, 1953) 24–5.

[209] On the original meaning of the public character of international law mentioned by E. Dumont in his 1802 translation of Bentham's *Principles of Morals and Legislation*, see *supra* note 45.

[210] See Permanent Court of Arbitration, *Russian Indemnity Case* (1912) 2 RIAA 829, 870. T.-J. Lawrence, *The Principles of International Law* (7th edn, MacMillan, London, 1923) 1–14; see L. Oppenheim, *International Law* (R.F. Roxburgh, ed) (3rd edn, Longmans, London, 1920 & 1921) 1. See J.L. Brierly, *The Law of Nations* (H. Waldock, ed) (6th edn, Clarendon, Oxford, 1963, first published 1930) 1, 1 and 41; See C. Rousseau, *Principes généraux du droit international public*, tome 1 (Pedone, Paris, 1944) 1. Rousseau subsequently qualifies the affirmation that international law only regulates relations between States: see 3. See, however, Kelsen for whom international law has no inherent 'domaine de validité matériel': H. Kelsen, 'Théorie générale du droit international public: problèmes choisis' (1932–IV) 42 RCADI 117–351, 182–3.

[211] G. Abi-Saab, 'Cours général de droit international public' (1987) 207 RCADI 9, 33. J. Verhoeven, Considérations sur ce qui est commun' (2008) 334 RCADI 15–434, 108; R. Y. Jennings, 'What is International Law and How Do We Tell it When We See it?' (1981) 37 *Annuaire Suisse de Droit international* 59.

[212] G. Buzzini, 'La Théorie des sources face au droit international général' (2002) 106 *Revue générale de droit international public* 581.

[213] R. Quadri, *Diritto internazionale pubblico* (Liguori, Naples, 1968) 107, referred to by Thirlway, *International Customary Law* (Sijthoff, Leiden, 1972) 40.

[214] See A. D'Amato, *The Concept of Custom in International Law* (Cornell UP, NY, 1971) 264; G. Schwarzenberger, *International Law*, vol. 1 (3rd edn, Stevens, London, 1957) 26. *Contra* Fitzmaurice,

theory of the sources of international law[215]—and fails to allow a distinction between sources of law and sources of obligation.[216] The source thesis has accordingly manifested itself in very different manners, be it sources *stricto sensu*,[217] formal validation,[218] or formal law-creating processes.[219] However, and whatever the ultimate terminology used, it seems hardly questionable, once again, that 20th century scholars have adhered in their great majority[220] to a formal law-ascertainment blueprint.

With formalism as a law-ascertainment mechanism having been dominant in the 20th century, most scholarly controversies—subject to a few exceptions in the inter-war period[221]—have revolved around the ambit, meaning, and authority of the list of admitted sources and the exhaustive character of article 38 of the Statute of the Permanent Court of International Justice and later of the International Court of Justice,[222] being a provision which, itself, is simply a list of the applicable law and which has never purported to exhaust the list of sources of international law.[223]

This dominance of formal law-ascertainment in the 20th century international legal scholarship has nevertheless not been synonymous with a total absence of non-

who construes customary international law as a source of law: G. Fitzmaurice, 'Some Problems Regarding the Formal Sources of International Law', in *Symbolae Verzijl* (Martinus Nijhoff, The Hague, 1958) 175.

[215] See *infra* 7.1 and 7.2.1.

[216] See the famous distinction between sources of obligation and sources of law drawn by Fitzmaurice: G. Fitzmaurice, ibid, 153–76, especially 157–8. According to Fitzmaurice, treaties are not actually sources of law, but only sources of obligations, the source of law being the principle *pacta sunt servanda.* For a criticism of that distinction as not a useful distinction to make, see M. Sørensen, 'Principes de droit international public: cours général' (1960–III) 101 RCADI 1–254, 53. See also the criticism of A. Pellet, 'Article 38', in A. Zimmermann et al. (eds), *The Statute of the International Court of Justice* (OUP, Oxford, 2002) 677, 703–4.

[217] For Condorelli, the term sources remains appropriate even with respect to customary international law. See Condorelli, 'Custom', in M. Bedjaoui (ed), *International Law: Achievements and Prospects* (Martinus Nijhoff, The Hague, 1991) 179–211, 186; see also G. Abi-Saab, 'La Coutume dans tous ses Etats', in *Essays in honor of Roberto Ago*, vol. I (Giuffrè, Milano, 1987) 58; C. Rousseau, *Principes généraux du droit international public*, tome 1 (Pedone, Paris, 1944) 108; on art. 38 as constituting a list of formal sources, see P. Dailler and A. Pellet, *Droit international public* (6th edn, LGDJ, Paris, 1999) 112.

[218] See A. D'Amato, 'What Counts as Law' in N.G. Onuf (ed), *Law-Making in the Global Community* (Carolina Academic Press, Durham, 1982) 83–107.

[219] See D.P. O'Connell, *International Law*, vol. 1 (2nd edn, Stevens, London, 1970) 7–8; see G. Schwarzenberger, *International Law*, vol. 1 (3d edn, Stevens, London, 1957) 25–7; R. Jennings, 'Law-Making and Package Deal', in Daniel Bardonnet (ed), *Mélanges Reuter: le droit international: unité et diversité* (Pedone, Paris, 1981) 347, 348.

[220] See however *infra* 4.2.3. regarding the New Haven Law School or the iconoclast approach of C. De Visscher, *Théories et Réalités en Droit International Public* (4th edn, Pedone, Paris, 1970) 67, 168–70.

[221] See the few general courses at the Hague Academy of Verdross, Bierly, Djuvara, Le Fur, or Gidel, referred to by M. Koskenniemi and which were dedicated to theoretical and philosophical topics: M. Koskenniemi, 'Repetition as Reform' (1998) 9 EJIL 405, 405.

[222] On the controversies during the drafting process of art. 38, see T. Skouteris, *The Notion of Progress in International Law Discourse* (LEI Universiteit, Leiden, 2008), later published as *The Notion of Progress in International Law Discourse* (T.M.C. Asser, The Hague, 2010).

[223] In the same vein, see A. Pellet, 'Article 38', A. Zimmermann et al. (eds), *The Statute of the International Court of Justice—A Commentary* (OUP, Oxford, 2006) 693–735.

formal law-identification. Indeed, almost all scholars, although they tried to rein in or hide its non-formal character, came to terms with the absence of formalism in custom-ascertainment.[224] In the second half of the 20th century, another form of deformalization gained currency through the concept of soft law, i.e. the idea that international law can originate in acts that are not formally identified as legal acts.[225] These non-formal law-ascertainment mechanisms enjoyed a wide acceptance as they provided room to reconnect international law with pluralized norm-making at the international level. In spite of their great indeterminacy and the correlative uncertainty which they generated, these two types of deformalization of law-ascertainment mechanisms were accepted because they were seen as welcome qualifications to the principled formalism of international law-ascertainment. Yet, notwithstanding such qualifications, the theory of the sources of international law continued to be devised along the lines of the source thesis.

For the sake of the argument made here, it is now of great import to note that, while overwhelmingly adhering to a source thesis, mainstream international legal scholarship in the 20th century—as well as in the early 21st century—remained very aloof from the theoretical debates about the foundations of formal law-ascertainment.[226] Apart from its critics, very few scholars ventured into a study of the ontology of formal law-ascertainment.[227] Although they do not always constitute the adequate outlet for an author's view on the theoretical foundations of formal law-

[224] For an examination of this form of deformalization, see *infra* 7.1 and 7.2.1.

[225] For an examination of this form of deformalization, see *infra* 5.1.

[226] In the same sense, see E. Jouannet, 'Regards sur un siècle de doctrine française du droit international' (2000) 46 AFDI 1–57. See generally, D. Kennedy, 'International Law and Nineteenth Century: History of an Illusion' (1996) 65 Nord. J. Int'l. L. 385, 387; D. Kennedy, 'A New Stream of International Legal Scholarship' (1988) 7 Wisconsin Int'l L. J. 1, 6; N. Purvis, 'Critical Legal Studies in Public International Law' (1991) 32 Harvard JIL 81, 84; M. Reisman, 'Lassa Oppenheim's Nine Lives' (1994) 19 Yale J. Int'l L. 255, 271; B. Kingsbury, 'The International Legal Order', NYU Law School Public Law & Legal Theory Research Paper No. 01–04 (2003), IILJ History and Theory of International Law Series, Working Paper No. 2003/1. See N. Onuf, 'Global Law-Making and Legal Thought', in N. Onuf (ed), *Law-Making in the Global Community* (Carolina Academic Press, Durham, 1982) 1, 13; See also A. D'Amato, 'The Need for a Theory of International Law' (Northwestern University School of Law, Public Law and Legal Theory Research Paper Series, 2007); A. D'Amato, 'What "Counts" as Law?' in N.G. Onuf (ed), *Law-Making in the Global Community* (Carolina Academic Press, Durham, 1982) 83, 83–107. D'Amato provided his own theory of the autonomy of the international legal system. See A. D'Amato, 'International Law as an Autopoietic System' in R. Wolfrum and V. Röben (eds), *Developments of International Law in Treaty Making* (Springer, Berlin, 2005) 335–99; See also T. Skouteris, *The Notion of Progress in International Law Discourse* (LEI Universiteit, Leiden, 2008) chapter 3, later published as *The Notion of Progress in International Law Discourse* (T.M.C. Asser, The Hague, 2010); M. Koskenniemi, 'Repetition as Reform'(1998) 9 EJIL 405; J. Klabbers, 'Constitutionalism and the Making of International Law' (2008) 5 NoFo 84, 94.

[227] A classical example is R. Jennings and A. Watts, *Oppenheim's International Law*, vol 1 (9th edn, Longman, London, 1992). This edition of Oppenheim has been criticized by M. Reisman, precisely for its lack of theoretical insights. See M. Reisman, 'Lassa Oppenheim's Nine Lives' (1994) 19 Yale J. Int'l L. 255, 271. See also the criticism of that edition by D.W. Greig, 'Oppenheim Revisited: An Australian Perspective' (1992) 14 Aust. YBIL 227.

ascertaining criteria,[228] most contemporary textbooks, for instance, clearly bespeak a lack of interest in the foundations of the source thesis.[229] Some do not even mention contestations of formal law-ascertainment and fail to explain why they open with an outline of theory of the sources.[230] Despite the fact that they offer their authors the possibility to expound their understanding of law, general courses at the Hague Academy—to take another example—rarely dwell upon the foundations of formal law-ascertainment in international law. As one author conceded, it seems undeniable that '(t)he search for an all-embracing general theory of international law has been abandoned in mainstream thought'.[231] It is this lack of interest of international legal scholars in the origins and foundations of formalism in international law that generated a severe dearth of legal theory devoted to that topic.

This dominant 'anti-theoretical'[232] posture of international legal scholarship can probably be explained by the growing self-assurance gained by international legal scholars who, after their branch of law was recognized as equal to other legal disciplines, no longer deemed it necessary to ponder and unravel the origin of their understanding of international law as a whole.[233] They preferred instead to focus on the study of the 'techniques'[234] of law-making and the search for some 'adjustments'[235] to the drawbacks of classical sources doctrines, especially their relationship with consent.[236] Others—especially in the English tradition of international law which had generally remained more pragmatic[237]—preferred to focus exclusively on practice. Their pragmatism proceeded from the idea that theory

[228] This remark has already been made by I. Scobbie who contends that one cannot expect complex theoretical arguments in textbooks. See I. Scobbie, 'Towards the Elimination of International Law: Some Radical Scepticism about Sceptical Radicalism' (1990) 61 BYBIL 352.

[229] See e.g. M. Shaw, *International Law* (5th edn, CUP, Cambridge, 2003) 48–64. See also M. Dixon, *Textbook on International Law* (6th edn, OUP, Oxford, 2007) 4–23.

[230] See I. Brownlie, *Principles of Public International Law* (7th edn, OUP, Oxford, 2008) 3–4; A. Cassese, *International Law* (2nd edn, OUP, Oxford, 2005); A. Aust, *Handbook of International Law* (CUP, Cambridge, 2005) 55.

[231] M. Shaw, *International Law* (5th edn, CUP, Cambridge, 2003) 61.

[232] The expression is from M. Koskenniemi, 'Repetition as Reform' (1998) 9 EJIL 405, 406. D. Kennedy, talking about the legal scholarship in general, refers to the 'legal culture's uneasiness about intellection'. See D. Kennedy, 'A Rotation in Contemporary Legal Scholarship' (2011) 12 *German Law Journal* 338, 338.

[233] T. O. Elias, 'Problems Concerning the Validity of Treaties' (1971–III) 133 RCADI 333–416, 341. See K. Zemanek, 'The Legal Foundations of the International System' (1997) 266 RCADI 9–335, 131.

[234] H. Thierry, 'Cours général de droit international public' (1990–III) 222 RCADI 9–186, 27 and 31.

[235] J. Verhoeven talks about 'accomodements'. See J. Verhoeven, 'Considérations sur ce qui est commun' (2008) 334 RCADI 9–434, 137.

[236] C. Tomuschat, 'Obligations Arising for States without or against Their Will' (1993) 241 RCADI 195–374, 216. and C. Tomuschat, 'General Course on Public International Law' (1999) 281 RCADI 9–438, 24. ; K. Zemanek, 'The Legal Foundations of the International System' (1997) 266 RCADI 9–335, 144.

[237] See e.g. R.Y. Jennings, 'General course of public international law' (1967–II) 121 RCADI 323, 329. (who said 'we need some list of sources if we are to make a beginning').

'provides no real benefits' and has the tendency to 'obscure the more interesting questions'.[238] Whatever the different motives behind this absence of scholarly appetite for investigations into the foundations of formal law-ascertainment,[239] the source thesis, in all its manifestations, was left without strong theoretical buttresses in theory of the sources of international law.

Such disinterest in the ontology of formal law-ascertainment in the international legal scholarship of the 20th and 21st centuries can prove particularly astounding, and to some extent paradoxical, since many international legal scholars who—while unanimously rejecting Hart's conception of international law and his denial of international law being a legal system[240]—unabashedly adhere to a Hartian version of the source thesis. Indeed, despite the fact that there is hardly any general work on public international law which does not mention Hart's theory of law,[241] and even though only a handful of scholars discard him as irrelevant,[242] very few scholars have actually ventured into exploring the foundations of formalism, whether

[238] I. Brownlie, 'International law at the fiftieth anniversary of the United Nations: general course on public international law' (1995) 255 RCADI 9–228, 30.

[239] For some additional reflections on the reasons behind the anti-theoretical stance of mainstream legal scholarship, see J. Klabbers, 'Constitutionalism and the making of international law' (2008) 5 NoFo 84, 95. See also D. Kennedy, 'A Rotation in Contemporary Legal Scholarship' (2011) 12 *German Law Journal* 338.

[240] See e.g. Brownlie, 'International law at the fiftieth anniversary of the United Nations: general course on public international law' (1995) 255 RCADI 9, 25; A. D'Amato, 'What "Counts" as Law?'in N.G. Onuf (ed), *Law-Making in the Global Community* (Carolina Academic Press, Durham, 1982) 83, 106; see also T. Franck, 'The Legitimacy of the International Legal System' (1988) 82 AJIL 751. More recently, see M. Payandeh, 'The Concept of International Law in the Jurisprudence of H.L.A. Hart' (2010) 21 EJIL 967.

[241] To name only a few, see the general courses of Dupuy 'L'unité de l'ordre juridique international—Cours général de droit international public' (2002) 297 RCADI 9–490; P. Weil 'Le droit international en quête de son identité: cours général de droit international public' (1992–VI) 237 RCADI 9–370; G. Abi-Saab 'Cours général de droit international public' (1987–VIII) 207 RCADI 9–463; I. Brownlie 'International law at the fiftieth anniversary of the United Nations: general course on public international law' (1995) 255 RCADI 9–228; O. Schachter, 'International Law in Theory and Practice: General Course in Public International Law' (1982–V) 178 RCADI 1–395.

[242] Brownlie discards Hart as too abstract and adopts a much more pragmatic conception of international law, drawing on the assumption that those in charge usually do not even understand law as a unitary concept. For Brownlie, there is not such a thing as a 'neat ultimate rule of recognition which provides an intellectual basis for a system of rules but a complex state of political fact': 'International law at the fiftieth anniversary of the United Nations: general course on public international law' (1995) 255 RCADI 9, 24. In a way that seems to indicate that Brownlie construed Hart's theory as a theory of obedience and not a theory of law-ascertainment, Brownlie also formulates the objection that the population may decide to abide by other rules of recognition: ibid, 25. For another rejection of Hart and the defence of a Kelsenian understanding of international law, see J. Kammerhofer, 'Uncertainty in the Formal Sources of International Law: Customary International Law and Some of its Problems' (2004) 15 EJIL 523, especially 543–7. His views are further elaborated in J. Kammerhofer, *Uncertainty in International Law: A Kelsenian Perspective* (Routledge, London, 2010) especially 205 and 224. (He particularly argues that, by placing the fact as the ultimate foundation of the system, Hartian perspective negates the possibility of an 'Ought'; from a Kelsenian perspective, a norm can base its validity only on a norm).

in their general work on international law[243] or in their studies devoted to the sources of international law.[244]

Although international legal scholarship has remained largely averse to investigations of the theoretical foundations of formal law-ascertainment, mention must nonetheless be made of a few notable exceptions. For instance, Gerald Fitzmaurice is probably one of the very few scholars who ventured into the roots of formal law-ascertainment, even though he stopped short of providing a fully-fledged conceptual framework for it. Indeed, even before the publication of Hart's *Concept of Law* and the subsequent flurry of theoretical discussion that its dissemination spawned, Fitzmaurice came close to preceding Hart in grounding formal law-ascertainment parameters in a rule of recognition, the validity of which is not an issue because it is external to the international legal order.[245] That contention, which admittedly is not always consistent or completely fathomable, had some strong and undisputable Hartian overtones. Still, the argument raised by Fitzmaurice did little to prod his contemporaries into the discussion.[246] Somewhat paradoxically, because of his anti-formalist stance, Georges Abi-Saab can probably also be credited with exploring the

[243] This is what I have deplored, in J. d'Aspremont, 'Hart et le Positivism postmoderne' (2009) 113 *Revue générale de droit international public* 635–54. It it noteworthy that even Prosper Weil, who had come to be seen as the living embodiment of the adherence to the source thesis for law-identification purposes and who had clearly indicated the Hartian origin of his source thesis, failed to clearly elucidate the theoretical roots of formal law-ascertainment. See P. Weil, 'Vers une normativité relative en droit international' (1982) *Revue générale de droit international public* 3; Weil artfully managed to propagate his source thesis in American legal scholarship: 'Towards Relative Normativity in International Law' (1983) 77 AJIL 413. Even in his general course he did not take pains to dwell upon the foundations of the formalism that he endorses. See P. Weil, 'Le droit international en quête de son identité: cours général de droit international public' (1992-VI) 237 RCADI 9–370, 131.

[244] For some more—sometimes diverging—attempts to transpose Hart's *Concept of Law* to sources of international law, and especially to theory of customary international law, see G.J.H. Van Hoof, *Rethinking the Sources of International Law* (Kluwer Law, The Hague, 1983); G.M. Danilenko, *Law-Making in the International Community* (Martinus Nijhoff, Dordrecht, 1993) 16; G.M. Danilenko, 'The Theory of International Customary International Law'(1998) 31 German YBIL 9–47; H. Meijers, 'How is International Law Made?—The Stage of Growth of International Law and the Use of Its Customary Rules' (1979) 9 NYIL 3; R.M. Walden, 'Customary International Law: A Jurisprudential Analysis' (1978) 13 Israel L. Rev. 86–102; see also M-H. Mendelson, 'The Formation of Customary International Law' (1998) 272 RCADI 159–410, especially 170 and 181–2 (although he equally borrows from Kelsen). Although her theory has some natural law overtones, see also S. Besson, 'Theorizing the Sources of International Law', in S. Besson and J. Tasioulas (eds), *The Philosophy of International Law* (OUP, Oxford, 2010) 163, 180–5.

[245] 'What is the conclusion? It is that the sources of international law cannot be stated, or cannot fully or certainly be stated, in terms of international law itself, and that there are and must be rules of law that have an inherent and necessary validity, in whose absence no system of law at all can exist or be originated. Such a rule, for instance, is the rule *pacta sunt servanda.* This rule does not require to be accounted for in terms of any other rule. It could neither not be, nor be other than what it is. It is not dependent on consent, for it would exist without it': G. Fitzmaurice, 'Some problems regarding the formal sources of international law' *Symbolae Verzijl* (Martinus Nijhoff, The Hague, 1958) 164.

[246] This statement was discussed and criticized by Thirlway, *International Customary Law and Codification* (Sijthoff, Leiden, 1972) 37.

foundations of law-ascertainment.[247] The work of Godefridus van Hoof[248] or Samantha Besson[249] and their use of the social thesis also constitute interesting—albeit limited—exceptions. All-in-all, investigations of the theoretical foundations of law-ascertainment have thus proved rather limited.

Leaving aside these few exceptions, it must be noted as well that the overall absence of comprehensive attention to the foundations of formalism in law-ascertainment does not mean that commentators did not deem it useful to expound the *reasons* behind their formal law-ascertainment model. This is what I have called earlier the politics of formalism.[250] Among others, mention can be made of Pierre-Marie Dupuy who defended formal law-ascertainment as a 'réducteur d'incertitude'.[251] Christian Tomuschat, for his part, promoted formalism on the basis of the authority of law and the promotion of the rule of law.[252] In the same vein, Gennady Danilenko pointed to the need to rein in manipulations of rules by States.[253] Some of the motives dovetail with the rationale of formal law-ascertainment that has been put forward in chapter 2.[254]

In the same vein, it must be indicated that the general tepidness towards the theoretical foundations of formalism has not prevented scholars from paying more attention to the *historical origins* of formalism. For instance, a number of commentators have advocated a Weberian conception of formalism, as illustrated by the work of Olivier Corten.[255] According to this view, the substitution of substantial validity by formal validity in the theory of the sources of international law, i.e. the source thesis, constitutes the culmination of rationality in modern political thinking in that it is the best tool with which to engage the legitimate dominance of those that are at

[247] Interestingly, some implicit references to the source thesis can be found in Abi-Saab's general course although he purported to reject the source thesis, see G. Abi-Saab, 'General Course' (1987-VIII) 207 RCADI 9–463, 41.

[248] See G.J.H. Van Hoof, *Rethinking the Sources of International Law* (Kluwer, The Hague, 1983) 288.

[249] S. Besson, 'Theorizing the Sources of International Law', in S. Besson and J. Tasioulas (eds), *The Philosophy of International Law* (OUP, Oxford, 2010) 163, 180–1.

[250] Cfr *supra* 2.2.

[251] Dupuy, 'L'unité de l'ordre juridique international—Cours général de droit international public' (2002) 297 RCADI 9, 26. He posited that law is 'd'abord une technique de régulation sociale, volontairement formalisée pour des raisons d'efficacité, de fiabilité, de sécurité, que l'on appelle la "sécurité juridique"'. Formalism, seen as a tenet of positivism, constitutes a 'réducteur d'incertitude': ibid, 30.

[252] C. Tomuschat, 'International law: ensuring the survival of mankind on the eve of a new century: general course on public international law' (1999) 281 RCADI 9–438, 26–9.

[253] G.M. Danilenko, *Law-Making in the International Community* (Martinus Nijhoff, Dordrecht, 1993) 16.

[254] Cfr *supra* 2.2.

[255] O. Corten, *Pour un positivisme juridique critique* (Pedone, Paris, 2008) 45 and 125. See, in particular, 66–7: 'L'essentiel est que les gouvernés croient que le droit offre un cadre de référence unique à interprétation objectivante, même si, en réalité, tel est loin d'être le cas. Si le droit est perçu comme se réduisant à un discours pouvant être interprété de manière variée, suivant les opinions politiques particulières, il perdrait l'essentiel de sa force de légitimation. Celle-ci suppose au contraire que soit maintenue, à tout le moins à l'égard de l'opinion publique, la fiction positiviste d'une neutralité, d'une objectivité et d'une unicité du droit, qualités qui s'opposeraient en tous points au particularisme, à la diversité et à la subjectivité'.

the helm of the decision-making processes of the international society.[256] While very enlightening for their historical and critical insights, these Weberian accounts of formalism have, however, fallen short, in my view, of providing sufficient theoretical foundations to formal law-ascertainment itself.[257]

The lack of interest paid by international legal scholars to the foundations of formal law-ascertainment in international law has generated an acute deficiency of legal theory devoted to that topic. As a result, formal law-ascertainment has been deprived of strong theoretical foundations and came to stand as an idol with feet of clay. It is argued here that it is this absence of any theoretical support for formal law-ascertainment in international law that created a prelude to the contemporary anti-formal approaches, which will be described in chapters 4 and 5.

3.2.3 Formal law-ascertainment in constitutionalist theory of international law

As stated above, it would be both an overgeneralization and erroneous to present the abovementioned broad depiction of the mainstream scholarship of the 20th century as encompassing all contemporary international legal scholarship. The mainstream theory of the sources of international law has, itself, been confronted with the emergence of various conceptualizations seeking to refine its approaches, including its law-ascertainment criteria. The most successful of these attempts has undoubtedly been the constitutionalist theory of international law, which is sometimes seen as a 'sub-discipline of public international law'.[258] Although international legal constitutionalism is too rich a stream to be considered a uniform approach to international law,[259] continuously oscillating between descriptive and normative approaches,[260] it can hardly be contested that various aspects of constitutionalist theory have started to

[256] For Weberian accounts of formalism in general, see M.J. Horwitz, 'The Rise of Legal Formalism' (1975) 19 Am. J. Legal Hist. 251. See also C.C. Goetsch, 'The Future of Legal Formalism' (1980) 24 Am. J. Legal Hist. 221. See also the remarks of U. Scarpelli, *Qu'est-ce que le positivisme juridique* (Bruylant/LGDJ, Paris,1996) 31 and 57. See generally, on the importance of Weber for the doctrine of source, the remarks of N. Onuf, 'Global Law-Making and Legal Thought', in N. Onuf (ed), *Law-Making in the Global Community* (Carolina Academic Press, Durham, 1982) 1, 36–9.

[257] See the review of O. Corten's study by J. d'Aspremont, 'Note de Lecture: O. Corten, Le discours du droit international, Paris Pedone, 2009' (2009) 4 *Revue générale de droit international public* 964–7.

[258] B. Fassbender, 'The Meaning of International Constitutional Law' in N. Tsagourias (ed), *Transnational Constitutionalism: International and European Perspectives* (CUP, Cambridge, 2007) 307, 308.

[259] On some tentative taxomomy, see N. Tsagourias, 'Introduction', in N. Tsagourias (ed), *Transnational Constitutionalism: International and European Perspectives* (CUP, Cambridge, 2007) 1, 8; see also the various contributions in J.L. Dunoff and J.P. Trachtman (eds), *Ruling the World? Constitutionalism, International Law, and Global Governance* (CUP, Cambridge, 2009). See also C. Walter, 'International Law in a Process of Constitutionalization', in P.A. Nollkaemper and J.E. Nijman, *New Perspectives on the Divide Between National and International Law* (OUP, Oxford, 2007) 191–5.

[260] The same point is made by B. Kingsbury and M. Donaldson, 'From Bilateralism to Publicness in International Law', *From Bilateralism to Community Interest: Essays in Honour of Judge Bruno Simma* (OUP, Oxford, 2011) (forthcoming) 79, 79.

infiltrate the whole spectrum of legal scholarship—as well as the judiciary[261]—and its progressive and reformist agenda has been embraced by a growing number of scholars.[262] Their impact in mainstream legal scholarship is such that one can reasonably wonder whether they have not in fact become the dominant approach in Western European international legal thinking.[263] To some extent, it has even become a common 'mindset' of contemporary scholars.[264]

Part of the success of international constitutionalism can certainly be traced back to the fact that it alleviates the fears fuelled by the fragmentation and pluralization of international law by offering some Kantian solace.[265] Constitutionalism certainly

[261] See the constitutionalist overtones of the decision Case T-306/01, *Yusuf and Al Barakaat International Foundation v. Council and Commission*, 21 September 2005 [2005] ECR II-3533; Case T-315/01, *Kadi v. Council and Commission*, 21 September 2005 [2005] ECR II-3649. On the constitutionalist aspects of that decision see J. d'Aspremont and Fr. Dopagne, 'Two Constitutionalisms in Europe: Pursuing an Articulation of the European and International Legal Orders' (2009) 69 ZaÖRV 939–78.

[262] For some classical examples of constitutionalist theories of international law, see C. Tomuschat, 'International Law: Ensuring the Survival of Mankind on the Eve of a New Century, General Course on Public International Law' (1999) 281 RCADI 9–438; H. Mosler, *The International Society as a Legal Community* (Sijthoff & Noordhoff, Alphen aan den Rijn, 1980). See in general J. Delbrück and U.E. Heinz (eds), *New Trends in International Lawmaking: International 'Legislation' in the Public Interest* (Duncker & Humblot, Berlin, 1996); J. Delbruck, 'Prospects for a "World (Internal) Law?": Legal Developments in a Changing International System'(2003) 9 Ind. J. Global Legal Studies 29–43; E. de Wet, 'The International Constitutional Order' (2006) 55 ICLQ 51–76, and E. de Wet, 'The Emergence of International and Regional Value Systems as a Manifestation of the Emerging International Constitutional Order' (2006) 19 LJIL 611–32; A. Peters, 'Compensatory Constitutionalism: The Function of Potential of Fundamental International Norms and Structure' (2006) 19 LJIL 579–610.

[263] For some examples of the influence of constitutionalism across the entire spectrum of international legal scholarship, see, for instance, P.-M. Dupuy, 'Some Reflections on Contemporary International Law and the Appeal to Universal Values: A Response to Martti Koskenniemi' (2005) 16 EJIL 131–7. See also P.-M. Dupuy, 'L'unité de l'ordre juridique international: cours général de droit international public' (2002) 297 RCADI 9–489, especially 218. On the question of the United Nations and the development of global values, see N. Schrijver, 'The Future of the United Nations' (2006) 10 *Max Planck Yearbook of United Nations Law* 1–34,and N. Schrijver, 'Les valeurs génerales et le droit des Nations Unies', in R. Chemain and A. Pellet (eds), *La Charte des Nations Unies, Constitution Mondiale?* (Pedone, Paris, 2006) 85–8; G. Abi-Saab, 'International Law and the International Community: The Long Road to Universality' in R.St J. MacDonald (ed), *Essays in Honour of Wang Tieya* (Martinus Nijhoff, The Hague, 1994) 31–41; V. Gowlland-Debbas, 'Judicial Insights into Fundamental Values and Interests of the International Community' in A.S. Muller, D. Rai, and J.M. Thuránszky (eds), *The International Court of Justice: Its Future Role After Fifty Years* (Martinus Nijhoff, The Hague, 1997) 327–66; See the constructivist account of P. Allott, 'The Concept of International Law' (1999) 10 EJIL 31–50, 35; J.I. Charney, 'International Lawmaking: Article 38 of the ICJ State Reconsidered', in J. Delbrück and E. Heinz (eds), *New Trends in International Lawmaking* (Duncker & Humblot, Berlin, 1996) 171–91, especially 189; J.I. Charney, 'Universal International Law' (1998) 87 AJIL 529–51; R. McCorquodale, 'An Inclusive International Legal System' (2004) 17 LJIL 477–504.

[264] M. Koskenniemi, 'Constitutionalism as Mindset: Reflection on Kantian Themes of International Law and Globalization' (2007) 8(1) *Theoretical Inquiries in Law* article 2. Compare with Fassbender, who deems that the transfer of constitutional ideas in international law has become 'uncontroversial': B. Fassbender, in N. Tsagourias (ed), *Transnational Constitutionalism: International and European Perspectives* (CUP, Cambridge, 2007) 307, 309.

[265] J. Klabbers, 'Setting the Scene', in J. Klabbers, A. Peters, and G. Ulfstein (eds), *The Constitutionalization of International Law* (OUP, Oxford, 2009) 1, 18; M. Koskenniemi, 'The Fate of Public International Law: Between Technique and Politics' (January 2007) 70(1) MLR 1–3, 19; B. Fassbender, 'The Meaning of International Constitutional Law' in N. Tsagourias (ed), *Transnational Constitutionalism: International and European Perspectives* (CUP, Cambridge, 2007) 307, 311; C. Tomuschat, 'International

also draws some influence from the groundwork laid by the liberal critique of mainstream schools of international law, which have paved the way for a greater amenability to the idea of a community. Indeed, the conceptualizations of international law described in the previous section have been berated by liberal scholars for being too State-centric and insufficiently amenable to the position of individuals.[266] In reaction, constitutionalism has grown as an attempt to 'humanize' the dominant state-centric conceptualization of international law[267] and promote a normative agenda of internationalism, substantive unity, and legal control of politics.[268] As a result, the vocabulary of constitutionalist conceptualizations of international law bears some undeniable resemblance to that of the liberal school of international law, with scholars of both schools seeing the international legal system as a community at work.

It must be acknowledged that constitutionalist conceptualizations of international law are not utterly new. The idea that there is a community at play behind international law has been with us for a long time.[269] Indeed, already in the late 19th century, some international lawyers shared a calling for a cosmopolitan sense of global public conscience.[270] More forceful endeavours to construe the international legal order as an international constitutional order with a view to promoting the substantive unity of international law and the rule of law were carved out in the first

Law: Ensuring the Survival of Mankind on the Eve of a New Century'(1999) 281 RCADI 9, 89. It should be noted, however, that constitutionalists do not reject the fragmentation associated with the multiplication of international judicial bodies, for this can constitute a step towards a more systemic implementation of the international rule of law. See A. Peters, 'Global Constitutionalism Revisited' (2005) 11 *International Legal Theory* 39, 65; I. de la Rasilla del Moral, 'At King Agramant's Camp—Old Debates, New Constitutional Times' (2010) 8 ICON 3; On some other reasons of the success of constitutionalism among international lawyers, see C. Schwöbel, 'The Appeal of the Project of Global Constitutionalism to Public International Lawyers', available at <http://papers.ssrn.com/sol3/papers.cfm?abstract_id=1713201>.

266 See among others, L. Henkin, *International Law: Politics and Values* (Martinus Nijhoff, The Hague, 1995); T.M. Franck, *Fairness in International Law and Institutions* (OUP, Oxford, 1995); F.R. Tesón, 'The Kantian Theory of International Law' (1992) 92 Colum. L. Rev. 53–102; A.-M. Slaughter, 'A Liberal Theory of International Law'(2000) 94 ASIL Proceedings 240–53; 'The Liberal Agenda for Peace: International Relations Theory and the Future of the United Nations' (1994) 4 Transnat'l L. & Contemp. Probs. 377–419; 'International Law in a World of Liberal States' (1995) 6 EJIL 503–38.

267 See e.g. C. Walter, 'International Law in a Process of Constitutionalization,' in Nollkaemper and J. E. Nijman, *New Perspectives on the Divide Between National and International Law* (OUP, Oxford, 2007) 191–215.

268 On the Agenda of constitutionalism, see W. Werner, 'The never-ending closure: constitutionalism and international law', in N. Tsagourias (ed), *Transnational Constitutionalism: International and European Perspectives* (CUP, Cambridge, 2007) 329, 330.

269 See the remarks of R. Collins, 'Constitutionalism as Liberal-Juridical Consciousness: Echoes from International Law's Past' (2009) 22 LJIL 251, 253–4; I. de la Rasilla del Moral, 'At King Agramant's Camp—Old Debates, New Constitutional Times' (2010) 8 ICON 3. On the criticisms of this idea, see generally B. Tamanaha, *General Jurisprudence of Law and Society* (OUP, Oxford, 2001).

270 On the sense of a global public consciousness in the work of Westlake, Bluntschli, Mancini, and Lorimer, see M. Koskenniemi, *The Gentle Civilizer of Nations: The Rise and Fall of International Law 1870–1960* (CUP, Cambridge, 2002), 11–97.

half of the 20th century.[271] These early constitutionalist approaches were emboldened by the liberal-cosmopolitan movement that arose in reaction to the Second World War, especially in Germany,[272] and to some extent in Anglo-Saxon scholarship, as is illustrated by the work of Wolfgang Friedmann[273] and Clarence Wilfred Jenks.[274] The appeal of the normative agenda of internationalism continued to grow in parallel with the formidable developments of international institutional law in the second half of the 20th century.[275]

Because of its strong Kantian and/or Grotian overtones and its resemblance to the liberal school of international law,[276] it could be tempting to categorize international constitutionalism as a critique of mainstream 20th century scholarship.[277] Certainly, international legal constitutionalism draws on some normative paradigms, most notably the existence of an international society that shares 'global values'.[278] They also embrace cosmopolitan features which were traditionally rejected.[279] For instance, Alfred Verdross—who is probably one of the most admired forebears of international legal constitutionalism[280]—contended that natural law and positive law do not necessarily exclude one another and construed *jus cogens* in terms of natural law.[281] In doing so, he attempted a synthesis between the positivism of his

[271] A. Verdross, *Die Verfassung, der Völkerrechtsgemeinschaft* (Springer, Berlin, 1926). On Verdross as one of the fathers of constitutionalism, see B. Fassbender, in N. Tsagourias (ed), *Transnational Constitutionalism: International and European Perspectives* (CUP, Cambridge, 2007) 307. See also I. de la Rasilla del Moral, 'At King Agramant's Camp—Old Debates, New Constitutional Times' (2010) 8 ICON 3.

[272] For an overview of the German legal scholarship in this respect, see S. Oeter, 'The German Influence on Public International Law', in Société française pour le droit international, *Droit International et diversité juridique, Journée franco-allemande* (Pedone, Paris, 2008) 39.

[273] W. Friedmann, *The Changing Structure of International Law* (Columbia UP, New York, 1964).

[274] C.W. Jenks, *The Common Law of Mankind* (Stevens, London, 1958).

[275] On constitutionalism bringing Friedmann's theory one step further, see the remarks of A. Peters, 'Global Constitutionalism Revisited' (2005) 11 *International Legal Theory* 39, 49.

[276] On the Kantian and Grotian dimensions of the liberal school of international law, see G. J. Simpson, 'Imagined Consent: Democratic Liberalism in International Legal Theory' (1994) 15 Aust. YBIL 103.

[277] See the remarks of J. Klabbers on the moralism behind constitutionalism, J. Klabbers, 'The Paradox of International Institutional Law' (2008) 5 IOLR 1–23, 16.

[278] For a criticism of that dimension of constitutionalist theories, see J. d'Aspremont, 'The Foundations of the International Legal Order' (2007) 18 FYIL 219–55. See also R. Collins, 'Constitutionalism as Liberal-Juridical Consciousness: Echoes from International Law's Past' (2009) 22 LJIL 251–87. Such a value-sceptic position is classically construed by modern natural lawyers as being that of a moral, minimalist. See e.g. A. Buchanan, *Justice, Legitimacy and Self-Determination. Moral Foundations for International Law* (OUP, Oxford, 2007) 38.

[279] On this point, see S.R. Ratner, 'From Enlightened Positivism to Cosmopolitan Justice: Obstacles and Opportunities', *From Bilateralism to Community Interest: Essays in Honour of Judge Bruno Simma* (OUP, Oxford, 2011) (forthcoming).

[280] See the remarks of N. Fassbender in N. Tsagourias (ed), *Transnational Constitutionalism: International and European Perspectives* (CUP, Cambridge, 2007) 312.

[281] See generally Verdross, *Die Verfassung der Völkerrechtsgemeinschaft* (Springer, Berlin, 1926). For a contemporary re-appraisal of Verdross, see E. Lagrange, 'Retour sur un classique : A. Verdross, Die Verfassung der Völkerrechtsgemeinschaft' (2008) 4 *Revue générale de droit international public* 973–84. See also the remarks of A. Orakhelashvili, *The Interpretation of Acts and Rules in Public International Law* (OUP, Oxford, 2008) 63 or A. Orakhelashvili, 'Natural Law and Justice', *Max Planck Encyclopedia of Public International Law*, available at <http://www.mpepil.com> para. 22.

master, Kelsen,[282] and the school of natural law. The features of natural law found in the writings of Verdross have not vanished in modern constitutionalist legal thinking.[283]

Despite the undeniable kinship between (early) constitutionalism and the natural law school, constitutionalist theory remains, from the standpoint of the argument made in this book, consistent with the formalism advocated in mainstream legal scholarship. Indeed, it has not put into question the formal law-ascertainment system upon which international law-identification rests in international legal scholarship. On the contrary, by trying to tame the perception of State-centrism in mainstream legal scholarship, the constitutionalist school of international law indirectly contributes to the reinforcement of the source thesis.

It will not come as a surprise that constitutionalism has stirred various criticisms coming from across the entire spectrum of the international legal scholarship.[284] Constitutionalism has been criticized as manifesting a vain idealism of unity and coherence.[285] Some critics have also pinpointed the hegemonic overtones of their agenda purportedly dedicated to the promotion of global values.[286] Others have bemoaned their striving for the reinvention of the sovereign authority at the international level[287] or their faith in international institutions as the bearers of progressive values.[288] In the same vein, constitutionalists have been criticized for attempting to find a substitute for sovereignty in an international system where choices are made by experts having recourse to technical vocabularies.[289] It has also been suggested that the formal unity pursued by international constitutionalists is a mirage luring scholars into believing that international law is more akin to constitutional law

[282] On some differences between Kelsen and Verdross, see B. Conforti, 'The Theory of Competence in Verdross' (1994) 5 EJIL 70–7. See also J. Kammerhofer, *Uncertainty in International Law: A Kelsenian Perspective* (Routledge, London, 2010) 210.

[283] On the idea that *jus cogens* is grounded in the values of natural law, see B. Simma, 'The Contribution of Alfred Verdross to the Theory of International Law' (1995) 6 EJIL 33—54, 53. On the various foundations of *jus cogens*, see R. Kolb, *Théorie du ius cogens international: essai de relecture du concept* (PUF, Paris, 2001); see also the remarks of R.P. Barnidge 'Questioning the Legitimacy of Jus Cogens in the Global Legal Order' (2008) 38 *Israel Yearbook on Human Rights* 199. On the severance of *jus cogens* from natural law, see A.Orakhelashvili, 'Natural Law and Justice', *Max Planck Encyclopedia of Public International Law*, available at <http://www.mpepil.com> para. 34.

[284] For an insightful overview of constitutionalism and its critiques, see N. Tsagourias (ed), *Transnational Constitutionalism: International and European Perspectives* (CUP, Cambridge, 2007) and in particular the contribution of W. Werner, 'The Never-ending Closure: Constitutionalism and International Law', at 329.

[285] A. Somek 'Kelsen Lives' (2007) 18 EJIL 451.

[286] J. D'Aspremont, 'The Foundations of the International Legal Order' (2007) 18 FYIL 219–55; See also M. Koskenniemi, according to whom constitutionalism and empire go well together even though constitutionalism is closely connected to transparency and accountability: M. Koskenniemi, 'The Politics of International Law: 20 Years Later' (2009) 20 EJIL 7–19, 17.

[287] See D. Kennedy, 'The International Style in Postwar Law and Politics' (1994) 1 Utah L. Rev. 7, 14.

[288] A. Orford, 'The Gift of Formalism' (2004) 15 EJIL 179–95, 191.

[289] M. Koskenniemi, 'The Fate of Public International Law: Between Technique and Politics' (January 2007) 70(1) MLR 1–30, 29; See also the criticism by M. Koskenniemi in 'Constitutionalism as Mindset Reflection on Kantian Themes of International Law and Globalization' (2007) 8(1) *Theoretical Inquiries in Law* article 2. See, however, Koskenniemi 'The Politics of International Law: 20 Years Later' (2009) 20 EJIL 7–19.

than private law, and that this may well end up cementing the fragmentation of the primary rules of international law.[290]

This is not the place to discuss these criticisms. For the purposes of this book, all that must be taken from the foregoing is the fact that constitutionalist scholars continue to adhere to the source thesis for the sake of law-ascertainment.[291] By trying to promote constitutional law—which they see as having successfully tamed sovereignty and protected the individual at the domestic level—at the international level, they have remained loyal to the necessity of identifying law through formal law-ascertainment standards. Hence, although their progressive and reformist agenda shows a clear normative position in favour of substantive unity and the subjection of politics to legal institutions,[292] many of them uphold formal law-identification and perpetuate the distinction between law and non-law. Even though, like most commentators in mainstream international legal scholarship, they have not taken pains to explain the foundations of formalism,[293] many of them have not concealed the reasons for their attachment to formal law-ascertainment and, in particular, its contribution to the authority of law, the viability of the legal system as well as the rule of law.[294]

290 J. Klabbers, 'Constitutionalism Lite' (2004) 1 IOLR 31. On the different conceptions of formal unity, see the interesting work of M. Prost, *The Concept of Unity in Public International Law*, Hart Monographs in Transnational and International Law (Hart, Oxford, 2011) (forthcoming).

291 In the same sense, see W. Werner, in N. Tsagourias (ed), *Transnational Constitutionalism: International and European Perspectives* (CUP, Cambridge, 2007) 329, 330. For J. Klabbers, much of the debate on constitutionalism in international law can be seen as a debate on sources in disguise. See J. Klabbers, 'Constitutionalism and the making of international law' (2008) 5 NoFo 84, 88. See also the remarks of S.R. Ratner, 'From Enlightened Positivism to Cosmopolitan Justice: Obstacles and Opportunities', *From Bilateralism to Community Interest: Essays in Honour of Judge Bruno Simma* (OUP, Oxford, 2011) (forthcoming) 2.

292 See e.g. B. Fassbender, in N. Tsagourias (ed), *Transnational Constitutionalism: International and European Perspectives* (CUP, Cambridge, 2007) 307, 320.

293 R. Collins, 'Constitutionalism as Liberal-Juridical Consciousness: Echoes from International Law's Past' (2009) 22 LJIL 251, especially 255 and 270.

294 C. Tomuschat, 'General Course on Public International Law' (1999) 281 RCADI 9–438, 26–9.

4

The Critiques of Formal Law-Ascertainment in the Theory of the Sources of International Law

In the same way that debates about the foundations of formalism in law-ascertainment in general legal theory trickled down into the theory of the sources of international law, the criticisms levelled against formal law-ascertainment in the former found a considerable echo in the latter. This is why it is necessary to start exploring the criticism of formal law-ascertainment in general legal theory (4.1), before turning to the corresponding criticisms in the theory of the sources of international law (4.2).

4.1 The Critiques of Formal Law-Ascertainment in General Legal Theory: A Sketch

As has been explained in the previous chapter, formalism is the direct consequence of the so-called source thesis whereby law is identified in accordance with its formal pedigree. The source thesis, although touched upon by scholastic scholars, was originally developed by Hobbes, Bentham, and Austin (this is what was called the *restrictive source thesis*). It was subsequently refined by Hart and his followers who contended that law-ascertaining criteria should be inferred from the practice of law-applying officials (this is what was called the *social thesis*). Before being sharpened by Hart, the source thesis suffered fierce criticisms by modern natural lawyers, which will be briefly recalled here (4.1.1). The subsequent critique of legal realists (4.1.2), the natural law-inspired critique drawn by Dworkin (4.1.3), and the critique associated with postmodernism (4.1.4) will then be given careful attention.

4.1.1 Modern natural law objections

As has already been explained, formalism emerged from the ruins of scholastic natural law theory. Despite having been the first to contemplate some form of formalism with which to identify law,[1] natural law theorists had espoused a

[1] J. Finnis. 'The Truth in Legal Positivism', in R.P. George (ed), *The Autonomy of Law: Essays of Legal Positivism* (OUP, Oxford, 1996) 195, 199; see also J. Finnis, 'On the incoherence of Legal positivism', in D. Patterson (ed), *A Companion to Philosophy of Law and Legal Theory*, (Blackwell, Oxford, 1999) 134, 136–9.

substantive conception of validity which was superseded by the utilitarian systematizations of the source thesis. Because the source thesis arose in reaction against the substantive validity theory of the scholastic natural law school, the source thesis was never the object of criticism by the ancestral natural law school.

Scholastic and subsequent Grotian natural law theories have later been taken up by modern natural law theorists. In my view, the source thesis has, however, remained mostly unchallenged by these (neo-)natural law approaches. Indeed, as is exemplified by Fuller's eight criteria of legality,[2] modern natural law criticisms have been primarily concerned with the determination of the essential—and mostly procedural—features of law.[3] More specifically, modern natural law has focused on the question of the authority of law and how to make law as perfect as possible to ensure compliance with it.[4] Modern natural law does not posit that law cannot be identified through the source thesis and does not necessarily reject formal law-ascertaining criteria.[5] It is no accident that Fuller's attachment to formalism may be the result of Wittgenstein's influence.[6] To a very large extent, therefore, it is fair to say that natural law theory and other theories of law promoting formalism as the basis for law-ascertainment do not necessarily contradict each other. The same is true of modern international natural law theory which, in this respect, strives not to be conflated with naturalism.[7]

[2] See the famous debate between Hart and Fuller in the *Harvard Law Review*: H.L.A. Hart, 'Positivism and the Separation of Law and Morals' (1958) 71(4) Harv. L. Rev. 593 and L. Fuller, 'Positivism and Fidelity to Law: A Reply to Professor Hart' (1958) 71(4) Harv. L. Rev. 631. See the symposium in the *New York University Law Review*: (2008) 83(4) NYULR; see also the account of that debate by F. Haldemann in 'Gustav Radbruch vs. Hans Kelsen: A Debate on Nazi Law' (June 2005) 18(2) *Ratio Juris* 170.

[3] As J. Brunnée and S.J. Toope, argue, it is not certain that the expression 'inner morality of law' used by Fuller was most adequate to describe his eight criteria of legality, for this has brought about a lot of confusion. See J. Brunnée and S.J. Toope, *Legitimacy and Legality in International Law. An Interactional Account* (CUP, Cambridge, 2010) 29.

[4] See F. Shauer, 'Positivism as Pariah', in R.P. George (ed), *The Autonomy of Law: Essays of Legal Positivism* (OUP, Oxford, 1996) 31, 38–9; K. Greenawalt, 'Too Thin and Too Rich', in R.P. George (ed), ibid, 1, 9; R. George Wright, 'Does Positivism Matter?' in R.P. George (ed), ibid, 57, 62; A.D. Cullison, 'Morality and the Foundations of Legal Positivism' (1985–1986) 20 *Valparaiso University Law Review* 61; Liam Murphy, 'Better to See Law This Way' (2008) 83 NYULR 1088, 1092; B. Bix, 'Natural Law Theory', in D. Patterson (ed), *A Companion to Philosophy of Law and Legal Theory* (Blackwell, Oxford, 1999) 223–40.

[5] J. Finnis, 'On the incoherence of legal positivism', in D. Patterson (ed), ibid, 134, 140: 'No natural law theory of law has ever claimed that in order to be law a norm must be required by morality, or that all legal requirements are also—independently of being validly posited as law—moral requirements'. It has even been argued that formalism is a common denominator of natural law and positivism. See E.J. Weinrib, 'Legal Formalism: On the Immanent Rationality of Law' (1988) 97 Yale L. J. 949 in D. Patterson, *Philosophy of Law and Legal Theory: An Anthology* (Blackwell, Oxford, 2003) 325–74, 361. See also the remarks of G. Fletcher, 'Comparative Law as a Subversive Discipline' (1998) 46 Am. J. Comp. L. 683, 685.

[6] L. Fuller, *The Morality of Law* (Revised edn, Yale UP, New Haven, 1969) 186.

[7] See A. Buchanan, *Justice, Legitimacy and Self-Determination. Moral Foundations for International Law* (OUP, Oxford, 2007) 4, 16, 21, and 66. (Buchanan states the difference between moral theory and naturalism). See also J. Brunnée and S.J. Toope, *Legitimacy and Legality in International Law. An Interactional Account* (CUP, Cambridge, 2010) 29 and 46.

It is not only that there is little contradiction between modern natural law theory and utilitarian theory based on the source thesis. There also are many convergences among them. For instance, Hart actually agreed with natural lawyers that unjust law has a much weaker claim to obedience than just law.[8] Moreover, utilitarians like Bentham and Hart have never denied that, as a matter of historical fact, the development of legal systems has been powerfully influenced by moral standards, and vice-versa.[9] In the same vein, it must be recalled that many supporters of the source thesis have espoused what has been called 'inclusive legal positivism' according to which it is not inconceivable that law-ascertaining rules themselves elevate moral norms into legal rules.[10]

Despite Hart's modest concession to natural lawyers through his inclusive positivist approach,[11] he fell short of embracing the classical natural law approach of a law-ascertainment based on the moral value of the command. It is true that Hart may have ignited some confusion in this respect by virtue of his argument related to the minimal conditions of viability of law, which he maladroitly labelled the 'minimum content of natural law'.[12] This assertion has been one of the most misunderstood parts of Hart's theory, for he gave the impression that the content of law could ultimately play a role in its identification.[13] In fact, Hart never departed from his purely formal law-ascertaining criteria. The reference to substantive criteria in his minimal content of natural law theory was only aimed at evaluating the sustainability of legal systems and, therefore, did not affect his adoption of the source thesis. This being said, the rift between modern natural law theory and theories based on the source thesis is much narrower than usually depicted. Accordingly, it is no surprise that modern natural law theory did little to challenge the role played by formalism in law-identification in general legal theory.

4.1.2 Legal realism

The first serious criticism of formalism came from legal realism. Legal realism emerged at the beginning of the 20th century and purported to provide novel methods of legal interpretation. In American jurisprudence, legal realism began to

[8] K. Greenawalt, 'Too Thin and Too Rich', in R.P. George (ed), *The Autonomy of Law: Essays of Legal Positivism* (OUP, Oxford, 1996) 1, 10. On the convergences between Hart and Fuller, see more specifically, N. Naffine, 'The Common Discourse of Hart and Fuller', in P. Cane (ed), *The Hart-Fuller Debate in the Twenty-First Century* (Hart, Oxford, 2010) 217–25.

[9] H.L.A. Hart, 'Positivism and the Separation of Law and Morals' (1958) 71(4) Harv. L. Rev. 593–629, 598–9.

[10] Cfr *supra* 3.1.3. On the objections against inclusive legal positivism by J. Raz and S. Shapiro, see *supra* note 82.

[11] As is well-known, in the postscript joined to the second edition of the *Concept of Law*, Hart almost exclusively addressed Dworkin's objections. It is on this occasion that he yielded to some of the objections raised by modern natural lawyers and elaborated on his inclusive legal positivism: H.L.A. Hart, *The Concept of Law* (2nd edn, OUP, Oxford, 1997) 238–76.

[12] H.L.A. Hart, ibid, 193.

[13] See for instance, L. May, 'Habeas Corpus and the Normative Jurisprudence of International Law' (2009) 23(2) LJIL 291–10.

thrive after the heyday of formalism came to an end in the first half of the 20th century. While Oliver Wendell Holmes had ushered in the realist critique of formalism,[14] it is probably Roscoe Pound who launched the first fully-fledged attack against formalism by criticizing accounts of adjudication which perceive the reasoning of judges in mechanical terms.[15] This critique was later extended by Karl Llewellyn, whose faith in functional pragmatism led him to reject formalism as unable to truly dictate any concrete result.[16]

Legal realism cannot be seen as adhering to one particular ideology or methodology. There are various strands, each with a different agenda and methodology[17]—with divergences revolving around what determines the judge's response to the facts of a particular case.[18] Realists proved averse to systematic theorizing and denied the existence of a realistic school.[19] Yet, all strands of realism seem permeated by predictive theory and an avowed pragmatism.[20] Indeed, the realist critique promoted a move away from formalism—understood as adjudicative neutrality and immanent intelligibility of legal arguments[21]—to ensure dynamic political change. Realist objections against neutral adjudication models (formalism) entailed rejections of what they saw as an 'abuse of logic'[22] or 'mechanical jurisprudence'.[23]

Although they primarily centred on formalism as adjudicative neutrality and immanent intelligibility of legal arguments, the realist critiques did not spare formalism in law-ascertainment. While some realist authors did not completely shed formal criteria of legality when it came to ascertaining law,[24] it is hard to deny, however, that the realist rejections against formalism as adjudicative neutrality brought about, albeit not explicitly, a rejection of formalism as law-ascertainment. Indeed, by adopting an external point of view,[25] legal realism advocated an ever-decreasing emphasis on words and an ever-increasing emphasis on observable

[14] O.W. Homes, 'The Path to Law' (1897) 10 Harv L. Rev. 457.

[15] R. Pound, 'Do We Need a Philosophy of Law' (1905) 5 *College Law Review* 339; R. Pound, 'Common law and Legislation' (1908) 21 Harv L. Rev. 383; R. Pound, 'The Theory of Judicial Decisions' (1923) 36 Harv L. Rev. 802.

[16] See for instance, K. Lewellyn, 'A Realistic Jurisprudence—the Next Step', in D. Patterson (ed), *Philosophy of Law and Legal Theory: An Anthology* (Blackwell, Oxford, 2003) 22, 22. For realism leading to radical empiricism, see A. Ross, *Introduction à l'empirisme juridique* (Bruylant/LGDJ, Brussels, 2004).

[17] For a mapping of the various stands of legal realism, see V. Nourse and G. Shaffer, 'Varieties of New Legal Realism: Can A New World Order Prompt A New Legal Theory', (2009) 95 Cornell. L. Rev. 61.

[18] See the taxonomy proposed by B. Leiter, 'Legal Realism', in D. Patterson (ed), *A Companion to Philosophy of Law and Legal Theory* (Blackwell, Oxford, 1999) 261, 271.

[19] B. Leiter, 'Legal Realism', in D. Patterson (ed), ibid, 261, 261.

[20] On pragmatism and legal realism, see I. Ward, *An Introduction to Critical Legal Theory* (Routledge, New York, 1998) 141.

[21] On this conception of formalism, cfr *supra* 2.1.2.

[22] A.J. Sebok, 'Misunderstanding Positivism' (1994–1995) 93 Mich. L. Rev. 2052, 2093.

[23] This is the famous expression of Roscoe Pound: 'Mechanical Jurisprudence'(1908) 8 Colum. L. Rev. 605.

[24] B. Leiter, 'Legal Realism', in D. Patterson (ed), *A Companion to Philosophy of Law and Legal Theory* (Blackwell, Oxford, 1999) 261, 263.

[25] See for instance, A. Ross, 'Le Concept de Droit selon Hart', in A. Ross, *Introduction à l'empirisme juridique* (Bruylant/LGDJ, Brussels, 2004) 183–89. On this particular point, see U. Scarpelli, *Qu'est-ce que le positivisme juridique* (Bruylant/LGDJ, Paris, 1996) 55.

behaviour.[26] Accordingly, a norm is a norm of law as long as it constitutes an accurate prediction of what a court will do.[27] In that sense, law ceases to be identified through its pedigree. Hence, law-identification boils down to a mere prediction of the behaviour of law-applying authorities, thereby shrouding law-ascertainment in great indeterminacy.

Legal realism has been the object of severe criticisms from various directions. The most stringent of these criticisms is that legal realism cannot completely forsake formal law-ascertainment, for there will always be a need for secondary rules conferring powers on law-applying officials whose behaviours constitute the law-ascertainment standards.[28] This is one of the reasons why, irrespective of the extraordinary legacy of legal realism, its rejection of formalism as law-ascertainment would probably have remained anecdotal[29] if it had not been taken up again by a new breed of legal realists.[30] Indeed, the gist of the realist critique of formalism as a theory of adjudication has subsequently been taken over by the policy-oriented school of jurisprudence, as well as those scholars affiliated to critical legal studies, and expanded.[31] These theories are examined below.[32] Another offspring of legal realism also ought to be mentioned: New Legal Realism. This new strand of legal realism has consolidated itself over the last decade and has been an increasingly successful approach to domestic law and international law.[33] Because international

[26] K. Lewellyn, 'A Realistic Jurisprudence—the Next Step', in D. Patterson (ed), *Philosophy of Law and Legal Theory: An Anthology* (Blackwell, Oxford, 2003) 22, 38.

[27] B. Leiter, 'Legal Realism', in D. Patterson (ed), *A Companion to Philosophy of Law and Legal Theory* (Blackwell, Oxford, 1999) 261, 262.

[28] One of the most famous and influential criticisms of legal realism has been elaborated by H.L.A Hart in *The Concept of Law* (2nd edn, OUP, Oxford, 1997) 136–37. See also N. Lacey, *A Life of H.L.A. Hart: The Nightmare and the Noble Dream* (OUP, Oxford, 2004). The criticisms formulated by Hart may explain why British legal scholars have remained rather indifferent to legal realism. On this point see N. Duxbury, 'Post-Realism and Legal Process', in D. Patterson, *A Companion to Philosophy of Law and Legal Process* (Blackwell, Oxford, 1999) 292.

[29] See the criticism of A. D'Amato, who argues that legal realism does not offer much of a research agenda when it comes to law-identification: A. D'Amato, 'The Need for a Theory of International Law', Northwestern University School of Law, Public Law and Legal Theory Research Paper Series (2007) 5.

[30] It is noteworthy that Hart himself praised some aspects of the legacy of legal realism: 'its main effect was to convince many judges, lawyers, practical and academic, of two things: first, that they should always suspect, although not always in the end reject, any claim that existing legal rules or precedents were constraints strong and complete enough to determine what a court's decision should be without other extra-legal considerations; secondly, that judges should not seek to bootleg silently into the law their own conceptions of the law's aims or justice or social policy or other extra-legal element required for decision but should openly identify and discuss them'. See. H.L.A. Hart, 'American Jurisprudence through English Eyes: The Nightmare and the Noble Dream' (1976–1977) 11 Ga. L. Rev. 969, 978.

[31] Interestingly, Hart somehow recognized this aspect of the legacy of legal realism, H.L.A. Hart, ibid, 978.

[32] Cfr *infra* 4.1.4, 4.2.3, and 4.2.4.

[33] See generally G. Shaffer, 'A New Legal Realism: Method in International Economic Law Scholarship', in C.B. Picker, et al. (eds), *International Economic Law—The State and Future of the Discipline* (Hart Publishing, Oxford, 2008) 29–42; H. Erlanger et al. 'New Legal Realism Symposium: Is it Time for a New Legal Realism?' (2005) 2 Wisconsin L. Rev. 335; S. Macaulay, 'The New Versus the Old Legal Realism: Things Ain't What They Used to Be' (2005) Wisconsin L. Rev. 365, 375; V. Nourse and G. Shaffer, 'Varieties of New Legal Realism: Can A New World Order Prompt A New Legal Theory' (2009) 95 Cornell L. Rev. 61.

economic law has been one of its most important breeding grounds, New Legal Realism is briefly analyzed below as well together with the manifestation of realism in international legal scholarship.[34] Finally, reference must be made to the realist scholarship which emerged in the field of international relations. Although sharing little kinship with legal realism, the realist strand of international relations scholarship generated a radical objection against international law that includes a rejection of formal identification of rules.[35] This realist critique is also—albeit briefly—examined below.[36]

4.1.3 Dworkin's famous attacks on the source and social theses

While, as has been shown above, both modern natural law theory and legal realism failed to provide a direct and compelling criticism of the source and social theses on which formal law-ascertainment is based, a more serious challenge was mounted by Ronald Dworkin, a former *protégé* of Hart himself, whom he succeeded as the Chair of Jurisprudence at Oxford.

The fierce debates between Dworkin and Hart are well-known and it would be of no avail to repeat them here. It suffices to recall that Dworkin's main objection to Hart's *source thesis* is that Hart's 'central notion of a single fundamental test for law forces us to miss the important roles of these standards that are not rules.'[37] Dworkin criticizes Hart by contending that law comprises numerous norms, the legal validity of which cannot be traced back to the sources of law identified by the rules of recognition. In other words, Dworkin, referring more particularly to his famous 'principles', holds that not all law is enacted as law and that even if it is not enacted as law it remains legally binding.[38]

Although it has been contested,[39] this aspect of Dworkin's theory[40] probably explains why his conception of law has sometimes been dubbed a 'weak natural law theory'[41] and why Hart himself considered Dworkin to be the contemporary version

[34] Cfr *infra* 4.2.2.

[35] The embodiment of the movement is probably H. Morgenthau. See *Politics Among Nations*, (2nd revised edn, Knopf, New York, 1954) 15–16; See R. Aron, *Paix et Guerre Entre des Nations* (Calmann-Lévy, Paris, 1984). On H. Morgenthau, see generally M. Koskenniemi, 'Image of Law and International Relations', in M. Byers (ed), *The Role of Law in International Politics: Essays in International Relations and International Law* (OUP, Oxford, 2000) 17–34, 28.

[36] Cfr *infra* 4.2.2.

[37] R. Dworkin, 'The Model of Rules', in D. Patterson (ed), *Philosophy of Law and Legal Theory: An Anthology* (Blackwell, Oxford, 2003) 46, 51.

[38] Ibid; see also R. Dworkin, *Taking Rights Seriously* (Harvard UP, Cambridge, 1977).

[39] J. Coleman and B. Leiter, 'Legal Positivism, in D. Patterson (ed), *A Companion to Philosophy of Law and Legal Theory* (Blackwell, Oxford, 1999) 241, 242.

[40] On Dworkin's criticisms of the source thesis, see A. Marmor, 'Legal Conventionalism' in J. Coleman (ed), *Hart's Postscript: Essays on the Postscript to 'The Concept of Law'* (OUP, Oxford, 2001) 193, 194.

[41] See K. Greenawalt, 'Too Thin and Too Rich', in R.P. George (ed), *The Autonomy of Law: Essays of Legal Positivism* (OUP, Oxford, 1996) 1, 5. In the same vein, see N. Onuf, 'Do Rules Say What They Do? From Ordinary Language to International Law' (1985) 26 Harvard JIL 385, 404; B. Bix, 'Natural Law Theory', in D. Patterson (ed), *A Companion to Philosophy of Law and Legal Theory* (Blackwell, Oxford, 1999) 223, 234–7.

of 'the Noble Dream'.[42] Hart's late turn to inclusive (soft) positivism was aimed at accommodating this part of Dworkin's criticism.[43]

Dworkin's criticisms have not been limited to the source thesis. Dworkin also discredits the *social thesis*, for, according to Dworkin, the criteria that make the rule of recognition must be accepted not only by officials but also by citizens.[44] More fundamentally, Dworkin rejects Hart's social thesis because it suffers from what has been called the *semantic sting*, that is 'the argument that unless lawyers and judges share factual criteria about the grounds of law there can be no significant thought or debate about what the law is'.[45] As has been explained above, for Hart, the language of law can be meaningful only if lawyers share the same tests, that is, if they abide by the same law-ascertaining criteria. If they disagree about these criteria, law ceases to be meaningful. For Dworkin, this makes Hart's theory incapable of explaining disagreements among lawyers. Lawyers disagree, according to Dworkin, because they have competing conceptions of some concepts. They rely upon substantively different understandings of the relevant concept, and they exchange arguments in support of one understanding or the other. Hart's idea that lawyers must share the same law-ascertainment tests makes such disagreement impossible because, according to Dworkin, an agreement about the law-ascertainment tests involves agreement about their correct application. This means that, for Dworkin, the basic standards about the ascertainment of rules necessarily entail criteria for their correct application, thereby making disagreement impossible. Dworkin concludes that Hart denies the possibility of disagreement and, accordingly, his theory is at odds with legal practice. In that sense, Hart's theory cannot account for the nature of legal disagreement. Genuine disagreements about the requirements of law would be impossible. As a consequence, Hart's theory cannot explain how law accomplishes what he considered to be its basic function, that is, to provide standards that guide behaviour.[46]

Dworkin's argument is not without clout. However, it is not certain that his objection clearly frustrates the social thesis. Indeed, Dworkin infers from the existence of an agreement on law-ascertaining criteria an agreement on their application. It is not certain that Hart clearly held such a position and went so far as to claim that the social thesis implies an agreement about the application of secondary rules. One can bemoan that Hart, in his postscript, denied that his theory suffers from the

[42] H.L.A. Hart, 'American Jurisprudence through English Eyes: The Nightmare and the Noble Dream' (1976–1977) 11 Ga L. Rev. 969, 983.

[43] Cfr *supra* 3.1.3.

[44] As is well-known, Hart denies that possibility. For Hart, it is implausible that most members of the public in a complex society will grasp and accept the criteria of recognition. It suffices that citizens display obedience. For Hart, the reasons why officials abide by the rule of recognition does not matter and is beside the point, so long as the officials engage in the sort of conduct that bespeaks commitment or supportiveness which sustains the operativeness of the legal system: H.L.A. Hart, *The Concept of Law* (2nd edn, OUP, Oxford, 1997) 59–60; 110–11.

[45] See R. Dworkin, *Law's Empire* (Fontana Press, London, 1986) 44–5.

[46] R. Dworkin, ibid, 32. On this point of disagreement, see the remarks of T. Endicott, 'Herbert Hart and the Semantic Sting' in J. Coleman (ed), *Hart's Postscript: Essays on the Postscript to 'The Concept of Law'* (OUP, Oxford, 2001) 39, 40–1.

so-called semantic sting and did not really take pains to reply to Dworkin's argument on this point.[47] His postscript is mostly directed at Dworkin's criticism of his source thesis. This being said, Dworkin's attack on the social thesis remains highly speculative, for Hart did not make clear that an agreement on how to apply law-ascertaining criteria is inherent in the social thesis.[48] Moreover, it must be acknowledged that Dworkin's argument was premised on his ambition to construct a theory of adjudication[49] which, if followed correctly, only yields answers to questions of American law.[50] Hart's social thesis, for its part, was not aimed at establishing a convincing theory of adjudication. It was simply meant to supplement the source thesis, which allows for the formal ascertainment of rules.[51] This does not mean, however, that Dworkin's and Hart's theories can be reconciled.[52] Rather it signifies that, like legal realist and modern natural law critiques of formalism, 'the debates between Dworkin and his opponents create the impression of being missed connections more often than responsive encounters.'[53]

4.1.4 Postmodern objections to the source and social theses

'Postmodernism' has become a catchword that embraces a host of different concepts and attitudes in general legal theory.[54] Among others, it has been associated with anti-liberal, post-structuralist, deconstructivist, and anti-universal approaches. It is also associated with a string of different paradigms like the rejection of reasoned

[47] H.L.A. Hart, *The Concept of Law* (2nd edn, OUP, Oxford, 1997) 246; See the remarks of Endicott who argues that Hart, in the postscript, seems 'mystified' by Dworkin's allegation: T. Endicott, ibid, 39, 40.

[48] See also Raz's criticisms of Dworkin's semantic sting argument. According to Raz, Dworkin is wrong to think that Hart and others were concerned with the meaning of the word 'law'. Dworkin's semantic sting argument is meant to show that certain concepts cannot be given a semantic account. For Raz, Dworkin's conclusion that certain concepts, the concept of law among them, cannot be explained rests on the claim that the application of concepts based on criteria cannot be subject to dispute, regarding what he calls 'pivotal cases'. See, J. Raz, 'Two Views of the Nature of the Theory of Law: A Partial Comparison' in J. Coleman (ed), *Hart's Postscript: Essays on the Postscript to 'The Concept of Law'* (OUP, Oxford, 2001) 1, especially 3 and 13.

[49] J. Coleman and B. Leiter, 'Legal Positivism', in D. Patterson (ed), *A Companion to Philosophy of Law and Legal Theory* (Blackwell, Oxford, 1999) 241, 242. In the same vein, see J. Beckett, 'Behind Relative Normativity: Rules and Process as Prerequisites of Law' (2001) 12 EJIL 627, especially 629.

[50] J. Raz 'Two Views of the Nature of the Theory of Law: A Partial Comparison' in J. Coleman (ed), *Hart's Postscript: Essays on the Postscript to 'The Concept of Law'* (OUP, Oxford, 2001) 1, 27–28.

[51] Cfr *supra* 3.1.3.

[52] J. Raz, ibid, 1, 36–7.

[53] M. Kramer, *In Defense of Legal Positivism: Law Without Trimmings* (OUP, Oxford, 1999) 128. See also J. Coleman, according to whom much of the debate between positivists and Dworkin 'appears rather foolish unless there is a version of positivism that makes Dworkin's criticisms, if not compelling, at least relevant': J. Coleman, 'Negative and positive positivism', in D. Patterson (ed), *Philosophy of Law and Legal Theory: An Anthology* (Blackwell, Oxford, 2003) 116, 119.

[54] D. Patterson argues that 'the discussion of postmodernism has fallen into the hands of those who use it as a vehicle for the propagation of specious ideas'. See D. Patterson, 'Postmodernism', in D. Patterson (ed), *A Companion to Philosophy of Law and Legal Theory* (Blackwell, Oxford, 1999) 375, 375.

narrative, the move away from universal grand theories, the deconstruction of 'metanarratives', the empowerment of the rule-applier, the politics of language, or general textual indeterminacy. In this book, the term is more simply used to refer generally to the critiques of law affiliated with critical legal studies and deconstructivism, which arose in the last quarter of the 20th century in general legal theory and which subsequently gained currency in the theory of the sources of international law.[55]

As the previous paragraphs have attempted to show, modern natural law and Dworkin's criticisms, albeit for very different reasons, have only modestly debilitated the place of formalism in general legal theory of law-ascertainment. This is why, in my view, the dominance of formal law-ascertainment theory had not been overturned, at least in Europe, until recently. It is argued here that the most serious challenge to the dominance of the source and social theses, which lie at the heart of formal law-ascertainment, came as a result of the emergence of a critique associated with deconstructivism[56] and critical legal studies.[57]

It must preliminarily be pointed out that the critical legal project has never identified itself as a separate, self-conscious, and monolithic movement,[58] producing one clear set of objections against formalism. Moreover, this critique, like many of its predecessors does not directly take aim at law and formal law-ascertainment. Yet, it is argued here that this postmodern critique has provided a breeding ground for the contemporary contestation of formal law-ascertainment, while simultaneously reviving the realist and policy-oriented critiques.

The heterogeneity of the sources of inspiration behind this critique undoubtedly constitutes one of its hallmarks. Indeed, this critique has been informed by philosophies as diverse as structuralism,[59] post-structuralism[60] like that of the Frankfurt

[55] The term is thus not reserved for the second generation of critical legal scholars but is used more broadly. For such a restrictive use of the word, see D. Kennedy, 'A Rotation in Contemporary Legal Scholarship' (2011) 12 *German Law Journal* 338, 356–61.

[56] See generally J. M. Balkin, 'Deconstruction', in D. Patterson (ed), *A Companion to Philosophy of Law and Legal Theory* (Blackwell, Oxford, 1999) 367–74.

[57] The word 'critical' in CLS is not mean to suggest criticizing but refers to a particular reasoning devised by theorists of the Frankfurt School. See D. Kennedy, 'Critical Theory, Structuralism and Contemporary Legal Scholarship' (1985–1986) 21 New Eng. L. Rev. 209, 216–17. On CLS, see generally R.M. Unger, 'The Critical Legal Studies Movement' (1983) 96 Harv. L. Rev. 561.

[58] D. Kennedy, 'Critical Theory, Structuralism and Contemporary Legal Scholarship' (1986) 21 New Eng. L. Rev. 209, 277. On the history of this movement, see M. Kelman, *A Guide to Critical Legal Studies* (Harvard UP, Cambridge,1987).

[59] As is explained by Kennedy, the tradition of structuralism in linguistics has been primarily influenced by Ferdinand de Saussure's distinction between synchronic and diachronic studies of language. See F. de Saussure, *Course in General Linguistics* (The Philosophical Library, New York, 1959). Before de Saussure, linguists had mostly studied the historical development of language. De Saussure considered his work to be 'diachronic' (i.e. meaning is produced by the relations among linguistic terms themselves rather than by history): D. Kennedy, ibid, 209, 249.

[60] The use of the work of post-structuralists is seemingly a distinctive feature of those seen as constituting the second generation of critical legal scholars. See D. Kennedy, 'A Rotation in Contemporary Legal Scholarship' (2011) 12 *German Law Journal* 338, 357.

School,[61] French deconstructivism,[62] and critical Marxism.[63] In spite of the contradictions between the various strands from which it drew inspiration[64] and although each of them had respectively gone out of fashion in their original circles,[65] thinkers as different as De Saussure, Foucault, Lévi-Strauss, Derrida, Lyotard, and Piaget[66] became the beacons for this new generation of legal theorists.

The divergences between their forebears did not, however, prevent this new generation from coming to share a common concern for the awareness of how observation is embedded in its context, and concurrently developing a type of relativism reminiscent of legal realism.[67] They all grew attuned to similar objectives, namely the study of the conceptual apparatus, reasoning techniques, legal ideals, and key images deployed by legal professionals when they make legal arguments.[68] Most of them premised their work on the assumption that 'both the observed objects and the observing subjects of science are socially constituted and... have to be analysed and interpreted within their historical-social context'.[69] This new generation of theorists accordingly embarked on a study of legal thought as much as legal history, for they sought to capture the changes over time in these conceptual apparatuses, reasoning techniques, legal ideals, and key images, with a view to unearthing the

[61] On the influence of the Frankfurt School on CLS, see generally, K. Tuori, *Critical Legal Positivism* (Aldershot, Ashgate, 2002). See also A. Arato and S. Piccone (eds), *The Essential Frankfurt School Reader* (Urizen Books, NY, 1978).

[62] On the relationship between CLS and French deconstructivism, see D. Kennedy, 'A Semiotics of Legal Argument' (1991) 42 Syracuse L. Rev. 75. See also D.Z. Cass, 'Navigating the Newstream: Recent Critical Scholarship in International Law' (1996) 65 Nord. J. Int'l. L. 341, 359.

[63] It is interesting how this critique has been amenable to Marxism, which has proved a remarkable and unique feature of theoretical thought in the US during the Cold War.

[64] According to Kennedy, it is impossible to combine structuralism with critical theory, each of them setting the other aside. As a result, both structuralism and critical legal theory fail to provide the sort of definitive security which legal scholars have sought. See D. Kennedy, 'Critical Theory, Structuralism and Contemporary Legal Scholarship' (1986) 21 New Eng. L. Rev. 209, 275 and 287. See also D. Kennedy, 'A Rotation in Contemporary Legal Scholarship' (2011) 12 *German Law Journal* 338, 353; For a similar argument, see J.M. Balkin, 'Deconstruction', in D. Patterson (ed), *A Companion to Philosophy of Law and Legal Theory* (Blackwell, Oxford, 1999) 367–74.

[65] D. Kennedy, *The Rise and Fall of Classical Legal Thoughts* (re-edited in 2006, Beard Books, Washington DC) at xxxii.

[66] Among them, Foucault is probably the one who has proved the most influential. See especially his text 'Nietzsche, Genealogy, History' in D. Bouchard and S. Simon (eds), *Language, Countermemory, Practice: Selected Essays and Interviews by Michael Foucault* (Cornell UP, NY, 1977) 139. On the relationship between Foucault and postmodernism, see I. Ward, *An Introduction to Critical Legal Theory* (Routledge, NY, 1998) 146.

[67] On the kinship between critical legal studies and legal realism, see see A.L. Paulus, 'International Law After Postmodernism' (2001) 14 LJIL 737. See also D.Z. Cass, 'Navigating the Newstream: Recent Critical Scholarship in International Law' (1996) 65 Nord. J. Int'l L. 341, 377. See K. Kress, 'Legal Indeterminacy', in D. Patterson (ed), *Philosophy of Law and Legal Theory: An Anthology* (Blackwell, Oxford, 2003) 253; D. Kennedy, 'Critical Theory, Structuralism and Contemporary Legal Scholarship' (1986) 21 New Eng. L. Rev. 209, especially 210; G. Fletcher, 'Comparative Law as a Subversive Discipline' (1998) 46 Am. J. Comp. L. 683, 690.

[68] D. Kennedy, *The Rise and Fall of Classical Legal Thoughts* (re-edited in 2006, Beard Books, Washington DC) at ix.

[69] G. Frankenberg, 'Critical Theory', *Max Planck Encyclopedia of Public International Law*, available at <http://www.mpepil.com> para. 2.

structures within the 'legal consciousness' of a legal profession.[70] Although some of the streams from which it borrowed sought to deflect attention away from the social context,[71] the scholars affiliated with this critique have instead concentrated on the social context in fervently advocating the need to 'dislodge the complacent everyday perception of reality'.[72] This new postmodern critique, despite being invoked by—and embodying—the 'political left' in support of its attack against the mainstream,[73] is not actually designed to pursue an agenda to persuade others with programmatic alternatives.[74] Its aim is not to convert lawyers to (post-)structuralism or deconstructivism.[75] This critique grew entirely in a self-reflective fashion in the sense that it seeks to undo the 'false consciousness' of mainstream scholarship[76] and tries to develop a valid form of knowledge, which avoids the pitfalls of both naturalism and positivism[77] by adding structuralist and critical techniques to the repertoire available for the understanding of law.[78]

As mentioned earlier, this critique did not directly take aim at law and formal law-ascertainment. The various strands of thinking which nurtured this critique had not produced any reflection about law and law-identification, as illustrated by structuralism[79] and the Frankfurt School.[80] The 'radical distance from the materials of legal culture'[81] inherent in the Frankfurt School, however, began to impact the legal academy with the rise of critical legal studies.[82] Because the critical legal studies movement itself has not yielded a single, monolithic body of thought and has been

[70] See the definition provided by D. Kennedy, *The Rise and Fall of Classical Legal Thoughts* (re-edited in 2006, Beard Books, Washington DC) 27.

[71] This is the case of structuralism. See D. Kennedy, 'Critical Theory, Structuralism and Contemporary Legal Scholarship' (1986) 21 New Eng. L. Rev. 209, 214.

[72] D. Kennedy, ibid, 209, 214.

[73] D. Kennedy, ibid, 209, 247. See also D. Kennedy, 'A Rotation in Contemporary Legal Scholarship' (2011) 12 *German Law Journal* 338, pp. 338–40.

[74] D. Kennedy, 'Critical Theory, Structuralism and Contemporary Legal Scholarship' (1985–1986) 21 New Eng. L. Rev. 209, 247.

[75] D. Kennedy, *The Rise and Fall of Classical Legal Thoughts* (re-edited in 2006, Beard Books, Washington DC) at xiv.

[76] D. Kennedy, 'Critical Theory, Structuralism and Contemporary Legal Scholarship' (1986) 21 New Eng. L. Rev. 209, 223; see also D. Kennedy, 'A Rotation in Contemporary Legal Scholarship' (2011) 12 *German Law Journal* 338, 355.

[77] D. Kennedy, 'Critical Theory, Structuralism and Contemporary Legal Scholarship' (1986) 21 New Eng. L. Rev. 209, 227.

[78] D. Kennedy, *The Rise and Fall of Classical Legal Thoughts* (re-edited in 2006, Beard Books, Washington DC) at xiv.

[79] According to Kennedy, it is not surprising that structuralism hardly produced any legal theory, for a structural legal theory is difficult to imagine. See however the few works that have been influenced by structuralism referred to by D. Kennedy, 'Critical Theory, Structuralism and Contemporary Legal Scholarship' (1986) 21 New Eng. L. Rev. 209, 267.

[80] H. Rottleuthner, 'The Contribution of the Critical Theory of the Frankfurt School to the Sociology of Law' in A. Podgorecki and C. Whelan (eds), *Sociological Approaches to Law* (Taylor & Francis, London,1981) 111.

[81] D. Kennedy, 'Critical Theory, Structuralism and Contemporary Legal Scholarship' (1986) 21 New Eng. L. Rev. 209, 245.

[82] See the foundation of the Conference on Critical Legal Studies (CCLS) in Madison, Wisconsin, in 1977.

evolving over time,[83] it is not possible to simply delineate the main common themes around which this new wave of thinking has been articulated. For the sake of the argument made here, it suffices to say that the critique affiliated with critical legal studies and deconstructivism endorsed the perception of the indeterminacy of law that had been brought into the spotlight by legal realists. Their technique of deconstruction further buttressed the conclusion that meaning is unstable and that all texts have multiple meanings that can conflict with one another. While falling short of advocating the complete indeterminacy of rules, as is sometimes contended by observers,[84] the critical legal project—at least the first generation thereof—brought it to a higher level, however, for it claimed to have identified additional sources of indeterminacy. Indeed, according to this critique, even the yardsticks to capture the meta-legal motives used by law-applying authorities themselves are beset by indeterminacy, simultaneously hampering the predictive and behavioural analysis advocated by legal realists, with whom it shared so many premises.[85]

By reinforcing the claim of the indeterminacy of law, this critique undoubtedly fostered the realist rejection of formalism as adjudicative neutrality and immanent intelligibility of legal arguments. It yielded a strong critique of formalism, which it saw as a legal technique at the hands of the judiciary to 'objectivize' the sphere of adjudication.[86] In doing so, it took particular aim at American liberalism, which had dominated American culture and politics since the Second World War, and the defence of objectivism and reasoned narrative.

Although it zeroed in on formalism as adjudicative neutrality and immanent intelligibility, the postmodern critique did not leave formalism as law-ascertainment untouched. The strong indeterminacy thesis which it promoted, as well as its repudiation of the foundations of the legal culture,[87] led to a consideration of the law-ascertainment blueprints as just as indeterminate and politically-informed as all other substantive legal rules. There are, of course, significant divergences of opinion on the consequences of the strong indeterminacy thesis put forward by this critique,[88] with some advocating a necessary reconstructive response,[89] while others

[83] On the difference between the first and second generation of critical legal scholars, see D. Kennedy, 'A Rotation in Contemporary Legal Scholarship' (2011) 12 *German Law Journal* 338.

[84] G. Binder, 'Critical Legal Studies', in D. Patterson (ed), *A Companion to Philosophy of Law and Legal Theory* (Blackwell, Oxford, 1999) 280, 281. See, however, P. Schlag ('"Le Hors de Texte, C'est Moi"—The Politics of Form and the Domestication of Deconstruction' (1990) 11 Cardozo L. Rev. 1631) who rejects any type of domestication of the deconstruction and the indeterminacy thesis.

[85] G. Binder, 'Critical Legal Studies', in D. Patterson (ed), ibid, 280, 281.

[86] See e.g. D. Kennedy, *The Rise and Fall of Classical Legal Thoughts* (re-edited in 2006, Beard Books, Washington DC) chapter I, especially 5.

[87] See M. Tushnet, 'Introduction to the Symposium "Perspectives on Critical Legal Studies"' (1984) 52 Geo. Wash. L. Rev. 239. See more generally, P. Schlag, '"Le Hors de Texte, C'est Moi"—The Politics of Form and the Domestication of Deconstruction' (1990) 11 Cardozo L. Rev. 1631; See also E.J. Weinrib, 'Legal Formalism: On the Immanent Rationality of Law' (1988) 97 Yale L. J. 949.

[88] On the tension between reconstructive enterprises and radical critical positions, see I. Ward, *Introduction to Critical Legal Theory* (Routledge, NY, 1998) 158.

[89] In this sense, deconstruction may become a 'technique' deployed by a self-conscious individual subject. See J. Balkin, 'Deconstructive Practice and Legal Theory' (1987) 96 Yale L. J. 743. This is often a tendency of the deconstruction supported by those scholars affiliated with critical legal studies.

maintaining a rather radical and uncompromising position on the indeterminacy thesis.[90] However, despite these discrepancies, formal law-ascertainment has not remained unaffected by the reinforced indeterminacy in the sense that formal law-ascertainment yardsticks have been equated to a set of artificial conventions that could be used by lawyers and scholars alike to ascertain legal rules according to their whims and interests.

Given its far-reaching consequences, it is not surprising that this postmodern critique became the subject of strong criticisms. In particular, it came to be seen as leading to a 'dead-end' and an 'intellectual desert', being nothing more than a 'planned campaign of social and cultural criticism'.[91] It was also castigated for being nihilistic—a criticism classically rebutted by critical scholars by virtue of a Nietzschean conception of nihilism that, according to them, was incarnated by legalism itself.[92] It has also been contended that the indeterminacy of law upon which this critique has grown was largely exaggerated.[93] It is not the aim of this section to discuss the various objections that have been levelled against this new stream of scholarship or to re-evaluate it. These debates have taken place elsewhere and are far too complex to be usefully recounted here. It simply suffices here to point out that this new postmodern critique came to cap several decades of—sometimes indirect—objections against the formal law-ascertainment.

Like all previous objections to the source thesis, this critique noticeably reached the international legal scholarship a few decades later. While domestic legal systems and specialized domestic legal literature remained rather unaffected and law-ascertainment was not invalidated by it, its impact on international legal scholarship has been far-reaching, for the scholarship inspired by this postmodern critique paved the way—although this has not always been consciously pursued—for the deformalization of international law-identification. It is precisely to the repercussions of these critiques in the theory of the sources of international law that we need to pay attention to now.

4.2 The Contestations of Formal Law-Ascertainment in the Theory of the Sources of International Law

Unsurprisingly, the various objections to the source thesis which have been mentioned above have also permeated international legal scholarship. International legal

[90] For a radical view and the rejection of any domestication of deconstruction, see more generally, P. Schlag, '"Le Hors de Texte, C'est Moi"—The Politics of Form and the Domestication of Deconstruction' (1990) 11 Cardozo L. Rev. 1631.

[91] R. Unger, *What Should Legal Analysis Become?* (Verso, London, 1996) 121.

[92] N. Purvis, 'Critical Legal Studies in Public International Law' (1991) 32 Harvard JIL 121. See also the new epilogue by M. Koskenniemi in *From Apology to Utopia* (CUP, Cambridge, 2005) 562.

[93] K. Kress, 'Legal Indeterminacy', reproduced in D. Patterson (ed), *Philosophy of Law and Legal Theory: An Anthology* (Blackwell, Oxford, 2003) 253, 253. See also the criticism of radical indeterminacy by MacCormick: N. MacCormick, 'The Concept of Law and the Concept of Law' in R.P. George (ed), *The Autonomy of Law: Essays of Legal Positivism* (OUP, Oxford, 1996) 163, 174.

scholars have not remained indifferent to the debates raging in general legal theory, and their conceptions of international law—in particular their understanding of the ascertainment of international legal rules—have been influenced by the abovementioned contestations of the source thesis. As a result, the objections vented against formalism in general legal theory found an echo in the theory of the sources of international law. The source thesis which had constituted the foundation of formalism in international legal scholarship, despite its dominance since the 19th century,[94] did not remain totally unchallenged.

It must be made clear that the discontent stirred by formalism did not necessarily manifest itself in the same ways in the theory of the sources of international law as in general legal theory, for reasons inherent in the specificities of international law. In the theory of the sources of international law, it often unfolded in a very idiosyncratic way, irrespective of the form that such a critique took in general legal theory. This is why there is no strict correlation between the criticisms of formal law-ascertainment in general legal theory and in the theory of the sources of international law; the specific structural features of international law made it impossible to simply transpose the objections against the source thesis devised in general legal theory in the context of international law.

The foregoing does not mean that the genealogy of the critique of formal law-ascertainment in international law is entirely alien to that which had pervaded the—sometimes indirect—critiques of formal law-ascertainment in general legal theory. As the following sections will show, some resemblances are perceptible. Be that as it may, although it is informed by them, the present chapter does not seek to draw any parallel with the classical critiques echoed in general legal theory. This is why I simply refer here to those streams of international legal scholarship which have expressly sought to overthrow the rule-based approach and tried to do away with the source thesis. Approaches which have put forward a—partial—abandonment of the source thesis by virtue of an adherence to some sort of substantive validity must first be evoked (4.2.1). Mention will then be made of the realist branch of International Relations Theory as well as the New Legal Realism (4.2.2) and the New Haven School (4.2.3). Finally, the powerful critique generated by those international legal scholars affiliated with critical legal studies and deconstructivism will be examined, as their critique has simultaneously yielded an anti-formalist movement in international legal scholarship and revived earlier critiques of formalism (4.2.4).

4.2.1 Remnants of substantive validity theory

Since the advent of the resolute rejection of naturalist theory in the 19th century, international law-identification models based on substantive validity have been very exceptional. Indeed, almost all the important and influential critiques of international law have been directed, not at formal law-ascertainment used in international law, but rather at the substance of the norms. These critiques have left formalism

[94] Cfr *supra* 3.2.1 and 3.2.2.

untouched. For instance, the creation of the *Institut de Droit international* in Ghent in 1873 reflected an effort to tame the Hegelian and sovereignty-oriented mindset among mainstream legal scholars with a view to promoting peace and humanity,[95] while simultaneously trying to elevate the voice and role of legal scholars in diplomatic circles. Far from putting into question the idea of progress associated with formal law-ascertainment, which was rife at that time, it actually contributed to its success. The later Soviet critique of the mainstream approach, although sometimes directed at an overly formal notion of law, was mainly directed at the content of international law rather than its identification.[96] The same is true with the Third World criticism of mainstream international law which, while promoting a more progressive development of international law, did not back away from the source thesis.[97]

Although revivals of substantive validity theory in international law have been scarce, some residues have nonetheless remained perceptible in international legal scholarship. They were generally rekindled by the First World War which—at least temporarily—put an end to the hopes that had been vested in the emerging theory of the sources of international law based on formalism. Only a few of the advocates of such substantive validity are mentioned here. Indeed, it is not necessary to expound on these critiques of formalism based on substantive validity, for their impact and legacy have been rather limited. Only a few examples need to be provided.

The *travaux préparatoires* of article 38 of the Statute of the Permanent Court of International Justice already bespoke an inclination for rules ascertained by virtue of substantive criteria. In particular, general principles of law, as originally designed by Baron Descamps to prevent *non liquet*, were informed by—and ascertained through—natural law principles.[98] That naturalistic understanding of general principles eventually gave ground to a compromise with the positivist position defended by Elihu Root,[99] although the difficulty of collecting representative data relating to

[95] See M. Koskenniemi, *The Gentle Civilizer of Nations* (CUP, Cambridge, 2002) 39.

[96] See G.I. Tunkin, *Droit international public: problemes théoriques* (Pedone, Paris, 1965) 54.

[97] See M. Bedjaoui, *Pour un nouvel ordre économique international* (Unesco, Paris, 1979) 108. See the English translation, *Towards a new international economic order* (Holmes & Meier, Paris, 1979). See the remarks of R. Bachand, 'La critique en droit international: Réflexions autour des livres de Koskenniemi, Anghie et Miéville' (2006) 19 *Revue québécoise de droit international* 8.

[98] *Permanent Court of International Justice, Advisory Committee of Jurists, Procès-verbaux of the proceedings of the Committee June 16th–July 24th 1920*, The Hague, 322–5. On this debate see M. Bos, *A Methodology of International Law* (T.M.C. Asser Instituut, Amsterdam/NY/Oxford, 1984) 68–75. A. Pellet, 'Article 38', in A. Zimmermann, et al. (eds), *The Statute of the International Court of Justice* (OUP, Oxford, 2002) 685–9. See also the Separate Opinion of Judge Cançado Trindade in the case pertaining to the *Pulp Mills (Argentina v. Uruguay)* before the ICJ, 20 April 2010, ICJ Rep. (2010) 3–6. On the Procès-verbaux, see generally, Jörg Kammerhofer, 'Introduction', in *Permanent Court of International Justice, Advisory Committee of Jurists, Procès-verbaux of the proceedings of the Committee June 16th–July 24th 1920 with Annexes (1920)* (Reprint 2006).

[99] Ibid.

domestic traditions often makes a return to substantive law-ascertainment criteria almost inevitable.[100]

Leaving aside the Statute of the International Court of Justice and turning more specifically to the international legal scholarship, it is worth mentioning that the scholar whose conceptualization of international law has been one of the most reminiscent of naturalist theory of substantial validity is undoubtedly Hersch Lauterpacht, who initiated what has been dubbed 'the Victorian school of international law'.[101] In the inter-war period, Lauterpacht belonged to a group of international lawyers with an open reformist agenda geared towards the rejection of the central character of sovereignty.[102] Lauterpacht never denied that Kant and Grotius were his spiritual fathers and the inspiration behind his cosmopolitan conceptualization of international law. Although he believed that State consent constitutes a formal source of law, he contended that much of international law follows the precepts of natural law, including secondary rules like the principle *Pacta sunt servanda*.[103] While he did not completely reject the source thesis, he still deemed it an insufficient law-ascertainment mechanism and found it inevitable to resort to natural law. Lauterpacht's natural law leanings are very well-illustrated by his re-writing of Oppenheim's *International Law*. The fifth edition of this classical treatise is a true transformation of the book, for it marks a real departure from the classical thesis on which legal positivism is based. It is true that some amendments in that direction had already been carved out by McNair in the fourth edition, but Lauterpacht's Grotian approach is manifest in the fifth edition.[104]

Although he still adhered to a rule-based approach, Roberto Ago also tried to partly do away with the source thesis by promoting a law-identification method based on some distinctive substantive elements of rules and on the function of law.[105]

[100] In the same vein, see M. Koskenniemi, 'The Pull of the Mainstream' (1990) 88 Mich. L. Rev. 1946, 1950.

[101] See also M. Koskenniemi, *The Gentle Civilizer of Nations* (CUP, Cambridge, 2002).

[102] See e.g. H. Lauterpacht, *The Function of Law in the International Community* (Clarendon, Oxford, 1933). On this point see J. Von Bernstorff, 'The Changing Fortunes of the Universal Declaration of Human Rights: Genesis and Symbolic Dimensions of the Turn to the Rights in International Law' (2008) 19 EJIL 903–924, 906.

[103] See the contemporary re-appraisal of Lauterpacht's Victorian approach by M. Koskenniemi, 'Lauterpacht: The Victorian Tradition in International Law' (1997) 8(2) EJIL 215–63; I. Scobbie, 'The Theorist as Judge: Hersch Lauterpacht's Concept of the International Judicial Function' (1997) 8 EJIL 264.

[104] 'Whatever may have been its merits in the past history of International Law, rigid positivism can no longer be regarded as being in accordance with existing International Law. Probably what has been described above as the Grotian school comes nearest to expressing correctly the present legal obligation': Oppenheim's *International Law* (H. Lauterpacht, ed) (5th edn, Longmans, London, 1935) 100.

[105] 'One must recognize that legality is not a quality conferred on norms because they were laid down by a given body, whichever that may be. What is of real value in the statement of the sociality of law is that law, as a social phenomenon . . . is manifested and operates in the life of society and that therefore one must look for it in society, and consider and understand it in relation to society and its needs. But this does not mean that "sociality" is the reason for "legal nature", that law is law because it is "created" by society, or because it is "the will of the social body", even in a metaphorical sense. One cannot say that society confers legality on its own norms or even if these norms are legal, that it is because society and its members want

Some remnants of models based on substantive validity were found in sociological approaches which provided that consistency with 'objective law' was a condition of validity of positive law. Objective law could, nonetheless, not be equated with natural law. For scholars like Georges Scelle, the difference between objective law and natural law lies in their origins. While natural law, as the product of reason, is immutable, objective law corresponds with social necessities which change with time and place and, accordingly, has an evolvable character.[106] Objective law, however, is 'given'[107] and its identification is thus not carried out through formal law-ascertaining criteria.[108] It is interesting to note that these scholars shared the same liberal and international project as some of those who espoused the source thesis for the identification of law but they simply took a different path.[109] For instance, the origin of Scelle's partial rejection of the source thesis is the fact that the State is simply a collective of individuals and therefore State-based law-identification criteria were not deemed to reflect the individual-centred society.[110] Since these sociological accounts of international law[111]—and the partial rejection of the source thesis that has accompanied them—have not survived their masters,[112] it probably is not necessary to further elaborate on this here.

and consider them as such. Legality is an attribute conferred, not by the society or by any other real or fictitious creating body but human thought which reflects on social phenomena; it is an attribute which is reserved for a certain category of norms, for a given group of judgments which it meets in social life because they, and they alone, are found to possess as a whole definite objective characteristics . . . The reason for their being legality and their being qualified as norms of law lies in the objective presence of these characteristics, which legal norms reveal in their structure and in their common functioning: not in an imaginary "laying down" or "creation" or "formulation" by "society"': R. Ago, "Positive Law and International Law"' (1957) 51 AJIL 691, 727–8.

[106] On that aspect of Scelle's theory, see the remarks of A. Orakhelashvili, 'Natural Law and Justice', *Max Planck Encyclopedia of Public International Law*, available at <http://www.mpepil.com> paras 22–3.

[107] A criticism by Kelsen of this concept of objective law is reproduced in C. Leben, *Controverses sur la Théorie Pure du Droit* (Panthéon-Assas/LGDJ, Paris, 2005) 66.

[108] See generally G. Scelle, *Précis de droit des gens, principes et systématique* (Dalloz, Paris, 2008). For a more recent account of G. Scelle's theory, see H. Thierry, 'The European Tradition in International Law: Georges Scelle' (1990) 1 EJIL 193; see also J. Nijman, *The Concept of International Legal Personality, An Inquiry into the History and Theory of International Law* (T.M.C. Asser, The Hague, 2004) 192; E. Jouannet, 'Regards sur un siècle de doctrine française du droit international' (2000) AFDI 1–57.

[109] See in particular the comparison between G. Scelle and H. Kelsen by C. Leben, *Controverses sur la Théorie Pure du Droit* (Panthéon-Assas/LGDJ, Paris, 2005) 12.

[110] G. Scelle, *Précis de droit des gens, principes et systématique* (Dalloz, Paris, 2008) preface, viii. On the political inspiration behind Scelle's project, see H. Thierry 'The European Tradition in International Law: Georges Scelle' (1990) 1 EJIL 193–209, 194.

[111] For an overview of the diverse sociological approaches to international law see A. Carty, 'Sociological Theories of International Law', *Max Planck Encyclopedia of Public International Law*, available at <http://www.mpepil.com>.

[112] See, however, the numerous sociological overtones of P. Allott's constructivist concept of international law, especially with respect to customary international law. See P. Allott, 'The Concept of International Law' (1999) 10 EJIL 31–50, 39. Such sociological accounts should not be conflated with recent attempts to ground the study of international law in its social context. See e.g. M. Hirsch, 'The Sociology of International Law: Invitation to Study International Rules and Their Social Context' (2005) 55 UTLJ 891. On the possible roles for sociology in the study of international law, see also A. Carty, 'Sociological Theories of International Law', *Max Planck Encyclopedia of Public International Law*, available at <http://www.mpepil.com> paras 42–6.

Similar overtones are also found in Charles de Visscher's humanist understanding of international law. The objectivist inclinations which he shared with sociological positivism made him a candidate for placement in the category of natural law. De Visscher was certainly not a fully-fledged natural lawyer and, indeed, cannot be easily categorized in any classical mapping of international legal scholarship.[113] However, his functionalist conception of law and its defence of the human ends of legal institutions are reminiscent of some naturalist methodologies.[114] This is especially true with respect to his take on customary international law.[115] According to de Visscher, customary international law boils down to a process of recognition by States that the rule in question corresponds with an implementation of the underlying basic principles of their society. In that sense, customary international law stems from the idea that States 'discover' pre-existing rules which reflect their social needs.[116]

The few conceptualizations of international law that have just been sketched out are illustrative of an understanding of law-ascertainment based on substantive validity. It is noteworthy that this resort to substantive validity has gone hand-in-hand with an attempt to demote the role played by the pedigree of the rule in its identification. It is true that, in retrospect, the impact of the few abovementioned conceptions has been modest,[117] as they have failed to durably influence international legal scholarship as a whole, especially when it comes to its adherence to the source thesis. Yet, these 'idealistic'[118] views have continued to sporadically infiltrate contemporary international legal scholarship, despite being themselves the target of some powerful objections by a new stream of critical thinking. The most contemporary uses of substantive validity in the international legal scholarship—as those found in Global Administrative Law or in Brunnée and Toope's interactional account of international law, as well as in international case-law—are analyzed below, for they have proved instrumental in the contemporary deformalization of law-ascertainment.[119] Attention must now be paid to the critiques of formalism which, informed by pragmatism and instrumentalism, have yielded a serious contestation to the use of formalism in international law-identification.

[113] See generally P.-M. Dupuy, 'The European Tradition of International Law: Charles de Visscher' (2000) 11 EJIL 871, especially 874.

[114] In the same sense, see F. Münch, 'A propos du droit spontané', in *Studi in onore di Giuseppe Sperduti* (Giuffrè, Milan, 1984) 160.

[115] C. de Visscher, 'La codification du droit international' (1925-I) 6 RCADI 325, 349–53.

[116] See the criticism by Thirlway of de Visscher's conception of customary international law in Thirlway, *International Customary Law and Codification* (Sijthoff, Leiden, 1972) 54.

[117] See the statement of the ICJ in *Southwest Africa* Case: 'a court of law can take account of moral principles only in so far as these are given sufficient expression in legal form' Second Phase, ICJ Rep. (1966) para. 49 (18 July 1966).

[118] F. Megret, 'International Law as Law', in J. Crawford and M. Koskenniemi (eds), *Cambridge Companion to International Law* (CUP, Cambridge, 2011) (forthcoming), available at <http://papers.ssrn.com/sol3/papers.cfm?abstract_id=1672824> 8–9.

[119] Cfr *infra* 5.1.

4.2.2 International realism: the turn to pragmatism

A sweeping challenge to the dominance of formalism in international legal scholarship came with the emergence in international theory—and mostly in international relations theory—of a new critique of international law. Indeed, international relations studies experienced the emergence of realist theories which, also barely affiliated with legal realism, brought about some severe criticism of formal law-ascertainment.[120]

International realism—sometimes also referred to as legal nihilism[121]—grew as a result of the profound disillusionment with war. It was premised on the equation of international law and international idealism. According to international realists, formal law-ascertainment leads to the exclusion from legal studies of phenomena that are crucial to any understanding of the law, namely, sociological, ethical, and political factors. Accordingly, they advocate a great scepticism towards the distinction between law and the power to dominate. Hence, rules cannot be reduced to what is binding. Instead, international norms among States are better identified in terms of the capacity to influence or dominate, not on the basis of formal criteria. According to these realist accounts, there are no legal or moral constraints on States. As a result, powerful States possess the freedom to act on instinct at their own leisure or liberty, and power boils down to the form of communication by which States interact and understand each other.[122] Despite the occasional invocation of Hart or Kelsen[123] and some obscure allusions to formality in the creation of law,[124] there is thus no place in international realism for law in a formal sense—what has often been dubbed by realists as naive and starry-eyed 'legalism'—and hence there is no place for law-ascertaining criteria. If the international arena is governed by some norms, they are those dictated by the most powerful States. Those norms are not identified by virtue of formal law-ascertaining criteria but exclusively stem from the exercise of powers on the international plane. A realist understanding of international law provides that law-ascertainment criteria—e.g. those devised by the Vienna Convention on the Law of Treaties—are only designed to clarify treaty obligations and fail to provide rules of recognition.[125] This rejection of formalism—itself informed by a turn to

120 See generally Abott, 'Modern International Relations Theory: A Prospectus for International Lawyers' (1989) 14 Yale J. Int'l L. 335–411, 338.

121 See the criticism of international legal realism by A. Buchanan, *Justice, Legitimacy and Self-Determination. Moral Foundations for International Law* (OUP, Oxford, 2007) 45.

122 A good illustration of realism is provided by the famous declaration of Dean Acheson in the 1963 ASIL Proceedings on the US quarantine of Cuba: 'the power, position and prestige of the United States had been challenged by another State; and law simply does not deal with such questions of ultimate power—power that comes close to the sources of sovereignty' (25 April 1963), (1963) 57 ASIL Proceedings, 13, 14. See generally, the account of realism by D. Kritsotis, 'The power of international law as a language' (1998) 34 Cal. W. L. Rev. 397–8.

123 See e.g. M.J. Glennon, 'How International Rules Die' (2005) 93 Geo. L. J. 939, especially 951 or 957.

124 J.E. Gersen and E. Posner, 'Soft Law', Chicago University, Public Law and Legal Theory Working Paper No. 213, March 2008, 44, available at <http://ssrn.com/abstract=1113537>.

125 J. Goldsmith and E. Posner, *The Limits of International Law* (OUP, Oxford, 2005).

pragmatism[126]—has manifested itself in many different ways and through many different voices.[127]

Although there are a wide variety of realist strands,[128] the abovementioned pragmatism of the realist approaches is often traced back to Hobbes' conceptualization of the state of nature.[129] The *realist school* has always centred on the Hobbesian 'state of nature' as a breeding ground for the contest for power.[130] Because Hobbes has been perceived as the precursor of so many radically opposite understandings of the international society[131]—and especially as the simultaneous precursor of the source thesis in general legal theory—it is important to stress that Hobbes, although he might have been 'guilty of gross and dangerous crudities',[132] did in fact recognize that international relations were not solely governed by a struggle for power. Indeed, he proved amenable to the role of common interests in international relations.[133] This is precisely what the *rationalist* approach of the English School has tried to demonstrate.[134] In that sense, it is argued here that Hobbes can hardly be seen as the

[126] M. Koskenniemi, 'What is International Law For?' in M. Evans, *International Law* (2nd edn, OUP, Oxford, 2006) 57, 67.

[127] The embodiment of the movement is probably H. Morgenthau who was a reformed international lawyer. H. Morgenthau, *Politics Among Nations* (4th edn, Alfred A. Knopf, NY, 1967). See also H. Morgenthau, 'Positivism, Functionalism and International Law' (1940) 34 AJIL 264; H. Morgenthau, *Scientific Man v. Power Politics* (Latimer, London, 1947). On H. Morgenthau, see generally M. Koskenniemi, 'Image of Law and International Relations', in M. Byers (ed), *The Role of Law in International Politics: Essays in International Relations and International Law* (OUP, Oxford, 2000) 17–34, 28. On the famous 'apostasy' of H. Morgenthau, see the comments of G. Simpson, 'The Situation on the International Legal Theory Front' (2000) 11 EJIL 449. See also R. Aron, *Paix et Guerre Entre des Nations* (Calmann-Lévy, Paris, 1984). See G. Kennan, *American Diplomacy, 1900–1950* (University of Chicago Press, Chicago, 1951); R. Niebuhr, *Moral Man and Immoral Society: A Study in Ethics and Politics* (Scribners, NY, 1932).

[128] A distinction if often made between realism and neo-realism. Kenneth Waltz, for instance, is said to be a neo-realist in the sense that he does not endorse the conservative and pessimistic analysis of men and favors a more top-down analysis of international relations based on the deficiencies of the international system, whereas Morgenthau, Kennan and Niebuhr construe the behaviour of States as a magnification of the flawed human nature. Neo-realists like Waltz are less averse to the role of international law. For an overview of the different strands of realism, see Keith L. Shimko, 'Realism, Neorealism and American Liberalism' (1992) 54 *The Review of Politics* 281–301.

[129] F. Megret, 'International Law as Law', in J. Crawford and M. Koskenniemi (eds), *Cambridge Companion to International Law* (CUP, Cambridge, 2011) (forthcoming), available at <http://papers.ssrn.com/sol3/papers.cfm?abstract_id=1672824> 9.

[130] Hans Morgenthau, *Politics Among Nations* (4th edn, Alfred A. Knopf, NY, 1967) 113.

[131] For a criticism of the idea that Hobbes has been the precursor of legal positivism, see S. Coyle, 'Thomas Hobbes and the Intellectual Origins of Legal Positivism' (2003) 16 CJILJ 243–70; see also D. Dyzenhaus, 'Hobbes and the Legitimacy of Law' (2001) 20 *Law and Philosophy* 461–98.

[132] G.E.G. Catlin, 'Thomas Hobbes and Contemporary Political Theory' (1967) 82 *Political Science Quarterly* 1–13.

[133] In the same vein, see L. May, *Crimes against Humanity: A Normative Account* (OUP, Oxford, 2005) 14–16. See also M.C. Williams, 'Hobbes and International Relations: A Reconsideration' (1996) 50 *International Organization* 213–36.

[134] H. Bull, *The Anarchical Society* (Macmillan, London, 1977) 4–5. On the appeal held by Grotius for Hedley Bull and the discrepancies between the former and the latter, see B. Kingsbury, 'A Grotian Tradition of Theory and Practice? Grotius, Law and Moral Skepticism in the Thought of Hedley Bull' (1998) 17 *Quinnipiac Law Review* 3–33; For a criticism of a moral reading of Hobbes, see T. Nagel, 'Hobbes's Concept of Obligation' (1959) 68 *The Philosophical Review* 68–83.

father of international realism and that his insight—as has been explained above[135]—is far more relevant to and supportive of the opposite view of an international legal order based on formal law-ascertainment.[136]

It is no surprise that the Cold War constituted the heyday of this sceptical account of formalism, and that international realism—at least as far as its influence in international legal scholarship is concerned—entered into an existential crisis in the wake of the fall of the Berlin Wall and the sudden faith in a global order that ensued.[137] Since this time, even in theory of international relations, other movements, such as regime theory and institutionalism, have gained more prominent roles.[138] Despite the attempted 'resuscitation'[139] of international realism in theory of international law by Jack Goldsmith and Eric Posner[140] and their attempt to elevate compliance into a law-ascertainment criterion, realist criticisms of the use of formal law-identification yardsticks in international law have failed to convince mainstream international legal scholars to back away from formal law-ascertaining criteria.[141] In that sense, international realists have proved much more successful in the theory of international relations than in the theory of international law. The failure of international realists—in contrast to legal realists—to mark international legal theory is partly the result of an obvious self-protection reflex by international legal scholars themselves,[142] and partly because of a few conflations like that between law-identification and compliance or the circularity of their argument about law-compliance.[143]

Before examining the challenges to formal law-ascertainment conveyed by the policy-oriented school and movements affiliated with critical legal studies which—

[135] Cfr *supra* 3.1.2.

[136] For a criticism of the neo-realist understanding of Hobbes, see D.W. Hanson, 'Thomas Hobbes' Highway to Peace' (1984) 38 *International Organization* 329–54. This is also what I have tried to defend elsewhere. See J. d'Aspremont, 'The Foundations of the International Legal Order' (2007) 18 FYIL 219–55.

[137] See the famous address by the President of the United States, 6 March 1991, 137 Cong. Rec. H1451–02, S2769–01 (1991). On this idea, see the remarks of G. Abi-Saab, 'A 'New World Order'? Some Preliminary Reflections' (1994) 7 Hague Y. B. Int'l L. 87.

[138] See e.g. R. Keohane, 'International Relations and International Law: Two Optics' (1997) 38 Harv. Int'l L. J. 487.

[139] See also A. D'Amato, 'The Need for a Theory of International Law', Northwestern University School of Law, Public Law and Legal Theory Research Paper Series, 6

[140] Jack Goldsmith and Eric Posner, *The Limits of International Law* (OUP, Oxford, 2005). For a criticism of their conception of law, see the very interesting contribution of A. Somek, 'Kelsen lives' (2007) 18 EJIL 409–51; For an empirical criticism of their work, see M. Scharf on the contemporary theories of compliance: M. Scharf, 'International Law in Crisis: A Qualitative Empirical Contribution to the Compliance Debate' (2009) 31 Cardozo L. Rev. 45.

[141] For a contemporary attempt to revive and modernize realism in international legal scholarship, see G. Shaffer, 'A Call for a New Legal Realism in International Law: The Need for Method', University of Minnesota Law School, Legal Studies Research Paper Series, Research Paper No. 09–02, available at <http://www.ssrn.com>.

[142] S.V. Scott, 'International Law as Ideology: Theorizing the Relationship between International Law and International Politics' (1994) 5 EJIL 313–325, 313.

[143] See for example, M.J. Glennon, 'How International Rules Die' (2005) 93 Geo. L. J. 939, especially 946.

contrary to international relations realism—can be seen as the offspring of legal realism, a word must still be said about the recent emergence of a new stream in the legal scholarship aimed at the modernization of legal realism and which has especially taken root in the literature about international economic law.[144] Indeed, a new group of legal scholars—which have denominated themselves the new legal realists, especially in the United States—take their cue from legal realists' plea for empirical research.[145] Yet, unlike legal realists who, despite advocating empirical research, did not conduct much empirical research themselves,[146] these scholars are actually and primarily engaged in empirical studies about law and international law.[147] In particular, they promote the empirical study of actors, institutions, and processes that give rise to international law as well as the reception and effects of international law. In doing so, they seek to complement quantitative analyses by a use of qualitative methods to understand how international law is made and received. Thus, they predominantly follow a bottom-up approach. This leads them to embrace a new interdisciplinary paradigm and create translations between law and social science which they want to be useful to legal academics and lawyers who are not always in a position to carry out empirical research themselves.[148]

Like legal realists, they, too, purport to translate their findings in practical tools which can be used by actors themselves with a view to promoting a stable (international) legal order.[149] Furthermore, they embrace the self-reflective distance and the scepticism towards doctrinal dogmatism advocated by the scholars affiliated with critical legal studies and deconstructivism.[150] Accordingly, legal scholars are instructed to remain constantly on guard for biases, and especially when they engage

[144] See generally G. Shaffer, 'A New Legal Realism: Method in International Economic Law Scholarship', in C.B. Picker, et al. (eds), *International Economic Law—The State and Future of the Discipline* (Hart, Oxford, 2008) 29–42; H. Erlanger, et al., 'New Legal Realism Symposium: Is it Time for a New Legal Realism?' (2005) Wisconsin L. Rev. 335; S. Macaulay, 'The New Versus the Old Legal Realism: Things Ain't What They Used to Be' (2005) Wisconsin L. Rev. 365, 375; V. Nourse and G. Shaffer, 'Varieties of New Legal Realism: Can A New World Order Prompt A New Legal Theory' (2009) 95 Cornell L. Rev. 61.

[145] On classical legal realism, see *supra* 4.1.2.

[146] S. Macaulay, 'The New Versus the Old Legal Realism: Things Ain't What They Used to Be' (2005) Wisconsin L. Rev. 365, 375. In that sense, they are to said to bear more resemblance to the 'Law and Society' movement than legal realists themselves. See G. Shaffer, 'A New Legal Realism: Method in International Economic Law Scholarship', in C.B. Picker, et al. (eds), *International Economic Law—The State and Future of the Discipline* (Hart, Oxford, 2008), 29–42, available at <http://www.ssrn.com/abstract=1105498> 8.

[147] See empirical research agenda of T. Ginsburg and G. Shaffer, 'Empirical Work in International Law', University of Minnesota Law School, Legal Studies Research Paper Series, Research Paper No. 09–32, available at <http://ssrn.com/abstract=1444448>.

[148] H. Erlanger, et al., 'New Legal Realism Symposium: Is it Time for a New Legal Realism?' (2005) Wisconsin L. Rev. 335, 336.

[149] G. Shaffer, 'A Call for a New Legal Realism in International Law: The Need for Method', University of Minnesota Law School, Legal Studies Research Paper Series Research Paper No. 09–02, available at <http://papers.ssrn.com/sol3/papers.cfm?abstract_id=1323912> 12.

[150] Cfr *supra* 4.1.4.

in empirical studies.[151] The awareness of the role of the social scientist as a human being and political being when carrying out empirical research is a lesson they overtly take from critical thinking.[152]

It is particularly interesting for the sake of the argument made in this book to note that these new (international) legal realists, although they not only look at international legal rules in the strict sense but also at other manifestations of the exercise of public authority at the international level,[153] do not simultaneously back away from formal law-identification. Their attempt to gauge the effects of the reception of international legal rules justifies that they remain receptive to formal law-ascertainment.[154] This is why New Legal Realism cannot be construed as a proper critique of formalism in the ascertainment of international legal rules—and hence there is no need to explore it further. Rather, New Legal Realism should be seen as one of the few contemporary attempts to bridge diverging strands of the international legal scholarship and, for that reason, certainly deserves the attention of international legal scholars.

4.2.3 The New Haven School: the turn to instrumentalism

The first most severe critique of formalism as a law-ascertainment mechanism in international law came, in my view, from the New Haven School (policy-oriented jurisprudence). This is because the authors of the New Haven School movement have carved out a new understanding of international law that does not presuppose a strict identification of international legal rules, thereby making formal law-ascertainment futile.[155]

The New Haven School builds upon the realist critique of formalism and concurs with its finding that formalism fails to offer a complete description of authoritative international decision-making, because international law cannot be reduced to a system of rules.[156] Like legal realism, New Haven is premised on the idea that international law is a form of social engineering that could be used as a tool to attain some given societal goals.[157] Although it shares the pragmatism of legal realism, New Haven nonetheless seeks to refine the realist critique and take it further for the

[151] G. Shaffer, 'A New Legal Realism: Method in International Economic Law Scholarship', in C.B. Picker, et al. (eds), *International Economic Law—The State and Future of the Discipline* (Hart, Oxford, 2008), 29–42, available at <http://www.ssrn.com/abstract=1105498> 9.

[152] H. Erlanger, et al., 'New Legal Realism Symposium: Is it Time for a New Legal Realism?' (2005) Wisconsin L. Rev. 335, 342.

[153] H. Erlanger, et al., ibid, 335, 343.

[154] H. Erlanger, et al., ibid, 335, 340.

[155] See generally, H.D. Lasswell and M.S. McDougal, *Jurisprudence for a Free Society: Studies in Law, Science, and Policy* (New Haven Press/Martinus Nijhoff Publishers, New Haven, 1992).

[156] M.S. McDougal, 'International law, power, and policy: a contemporary conception' (1953-I) 82 RCADI 133–259, 162–4; R.A. Falk, Casting the Spell: The New Haven School of International Law' (1995) 104(7) Yale L.J. 1991.

[157] See the remarks of I. Scobbie, 'Wicked Heresies or Legitimate Perspectives?', in M. Evans, *International Law* (2nd edn, OUP, Oxford, 2006) 94.

realization of a certain normative agenda.[158] This is why, despite kinship with legal realism being undeniable, New Haven also has some affinity with natural law theory.[159] Indeed, it takes the perspective of the decision-maker,[160] and not that of the rule-user, and aims at providing the world's decision-making processes with rational criteria to achieve the right law.[161]

In particular, the New Haven School perceives law as a collection of competing norms between which choices must be made. According to Myles S. McDougal, international law is

> a comprehensive process of authoritative decision in which rules are continuously made and remade; ... the function of the rules of international law is to communicate the perspectives (demands, identifications and expectations) of the peoples of the world about this comprehensive process of decision; and ... the national application of these rules in particular instances requires their interpretation, like that of any other communication, in terms of who is using them, with respect to whom, for what purposes (major and minor), and in what context.[162]

Worded differently, international law is 'a flow of decision in which community prescriptions are formulated, invalidated and in fact applied'.[163] In the same vein, Rosalyn Higgins sees international law as 'the whole process of competent persons making authoritative decisions in response to claims which various parties are pressing upon them, in respect of various views and interests'.[164] In sum, international law is accordingly regarded as a comprehensive process of decision-making rather than as a defined set of rules and obligations.[165]

Because international law is construed as the product of a social process, the New Haven approach minimizes the role played by rules. Thereby, it is said to be an anti-rule-based approach.[166] From the perspective of New Haven, rule-based approaches offer little insight into the structures, procedures, and types of decision that take place in the contemporary world community. The New Haven School thus backs

[158] I. Scobbie, 'Wicked Heresies or Legitimate Perspectives?', in M. Evans (ed), *International Law* (2nd edn, OUP, Oxford, 2006) 83, 94; see also A. D'Amato, 'The Need for a Theory of International Law', Northwestern University School of Law, Public Law and Legal Theory Research Paper Series, 6.

[159] M. Reisman has not concealed the natural law origins of this approach. See M. Reisman, 'The Views from the New Haven School of International Law' (1992) 86 ASIL Proceedings 118.

[160] M. Reisman, ibid, 118, 119.

[161] M.S. McDougal, 'Law as a Process of Decision: A Policy-oriented Approach to Legal Study' (1956) 1 *Natural Law Forum* 53.

[162] M.S. McDougal, 'A Footnote' (1963) 57 AJIL 383.

[163] M.S. McDougal, 'International Law, Power, and Policy: A Contemporary Conception' (1953-I) 82 RCADI 133–259, 181.

[164] R. Higgins, 'Policy Considerations and the International Judicial Process' (1968) 17 ICLQ 58, 59.

[165] See M.S. McDougal, 'International Law, Power and Policy' (1952) 83 RCADI 133; M.S. McDougal, et al., 'Theories about International Law: Prologue to a Configurative Jurisprudence' (1968) 8 Va. J. Int'l L. 188; M.S. McDougal, 'International Law and the Future' (1979) 50 Miss. L. J. 259; H. Lasswell and M.S. McDougal, *Jurisprudence for a Free Society: Studies in Law, Science and Policy* (New Haven Press/Martinus Nijhoff Publishers, New Haven, 1992); M.S. McDougal and W.M. Reisman, *International Law in Contemporary Perspective* (Foundation, New Haven, 1980) 5.

[166] See M.S. McDougal, 'Some Basic Theoretical Concepts about International Law: A Policy-Oriented Framework of Inquiry' (1960) 4 *Journal of Conflict Resolution* 337–54.

away from the source thesis, for there is no need to draw a distinction between law and non-law. International law being a process, there is no discontinuity between law and non-law.[167] Hence, law-ascertainment becomes pointless. As Michael Reisman explains, 'New Haven believes that a useful theory about law must avoid the temptation, so common in conventional legal method, to drastically reduce the universe of variables to a text or a few purportedly key social factors'.[168] The New Haven School thus attempts to de-emphasize the distinction between law and non-law and promote a conception of the relationship between law and non-law as a continuum, thereby making formal law-ascertainment mechanisms entirely unnecessary.[169]

This rejection of the source and social theses and the idea that there is a continuum between law and non-law is entirely inspired by the goals pursued by the New Haven School. By advocating a conception of law as a social process, the abovementioned authors aimed at a self-empowerment, for they see themselves as an intrinsic part of that process. In that sense, their process-based conception of law goes hand-in-hand with a more inclusive understanding of the responsibilities of lawyers. Among these new tasks, lawyers ought to contribute to the training of policy-makers for the achievement and promotion of eight constituent values they construe as essential in a free society dedicated to the promotion of human dignity.[170] This is why, in the view of New Haven, law is not only a limit on effective power but also a tool for promoting both order and certain values pertaining to human dignity. As Reisman puts it, 'jurisprudence is a theory about making social choices' and '(t)he primary jurisprudential and intellectual tasks are the prescription and application of policy in ways that maintain community order and, simultaneously, achieve the best possible approximation of the community's social goals'.[171] The pursuit of certain societal values through a process-based conception of international law explains why the New Haven School approach is often seen as a turn towards instrumentalism.[172]

[167] R. Higgins, *Problems and Process: International Law and How We Use It* (OUP, Oxford, 1995) 8–10. See also R. Higgins, 'The Identity of International Law', in B. Cheng (eds), *International Law: Teaching and Practice* (Stevens, London, 1982) 27–44.

[168] M. Reisman, 'The View from the New Haven School of International Law' (1992) 86 ASIL Proceedings 118, 121. See also R. Higgins, according to whom 'To remain "legal" is not to ignore everything that is not rules. To remain "legal" is to ensure that decisions are made by those authorized to do so, with important guiding reliance on past decisions, and with available choices being made on the basis of community interests and for the promotion of common values': R. Higgins, ibid, 9.

[169] The rejection of formalism is not the only 'victim' of the process-based approach of New Haven. The Policy-Oriented School also led to a rejection of the concept of international legal personality (ILP) and put the focus on 'participants' rather than 'legal subjects'. See e.g. R. Higgins, ibid, 49–50. On this aspect of New Haven, see J. Nijman, *The Concept of International Legal Personality: An Enquiry Into the History and Theory of International Law* (T.M.C. Asser, The Hague, 2004) 332–3.

[170] See H. Lasswell and M.S. McDougal, 'Legal Education and Public Policy-Professional Training in the Public Interest (1943) 52 Yale L. J. 203, 206.

[171] M. Reisman, 'The View from the New Haven School of International Law' (1992) 86 ASIL Proceedings 118, 120.

[172] O. Schachter, 'International Law in Theory and Practice' (1982-V) RCADI 178 1–395, 40; M. Koskenniemi, 'What is International Law For?' in M. Evans, *International Law* (2nd edn, OUP, Oxford, 2006) 57, 57.

While it successfully prompted a new wave of interest in process-based approaches and the cross-disciplinary perspectives that it involves, the New Haven School approach quickly became the object of criticism. To my understanding, some of these objections explain why the policy-oriented approach has failed to significantly overturn the adherence to formal law-ascertainment found in mainstream international legal scholarship, at least until recently.[173] Most of the criticism levelled at the process-based approach of New Haven is based on the suspicion that it was in collusion with the American foreign policy decision-makers. According to that view, the New Haven School places a veil of legitimacy over ideological American foreign policy.[174] In that sense, the New Haven School proves vulnerable to the same criticisms as naturalism.[175] It has also been claimed that the New Haven approach does not provide enough guidance as to whether a behaviour is wrongful or not.[176] Because the policy-oriented schools construe the 'authoritative' character of the process so broadly, international law ends up indiscriminately encompassing any decision made by any international decision-maker,[177] thereby fuelling a lot of uncertainty. Such uncertainty strips international law of the 'certainty required for meaningful accountability'.[178] The resulting arbitrariness cannot be avoided without returning to a rule-based approach.[179]

While it is not the aim of this chapter to discuss these main objections formulated against the policy-oriented school,[180] what matters here is to realize that New Haven only offers a short respite to the problem of law-ascertainment.[181] The shift from the source to the process brought about by New Haven does not offer a satisfactory

[173] See the remarks by R.A. Falk, according to whom New Haven cannot survive the vision of its founders: R.A. Falk, 'Casting the Spell: The New Haven School of International Law' (1995) 104 Yale L.J. 1991, 1997.

[174] This has been famously explained by J. Hathaway, 'America, Defender of Democratic Legitimacy' (2000) 11 EJIL 121–34. See also J. Hathaway, *Rights of Refugees under International Law* (CUP, Cambridge, 2005) 20. In the same sense, see R.A. Falk, ibid, 1997; see also C. Tomuschat, 'General Course on Public International Law' (1999) 281 RCADI 9–438, 26–9.

[175] N. Purvis, 'Critical Legal Studies in Public International Law' (1991) 32 Harvard JIL 81, 86; see also J. Hathaway, 'America, Defender of Democratic Legitimacy' (2000) 11 EJIL 121–34, 129 or J. Hathaway, *Rights of Refugees under International Law* (CUP, 2005) 21.

[176] J. Hathaway, ibid, 22. See the tentative rebuttal of that type of criticism by R. Higgins, *Problems and Process: International Law and How We Use It* (OUP, Oxford, 1995) 8.

[177] A. D'Amato, 'Is International Law Really Law?' (1984–1985) 79 Northwest. U. L. Rev. 1293, 1302.

[178] J. Hathaway, *Rights of Refugees under International Law* (CUP, Cambridge, 2005) 18.

[179] M. Koskenniemi, 'International Law in a Post-Realist Era' (1995) 16 Aust. YBIL 1.

[180] For other criticisms of New Haven see P. Allott, 'Language, Method and the Nature of International Law' (1971) 45 BYBIL 79–135, 123–5; G. Fitzmaurice, '*Vae Victis* or Woe to the Negotiator? Your Treaty or Our Interpretation of It' (review essay) (1971) 65 AJIL 372, 370–3; J. Boyle, 'Ideals and Things: International Legal Scholarship and the Prisonhouse of Language' (1985) 26 Harvard JIL 327, 349; S.J. Toope, 'Confronting Indeterminacy: Challenges to International Legal Theory' (1990) 19 *Proceedings of the Canadian Council of International Law* 209;P.R. Trimble, 'International Law, World Order and Critical Legal Studies' (1990) 42 Stan. L. Rev. 811. For a tentative rebuttal of these criticisms, see R. Higgins, 'The Identity of International Law', in B. Cheng (eds), *International Law: Teaching and Practice* (Stevens, London, 1982) 37–42.

[181] G. Abi-Saab, 'Cours général de droit international public' (1987-VIII) 207 RCADI 9–463, 39–49; I. Brownlie, 'International law at the fiftieth anniversary of the United Nations: general course on public

solution in terms of law-ascertainment because New Haven does not provide any criteria to formally ascertain the decision-making *process* itself. As a result, the norms adopted through that process are not formally identifiable.[182] This is not to say that process-based conceptions of law necessarily preclude law-ascertainment. If the process in which the rules in question originate has been formalized, it can be a formal law-ascertainment yardstick for these rules. This is so, for instance, in the case of international judicial proceedings, which I examine in chapter 7.[183] Such judicial proceedings are themselves clearly identifiable through formal criteria and hence the rules which they generate can be formally ascertained. However, because the norm-making process envisaged by New Haven, although authoritative, is not formally defined, it can be argued that the process-based approach of New Haven leads to a deformalization of law-ascertainment.

Mindful of the drawbacks inherent in the New Haven approach, some commentators have tried to reconcile the process-based approach of the New Haven School and the mainstream rule-based approach.[184] According to Higgins, such a reconciliation is not possible; one necessarily has to chose between a rule-based and a process-based approach.[185] The inextricable return to formalism which pervades these tentative reconciliations seems to underpin her conclusion.[186] It is argued here that, unless New Haven scholars recognize that process-based approaches reintroduce formal law-identification by the back door, i.e. through the formal identification of the process, policy-oriented jurisprudence—at least in its most radical forms–cannot accommodate formal law-ascertainment. If this is true, New Haven, irrespective of its undeniable descriptive virtues,[187] cannot be seen as offering any

international law' (1995) 255 RCADI 9–228, 29; G.J.H. Van Hoof, *Rethinking the Sources of International Law* (Kluwer, Deventer, 1983) 283.

182 In the same vein, see G.J.H. Van Hoof, ibid, 283.

183 Cfr *infra* 7.2.4.

184 See G. Abi-Saab, 'Cours general de droit international public' (1987-VIII) 207 RCADI 9–463, 39: According to Koskenniemi, this was also the ambition of Virally in his general course (M. Virally, 'Panorama du droit international contemporain: cours général de droit international public' (1983-V) 183 RCADI 9–382) and Schachter in his general course ('International Law in Theory and Practice: General Course in Public International Law' (1982-V) 178 RCADI 1–395). See M. Koskenniemi, *From Apology to Utopia* (CUP, Cambridge, 2005) 159. See also O. Schachter, 'Towards a Theory of International Obligation' (1967–1968) 8 Va. J. Int'l L. 300. According to Higgins, it is highly questionable that these authors have attempted to float a conciliatory understanding of international law. See R. Higgins, *Problems and Process: International Law and How We Use It* (OUP, Oxford, 1995) 8. See also the earlier attempts by C.W. Jenks, *The Common Law of Mankind* (Stevens, London, 1955) or G.J.H. Van Hoof, *Rethinking the Sources of International Law* (Kluwer, Deventer, 1983) 44.

185 R. Higgins, ibid, 8.

186 For instance, O. Schachter claimed that international law was not only a body of rules but also a set of purposive activities: O. Schachter, 'International Law in Theory and Practice: General Course in Public International Law' (1982-V) 178 RCADI 1–395, 23. Accordingly, he sought to reconcile process-based and rule-based approaches: ibid, 58. However, despite pointing out the abuse of the rule-based approach, he still adhered to it: ibid, 60–73. Thus Schachter construed the doctrine of sources as the 'principal intellectual instrument in the last century for providing objective standards of legal validation': ibid, 60.

187 I have tried to shed some light on the formidable descriptive virtues of New Haven elsewhere. See J. d'Aspremont, 'Non State-Actors: Oscillating between Concepts and Dynamics', in J. d'Aspremont (ed), *Participants in the International Legal System—Multiple Perspectives on Non-State Actors in International*

satisfactory law-ascertainment mechanisms,[188] thereby leaving law-determination in limbo.[189]

4.2.4 Critical legal studies and deconstructivism in international law: international law as a language

For a few decades, New Haven proved the most powerful critique of formal international law-ascertainment. It was, however, to be overtaken in the last two decades of the 20th century by a new stream of critique which, although not primarily directed at formalism in the theory of law-ascertainment, generated a powerful objection against it. In fact, critical legal studies and deconstructivism reached international legal scholarship a decade after they emerged in domestic law circles.[190] Critical legal studies and deconstructivism bred a new generation of international legal scholars[191] who astutely reinvigorated interest in theory of international law and provided a refreshing and thought-provoking re-evaluation of the classical formal law-ascertainment yardsticks of the mainstream scholarship.[192] Although this new strand has its intellectual roots in 20th century European philosophy, it particularly flourished in the United States[193] where it distanced itself from the previous American critique of the mainstream scholarship which had been offered by the policy-oriented jurisprudence.[194] The latter was dedicated to the realization of a free society and saw international law as a collection of competing norms between which choices must be made. New Haven sought to promote and reinforce the role of lawyers in the political establishment. The critical legal project is much more agnostic, for it seeks—at least expressly—neither the promotion of a given agenda nor the preservation of the authority of international lawyers in the political establishment. Moreover, this critique is geared up to transparency and pluralism, for it seeks to avoid the artificial rigour generated by New Haven to pursue

Law (Routledge, London, 2011) 1. For a good illustration of the descriptive insights of New Haven, see C. Steer, 'Non-State Actors in International Criminal Law', in J. d'Aspremont (ed), ibid, 295.

188 See also the criticisms of F. Kratochwil, *Rules Norms and Decisions: On the Conditions of Practical and Legal Reasoning in International Relations and Domestic Affairs* (CUP Cambridge, 1989) 194–200.

189 On the rationale of formalism, cfr *supra* 2.2.

190 For some discussion of early international legal scholarship, see D. Kennedy, 'Theses about International Law Discourse' (1980) 23 German YBIL 353 and D. Kennedy, 'The Sources of International Law' (1987) 2 Am. U. J. Int'l L. & Pol'y 1.

191 M. Koskenniemi expressly indicated that he borrowed the structuralist distinction between langue/parole (deep structure and surface) and described international law as a language constructed of binary oppositions that represent possible (contradictory) responses to international legal problems. To this matrix, he added a deconstructive approach to show that the binary structures of the language of international law are interminably constructed and deconstructed through predictable and highly formal argumentative patterns, allowing any substantive outcomes. See eg. M. Koskenniemi, 'Letters to the Editors of the Symposium' (1999) 93 AJIL 351, 355.

192 Interestingly, these scholars will usually deny that they can be categorized as belonging to any of these movements. See eg. M. Koskenniemi, 'Letters to the Editors of the Symposium' (1999) 93 AJIL 351.

193 N. Purvis, 'Critical Legal Studies in Public International Law' (1991) 32 Harvard JIL 81–127, 89.

194 B.S. Chimni, *International Law and World Order: A Critique of Contemporary Approaches* (Sage, London, 1993); M. Koskenniemi, 'International Law in a Post-Realist Era' (1995) 16 Aust. YBIL 1.

a given agenda.[195] Yet, like New Haven, this critique is undeniably indebted to legal realism from which it borrows several characteristics, including a de-emphasis on words, a move away from formalism in legal argumentation, and a corresponding, ever-increasing emphasis on the social consequences of law.[196]

Although originally thriving in the United States, this 'new stream' quickly disseminated around the world and many 'Schools' became breeding grounds for critical thinking in the area of international law, especially in the Anglo-Saxon world. This new postmodern critique of the abovementioned mainstream conception of international law rapidly turned too diverse and too diffuse for it to be the object of a comprehensive account within the framework of this book. Furthermore, putting it into a single box would be misleading and at loggerheads with the essence of that critique. Indeed, it is not at all a self-conscious, separate, and unified movement, that can be construed as the mere continuation of critical legal studies that first arose in general legal theory.[197] While it certainly is indebted to this stream of thinking—in particular the Frankfurt School—this critique grew independently from the authors of the critical legal studies movement. Moreover, it manifested itself in very different forms.[198] Some of these theories have embraced the cause of groups or interests not represented in traditional doctrines,[199] as illustrated by the feminist[200] and Third World[201] critiques of mainstream scholarship. The 'self-dissolution' of the

[195] S. Ratner and A.-M. Slaughter, 'Appraising the Methods of International Law: A Prospectus for Readers' (1999) 93 AJIL 292, 299.

[196] On the kinship between CLS and realism, see A.L. Paulus, 'International Law After Postmodernism' (2001) 14 LJIL 737. See also D.Z. Cass, 'Navigating the Newstream: Recent Critical Scholarship in International Law' (1996) 65 Nord. J. Int'l L. 341, 377. See K. Kress, 'Legal Indeterminacy' in D. Patterson (ed), *Philosophy of Law and Legal Theory: An Anthology* (Blackwell, Oxford, 2003) 253, 253.

[197] Cfr *supra* 4.1.4.

[198] Cfr for instance the mild form of deconstruction attributed to Martti Koskenniemi *supra* 2.1.2.

[199] M. Koskenniemi, 'International Legal Theory and Doctrine', *Max Planck Encyclopedia of Public International Law*, available at <http://www.mpepil.com> para. 14.

[200] C. Chinkin, et al. 'Feminist Approaches to International Law' (1991) 85 AJIL 613. See the criticisms of feminist theories by F.R. Tesón, 'Feminism and International Law: A Reply' (1994) 33 Va J. Int'l L. 647 and A. D'Amato, 'Book Review of R. Cook (ed), *Human Rights of Women: National and International Perspectives*' (1994) 89 AJIL 840. See also the criticism of B. Kingsbury, 'The International Legal Order', IILJ Paper Series, 19.

[201] These are the so called TWAIL (Third World Approaches to International Law). See generally M. Mutua, 'What is TWAIL?' (2000) 94 ASIL Proceedings 31. See A. Anghie and B.S. Chimni, 'Third World Approaches to International Law and Individual Responsibility in International Conflicts' (2003) 2 *Chinese Journal of International Law* 77; K. Mickelson, 'Taking Stock of TWAIL Histories' (2008) 10 *International Community Law Review* 355. See also M. Gallié, 'Les Théories tiers-mondistes du droit international (TWAIL): un renouveau?' (2008) 39 *Etudes internationales* 17; H. Charlesworth, 'Feminist Ambivalence about International Law' (2005) 11 *International Legal Theory* 1; K. Mickelson, 'Rhetoric and Rage: Third World Voices in International Legal Discourse' (1998) 16 Wisconsin Int'l L. J. 353; U. Baxi, 'What may the Third World expect from International Law' (2006) 27 *Third World Quarterly* 713; A. Anghie, *Imperialism, Sovereignty and the Making of International Law* (CUP, Cambridge, 2004); D.P. Fidler, 'Revolt against or from within the West—TWAIL, the Developing World, and the Future Direction of International Law' (2003) 2 *Chinese Journal of International Law* 29; M. Khosla, 'The TWAIL Discourse: The Emergence of a New Phase' (2007) 9 *International Community Law Review* 291; O.C. Okafor, 'Newness, Imperialism, and International Legal Reform in Our Time: a TWAIL Perspective' (2005) 43 Osgoode Hall L. J. 17.

so-called 'New Approaches to International Law' (NAIL), which was once the banner under which all these critiques identified themselves,[202] has illustrated the impossibility of an all-embracing categorization. While not constituting a movement in itself, the authors adhering to this critique have also resented being seen as embracing one given method,[203] and have thereby sought to avoid any pigeonholing from the standpoint of methodology.

Because of the heterogeneity of this critique, the ensuing considerations cannot be anything but concise and slightly overgeneralizing. However, the difficulty of capturing and mapping critical approaches in international law does not prevent the following paragraphs from pinpointing some of the elements in this critique which, as the following chapters will demonstrate, have—albeit inadvertently—sowed the seeds of a more general deformalization of international law-ascertainment which some of these authors did not always completely envisage.

There is little doubt that the acknowledgement of the role of 'politics' in legal argumentation—a characteristic it shares with legal realism—lies at the heart of this stream of international legal scholarship which is intent on redeeming international law as a political project.[204] As such, these scholars have not taken issue with the political, but rather with the techniques used by international legal scholars to repress the political. This is why they have engaged in striving for a politicization of international law, i.e. putting the political debate at the centre of international law rather than displacing it through formal mechanisms. The critical legal project in international law thus rests on the assumption that international law struggles to be political.[205] International law is accordingly construed as a political project which, by resorting to various problem-solving techniques, including formal law-ascertainment mechanisms, has purported to 'displace' the political debate.[206] In particular, formalism—construed as 'standardization'—simply relocates the problem of politics to a different place within the doctrine instead of resolving it.[207]

For these scholars, international law, despite using such complicated techniques, has failed as a political project that purports to displace politics. Indeed, according to their view, mainstream international legal scholarship has only artificially skirted

[202] T. Skouteris, 'Fin de NAIL: New Approaches to International Law and its Impact on Contemporary International Legal Scholarship' (1997) 10 LJIL 415.

[203] See the so-called 'incident' on the occasion of the special symposium in the American Journal of International Law, M. Koskenniemi, 'Letter to the Editors of the Symposium' (1999) 93 AJIL 352. See also D. Kennedy, 'When Renewal Repeats: Thinking Against the Box' (1999–2000) 32 NYU JILP 335, 497.

[204] D. Kennedy, 'A New World Order: Yesterday, Today and Tomorrow' (1994) 4 Transnat'l L. & Contemp. Probs. 370 and 374.

[205] D. Kennedy, 'A New Stream of International Legal Scholarship' (1988–1989) 7 Wisconsin Int'l L. J. 1, 7.

[206] M. Koskenniemi, 'The Legacy of the Nineteenth Century', in D. Armstrong et al. (eds), *Routledge Handbook of International Law* (Routledge, London, 2009) 141, 151–2.

[207] T. Skouteris, *The Notion of Progress in International Law Discourse* (LEI Universiteit, Leiden, 2008) 127, later published as *The Notion of Progress in International Law Discourse* (T.M.C. Asser, The Hague, 2010).

philosophical debates through pragmatism[208] and has resorted to an 'obsessive repetition of a rather simple narrative structure'.[209] According to international legal scholars affiliated with critical legal studies and deconstructivism, the only answer found by mainstream scholars to overcome these contradictions is 'repetition'.[210] This repetition has served to hide the fundamental contradictions which riddle the problem-solving techniques purported to displace political debate. The most fundamental contradiction that besets international law as a political project pertains to the idea that international law is simultaneously independent of and embedded in the sovereign will of States.[211]

Instead of simply repeating ancestral formal standards which have hidden the contradictions inherent in international legal arguments, the critical legal project aims at unearthing—in a very astute manner which avoids spurring a revitalization of the natural law tradition against the background of which that approach emerged—the projects pursued by mainstream scholars who feign to ignore these contradictions for the sake of pragmatism.[212] It does not pursue any particular doctrinal, political, or institutional reform.[213] Rather, it simply seeks to reveal the contextual character of the authority of the mechanisms used to displace political debate. Questioning their authority is supposed to ignite a new move towards meaningful theoretical inquiry in international legal scholarship, for scholars can no longer rely on repetition and tradition.[214] History and genealogy have constituted important tools to scrutinize an authority in a given context.

There is no doubt that these scholars have wielded these hermeneutical instruments with great talent.[215] The mapping of the discipline which they have provided has been remarkable and enlightening for all scholars, whatever their affiliation may be. Even more important than the sterling findings of their research, their historical and genealogical deconstruction of the vocabularies of international law has given rise to a much greater self-reflective consciousness in the discipline—which these

[208] D. Kennedy, 'A New Stream of International Legal Scholarship'(1988–1989) 7 Wisconsin Int'l L. J. 1, 28.

[209] Ibid, 2.

[210] Ibid, 30–2.

[211] As Kennedy explains: 'The discipline's central Twentieth Century riddle—how can public order be created among sovereigns—was solved by the private law analogy: sovereigns could create a public order by consent, by contract, without compromising their autonomy or needing to rely on an international government', see D. Kennedy, 'A New World Order: Yesterday, Today and Tomorrow' (1994) 4 Transnat'l L. & Contemp. Probs 329–75, 370; See also D. Kennedy, 'A New Stream of International Legal Scholarship' (1988–1989) 7 Wisconsin Int'l L. J. 1.

[212] D. Kennedy, 'The Disciplines of International Law and Policy'(1999) 12 LJIL 34–5.

[213] D. Kennedy, 'When Renewal Repeats: Thinking Against the Box' (1999–2000) 32 NYU JILP 335, 460. The work of M. Koskenniemi seems to contrast with that of D. Kennedy in this respect. On the 'culture of formalism', cfr *supra* 2.1.2.

[214] D. Kennedy, 'A New Stream of International Legal Scholarship' (1988–1989) 7 Wisconsin Int'l L. J. 1, 6.

[215] D. Kennedy, 'The Disciplines of International Law and Policy' (1999) 12 LJIL 87. See also M. Koskenniemi, *The Gentle Civilizer of Nations: The Rise and Fall of International Law 1870–1960* (CUP, Cambridge, 2002).

scholars, to their great credit, do not balk at applying to themselves.[216] Unearthing the agendas and the stories behind the various vocabularies of the international legal scholarship is nowadays growing more and more common, even among those who do not share the ambitions sought by this new generation of legal scholars. This 'attitude' has required resorting to interdisciplinarity,[217] and, most notably, some sociological insights.

Seen in this light, the postmodern critique of mainstream conceptions of international law has, to a large extent, been a *critique of the discipline* and of the manner in which the discipline constructs itself and its relations with the world.[218] It has sought to destabilize international lawyers' faith in the objectivity and neutrality of their professional routine and create an 'identity-crisis' among them with a view to prompting their emancipation.[219] Since it accordingly targets the discipline itself rather than its object, it can be seen as a movement of contestation of this imaginary 'invisible college'[220] and, hence, closely associated with 'opposition' within the discipline.

This 'insurgent' movement has undoubtedly had a dramatic impact on international legal scholarship. That does not mean that these critical approaches have not been unchallenged. To mention but a few objections levelled against them—and without prejudging their exactitude, one can recall that critical approaches have been chastised for stirring discord at a time when fragmentation has required unity among legal scholars.[221] They have also been castigated for their navel-gazing attitude and their self-indulgent conversations, as well as for failing to provide concrete solutions to legal issues.[222] In the same vein, critical approaches have also been criticized for not offering an approach that facilitates the teaching of international law.[223] Likewise, those scholars affiliated with the process-based critique of the mainstream formal model have unsurprisingly bemoaned the fact that critical approaches cannot assist law in the achievement of political goals.[224] As is well-known, this critique has also been berated for leading to utter relativism and precluding language from

[216] E.g. Koskenniemi acknowledges that deconstructivism itself is only a cultural or historical convention, that is 'a style with an emancipatory potential which . . . is always in danger of being transformed into a means of status quo legitimation': M. Koskenniemi, 'Letters to the Editors of the Symposium' (1999) 93 AJIL 351, 360.

[217] On the possible change of opinion of M. Koskenniemi on the use of multidisciplinarity, see M. Koskenniemi, 'Politics of International Law, 20 Years Later' (2009) 20 EJIL 7–19.

[218] M. Koskenniemi, 'International Legal Theory and Doctrine', *Max Planck Encyclopedia of Public International Law*, available at <http://www.mpepil.com> para. 14.

[219] On this point, see the remarks of J. von Bernstorff, 'Sisyphus was an international lawyer. On Martti Koskenniemi's "From Apologia to Utopia" and the place of law in international politics' (2006) 7 *German Law Journal* 1015, 1023–6.

[220] On this image, see O. Schachter, 'The Invisible College of International Lawyers' (1977) 72 Northwest. U. L. Rev. 217.

[221] P.-M. Dupuy, 'Some Reflections in Contemporary International Law and the Appeal to Universal Values: A Response to Martti Koskenniemi' (2005) 16 EJIL 131, 137.

[222] See e.g. N. Oluf, 'The Constitution of International Society' (1994) 5 EJIL 1–19, 6.

[223] P. Wrange, 'An Open Letter to My Students' (1996) 56 Nord. J. Int'l L. 569–95, 571.

[224] R. Higgins *Problems and Process: International Law and How We Use It* (OUP, Oxford, 1995) 9.

becoming a vehicle of knowledge.[225] Finally, this critique has been faulted for its assumption that international law is not the vindication of authority over power.[226] Although many of these criticisms are probably slightly overblown, it is not the intention of this book to evaluate each of them. Rather, it is of great import to appraise the extent to which the critical legal project has furthered the abovementioned objections against formal law-ascertainment in the theory of the sources of international law.

For scholars affiliated with critical legal studies and deconstructivism, formalism—which they mainly construe as a technique of legal argumentation—constitutes a political project that aims at controlling the content of norms through abstract categories.[227] More particularly, formalism provides 'the shared surface... on which political adversaries recognize each other as such and pursue their adversity in terms of something shared, instead of seeking to attain full exclusion... of the other'.[228] In the eyes of the critical legal project, formal legal argumentation has failed to fulfil this ambition.

As was said earlier, this critique has primarily been directed at formalism in legal argumentation. The work of postmodern scholars has, nonetheless, simultaneously—and sometimes inadvertently—delivered a fundamental critique of formal law-ascertainment models as well. In particular, when applied to law-ascertainment in particular, this critique of formalism ends up equating formal law-ascertainment criteria with a problem-solving tactic purported to avoid theoretical controversies and indeterminacy,[229] an attempt that, in the view of these scholars, has similarly failed.[230] This failure of formal law-ascertainment is to be traced back to the fact that formal law-identification criteria can equally ascertain norms as law or non-law. Indeed, because such criteria remain beset by indeterminacy, they cannot do away with an inescapable margin of political discretion.[231] As problem-solving tactics, formal law-ascertainment like formal legal argumentation, remains inextricably apologetic or utopian.[232]

[225] This is a classical criticism leveled against scholars associated with deconstructivism and critical legal studies. See the remarks on the association between CLS and Relativism: M. Koskenniemi, the New Epilogue in *Apology to Utopia* (CUP, Cambridge, re-issued 2005). See also O. Korhonen, 'New International Law: Silence, Defence or Deliverance' (1996) 7 EJIL 1–28.

[226] R. Higgins, *Problems and Process: International Law and How We Use It* (OUP, Oxford, 1995) 15.

[227] D. Kennedy, 'A New Stream of International Legal Scholarship' (1988–1989) 7 Wisconsin Int'l L. J. 1, 30.

[228] M. Koskenniemi, 'What is International Law For?' in M. Evans, *International Law* (2nd edn, OUP, Oxford, 2006) 57, 77.

[229] M. Koskenniemi, 'Letters to the Editors of the Symposium' (1999) 93 AJIL 351, 354.

[230] T. Skouteris, *The Notion of Progress in International Law Discourse* (LEI Universiteit, Leiden, 2008), chapter 3, later published as *The Notion of Progress in International Law Discourse* (T.M.C. Asser, The Hague, 2010). According to Skouteris, 'the success of the doctrine of sources cannot be attributed to its (alleged) claim of bringing closure to the perennial questions of law making and law-ascertainment. Sources talk, however, manage to capture the fantasy of an entire profession as a means of moving forward with the discipline. The idea was that, if only one was able to devise a set of finite, universally applicable formal categories of legal norms, one would be able to end the problems of indeterminacy' (at 81).

[231] M. Koskenniemi, *From Apology to Utopia* (CUP, Cambridge, 2005) 189–97.

[232] M. Koskenniemi, 'The Politics of International Law' (1990) 1 EJIL 4, 20–7; D. Kennedy, 'A New Stream of International Legal Scholarship' (1988–1989) 7 Wisconsin Int'l L. J. 1, 30. On the differences between Koskenniemi's and Kennedy's denunciations of the contradictions in a formal understanding of

Another objection against formal law-ascertainment is that the repetition of a highly technical language used to overcome the contradictions in law-ascertainment transforms international law into a set of sophisticated vocabularies which are mastered by only a few well-trained lawyers.[233] In that sense, law-identification leads to a system ruled by experts. This paves the way for a managerial understanding of the problems susceptible to a legal solution. Experts of these techniques have grown in different subspecialties, each of them using different formal law-identification categories (environmental law, human rights law, etc).[234] These objections against law-ascertainment encountered in the critical legal project have mostly been directed at the source thesis.[235] Yet, that does not mean that this critique has spared the social thesis.[236] Indeed, these scholars have usually endorsed the idea that practice cannot be cognized without pre-defined categories,[237] and hence, there cannot be a non-normative empirical study of international law.[238] Formal law-ascertainment, because it provides a way to cognize the practice, is bound to be normative. This—to some extent indirect—challenge to the source and social theses explains why the postmodern critique can be seen, in my view, as having come to reinforce the idea that formal ascertainment of international legal rules is beset by contradictions and is unable to fulfil the functions allocated to it.

This being said, it must be recalled that some support for a 'culture of formalism' has been expressed in the critical legal project.[239] While this notion, as has been explained above,[240] is utterly different from the conception of formalism espoused here and is not centred on law-ascertainment, it can be argued that the underlying motives of the call for a 'culture of formalism' are not at odds with the rationale of formal law-ascertainment.[241] Yet, despite some similarity of motives, this attempt to ensure the universality of legal argumentation has done little to rein in the powerful and compelling objections against formal law ascertainment that have—sometimes inadvertently—accompanied the critical legal project.

It is worth noting in particular that, in the present state of international legal scholarship, the critique of formal law-ascertainment generated by the critical approaches described here has been met either by an all-out and uncritical enthusiasm or by a dismissive and unmotivated rejection. In other words,

law, see D. Kennedy, 'When Renewal Repeats: Thinking Against the Box' (1999–2000) 32 NYU JILP 335, 407. Kennedy emphasized that Koskenniemi's account, while echoing Kennedy's earlier work, has the advantage of dynamism, for one moves repeatedly from apology to utopia.

233 M. Koskenniemi, 'The Fate of Public International Law: Between Technique and Politics' (January 2007) 70 MLR 1.

234 M. Koskenniemi, 'Politics of International Law: 20 Years Later' (2009) 20 EJIL 7–19.

235 On the concepts of source and social theses, cfr *supra* 2.1.

236 See the remarks of M. Koskenniemi, 'Repetition as Reform' (1998) 9 EJIL 405.

237 On the foundations of critical legal studies and the origin of some of its main tenets in general legal theory, see *supra* 4.1.4.

238 On this aspect of critical legal project in international law, see J. Beckett, 'Rebel Without a Cause? Martti Koskenniemi and the Critical Legal Project' (2006) 7 *German Law Review* 1045, 1074.

239 Cfr *supra* 2.1.2.

240 Cfr *supra* 2.2.

241 On the rationale of formalism, cfr *supra* 2.2.

international legal scholars have balked at engaging with that critique of formalism. To a certain extent, this lack of engagement by international legal scholars with the overall rejection of formalism presented by the postmodern critique has reinforced the critique of law-ascertainment that indirectly accompanies the critical legal project. It is accordingly not utterly surprising that the success of the critical legal project in international legal scholarship—which itself has rekindled some of the earlier critiques of formalism mentioned here—has coincided—without being the immediate cause thereof—with a serious move away from formal law-ascertainment in the theory of the sources of international law. This is why this concise genealogy of the critiques of formalism must now be followed by a sketch of the current manifestations of deformalization of law-identification witnessed in the theory of the sources of international law.

5

Deformalization of Law-Ascertainment in Contemporary Theory of the Sources of International Law

It seems difficult to dispute that the success of the critiques spelled out in chapter 4 is interwoven with the relative indifference, described in chapter 3, of international legal scholars towards the theoretical foundations of law-ascertainment.[1] Likewise, there are some good reasons to think that the extent to which these critiques have contributed to the contemporary move away from formal law-ascertainment in the theory of the sources of international law—this is what I call the deformalization of law-ascertainment[2]—has been reinforced by the rapid pluralization undergone by contemporary international norm- and law-making processes which has accompanied the unprecedented development of international law and globalization in the 20th and 21st centuries.[3] In other words, it is not a coincidence that the growing abandonment of formal law-identification criteria in the

[1] On this indifference of international legal scholars towards theory, see generally E. Jouannet, 'Regards sur un siècle de doctrine française du droit international' (2000) AFDI 1–57. See generally, D. Kennedy, 'International Law and Nineteenth Century: History of an Illusion' (1996) 65 Nord. J. Int'l L. 385, 387; D. Kennedy, 'A New Stream of International Legal Scholarship' (1988–1989) 7 Wisconsin Int'l L. J. 1, 6; N. Purvis, 'Critical Legal Studies in Public International Law' (1991) 32 Harvard JIL 81, 84; M. Reisman, 'Lassa Oppenheim's Nine Lives' (1994) 19 Yale J. Int'l L. 255, 271; B. Kingsbury, 'The International Legal Order', NYU Law School Public Law & Legal Theory Research Paper No. 01–04 (2003), IILJ History and Theory of International Law Series, Working Paper No. 2003/1. See. N. Onuf, 'Global Law-Making and Legal Thought', in N. Onuf (ed), *Law-Making in the Global Community*, (Carolina Academic Press, Durham, 1982) 1, 13; See also A. D'Amato, 'The Need for a Theory of International Law', Northwestern University School of Law, Public Law and Legal Theory Research Paper Series (2007); A. D'Amato, 'What "Counts" as Law?' in N.G. Onuf (ed), ibid, 83–107. D'Amato provided his own theory of the autonomy of the international legal system. See A. D'Amato, 'International Law as an Autopoietic System' in R. Wolfrum and V. Röben (eds), *Developments of International Law in Treaty Making* (Springer, Berlin, 2005) 335 (see the criticism of D'Amato's theory by A. Pellet, 'Complementarity of International Treaty Law, Customary Law and Non-Contractual Law-Making' in the same volume, 409–14). See also T. Skouteris, *The Notion of Progress in International Law Discourse* (LEI Universiteit, Leiden, 2008), chapter 3, later published as *The Notion of Progress in International Law Discourse* (T.M.C. Asser, The Hague, 2010). M. Koskenniemi, 'Repetition as Reform' (1998) 9 EJIL 405; J. Klabbers, 'Constitutionalism and the Making of International Law' (2008) 5 NoFo 84, 94.

[2] The meaning of deformalization in this book thus departs from the use of that concept to refer to norm-making by informal non-territorial networks. See M. Koskenniemi, 'Constitutionalism as a Mind-set: Reflections on Kantian Themes about International Law and Globalization' (2007) 8 *Theoretical Inquiries in Law* 9, 13. On the concepts of formalism and deformalization, see *supra* 2.1.1.

[3] On the concept of normative order, see generally N. MacCormick, *Institutions of Law: An Essay in Legal Theory* (OUP, Oxford, 2008) 11–20.

international legal scholarship has taken place against the backdrop of the dramatic pluralization of norm-making at the international level, for the latter has conveyed the impression that formal law-ascertainment was no longer attuned to contemporary realities. This phenomenon has already been described above.[4] The following paragraphs only aim at depicting some of the manifestations of the deformalization of law-ascertainment currently witnessed in the international legal scholarship against the backdrop of this contemporary pluralization of international norm- and law-making processes. I start by expounding on some of the most common forms of non-formal law-ascertainment yardsticks which are used by international legal scholars and international lawyers (5.1). I then explain how this has generated a general acceptance of the idea of softness of legal concepts (5.2). I eventually say a few words on the various agendas pursued by each of these different types of deformalization (5.3).

5.1 The Various Manifestations of Deformalization of Law-Ascertainment in Contemporary International Legal Scholarship

The contemporary rejection of formalism in international law-identification has proved a complex phenomenon and has manifested itself in many ways. A systematic account of all the manifestations of deformalization of international law-ascertainment would certainly exceed the ambit of this book. However, it is necessary to flag its most common expressions in the theory of the sources of international law.

Contemporary persistence of substantive validity

Despite being the object of the compelling objections raised by international legal scholars affiliated with deconstructivism and critical legal studies, uses of substantive validity have continued to infuse the theory of the sources of international law. Very illustrative of that persistence of substantive validity are those scholars who, faced with the impossibility of resorting to formal identification criteria of customary international law, have designed a theory of customary international law informed by moral or ethical criteria.[5] According to this view, customary international rules ought to be ascertained by virtue of some fundamental ethical principles, a theory of custom-ascertainment based on substantive criteria which, albeit admitting the

[4] Cfr *supra* 1.

[5] See J. Tasioulas, 'Customary International Law and the Quest for Global Justice' in A. Perreau-Saussine and J.-B, Murphy (eds), *The Nature of Customary Law* (CUP, Cambridge, 2007) 307; J. Tasioulas, 'In Defence of Relative Normativity: Communitarian Values and the Nicaragua Case' (1996) 16 OJLS 85; See also B.D. Lepard, *Customary International Law, A New Theory with Practical Applications* (CUP, Cambridge, 2010) especially 77. This echoes some isolated proposals made at the time of the drafting of art. 38. See e.g. the Argentinian amendment to draft art. 38, according to which customary international law should be construed as 'evidence of a practice founded on principles of humanity and justice, and accepted as law', League of Nations, *Documents Concerning the Action Taken by the Council of the League of Nations under article 14 of the Covenant and the Adoption of the Assembly of the Statute of the Permanent Court* (1921) 50. For a criticism of this understanding of custom, see J. Beckett, 'Behind Relative Normativity: Rules and Process as Prerequisite of Law' (2001) 12 EJIL 627.

possible fluctuating character of these criteria, is reminiscent of theories of substantive validity.[6]

Reference must also be made to some radical contemporary liberal scholars[7] and especially those who have been qualified as 'anti-pluralists'.[8] Indeed, the Kantian foundations of their understanding of international law have led some of them to resuscitate the classical kinship between morality and international law.[9] It is fair to say that, in doing so, these scholars have rejected the source thesis and embraced a law-identification blueprint based on substantive validity.[10]

International case-law is occasionally pervaded by naturalist conceptions of law-ascertainment as well. A good illustration is provided by the conception of customary international law advocated by the International Tribunal for the Former Yugoslavia which, although admittedly its case-law is not fully consistent on this point, has deemed that 'demands of humanity or the dictates of public conscience' could be conducive to the creation of a new rule of customary international law, even when practice is scant or non-existent.[11]

It seems that a conception of law based on substantive validity—and hence on a substance-based conception of law-ascertainment—is not entirely absent from Global Administrative Law (GAL). It is true that GAL is not directly concerned with traditional forms of international law-making.[12] It, however, is not entirely exclusive of it,[13] among other reasons because GAL still partially rests on 'formal sources' which include classical sources of public international law.[14] This is why it is noteworthy that, despite claiming that he espouses a Hartian inclusive legal positivism[15]—that is the idea that the rules of recognition can recognize some substantive principles as legal principles—Benedict Kingsbury, for instance, in his attempt to develop (formal) institutional procedures, principles and remedies, advocates that the

[6] See J. Beckett, ibid, 627, 648.

[7] Liberalism in American legal scholarship is often associated with the exodus of the German legal science which enriched the expanding US legal scholarship. In that sense, the Kantian-grounded liberal cosmopolitan views of many of the most important educational institutions of US elites was considerably reinforced by this influx of scholars: S. Oeter, 'The German Influence on Public International Law', in Société française pour le droit international, *Droit International et diversité juridique, Journée franco-allemande* (Pedone, Paris, 2008), 38.

[8] G. Simpson, 'Two Liberalisms' (2001) 12(3) EJIL 537–71.

[9] The most famous example is Tesón, 'The Kantian Theory of International Law' (1992) 92 Colum. L. Rev. 53. See also F. Tesón, *A Philosophy of International Law* (Westview, Boulder, 1998). On Tesón's understanding of international law, see G.J. Simpson, 'Imagined Consent: Democratic Liberalism in International Legal Theory' (1994) 15 Aust. YIBL 103, 116. For a criticism of Tesón from a natural law standpoint, see A. Buchanan, *Justice, Legitimacy and Self-Determination. Moral Foundations for International Law* (OUP, Oxford, 2007) 17–18.

[10] For a criticism, see P. Capps, 'The Kantian Project in Modern International Legal Theory' (2001) 12(5) EJIL 1003.

[11] *Prosecutor v Kupreskic*, Case No. IT-95–16-T, 14 janvier 2000, para. 527.

[12] Cfr *supra* 1.3.

[13] See e.g. B. Kingsbury and L. Casini, 'Global Administrative Law Dimensions of International Organizations Law' (2009) 6 IOLR 319–58.

[14] B. Kingsbury, N. Krisch, and R. Stewart, 'The Emergence of Global Administrative Law' (2005) 68 LCP 16, 29-30.

[15] B. Kingsbury, 'The Concept of "Law" in Global Administrative Law' (2009) 20 EJIL 23.

principle of publicness[16]—and the substantive tenets behind it—constitutes a necessary element in the concept of law irrespective of the rule of recognition,[17] a position partly reminiscent of Lauterpacht.[18] Whilst not strictly moral in content, the allegedly inherent quality of publicness of law advocated by Kingsbury has a strong normative dimension which inevitably brings about a deformalization of law-ascertainment.[19] Unsurprisingly, Kingsbury expressly acknowledges that his own conception of publicness runs in the opposite direction from Hart which inspires the theory of formal ascertainment defended here.[20]

Brunnée and Toope's transposition of Fuller's theory to international law can also be seen as constituting the expression of a substantive validity theory leading to a deformalization of law-ascertainment.[21] Although, as has been argued above,[22] modern natural law theory in international law has been, like most modern natural law theory, more concerned with the authority of law than the identification of international legal rules, these two authors have made use of Fuller's eight procedural criteria in a way that leads them to elevate the 'fidelity to law' into a law-ascertainment criterion. Indeed, Fuller's eight criteria of legality, in their view, 'are not merely signals, but are conditions for the existence of law'[23] They 'create legal obligation'.[24] Yet, it must be made clear that Fuller's criteria of legality, in the eyes of these authors, are not themselves the direct law-ascertaining criteria. They are solely 'crucial to generating a distinctive legal legitimacy and a sense of commitment... among those to whom law is addressed'.[25] In that sense, it is rather the 'fidelity to law'—in other words, the sense of obligation—that is the central indicator by which international legal rules ought to be identified. In that sense, Brunnée and Toope's theory comes down to a blended mix of substantive validity and effect-based conception of international law. The deformalization of law-ascertainment conveyed by their theory is thus as much the result of their resort to substantive validity as to a theory of international law whereby law is restricted to what generates a sense of obligation among the addressees of its rules. This is why it ought also to be mentioned as an illustration of the contemporary effect- (or impact-)based conception of international law-ascertainment.

[16] Ibid. ('Only rules and institutions meeting these publicness requirements immanenent in public law... can be regarded as law')

[17] B. Kingsbury, ibid, 23–57, 31

[18] This point is also made by A. Somek, 'The Concept of "Law" in Global Administrative Law' (2009) 20 EJIL 984–95, especially 991. See also the remarks of M-S. Kuo, 'The Concept of "Law" in Global Administrative Law' (2009) 20 EJIL 997–1004.

[19] B. Kingsbury and M. Donaldson, 'From Bilateralism to Publicness in International Law', *From Bilateralism to Community Interest: Essays in Honour of Judge Bruno Simma* (OUP, Oxford, 2011) (forthcoming) 79, 86.

[20] B. Kingsbury and M. Donaldson, ibid, 79, 89.

[21] See J. Brunnée and S.J. Toope, *Legitimacy and Legality in International Law. An Interactional Account* (CUP, Cambridge, 2010).

[22] Cfr *supra* 4.1.1.

[23] Ibid, 41.

[24] Ibid, 7.

[25] See J. Brunnée and S.J. Toope, *Legitimacy and Legality in International Law. An Interactional Account* (CUP, Cambridge, 2010) 7.

The few limited expressions of theory of substantive validity reported here undoubtedly contribute to the contemporary deformalization of law-ascertainment, as the ethical or moral law-identification criteria which they resort to do not constitute formal law-identification indicators.

Effect- or impact-based conceptions of international law-ascertainment

The most common non-formal law-ascertainment blueprint is found in *effect- (or impact-)based* conceptions of international law which have been embraced by a growing number of international legal scholars.[26] For these scholars, what matters nowadays is 'whether and how the subjects of norms, rules, and standards come to accept those norms, rules and standards... [and] [i]f they treat them as authoritative, then those norms can be treated as... law'.[27] In their view, any normative effort to influence international actors' behaviour, at least if it materializes in the adoption of an international instrument, should be considered to be comprised in international law. Such an effect- (or impact-)based conception of international law—which entails a shift from the perspective of the norm-maker to that of the norm-user—has itself taken various forms. For instance, it has led to conceptions whereby compliance is elevated to the law-ascertaining yardstick.[28] It has also materialized in behaviourist approaches to law where what seems to be crucial is only the 'normative ripples' that norms can produce.[29] Whatever its actual manifestation,

[26] For a few examples see, J.E. Alvarez, *International Organizations as Law-makers* (OUP, NY, 2005); J. Brunnée and S.J. Toope, 'International Law and Constructivism, Elements of an International Theory of International Law' (2000–2001) 39 Colum. J. Transnat'l L. 19–74, 65. These effect-based approaches must be distinguished from the subtle conception defended by Kratochwil based on the *principled rule-application* of a norm which refers to the explicitness and contextual variation in the reasoning process and the application of rules in 'like' situations in the future. See F. Kratochwil, *Rules Norms and Decisions: On the Conditions of Practical and Legal Reasoning in International Relations and Domestic Affairs* (CUP, Cambridge, 1989) 206–8. See also F. Kratochwil, 'Legal Theory and International Law', in D. Armstrong (ed), *Routledge Handbook of International Law* (Routledge, NY, 2009) l, 58.

[27] On that approach, see the remarks of J. Klabbers, 'Law-making and Constitutionalism' in *The Constitutionalization of International Law* (OUP, Oxford, 2009) 98.

[28] See e.g. J. Brunnée and S.J. Toope, 'International Law and Constructivism, Elements of an International Theory of International Law' (2000–2001) 39 Colum. J. Transnat'l L. 19–74, 68: 'We should stop looking for the structural distinctions that identify law, and examine instead the processes that constitute a normative continuum bridging from predictable patterns of practice to legally required behavior'. The same authors argue: 'Once it is recognized that law's existence is best measured by the influence it exerts, and not by formal tests of validity rooted in normative hierarchies, international lawyers can finally eschew the preoccupation with legal pedigree (sources) that has constrained creative thinking within the discipline for generations' (ibid, 65). As has been argued above, their interactional account of international law is nonetheless based on both substantitve validity and the impact of rules on actors. For a more elaborated presentation of their interaction theory, see J. Brunnée and S.J. Toope, *Legitimacy and Legality in International Law. An Interactional Account* (CUP, Cambridge, 2010).

[29] J.E. Alvarez, *International Organizations as Law-makers* (OUP, NY, 2005). Alvarez argues, 'Although we have turned to such institutions for the making of much of today's international law, the lawyers most familiar with such rules remain in the grip of a positivist preoccupation with an ostensibly sacrosanct doctrine of sources, now codified in article 38 of the Statute of the International Court of Justice, which originated before most modern IOs were established and which, not surprisingly, does not mention them': J.E. Alvarez, *International Organizations as Law-makers* (OUP, NY, 2005) x. He adds, '[W]e continue to pour an increasingly rich normative output into old bottles labeled treaty, custom, or

there is no doubt that effect- (or impact-)based conceptions of law-ascertainment have grown widespread in the contemporary international legal scholarship.

The use of the effect or impact of norms to identify rules is not only witnessed in studies about the traditional forms of international law-making. Mention must again be made here of two well-known research projects which, although not directly centred on international law but on the new forms of contemporary norm-making, show how international norms are being ascertained by virtue of their effect or impact: the Heidelberg research project on the Exercise of Public Authority by International Institutions and—the already discussed—Global Administrative Law project.[30] It is true that, because of the specificities of the normative phenomenon with which these two projects deal, the use of a non-formal yardstick of norm-identification in these cases proves absolutely indispensable. Yet, they provide an insightful illustration of how, outside the classical remit of international law, effect- (or impact-)based conceptions of norm-ascertainment have also been thriving.

Some very subtle and elaborate forms of effect- (or impact-)based norm-ascertainment models informed by the need to continuously ensure the legitimacy of the exercise of public authority at the international level have, for instance, been defended by Armin von Bogdandy, Philipp Dann, and Matthias Goldmann within the framework of the Heidelberg research project on the Exercise of Public Authority by International Institutions. Their model of norm-ascertainment is not strictly based on the impact of the norms that they examine but rather on the expected impact that these norms create.[31] Drawing on such an expectations-based conception to capture normative production outside the traditional international law-making blueprint, these scholars have attempted to devise 'general principles of international public authority'[32] with a view to fostering 'both the effectiveness and the legitimacy of international public authority.[33] These endeavours have not gone as far as claiming that any exercise of international public authority should be construed as law. The use of non-formal criteria is designed to capture norms which are precisely

(much more rarely) general principles. Few bother to ask whether these state-centric sources of international law, designed for the use of judges engaged in a particular task, remain a viable or exhaustive description of the types of international obligations that matter to a variety of actors in the age of modern IOs': J.E. Alvarez, ibid, x-xi. He exclusively focuses on the normative impact and 'the ripples' of norms: see J.E. Alvarez, ibid, xiii, 63, 122. A similar account can be found in D.J. Bederman, 'The Souls of International Organizations: Legal Personality and the Lighthouse at Cape Spartel' (1996) 36 Va. J. Int'l L. 275, 372; N. White, 'Separate but Connected: Inter-Governmental Organizations and International Law' (2008) 5 IOLR 175–95, especially 181–6.

30 Cfr *supra* 1.3.

31 See also M. Goldmann, 'Inside Relative Normativity: From Sources to Standard Instruments for the Exercise of International Public Authority' (2008) 9 *German Law Journal* 1865 and A. von Bogdandy, P. Dann, and M. Goldmann, 'Developing the Publicness of Public International Law: Towards a Legal Framework for Global Governance Activities' (2008) 9 *German Law Journal* 1375.

32 A. von Bogdandy, et al., ibid, 1375–400. With respect to the development of 'standard instruments', see A. von Bogdandy, 'General Principles of International Public Authority: Sketching a Research field' (2008) 9 *German Law Journal* 1909–1939. See M. Goldmann, 'Inside Relative Normativity: From Sources to Standard Instruments for the Exercise of International Public Authority' (2008) 9 *German Law Journal* 1865–1908.

33 M. Goldmann, ibid, 1865–1908, 1867.

not, strictly speaking, international legal rules and which, on the basis of formal criteria, could not be identified. However, their 'legal conceptualization'[34] echoes a deformalization of norm-identification[35] necessary to ensure the legitimacy of the exercise of international public authority.[36]

Interestingly, the deformalization of law-identification that inevitably accompanies the conceptualization at the heart of this project is meant to be only temporary, since the ultimate aim of these scholars is to re-formalize the identification of those 'alternative instruments'.[37] Indeed, it is of the utmost importance to highlight that, despite the deformalization at the heart of the net by virtue of which they capture their object of study, the ambition of these scholars has remained the elaboration of formal 'principles of international public authority'[38] in order to foster 'both the effectiveness and the legitimacy of international public authority'.[39] Their use of non-formal criteria has thus been designed to apprehend normative activities which are not, strictly speaking, international legal rules and which, on the basis of formal criteria, could not be identified. Their ultimate aim has nonetheless remained a 'legal conceptualization' to an extent necessary to ensure the legitimacy of the exercise of international public authority. In that sense, the deformalization of law-identification inherent in their attempt to capture new forms of exercises of public authority has been accompanied by a reformalization of those 'alternative instruments' and, in the same vein as Global Administrative Law, an attempt to devise formal principles of public authority.

While also constituting an expression of substantive validity theory—as has been discussed above,[40] Global Administrative Law (GAL) must be again mentioned here. Indeed, although it is geared towards the development of institutional procedures, principles, and remedies, which encompass formal mechanisms of application of GAL,[41] it captures the normative product of these processes through an effect- (or impact-)based conception of norm-ascertainment. In particular, GAL is premised on the idea that, regarding these alternative modes of norm-making, problems of law-ascertainment cannot be fully resolved.[42] This certainly is not surprising, since the

[34] M. Goldmann, ibid, 1865.

[35] A. von Bogdandy, P. Dann, and M. Goldmann 'Developing the Publicness of International Law' (2008) 9 *German Law Journal* 1375–1400, 1376.

[36] M. Goldmann, 'Inside Relative Normativity: From Sources to Standard Instruments for the Exercise of International Public Authority' (2008) 9 *German Law Journal* 1867–8.

[37] Ibid.

[38] A. von Bogdandy, P. Dann, and M. Goldmann 'Developing the Publicness of International Law' (2008) 9 *German Law Journal* 1375–1400. With respect to the development of 'standard instruments', see A. von Bogdandy, 'General Principles of International Public Authority: Sketching a Research field' (2008) 9 *German Law Journal* 1909–1939. See M. Goldmann, 'Inside Relative Normativity: From Sources to Standard Instruments for the Exercise of International Public Authority' (2008) 9 *German Law Journal* 1865–1908.

[39] M. Goldmann, ibid, 1865–1908, 1867.

[40] Cfr *supra* 5.1.

[41] B. Kingsbury, N. Krisch, and R. Stewart, 'The Emergence of Global Administrative Law' (2005) 68 LCP 16, 27.

[42] See B. Kingsbury, et al., ibid, 15–61, 29; C. Harlow, 'Global Administrative Law: The Quest for Principles and Values' (2006) 17 EJIL 197-214. According to Kingsbury, GAL rests on an 'extended

norms created through the processes concerned cannot be ascertained through the classical theory of the sources.[43] GAL accordingly resorts to non-formal yardsticks, and in particular effect- (or impact-)based criteria, to identify what it considers a normative product.[44] As was said above, these principles to which these alternative norms are subjected are themselves identified through substance-based criteria, and especially by virtue of the principle of publicness.[45] Although some of its leading figures have curiously professed that GAL bespeaks a Hartian conception of law,[46] GAL can thus be understood as resting on a subtle use of both effect- (or impact-) and substance-based norm-ascertainment indicators.

This being said, it must be recalled that GAL has simultaneously sought the development of formal institutional procedures, principles, and remedies, which encompass formal mechanisms of the application of GAL.[47] The emerging rules it refers to accordingly encapsulate formal procedures and standards for regulatory decision-making outside traditional domestic and international frameworks.[48] In that sense, it promotes a formalization of global processes.[49] Whilst the source of GAL and the practice it seeks to apprehend involve deformalization, its object thus remains the development of formal rules and procedures.

If we leave aside these two specific research projects dedicated to the new pluralized forms of norm-making at the international level, it is noteworthy that, however nuanced and detailed they may be, effect- (or impact-)based models of norm-ascertainment are generally grounded in a two-fold deformalization of law-ascertainment. First, the impact that the rule bears has not been subject to formal identification for it necessitates that one looks at the behaviour of actors—an approach which Judge Ago had famously criticized in his notable Separate Opinion

Hartian conception of law' which elevates publicness to a constitutive element of law. According to that view, publicness is a necessary element in the concept of law under modern democratic conditions. By publicness, Kingsbury means the claim made for law that it has been wrought by the whole society, by the public, and the connected claim that law addresses matters of concerns to the society as such. See B. Kingsbury, 'The Concept of Law in Global Administrative Law' (2009) 20(1) EJIL 23–57, 31.

[43] B. Kingsbury, ibid, 23–57, 25–26.

[44] 'The legal mechanisms, principles and practices, along with supporting social understandings, that promote or otherwise affect the accountability of global administrative bodies, in particular by ensuring that these bodies meet adequate standards of transparency, consultation, participation, rationality and legality and by providing effective review of the rules and decisions these bodies make': B. Kingsbury, ibid, 23–57, 25.

[45] B. Kingsbury, ibid, 23–57, 31.

[46] B. Kingsbury, ibid, 23–57; see also B. Kingsbury, 'Global Administrative Law Dimensions of International Organizations Law', Public Law & Legal Theory Research Paper Series, Working Paper No. 10-04, January 2010, available at <http://www.ssrn.com>.

[47] B. Kingsbury, N. Krisch, and R. Stewart, 'The Emergence of Global Administrative Law' (2005) 68 LCP 16, 27.

[48] S. Chesterman, 'Global Administrative Law', Working Paper for the S.T. Lee Project on Global Governance (2009), New York University Public Law and Legal Theory Working Papers, Paper 152, available at <http://lsr.nellco.org/nyu_plltwp/152>, 4.

[49] In the same vein, see S. Chesterman, ibid, 3-4.

in the *Nicaragua* case at the jurisdictional stage.[50] Second, the actors whose behaviour is impacted have also remained free of any formal definition—which is hardly surprising, for even the State in mainstream theory has proven to be indefinable through formal criteria.[51] All-in-all, effect- (or impact-)based identification of international law has thus been synonymous with non-formal law-ascertainment.

Interestingly, and somewhat paradoxically, all the abovementioned effect- (or impact-)based approaches to law-ascertainment have borne a resemblance to the compliance-based conceptions of international law found in realist theories according to which law only exists to the extent to which it is complied with.[52] It is equally noteworthy that the undeniable success of these effect- (or impact-)based conceptions of law-ascertainment in contemporary legal scholarship has not been without consequence for the general research agenda of international legal scholars, since effect- (or impact-)based conceptions have revived interest in the theory of the fairness of law. Indeed, it is uncontested that the fairness or the justness of a rule encourages compliance by those subjected to it[53]—a contention also at the heart of modern natural law theories examined above[54] For this reason, effect- (or impact-) based accounts have also kindled a need to bolster the legitimacy of international legal rules. The attention accordingly devoted to the question of the legitimacy of international law—which has been directly shored up by the reinforcement of effect- (or impact-)based law-ascertainment theories—has further deflected the attention of international legal scholars away from the problems inherent in the effect- (or impact-)based conceptions of law, especially from the standpoint of law-ascertainment.[55]

The repercussions of effect- (or impact-)based law-ascertainment on the theory of legitimacy is not limited to a reinforced interest in the latter. Effect- (or impact-) based identification of international legal rules has also spawned a shift in the central paradigm in the theory of legitimacy. Indeed, because effect- (or impact-) based law-ascertainment models entail a deformalization of law-ascertainment, formal law-identification can no longer constitute a source of the legitimacy of rules. The legitimacy of international legal rules—which is sought to secure greater compliance—is, in turn, sought in their content. This shift in the central paradigm of legitimacy can, potentially, lead to a return to substance-based identification of

[50] See Separate Opinion of Judge Ago, ICJ Rep. (1984) 527 ('A ce sujet je dois faire... une reserve expresse quant à l'admissibilité de l'idée même que l'exigence d'un acte formel d'acceptation puisse être remplacée... par une simple conduite de fait...').

[51] Cfr *supra* 2.1.1.

[52] J. Goldsmith and E. Posner, *The Limits of International Law* (OUP, Oxford, 2005). For a criticism of their conception of law, see the very interesting contribution of A. Somek, 'Kelsen lives' (2007) 18 EJIL 409–51. Some aspects of this conception have been discussed above. Cfr *supra* 4.2.2.

[53] See the famous account made by T. Franck, *The Power of Legitimacy Among Nations* (OUP, Oxford 1990) 25.

[54] Cfr *supra* 4.1.1.

[55] Cfr *supra* 2.2.

law.[56] The naturalistic overtones of such an outcome—of which supporters of effect- (or impact-)based law-ascertainment models are not always aware—confirms the significant extent of the deformalization of law-ascertainment that they bring about.

Process-based conceptions of international law-identification and other manifestations of the deformalization of international law-ascertainment

The effect- (or impact-)based conceptions of international law do not constitute the exclusive manifestation of the deformalization of law-ascertainment in contemporary legal scholarship. Indeed, the general scepticism vented against formal law-ascertaining criteria has also led to a revival of *process-based* law-identification. This revival of process-based critique of mainstream conceptions of international law has no doubt re-kindled the deformalization of law-ascertainment advocated by the New Haven School.[57] Such a resuscitation of New Haven has occasionally been expressed in functionalist terms.[58] Whatever its ultimate manifestation, process-based approaches have come with a great deformalization of law-ascertainment, for it has generally proved very difficult to formally ascertain the process by which international legal rules are identified.[59]

There are other, more marginal, expressions of the deformalization of law-ascertainment in the contemporary international legal scholarship.[60] For instance, it has sometimes been argued that the purpose of the rule should be turned into a law-ascertaining criterion.[61] While these—more isolated—approaches cannot be discussed here, they ought at least to be mentioned because they further illustrate the general deformalization of law-ascertainment currently at play in the contemporary international legal scholarship.

[56] For an even more radical position, see M. Virally, 'A Propos de la "Lex Ferenda"', in Daniel Bardonnet (ed), *Mélanges Reuter: le droit international: unité et diversité* (Pedone, Paris, 1981) 521–33, p. 530.

[57] For a classical example of this type of deformalization, see R. Higgins, *Problems and Process: International Law and How We Use It* (OUP, Oxford, 1995) 8–10. For another illustration of the contemporary tendency to identify the law through processes, see P.S. Berman, 'A Pluralist Approach to International Law' (2007) 32 Yale J. Int'l L. 301. For a hybrid law-ascertainment approach based on both effect and processes, see H.G. Cohen, 'Finding International Law: Rethinking the Doctrine of Sources' (2007) 93 Iowa L. Rev. 65. The New Haven approach to law-ascertainment has been examined above. Cfr *supra* 4.2.3.

[58] See D.M. Johnston, 'Functionalism in the Theory of International Law' (1988) 26 Canadian YBIL 3, especially 30–1.

[59] On the difficulty to formally ascertain processes, see G. Abi-Saab, 'Cours général de droit international public' (1987-VIII) 207 RCADI 9–463, 39–49; Brownlie 'International law at the fiftieth anniversary of the United Nations: general course on public international law' (1995) 255 RCADI 9–228, p. 29; G.J.H. Van Hoof, *Rethinking the Sources of International Law* (Kluwer, Deventer, 1983) 283.

[60] For a more precise and systematic taxonomy of these other approaches, see J. Klabbers, 'Law-Making and Constitutionalism' in *The Constitutionalization of International Law* (OUP, Oxford, 2009) 94.

[61] This is what J. Klabbers has described the 'Functionalist turn'. For examples, see J. Klabbers, ibid, 99.

5.2 The Softness of International Law

Irrespective of how deformalization of law-identification actually manifests itself, the rejection of formal law-ascertainment has generated the acceptance among international legal scholars of the existence of a grey area where it is not possible to distinguish law from non-law. More particularly, international law is increasingly seen as a *continuum* between law and non-law, and formal law-ascertainment as no longer being capable of capturing legal phenomena in the international arena. This has gone hand-in-hand with a conflation between legal acts and 'legal facts' (*faits juridiques*)[62] in the theory of the sources of international law[63] and an espousal of the overall softness of legal concepts.[64] Indeed, the theory of the softness of international law has been gaining currency in international legal scholarship. It has been argued that not only has law become soft, but so have governance,[65] law-making,[66] international organizations,[67] enforcement,[68] and even—from a critical legal perspective—international legal arguments.[69] This general idea of softness—and especially the softness of the instrument (*instrumentum*) in which international legal rules can allegedly be contained[70]—has commonly originated in the abovementioned presupposition that the binary nature of law is ill-suited to accommodate the growing complexity of contemporary international relations, and that international law comprises a very large grey area where there is no need to define law and non-

[62] The term 'legal fact' is probably not the most adequate to translate a concept found in other languages. It however seems better than 'juridical fact'. I have used the former in earlier studies about this distinction. See J. d'Aspremont, 'Softness in International Law: A Self-Serving Quest for New Legal Materials' (2008) 19 EJIL 1075–93.

[63] For an early systematization of the distinction between legal acts and legal facts, see D. Anzilotti, *Cours de droit international, premier volume: introduction—theories générales*, translated by G. Gidel (1929). See also Morelli, 'Cours général de droit international public' (1956-I) 89 RCADI 437–604, p. 589. J-P. Jacqué, 'Acte et norme en droit international' (1991-II) 227 RCADI 357–417, p. 372. See also M. Virally, *La pensée juridique* (LDGJ, Paris, 1960) 93; G. Abi-Saab, 'Les sources du droit international. Essai de déconstruction', in *Le Droit international dans un monde en mutation: liber amicorum en hommage au Professeur Eduardo Jimenez de Arechaga* (Fundación de Cultura Universitaria, Montevideo, 1994) 29–49, p. 40.

[64] I have studied that phenomenon in greater depth elsewhere. See J. d'Aspremont, 'Softness in International Law: A Self-Serving Quest for New Legal Materials' (2008) 19 EJIL 1075–93.

[65] K.W. Abbott and D. Snidal, 'Hard and Soft Law in International Governance' (2000) 54 *International Organization* 421–56.

[66] P.-M. Dupuy, 'Soft Law and the International Law of the Environment' (1990–1991) 12 Mich. J. Int'l L. 420–35, especially p. 424.

[67] J. Klabbers, 'Institutional Ambivalence by Design: Soft Organizations in International Law' (2001) 70 Nord. J. Int'l L. 403–21.

[68] O. Yoshida, 'Soft Enforcement of Treaties: The Montreal Protocol's Noncompliance Procedure and the Functions of Internal International Institutions' (1999) 95 Colo. J. Int'l Envtl. L. & Pol'y 95; A.E. Boyle, 'Some reflections on the relationship of treaties and soft law' (1999) 48 ICLQ 901, especially p. 909.

[69] D. Kennedy, 'The Sources of International Law' (1987) 2 Am. U. J. Int'l L. & Pol'y 1, especially 20–1.

[70] On the distinction between *instrumentum* and *negotium*, cfr *infra* 7.2.2.

law.[71] Norms enshrined in soft instruments, e.g. political declarations, codes of conduct, and gentlemen's agreements, are considered as part of this continuum between law and non-law.

In the traditional theory of the sources of international law, norms enshrined in a non-legal instrument (i.e. those norms with soft *instrumentum*) can still produce legal effects. For instance, they can partake in the *internationalization of the subject-matter,*[72] provide guidelines for the interpretation of other legal acts,[73] or pave the way for further subsequent practice that may one day be taken into account for the emergence of a norm of customary international law.[74] Yet, if only the formal pedigree were to be the law-ascertainment criterion, they would simply be legal facts. Nonetheless, the international legal scholarship has manifested a strong tendency to construe these legal facts as law, properly so-called.[75]

I will explain in chapter 7 why classical international law-ascertainment yardsticks prove highly unsatisfactory.[76] However inadequate the mainstream theory of the sources of international law may be to capture the complexities of contemporary norm-making at the international level, the softness inherent in the growingly accepted idea of a grey area and the elevation of the norms enshrined in non-legal instruments—which are at best legal facts—into international legal rules reinforce the current deformalization of the ascertainment of international legal rules

[71] On this point see particularly L. Blutman, 'In the Trap of a Legal Metaphor: International Soft Law' (2010) 59 ICLQ 605, 613–14.

[72] On this question, see J. Verhoeven, 'Non-intervention: affaires intérieures ou "vie privée"?' *Mélanges en hommage à Michel Virally: Le droit international au service de la paix, de la justice et du développement* (Pedone, Paris, 1991) 493–500; R. Kolb, 'Du domaine réservé—Réflexion sur la théorie de la compétence nationale' (2006) 110 *Revue générale de droit international public* 609–10; F.B. Sloan, 'General Assembly Resolutions Revisited (Forty Years Later)' (1987) 58 BYBIL 124.

[73] See A. Aust, 'The Theory and Practice of Informal International Instruments' (1986) ICLQ 35, 787–812; R.-J. Dupuy, 'Declaratory Law and Programmatory Law: From Revolutionary Custom to "Soft Law"' in R. Akkerman et al. (eds), *Declarations of Principles. A Quest for Universal Peace* (Sijthoff, 1977) 247, p. 255. U. Fastenrath, 'Relative Normativity in International Law' (1993) 4 EJIL 305–40. See O. Schachter, 'The Twilight Existence of Non-Binding International Agreements' (1977) 71 AJIL 296.

[74] This is, for instance, the intention of art. 19 of the ILC articles on Diplomatic Protection on the 'recommended practice' by States, *Official Records of the General Assembly*, Sixty-first Session, Supplement No. 10 (A/61/10).

[75] A. Boyle and C. Chinkin, *The Making of International Law* (OUP, Oxford, 2007) 211–29; V. Lowe, *International Law* (OUP, Oxford, 2007) 96–7. A.T. Guzman, 'The Design of International Agreements' (2005) 16 EJIL 579–612. Pellet has hinted at the idea of a 'dégradé normatif': A. Pellet, 'Le "bon droit", et l'ivraie—plaidoyer pour l'ivraie' in *Mélanges offerts à Charles Chaumont, Le droit des peuples à disposer d'eux-mêmes. Méthodes d'analyse du droit international* (Pedone, Paris, 1984) 465–93, especially 488. See also G. Abi-Saab, 'Eloge du 'droit assourdi' in *Nouveaux itinéraires en droit: Hommage à François Rigaux* (Bruylant, Brussels, 1993) 59, 62–3; R.R. Baxter, 'International Law in "Her Infinite Variety"' (1980) 29 ICLQ 549; R. Ida, 'Formation des normes internationales dans un monde en mutation. Critique de la notion de Soft Law', *Mélanges en hommage à Michel Virally: Le droit international au service de la paix, de la justice et du développement* (Pedone, Paris, 1991) 333, p. 336; M. Virally, 'La distinction entre textes internationaux de portée juridique et textes internationaux dépourvus de portée juridique, Rapport provisoire à l'Institut de droit international' (1983) 60 *Annuaire de L'Institut de Droit International* 166, p. 244; O. Elias and C. Lim,'General principles of law', 'soft' law and the identification of international law' (1997) 28 Netherlands YBIL 45.

[76] Cfr *infra* 7.2.

described in the previous section.[77] Softness can thus be seen here as constituting an integral part of the contemporary deformalization of international law-ascertainment.[78]

5.3 The Diverging Agendas Behind the Deformalization of Law-Ascertainment

The abovementioned manifestations of the deformalization of law-ascertainment have been informed by very different agendas.[79] Similar conceptions of law-ascertainment sometimes even serve very opposite agendas. This is well-illustrated by the use of effect- (or impact-)based conceptions by some of the abovementioned scholars[80] and behavioural conceptions defended by (neo-)realists who, although resorting to somewhat comparable conceptions of law-identification, have been pursuing radically different objectives. It certainly is not the aim of the following paragraphs to identify each of the motives that lie behind the various understandings of law-ascertainment which have been mentioned in this chapter. I only sketch out here some of the main objectives that scholars may have been—sometimes unconsciously—pursuing by deformalizing the ascertainment of international legal rules. I subsequently formulate some critical remarks. The presentation of the agenda of deformalization of law-ascertainment attempted in the following paragraph takes an external point of view. It leaves aside the motives animating international actors engaged in international norm-making processes and those behind their choices regarding the nature of the norm which they seek to create.[81]

Programming the future development of international law

The most common driving force behind the deformalization of law-ascertainment pertains to what I call the *programmatic* virtue of the use of non-formal law-

[77] C.M. Chinkin, 'The Challenge to Soft Law, Development and Change in International Law' (1989) 38 ICLQ 850, p. 865.

[78] I have expounded on the idea of softness of international law elsewhere. See J. d'Aspremont, 'Softness in International Law: A Self-Serving Quest for New Legal Materials' (2008) 19 EJIL, 1075–93. See also J. d'Aspremont, 'Les dispositions non-normatives des actes juridiques conventionnels' (2003) 36 *Revue Belge de Droit International* 492.

[79] I have mentioned some of these agendas in previous works: J. d'Aspremont, 'Softness in International Law: A Self-Serving Quest for New Legal Materials' (2008) 19(5) EJIL 1075. See also J. d'Aspremont, 'La Doctrine du Droit international et la tentation d'une juridicisation sans limite' (2008) 112 *Revue générale de droit international public* 849–66.

[80] Cfr *supra* 5.1.

[81] On the reasons why international actors prefer soft law to hard law and vice-versa, see generally H. Hillgenberg, 'A Fresh Look at Soft Law' (1999) 10 EJIL 499, 501–2; See also the insightful three-tiered analysis of K. Raustiala, 'Form and Substance in International Agreements' (2005) 99 AJIL 581, 591–601; D. Carreau, *Droit International* (8th edn, Pedone, Paris, 2004) 205; G. Shaffer and M. Pollack, 'Hard vs. Soft Law: Alternatives, Complements and Antagonists in International Governance' (2010) 94 Minn. L. Rev. 706, p. 717–21.

ascertainment criteria.[82] I hereby refer to the use by international lawyers of non-formal criteria of law-identification with the hope of contributing to the subsequent emergence of new rules in the *lex lata*. Thus I have in mind the identification of rules which, although not strictly speaking legal rules, are seen as constituting an experimental ground for future legal rules whose emergence is deemed desirable.[83] The resort to non-formal law-ascertainment is meant, in this case, to be conducive to the subsequent emergence of new rules. This programmatic attitude is rife in the area of human rights law and environmental law.[84]

Promoting the expansion of international law

Programming the further crystallization of formally ascertainable rules is not the only driving force behind the abovementioned deformalization of law-ascertainment. The latter is also widely informed by the idea that international law is necessarily good and should therefore be expanded. There is indeed a widespread tendency among international lawyers to consider that any international legal rule is better than no rule at all, and that the development of international law should be promoted as such.[85] This faith in the added value of international law in comparison to other social norms is often accompanied by the belief that the cost of non-compliance necessarily outweighs the benefit thereof. Seen in this light, international law is conceived as an essential condition of any systematized form of an international community[86] and any new legal rule is deemed a step towards a greater integration of that community away from the anarchical state of nature.[87] Accordingly, deformalizing international law-ascertainment is seen as instrumental in expanding the realm of the international community with a view to promoting what is seen as progress.[88]

[82] This argument has also been made by L. Blutman, 'In the Trap of a Legal Metaphor: International Soft Law' (2010) 59 ICLQ 605, 617–18. In the same vein, see M. Reisman, 'Soft Law and Law Jobs' (2011) 2 *Journal of International Dispute Settlement* 25, 25–6.

[83] For an avowed programmatic use of soft law and customary international law, see R.-J. Dupuy, 'Droit déclaratoire et droit programmatoire de la coutume sauvage a la "soft law"' in *Société française pour le droit international, L'élaboration du droit international public, Colloque de Toulouse* (1974) (Pedone, Paris, 1975) 132–48; see also A. Pellet, 'Complementarity of International Treaty Law, Customary Law and Non-Contractual Law-Making' in R. Wolfrum and V. Röben (eds), *Developments of International Law in Treaty Making* (Springer, Berlin, 2005) 409, p. 415; U. Fastenrath, 'Relative Normativity in International Law' (1993) 4 EJIL 305, p. 324; See also F. Sindico, 'Soft Law and the Elusive Quest for Sustainable Global Governance' (2006) 19 LJIL 829, p. 836.

[84] See e.g. A. Pellet, 'The Normative Dilemma: Will and Consent in International Law-Making' (1988–1989) 12 Aust. YBIL 22, p. 47.

[85] This was insightfully highlighted by J. Klabbers, 'The Undesirability of Soft Law' (1998) 67 Nord. J. Int'l L. 381–91, p. 383.

[86] See e.g. G.G. Fitzmaurice, 'The general principles of international law considered from the standpoint of the rule of law' (1957-II) 92 RCADI 1, 38; G. Abi-Saab, 'Cours général des droit international public' (1987-VIII) 207 RCADI 9–463 p. 45.

[87] On the various dimensions of this enthusiasm for the international, see D. Kennedy, 'A New World Order: Yesterday, Today and Tomorrow' (1994) 4 Transnat'l L. & Contemp. Probs. 329–75, p. 336.; See also S. Marks, *The Riddle of All Constitutions* (OUP, Oxford, 2000) 146.

[88] On the idea of progress see T. Skouteris, *The Notion of Progress in International Law Discourse* (LEI Universiteit, Leiden, 2008), chapter 3, later published as *The Notion of Progress in International Law Discourse* (T.M.C. Asser, The Hague, 2010).

While the idea that international law is necessarily good and should be preferred to non-legal means of regulation can be seriously questioned, it helps explain how the use of non-formal international law-ascertainment has turned into a tool to expand international law. Using non-formal law-identification criteria is yet another strategy which comes to complement the existing interpretative instruments devised by international lawyers to expand international law.[89]

Accountability for the exercise of public authority

As was said above,[90] most of the international normative activity nowadays unfolds outside the traditional framework of international law, and generates norms which do not qualify as international legal rules according to the traditional law-ascertainment criteria of mainstream theory of the sources of international law. Yet, international legal scholars have been prompt to see in these new forms of norm-making at the international level a phenomenon that they ought to come to grips with and could not leave aside. It is particularly by virtue of a preoccupation with the accountability deficit generated by the sweeping impact that such norms could bear on international and national actors, that international legal scholars have increasingly tried to encompass these new phenomena in the remit of international legal studies. Encapsulating these new normative phenomena has required the use of non-formal law-ascertainment. Some of them have even been exclusively focused on this pluralization of norm-making at the international level with a view to designing instruments addressing this accountability deficit. While American liberal scholars and their interest in governmental networks may have been the first to seriously engage in such an endeavour,[91] they were quickly followed by others, as is illustrated by NYU's Global Administrative Law[92] or the Max Planck Institute's study of the International Exercise of International Public Authority'.[93] Whilst, strictly speaking, the latter have not zeroed in on traditional international legal rules,[94] they are symptomatic of the contemporary use of non-formal law-ascertainment criteria as part of an endeavour to address accountability deficit.

[89] On the use of treaty interpretation to expand international law, see L. Lixinski, 'Treaty Interpretation by the Inter-American Court of Human Rights: Expansionism at the Service of the Unity of International Law' (2010) 21 EJIL 585–604.

[90] Cfr *supra* 1.1.

[91] See e.g. M. Slaughter, *A New World Order* (Princeton UP, Princeton, 2004). See also A.-M. Slaughter, 'Global Government Networks, Global Information Agencies, and Disaggregated Democracy' (2003) 24 Mich. J. Int'l L. 1041.

[92] See B. Kingsbury, N. Krisch, and R. Steward, 'The Emergence of Global Administrative Law' (2005) 68 *Law and Contemporary Problems* 15–61, p. 29; C. Harlow, 'Global Administrative Law: The Quest for Principles and Values' (2006) 17 EJIL 197–214; B. Kinsgbury, 'The Concept of Law in Global Administrative Law' (2009) 20(1) EJIL 23–57.

[93] See also M. Goldmann, 'Inside Relative Normativity: From Sources to Standard Instruments for the Exercise of International Public Authority' (2008) 9 *German Law Journal* 1865 and A. von Bogdandy, P. Dann, and M. Goldmann, 'Developing the Publicness of Public International Law: Towards a Legal Framework for Global Governance Activities' (2008) 9 *German Law Journal* 1375.

[94] Cfr *supra* 1.3.

A self-serving quest for new legal materials

Deformalization of law-ascertainment also has some roots in the—conscious or unconscious—quest of international legal scholars to *stretch the frontiers of their own discipline.* In that sense, deformalization of law-identification could be a means to alleviate the unease that has followed the sweeping development of international legal scholarship. Indeed, there is no doubt today that international law has acquired an unprecedented importance in legal discourse and has proven to be a paramount component of legal studies. Hence, universities and research institutes have significantly increased the number of staff charged with teaching and research in the field of international law. At the same time, many people have 'discovered' their calling for international law. International law is now studied to an unprecedented extent. As a result, the international legal scholarship has mushroomed and the number of research projects and publications on international law has soared. There is little doubt that we presently face a proliferation of international legal thinking.[95] Although the foregoing may be seen as an encouraging and cheerful development,[96] it has not come about without problems. Because scholars are so numerous today, it is much harder for each of them to find their niche and distinguish themselves. As a result, there are fewer unexplored fields and less room for the original findings that are sometimes commanded by incongruous institutional constraints when not driven by mere vanity.[97] This makes it much harder to make one's mark today than it was at a time when international legal thinking was still in its infancy. The greater difficulty in finding a niche has pushed scholars into fiercer competition and ignited a feeling of constriction, as if their field of study had grown too narrow to accommodate all of them. This battle within the profession has simultaneously been fostered by a battle among professions and, in particular, the growing interest of non-legal disciplines in subjects classically deemed to be within the exclusive ambit of legal scholarship.[98]

Against that backdrop, many scholars have chosen to carry out an extension of the limits of classical international law by 'legalizing' objects that intrinsically lie outside

[95] This is why I have expounded on in J. d'Aspremont, 'Softness in International Law: A Rejoinder to Tony D'Amato' (2009) 20 EJIL 911–17. See also J. d'Aspremont, 'La doctrine du droit international face à la tentation d'une juridicisation sans limites' (2008) 112 *Revue générale de droit international public* 849–66. See also K. Raustiala, 'Form and Substance in International Agreements' (2005) 99 AJIL 581, 582 (he contends that 'pledges are smuggled in into the international lawyer's repertoire by dubbing them soft law').

[96] The variety and richness of scholarly opinions is often seen as one positive consequence of the unforeseen development of legal scholarship. See the remarks of B. Stephens on the occasion of the panel on 'Scholars in the Construction and Critique of International Law' held on the occasion of the 2000 ASIL meeting, (2000) 94 ASIL Proceedings 317, 318.

[97] See *contra* D. Kennedy, 'A New World Order: Yesterday, Today and Tomorrow' (1994) 4 Transnat'l L. & Contemp. Probs. 329–75, 370.

[98] On the battle for controlling the production of discourse, see generally M. Foucault, 'The Order of Discourse' in R. Young (ed), *Untying the Text: a Post-Structuralist Reader* (Routledge, London, 1981) 52.

the limits of international law through the use of non-formal law-ascertainment criteria. The use of non-formal law-ascertainment criteria, in this context, has helped scholars find new extra raw material and opened new avenues for legal research.[99]

Creative argumentation before adjudicative bodies

Finally, mention must be made of the abiding and inextricable inclinations of advocates and counsel in international judicial proceedings to take some liberties with the theory of the sources of international law.[100] To them, formal law-ascertainment frustrates creativity.[101] Deformalizing law-ascertainment conversely provides them with some leeway to stretch the limits of international law and unearth rules that support the position of the actors which they represent.[102] The use of non-formal law-ascertainment criteria thus offers more room for creative argumentation. This tendency—which is somewhat inevitable—does not seem to contradict any standard of conduct elaborated by the profession.[103] It usually manifests itself in cases where applicable rules are scarce.[104] It commonly materializes in the invocation of soft legal rules,[105] or the use of a very liberal ascertainment of custom and general principles of law.[106]

Remarks on the agendas of deformalization

The foregoing shows that deformalization of law-ascertainment stems from a host of different agendas which may, at times, seem contradictory. Subject to the occasional self-serving quest for new materials pursued by some scholars to nourish and expand their own areas of study, it is fair to say that deformalization of international law-ascertainment has usually been undertaken out of a sense of justice or collective interest. I do not intend to appraise each of these agendas. Yet, a word must be said

[99] For an illustration of that phenomenon, see e.g. D. Johnston, 'Theory, Consent and the Law of Treaties' (1988–1989) 12 Aust. YBIL 109.

[100] See generally S. Rosenne 'International Court of Justice: Practice Direction on Agents, Counsel and Advocates', in S. Rosenne (ed), *Essays on International Law and Practice* (Nijhoff, Leiden, 2007) 97–104; J.-P. Cot, 'Appearing "for" or "on behalf of" a State: the Role of Private Counsel before International Tribunals' in N. Ando, et al. (eds), *Liber Amicorum Judge Shigeru Oda*, vol 2 (Kluwer, The Hague, 2002) 835–47; J.P.W. Temminck Tuinstra, *Defence Counsel in International Criminal Law* (T.M.C. Asser, The Hague, 2009); U. Draetta, 'The Role of In-House Counsel in International Arbitration' (2009) 75 *Arbitration* 470–80.

[101] Interestingly, the same argument has been made as far as legal scholars are concerned. See J. Brunnée and S.J. Toope, 'International Law and Constructivism, Elements of an International Theory of International Law' (2000–2001) 39 Colum. J. Transnat'l L. 19–74, 65.

[102] I owe this argument to an interesting discussion with Alan Boyle.

[103] See *The Hague Principles on Ethical Standards for Counsel Appearing before International Courts and Tribunals* elaborated by the The Study Group of the International Law Association on the Practice and Procedure of International Courts and Tribunals, 2010, available at <http://www.ucl.ac.uk/laws/cict/docs/Hague_Sept2010.pdf>; see also Jan Paulsson, 'Standards of conduct for counsel in international arbitration' (1992) 3 Am. Rev. Int'l Arb. 214–22.

[104] For a recent example, see e.g. the Memorial of Argentina of 15 January 2007 in the case *Pulp Mills on the River Uruguay (Argentina v. Uruguay)* 132–42, available at <http://www.icj-cij.org/docket/index.php?p1=3&p2=3&code=au&case=135&k=88;>.

[105] Cfr *supra* 5.2.

[106] Cfr *infra* 7.1. and 7.2.1.

about the two most common of them, namely the programmatic attitude geared towards the emergence of new rules of international law[107] and the quest for greater accountability through non-formal law-identification.[108]

I cannot help voicing some strong reservations about the idea that the use of non-formal law-ascertainment criteria contributes to the facilitation of the emergence of new and desirable rules of international law. More specifically, I doubt that experimenting with a new rule of international law through the use of non-formal law-ascertainment criteria really helps such a norm to actually become a rule of international law. In my view, it is not true that international law is a behavioural model to which addressees grow accustomed and finally abide by. International legal rules do not exist simply because States and other addressees become habituated to being bound by them and eventually accept it. On the contrary, the use of non-formal criteria to experiment with the expansion of international law in areas where it would not be identified as such on the basis of formal law-ascertainment yardsticks may even prove counter-productive. Indeed, it may fuel strong opposition by the actual international law-makers and law-addressees. Furthermore, the illusory state of international law that is conveyed through the use of non-formal law-ascertainment may obfuscate the need to lobby for the adoption of new rules. In fact, the use of non-formal law-ascertainment criteria may bring about a feeling that the adoption of legal or non-legal regulations is no longer necessary. It can simultaneously dim the awareness of the possibility of resorting to non-legal instruments—which may prove more effective—to achieve the same political end.[109]

While the need to ensure changes to actual international legal rules is not itself condemned here, it must be pointed out that the plea for some elementary formalism in law-identification—which is more systematically spelled out in chapter 7—should not necessarily be perceived as coming at the expense of a critical evaluation of existing rules and the progressive development or change of international law in areas where States are usually loath to being bound by stricter rules. On the contrary, rather than an impediment, formal law-identification—as was already cogently demonstrated by Bentham[110]—is a necessary condition to sustain the possibility of both critical evaluation of and change to actual international legal rules.

Turning to the separate idea that deformalization of international law-ascertainment can help allay accountability deficits inherent in the exercise of public authority outside the traditional framework of international law, I am of the opinion that this underlying motive of the contemporary deformalization of law-ascertainment is barely more convincing than the idea of programming the progressive development of international law. Indeed, it is to be questioned whether bringing these new forms of the exercise of public authority into the remit of international law clearly helps to

[107] Cfr *supra* 5.3.

[108] Cfr *supra* 5.3.

[109] In the same vein, see W.M. Reisman, 'The Cult of Custom in the Late 20th Century' (1987) 17 Cal. W. Int'l L. J. 133, p. 136.

[110] Cfr *supra* 3.1.2.

foster accountability. Why would accountability be more efficiently achieved if a norm-making process or an exercise of public authority is brought within the remit of international law? In other words, why would international law provide a better framework of accountability, since international law itself already lacks binding and generally available accountability mechanisms? Accountability mechanisms being significantly underdeveloped in international law, one may especially wonder whether bringing this normative activity in the remit of international law really serves its avowed objective. Moreover, it is not certain that the accountability mechanisms that could be found in international law would be the most effective. International actors have consciously and purposely placed such a normative activity outside the traditional framework of international law with a view to eluding the—already underdeveloped—mechanisms of accountability provided by international law. If legal scholars, analysts, or theorists were to succeed in their attempt to bring these forms of the exercise of public authority in the remit of international law, it can be anticipated that international actors would, in turn, again create new normative tools and use other norm-making channels which allow them to evade accountability.

In sum, it remains to be seen whether any of these—albeit lofty—objectives can be fully achieved by deformalizing international law-ascertainment. It is not only that the use of non-formal law-identification criteria does little to actually change the *lex lata* or foster accountability mechanisms. It is also that it comes with a very high cost in terms of normativity (and authority) of international law, meaningfulness of the international legal scholarship, possibility of a critique of international legal rules, and the rule of law.[111]

[111] This has been discussed above. Cfr *supra* 2.2.

6

Lessons from the Discontent with Formalism

The deformalization of law-ascertainment in international law described in chapter 5, which is currently witnessed in the context of the current pluralization of international norm-making processes, bespeaks a great unease towards formal law-ascertainment. It is argued here that such a deformalization cannot be demoted to a simple cyclical swing of a pendulum caused by a time of anxiety. Indeed, as was described in chapter 5, deformalization of law-ascertainment has reached such unprecedented heights in the theory of the sources of international law that, although the foundations of the source thesis in international law have been the object of little attention or critical appraisal in international legal scholarship—in contrast to general legal theory—shedding some light on the theoretical foundations of formal law-ascertainment and transposing it to the theory of the sources of international law would do little to revive the consensus about the need for some elementary formalism in international law.

The futility of a mere restatement of the foundations of the source thesis for the sake of its application in international law is also underpinned by the growing acknowledgement of the limits of formalism when applied to international law. The limits of formal law-ascertainment have been particularly revealed by the successive waves of contestations against formal law-ascertainment described in chapter 4. It cannot be contested that these various generations of discontent, while occasionally echoing some eclectic as well as prudent support for formalism,[1] have faulted some aspects of formalism—even in the theory of law-ascertainment—and laid bare some contradictions of the formalistic posture embraced by default—at least until recently—by many international legal scholars.[2]

For these reasons, the current abandonment of formal ascertainment of international legal rules calls not only for a better theoretical understanding of the foundations of formalism, but also for its *revitalization*. Such a rejuvenation necessitates that attention be paid to some of the critiques outlined in chapter 4. I am of the opinion that formalism in international law-ascertainment can only outlive the critiques as well as the challenges inherent in the current pluralization of international norm-making processes and remain a useful theoretical framework in which to construct international law if it learns from the various critiques mentioned in chapter 4. I will

[1] Cfr *supra* 2.1.2 and 4.2.4. [2] Cfr *supra* 4.2.4.

also show in the following chapter that revisiting formalism simultaneously requires that some of the illusions of formalism permeating the current theory of the sources in international law be dispelled.[3]

This chapter elaborates on the lessons learnt from some of the objections formulated against the classical theory of the sources of international law as these objections help critically appraise the limits of the source and social theses.[4] In particular, it will be explained that it is only once we assume formalism as a political project, and accept the relative indeterminacy of formal law-ascertainment criteria as well as the normative character of the empirical methodology inherent in the social thesis, that we can engage in its rejuvenation in the context of international law.

The first lesson that ought to be learned from postmodern critique—and its predecessors—pertains to the recognition of the indeterminacy of language—understood as more than a mere repetition of the idea that meaning always is constructed—that inevitably infuses formal law-ascertainment (6.1). The indeterminacy of language leads to the second major lesson of the abovementioned critiques, i.e. the political character of formalism at the level of law-ascertainment (6.2). Eventually, I endorse the idea which infuses the postmodern critique that empirical methodology inherent in the social thesis is necessarily normative, for any social practice is a social construct which rests on a practice that cannot be directly observed without predefined conceptual tools (6.3). It will simultaneously be shown that these compelling findings do not constitute obstacles to the rejuvenation of formal law-ascertainment in the theory of the sources of international law put forward in chapters 7 and 8.

6.1 Assuming Indeterminacy of Law-Ascertainment Criteria

Legal realism had long ago proved that law is beset by indeterminacy and that its language is insufficient to provide a determinate answer to problems which it is purported to apply to, thereby endowing law-applying authorities with a leeway that allows them to make decisions according to their understanding of justice. Because legal realists assert that law is fundamentally indeterminate, they called for an ever-decreasing emphasis on words and a correlative ever-increasing emphasis on observable behaviour.[5] The critical legal project has extended such findings to legal

[3] Cfr *infra* 7.1.

[4] In doing so, I depart here from comments I had made earlier about the international legal scholarship affiliated with deconstructivism and critical legal studies where I misread (or totally ignored) some aspects of the critical legal project with which I now find myself in agreement with. See J. d'Aspremont, 'Uniting Pragmatism and Theory in International Legal Scholarship: Koskenniemi's From Apology to Utopia Revisited' (2006) 19 *Revue québécoise de droit international* 353–60.

[5] K. Lewellyn, 'A Realistic Jurisprudence—the Next Step' in D. Patterson (ed), *Philosophy of Law and Legal Theory: An Anthology* (Blackwell, Oxford, 2003) 22, 38; See the criticism of Realists in H.L.A. Hart, 'American Jurisprudence Through English Eyes: The Nightmare and the Noble Dream' (1976–1977) 11 Ga. L. Rev. 969. See *supra* 4.1.

argumentation in general.[6] They have not bemoaned indeterminacy, which is not seen as a bad thing. They have simply claimed that indeterminacy has to be assumed by resisting the temptation to artificially suppress it. Turning to formalism—which they primarily understood as formal legal argumentation, scholars affiliated with critical legal studies and deconstructivism have concluded that, because of this inescapable indeterminacy, the political project behind formalism has failed. Formal law argumentation can produce diametrically opposed solutions to any legal problem and, as a result, formal analysis has been unable to displace the political discourse,[7] even when there is no semantic ambivalence.[8] Even though, on the whole, the debate in the critical literature about the indeterminacy of international law is somewhat confusing because it oscillates between several types of formalism,[9] indeterminacy has also been seen as one of the causes of the failure of formalism at the level of law-ascertainment.

The account of formalism made here does not call into question the finding of indeterminacy as regards legal argumentation in general. With respect to formal law-ascertainment, it similarly concurs with the idea that any formal indicator is inevitably riddled with indeterminacy. Indeed, it cannot be contested that the indeterminacy of language has inevitably contaminated the language of law, including formal law-ascertainment criteria.[10] Most commonly, indeterminacy simply stems from the openness of the ordinary language through which the prescriptions of law are conveyed. Likewise, law being the product of human thought,[11] it is—like any other language—inescapably beset by ambiguities. These ambiguities may have been desired because they were the only manner in which the consensus reached by lawmakers could be translated into anything written. They can also be inherent in the connotation or the denotation of words.[12] Whatever its source, indeterminacy creates space for legal argumentation and diverging opinions as to the exact meaning of a given rule, including secondary rules.

It is also recognized here that the use of formal indicators does little to contain the contagion of indeterminacy in the transposition from ordinary language to the language of law. Because it subjects law-identification to formal categories described in ordinary language, the source thesis is itself saddled with such indeterminacy. Being pervaded by indeterminacy while making law-identification dependant on a formal language, formalism at the level of law-ascertainment could even be seen as a Trojan horse

[6] For Koskenniemi, all the doctrines of sources are indeterminate because they tell us that the law can be found in State behaviour and that such a behaviour reflects either consent or justice, while presupposing that neither of them can be captured in a manner that preserves the objectivity necessary to distinguish law from politics. See M. Koskenniemi, *From Apology to Utopia* (CUP, Cambridge, 2005) 387.

[7] M. Koskenniemi, ibid, 189–97.

[8] M. Koskenniemi, ibid, 590.

[9] On some of the main understandings of formalism, cfr *supra* 2.1.

[10] In the same vein, J. Kammerhofer, *Uncertainty in International Law: A Kelsenian Perspective* (Routledge, London, 2010) 117–18.

[11] In the same vein, R. Ago, 'Positive Law and International Law' (1957) 51 AJIL 691–733, 727–8.

[12] On the distinction between ambiguity (words' connotation) and vagueness (words' denotation), see the work of Michael Thaler as reported by J. Kammerhofer, *Uncertainty in International Law: A Kelsenian Perspective* (Routledge, London, 2010) 118.

that contributes to the more general infiltration of indeterminacy in international law as a whole. Interestingly, and contrary to what is often believed,[13] supporters of formal law-ascertainment have never denied that, not only is formal law-ascertainment itself riddled by indeterminacy,[14] it also contributes to the general indeterminacy of law.[15] In making such a claim, they recognize the correlative empowerment of law-applying authorities to make decisions by resorting to non-legal criteria, even when it comes to distinguishing law from non-law.[16]

The claim of the indeterminacy of law, including that of law-ascertainment criteria, has already been sufficiently discussed in the literature.[17] As far as the principle is concerned, it is rarely the object of disagreement—the question no longer being whether law is determinate but whether law-applying authorities are endowed with sufficient legitimacy to wield the powers left to them as a result of the indeterminacy of law.

Recognizing the indeterminacy of formal law-ascertainment mechanisms does not, however, preclude formalism at the level of law-ascertainment.[18] While coming to terms with this indeterminacy and the absence of a true meaning of the units of the language of law, it is defended here that, despite being beset by indeterminacy, formal law-ascertainment can still provide sufficient indications as to what is law and what is not law.[19] It is true that this relative determinacy that formalism can provide

[13] Despite this concession, it is true that supporters of formalism have not always come to terms with the indeterminacy of law, for, in legal scholarship, formalism has often been associated with the possibility of immanent rationality and objectivity in law. See E.J. Weinrib, 'Legal Formalism, On the Immanent Rationality of Law' (1997–1998) 97 Yale L. J. 949. It is precisely because formalism has been sometimes associated with such immanent rationality and objectivity that it has become a prime target of legal realists—who dubbed it as naïve and starry-eyed legalism (cfr *supra* 4.1.1). The legal realist critique has probably had an impact on the later recognition by the aforementioned positivists of the indeterminacy of law and formal law-ascertainment.

[14] O. Corten, *Le discours du droit international: Pour un positivisme critique* (Pedone, Paris, 2009). See also A.L. Paulus, 'International Law After Postmodernism' (2001) 14 LJIL 754.

[15] J. Raz, *Authority of Law* (Clarendon, Oxford, 1983) 73. See H.L.A. Hart, *The Concept of Law* (2nd edn, OUP, Oxford, 1997) 128.

[16] H. Kelsen, 'La Théorie Pure dans la Pensée Juridique' in C. Leben and R. Kolb (eds), *Controverses sur la Théorie Pure du Droit* (LGDJ, Paris, 2005) 173; H.L.A. Hart, ibid, 136. See also H.L.A. Hart and A.M. Honore, *Causation in the Law* (Clarendon Press, Oxford, 1959) 5; N. Bobbio, *Essais de théorie du droit* (Bruylant/LGDJ, Paris, 1998) 10 and 38. Bobbio, for instance, never denied that, as a result of the lingering indeterminacy in formalism, interpretation could not be neutral and can include political decision-making. Although he denied the possibility of a judge resorting to non-legal principles as such without making them legal principles, Raz also defended that judicial discretion—which is nurtured by the indeterminacy of law—is a necessary complement to formalism, for indeterminacy originates in formal law-ascertainment: J. Raz, *Authority of Law* (Clarendon, Oxford, 1983) especially 41–52. See, more generally, L. Murphy, 'The Political Question of the Concept of Law' in J. Coleman (ed), *Hart's Postscript: Essays on the Postscript to 'The Concept of Law'* (OUP, Oxford, 2001) 371, 393.

[17] See the interesting take on indeterminacy offered by J. Waldron, *Law and Disagreement* (OUP, Oxford, 1999).

[18] This claim was already made by Hart: H.L.A. Hart, *The Concept of Law* (2nd edn, OUP, Oxford, 1997) 138.

[19] For an illustration of similar debates in general legal theory, see the criticism by Kress: K. Kress, 'Legal Indeterminacy', reproduced in D. Patterson (ed), *An Anthology of Philosophy of Law and Legal Theory* (Blackwell, Oxford, 2003) 253, 253.

when it comes to distinguishing law from non-law does not deprive law-applying authorities of the large margin of discretion they enjoy when determining what constitutes an international legal rule. Likewise, it is not contested that formalism does not prevent the existence of borderline cases where law-applying authorities necessarily enjoy an almost unfettered discretion. Yet, indeterminacy does not *per se* preclude the existence of some elementary indicators as to what is law and what is non-law.[20]

The possibility of maintaining formal law-ascertainment criteria despite their indeterminacy lies, first, in the fact that their indeterminacy is more restricted than what is often asserted. As will be shown below, the social practice of law-applying authorities, in most instances, is instrumental in providing an elementary meaning to formal law-identification mechanisms and reining in radical indeterminacy. This is the role ascribed to the so-called social thesis which is analyzed below.[21] It is true that grounding law-ascertainment in the practice of law-applying authorities probably proves more difficult in international law. Indeed, the international legal order is not endowed with wide-ranging institutional and vertical structures which would systematically put an authority in a position to make a pronouncement on where the limit between law and non-law lies. The social practice found at the international level is probably more limited than that which can be found in domestic legal orders. Moreover, as will be explained below, the few pronouncements about the formal limits of international law by international law-applying authorities predominantly fall short of defusing controversies and providing sufficient guidance to enable a consistent practice of law-ascertainment to emerge.[22] This being said, it must be acknowledged that international law is nowadays applied by an increasing number of authorities, including regional and domestic ones. Although these law-applying authorities can be organs of a legal order separate from the international legal order whose relationship with the latter must often be analyzed in rather dualistic terms, they nowadays contribute significantly to the practice of law-ascertainment and can offset the scant, erratic, and patchy social practice presented by universal international law-applying authorities.[23] A final factor helps make up for the limited social practice of law-ascertainment at the international level. Indeed, as will be explained below, commentators undoubtedly contribute to the clarification and unearthing of the rare social practice of law-ascertainment. While their contribution is certainly not neutral, they help locate and lay bare the little social practice that exists at the international level.[24] It will be demonstrated that the international legal order provides at least the possibility of a significant social practice which helps stem the indeterminacy of law-ascertainment mechanisms that is perpetuated by formalism itself.[25]

Tempering the indeterminacy of law-ascertainment indicators by virtue of the social thesis surely reintroduces some limited normativity, for practice is necessarily

[20] In the same vein, see J. Klabbers, *The Concept of Treaty in International Law* (Kluwer, The Hague, 1996) 12. See also H.L.A. Hart, *The Concept of Law* (2nd edn, OUP, Oxford, 1997) 148.

[21] Cfr *infra* 8. [22] Cfr *infra* 7.2.2. [23] Cfr *infra* 8.3.

[24] Cfr *infra* 8.3. [25] Cfr *infra* 8.3 and 8.4.

a social construct which requires abstract predefined categories.[26] Likewise, such a move bestows a sociological role on legal scholars. This social practice—and the theoretical issues which come with it—will be subsequently analyzed.[27] All that matters here is to point out that, even though the political character of formalism and the indeterminacy of formal law-ascertainment in international law cannot be denied, formalism, as a political project, has the potential to rest on a sufficient social practice that allows it to contain indeterminacy, which allows it to remain a central yardstick for the ascertainment of international legal rules.

6.2 The Politics of Formal Law-Ascertainment

To understand the political character of formalism, it is of preliminary importance to point out the extent to which the political dimension of formalism is interwoven with the finding of the indeterminacy of law. Even though the extent of the indeterminacy of law can itself be subject to debate, it cannot be denied that law, including its formal law-ascertainment mechanisms, is inextricably indeterminate. Such indeterminacy inevitably condemns (international) lawyers to making choices. Indeed, if law is indeterminate because its commands are conveyed through a language which is itself indeterminate, (international) lawyers invariably face the question of what they ought to do with such indeterminacy.[28] This choice can be presented as follows. On the one hand, (international) lawyers can choose to live in total indeterminacy—that is the option sometimes dubbed relativistic and nihilistic[29]—and reject any rationality, for it would necessarily be illusive. On the other hand, they can come to terms with the indeterminacy and strive to disambiguate legal rules. It is well-known that this alternative has constituted the essence of the debate between some strands of the critical approaches—which contend that the first type of nihilism is to be preferred to the nihilism that flows from the illusion of objectivity in the legal discourse[30]—and more positivist, Grotian and/or Kantian understandings of international law which consider that the function they assign to international law can only be achieved if it is disambiguated.[31] Even within the critical legal projects, there have been attempts to preserve the possibility of legal

[26] J. Beckett, 'Countering Uncertainty and Ending Up/Down Arguments: Prolegomena to a Response to NAIL' (2005) 16 EJIL 213.

[27] Cfr *infra* 8.

[28] S. Marks, *The Riddle of All Constitutions* (OUP, Oxford, 2003) 144.

[29] It is not entirely certain that accepting utter indeterminacy really amounts to nihilism. It should be recalled that, for Nietzsche, the submission to a ready-made set of values or ideologies constitutes, in itself, nihilism. See generally, G.B. Smith, *Nietzsche, Heidegger, and the Transition to Postmodernity* (University of Chicago Press, Chicago, 1996); D. Detmer, 'Heidegger and Nietzsche on "Thinking in Values"' (1989) 23 *Journal of Value Inquiry* 275–83. See my comments on this aspect in J. d'Aspremont, 'The Foundations of the International Legal Order' (2007) 18 FYBIL 219–55.

[30] Koskenniemi tried to substantiate its defence in the epilogue that he added in the reissue of *From Apology to Utopia* (CUP, Cambridge, 2005) 562–617.

[31] I have myself earlier rejected the acceptance of indeterminacy proposed by the critical approaches before subsequently changing my opinion. See J. d'Aspremont, 'Uniting Pragmatism and Theory in

argumentation.[32] Notwithstanding the specific answer given by each stream of the legal scholarship, there is little doubt that this existentialist question about the disambiguation of law will abidingly continue to fuel scholarly debates[33] without being possibly clinched by any argument of authority.[34] Moreover, making the choice for disambiguation of law will not, in itself, depoliticize the ensuing posture that can be adopted. If international legal scholars choose to work towards the disambiguation of law, they will subsequently face a new political choice. Indeed, each mode of disambiguation will itself boil down to a political decision, for there are political stakes associated with each mode of disambiguation,[35] especially when no authority can decisively clinch the issue for practical purposes.[36] In that sense, formalism in the theory of law-ascertainment only constitutes one of the several political options available to (international) lawyers—and particularly legal scholars—who decide to assume the indeterminacy of law.

There may be a string of different reasons motivating the political choice of formalism. Unearthing the political motives behind the choice of formalism—and the political agenda which corresponds with them—is no doubt of great interest to international legal scholars, even though this is, arguably, more a matter pertaining to the sociology of international law than to the theory of the sources of international law. Whilst it is not my ambition here to elaborate on the political motives of an espousal of formalism in its various manifestations, it is interesting to recall that that formalism in its most common understanding, i.e. in legal argumentation,[37] has usually been celebrated for its ability to provide predictability in judicial decisions,[38] accessibility of legal prescripts to their addressees and legal certainty,[39] order and

International Legal Scholarship: Koskenniemi's From Apology to Utopia revisited' (2006) 19 *Revue québecoise de droit international* 353–60, also available on <http://www.globallawbooks.org>.

[32] See the 'culture of formalism' put forward by Martti Koskenniemi and discussed *supra* 2.1.2.

[33] According to D'Amato, indeterminacy constitutes the 'key issue in legal scholarship today': A. D'Amato, 'Pragmatic Indeterminacy' (1990) 85 Northwest. U. L. Rev. 148, 148. See also Kammerhofer, *Uncertainty in International Law: A Kelsenian Perspective* (Routledge, London 2010) 260–1.

[34] T. Campbell, *The Legal Theory of Ethical Positivism* (Aldershot, Darmouth, 1996); O. Korhonen, 'New International Law: Silence, Defense or Deliverance' (1996) 7 EJIL 1–28, 21. On the existence of that choice, see also O. Corten, *Méthodologie du droit international public* (Editions de l'Université de Bruxelles, Brussels, 2009) 44 and 56.

[35] L. Murphy, 'Better to see Law this Way' (2008) 83 NYU LR 1104; L. Murphy, 'The Political Question of the Comcept of Law' in J. Coleman (ed), *Hart's Postscript: Essays on the Postscript to 'The Concept of Law'* (OUP, Oxford, 2001) 371. See also L. Murphy, 'Concepts of Law' (2005) 30 Australian J. Leg. Phil. 1. See U. Scarpelli, *Qu'est-ce que le positivisme juridique* (Bruylant/LGDJ, Paris,1996) 57; F. Schauer, 'Postivism as Pariah', in R.P. George (ed), *The Autonomy of Law: Essays of Legal Positivism* (OUP, Oxford, 1996) 31, 34; J. Waldron, 'Normative (or Ethical) Positivism' in J. Coleman (ed), *Hart's Postscript: Essays on the Postscript to the Concept of Law* (OUP, Oxford, 2001) 410, 411–33; J. Beckett, 'Behind Relative Normativity: Rules and Process as Prerequisites of Law' (2001) 12 EJIL 627, 648; J. Beckett, 'Countering Uncertainty and Ending Up/Down Arguments: Prolegomena to a Response to NAIL' (2005) 16 EJIL 213, 214–19.

[36] B. Kingsbury, 'The Concept of Law in Global Administrative Law' (2009) 20(1) EJIL 23–57, 26.

[37] On this understanding of formalism, cfr *supra* 2.1.2.

[38] N. Bobbio, *Essais de théorie du droit* (Bruylant/LGDJ, Paris, 1998) 29.

[39] J. Raz, 'The Rule of Law and its Virtue', in J. Raz (ed), *The Authority of Law—Essays on Law and Morality* (Clarendon, Oxford, 1979) 213–14.

peace,[40] self-government and individual freedom,[41] and separation between law and morals, which correlatively allows a moral evaluation of law[42] and excludes any justification of non-conformity with law on non-formal grounds.[43] Widely discussed in general legal theory, these benefits of formalism in general have resonated in international legal scholarship.[44] On the occasion of the discussion of the benefits of this type of formalism, attention has also been paid to its costs.[45] Leaving aside the fundamental contradictions unearthed by critical thinking,[46] it has been said, for instance, that formal legal argumentation reduces the flexibility and the range of solutions available in each situation and prevents principles from being adapted to the context of their application. This downside of formalism in legal argumentation has often been stigmatized in American legal scholarship which, as is explained above, has generally been more inclined to reject formalism in legal argumentation.[47] Likewise, formal legal argumentation has been seen as preventing rules from evolving and accommodating unforeseen situations, notably the challenges posed by the growing pluralization of international norm-making and the growing number of informal exercises of public authority at the international level. It could also be said that formalism runs against a healthy pluralism.[48] More anecdotally, it has been contended that formal legal argumentation tarnishes the appeal of international law in the sense that international law without politics would be 'boring'.[49]

[40] According to L. Oppenheim as interpreted by Kingsbury: B. Kingsbury, 'Legal Positivism as Normative Politics: International Society, Balance of Power and Lassa Oppenheim's Positive International Law' (2002) 13(2) EJIL 401–37.

[41] See the remarks of B. Kingsbury, 'The Concept of Law in Global Administrative Law' (2009) 20(1) EJIL 23–57, 28.

[42] See our remarks on J. Bentham *supra* 3.1.2; J. Raz, *The Authority of Law* (Clarendon, Oxford, 1983) 51; W. Twining *General Jurisprudence: Understanding Law from a Global Perspective*, (CUP, Cambridge, 2009) 27. Scarpelli, *Qu'est-ce que le positivisme juridique* (Bruylant/LGDJ, Paris, 1996) 87.

[43] J. Raz, ibid, 41 and 52; N. MacCormick, 'The Concept of Law and the "Concept of Law"' in R.P. George (ed), *The Autonomy of Law: Essays of Legal Positivism* (OUP, Oxford, 1996) 163, 169; G. Postema, 'Law's Autonomy and Public Practical Reason', in R.P. George (ed), ibid, 79, 93; N. Bobbio, *Essais de théorie du droit* (Bruylant/LGDJ, Paris, 1998) 38.

[44] For a few examples of scholars who engaged in reflections about the motives of formalism, see P.-M. Dupuy, 'L'unité de l'ordre juridique international: cours général de droit international public', (2002) 297 RCADI 9–489, 26, 30, 200–2; J. Hathaway, *Rights of Refugees Under International Law* (CUP, Cambridge, 2005) 18–24; O. Corten, *Le discours du droit international: pour un positivisme critique* (CERDIN, Paris, 2009) 66.

[45] On the political agenda of those schools of thought which have backed away from formalism, see D. Kennedy, 'When Renewal Repeats: Thinking Against the Box' (1999–2000) 32 NYU JILP 335, 445–7.

[46] Cfr *supra* 4.1.4. and 4.2.4.

[47] In that sense, see R.H. Pildes, 'Conflicts Between American and European Views: The Dark Side of Legalism' (2003–2004) 44 Va. J. Int'l L. 145, 154; see also E. Jouannet, 'French and American Perspectives on International Law: Legal Cultures and International Law' (2006) 58 Maine L. Rev. 292.

[48] See e.g. N. Krisch, *Beyond Constitutionalism—The Pluralist Structure of Postnational Law* (OUP, Oxford, 2010), 3–14 and 69–105. On the specific question whether Hart's theory can sustain legal pluralism, see J. Waldron, 'Legal Pluralism and the Contrast Between Hart's Jurisprudence and Fuller's', in P. Cane (ed), *The Hart-Fuller Debate in the Twenty-First Century* (Hart, Oxford, 2010) 135–55 and M. Davies, 'The Politics of Defining Law', in P. Cane (ed), ibid, 157–67.

[49] L. Mälksoo, 'The Science of International Law and The Concept of Politics' (2005) 76 BYBIL 383, 500.

This is not the place to discuss whether the perceived benefits of formal legal argumentation are justified and whether they outweigh its alleged costs. They have been widely discussed in general legal theory and some of them were mentioned in chapters 3 and 4. Moreover, it is far from certain that the benefits and drawbacks of formalism in legal argumentation are strictly relevant as far as formalism at the level of law-ascertainment is concerned. The reasons why formal law-ascertainment should be promoted have already been depicted in chapter 2.[50] I have essentially argued that some elementary formalism is necessary at the level of law-ascertainment to preserve the normative character of international law, without which international law would fail to realize most of the possible goals ascribed to it and would be stripped of authority, legitimacy, and efficacy. I have also contended that formalism helps preserve the significance of scholarly debates about international law as well as the possibility of a critique of international legal rules. The contribution of formal law-ascertainment to the international rule of law has also been mentioned. It would be of no avail to revert to this discussion now. I simply deem it necessary to indicate that, as the foregoing has hopefully demonstrated, the political motives behind the plea for formal law-ascertainment that is made here is alien to those of some of the classical positivist accounts of international law. For instance, Oppenheim's formalism has not been entirely alien to the normative goals of peace, order, justice, and the control of violence.[51] It could also be argued that even Kelsen, in his attempt to purify legal theory, was striving—although in a more subtle manner—to counter Hegelian individualism and its transposition by Jellinek in international legal scholarship, with a view to promoting the idea of an international rule of law and pacifying relations among States.[52] In that sense, Kelsen's Pure Theory of Law not only rests on a neo-Kantian premise but is also directed at a neo-Kantian vision of the international society.[53] The choice of formalism at the level of law-ascertainment that is advocated here is not a choice for such a destiny of the international society. According to the argument made here, formal law-ascertainment is, more modestly, nothing more than a political choice for the preservation of the normative character of international law, the meaningfulness of the international legal scholarship, the possibility of a critique of law, and the rule of law.

Whatever the ultimate motive may be for espousing formal law-ascertainment in the theory of the sources of international law, one of the lessons learnt from the

[50] Cfr *supra* 2.2.

[51] This has been brilliantly shown by B. Kingsbury: B. Kingsbury, 'Legal Positivism as Normative Politics, International Society, Balance of Power and Lassa Oppenheim's Positive International Law' (2002) 13 EJIL 401–36.

[52] See for instance H. Kelsen, 'Les rapports de système entre le droit interne et le droit international public' (1926-IV) 14 RCADI 227–331, 324.

[53] The same argument is made by many authors. See, for instance, F. Rigaux, 'Hans Kelsen on International Law' (1998) 9 EJIL 325–43, 326; see N. Bobbio and D. Zolo, 'Hans Kelsen, the Theory of Law and the International Legal System: A Talk' (1998) 9 EJIL 355–67; D. Zolo, 'Hans Kelsen: International Peace through International Law' (1998) 9 EJIL 306–24. This seems corroborated by his conclusion in the Oliver Wendell Holmes Lectures, cited by F. Rigaux, 'Hans Kelsen on International Law' (1998) 9 EJIL 325–43, 337. See also C. Leben (ed), *Hans Kelsen—Ecrits français de droit international* (PUF, Paris, 2001) 19.

various waves of critiques described in chapter 4 is that, as formalism arises from a political choice, this choice must be made with awareness of the costs and benefits of formalism. If we accept the absence of any authority-based necessity of formalism and condemn the aforementioned habit of hiding behind the formalistic attitude that has prevailed by default until recently in mainstream international legal scholarship, formalism in the theory of law-ascertainment must be *freely and consciously chosen*. In other words, once it is acknowledged that formalism in the theory of law-ascertainment boils down to a political choice which is not dictated by any argument of authority or habit, all that matters is to ensure that the choice of formalism is free and duly informed. The rejuvenation of formal law-ascertainment in the theory of the sources of international law attempted in chapters 7 and 8 thus rests on a choice whose political character is entirely assumed.

6.3 Normativity and Empirical Methodology

Drawing on the—more or less uncontested—idea that law is a certain way of making sense of reality, not a bare fact,[54] some of the critiques mentioned in chapter 4 have contended that law cannot be the direct object of observation. In that sense, these critiques have faulted the idea that law can be reduced to a practice which can be subject to non-normative observation. Like the cognition of any practice, the observation of the practice of law requires that law be preliminarily defined. The argument made here concurs with this idea. There is little doubt that formal law-ascertainment is a way of cognizing the practice of law. The model of formal law-ascertainment grounded in the social thesis that is defended here necessarily presupposes a construction through which practice of law-applying authorities can be captured. The rejuvenation of the theory of formal law-ascertainment initiated in this book, although not being a general theory of law,[55] inevitably has a normative dimension. The argument made here accordingly backs away from any claim that the empirical methodology inherent in the social thesis is non-normative.

Despite having an inevitable normative dimension, the social thesis nonetheless cannot be conflated with naïve objectivism. Indeed, it will be shown that, being entirely dependent on contingent and fickle communitarian semantics and making the quest for validity of international law as a whole utterly moot—at least for the sake of law-ascertainment,[56] the model of formal law-ascertainment presented here

[54] See the famous and oft-quoted assertion by P. Allott, *Eunomia* (OUP, Oxford, 2001) xxvii: 'We make the human world, including human institutions through the power of the human mind. What we have made by thinking we can make new by new thinking'. On this point, see the remarks of J. Beckett, 'Countering Uncertainty and Ending Up/Down Arguments: Prolegomena to a Response to NAIL' (2005) 16 EJIL 213, especially 214–16.

[55] See *supra* 1 and 2.1.1.

[56] Cfr *infra* 8.2 and 8.4.

does not presuppose any objectivism or naturalism[57] and, hence, does not constantly oscillate between the two contradictory positions of apology and utopia.[58]

As the foregoing has attempted to demonstrate, the abovementioned lessons learnt from the discontent towards formalism outlined in chapter 4 do not necessarily entail forsaking the main tenets of formal law-identification which have been described in chapter 3 but rather help revitalize it. The formal law-ascertainment model that is presented in the next two chapters still rests on an identification of international legal rules through formal indicators (the source thesis), which are themselves rooted in the social practice of law-applying authorities (the social thesis). It will be shown that the source and social theses, even if they cannot do away with indeterminacy and inevitably have a normative dimension, still constitute the twin linchpins of any model of formal law-identification in the theory of the sources of international law, even in a world of pluralized norm-making processes.

[57] It will be recalled that the scholars who espouse a Kelsenian understanding of law however argue that the social thesis presupposes the same type of absolute and external standard as natural law does. See e.g. J. Kammerhofer, *Uncertainty in International Law. A Kelsenian Perspective* (Routledge, London, 2010) 226. For a discussion of that point see *infra* 8.2 and 8.4.

[58] This contradiction is described in M. Koskenniemi, *From Apology to Utopia* (CUP, Cambridge, 2005) 303.

7

The Configuration of Formal Ascertainment of International Law: The Source Thesis

This chapter examines the current law-ascertainment yardsticks in the mainstream theory of the sources of international law with a view to flagging up and addressing some of their flaws. It simultaneously endeavours to refresh law-ascertainment criteria in contemporary international law. Such a revitalization is attempted on the basis of the theoretical model mentioned above, according to which rules are ascertained through their pedigree (the source thesis). This chapter first expounds on how the source thesis has materialized in the theory of the sources of international law, showing that, to a large extent, the formal character of law-ascertainment has been fabricated. It then tries to shed some light on possible avenues for a rejuvenation of the source thesis in the theory of sources of international law. In particular, drawing on some practical examples, a plea is made for a move away from the law-ascertaining role of intent.

As has been explained in the previous chapters,[1] the so-called source thesis refers to the idea that law is identified by its pedigree, itself defined in formal terms, and that, as a result, identifying the law boils down to a formal pedigree test.[2] Because the pedigree is defined in formal terms, the source thesis entails formal law-ascertainment. The categorization of the pedigree requires formalization which itself necessitates the use of ordinary language. This is why, as was indicated earlier,[3] formalism at the level of law-ascertainment, and in particular the identification of rules through their pedigree (the source thesis) cannot completely elude indeterminacy. Yet, as will be demonstrated here, it is only possible for a social practice of law-ascertainment by law-applying authorities to provide a relative determinacy to formal categories on which any formal model of law-identification is based if standards of pedigree of international rules are fashioned in a manner that lends limited room to indeterminacy. It is argued here that the source thesis in the mainstream theory of the sources of international law—as it is embodied in the model provided by article 38 of the Statute of the International Court of Justice (ICJ Statute) and the accompanying

[1] See in particular *supra* 2.1.1.

[2] On the source thesis, see generally. J. Raz, 'Legal Positivism and the Sources of Law', in J. Raz, *The Authority of Law: Essays on Law and Morality* (Clarendon, Oxford, 1983) 37–52.

[3] Cfr *supra* 6.1.

source doctrines inspired by analogies with domestic rules[4]—fails to offer a satisfactory blueprint for law-ascertainment in international law.

Even though the following paragraphs will present a model of formal law-ascertainment that, to a significant extent, departs from the source doctrines which accompany article 38, it must first be acknowledged that providing a model for law-ascertainment has never been the function of article 38. Indeed, article 38 has never been more than a provision that modestly aims to define the law applicable by the International Court of Justice (ICJ).[5] Moreover, article 38 has never purported to provide an exhaustive list of the sources of international law. And that list was not considered very helpful anyway, even by the authors of the Statute.[6] In that sense, the frenzy that this provision has always stirred up in international legal scholarship is somewhat ill-grounded. Yet, because it offers a handy toolbox for international lawyers in need of a list of sources of international law endowed with some elementary authority, and because of the sophisticated source doctrines that have accompanied it, this provision—although it has not been the only conventional provision to list the sources of international law[7]—has been the lens through which law-identification in international law has been—almost exclusively—construed, and on the basis of which several generations of international lawyers have been trained.

Given that the list of sources contained in article 38 of the ICJ Statute has been misguidedly elevated into the overarching paradigm of all source doctrines in international law, it should not come as a surprise that the formal law-ascertainment model that it is said to offer has been unanimously deemed unsatisfactory.[8] Reviewing all the weaknesses of which that provision has been accused is not indispensable

[4] M. Koskenniemi, 'The Legacy of the Nineteenth Century', D. Armstrong (ed), *Handbook of International Law* (Routledge, London, 2009) 141, 151. See also P.-M. Dupuy, for whom the source thesis is borrowed from domestic legal theories: P.-M. Dupuy, 'Théorie des sources et coutume en droit international contemporain' in *Le Droit international dans un monde en mutation: liber amicorum en hommage au Professeur Eduardo Jimenez de Arechaga* (Fundación de Cultura Universitaria, Montevideo, 1994) 51, 58.

[5] In the same sense, Condorelli, 'Custom', in M. Bedjaoui (ed), *International Law: Achievements and Prospects* (Martinus Nijhoff, The Hague, 1991) 179–211, 184; G. Fitzmaurice, 'Some Problems Regarding the Formal Sources of International Law', in *Symbolae Verzijl* (Martinus Nijhoff, The Hague, 1958) 173.

[6] See the authors and the documents cited by O. Spiermann, *International legal argument in the Permanent Court of International Justice, The Rise of the International Judiciary* (CUP, Cambridge, 2005) 207.

[7] See art. 7 of the XII Hague Convention Relative to the Creation of an International Prize Court of 28 October 1907 (never ratified): 'If a question of law to be decided is covered by a treaty in force between the belligerent captor and a Power which is itself or whose subject or citizen is a party to the proceedings, the Court is governed by the provisions in the said treaty. In the absence of such provisions, the Court shall apply the rules of international law. If no generally recognized rule exists, the Court shall give judgment in accordance with the general principles of justice and equity'.

[8] Using art. 38 as it stands has been deemed 'absurd'. See R. Jennings, 'The Identification of International Law' in in B. Cheng (ed), *International Law: Teaching and Practice* (Stevens, London, 1982) 3, 9. See also the criticisms by P. Haggenmacher, 'La doctrine des deux elements du droit coutumier dans la pratique de la Cour internationale' (1986) 90 *Revue générale de droit international public* 5–125, 25–6.

for the sake of the argument made here. Each textbook of international law begins its study of the sources of international law by listing the drawbacks of that provision, the usual targets being its non-exhaustive character[9] or its obsolete—and almost politically incorrect—distinction between civilized States and others.[10] It is argued here that law-ascertainment in international law must be conceived independently from article 38, which was not only conceived to serve another purpose, but also leaves too much room for non-formal law-ascertainment.

Leaving aside article 38 of the ICJ Statute, the following paragraphs address the structural flaws of the current formal law-ascertainment blueprint in international law with a view to offering a refreshed model of law-ascertainment in the theory of the sources of international law. This revitalization of formalism starts by shedding some of the mirages of formalism that shroud the traditional theory of the sources and which have allowed legal scholarship to live in an illusion of relative certainty regarding the identification of international legal rules (7.1). It will then be argued that this formal law-ascertainment model goes hand-in-hand with the incorporation of international legal rules in a written instrument. The argument made here particularly takes aim at those conceptualizations of the sources of international law that allow rules to be made through oral agreements or oral promises. After commenting on the sources of international law which do not necessitate a written instrument for identification purposes, attention will turn to the ascertainment of international legal acts, namely treaties, written promises, and acts of international organizations. On that occasion, the limits and drawbacks of the current model used to ascertain international legal acts will be scrutinized with a view to demonstrating that the current theory of the sources of international law, because of the prominent law-ascertaining role of intent, is insufficient to ensure the formal ascertainment of international legal rules (7.2). An attempt will thus be made to spell out a refreshed configuration of international law-ascertainment beyond intent (7.3).

[9] On unilateral acts as sources of rights and obligations, see E. Suy, *Les actes juridiques unilatéraux en droit international public* (LGDJ, Paris, 1962); E. Suy, 'Unilateral Acts of States as a Source of International Law: some New Thoughts and Frustrations' in *Droit du pouvoir, pouvoir du droit: mélanges offerts à Jean Salmon* (Bruylant, Brussels, 2007) 631–42. See also J. d'Aspremont, 'Les travaux de la Commission du droit international relatifs aux actes unilatéraux des Etats' (2005) 109 *Revue générale de droit international public* 163–89. See the contribution of V. Rodríguez Cedeño, et al., 'Unilateral acts of States', in the *Max Planck Encyclopedia of International Law* (OUP, Oxford, 2008). See also C. Goodman, 'Acta Sunt Servanda ? A Regime for Regulating the Unilateral Acts of States at International Law (2006) 25 Aust. YBIL 43.

[10] B. Vitanyi, 'Les positions de la doctrine concernant le sens de la notion de principes généraux de droit reconnus par les nations civilisées' (1982) 86 *Revue générale de droit international public* 54–5; Y. Ben Achour, *Le rôle des civilisations dans le système (droit et relations internationales)* (Bruylant, Brussels, 2003) 129. See also G. Abi-Saab, 'Cours général de droit international public' (1987-VIII) 207 RCADI 9–463, 56. For a suggested renewal of the meaning of the reference to civilized nations, see the remarks of E.-U. Petersmann, 'Constitutionalism and International Adjudication: How to Constitutionalize the U.N. Dispute Settlement System' (1999) 31(4) NYU JILP 753–90, 762.

7.1 Dispelling the Illusion of Formalism Accompanying Formal Evidentiary, Law-Making, and Content-Determining Processes

Despite the fact that formalism has been embraced as a central paradigm of the ascertainment of international legal rules in the mainstream theory of the sources of international law—as has been explained in chapter 3—the theory of the sources provides for the use of non-formal law-ascertainment. Indeed, the mainstream theory of the sources of international law recognizes the existence of rules of international law originating in customary international law, general principles of law, oral agreement, or an oral promise. These sources of international legal rules do not rest on any formal law-ascertainment mechanisms, for these rules are not identified on the basis of formal criteria. Yet, the non-formal character of these law-ascertainment mechanisms has occasionally been dimmed by other forms of formalism which are alien to law-ascertainment. Indeed, as described in chapter 3, international legal scholars, since the advent of formalism, have relentlessly cloaked the making, evidence, and interpretations of the rules of international law with a veil of formalism. This has allowed the international legal scholarship to live with an illusion of formal law-ascertainment, even with respect to those legal rules which are not identified by virtue of formal indicators. There is no doubt that this illusion has been instrumental in the critiques mentioned in chapter 4. It is accordingly necessary to draw a preliminary distinction between the formalization of law-ascertainment and the veil of formalism that shrouds the *making*, the *evidence*, or the *determination of the content* of the rules. The following paragraphs thus distinguish between formal law-ascertainment and formal evidence of law, formal law-making process, and formal determination of the content of the rules. To shed light on such distinctions, it will suffice to mention a few of the classical sources of international law. There is no need to systematically review each of the traditional sources of international law classically recognized as such in the mainstream theory of the sources of international law.

Distinguishing formal law-ascertainment and formal evidence of law: customary international law

As was explained above,[11] ascertainment of law and evidence of law, whilst being two distinct intellectual operations, are inevitably interconnected. Indeed, evidence of law entails that the law-ascertainment criteria of the rule—which are defined *in abstracto*—be verified *in concreto*, that is for the sake of the specific situation in which the existence of a legal rule must be evidenced. Evidence of law accordingly calls upon the authority or the individual applying or invoking the rule to demonstrate the actual existence of indicators which themselves ascertain the existence of the rule. The close kinship between ascertainment of law and evidence of law does not mean, however, that if the ascertainment of a rule is non-formal, its evidence cannot be

[11] Cfr *supra* 2.1.1.

made formal. At least theoretically, one can well prove the existence of a rule through a formal evidentiary process although the rule concerned is ascertained by virtue of non-formal criteria. It is, therefore, not surprising that formal evidentiary processes have been devised to offset the uncertainties associated with the non-formal character of the ascertainment-mechanism of a rule. The way in which customary international law has been conceptualized in the theory of the sources of international law is very illustrative of such an endeavour to compensate non-formal law-ascertainment by a formal evidentiary process.[12] The example of customary international law simultaneously shows how difficult it actually is to effectively counterbalance the non-formal character of law-ascertainment by a formal evidentiary process. While the non-formal nature of custom-ascertainment is analyzed later, together with these rules that are ascertained short of any written instrument,[13] the following paragraphs depict how international legal scholars have striven to formalize the evidence of custom and the extent to which such an endeavour foundered.

International lawyers and scholars have long tried to develop a *formalization of the evidence* of customary international law.[14] Seen in this light, the theory of customary international law can be said to be nothing more than a formal 'programme for evidence'.[15] Such formalization of the evidence of custom elevates the two constitutive elements of custom into two evidentiary indicators which the law-applying authority are called upon to verify *in concreto*. This means that, when applying customary international law, the authority in question must preliminarily prove its existence through a two-step formal process which will be reflected in its decision. Such a formalization of the evidence of custom thus rests on the presupposition of a (general or regime-specific) secondary rule imposing obligations on international law-applying authorities as to how they must prove the existence of customary rules.[16]

This approach has undoubtedly conveyed the hope among international lawyers that the behaviour of law-applying authorities could be predicted despite the highly

[12] For a similar distinction between ascertainment of customary rules and evidence of customary rules, see P. Daillier, M. Forteau, and A. Pellet, *Droit international public* (8th edn, LGDJ, Paris, 2009) 364.

[13] Cfr *infra* 7.2.1.

[14] This also is the opinion of J.-A. Barberis, 'La Coutume est-elle une source de droit international?' in *Mélanges en hommage à Michel Virally: Le droit international au service de la paix, de la justice et du deíveloppement* (Pedone, Paris, 1991) 43–52, 44 and 50–1; P.-M. Dupuy, 'Théorie des sources et coutume en droit international contemporain' in *Le Droit international dans un monde en mutation: liber amicorum en hommage au Professeur Eduardo Jimenez de Arechaga* (Fundación de Cultura Universitaria, Montevideo, 1994) 51, 54; See also Brownlie, *Principles of Public International Law* (6th edn, OUP, Oxford, 2003) 8 (for whom, after all, it only is a question of proof). See also B. Stern, 'La Coutume au coeur du droit international, quelques réflexions', in D. Bardonnet (ed), *Mélanges Reuter: le droit international: unité et diversité* (Pedone, Paris, 1981) 479–99, 483; B. Cheng also construes usage as only evidential. See B. Cheng, 'On the Nature and Sources of International Law', in B. Cheng (ed), *International Law: Teaching and Practice* (Stevens, London, 1982) 203, 223. See also A. Pellet, 'Cours Général: Le droit international entre souveraineté et communauté internationale—La formation du droit international' (2007) 2 *Anuário Brasileiro de Direito Internacional* 12–75, 63.

[15] M. Bos, *A Methodology of International Law* (T.M.C. Asser Instituut, Amsterdam/NY/Oxford, 1984) 224.

[16] In the same vein, see J. Raz, *The Authority of Law* (Clarendon, Oxford, 1983) 96.

indeterminate character of custom-ascertainment. In that sense, the formalization of the evidence of customary international law has sometimes contributed to the emergence of a sense of greater adjudicative neutrality[17] in international legal argumentation and international legal adjudication.[18] Interestingly, such a formalization of the evidentiary process of customary international law can probably be deemed to correspond more closely with the conceptualization of customary international law enshrined in article 38 of the ICJ Statute which provides for a method to evidence the existence of customary international law.[19]

This being said, it would be an exaggeration to claim that this formal evidentiary model of customary international law has proved entirely satisfactory. International legal scholars themselves have been divided as to the parity existing between these two evidentiary elements.[20] Moreover, the evidentiary practice of judicial bodies has provided little consistency,[21] seesawing between the psychological[22] and the material elements.[23] More importantly, the formalism in legal argumentation and legal adjudication brought about by the formalization of the evidence of customary international law has not allayed the indeterminacy of custom-ascertainment itself and the defective normative character of customary rules.[24]

It is argued here that deficiencies of the formal programme for evidence of custom are, to a large extent, to be traced back to the non-formal character of custom-ascertainment which will be examined below.[25] The fruitless attempts to formalize evidence of custom show the need to distinguish between custom-ascertainment and evidence of custom, as the latter does not in itself formalize the former. What a formal evidentiary process formalizes is only the legal reasoning of the law-applying authority called upon to apply a rule of customary international law. The resulting formalism found in the legal reasoning inherent in the formal evidence of custom

[17] Cfr *supra* 2.1.2.

[18] On the different meanings of formalism, see *supra* 2.1.

[19] In the same vein, see S. Sur, 'La Coutume internationale' (1989) 3 *Juris-Classeur de Droit International*, Fascicule 13, 15. See also A. Pellet, 'Article 38', in A. Zimmermann, C. Tomuschat, and K. Oellers-Frahm (eds), *The Statute of the International Court of Justice* (OUP, Oxford, 2002) 677, 749.

[20] Part of the debate between the traditional custom and the new custom can also be interpreted along these lines. See the account by A.E. Roberts, 'Traditional and Modern Approaches to Customary International Law: A Reconciliation' (2001) 95 AJIL 757.

[21] See the remarks and criticisms of A. D'Amato, 'Trashing Customary International Law', (1987) 81 AJIL 101, 102–3; T. Franck, 'Some observations on the ICJ's Procedural and Substantive Innovations' (1987) 81 AJIL 161–21, 118–19; J. Verhoeven, 'Le droit, le juge et la violence. Les arrêts Nicaragua c. Etats-Unis' (1987) 91 *Revue générale de droit international public* 1159–239, 1209; A. Pellet, 'Article 38', in A. Zimmermann, C. Tomuschat, and K. Oellers-Frahm (eds), *The Statute of the International Court of Justice* (OUP, 2002) 677, 760.

[22] See also *ICJ, Military and Paramilitary Activities in and against Nicaragua (Nicaragua v. United States of America)*, Merits, ICJ Rep. (1986).

[23] ICJ, *North Sea Continental Shelf*, ICJ Rep. 3 (1969) 35, 42–3, paras 53–75.

[24] On the problems of ascertainment and normativity of customary international law, see M. Prost, *Unitas multiplex—Les unités du droit international et la politique de la fragmentation* (McGill University, Montreal, 2008) 154, available at <http://digitool.library.mcgill.ca/>; P. Daillier, M. Forteau, and A. Pellet, *Droit international public* (8th edn, LGDJ, Paris, 2009) 349: T. Guzman, 'Saving Customary International Law' (2005) 27 Mich. J. Int'l L. 115, especially 157–59.

[25] Cfr *infra* 7.2.1.

certainly helps foster the legitimacy of the law-applying authority concerned and that of its decision. However, such a formalism is not immune from the criticisms raised by the modern critiques of formalism described in chapter 4, which have mostly taken aim at the idea of formal legal reasoning.[26]

Distinguishing formal law-ascertainment and formal law-making procedures: agreements in simplified form

As has been explained earlier in this book,[27] formal law-ascertainment means that law is identified by virtue of formal indicators. These criteria can be of various kinds. In the theory of the sources of international law, formal law-ascertainment has manifested itself through either a theory of the sources *stricto sensu*,[28] formal validation,[29] or formal law-creating processes.[30] It must be noted that, however it has actually manifested itself in the theory of the sources of international law, formal law-ascertainment has generally been construed as independent from the procedure through which the law is made. Indeed, as a matter of principle, law can be ascertained through formal criteria without having been made subject to a formal procedure. It is true that international treaties often originate in a very formal procedure, the various aspects of which have been the object of a string of rules in the Vienna Convention on the Law of Treaties ('the Vienna Convention'),[31] starting with the production of full powers by the competent authority and ending with registration. However, it is not always the case that treaties are formally made and a treaty can be adopted through a highly non-formal procedure. The use of non-formal treaty-making could even be said to be on the rise.[32] The best illustration thereof is offered by the accepted practice of agreements in simplified form (*accords en forme simplifiée*). Agreements in simplified form are proper treaties, although they originate in an ad hoc and often non-formal procedure which departs from the

[26] On this conception of formalism, cfr *supra* 2.1.2.

[27] Cfr *supra* 2.1.1.

[28] For Condorelli, the term sources remain appropriate even with respect to customary international law. See Condorelli, 'Custom', in M. Bedjaoui (ed), *International Law: Achievements and Prospects* (Martinus Nijhoff, The Hague, 1991) 179–211, 186; see also G. Abi-Saab, 'La coutume dans tous ses états ou le dilemme du développement du droit international général dans un monde éclaté', in *Essays in honor of Roberto Ago* (Giuffrè, Milan, 1987) 58; C. Rousseau, *Principes généraux du droit international public*, tome 1 (Pedone, Paris, 1944) 108.

[29] See A. D'Amato, 'What 'Counts' as Law?' in N.G. Onuf (ed), *Law-Making in the Global Community* (Carolina Academic Press, Durham, 1982) 83.

[30] See D.P. O'Connell, *International Law*, vol. 1 (2nd edn, Stevens, London, 1970) 7–8; see G. Schwarzenberger, *International Law*, vol. 1 (3rd edn, Stevens, London, 1957) 25–7; Jennings, 'Law-Making and Package Deal', in D. Bardonnet (ed), *Mélanges Reuter: le droit international: unité et diversité* (Pedone, Paris, 1981) 347, 348.

[31] See in particular arts 11–17 and the comments thereto.

[32] C. Lipson, 'Why are some international agreements informal' (1991) 45 *International Organization* 495; M. Fitzmaurice, 'The Identification and Character of Treaties and Treaty Obligations between States in International Law' (2003) 73 BYBIL 141, 142; G.M. Danilenko, *Law-Making in the International Community* (Martinus Nijhoff, Dordrecht, 1993) 55. Such a finding was already made by M. Lachs, 'Some Reflections on Substance and Form of International Law', in W. Friedmann, L. Henkin, and O. Lissitzyn (eds), *Transnational Law in a Changing Society, Essays in Honor of P. Jessup* (Columbia UP, NY, 1972) 99.

traditional and solemn treaty-making procedure, and are usually not subject to registration with the Secretariat of the United Nations.[33] It is precisely the non-formal character of their making, especially at the domestic level, that has resulted in agreements in simplified form being so enticing.[34] Despite the non-formal character of the procedure through which they are made, agreements in simplified form are nevertheless ascertained through the (quasi-) formal law-ascertainment criteria applicable to treaties. The foregoing underpins the utmost relevance of such a distinction between the (non-)formal character of the law-making procedure and the (non-) formal character of the ascertainment of the rule concerned. It is argued here that such a distinction remains particularly necessary as the need for non-formal law-making procedures continues to grow unabated in a globalized world where changes are wide-ranging, more sudden, and less predictable. In this context, it is argued that deformalization of law-making procedures ought not necessary to entail deformalization of law-ascertainment.

Interestingly, the inconsequentiality of the formal character of international law-making procedures for the identification of international legal acts seems to be confirmed by the case-law of the ICJ[35] and is commonly accepted in international legal scholarship.[36] It is true that the case-law of the ICJ has sometimes appeared to lend limited support to the idea that formal elements of law-making procedures constitute necessary conditions for an act to be a legal act. For instance, the nebulous wording in the ICJ decision in the oft-discussed *Qatar v. Bahrain* case could be interpreted as supporting the idea that signature of the agreement is a law-ascertainment criterion.[37] Likewise, in the decision of the *Nuclear Test* case, some ambiguity shrouds the

[33] On agreements in simplified form, see C. Chayet, 'Les accords en forme simplifiée' (1957) 3 AFDI 205–26; F.S. Hamzeh, 'Treaties in simplified form—modern perspective' (1968–69) 43 BYBIL 179–89; J. Salmon, 'Les Accords non formalizes ou 'solo consensu' (1999) 45 AFDI 1–28, 22; P. Gautier, *Les accords informels et la Convention de Vienne sur le droit des traités entre Etats, Mélanges Jean Salmon: Droit du pouvoir, pouvoir du droit* (Bruylant, Brussels, 2007) 425–54; see also P. Gautier, *Essai sur la définition des traités entre Etats* (Bruylant, Brussels, 1993) 149–309. For an earlier recognition of agreement in simplified form, see the 1935 codification of the law of treaties by the Harvard Research (1935) 29 AJIL Sup. 697–698 (although it excluded simple exchange of notes from its definition of treaty).

[34] A. Aust, 'The theory and practice of informal international instruments' (1986) 35 ICLQ 787, 811. J. Klabbers, *The Concept of Treaty in International Law* (Kluwer, The Hague, 1996) 29; M. Fitzmaurice, 'The Identification and Character of Treaties and Treaty Obligations Between States in International Law' (2003) 73 BYBIL 141, 142.

[35] ICJ, *Aegean Sea Continental Shelf (Greece v. Turkey)*, Judgment of 19 December 1978, paras 95–107 (emphasis is put on the intent as reflected in the actual terms and the context of the agreement). More recently, see the laconic decision of the Court regarding the nature of the *Maroua Declaration adopted by Cameroon and Nigeria in Land and Maritime Boundary between Cameroon and Nigeria (Cameroon v. Nigeria: Equatorial Guinea intervening)* 10 October 2002, para. 263: 'The Court considers that the Maroua Declaration constitutes an international agreement concluded between States in written form and tracing a boundary; it is thus governed by international law and constitutes a treaty in the sense of the Vienna Convention on the Law of Treaties (see Art. 2, para. l), to which Nigeria has been a party since 1969 and Cameroon since 1991, and which in any case reflects customary international law in this respect'.

[36] See e.g. the remarks of P. Gautier, *Essai sur la définition des traités entre Etats* (Bruylant, Brussels, 1993) 58.

[37] ICJ, *Maritime Delimitation and Territorial Questions between Qatar and Bahrain (Qatar v. Bahrain)*, Judgment of 1 July 1994, para. 27: 'The Court does not find it necessary to consider what might have been the intentions of the Foreign Minister of Bahrain or, for that matter, those of the Foreign Minister of

issue of the place of 'publicity' in the ascertainment of legal promises.[38] Within the framework of the work done by the International Law Commission (ILC) on unilateral acts, similar opinions have been heard as to the importance of publicity in the ascertainment of legal promises,[39] although the ILC eventually decided otherwise.[40] However, these few—limited—departures from the common rejection of formalism in the law-making procedure as an element of law-ascertainment fell short of reversing it and the mainstream theory of the sources of international law has globally remained averse to the ascertaining role of formal procedures—although it has been recognized that material and procedural indicators could play a supplementary role in this regard.[41] These few examples simply bespeak the international lawyers' temptation to take refuge in procedures to elude the difficulties inherent in law-ascertainment.

The abovementioned temptation to elevate formalism of the law-making procedure into a formal law-ascertainment criterion probably stems from their evidentiary weight as to the presence of a will to make law. As was just indicated, there is little doubt that the formal steps of the law-making procedure can constitute useful indicators of such an intent, although their evidentiary importance has been scaled down by the ICJ for international treaties.[42] This is certainly true with respect to the international registration of treaties, which factually provides a presumption of intent.[43] Moreover, it cannot be excluded that, within a specific legal order and

Qatar. The two Ministers signed a text recording commitments accepted by their Governments, some of which were to be given immediate application. Having signed such a text, the Foreign Minister of Bahrain is not in a position subsequently to say that he intended to subscribe only to a "statement recording a political understanding", and not to an international agreement'. This has led some scholars to see that decision as 'a further step along the path of the gradual erosion of specific consent as the basis of the Court's jurisdiction'. See E. Lauterpacht, '"Partial" Judgments and the Inherent Jurisdiction of the International Court of Justice', in V. Lowe and M. Fitzmaurice (eds), *Fifty Years of the International Court of Justice: Essays in Honour of Sir Robert Jennings* (CUP, Cambridge, 1996) 465, 467; in the same vein see M. Fitzmaurice, 'The Identification and Character of Treaties and Treaty Obligations Between States in International Law' (2003) 73 BYBIL 141, 170.

[38] See ICJ, *Nuclear Tests* case *(Australia v. France)*, 20 December 1974, para. 43: 'An undertaking of this kind, if given publicly, and with an intent to be bound, even though not made within the context of international negotiations, is binding'.

[39] Second report of the Special Rapporteur, A/CN.4/500, § 55. On this question, see C. Goodman, 'Acta Sunt Servanda ? A Regime for Regulating the Unilateral Acts of States at International Law (2006) 25 Aust. YBIL 43, especially 58–9.

[40] See recommendation n°1 of the ILC working group, ILC Report (2003), A/58/10, §306.

[41] See generally, J. Klabbers, *The Concept of Treaty in International Law* (Kluwer, The Hague, 1996) 68–86. See P. Gautier, *Essai sur la définition des traités entre Etats*, (Bruylant, Brussels, 1993) 78–85. This is further analyzed below; M. Fitzmaurice, 'The Identification and Character of Treaties and Treaty Obligations Between States in International Law' (2003) 73 BYBIL 141, 149–56. Cfr *infra* 7.2.4.

[42] ICJ, *Aegean Sea Continental Shelf (Greece v. Turkey)*, Judgment of 19 December 1978, para. 95–107 (where the emphasis was put on actual terms and context); In *Maritime Delimitation and Territorial Questions between Qatar and Bahrain (Qatar v. Bahrain)*, Judgment of 1 July 1994, para. 28, the Court interestingly held that 'The Court therefore cannot infer from the fact that Qatar did not apply for registration of the 1990 Minutes until six months after they were signed that Qatar considered, in December 1990, that those Minutes did not constitute an international agreement'.

[43] H. Lauterpacht proposed to enshrine such presumption in the articles about the law of treaties. See 'First Report' (1953) II *Yearbook of the ILC* 97–8. On the significance of registration, see generally D.N.

among certain States, the legal effects of a treaty are conditioned upon a formal procedural requirement.[44] That does not mean, however, that the (non-)formal character of the law-making procedure must be conflated with the (non-)formal nature of the ascertainment of the rules which are generated therefrom. As was already said, a rule that is identified through formal law-ascertainment criteria can very well originate in a non-formal law-making procedure and, conversely, a rule ascertained through non-formal criteria could have been generated by a very formal procedure.

Distinguishing formal law-ascertainment and formal determination of the content of rules: principles of interpretation of international law

It is argued here that the criteria on the basis of which international legal rules are ascertained are not necessarily the same as those through which the *content* of law is determined. This means that the yardstick to distinguish between law and non-law may differ from that used, once a legal rule has been ascertained, to determine the scope of the legal obligation that the rule in question imposes.[45] This distinction is of fundamental import as is explained in this section.

Because there is no application of law without interpretation,[46] the question of the determination of the content of international legal rules arises each time one is called upon to apply a rule. This means that the question of the interpretation of law is permanent. It imbues any process of legal reasoning. Yet, because of the indeterminacy of language, the interpretation of law is necessarily accompanied by a wide discretionary power of the authority in charge of the application of the rule concerned. It is with a view to reining in and legitimizing the use of the discretionary powers of law-applying authorities and simultaneously limiting the fluctuations of expectations of addressees as to the meaning (and effects) of rules, that interpretation has been subject to formal limits. In international law, this has taken the form of formal rules of interpretation which, as far as international treaties are concerned, are enshrined in articles 31 to 33 of the Vienna Convention, which were themselves

Hutchinson, 'The Significance of the Registration and Non-Registration of an International Agreement in Determining Whether or Not it is a Treaty' (1993) *Current Legal Problems* 257–90.

44 See art. 18 of the Covenant of the League of Nations: 'Every treaty or international engagement entered into hereafter by any Member of the League shall be forthwith registered with the Secretariat and shall as soon as possible be published by it. No such treaty or international engagement shall be binding until so registered'. For one of the very few applications of such sanction, see the decision of the French-Mexican Claims Commission of 19 October 1928 in the case of *Pablo Najera*, RIAA, vol. V, 468–73.

45 In the same vein, see A. Orakhelashvili, *The Interpretation of Acts and Rules in Public International Law* (OUP, Oxford, 2008) 285–6; J. Beckett, 'Behind Relative Normativity: Rules and Process as Prerequisites of Law' (2001) 12 EJIL 627–50; J. Beckett, 'Countering Uncertainty and Ending Up/Down Arguments: Prolegomena to a Response to NAIL' (2005) 16 EJIL 213, 217; O. Corten, *Méthodologie du droit international public* (Editions de l'Université de Bruxelles, Brussels, 2009) 213. See *contra* P. Reuter, 'Traités et transactions. Réflexions sur l'identification de certains engagements conventionnels', in *Essays in honor of Roberto Ago* (Giuffrè, Milan, 1987) 399.

46 As famously stated by G. Scelle. See G. Scelle, *Précis de droit des gens principes et systématique*, vol. II (Sirey, Paris, 1934) 488. See also G. Schwarzenberger, 'Myths and Realities in Treaty Interpretation' (1968) 9 Va. J. Int'l L. 1, 8.

informed by some earlier scholarly work.[47] Although it has proved less successful, a similar endeavour has also been undertaken for unilateral acts and promises,[48] which the ICJ did not see as being necessarily governed by the same principles as international treaties.[49]

As far as the interpretation of international treaties is concerned, the adoption of these rules has been deemed a feat.[50] It was intended to replace the sovereignty-protective principles of interpretation devised by international courts in the first half of the 20th century[51] by a toolbox of allegedly neutral principles.[52] Leaving aside the legitimacy that these rules bestow upon the legal reasoning of law-applying authorities, the paradox nonetheless is that, while they constitute some of the rules of the Vienna Convention to which reference is most frequently made,[53] they are actually of limited help, for, in my view, the actual leeway of law-applying authorities remains almost unfettered.[54] The exercise of that discretion has simply been made more

[47] See (1956) 46 *Annuaire de l'Institut de droit international* 364–5. See also <http://www.idi-iil.org/>. A.D. McNair, *The Law of Treaties* (Clarendon, Oxford, 1961) 466; See L. Siorat, *Le Problème des lacunes en droit international. Contribution à l'étude des sources du droit et de la fonction judiciaire* (LGDJ, Paris, 1958) 134. C. Rousseau, *Principes généraux du droit international public*, tome I (Pedone, Paris, 1944) 676. See also P. Verzijl, *Georges Pinson* case (1927–8) AD No. 292, cited by C. McLachlan, 'The Principle of Systemic Integration and Article 31(3)(c) of the Vienna Convention' (2005) 54 ICLQ 279, 279. On the work of the ILC, see M.S. McDougal, 'The International Law Commission's Draft Articles upon Interpretation: Textuality Redivivus' (1967) 61 AJIL 992–1000.

[48] See the *Fourth report on Unilateral Acts of States*, A/CN.4/519, §§101–54 and *Fifth report on Unilateral Acts of States*, A/CN.4/525, add.1, §§120–35. See the comments of J. d'Aspremont, 'Les travaux de la Commission du droit international sur les actes unilatéraux des Etats' (2005) 109 *Revue générale de droit international public* 163–89. See the contribution of V. Rodríguez Cedeño, et al., 'Unililateral acts of States', in the *Max Planck Encyclopedia of International Law* (OUP, Oxford, 2008). See also C. Goodman, 'Acta Sunt Servanda ? A Regime for Regulating the Unilateral Acts of States at International Law (2006) 25 Aust. YBIL 43 or A. Orakhelashvili, *The Interpretation of Acts and Rules in Public International Law* (OUP, Oxford, 2008) 465–86.

[49] See ICJ, Advisory Opinion on the *Accordance with international law of the unilateral declaration of independence in respect of Kosovo*, 22 July 2010, available at <http://www.icj-cij.org> para. 94.

[50] P. Reuter, *Introduction au droit des traités* (Armand Colin, Paris, 1972) 103. See P.Daillier and A. Pellet, *Droit international public* (6th edn, LGDJ, Paris, 1999) 262.

[51] PCIJ, *Interpretation of Article 3, Paragraph 2, of the Treaty of Lausanne*, Advisory Opinion, 1925 PCIJ Series B, No. 12, 7, 25.

[52] On the rebuttal of that idea, see L. Crema, 'Disappearance and New Sightings of Restrictive Interpretation(s)' (2010) 21 EJIL 681–700.

[53] See e.g. ICJ, Arbitral Award of 31 July 1989 *(Guinea-Bissau v. Senegal)*, Judgment, ICJ Rep. (1991) 69–70, para. 48; *Land, Island and Maritime Frontier Dispute (El Salvador/Honduras: Nicaragua intervening)*, Judgment, ICJ Rep. (1992) 582–3, para. 373, and 586, para. 380; *Territorial Dispute (Libyan Arab Jamahiriya/Chad)*, Judgment, ICJ Rep. (1994) 21–2, para. 41; *Maritime Delimitation and Territorial Questions between Qatar and Bahrain (Qatar v. Bahrain)*, Jurisdiction and Admissibility, Judgment, ICJ Rep. (1995) 18, para. 33.

[54] See Lauterpacht, 'Restrictive Interpretation and the Principle of Effectiveness in The Interpretation of Treaties' (1949) 26 BYBIL 48–85, 53: 'In a sense, the controversy as to the justification of rules of interpretation partakes of some degree of artificiality as it tends to exaggerate their importance. For as a rule they are not the determining cause of judicial decision, but the form in which the judge cloaks a result arrived at by other means. It is elegant—and it inspires confidence—to give the guard of an established rule of interpretation to a conclusion reached as to the meaning of a . . . treaty. But it is a fallacy to assume that the existence of these rules is a secure safeguard against arbitrariness or impartiality. The very choice of any single rule or of a combination or cumulation of them is the result of a judgment arrived at, independently

formal with the hope of making the outcome therewith more legitimate. Nothing is more illustrative than the case-law of the international tribunals pertaining to the principle of systemic integration, despite this principle making interpretation less contingent on the intent of the lawmakers and more dependent on existing formal legal instruments.[55] Be that as it may, the existence of the formal principles of interpretation shrouds law-application with a veil of formalism. These rules purport to provide a formal methodology to the interpretation of international legal rules.[56] In that sense, formalism in interpretation is an expression of the theory of adjudicative neutrality and immanent intelligibility of legal arguments,[57] whereby interpretation is meant to provide certainty in the behaviour of law-applying authorities.[58]

Rule-scepticism and legal realism,[59] as well as subsequent approaches to international law associated with deconstructivism and critical legal studies,[60] have already long

of any rules of construction, by reference to considerations of good faith, of justice, and of public policy within the orbit of the express or implied intention of the parties or of the legislature'. See also J.H.H. Weiler, 'The Interpretation of Treaties—A Re-examination Preface' (2010) 21(3) EJIL 507.

[55] See e.g. ICJ, *Oil Platforms*, decision of 6 November 2003, ICJ Rep. (2003) para. 78; See the criticisms of P. d'Argent, 'Du commerce à l'emploi de la force: l'affaire des plates-formes pétrolières (arrêt sur le fond)' (2003) 49 *Annuaire français de droit international* 266, 655–78; See the Opinion of Judge Buergenthal, Judge Higgins, or the Opinion of Judge Kooijmans, ICJ Rep. (2003); See C. McLachlan, 'The Principle of Systemic Integration and Article 31(3)(c) of the Vienna Convention' (2005) 54 ICLQ 279. Compare with the more reasonable use of that principle in the case *Djibouti v. France,* ICJ Rep. (1999) paras 113–14. For other uses of the principles of systemic integration in the international case-law, see *Arbitration regarding the Iron Rhine Railway, (Kingdom of Belgium v. Kingdom of the Netherlands)* 24 May 2005, available at <http://www.pca-cpa.org> paras 58 and 79. See the remarks of P. d'Argent, 'De la fragmentation à la cohésion systémique: la sentence arbitrale du 24 mai 2005 relative au Rhin de fer (Ijzeren Rijn)' in *Droit du pouvoir, pouvoir du droit, Liber amicorum Jean Salmon* (Bruylant, Brussels, 2007) 1113–37. See the very restrictive interpretation by the WTO Appellate Body in the *EC-Measures Affecting the Approval and Marketing of Biothech Products* WT/DS291/R; WT/DS292/R; WT/DS293/R, 29 September 2006, para. 7.68: 'Indeed, it is not apparent why a sovereign State would agree to a mandatory rule of treaty interpretation which could have as a consequence that the interpretation of a treaty to which that State is a party is affected by others of international law which that State has decided not to accept'. On this point, see the remarks of B. Simma, 'Universality of International Law from the Perspective of a Practitioner' (2009) 20 EJIL 265–97, 276–7. On that principle, see also the remarks of J. d'Aspremont, 'The Systemic Integration of International Law by Domestic Courts: Domestic Judges as Architects of the Consistency of the International Legal Order', in A. Nollkaemper and O.K. Fauchald (eds), *Unity or Fragmentation of International Law: The Role of International and National Tribunals* (Hart, Oxford, 2011) (forthcoming).

[56] See generally S. Sur, *L'interprétation en droit international public* (LGDJ, Paris, 1974). See also J.-M. Sorel, 'Article 31', in P. Klein and O. Corten (eds), *Les Conventions de Vienne sur le Droit des Traités. Commentaire article par article* (Bruylant, Bruxelles, 2006) 1289–338; A. Orakhelashvili, *The Interpretation of Acts and Rules in Public International Law* (OUP, Oxford, 2008) 301–92; J. Kammerhofer, *Uncertainty in International Law: A Kelsenian Perspective* (Routledge, London, 2010) 92.

[57] On this conception of formalism, cfr *supra* 2.1.2.

[58] See E.J. Weinrib, 'Legal Formalism: On the Immanent Rationality of Law' (May 1988) 97(6) Yale L. J. 949–1016; S.V. Scott, 'International Law as Ideology: Theorizing the Relationship between International Law and International Politics' (1994) 5 EJIL 313–25, especially 322.

[59] On the realist criticisms of formalism as a theory of legal reasoning in adjudication, see generally A.J. Sebok, 'Misunderstanding Positivism' (1994–1995) 93 Mich. L. Rev. 2054 especially. 2071. See also *supra* 4.1.2.

[60] See e.g. D. Kennedy, 'The Disciplines of International Law and Policy' (1999) 12 LJIL 84; D. Kennedy, 'When Renewal Repeats: Thinking Against the Box' (1999–2000) 32 NYU JILP 335. M.

demonstrated the illusory character of formalism in law-interpretation[61] and shed some light on the 'abuse of logic',[62] the 'abuse of deduction',[63] and the 'mechanical jurisprudence'[64] inherent in such a formal determination of the content of legal rules. This is why it is so important to stress that the formalism accompanying formal interpretation of international legal rules is fundamentally different from formalism in law-ascertainment. Indeed, formal determination of the content of rules, i.e. formalism in interpretation, should be clearly distinguished from formal law-ascertainment. Subjecting a rule to formal ascertainment does not mean that its content must necessarily be determined through formal interpretative processes. The opposite is also true. The content of rules which are identified through non-formal ascertainment processes can remain subject to formal principles of interpretation. In international law, for instance, it is commonly agreed that the principles of interpretation designed by the Vienna Convention are customary international law[65] and apply to oral agreements, despite the latter being identified through non-formal ascertainment standards.

It is true that if a criterion like the intent of the parties is elevated into a law-ascertainment indicator, and if that intent is to be inferred from the instrument, interpretation of the content of the instrument will be necessary to unearth the intent and thus to assess whether the rule is a legal rule.[66] This, however, is a consequence of the use of intent as a law-identification criterion.[67] As such, law-ascertainment and interpretation of the content of rules are two distinct operations. The distinction is important, for the law-ascertainment criteria of a rule can be free of any formalism while the determination of its content may be subject to formal principles

Koskenniemi, *The Gentle Civilizer of Nations: The Rise and Fall of International Law 1870–1960* (CUP, Cambridge, 2002) 502. M. Koskenniemi, *From Apology to Utopia* (CUP, Cambridge, 2005) 306. N. Purvis, 'Critical Legal Studies in Public International Law' (1991) 32 Harvard JIL 81; T. Skouteris, 'Fin de NAIL: New Approaches to International Law and its Impact on Contemporary International Legal Scholarship' (1997) 10 LJIL 415; T. Skouteris, *The Notion of Progress in International Law Discourse* (LEI Universiteit, Leiden, 2008) chapter 3; For a similar interpretation of formalism from the vantage point of critical legal studies, see I. Scobbie, 'Towards the Elimination of International Law: Some Radical Scepticism about Sceptical Radicalism' (1990) 61 BYBIL 339–62, 345.

[61] Cfr *supra* 7.1.

[62] A.J. Sebok, 'Misunderstanding Positivism' (1994–1995) 93 Mich. L. Rev. 2054, 2093.

[63] D. Kennedy, *The Rise and Fall of Classical Legal Thoughts* (re-edited in 2006, Beard Books, Washington DC) at xviii.

[64] This is the famous expression of Roscoe Pound, 'Mechanical Jurisprudence' (1908) 8 Colum. L. Rev. 605.

[65] See generally J.M. Sorel, 'Article 31' in P. Klein and O. Corten (eds), *Les Conventions de Vienne sur le Droit des Traités. Commentaire article par article* (Bruylant, Bruxelles, 2006) 1289–334; M.E. Villiger, *Customary International Law and Treaties: A Study of their Interactions and Interrelations with Special Consideration of the 1969 Vienna Convention on the Law of Treaties* (Nijhoff, Dordrecht, 1985) 334–43; see ICJ, *Territorial Dispute (Libyan Arab Jamahiriya/Chad)* ICJ Rep. (1994) 6; *Kasikili/Sedudu Island (Botswana/Namibia)* ICJ Rep. (1999) 1059; *LaGrand (Germany v. United States of America)* ICJ Rep. (2001) 501, para. 99. See *Affaire concernant l'apurement des comptes entre le Royaume des Pays-Bas et la République Française en application du Protocole du 25 septembre 1991 additionnel à la Convention relative à la protection du Rhin contre la pollution par les chlorures du 3 décembre 1976 (The Netherlands v. France)*, Award of 12 March 2004, UNRIAA, vol. XXV, 312, para. 103.

[66] O. Corten, *Méthodologie du droit international public* (Editions de l'Université de Bruxelles, Brussels, 2009) 213–14.

[67] Cfr *infra* 7.2.3.

of interpretation and vice-versa. This is also the reason why formal law-ascertainment—which is exclusively discussed in this book—does not contribute to the delineation of the entire phenomenon of law and falls short of providing precise indication as to the content of law.[68]

7.2 Ascertainment of International Legal Rules in Traditional Source Doctrines and Case-Law

The previous paragraphs have been aimed at laying bare some of the illusions of formal law-ascertainment mistakenly associated with formal evidentiary processes, formal law-making procedures, and formal determination of the content of international legal rules in the mainstream theory of the sources of international law. I am now turning to the current state of formal ascertainment of international legal rules in mainstream theory of the sources. As has been explained above,[69] international legal rules have commonly been ascertained through their sources. Main sources of international law include treaties, unilateral promises, customary law, and general principles of law. It is not the aim of this section to review them all. A distinction will, more simply, be drawn between those rules of international law that are ascertained by virtue of the instrument in which they are enshrined (7.2.2) and those that are not (7.2.1) with a view to demonstrating that formal law-ascertainment has only proved possible as regards the former. Yet, it will be shown that, in traditional sources doctrines, even those rules ascertained by virtue of the instrument in which they are contained still necessitate resorting to non-formal indicators, thereby showing the limits of formal law-ascertainment as is currently fashioned in the mainstream theory of the sources of international law (7.2.3 and 7.2.4).

7.2.1 Rules ascertained short of any written instrument: custom, general principles of law, oral treaties, and oral promises

International law has long recognized the existence of rules that are not enshrined in a written instrument, as is illustrated by the general acceptance that customary international law, general principles of law, or oral agreements and promises can generate rules of international law. These rules usually correspond with the category of rules dubbed by international legal scholars 'non-treaty law'.[70] As a result, the rules originating in these sources are not ascertained on the basis of a written instrument but by virtue of indicators found elsewhere. It will be shown here that

[68] For a more ambitious attempt to describe the 'complete phenomenon of law', see M. Bos, *A Methodology of International Law* (T.M.C. Asser Instituut, Amsterdam/NY/Oxford, 1984) 2.

[69] Cfr *supra* 3.2.2.

[70] See e.g. D. Bodansky, 'Prologue to a Theory of Non-Treaty Norms', in M. Arsanjani, et al. (eds), *Looking to the Future: Essays on International Law in Honor of W. Michael Reisman* (Brill, Leiden, 2011) 119–34; see also H. Hillgenberg, 'A Fresh look at Soft Law' (1999) 10 EJIL 499. See also the distinction by P. Daillier, M. Forteau, and A. Pellet between conventional modes of law-making and non-conventional modes of law-making (the latter including voluntary and spontaneous modes of law-making). See P. Daillier, M. Forteau, and A. Pellet, *Droit international public* (8th edn, LGDJ, Paris, 2009) 365.

these indicators fail to be formal. Customary international law being one of the most controversial and commented on sources of international legal rules that are ascertained short of any written instrument, this will be focused on here. Yet, a few words will still be said about general principles of law, oral treaties, and oral promises.

Customary international law

Customary international law is the embodiment of these rules which are ascertained short of any written instrument. The fact that the *opinio juris*—and practice if one believes that the latter can ever manifest itself in written form—materialize in a written instrument does not in itself make the identification of customary rules dependent on the existence of a written instrument. In such a case, the written manifestation of the constitutive element of custom cannot be equated with the law-ascertainment yardstick, for it simply is the evidence of one of the constitutive elements.

I have already shown that attempts to formalize evidence of custom have foundered.[71] I have then argued that such a failure to formalize custom evidentiary process was to be traced back to the deeply non-formal nature of custom-ascertainment. Indeed, as the following paragraphs will now try to demonstrate, it seems difficult to deny that the conceptualization of the ascertainment of customary international law in mainstream scholarship has always rested on non-formal criteria.[72] Indeed, in the mainstream theory of the sources of international law, the ascertainment of customary international law is considered *process-based*.[73] More specifically, according to traditional views, customary international rules are identified on the basis of a *bottom-up crystallization process* that necessitates a concurring and constant behaviour of a significant amount of States accompanied by their belief (or intent) that such a process corresponds with an obligatory command of international law.[74] The possible contradictions associated with this widespread two element-conceptualization of customary international law are well-known.[75] It seems

[71] Cfr *supra* 7.1 and 7.2.1.

[72] On the discussion about customary international law in the League of Nations' Committee of Jurists during the drafting of the Statute of the PCIJ, see P. Haggenmacher, 'La doctrine des deux éléments du droit coutumier dans la pratique de la Cour internationale' (1986) 90 *Revue générale de droit international public* 5–126, 18–32. See also T. Skouteris, *The Notion of Progress in International Law Discourse* (LEI Universiteit, Leiden, 2008).

[73] For a classical example, see Daillier and Pellet, *Droit international Public* (6th edn, LGDJ, Paris, 1999) 318. On the various conceptualizations of customary international law as a process, see the remarks of R. Kolb, 'Selected Problems in the Theory of Customary International Law' (2003) 50 NILR 119–50.

[74] On the emergence of the subjective element in the theory of custom in the 19th century, see P. Guggenheim, 'Contribution à l'Histoire des Sources du Droit des Gens' (1958) 94 RCADI 1–84, 36–59. A. D'Amato, *The Concept of Custom in International Law* (Cornell UP, NY, 1971) 44–50.

[75] See the famous contradiction highlighted by Sørensen, 'Principes de droit international public' (1960-III) 101 RCADI 1–254, 50 ('Si l'on définit l'élément subjectif de telle sorte que l'agent de l'Etat doit avoir la conviction de se conformer ou d'obéir à ce qui est déjà le droit, on présuppose l'existence antérieure des règles juridiques, et la coutume, par conséquent, ne peut pas être le processus par lequel le droit est créé. Si d'autre part, on rejette la conception d'un droit préexistant, tout en exigeant que la pratique, dès le début, soit basée sur la conviction d'une obligation ou d'une autorisation d'agir, on exige en effet, comme base de la coutume, que l'agent se trouve en erreur'). In the same sense, see D'Amato, ibid, 7. On this paradox, see the comments of R. Kolb, 'Selected Problems in the Theory of Customary International Law' (2003) 50 NILR 119, 137.

more important to emphasize here that neither the behaviour of States nor their beliefs can be captured or identified by formal criteria.[76] As a result, ascertainment of customary international law does not hinge on any standardized pedigree. Like other process-based models of law-identification,[77] custom-identification eschews formal ascertainment and follows a fundamentally non-formal ascertainment pattern.[78] This is why custom-identification has often been deemed an 'art'[79] and why some authors have been loath to qualify customary law as a proper 'source' of international law.[80]

It is true that, in the case of custom, non-formal law-ascertainment has been perceived as a means to favour the emergence of legal rules even in the absence of solemn treaty-making. Indeed, customary international law, while having constituted a crucial source of rules in the early development of international law and provided the international legal system with some necessary elementary principles that ensure its viability,[81] has continued to be construed as a source of rules that does not require the solemnity of treaty-making and can even abide the silence or inaction

[76] In the same vein, M. Koskenniemi, *From Apology to Utopia* (CUP, Cambridge, 2005) 388. See also S. Zamora, 'Is There Customary International Economic Law?' (1989) 32 German YBIL 9, 38; For a classical example of the difficulty to capture the practice, see ICJ, *Case concerning the Dispute Regarding Navigational and Related Rights (Costa Rica v. Nicaragua)*, 13 July 2009, ICJ Rep. (2009) para. 141. On the particular difficulty of establishing the practice of abstention, see PCIJ, *Lotus*, Series A, No. 10 (1927), 28 or ICJ, *Military and Paramilitary Activities in and against Nicaragua (Nicaragua v. United States of America)*, Merits, ICJ Rep. (1986) para. 188. Distinguishing the two constitutive elements of customary law has even occasionally been seen as infeasible to some scholars. The literature on whether declarations or treaties constitute state practice or *opinio juris* has been controversial. See e.g. A. D'Amato, *The Concept of Custom in International Law* (Cornell UP, NY, 1971) 88–90. D'Amato argues that statements can only be *opinio juris*. Compare with M. Akehurst, 'Custom as a Source of International Law' (1974–75) 47 BYBIL 1–53, 35. For a defence of the classical two element-doctrine, see *contra* S. Donaghue, 'Normative Habits, Genuine Beliefs and Evolving Law: Nicaragua and the Theory of Customary International Law' (1995) 16 Aust. YBIL 327. See also J. Tasioulas, 'Opinio Juris and the Genesis of Custom: A Solution to the "Paradox"' (2007) 26 Aust. YBIL 199.

[77] See above the process-based ascertainment of international legal rules defended by the New Haven Law School, cfr *supra* 4.2.3.

[78] M.H. Mendelson, 'The Formation of Customary International Law' (1998) 272 RCADI 159–410, 172; G. Buzzini, 'La Théorie des sources face au droit international général', (2002) 106 *Revue générale de droit international public* 581; this also is what leads R. Kolb to contend that art. 38 does not lay down an entirely formal system of sources. See R. Kolb, *Réflexions de philosophie du droit international. Problèmes fondamentaux du droit international public: Théorie et Philosophie du droit international* (Bruylant, Brussels, 2003) 51. It is interesting to note that Bodansky, for his part, follows a different reasoning in that he seems to deny that custom is a formal source of law because custom-ascertainment does not necessarily hinge on the existence of criteria defined by a secondary rule of international law but may also more crudely originate in direct States' acceptance. See D. Bodansky, 'Prologue to a Theory of Non-Treaty Norms', in M. Arsanjani, et al. (eds), *Looking to the Future: Essays on International Law in Honor of W. Michael Reisman* (Brill, Leiden, 2011) 119, 128–9.

[79] M.W. Janis, *An Introduction to International Law* (2nd edn, Little, Brown & Co, Boston, 1993) 44.

[80] See the discussion in H. Thirlway, *International Customary Law and Codification* (Sijthoff, Leiden, 1972) 25–30. See also the remarks by Condorelli, 'Custom', in M. Bedjaoui (ed), *International Law: Achievements and Prospects* (Martinus Nijhoff, The Hague, 1991) 179–211, 186.

[81] This is what has fuelled part of the criticisms related to the democratic deficit of custom-making processes. P. Kelly, 'The Twilight of Customary International Law' (2000) 40 Va J. Int'l L. 449, 519 and led to the rejection of customary principles by socialist and new States. See L. Henkin, *How Nations Behave* (2nd edn, Columbia UP, NY, 1979) 121.

of States. In that sense, subjecting customary international law to a purely formal identification process would run *contra* to its *raison d'être* and would deprive it of its distinctive character. And so, the non-formal character of custom-ascertainment lies in the essence of customary international law, which is meant to be responsive to fluid social contexts as well as to the fluctuation of States' interests and behaviours.[82]

Although it corresponds with the essence of custom, the non-formal character of the ascertainment of customary international law has generated some severe predicaments which are very illustrative of the difficulties associated with non-formal law-ascertainment.[83] Not only does the non-formal nature of custom-ascertainment, as has been demonstrated by scholars affiliated with deconstructivism and critical legal studies,[84] bring about a constant move in law-ascertainment between State conduct (*apologism*) and normative beliefs (*utopianism*), but above all, the process-based elements of custom fail to provide a reliable yardstick to distinguish between law and non-law.[85] The non-formal character of custom-ascertainment accordingly condemns such rules to being dangerously indeterminate, at least as long as they have not been certified by a law-applying authority.[86] During that period of uncertainty, customary international rules *often lack normative character* and, hence, their authority is gravely enfeebled.

[82] For a multidisciplinary, historical, and comparative examination of custom's enduring place in both domestic and international law, see D.J. Bederman, *Custom as a Source of Law* (CUP, Cambridge, 2010).

[83] See B. Stern, 'La Coutume au coeur du droit international, quelques réflexions', in D. Bardonnet (ed), *Mélanges Reuter: le droit international: unité et diversité* (Pedone, Paris, 1981) 479, 479. Stern writes: 'il est clair que la coutume dérange'. See also G. Abi-Saab, 'La Coutume dans tous ses Etats', in *Essays in honor of Roberto Ago*, vol. I (Giuffrè, Milano, 1987) 58. Abi-Saab qualifies customary law as 'processus mystérieux' and 'enigma permanente'; see also J. Kammerhofer, 'Uncertainty in the Formal Sources of International Law: Customary International Law and Some of its Problems' (2004) 15 EJIL 523–53 or A. Orakhelashvili, *The Interpretation of Acts and Rules in Public International Law* (OUP, Oxford, 2008) 51 and 70.

[84] This has been insightfully demonstrated by M. Koskenniemi: M. Koskenniemi, *From Apology to Utopia* (CUP, Cambridge, 2005) 388–473. He argues that the doctrine of custom is indeterminate because of its circular character which stems from its assumption of behaviour as evidence of *opinio juris* and the latter as evidence of the custom-making behaviour. See especially 437–8. See also M. Koskenniemi, 'The Normative Force of Habit; International Custom and Social Theory' (1990) 1 FYBIL 77–153 or see also M. Koskenniemi, 'The Pull of the Mainstream' (1990) 88 Mich. L. Rev. 1946, especially 1947 and 1953.

[85] P.-M. Dupuy, 'Théorie des sources et coutume en droit international contemporain' in *Le Droit international dans un monde en mutation: liber amicorum en hommage au Professeur Eduardo Jimenez de Arechaga* (Fundación de Cultura Universitaria, Montevideo, 1994) 51, 61. See also the very radical criticism by P. Kelly, 'The Twilight of Customary International Law' (2000) 40 Va J. Int'l L. 449, according to whom it is a 'matter of taste'; See S. Zamora, 'Is There Customary International Economic Law?' (1989) 32 German YBIL 9, 38.

[86] This is why Kelsen argued that *opinio juris* is a fiction to disguise law-creating powers of judges. See H. Kelsen, 'Théorie du droit international coutumier' (1939) 1 *Revue générale de droit international public* 253–74. This indeterminacy and the correlative leeway of judges have led some scholars to call for an abandonment of custom as a source of customary international law. See N.C.H. Dunbar, 'The Myth of Customary International Law' (1983) Aust. YBIL 1. See also the remarks of D. Carreau, *Droit International* (8th edn, Pedone, Paris, 2004) 263; For a criticism of this position, see *contra* J. Tasioulas, 'Opinio Juris and the Genesis of Custom: A Solution to the "Paradox"' (2007) 26 Aust. YBIL 199.

The uncertainty inherent in the non-formal nature of custom-ascertainment has hardly been alleviated by international judicial practice, for the latter has been unable to offset the absence of formal law-ascertainment criteria by a consistent and intelligible reading of the custom-making process.[87] Obviously, codification, because it lays down customary international law in a written document which is often subsequently endowed with a legal character, is the most effective manner in which the downsides of non-formal custom-ascertainment can be averted. This is the very reason why international lawyers and lawmakers have long striven to codify customary international law. Yet, as practice has demonstrated, codification of customary international law, whether undertaken by private groups or public authorities,[88] has often proved unachievable.[89] The ILC's difficulty in drawing a line between progressive development and codification[90] has illustrated the extent to which codifying custom cannot be severed from law-making. Bound with law-making, codification of customary international law is made even more difficult, thereby offering nothing more than a short-lived relief to the drawbacks inherent in the non-formal character of custom-ascertainment.

It should not be surprising that, given the difficulty of properly codifying customary law, the abiding predicaments yielded by the non-formal character of the identification of customary international law have prodded attempts to reshape custom-ascertainment into a formal operation. In particular, ambitious attempts to endow custom-ascertainment with formal trappings have materialized themselves in spectacular scholarly efforts put into the elaboration and streamlining of the above-mentioned subjective and objective elements of custom.[91] Indeed, the two elements of customary international law have been the object of much scholarly refinement, and codes have been established to decipher or articulate the beliefs and the behaviours of States.[92] A fair number of these scholarly refinements have conveyed

[87] Compare ICJ, *Military and Paramilitary Activities in and against Nicaragua (Nicaragua v. United States of America)*, Merits, ICJ Rep. (1986) para. 188. and *North Sea Continental Shelf (Federal Republic of Germany/Denmark; Federal Republic of Germany/Netherlands)*, ICJ Rep. (1969) para. 42.

[88] On the retreat of private initiatives in the codification of customary international law, see generally N. Onuf, 'Global Law-Making and Legal Thought', in N. Onuf (ed), *Law-Making in the Global Community* (Carolina Academic Press, Durham, 1982) 1, 22.

[89] On codification in general see M. Sahovic, 'Le rôle et les méthodes de la codification et du développement progressif du droit international', in *Le Droit international 2* (IHEI Pedone, Paris, 1982) 71–126; M. Diez de Velasco Vallejo, 'Législation et codification dans le droit international actuel', *Essays in honor of Roberto Ago*, vol. I (Giuffrè, Milano, 1987) 247–59; J. Sette-Camara, 'The ILC Discourse and Method', *Essays in honour of Roberto Ago* (Giuffré, Milan, 1987) 467–502; P. Daillier, M. Forteau, and A. Pellet, *Droit international public* (8th edn, LGDJ, Paris, 2009) 367.

[90] See J. d'Aspremont, 'Les travaux de la Commission du droit international sur les actes unilatéraux des Etats' (2005) 109 *Revue générale de droit international public*, 163–89; see also M. Virally, 'A Propos de la "Lex Ferenda"', in D. Bardonnet (ed), *Mélanges Reuter: le droit international: unité et diversité* (Pedone, Paris, 1981) 521–33, 520.

[91] G. Abi-Saab has compared the formalization through the two elements to a family history on a newborn on his state of health. See G. Abi-Saab, 'La coutume dans tous ses états ou le dilemme du développement du droit international général dans un monde éclaté', in *Essays in honor of Roberto Ago*, vol. I (Giuffrè, Milan, 1987) 59.

[92] A typical example is the attempt to define those authorities that have the capacity to express the subject element on behalf of the State. See e.g. K. Strupp, 'Les règles générales du droit de la paix' (1934/I)

the idea that custom is a formal source of law whose rules are identified on the basis of formal criteria.[93]

The illusion of formalism in custom-ascertainment has also been a consequence of the attempted proceduralization of the custom-making process inherent in the much-discussed theory of the 'persistent objector', devised by legal scholars[94] and subsequently followed by judicial bodies.[95] Indeed, and whatever its inconsistencies,[96] the persistent objector rule bespeaks an idea that the making of customary international law is a somewhat formal process from which States can formally decide to withdraw,[97] thereby lending support to the idea that custom can be—at least partly—ascertained through formal identification of the custom-making process.

47 RCADI 259–595, 313–15; G.J.H. Van Hoof, *Rethinking the Sources of International Law* (Kluwer, Deventer, 1983) 107–8. A. D'Amato, *The Concept of Custom in International Law* (Cornell UP, NY, 1971) 50–1. H. Thirlway, *International Customary Law and Codification* (Sijthoff, Leiden, 1972) 58; Akehurst, 'Custom as a Source of International Law' (1974–75) 47 BYBIL 1–53, 8–10; C. Rousseau, *Principes Généraux du droit international public*, vol. 1 (Pedone, Paris, 1944) 845–55. See also the 'sliding scale' theory of F.L. Kirgis, 'Custom on a Sliding Scale' (1987) 81 AJIL 146. See also the use of 'game theory' to refine the articulation of these two elements. See e.g. Brian D. Lepard, *Customary International Law, A New Theory with Practical Applications* (CUP, Cambridge, 2010) or N. Petersen, 'The Role of Consent and Uncertainty in the Formation of Customary International Law', *Working paper of the Max Planck Institute for Research on Collective Goods Bonn 2011/4*, available at <<http://ssrn/abstract=1761142>.

[93] On the idea that customary international law is a formal source of law, see E. Suy, *Les actes juridiques unilatéraux en droit international public* (LGDJ, Paris, 1962) 5; see G.M. Danilenko, *Law-Making in the International Community* (Martinus Nijhoff, Dordrecht, 1993) 30. It is interesting to note that P. Daillier, M. Forteau, and A. Pellet, for their part, argue that customary international law is a formal source of law because it originates in a law-creating process which is governed by international law and is itself formal. See *Droit international public* (8th edn, LGDJ, Paris, 2009) 353 and 355.

[94] See G. Fitzmaurice, 'The General Principles of International Law Considered from the Standpoint of the Rules of Law' (1957 II) 92 RCADI 1–227, 49–50.

[95] ICJ, *Fisheries case (UK v. Norway)*, 18 December 1951, ICJ Rep. (1951) 116, 131; ICJ, *Asylum case (Colombia v. Peru)*, 20 November 1950, 266, 277–78. It has also been endorsed by regional bodies. See e.g. Inter-American Commission of Human Rights, *James Terry Roach and Jay Pinkerton v. United States*, No. 9647, resolution 387, 22 September 1987, Inter-Am. Ct H.R. Annual Report, 1986–7, OAS Doc. No. OEA/Ser.1/V.II.71, Doc. 9, Rev. 1, para. 52.

[96] P. Dumberry, 'Incoherent and Ineffective: The Concept of Persistent Objector Revisited', (2010) 59 ICLQ 779–802. P.-M. Dupuy, 'A propos de l'opposabilité de la coutume générale: enquête brève sur l'objecteur persistant', in *Le droit international au service de la paix, de la justice et du développement. Mélanges offerts à Michel Virally* (Pedone, Paris, 1991) 257–72; See also J. Charney, 'The persistent objector rule and the developments of CIL' (1985) 56 BYBIL 1; P.-M. Dupuy, 'L'unité de l'ordre juridique international: cours général de droit international public' (2002) 297 RCADI 9–489, 174. O. Barsalou,'La doctrine de l'objecteur persistant en droit international' (2006) 19 *Revue québécoise de droit international* 1–18; See also H. Charlesworth, 'Customary International Law and the Nicaragua Case' (1984–1987) 11 Aust. YBIL 1, 3; C.A. Bradley and M. Gulati, 'Withdrawing from International Custom' (2010) 120 Yale L. J. 202. For a defence of the persistent objector principle, see *contra* T.L. Stein, 'The Approach of the Different Drummer: The Principle of the Persistent Objector in International Law' (1985) 26 Harv. Int'l L. J. 457.

[97] On the idea that the theory of persistent objector betrays an attempt to formalize customary process, see P.-M. Dupuy, 'Théorie des sources et coutume en droit international contemporain' in *Le Droit international dans un monde en mutation: liber amicorum en hommage au Professeur Eduardo Jimenez de Arechaga* (Fundación de Cultura Universitaria, Montevideo, 1994) 51, 61.

It is argued here that neither the extreme refinement of the two ascertainment criteria of custom nor the latent proceduralization associated with the theory of the persistent objector have sufficed to ensure formal-custom-identification.[98] The extreme refinement of the two criteria of custom in international legal scholarship has not metamorphosed custom-ascertainment into a formal process. In the same vein, the proceduralization of custom-making that accompanies the theory of the persistent objector has proved too controversial to be taken seriously.[99] All those attempts to formalize the ascertainment of customary international law have thus failed,[100] and custom-ascertainment has remained dominantly conceived as process-based.[101]

It is true that, like other process-based models of law-ascertainment,[102] the identification of customary international law can, at least theoretically, be subject to some limited formalization of the process on which it rests.[103] Formalizing that process, however, has proved unfeasible for it has not been possible to identify patterns in the process of the creation of custom, other than the two abovementioned elements, and that process has, to a large extent, remained unfathomable.[104] Given the impossibility of identifying the process of creating custom, only its *institutionalization* could allow this process to be captured in formal terms. In the case of custom, institutionalization would probably entail the recognition of a rule-making

[98] One of the most famous objections to this formal conception of customary international law has been offered by R. Ago who has construed custom as 'spontaneous law'. See R. Ago, 'Science Juridique et Droit International' (1956) 90 RCADI 851–958, 936–41; See also Ago, 'Diritto positivo e diritto internazionale', in *Comunicazioni e Studi* VII (Università di Milano, Milano, 1955) 44; Some support for Ago's conception of custom has been expressed by B. Stern, 'La Coutume au Coeur du droit international, quelques réflexions', in D. Bardonnet (ed), *Mélanges Reuter: le droit international: unité et diversité* (Pedone, Paris, 1981) 479, at 484. For another type of criticism, see M. Virally, *La pensée juridique* (LDGJ, Paris, 1960) 160–2.

[99] See *supra* note 96 the criticisms by Dumberry and Dupuy. The approach based on spontaneous law has been the object of some qualifications by G. Abi-Saab, 'La coutume dans tous ses états ou le dilemme du développement du droit international général dans un monde éclaté', in *Essays in honor of Roberto Ago*, vol. I (Giuffrè, Milan, 1987) 60.

[100] In the same vein, see P.-M. Dupuy, 'L'unité de l'ordre juridique international: cours général de droit international public' (2002) 297 RCADI 9–489, 166–7; P.-M. Dupuy, 'Théorie des sources et coutume en droit international contemporain' in *Le Droit international dans un monde en mutation: liber amicorum en hommage au Professeur Eduardo Jimenez de Arechaga* (Fundación de Cultura Universitaria, Montevideo, 1994) 51, 61–3; See R. Jennings, 'The Identification of International Law' in B. Cheng (ed), *International Law: Teaching and Practice* (Stevens, London, 1982) 3, 9; R. Ago, 'Science juridique et droit international' (1956-II) 90 RCADI 851, 939; H. Charlesworth, 'Customary International Law and the Nicaragua Case' (1984–1987) 11 Aust. YBIL 1, 27; G. Buzzini, 'La Théorie des sources face au droit international général' (2002) 106 *Revue générale de droit international public* 581.

[101] For a study of the various driving forces behind that process, see M. Byers, *Custom, Powers and the Power of Rules* (CUP, Cambridge, 1999). See the comments of G. Simpson, 'The Situation on the International Legal Theory Front: The Power of Rules and the Rule of Power' (2000) 11 EJIL 439–64.

[102] See *supra* 4.2.2.

[103] On this approach, see generally G. Abi-Saab, 'La coutume dans tous ses états ou le dilemme du développement du droit international général dans un monde éclaté', in *Essays in honor of Roberto Ago*, vol. I (Giuffrè, Milan, 1987) 59–60.

[104] See the remarks of S. Sur, 'La Coutume internationale' (1989) *Juris-Classeur de Droit International*, Fascicule 13, 14.

role bestowed upon judges whose functions are classically exclusively evidentiary and cognitivistic,[105] thereby elevating international—and to a lesser extent domestic[106]—judges into a law-making organ of the international community.[107] Such a formalization of the custom-making process, although more congruent with actual practice of adjudication on the basis of customary principles, has unsurprisingly fuelled much unease in the international legal scholarship, for it—expressly—transforms customary international law into a judge-made law. While international lawyers are usually ready to recognize the role of international courts and tribunals in the progressive development of primary rules of international law, the idea that courts and tribunals are expressly endowed with custom-making power is not yet accepted.[108]

Since formalization of the custom-making *process* through institutionalization has proved inconceivable, international legal scholarship has engaged in other ventures to endow the process of custom-ascertainment with some formal trappings. What has been designated as 'new custom' or 'modern custom'[109] embodies such penultimate endeavours. According to the 'new custom' theory, customary international law is said to originate in a conscious process taking place within the framework of universal intergovernmental bodies[110] and ignited by the deliberate will to create a

[105] On the custom-generating role of courts, see generally, N. Onuf, 'Global Law-Making and Legal Thought', in N. Onuf (ed), *Law-Making in the Global Community* (Carolina Academic Press, Durham, 1982) 1, 21–2.

[106] See, however, the argument of R. Falk, according to which domestic courts are in a better position to ascertain customary law for they can more authoritatively capture State practice: R. Falk, *The Role of Domestic Courts in the International Legal Order* (Syracuse UP, Syracuse, 1964) 19–20.

[107] See Kelsen, in C. Leben, *Hans Kelsen, Ecrits français de droit international* (PUF, Paris, 2001) 77. See also the recognition of that law-making role by L.V. Prott, *The Latent Power of Culture and the International Judge* (Professional Books, Abingdon, 1979) 77–8.

[108] This is one of the reasons why Kelsen rejected the subjective element in the theory of customary law, for he contended that *opinio juris* is a fiction to disguise law-creating powers of judges. See Kelsen, 'Théorie du droit international coutumier' (1939) 1 *Revue générale de droit international public* 253–74. For another classical rejection of the law-making power of international judges, see G. Fitzmaurice, 'Judicial Innovation—Its Uses and Its Perils' in R.Y. Jennings (ed), *Essays in Honour of Lord McNair* (Stevens, London, 1965) 24 or G. Fitzmaurice, 'The General Principles of International Law Considered from the Standpoint of the Rules of Law' (1957 II) 92 RCADI 1–227; See also D. Akande, 'Nuclear Weapons, Unclear Law? Deciphering the Nuclear Weapons Advisory Opinion of the International Court' (1997) 68 BYBIL 165, 213–15. See *contra* the famous position of H. Lauterpacht, *The Function of Law in the International Community* (Clarendon, Oxford, 1933) 319–20. On the more specific question of law-making by international criminal tribunals, see S. Darcy and J. Powderly (eds), *Judicial Creativity at the International Criminal Tribunals* (OUP, Oxford, 2011) and in particular the contribution of F. Raimondo, 'General Principles of Law, Judicial Creativity and the Development of International Criminal Law', 45–59.

[109] For an illustration, see J. Charney, 'Universal International Law' (1993) 87 AJIL 529. See also C. Tomuschat, 'Obligations arising for states without or against their will' (1993-IV) 241 RCADI 195–374, 269. The theory of 'new custom' has been insightfully analyzed by Abi-Saab: G. Abi-Saab, 'La Coutume dans tous ses états ou le dilemme du développement du droit international général dans un monde éclaté', in *Essays in Honor of Roberto Ago* (Giuffrè, Milan, 1987) 62–5; See the tentative reconciliation between this modern custom and the traditional custom by A.E. Roberts, 'Traditional and Modern Approaches to Customary International Law: A Reconciliation' (2001) 95 AJIL 757.

[110] See generally S. Schwebel, 'The Effects of Resolutions of the UN General Assembly on Customary International Law' (1979) ASIL Proceedings 301; M. Bos, 'The Recognized Manifestations of International Law, A New Theory of the Sources' (1977) 20 German YBIL 9; K. Skubiszewski, 'Resolutions of the

new rule. It can also manifest itself by the absence of objection.[111] This custom-making process is more deductive than the classical inductive blueprint of customary international law,[112] for the classical subjective element allegedly takes precedence over actual practice.[113] Also, it is more normative in the sense that it is directed towards the promotion of moral considerations.[114]

Such an understanding of customary international law has been subject to very scathing criticisms, mostly because of its inconsistency with practice.[115] This is not the place to discuss these objections, however. For the sake of the argument made in this book, all that matters is to indicate that, should it be upheld both in practice and in theory, the formalization of the ascertainment-process of custom implied by this 'new custom' remains insufficient to formalize the custom-making process.[116] Leaving aside the satisfaction that such a conceptualization can provide to lawyers, the

UN General Assembly and Evidence of Custom', in *Essays in honor of Roberto Ago*, vol. I (Giuffrè, Milan, 1987) 503–13.

[111] See e.g. the conception of customary international law defended by the Special Tribunal for Lebanon, Appeals Chamber, *Decision on Appeals of Pre-Trial Judge's Order Regarding Jurisdiction and Standing*, CH/AC/2010/02, 10 November 2010, para. 47. Such a conception of *opinio juris* clearly runs against the traditional view expressed by the PCIJ in the *Lotus* case, PCIJ, Ser. A, No. 10, 1927, 28.

[112] For the classical inductive process, see ICJ, *Delimitation of the Maritime Boundary of the Gulf of Maine (Canada/United States of America)* ICJ Rep. (1984) 246 (Judgment of 12 October).

[113] B. Cheng also construes usage as only evidential. See B. Cheng, 'On the Nature and Sources of International Law', in B. Cheng (ed), *International Law: Teaching and Practice* (Stevens, London, 1982) 203, 224. B. Cheng is said to be the author who coined the expression 'instant custom' which can be seen as one manifestation of this new custom. See B. Cheng, 'United Nations Resolution on Outer Space: "Instant" International Customary Law?' (1965) 5 Indian J. Int'l L. 23. See also Judge Tanaka's dissenting opinion in the *South West Africa* (*Ethiopia v. South Africa; Liberia v. South Africa*), (Second Phase), ICJ Rep. (1966) 6, 291.

[114] For a few examples of such conceptualizations of customary international law, see Henkin, 'Human Rights and State "sovereignty"' (1995–96) 25 Ga. J. Int'l. & Comp. L. 31–45, 34–5; Meron, *Human Rights and Humanitarian Norms as Customary International Law* (OUP, Oxford, 1989) 2; R.B. Lillich, 'The Growing Importance of Customary International Human Rights Law' (1995–96) 25 Ga. J. Int'l. & Comp. L. 1–30, 8.

[115] See e.g. R. Jennings, 'The Identification of International Law', in B. Cheng (ed), *International Law: Teaching and Practice* (Stevens, London, 1982) 3, 6; P.-M. Dupuy, 'Théorie des sources et coutume en droit international contemporain' in *Le Droit international dans un monde en mutation: liber amicorum en hommage au Professeur Eduardo Jimenez de Arechaga* (Fundación de Cultura Universitaria, Montevideo, 1994) 51, 68; see A. D'Amato, 'Trashing Customary International Law' (1987) 81 AJIL 101; P.P. Kelly, 'The Twilight of Customary International Law' (2000) 40 Va J. Int'l L. 449, 451; F. Münch, 'A propos du droit spontané', in *Studi in onore di Giuseppe Sperduti*, (Giuffrè, Milan, 1984) 149–62; D. Vignes, 'La Coutume surgie de 1973 à 1982 n'aurait-elle pas écartée la codification comme source principale du droit de la mer?', in *Liber Amicorum honouring Ignaz Seidl-Hohenveldern, Law of Nations Law of International Organizations World's Economic Law* (Carl Heymanns Verlag KG, Cologne, 1988) 635–43. See also G. Ladreit de Lacharrière, 'Aspects du relativisme du droit international', in A. Bos and H. Siblesz (eds), *Realism in Law-Making, Essays on international law in honour of Willem Riphagen* (Martinus Nijhoff, Dordrecht, 1986) 89–99; B. Simma and P. Alston, 'The Sources of Human Rights Law: Custom, Jus Cogens and General Principles' (1988–1989) 12 Aust. YBIL 82.

[116] In the same sense, see G. Abi-Saab, 'La coutume dans tous ses états ou le dilemme du développement du droit international général dans un monde éclaté', in *Essays in honor of Roberto Ago*, vol. I (Giuffrè, Milan, 1987) 63–4.

making of such 'new customs' is no less contingent upon the fickle driving forces of the multilateral political decision-making processes and the will of States than 'traditional custom'. As a result, the ascertainment of such new customs is barely less indeterminate than that of its classical custom. Moreover, this new custom, because it puts the emphasis on the *opinio juris*, is often tinged with a taste of substantive validity,[117] which in itself fosters the resort to meta-principles for the identification of international legal rules, as is illustrated by some international case-law.[118] All-in-all, this concept of new custom thus does little to abate the predicaments associated with the non-formal ascertainment of customary international law.

As the debate about customary international law—cursorily depicted here—shows, in the absence of formal law-ascertainment criteria only the evidence of such a rule can be subject to formalism. As had been explained above,[119] the attempted formalization of the evidence of customary international law has done little to offset the indeterminacy inherent in the non-formal character of custom-ascertainment which has been described here. Leaving aside the formalization brought about by the codification of custom, only the institutionalization of the custom-making process allows the preservation of the normative character of customary international law. Such an institutionalization of customary international law would, however, require acceptance that law-applying authorities have custom-making powers which go beyond their traditional cognitivistic tasks, an idea that courts themselves usually balk at espousing.[120] This is why customary international law, unless it undergoes a radical formalization in the form of written transposition,[121] will long continue to constitute one of best illustrations of the cost associated with non-formal law-ascertainment in terms of the normative character of the rules concerned.[122]

[117] Cfr *supra* 5.1.

[118] See e.g. ICTY, Case No. IT-95–16-T, 14 January 2000, para. 527. On the approach of the ICTY towards customary international law, see the remarks of R.B. Baker, 'Customary International Law in the 21st Century' (2010) 21 EJIL 173–204.

[119] Cfr *supra* 7.1.

[120] Art. 38 of the ICJ Statute lends support to a strictly cognitivistic task of international courts. In the same vein, see ICJ, Advisory Opinion on the *Legality of the Threat or Use of Nuclear Weapons*, ICJ Rep. (1996-I) 237, para. 18 (according to which the Court 'states the existing law and does not legislate' and this is so 'even if, in stating and applying the law, the Court necessarily has to specify its scope and sometimes not its general trend'). On this debate, cfr *infra* chapter 8 note 48.

[121] A radical formalization has been put forward by D'Amato through the concept of *articulation* which ought to replace the two-element doctrine by an objective validator that will usually take the form of a written statement. While D'Amato's approach undoubtedly offers a useful model to formalize custom-ascertainment, it has failed to generate consensus. See e.g. the criticisms of that understanding in H. Thirlway, *International Customary Law and Codification* (Sijthoff, Leiden, 1972) 51–4; some measured support for D'Amato's theories is provided by N. Onuf, 'Global Law-Making and Legal Thought', in N. Onuf (ed), *Law-Making in the Global Community* (Carolina Academic Press, Durham, 1982) 1, 18.

[122] On the normative deficiencies of custom, see the remarks of A. Somek, 'Defective Law', *University of Iowa Legal Studies Research Paper* No. 10–33 (2010) available at <http://papers.ssrn.com/sol3/papers.cfm?abstract_id=1678156>.

General principles of law

Similar conclusions hold with respect to *general principles of law*. Mention of general principles has already been made on several occasions above.[123] It is only necessary here to recall that general principles were originally designed by Baron Descamps as a tool against *non liquet* that includes the resort to natural law principles before being subsequently re-construed as an emanation of domestic traditions. These domestic traditions from which general principles supposedly emanate often find a written expression in domestic constitutions, legislation, or case-law. Yet, as in the case of custom-identification, these written instruments do not constitute the basis on which general principles are ascertained. Their existence will be established by virtue of the convergence of these domestic traditions as is evaluated by the judge applying it. Moreover, as was explained above, the difficulty of collecting representative data of domestic traditions will simultaneously make a return to substantive law-ascertainment criteria almost inevitable,[124] thereby further moving the ascertainment of general principles away from the formal law-ascertainment by virtue of a written instrument.[125] It thus seems hardly disputable that the ascertainment of general principles of law is devoid of any formal character.[126]

Oral treaties

It is unanimously recognized that oral agreements can constitute a proper source of rights and obligations. The acceptance of oral agreements as a source of law dates back to the classical theory of the sources of international law.[127] Despite its scarcity in contemporary practice,[128] such sources are still accepted by international lawyers

[123] Cfr *supra* 4.2.1.

[124] In the same vein, see M. Koskenniemi, 'The Pull of the Mainstream' (1990) 88 Mich. L. Rev. 1946, 1950.

[125] For some additional critical remarks about general principles, see generally, B. Vitanyi, 'Les positions doctrinales concernant le sens de la notion de 'principes généraux reconnus par les nations civilisées' (1982) 86 *Revue générale de droit international public* 46; R. Kolb, 'Principles as Sources of International Law (With Special Reference to Good Faith)' (2006) 53 NILR 1; A. Cassese, *International Law* (2nd edn, OUP, Oxford 2005) 188; V. Degan, *Sources of International Law* (Kluwer Law International, The Hague, 1997) 14; A. Pellet, 'Article 38', in A. Zimmermann, C. Tomuschat, and K. Oellers-Frahm (eds), *The Statute of the International Court of Justice* (OUP, Oxford, 2002) 764–73.

[126] The illusion of formalism behind the general principles of law is well-illustrated by the scholarly debates reported in the seminal work of L. Siorat, *Le Problème des lacunes en droit international. Contribution à l'étude des sources du droit et de la fonction judiciaire* (LGDJ, Paris, 1958) 262. See also C. Rousseau, *Principes généraux du droit international public*, tome I (Pedone, Paris, 1944) 890–929. See also the Separate Opinion of Judge Cançado Trindade in the case pertaining to the *Pulp Mills (Argentina v. Uruguay)* before the ICJ, 20 April 2010, ICJ Rep. (2010) 6. For a similar criticism of the formalism of general principles, see M. Koskenniemi, 'The Pull of the Mainstream' (1990) 88 Mich. L. Rev. 1946, 1950.

[127] See De Martens, *Droit des gens* (Aillaud, Paris, 1831) 541. See also the mention of Grotius by P. Gautier, *Essai sur la définition des traités entre Etats* (Bruylant, Brussels, 1993) 85.

[128] See the oral declaration on the occasion of the signature of the Agreement on the Resolution of practical problems with respect to Deep Seabed Mining Areas, 14 August 1987, ILM (1987) 1508. On the quasi-inexistence of oral agreements in the practice, see A. Aust, *Modern Treaty Law and Practice* (CUP, Cambridge, 2007) 9; F. Capotorti, 'Cours general de droit international public' (1994-IV) 248 RCADI

nowadays.[129] The possibility of oral agreements is expressly recognized in the Vienna Convention. Indeed, although the Vienna Convention is not applicable to oral agreements, its article 3 expressly reserves the binding force of these agreements and the application of the rules of the Convention to them.[130] Unless recorded in writing, oral agreements cannot be ascertained by virtue of a written instrument and law-identification hinges on non-formal criteria like the orally expressed intent.[131] Such an indicator does not qualify as a formal indicator. It is therefore no surprise that such a law-ascertainment criterion has come with the difficulties commonly associated with non-formal law-ascertainment.[132] These difficulties have been deemed sufficiently serious to justify the omission of oral agreements from the various enterprises of codification of the law of treaties. Indeed, the 1928 Havana Convention on Treaties,[133] the codification undertaken by the Harvard Research in International Law in the 1930s,[134] and that undertaken by the ILC[135] in the 1960s have all excluded oral agreements from the ambit of their project.[136]

9–343, 153. Even in 1889, Baron Lambermont's award in the case of the Island of Lamu oral agreements was deemed odd as not reflecting international usages. See 'Arbitral sentence of Baron Lambermont in the Island of Lamu dispute' (1890) XXII *Revue de droit international et de législation comparée* 349–60.

[129] A. Aust, *Modern Treaty Law and Practice* (2nd edn, CUP, Cambridge, 2007) 9; P. Gautier, *Essai sur la définition des traités entre Etats* (Bruylant, Brussels, 1993) 85–8. See also P. Gautier, 'Article 2', in P. Klein and O. Corten (eds), *Les Conventions de Vienne sur le Droit des Traités. Commentaire article par article* (Bruylant, Bruxelles, 2006) 45, 55–6. See also Y. Bouthillier and J-F. Bonin, 'Article 3', in P. Klein and O. Corten (eds), ibid, 97, 103–5.

[130] Art. 3: 'International agreements not within the scope of the present Convention: The fact that the present Convention does not apply to international agreements concluded between States and other subjects of international law or between such other subjects of international law, or to international agreements not in written form, shall not affect: (a) the legal force of such agreements; (b) the application to them of any of the rules set forth in the present Convention to which they would be subject under international law independently of the Convention; (c) the application of the Convention to the relations of States as between themselves under international agreements to which other subjects of international law are also parties'.

[131] A. Aust, *Modern Treaty Law and Practice* (2nd edn, CUP, Cambridge, 2007) 9; P. Gautier, *Essai sur la définition des traités entre Etats* (Bruylant, Brussels, 1993) 85–8.

[132] The Harvard Research, for instance, voiced strong misgivings towards oral agreements. See the 1935 codification of the law of treaty by the Harvard Research (1935) 29 AJIL Sup. 691 ('Without the instrument, there is no evidence of an agreement, there is nothing to be interpreted or applied; in short there is no treaty apart from the instrument which records its stipulations'). This was already bemoaned by Rousseau, *Principes Généraux du droit international public*, vol. 1 (Pedone, Paris, 1944) 143. During the debates at the ILC, several members voiced the support for the idea that there cannot be a binding agreement without an instrument. See *Yearbook of the International Law Commission*, vol. I (1950) 64. See also the remarks by P. Reuter, *Introduction au Droit des Traités* (3rd edn, PUF, Paris, 1995) 27.

[133] Cited in (1935) 29 AJIL Sup 690.

[134] Ibid.

[135] On the reasons why the ILC decided not to include oral agreements in the scope of application of its articles, see ILC Rep. A/4169 (F) (A/14/9), 1959, chp. II, paras 8–20, 94–6; ILC Rep. A/5209 (F) (A/17/9), 1962, chp. II, paras 11–23, 178.

[136] Art. 2.1 VCLT: 'For the purposes of the present Convention: (a) "treaty" means an international agreement concluded between States in written form and governed by international law, whether embodied in a single instrument or in two or more related instruments and whatever its particular designation'.

Oral promises

Similar conclusions can be drawn as regards *oral promises* which came to be recognized as a source of law by the Permanent Court of International Justice in its decision in the famous *Eastern Greenland* case.[137] The ICJ confirmed the status of oral agreements as a source of international legal rules.[138] As in the case of oral agreements, the absence of a written instrument has inextricably barred promise-ascertainment from being based on formal criteria. Interestingly, the wording of the *Nuclear Test* case lent some support to the idea that 'publicity' plays a role in the ascertainment of legal promises,[139] an opinion also heard within the framework of the work of the ILC on unilateral acts.[140] The dominant opinion remains, however, that oral promises do not require publicity and that they are ascertained only by virtue of a non-formal indicator, i.e. the intent of their author.[141] The use of a non-formal criterion to ascertain oral promises has occasionally prompted some scholars to endow unilateral commitments made orally with some limited element of formalization, for instance through the construction of *pacta tertiis* (*stipulation pour autrui*).[142] As in the case of customary international law,[143] it is not certain that any of these endeavours has been successful in alleviating the problems inherent in the non-formal character of oral promise-ascertainment of formal law-ascertainment criteria.

Concluding remarks on legal rules ascertained short of any written instrument

The foregoing shows that, according to the mainstream theory of the sources of international law, there thus is a wide array of rules in international law which are ascertained short of any written instrument. In these instances, the law-ascertainment

[137] ICPJ, *Eastern Greenland* case, Series A/B, No. 53, 71.

[138] See ICJ, *Nuclear Tests* case *(Australia v. France)*, 20 December 1974, para. 43.

[139] See ICJ, *Nuclear Tests* case, ibid, para. 43: 'An undertaking of this kind, if given publicly, and with an intent to be bound, even though not made within the context of international negotiations, is binding'.

[140] Second report of the Special Rapporteur, A/CN.4/500, §55. On this question, see C. Goodman, 'Acta Sunt Servanda ? A Regime for Regulating the Unilateral Acts of States at International Law (2006) 25 Aust. YBIL 43, especially 58–9. The ILC eventually decided not to elevate publicity to a promise-ascertainment criterion. See recommendation n° 1 of the ILC working group, ILC Rep. (2003), A/58/10, § 306.

[141] On that point, see generally E. Suy, *Les actes juridiques unilatéraux en droit international public* (LGDI, Paris, 1962) 28; Harvard Research codification of the law of treaties (1935) 29 AJIL Sup 730; See also J. d'Aspremont, 'Les travaux de la Commission du droit international relatifs aux actes unilatéraux' (2005) 109 *Revue générale de droit international public* 163–89.

[142] On this debate see J.-P. Jacqué for whom there is no difference between promise and a treaty providing rights for third States. See Jacqué, 'A propos de la promesse unilatérale', D. Bardonnet (ed), *Mélanges Reuter: le droit international: unité et diversité* (Pedone, Paris, 1981) 327–45. See also the remarks of P. Gautier, *Essai sur la définition des traités entre Etats* (Bruylant, Brussels, 1993) 42. A common example of that approach is provided by ICJ, *Military and Paramilitary Activities in and against Nicaragua (Nicaragua v. United States of America)*, Merits, ICJ Rep. (1986). For the very opposite view, according to which conduct could suffice to demonstrate intention, see. K. Skubiszewski, 'Unilateral Acts of States', in M. Bedjaoui (ed), *International Law: Achievements and Prospects*, (UNESCO, Paris, 1991) 221–40, 223.

[143] Cfr *supra* 7.1 and 7.2.1.

criteria are practice, *opinio juris*, convergence of domestic traditions, or orally expressed intent. None of them is a formal identification criterion. Although material or procedural indicators can potentially play a supplementary ascertaining role as will be explained below,[144] the lack of written instrument in which the rule is enshrined constitutes a fundamental obstacle to formal law-identification.

It should be made absolutely clear that such a finding does not necessarily entail a call for the abolishment of these sources of international law.[145] Rather, it merely shows that recognizing customary international law, general principles of law, oral treaties, and oral promises as a source of international legal rules should stem from a conscious choice, i.e. a choice for non-formal law-ascertainment informed by an awareness of its costs, especially in terms of the normative character of the rules produced thereby.[146]

7.2.2 Rules ascertained by virtue of a written instrument: written treaties and other international legal acts

Rules that are identified by virtue of a written instrument are those originating in written treaties and all other international legal acts, including written promises and legal acts of international organizations. According to the most common theory of the sources of international law, an international treaty, written promise, or act of an international organization usually contains what its author(s) has wished. Indeed, it is to achieve a given purpose that one or several actors will make a norm and will possibly elevate it into a legal rule. The norm is classically called the *negotium*. If they enshrine the norm in a written instrument, the act which enshrines the norm is classically called the *instrumentum*. In that sense, the *instrumentum* is the 'container'.[147] The mainstream position provides that the authors of the legal act have

[144] Cfr *infra* 7.2.4.

[145] Contrast with the challenge to the binding effect of customary international law by C.A. Bradley and M. Gulati, 'Withdrawing from International Custom' (2010) 120 Yale L. J. 202, See the criticism by A. Roberts, 'Who Killed Article 38(1)(b)? A Reply to Bradley and Gulati', available at <http://ssrn.com/abstract=1607753>.

[146] Cfr *supra* 2.2.

[147] Such a distinction was already made by Kelsen, 'Theorie du droit international public' (1953-III) 84 RCADI, 1–203, 136. This distinction was also made by the special rapporteur Brierly of the ILC on the Law of Treaties: 'A certain linguistic difficulty must... inevitably pervade the framing of rules for the conclusion of treaties. This is especially the case when the term "treaty" is used primarily to connote the instrument or document embodying a binding agreement rather than the agreement itself.... It is innocuous provided that it does not obscure the real nature of treaty, which is a legal act or transaction, rather than a document', A/CN.4/32, *Yearbook of the International Law Commission*, vol. II (1950) para. 30. See also the report of Fitzmaurice, A/CN.4/101, *Yearbook of the International Law Commission*, vol. II (1956) article 14 and commentary No. 24. See also the dissenting opinion of Judge Basdevant, ICJ, Ambatelios, 1 July 1952, ICJ Rep. (1952) 169; See also 1935 codification of the Harvard Research (1935) 29 AJIL Sup 690. Some authors have preferred the words *actum* and *actus* to draw such a distinction between the content of the act and the instrument where it is enshrined: see J. Dehaussy, cited by J.-P. Jacqué, *Elements pour une théorie de l'acte juridique en Droit international public* (LDGJ, Paris, 1972) 52. Jacqué, however, draws a distinction between, on one hand, the *negotium-instrumentum* dichotomy, which are two constitutive elements of the legal act, and the *act-norm* dichotomy on the other hand. See

complete control over both the *negotium* and the *instrumentum*. In that sense, they determine both the content and the container.[148]

From the standpoint of the theory of law-ascertainment, it is fundamental to point out that *both the content and the container can potentially serve as a formal signpost that indicates whether the norm in question is an international legal rule.* Indeed, theoretically speaking, the pedigree of the legal rule could be sought in either a pre-defined given content or in a pre-defined type of container. This being said, it is noteworthy that, next to written treaties, there are many different kinds of international legal acts. International legal acts are very numerous, ranging from certain decisions of international organizations to judicial awards and decisions.[149] Each type of legal act is governed by a different type of regime and there is no such thing as a truly unitary legal regime of international legal acts.[150] In that sense, there are as many different regimes of legal acts as there are types of legal acts. Yet, despite this diversity, there is still a common denominator as to the main element of the ascertainment of most of these international legal acts, including written treaties: the decisive criterion to determine the nature of the rule is never sought in the *negotium* but only in the *instrumentum*, which provides the law-ascertainment indicator. Indeed, in mainstream theory of the sources of international law, it is upon the container (*instrumentum*) that the law-ascertainment role has been bestowed. In particular, the formulation of clear obligations has not been considered a *constitutive element* of any legal act.[151] It is true that, in the international legal scholarship, some authors have attempted to elevate the content of a norm into a formal criterion to ascertain international legal rules, the most famous of them being Hersch Lauterpacht.[152]

J.-P. Jacqué, *Elements pour une théorie de l'acte juridique en Droit international public* (LDGJ, Paris, 1972) 47–56.

[148] In the same vein, K. Raustiala, 'Form and Substance in International Agreements' (2005) 99 AJIL 581; H. Hillgenberg, 'A Fresh Look at Soft Law' (1999) 10 EJIL 499, 504–5. For a criticism of the correlative idea that States can freely decide to activate or not international law, see J. Klabbers, *The Concept of Treaty in International Law* (Kluwer, The Hague, 1996) and J. Klabbers, 'Not Re-Visiting the Concept of Treaty', in A. Orakhelashvili and S. Williams (eds), *40 Years of the Vienna Convention on the Law of Treaties* (BIICL, London, 2010). On the choice between law and non-law, see J. Klabbers, 'The Commodification of International Law' (2006) *Select Proceedings of the European Society of International Law*, vol. 1 (Hart, Oxford, 2008) 341–58. See also the account of the cost and benefits of non-law by C. Lipson, 'Why are some international agreements informal' (1991) 45 *International Organization* 495.

[149] See the typology of all the different international legal acts by Jacqué: J.-P. Jacqué, *Elements pour une théorie de l'acte juridique en Droit international public* (LDGJ, Paris, 1972) 311–477.

[150] P. Reuter, 'Principes de droit international public' (1961) 103 RCADI 425, 459–60; J.-P. Jacqué, *Elements pour une théorie de l'acte juridique en droit international public* (LDGJ, Paris, 1972) 18–20.

[151] For a classical example, see Rousseau, *Principes Généraux du droit international public*, vol. 1 (Pedone, Paris, 1944) 156–7; Basdevant, 'Règles générales du droit de la paix' (1936) 58 RCADI 471–692, 208.

[152] Separate Opinion of Judge Lauterpacht to the ICJ Decision of 6 July 1957 in the case concerning *Certain Norwegian Loans*, ICJ Rep. (1957) 48: 'An instrument in which a party is entitled to determine the existence of its obligation is not a valid and enforceable legal instrument of which a court of law can take cognizance. It is not a legal instrument. It is a declaration of a political principle and purpose'; See also his Dissenting Opinion to the ICJ decision of 21 March 1959 in the *Interhandel* case, ICJ Rep. (1959) 116. This also permeates his work as Special Rapporteur on the Law of Treaties of the International Law Commission. See generally *ILC Report*, A/2456 (A/8/9), 1953, chp. V(II)(i), para 164 and *ILC Report*, A/

Likewise, it has sometimes been contended that the objective function of the norm, rather than the instrument, should be considered the criterion to distinguish law from non-law.[153] However—and despite some ambiguous wording of the ICJ once hinting at the opposite,[154] this understanding of law-ascertainment has remained isolated. The *instrumentum* has usually been preferred to the *negotium* as the basis for the ascertainment of written treaties and other international legal acts.[155]

As a result, the *negotium* has been left without any law-ascertainment effect in the theory of the sources of international law. Legal acts whose content is totally non-normative, that is acts that fail to provide any precise directive as to which behaviour its authors are committed to follow, can still qualify as international legal rules.[156]

2693 (A/9/9), 1954, chp. I (III), para. 8. See also 1935 codification of the law of treaty by the Harvard Research (1935) 29 AJIL Sup. 692; P. Gautier, *Essai sur la définition des traités entre Etats* (Bruylant, Brussels, 1993) 63–74. Interestingly, some of these scholars have even subsequently relented from this view. Compare J.-P. Jacqué, *Elements pour une théorie de l'acte juridique en Droit international public* (LDGJ, Paris, 1972) 69–70 and J-P. Jacqué, 'Acte et norme en droit international' (1991-II) 227 RCADI 357–417, 383.

153 See R. Ago, 'Positive Law and International Law' (1957) 51 AJIL 691, in particular 727–8: 'Certain norms can be qualified as legal because of characteristics belonging objectively to the norms themselves because of their function as norms of law and not as a mere reflection of their origin'.

154 See ICJ, *Maritime Delimitation and Territorial Questions between Qatar and Bahrain (Qatar v. Bahrain)*, 1 July 1994, para. 25: 'the Minutes are not a simple record of a meeting, similar to those drawn up within the framework of the Tripartite Committee; they do not merely give an account of discussions and summarize points of agreement and disagreement. They enumerate the commitments to which the Parties have consented. They thus create rights and obligations in international law for the Parties. They constitute an international agreement'. On this point, see the Dissenting Opinion of Judge Oda, ICJ Rep. (2004) 133.

155 For a classical affirmation of that position, see P. Reuter, *Introduction au Droit des Traités* (3d edn, PUF, Paris, 1995) 30. For a criticism of that conceptual construction according to which States, through the choice of *instrumentum*, can freely decide to activate or not international law, see J. Klabbers, *The Concept of Treaty in International Law* (Kluwer, The Hague, 1996) (who argues that once States have reached agreement, international law will attach certain legal effects to such agreements without it being a matter of choice to for the parties). More recently, see J. Klabbers, 'Not Re-Visiting the Concept of Treaty', in A. Orakhelashvili and Sarah Williams (eds), *40 Years of the Vienna Convention on the Law of Treaties* (BIICL, London, 2010).

156 Numerous treaties nowadays enshrine such a soft *negotium*. One of the most obvious examples is provided by the 1995 Framework Convention on the protection of national minorities of the Council of Europe, which deliberately falls short of defining the concept of minorities, leaving it to the parties to determine whether there are national minorities on their territory. See the Explanatory Report of the Convention, para. 12, available at <http://conventions.coe.int>. See also the declaration of 11 May 1995 by Germany or the declaration of 23 March 1998 by Slovenia, available at <http://conventions.coe.int>. On the legal problems generated by these convention instruments, see generally J. d'Aspremont 'Les réserves aux traités. Observations à la lumière de la Convention-cadre du Conseil de l'Europe pour la protection des minorités nationales' in *Les Minorités, Recueil des travaux de l'Association Henri Capitant*, tome LII/2002 (UNAM, Mexico City, 2002) 487–514. Another example of instruments with a soft *negotium* is provided by those agreements which are not self-sufficient, in the sense that they require complementary instruments for their scope to be fully defined. This is commonly the case of framework conventions which abound in the field of environmental law or nuclear non-proliferation. These types of soft *negotium* usually come with provisions that require the parties to adopt complementary instruments (*pacta de contrahendo* or *de negociando*) that will flesh out the directives contained in the original instrument. For an example of this sort of provision, see for instance art. III.4 of the non-proliferation treaty. See the illustrations provided by A. Kiss, 'Les traités-cadres: une technique juridique caractéristique du droit international de l'environnement '(1993) 39 *Annuaire français de droit international* 792. See also, R.–J. Dupuy, 'Declaratory Law and

I have elsewhere dubbed these sorts of international legal rules 'rules with a *soft negotium*'[157] and argued that, if the concept of 'soft law' is to make any sense, it is in connection therewith.[158] It is not necessary to revert to that demonstration here.

This *instrumentum*-based ascertainment of international legal acts and treaties is not only doctrinal. It is also strictly followed by international law-applying authorities, and especially the ICJ. For instance, in the *North Sea Continental Shelf* case, the Court deemed that the principle of equidistance enshrined in article 6 of the 1958 Convention on the Continental Shelf was not normative but did not challenge its legal character.[159] Likewise, in the case pertaining to the *Military and Paramilitary Activities in Nicaragua*, the Court, despite contending that article 3(d) of the Charter of the Organization of American States[160] does not provide for any sort of obligation to the parties,[161] did not reject its legal character. The same is true with respect to its judgment on the preliminary objections in the *Oil Platforms* case. In that case, although it considered that article I of the 1955 Treaty of Amity, Economic Relations and Consular Rights between Iran and the United States according to

Programmatory Law: From Revolutionary Custom to "Soft Law"', in R. Akkerman et al. (eds), *Declarations on Principles. A Quest for Universal Peace* (A.W. Sijthoff, Leyden, 1977) 247, 254; See also the advisory opinion of the ICJ on the *International Status of South-West Africa*, 11 July 1950, ICJ Rep. 128, especially 140.

[157] This is what has been called by some authors 'conventional resolutions'. See R.-J. Dupuy, ibid, 247, 252. It has also been seen as an instrument with a "soft formulation". See A. Boyle and C. Chinkin, *The Making of International Law* (OUP, Oxford, 2007) 220. On 'preambles' which can be considered to be soft *negotium*, see E. Suy, 'Le Préambule', in E. Yakpo and T. Boumedra (eds) *Liber Amicorum M. Bedjaoui* (Kluwer, The Hague, 1999) 253–69.

[158] J. d'Aspremont, 'Softness in International Law: A Self-Serving Quest for New Legal Materials' (2008) 9 EJIL 1075. Baxter is probably the first author to have interpreted soft law in this sense. See 'International Law in "Her Infinite Variety"' (1980) 29 ICLQ 549; H. Hillgenberg, 'A Fresh look at Soft Law' (1999) 10 EJIL 499, 499–515, especially 500; T. Gruchalla-Wesierski, 'A Framework for Understanding "Soft Law"' (1984) 30 McGill L. J. 37–88, 39; A.E. Boyle, 'Some Reflections on the Relationship of Treaties and Soft Law' (1999) 48 ICLQ 901; G. Abi-Saab, 'Eloge du 'droit assourdi'—Quelques réflexions sur le rôle de la soft law en droit international contemporain', in *Nouveaux itinéraires en droit: Hommage à François Rigaux* (Bruylant, Brussels, 1993) 59, 61. More recently, see A. Boyle and C. Chinkin, *The Making of International Law* (OUP, Oxford, 2007) 220; G. Abi-Saab, 'Cours général de droit international public' (1987-VIII) 270 RCADI 9–463, 209–13; J. d'Aspremont, 'Les dispositions non-normatives des actes juridiques conventionels' (2003) 36 *Revue Belge de Droit International* 496–522, 520; See however, V. Lowe, *International Law* (Clarendon, Oxford, 2007) 96 (who rejects the use of soft law to refer to legal acts with a soft content). For a criticism of the concept of soft law in the sense of soft *negotium*, see K. Raustiala, 'Form and Substance in International Agreements' (2005) 99 AJIL 581, 589.

[159] ICJ Rep. (1969) para. 72. In that particular instance, this finding led the Court to conclude that this rule could not crystallize or generate a rule of customary international law. For an analysis of this aspect of the case, see J. d'Aspremont, 'Les dispositions non-normatives des actes juridiques conventionnels' (2003) 36 *Revue Belge de Droit International* 496–522, 518. See also A. Boyle and C. Chinkin, *The Making of International Law* (OUP, Oxford, 2007) 221.

[160] Art. 3(d) OAS Charter reads: 'The Solidarity of the American States and the high aims which are sought through it require the political organization of those States on the basis of the effective exercise of representative democracy'.

[161] ICJ Rep. (1986) para. 259–61. For an analysis of this aspect of the case, see J. d'Aspremont, 'Les dispositions non-normatives des actes juridiques conventionnels' (2003) 36 *Revue Belge de Droit International* 496–522, 518.

which 'there shall be firm and enduring peace and sincere friendship' did not contain any obligation, it did not disqualify it as an international legal rule.[162]

According to the model of formal law-ascertainment in international law presented here, the container (*instrumentum*) of the rule is thus where the element that allows a distinction between law and non-law must be sought. In other words, the classical understanding of the source thesis in the theory of the sources of international law shows—leaving aside customary international law, general principles, and oral treaties and oral promises, which remain identified on the basis of non-formal criteria[163]—that international legal rules are ascertained through the pedigree provided by the written instrument in which it is enshrined. Resorting to the *instrumentum* for the sake of law-identification constitutes the basis—still useful in my view—for formal ascertainment of international legal rules contained in international treaties and other international legal acts. Yet, as it will now be explained, actual formal law-identification of treaties and other international legal acts has remained frustrated in mainstream theory of the sources by the ultimate role bestowed upon intent in the identification of treaties and other international legal acts, despite law-ascertainment being operated on the basis of the *instrumentum*.

7.2.3 Deficiencies of formal law-identification in traditional source doctrines: the lingering law-ascertaining role of intent

It is argued here that, even though the abovementioned model of formal law-ascertainment based on the *instrumentum* lays down an adequate framework for formal law-ascertainment, this classical model has proved unsatisfactory when it comes to determine those indicators contained in the written instrument that make the rules enshrined therein international legal rules. This is particularly true with respect to the identification of international treaties and unilateral promises in international law.

It surely is not the place to re-evaluate the literature found in the collection of existing books and articles devoted to the definition of international legal acts, and in particular international treaties and unilateral acts.[164] It suffices to mention the uncontroversial finding that the identification of international treaties and unilateral promises remains very precarious in the mainstream theory of the sources of international law, despite attempts to codify their regime.[165] Indeed, law-ascertainment of written treaties and written unilateral promises is made exclusively

[162] ICJ Rep. (1996) paras 28 and 31.

[163] Cfr *supra* 7.2.1.

[164] For an insightful reconsideration of that literature, see J. Klabbers, *The Concept of Treaty in International Law* (Kluwer, The Hague, 1996).

[165] On the regime governing international treaties, see the Vienna Conventions on the Law of Treaties of 1969 and 1986 and the commentary of P. Klein and O. Corten (eds), *Les Conventions de Vienne sur le Droit des Traités. Commentaire article par article* (Bruylant, Bruxelles, 2006). On the unsuccessful codification of the legal regime of unilateral acts, see the work of the ILC and the comments of J. d'Aspremont, 'Les travaux de la Commission du droit international relatifs aux actes unilatéraux' (2005) 109 *Revue générale de droit international public* 163–89.

dependent on the intent of the authors of these acts. For instance, as far as treaties are concerned, it is well-known that the yardstick purportedly provided by the Vienna Convention ('governed by international law') is of little use, for it only refers to the consequence of an agreement being identified as a legal agreement rather than its ascertainment as a legal agreement.[166] Although the Vienna Convention is silent as to the decisive treaty-ascertainment criterion, it is uncontested in the view of the ILC that the legal nature of an act hinges on the intent of the parties. Indeed, apart from Fitzmaurice who sought to make it an explicit criterion,[167] the ILC and its Special Rapporteurs took it for granted and did not deem it necessary to specify it in their definition of a treaty.[168] This opinion is shared by most international legal scholars.[169] The same is true with respect to unilateral written declarations, which are considered to enshrine an international legal rule if their authors' intent to be bound can be demonstrated.[170]

This mainstream position as to the decisive criterion for the determination of the nature of the written instrument significantly changes the nature of the ascertainment of legal acts. Indeed, while the general framework of the ascertainment of international legal acts described above provides the foundation for a law-identification centred on the written instrument in which the rule is incorporated, the nature of that instrument is thus ultimately identified through the material source of law, i.e. the intent of its author. In other words, although law-ascertainment remains, on the surface, formal because it hinges on the existence of a written instrument, the legal nature of that instrument is itself determined on the basis of a non-formal criterion: *intent*.[171]

It is argued here that nothing could be more at loggerheads with formal law-identification than the intent-based law-ascertainment criterion that does not require

166 Fitzmaurice had explicitly made a distinction between the law-ascertainment criterion and the consequence of an agreement being ascertained as a treaty. See *ILC Report*, A/3159 (F) (A/11/9), 1956, chp. III(I), para. 34.

167 *ILC Report*, A/3159 (F) (A/11/9), 1956, chp. III(I), para. 34.

168 *ILC Report*, A/6309/Rev.1 (F) (A/21/9), 1966, part I(E), paras 11–12, and part II, chp. II, paras 9–38.

169 Among others, see A. Aust, *Modern Treaty Law and Practice* (2nd edn, CUP, Cambridge, 2007) 20; R. Jennings and A. Watts (eds), *Oppenheim's International Law*, vol. 1 (9th edn, Longman, London, 1992) 1202; J. Klabbers, *The Concept of Treaty in International Law* (Kluwer, The Hague, 1996) 68; M. Fitzmaurice, 'The Identification and Character of Treaties and Treaty Obligations Between States in International Law' (2003) 73 BYIBL 141, 145 and 165–6; A. Orakhelashvili, *The Interpretation of Acts and Rules in Public International Law* (OUP, Oxford, 2008) 59. See also the general remarks of I. Seidl-Hohenveldern, 'Hierarchy of Treaties', in J. Klabbers and R. Lefeber, *Essays on the Law of Treaties. A Collection of Essays in Honour of Bert Vierdag* (Martinus Nijhoff, 1998) 7. See J.-P. Jacqué, *Elements pour une théorie de l'acte juridique en Droit international public* (LDGJ, Paris, 1972) 121; See C. Chinkin, 'A Mirage in the Sand? Distinguishing Binding and Non-Binding Relations Between States' (1997) 10 LJIL 223–47.

170 ICJ, *Nuclear Tests* case *(Australia v. France)*, 20 December 1974, para. 43: 'When it is the intention of the State making the declaration that it should become bound according to its terms, that intention confers on the declaration the character of a legal undertaking'. See E. Suy, *Les actes juridiques unilatéraux en droit international public* (LGDJ, Paris, 1962) 28.

171 See e.g. A. Orakhelashvili, *The Interpretation of Acts and Rules in Public International Law* (OUP, Oxford, 2008) 59–60. See the other examples mentioned in 3.2.2.

intent to materialize in a linguistic or a material sign. Indeed, such a criterion ultimately bases the identification of international legal acts on a fickle and indiscernible psychological element and inevitably brings about the same difficulties as those encountered in the ascertainment of oral promises and oral treaties. Despite making a detour through a formal instrument for the identification of legal rules, the ascertainment of international legal acts cannot, in the end, evade the non-formal character of ascertainment inherent in the necessity to establish the intent. By the same token, the use of intent as a law-ascertainment criterion, at least if intent is to be unearthed from the content of the rules and not from procedural and material indicators,[172] leads to a conflation between law-ascertainment and the interpretation of the content of the rules[173] and necessitates the use of the rules of interpretation of the content of rules for an operation which is intrinsically alien to it.[174]

It is true that the intent upon which the identification of international legal acts depends should be distinguished from another type of intent. Indeed, the intent of international lawmakers has multiple implications in the classical sources doctrine. Intent determines whether the rule in question is law or not. Intent is also instrumental in the determination of the extent of the rights and obligations provided by the rule. It is this dimension of intent that the criteria laid down in article 31 of the Vienna Convention are aimed at capturing. A distinction must thus be drawn between intent as to the nature of the norm and intent as to the extent (and content) of the rule. As far as law-ascertainment is concerned, only *the intent to make law* matters.[175] The intent as to the content of the law is of no relevance to the determination of the nature of the international legal act in which the rule is incorporated.

Although the intent to make law and the intent as to the content of the law ought to be distinguished, it is noteworthy that the criteria devised to determine these two types of intent have followed a rather similar pattern in the theory of the sources of international law, oscillating between the intent as it is expressed (*volonté déclarée*) and the allegedly original or actual intent (*intention réelle*).[176] According to the blueprint provided by article 31 of the Vienna Convention, the establishment of the intent as to the content of the rule hinges—in order of their importance—on its terms, its object and purpose, and, ultimately, the context in which it is made.[177]

[172] On the use of material and procedural indicators, see 7.2.4.

[173] Cfr *supra* 7.1.

[174] In the same vein, see O. Corten, *Méthodologie du droit international public* (Editions de l'Université de Bruxelles, Brussels 2009) 213–14. See also *supra* 7.1.

[175] J.-P. Jacqué, *Elements pour une théorie de l'acte juridique en droit international public* (LDGJ, Paris, 1972) 121.

[176] See J.-P. Jacqué, ibid, 113. See also J. Kammerhofer, *Uncertainty in International Law: A Kelsenian Perspective* (Routledge, London, 2010) 88. For a relativization of this distinction, see P. Reuter, *Introduction au Droit des Traités* (3rd edn, PUF, Paris, 1995) 27.

[177] Art. 31—'General rule of interpretation: 1. A treaty shall be interpreted in good faith in accordance with the ordinary meaning to be given to the terms of the treaty in their context and in the light of its object and purpose. 2. The context for the purpose of the interpretation of a treaty shall comprise, in addition to the text, including its preamble and annexes: (a) any agreement relating to the treaty which was made between all the parties in connection with the conclusion of the treaty; (b) any instrument which was

Thus, to determine the content of a conventional rule, the *volonté déclarée* is the overarching criterion, only seconded by the *intention réelle*. Interestingly, according to the case-law of the ICJ, manifestations of intent to make law are classically sought in the terms of the *instrumentum*,[178] that is in the *volonté déclarée*. However, because the *volonté déclarée* as reflected in the terms of the *instrumentum* can be beset by uncertainty, attention has also been paid to the *intention réelle* that manifests itself in the *circumstances* of the adoption of the legislation concerned.[179]

Leaving aside this resemblance between the criteria devised for the determination of the intent to be bound and the intent as to the scope of the obligation, it must only be stressed here that, even taken together, these criteria have failed to provide a firm and reliable yardstick to capture the intent of the lawmakers to make law. The identification of a treaty or a unilateral promise has remained a deeply speculative operation aimed at reconstructing the author(s)' intent.[180] The intent-based ascertainment of international legal acts has yielded contradictions which may partly explain why international legal scholars have been lured by the effect- (or impact-) based or process-based models of law-ascertainment presented in chapter 5. Indeed, as with any formalization of evidence, the attempt to formalize the establishment of law simultaneously fosters the formalism in legal reasoning of law-applying authorities without easing the indeterminacy of law-ascertainment criteria.[181] As this book is not concerned with formalism in legal reasoning, it is only of consequence to point out that, whatever its consequences for legal reasoning, the intent-based criteria of ascertainment of international legal acts fall short of ensuring a formal identification of international legal rules.

It is worthy of mention that the inevitable non-formal character of law-ascertainment associated with the establishment of the intent to be bound in order to determine the nature of international acts has prodded international lawyers, including international judges, to devise similar attitudes to those witnessed in the context of customary international law.[182] Indeed, confronted with the impossibility of

made by one or more parties in connection with the conclusion of the treaty and accepted by the other parties as an instrument related to the treaty. 3. There shall be taken into account, together with the context: (a) any subsequent agreement between the parties regarding the interpretation of the treaty or the application of its provisions; (b) any subsequent practice in the application of the treaty which establishes the agreement of the parties regarding its interpretation; (c) any relevant rules of international law applicable in the relations between the parties. 4. A special meaning shall be given to a term if it is established that the parties so intended.' See the remarks of A. Aust, *Modern Treaty Law and Practice* (2nd edn, CUP, Cambridge, 2007) 234.

[178] ICJ, *Aegean Sea Continental Shelf (Greece v. Turkey)*, Judgment of 19 December 1978, paras 95–107 (emphasis is put on the actual terms and circumstances).

[179] As regards the identification of international treaties, see ICJ, *Aegean Sea Continental Shelf*, ibid, paras 95–107: emphasis is put on the actual terms and circumstances.

[180] In the same vein see J. Klabbers, *The Concept of Treaty in International Law* (Kluwer, The Hague, 1996) 11. See also the remarks of G.M. Danilenko, *Law-Making in the International Community* (Martinus Nijhoff, Dordrecht, 1993) 57 (who pleads for the necessity of a formal act of acceptance).

[181] See C. Chinkin, 'A Mirage in the Sand? Distinguishing Binding and Non-Binding Relations Between States' (1997) 10 LJIL 244–7. M. Koskenniemi, *From Apology to Utopia* (CUP, Cambridge, 2005) 585.

[182] These attitudes have been described above. See *supra* 7.1 and 7.2.1.

establishing the intent to be bound on the basis of formal criteria, international scholars and judges have, again, engaged in a formalization of the evidentiary process.[183] This has particularly been the tendency of the ICJ, which has striven to devise something of a methodology for ascertaining the intent of the parties.[184] The methodology used by the Court, on top of lacking clear consistency, has failed to alleviate the problems inherent in the establishment of intent. This is why we have been left in a bind when it comes to establishing the intent with a view to distinguishing law from non-law.[185] The difficulty of systematizing intent probably explains why, more recently, the Court seems to have backed away from attempting to offer a clear methodology in this respect, as is illustrated by its decisions in the case of the *Land and Maritime Boundary between Cameroon and Nigeria*[186] and the case of *Pulp Mills on the River Uruguay.*[187]

7.2.4 A limited abatement: the translation of intent in the use of material or procedural indicators

In most domestic and regional legal systems the use of material and procedural indicators, be they sanction, certification, seal, or publication, plays a paramount law-ascertaining role. Given the low institutionalization of the international legal system, such material and procedural signs are less systematically used and their role is therefore more limited. Yet, in international law, the use of material or procedural indicators is not totally absent as the resort to such signs undoubtedly helps assuage problems inherent in the law-ascertaining role of intent.[188] Indeed, when it comes to

[183] See e.g. K. Widdows 'On the Form and Distinctive Nature of International Agreements' (1976–7) 7 Aust. YBIL 114. On this point, see the remarks of M. Fitzmaurice, 'The Identification and Character of Treaties and Treaty Obligations Between States in International Law' (2003) 73 BYBIL 141, 145.

[184] As regards the identification of international treaties, see ICJ, *Aegean Sea Continental Shelf (Greece v. Turkey)*, Judgment of 19 December 1978, paras 95–107: emphasis is put on the actual terms and circumstances. Compare *Maritime Delimitation and Territorial Questions between Qatar and Bahrain (Qatar v. Bahrain)*, Judgment of 1 July 1994. Regarding the identification of unilateral promise, see ICJ, *Nuclear Tests (Australia v. France)*, 20 December 1974, para. 43; *Military and Paramilitary Activities in and against Nicaragua (Nicaragua v. United States of America)*, Merits, ICJ Rep. (1986). See ICJ, *Burkina-Faso Mali.* See the remarks of J. Klabbers, 'Qatar v. Bahrain: the concept of "treaty" in international law' (1995) 33 ARV 361–76.

[185] See generally J. Klabbers, *The Concept of Treaty in International Law* (Kluwer, The Hague, 1996) especially 245–50.

[186] See the laconic consideration of the Court regarding the nature of the Maroua Declaration adopted by Cameroon and Nigeria in Land and Maritime Boundary between Cameroon and Nigeria *(Cameroon v. Nigeria: Equatorial Guinea intervening)*, 10 October 2002, para. 263 ('The Court considers that the Maroua Declaration constitutes an international agreement concluded between States in written form and tracing a boundary; it is thus governed by international law and constitutes a treaty in the sense of the Vienna Convention on the Law of Treaties (see Art. 2, para. l), to which Nigeria has been a party since 1969 and Cameroon since 1991, and which in any case reflects customary international law in this respect').

[187] ICJ, *Pulp Mills on the River Uruguay (Argentina v. Uruguay)*, Judgment of 20 April 2010, para. 138.

[188] See generally, J. Klabbers, *The Concept of Treaty in International Law* (Kluwer, The Hague, 1996) 68–86. See P. Gautier, *Essai sur la définition des traités entre Etats*, (Bruylant, Brussels, 1993) 78–85; M. Fitzmaurice, 'The Identification and Character of Treaties and Treaty Obligations Between States in International Law' (2003) 73 BYBIL 149–56.

treaty-making, States are most of the time mindful of the frontier between a legal instrument and a non-legal instrument,[189] as is illustrated by the recent contemporary practice of international law-making in relation to global-warming and climate change.[190] This is why they generally take pains to ensure that the law-making procedure employed or the instrument finally adopted indicates what they intended regarding the legal or non-legal nature of the rules they have agreed on.[191] For instance, the requirement that the instrument be ratified to enter into force[192] will usually be considered an indication that they intended the agreement to be of a legal nature. Likewise, States can accompany the making of the norm with sufficient solemn signs or material indicators, like a solemn signature ceremony. Through material or procedural indicators, international lawmakers often make sure to show the nature of the instrument of regulation that they adopt.

The abatement to the indeterminacy inherent in the law-ascertaining role of intent offered by the use of material and procedural pointers nonetheless remains limited. Indeed, despite the usual awareness of lawmakers of what is law and non-law in treaty-making processes, and their intent to translate their will in material or procedural acts, not all instruments or norm-making processes reveal the intent of the author of the norms as to their legal nature. On the contrary, it happens regularly that international agreements, in spite of the use of material and procedural indicators, prove very evasive and ambiguous as to the intent of their authors regarding their nature.[193]

Moreover, even in the presence of material or procedural indicators, treaties and other international legal acts can still fail to contain any clear pointer as to the intent of their authors. Indeed, the ambiguity as to the nature of the act may be consciously sought by the authors of the norm, for, if embroiled in a dispute, they may one day benefit from the absence of an express indication as to the nature of the instrument

[189] In the same vein, D. Shelton, 'Soft Law' in D. Armstrong (ed), *Handbook of International Law* (Routledge, London, 2009) 68, 78 or K. Raustiala, 'Form and Substance in International Agreements' (2005) 99 AJIL 581, 887; A. Aust, who argues that such clear awareness is reflected in the terminology of agreements: A. Aust, *Modern Treaty Law and Practice* (2nd edn, CUP, Cambridge, 2007) 33; C. Lipson, 'Why are some international agreements informal' (1991) 45 *International Organization* 495.

[190] See e.g. the conscious choice of a majority of States during the negotiating process about a new framework to tackle global-warming in the second half of 2009, whereby States decided that any agreement they could reach would take the form of a political agreement and not an international legal act. See H. Cooper and B. Knowlton, 'Leaders delay action on climate agreement', *International Herald Tribune*, 16 November 2009, 1.

[191] See the remarks by Jacqué: J.-P. Jacqué, *Elements pour une théorie de l'acte juridique en droit international public* (LDGJ, Paris, 1972) 128. See also J. Klabbers, *The Concept of Treaty in International Law* (Kluwer Law International, The Hague, 1996) 68–86. See P. Gautier, *Essai sur la définition des traités entre Etats* (Bruylant, Brussels, 1993) 78–85. This choice between law and non-law has been called by J. Klabbers the 'Commodification of International Law'. See J. Klabbers, 'The Commodification of International Law' (2006) *Select Proceedings of the European Society of International Law*, vol. 1 (Hart, Oxford, 2008) 341–58.

[192] See art. 14 of the 1969 Vienna Convention.

[193] See the call of K. Widdows for a greater use of labels by States in their treaty-making practice 'On the Form and Distinctive Nature of International Agreements' (1976–7) 7 Aust. YBIL 114, 128.

and deny that they ever intended to be bound by a legal rule.[194] Furthermore, it may well be that the authors of the norm have used one of the abovementioned material or procedural signs but these signs prove too uncertain to constitute evidence of intent to make law.[195] This is well-illustrated by the case-law of the ICJ.[196] Eventually, the current trend of resorting to non-formal and fast norm-making processes at the international level entails an increasingly limited use of evidentiary signs of their intent by the authors of international norms, thereby leaving the ascertainment of treaties and other international legal acts further in limbo. This is why it often happens that international treaties and other international legal acts do not reveal the intent of the parties.

It will thus not come as a surprise that this limited role of material and procedural indicators in international law-making hardly curbs the speculative character of intent-based law-ascertainment. This is a reason why suggestions have been made to abandon intent as a criterion of legal act-ascertainment.[197] There is much truth and merit to this suggestion. Such propositions, however, have yet to be endorsed and substantiated by the international legal scholarship and law-applying authorities. It is the aim of the following paragraphs to complement these propositions and propose some avenues through which we can go beyond the intent-based ascertainment of international legal acts. The ambition here is not to revamp the theory of the sources of international law but, more modestly, to provide a framework for the revitalization of the current configuration of the source thesis in international law by severing the ascertainment of legal acts from intent, the latter being construed as nothing more than a material source of law and not a law-ascertainment criterion. It will be shown that, although the framework put forward here remains, to a large extent, a theoretical construction, some underpinnings for the use of written linguistic indicators as law-ascertainment criteria can already be found in contemporary practice.[198]

[194] See e.g. ICJ, *Maritime Delimitation and Territorial Questions between Qatar and Bahrain (Qatar v. Bahrain)*, 1 July 1994, paras 21–30. See the remarks of C. Chinkin, 'A Mirage in the Sand? Distinguishing Binding and Non-Binding Relations Between States', (1997) 10 LJIL 223–47. See also M. Koskenniemi, *From Apology to Utopia* (CUP, Cambridge, 2005) 585.

[195] See the Separate Opinion of Judge Ago appended to the judgment of 26 November 1984 of the ICJ, *Military and Paramilitary Activities in and against Nicaragua*, para. 31; This opposite is also true. There are many international instruments carved in the form of international treaties or adopted as a result of solemn procedures which have not been intended to be legal instruments. See e.g. 1975 Helsinki Final Act, available at <http://www.osce.org/mc/39501>; see also the Charter of Economic Rights and Duties of States, Resolution of the General Assembly 3281 (XXIX), A/RES/29/3281, 12 December 1974.

[196] ICJ, *Aegean Sea Continental Shelf (Greece v. Turkey)*, Judgment of 19 December 1978, paras 95–107; ICJ, *Maritime Delimitation and Territorial Questions between Qatar and Bahrain (Qatar v. Bahrain)*, Judgment of 1 July 1994, para. 28.

[197] J. Klabbers, *The Concept of Treaty in International Law*, (Kluwer, The Hague, 1996) especially 245–50.

[198] Cfr *infra* 7.3.2.

7.3 Devising Formal Law-Ascertainment of International Legal Rules Beyond Intent

As the previous sections have shown, the ascertainment of rules originating in customary law, general principles, oral promises, and oral agreements cannot be made formal despite scholarly endeavours in this regard. When it comes to treaties and other international legal acts which are included in a written instrument, it has been explained that both the content (*negotium*) and the container (*instrumentum*) can potentially serve as a formal signpost that indicates whether the norm in question is an international legal rule. Yet, in the mainstream source doctrines presented above,[199] it has been shown that it is upon the container (*instrumentum*) that a law-ascertaining role has been bestowed, thereby laying down a solid framework for formal law-ascertainment.

In my opinion, the abovementioned classical pattern that grounds the ascertainment of treaties and other international legal acts in the *instrumentum* still provides an adequate framework for formal law-ascertainment in international law. Indeed, whether we frame the discussion in terms of 'sources',[200] 'objective validators',[201] or 'formal law-creating processes',[202] the need to ground formal law-ascertainment in the written instrument in which the rule is enshrined ought to remain, in my view, unchallenged. In that sense, the use of the *instrumentum* should continue to be favoured as the basis on which legal rules originating in treaties and other international legal acts are ascertained, for it constitutes the only possible framework for the formal ascertainment of international legal rules.

Because the formal character of law-ascertainment inherent in the use of the *instrumentum* has been distorted in mainstream theory by the subsequent resort to intent as the decisive law-identification criterion, I nonetheless submit that we should back away from classical theory of the sources of international law with respect to the ultimate intent-based law-ascertainment criterion of treaties and other international legal acts. While such a plea for a move away from intent as a direct law-ascertainment criteria, as was indicated above, is not unheard in the international legal scholarship,[203] I more specifically contend that intent as a law-ascertainment criterion ought to be replaced, in practice as well as in our doctrines of sources, by a systematic use of *written linguistic indicators* in the making of treaties and other

[199] Cfr *supra* 7.2.1.

[200] This corresponds with the mainstream approach to law-ascertainment. Cfr *supra* 3.2.2.

[201] A. D'Amato, 'What "Counts" as Law?' in N.G. Onuf (ed), *Law-Making in the Global Community* (Carolina Academic Press, Durham, 1982) 83–107.

[202] See D.P. O'Connell, *International Law*, vol. 1 (2nd edn, Stevens, London, 1970) 7–8; see G. Schwarzenberger, *International Law*, vol. 1 (3rd edn, Stevens, London, 1957) 25–7; Jennings, 'Law-Making and Package Deal', in D. Bardonnet (ed), *Mélanges Reuter: le droit international: unité et diversité* (Pedone, Paris, 1981) 347, 348.

[203] J. Klabbers, *The Concept of Treaty in International Law* (Kluwer, The Hague, 1996) especially 245–50.

international legal acts with a view to ensuring a better distinction between law and non-law.

It should be made clear that claiming the systematic use of written linguistic indicators in the making of treaties and other international legal acts does not mean that, strictly speaking, formal law-identification must necessarily be associated with the *instrumentum*, that is the written instrument when the norm concerned is enshrined. First, theoretically speaking, the written instrument which contains the linguistic indicators does not necessarily need to be the same instrument as the one which enshrines the rule. However, practice shows that authors of norms classically do not elaborate two written instruments, one enshrining the norm, the other containing the indicator as to the nature of the norm. Second, as has been explained earlier,[204] formal ascertainment of international legal rules can potentially be achieved through the use of indicators which do not take a written form. Indeed, linguistic indicators can be orally formulated and not translated in writing. Likewise, formal law-ascertainment can be realized through the use of material indicators. While recognizing the possibility of formal ascertainment of international legal rules through the use of non-written indicators, it nonetheless is argued here that written linguistic indicators should play the predominant role in law-ascertainment for they constitute a more reliable and effective yardstick than oral linguistic indicators or material indicators (7.3.1), especially at a time of growing deformalization and pluralization of international norm-making processes. An illustration borrowed from contemporary practice is made (7.3.2). Finally, it is explained why the use of written linguistic indicators as direct law-ascertainment criterion, although sometimes being practically indistinguishable from formal evidence of intent, constitutes a conceptual shift which allows a move away from intent-based law-ascertainment (7.3.3).

7.3.1 The use of written linguistic indicators to ensure formal law-ascertainment of international legal rules

As was explained above, international lawmakers often resort to an array of textual, material, and procedural signs that indicates their intent to elevate the norm they agree on into a rule of international law applicable among them.[205] It has been shown above why these indicators have proved insufficient and too unsystematic to ensure formal ascertainment of treaties and other international legal acts. This is why it is argued here that only the systematic use of written linguistic indicators can ensure formal law-ascertainment in international law. Indeed, it is defended here that written linguistic pointers are more efficacious than any other pointers when it comes to fulfilling any of the abovementioned rationales of formalism in the theory of the sources of international law—that is, to guarantee the normative character of international law, the possibility of a critique of international legal rules, the preservation of a meaningful scholarly debate, or the international rule of law.

[204] Cfr *supra* 2.1.1. [205] Cfr *supra* 7.2.4.

Interestingly, it is because written linguistic indicators are the most effective and reliable law-ascertaining pointer that States happen to consciously avoid using them when they want to keep the frontiers between law and non-law in the midst.[206]

Linguistic pointers can be oral or written. In that sense, ascertainment of a rule would still be formal even if carried out through oral law-ascertaining indicators expressed during the making process of the norm concerned. However, it is argued here that, short of any written record, law-ascertaining indicators will be extremely short-lived and unavailable the moment the nature of the rule becomes uncertain. In that sense, if the linguistic indicator as to the nature of the rule is not enshrined in a written instrument, it will not be able to fulfil its role of law-ascertaining indicator. Moreover, it must be realized that the use of oral linguistic indicators does not correspond with the practice, for situations where authors of a norm do not record it in a written instrument are extremely scarce. This is especially well-illustrated by the practice pertaining to oral agreements and oral promises.[207]

Because written indicators emerge, in my view, as the most reliable and efficacious law-ascertainment criterion in comparison to others, the argument made here presupposes that the rule is contained in a written instrument, i.e. the *instrumentum*. In the absence of a written instrument in which it is enshrined, the pedigree of the norm cannot be determined on the basis of written linguistic indicators. It is the written instrument in which the rule is incorporated that contains the formal indicator as to the nature of the norm. It is true, as has just been explained, that linguistic indicators can be provided by a written instrument which does not itself enshrine the rule concerned. In other words, it may be that the *instrumentum* and the written instrument that contains the law-ascertaining linguistic indicators are two different things. Although this proves theoretically possible, practice shows that authors of norms, when they take pains to include law-ascertaining indicators, incorporate them in the same instrument as the one containing the norm concerned. This is why I repeat that the current model of ascertainment of treaties and other international legal acts based on the *instrumentum* should be preserved. Yet, rather than identifying the rules originating therein on the intent expressed in the *instrumentum*, linguistic indicators—however symptomatic of an intent to be bound they may be—should be designed and systematically encapsulated in the instrument as to clearly indicate the nature of these rules. And they should be elevated into the primary law-ascertainment criterion of international treaties and the other international legal acts.

Even if I am of the opinion that written linguistic indicators should be endowed with the main law-ascertaining role, it cannot be excluded that material and procedural indicators continue to play an auxiliary role in the ascertainment of international legal rules. Formal law-ascertainment on the basis of written linguistic indicators and ascertainment by virtue of material or procedural indicators cannot

[206] Cfr *supra* 2.2.

[207] See the practice described by P. Gautier, 'Article 2', in P. Klein and O. Corten, *Les Conventions de Vienne sur le Droit des Traités: commentaire article par article* (Bruylant, Bruxelles, 2006) 53–6. On oral treaties and promises, cfr *supra* 7.2.1.

always be clearly distinguished, for the use of material or procedural indicators often goes hand-in-hand with the adoption of written instruments where the rule adopted is enshrined, as is illustrated by treaty-making practice.[208] To the extent that we concede a rule-making power to the judiciary,[209] this is also the case with rules produced by the international judiciary. Indeed, the rules of international law originating in *judgments, awards,* and *orders* of international tribunals are partly ascertained through material and procedural criteria.[210] It is, therefore, not surprising that the ascertainment of the rules of international law that originate in such adjudicatory processes has not suffered from indeterminacy as much as customary international law, oral treaties, or promises. Certainly, the content of judgments, orders, or awards remains beset by the same indeterminacy as any other international legal rules. Yet, leaving aside any possible subsequent challenge to their validity,[211] their identification as a judgment, order, or award rarely stirs much controversy thanks to the law-ascertaining role of the material and procedural features of the 'making' of such rules.

Whether or not they are supplemented by procedural and material signposts, linguistic indicators do not need to be sophisticated. On the contrary, they should be as simple as possible to contain the indeterminacy inherent in ordinary language and leave as little doubt as possible as to the nature of the instrument concerned. Such simplicity does not necessarily imply universality and uniformity. All the different international legal acts do not necessarily need to be ascertained through the same indicators. It is true that multiplication of indicators would bear the risk of promoting the culture of managerialism deplored by some scholars associated with critical legal studies and deconstructivism,[212] for each set of indicators could become the esoteric technique of a small circle of experts. That risk should nonetheless not be exaggerated. Notwithstanding the streamlining role played by legal scholars,[213] those linguistic indicators would remain primarily carved out by lawmakers themselves.

[208] Cfr *supra* 7.2.4.

[209] On this debate, see, among others, the position of Kelsen described *supra* 3.1.3.

[210] International legal rules produced through judiciary processes will usually be found in the operative part (*dispositif*) of international judicial decisions producing international legal rules. That does not mean that the entire *dispositif* will be rule-creating. As I have explained elsewhere, contemporary practice indicates a greater leaning of international tribunals to make recommendation in the *dispositif* of their decision. See J. d'Aspremont, 'The recommendations made by the International Court of Justice' (2007) 56 ICLQ 185–98; see the reaction of H. Thirlway, 'The Recommendation made by the International Court of Justice: A Sceptical View' (2009) 58 ICLQ 151–62.

[211] See e.g. ICJ, *Case concerning the Arbitral Award made by the King of Spain on 23 December 1906*, 18 November 1960, ICJ Rep. (1960); see also ICJ, Arbitral Award of 31 July 1989 *(Guinea-Bissau v. Senegal)*, 12 November 1991, ICJ Rep. (1991) 75. For a general theory of the grounds of invalidity, see J. Verhoeven, 'Les nullités du droit des gens', in *Droit international* 1, Institut des Hautes Etudes Internationales de Paris (eds), (Pedone, Paris, 1981) 1–110. For some classical works on this topic, see R.Y. Jennings, 'Nullity and Effectiveness in International Law', in *Essays in honour of Lord McNair*, (Stevens, London, 1965) 64–87; E. Lauterpacht, 'The Legal Effects of International Organisations', in *Essays in honour of Lord McNair* (Stevens, London, 1965) 88–121.

[212] See M. Koskenniemi, 'The Politics of International Law: 20 Years Later' (2009) EJIL.

[213] Cfr *infra* 8.3.

However diverse these lawmakers may be growing in the future,[214] it is likely that they would stick to a rather homogenous string of linguistic indicators for the ascertainment of legal acts.

It should also be made clear that the elaboration of given linguistic indicators along the lines suggested here does not prejudge nor require the existence of a given anatomy or design of the legal act. Once it is recognized that it is the linguistic indicators that determine whether the act is legal or not, it is not even necessary that the overall anatomy or design of international legal acts be subject to any sort of formalization.[215]

This plea for the use of written linguistic indicators in the elaboration of international rules for the sake of law-ascertainment may sound odd at a time when international affairs seem to require a greater deformalization of norm-making processes. However, as has been shown above,[216] the use of specific linguistic indicators for the sake of law-ascertainment is not at loggerheads with the use of non-formal norm-making procedures. It has been sufficiently explained above that the resort to written linguistic indicators contemplated here does not require international legal acts to be devised in accordance with a strictly defined procedure.[217] On the contrary, elaborating precise linguistic indicators for the identification of international legal acts is precisely what allows the use of increasingly non-formal law-making procedures while simultaneously preserving the possibility of distinguishing law from non-law. In other words, it is argued here that the contemporary deformalization of law-making processes will only prove sustainable if accompanied by the creation of a set of specific linguistic indicators for the identification of international legal acts.

In my view, a use of such written linguistic indicators in the making of treaties and other international legal acts along the lines that have been spelled out here would allow the emergence of a law-making language through which the subjects of international law—whomever they may be—make reasonably clear where the frontier between law and non-law lies. The use of such indicators would certainly not keep all the indeterminacy at bay. Depending on the precision and simplicity of such indicators, controversies cannot be excluded. However, as is exemplified by the practice of the Security Council mentioned below,[218] the use of simple linguistic indicators can significantly help rein in the indeterminacy inherent in the difficulty of drawing a line between law and non-law.

[214] See generally J. d'Aspremont (ed), *Participants in the International Legal System—Multiple Perspectives on Non-State Actors in International Law* (Routledge, London, 2011).

[215] See *contra* the League of Nations Advisory and Technical Committee on Communications and Transit: 'The Committee takes the opportunity of emphasizing the desirability, when drawing up Conventions concluded under League auspices, including those framed by the International Labour Organization, of always trying to draft texts as uniformly as the varied nature of the subject dealt with permits' (1930) *League of Nations Official Journal* 1856, cited by the Harvard Research (1935) 29 AJIL Sup 728.

[216] Cfr *supra*. 7.1.

[217] Cfr *supra* 2.1.2 and 7.1.

[218] Cfr *infra* 7.3.2.

The theoretical foundations of such linguistic indicators, as well as the determination of who should devise it, must still be discussed. Such an undertaking is left for the last part of this book which is aimed at clarifying and unravelling the social thesis in the theory of the sources of international law.[219]

7.3.2 The use of written linguistic indicators in contemporary practice

Although the mainstream theory of the sources either rests on some illusions of formalism[220] or distorts the formal ascertainment of treaties and other international legal acts by an ultimate resort to intent even in the case of rules ascertained by virtue of the *instrumentum*,[221] contemporary practice already manifest in the use of written linguistic standards, not as evidence of intent but as a law-ascertainment sign. Because such—well-known—practice shows that the abovementioned construction is not only a purely theoretical exercise, it is useful to recall it in the following paragraphs.

The use of written linguistic indicators is witnessed in the practice pertaining to how legal acts of some *international organizations* are sometimes ascertained. Indeed, the making of legal acts of some international organizations has been subject to a great degree of formalism[222] which has manifested itself in the use of written linguistic indicators for its identification. If one takes the example of those resolutions of the Security Council that are supposed to create international legal obligations,[223] it is noteworthy that the identification of the rules that they can generate has escaped the considerable indeterminacy which afflicts the identification of other international legal acts. The Charter of the United Nations empowers the Security Council to adopt legally binding decisions, which do not necessarily include the use of force, upon Member States for the maintenance of peace and security.[224] While such acts were scarce during the Cold War,[225] they have proliferated since the early 1990s. Together with their multiplication, the practice has manifested itself in the emergence of a very specific and consistent language indicative of the will of the Council to enshrine international legal rules in the resolutions. Indeed, it is common practice nowadays that the Council, when it seeks to impose a legal obligation upon Member States within the framework of Chapter VII, adopts a resolution that starts by making the finding that there has been a breach of or threat to the peace, or an act of aggression. The resolution then expressly indicates that the Council is acting under Chapter VII, and finally mentions the wording 'decides' before formulating the obligation imposed on the Member States. There has been much disagreement as to whether the power of the Council to create legal obligations binding the Member

219 Cfr *infra* chapter 8.

220 Cfr *supra* 7.1.

221 Cfr *supra* 7.2.

222 See generally J.-P. Jacqué, *Elements pour une théorie de l'acte juridique en droit international public* (LDGJ, Paris, 1972) 122, 129–30.

223 The Security Council may adopt decisions of another type. See e.g. art. 94(2) UN Charter.

224 See in particular arts 25 and 41 of the UN Charter.

225 See e.g. Res. 232 (1966), 253 (1968), and 418 (1977).

States is limited to Chapter VII or extends beyond it by virtue of article 25—in which case it is not necessary that the Council makes an express finding that there has been a threat to or breach of the peace, or an act of aggression.[226] Irrespective of the question whether the power of imposing binding obligations upon the Member States is limited to its powers under Chapter VII of the Charter, contemporary practice has left little uncertainty as to when a resolution of the Security Council is a legal rule thanks to the language of 'decision'.[227] Once the Council has decided to impose legal obligations on one, several or all member States, it makes use of these very specific textual indicators that will elevate its directives to the status of international law, at least within the framework of the UN Charter.[228]

This very mundane and oft-discussed example sufficiently illustrates that the determination of the nature of an international legal act does not necessarily need to be based on a fickle and impalpable criterion such as the intent of the author of the act. Simple linguistic indicators can determine the nature of the rules adopted by international organizations with reasonable certainty.

7.3.3 Written linguistic indicators as law-ascertainment criteria and the move away from intent

The practice of resorting to written linguistic indicators that has been advocated here should certainly not be seen as *another way to formalize the evidence of intent.*[229] Law-ascertainment and evidence of law are two distinct operations and the formalization of one does not bring about a formalization of the other.[230] The purpose of the use of such formal indicators is thus not the formalization of evidence of intent. As a result of the model of law-ascertainment that has been put forward here, the search for

[226] The latter is the opinion of the ICJ. See ICJ, *Opinion of 21 June 1971 on the Legal Consequences for States of the Continued Presence of South Africa in Namibia (Southwest Africa)* notwithstanding Security Council Resolution 276 (1970), ICJ Rep. (1971) 53, no. 112–16. For a criticism of that position, see B. Conforti, *The Law and Practice of the United Nations* (3rd edn, Martinus Nijhoff, Leiden, 2005) 295. Contrast the remarks of Higgins, 'The Advisory Opinion on Namibia: Which UN Resolutions are Binding under Article 25 of the Charter?' (1972) 21 ICLQ 270.

[227] On this practice, see N. Angelet and E. Suy, 'Article 25', in J.-P. Cot, A. Pellet, and M. Forteau, *La Charte des Nations Unies, Commentaire article par article* (3rd edn, Economica, Paris, 2005) 914–15.

[228] See the advisory opinion of the ICJ on *Accordance with International Law of the Unilateral Declaration of Independence by the Provisional Institutions of Self-Government of Kosovo* of 22 July 2010, para. 88 (not yet published, available at <http://www.icj-cij.org>) which seems to consider that resolution 1244 (1999) of the Security Council constitutes international law and is thus not only law within the exclusive framework of the UN Charter. On this debate, see generally L. Focsaneanu, 'Le droit interne de l'Organisation des Nations Unies' (1975) 3 *Annuaire Français de Droit International* 315–49; See also J. d'Aspremont and F. Dopagne, 'Two Constitutionalisms in Europe: Pursuing an Articulation of the European and International Legal Orders' (2008) 68 ZaÖRV 939–78.

[229] For an example of such a use of written linguistic indicators, see the Separate Opinion of Judge Ago appended to the judgment of 26 November 1984 of the ICJ, *Military and Paramilitary Activities in and against Nicaragua (Nicaragua v. United States of America)*, para. 31.

[230] On the distinction between formalization of evidence and formalization of ascertainment, cfr *supra* 2.1 and 7.1.

intent becomes vain as the law-applying authority only needs to verify *in concreto* the existence of those written linguistic indicators which ascertain the law *in abstracto*.

It is true that, irrespective of which actors actually are in a position to make international legal rules, the use of written linguistic law-ascertainment indicators necessarily reflects some law-making intent of the author(s) of the rules concerned. Indeed, the use of law-ascertainment indicators—subject to errors—flows from a conscious choice and it is because the lawmakers want to make law that they will resort to these pointers. Yet, the fact that intent remains a material source of law does not necessarily mean that international legal rules must continue to be ascertained on the basis of intent. On the contrary, the law-ascertainment model that is put forward here gives rise to the possibility to sever the theory of the sources of international law from intent. Even though the use of written linguistic standards necessarily reflects an intent, these written linguistic indicators are meant to be self-sufficient pointers to ascertain legal rules. While preserving some importance—at least according to the current rules on interpretation[231]—as to the determination of the content of rules,[232] intent, in the law-ascertainment model presented above, accordingly becomes of no relevance to ascertain rules and is simply demoted to a material source of law.

What is at stake here is thus a complete reversal of our theoretical perspectives which allows the ascertainment of treaties and other international legal acts to do away with the speculations inherent in the establishment of intent and makes it exclusively dependent on the use of linguistic indicators. Keeping such speculations at bay, in turn, facilitates greater consistency in the practice of law-ascertainment of law-applying authority, thereby reinforcing the possibility of a social practice able to rein in indeterminacy—as will be explained below.[233] Finally, looking at linguistic indicators, not as an evidentiary process or a tool to evidence intent to make law but as a self-sufficient law-ascertainment criterion, permits a move away from a purely intent-based system of law-identification and paves the way for an international legal system where States' intent, although inevitably instrumental in the making of international law, ceases to be the central parameter on the basis of which rules of that system are identified.

7.4 Concluding Remarks: From the Source Thesis to the Social Thesis

This chapter has shown that we first need to shed the illusions of formalism in some of the classical sources of international law and unearth the non-formal character of the ascertainment of the rules originating therein. Dispelling the mirage of formal law-ascertainment that accompanies the evidence of customary international law, the making of international law, or the interpretation of international legal rules is a

[231] On the attempt to formalize interpretation, cfr *supra* 7.1.

[232] On the distinction between intent in determining the scope (and content) of a rule and intent in law-ascertainment cfr *supra* 7.2.3.

[233] This is the social thesis which will be studied below. Cfr *infra* chapter 8.

prerequisite if one wants to understand the ascertaining role that formalism can play in the theory of the sources of international law. Drawing on this finding, this chapter has revisited formal law-ascertainment criteria in the case of international legal acts, namely international treaties, unilateral promises, and other international legal acts, with a view to unearthing the current contradictions pertaining to the ascertainment criteria of international legal acts as they presently stand, and especially the fact that their identification is ultimately entirely dependent upon non-formal mechanisms grounded in the elusive intent of the law-maker. It has been more specifically argued here that only the abandonment of intent as law-ascertainment yardstick by using written linguistic indicators allows the ascertainment of international legal rules to be truly formal, thereby improving the normativity of the rules of international law while ensuring the possibility of a critique of law, the possibility of a meaningful scholarly debate, and some elementary respect for the rule of law. The previous sections have simultaneously attempted to rein in the indeterminacy that riddles formal law-ascertainment by stripping it of some of the law-ascertainment criteria that perpetuate indeterminacy.

It is true that scholars and theorists do not have control over how international actors actually make law. For instance, as was explained above,[234] resorting to non-formal criteria is sometimes the result of a conscious move by international actors to nurture the ambiguity regarding the frontiers of law. The purposed attempts by international actors to obscure the distinction between law and non-law constitutes yet another reason why the theory of the sources designed by international legal scholars should not cultivate such harmful ambiguities.

The theoretical model of law-ascertainment presented here has yet to provide an indication as to its ontology. Indeed, formalism in law-ascertainment, as construed here, is not self-sufficient. Since formal law-ascertainment is shaped through ordinary language, it would remain inextricably beset by the indeterminacy of language if it were not grounded in the social practice of those applying it. Moreover, the call for the use of linguistic indicators allowing the identification of international legal rules that has been formulated above also requires that we agree upon those who participate in the formulation of such linguistic indicators. This is the object of the following chapter, which will disentangle the 'social thesis' component of the model of law-ascertainment envisaged here.

The social practice spelled out in the following chapter will contribute to a further mitigation of the indeterminacy of law-ascertainment criteria. The mitigating effect that the social thesis can play on the indeterminacy of the formal categories of the source thesis can relieve formal law-ascertainment from the burden of indeterminacy that prevents it from being a reliable mechanism for the identification of international legal rules. The following chapter will also shed light on the determination of those who are engaged in the elaboration of the linguistic indicators needed to ensure the formal ascertainment of international legal rules. Finally, this study of social practice in the context of the sources of international law will help unravel the

[234] Cfr *supra* 1.3 and 2.2.

question of the foundations of those formal law-ascertainment criteria. It will be more specifically demonstrated that, by virtue of the social thesis, clarifying the foundations of the abovementioned law-ascertainment criteria proves nonessential. At least for the sake of law-ascertainment, it ceases to be necessary to think of formal law-ascertainment criteria in terms of 'rules' or 'meta-principles',[235] for they originate, not in a formal rule, but in a social practice. By rooting the abovementioned law-ascertainment criteria in a social practice, the social thesis described below expunges any question of the validity of these criteria. While the existence of each rule of the international legal system ought to be appraised in the light of the abovementioned law-ascertainment criteria, the existence of these criteria no longer needs to be tested on the basis of superior rules. Being grounded in social practice, these law-ascertainment criteria allow the international legal order—which they help delineate—to be—at least from the vantage point of law-ascertainment—a self-standing set of rules, the existence of which is dependent on facts.

[235] In the same vein, see G. Fitzmaurice, 'Some Problems Regarding the Formal Sources of International Law', in *Symbolae Verzijl* (Martinus Nijhoff, The Hague, 1958). See *contra* H. Kelsen, *supra* 3.1.3. See also J. Kammerhofer, 'Uncertainty in the Formal Sources of International Law: Customary International Law and Some of Its Problems' (2004) 15 EJIL 523, 544. See also the dissenting opinion of Judge Oda in *Maritime Delimitation and Territorial Questions between Qatar and Bahrain (Qatar v. Bahrain)*, Judgment of 1 July 1994, para. 13. On this debate, see A. Truyol y Serra, 'Théorie du droit international public—Cours général' (1981-IV) 173 RCADI 13, especially 127–30. See also the remarks of H. Thirlway, *International Customary Law and Codification* (Sijthoff, Leiden, 1972) 37–40.

8

The Foundations of Formal Ascertainment of International Law: The Social Thesis

The previous chapter has tried to refresh the formal ascertainment of international legal rules and dispel some of the illusions of formalism that permeate mainstream theory of the sources in international law. It has opened some avenues to revitalize the current law-ascertainment criteria in international law by moving away from intent. Yet, the abovementioned model of formal law-ascertainment is not self-sufficient, for it does not provide any indication as to the foundations of such formal law-ascertainment blueprint. Indeed, any set of formal yardsticks of law-ascertainment shaped through ordinary language would remain inextricably beset by the indeterminacy of language if it were not grounded in the social practice of those who apply them. This chapter thus turns to the foundations of law-ascertainment in the theory of the sources of international law and, trying to offset the anti-theoretical bent of the international legal scholarship, demonstrates the possibility of constructing a theory of formal law-ascertainment grounded in the social practice of law-applying authorities. In other words, it explains how the source thesis presented in the chapter 7 can itself be rooted in the social practice of law-applying authorities (the social thesis).

As was indicated above,[1] such an understanding of the foundations of formalism corresponds with Hart's and his followers' so-called social thesis. Indeed, according to Hart's theory which was described in chapter 3, the social thesis purports to provide foundations to law-ascertainment criteria—which, in Hart's theory, are embodied by the rule of recognition. This understanding of the foundations of formal law-ascertainment criteria, although devised for domestic legal systems, proves equally insightful for the ascertainment of international legal rules. It has been shown in chapter 3 that international lawyers and scholars, while proving very amenable to Hart's source thesis (and especially the rule of recognition), curiously paid very little attention to his idea that the social practice provides the foundations of formal law-ascertainment.[2] It is the ambition of the following paragraphs to demonstrate the relevance of the social thesis for the ascertainment of international legal rules. It is acknowledged, however, that the application of the social thesis to

[1] Cfr *supra* 2.1.1 and 3.1.3.

[2] Dupuy is among those who has been the most explicit on this point. See P.-M. Dupuy, 'L'unité de l'ordre juridique international: cours général de droit international public' (2002) 297 RCADI 9–489, 200. He argues on p. 201 that law is a language which 'repose sur des conventions, c'est-à-dire sur des significations acceptées par tous ceux qui doivent l'employer'.

international law does not come without problems and will have to be tailored to fit the international context. For example, the concept of a law-applying authority must no doubt be reconceptualized. One cannot simply mechanically transpose Hart's social thesis to the theory of the sources of international law. Subsequent amendments to the social thesis devised by Hart's followers will also prove of relevance here.

This chapter starts by explaining how the meaning of law-ascertainment criteria can be grounded in social practice without falling into the pitfall of objectivism. In doing so, it borrows from Wittgenstein's recourse to communitarian semantics produced by law-applying authorities (8.1). Because of the fragmented and horizontal character of the international legal order, the concept of law-applying authorities whose practice is generative of law-ascertainment practice will necessitate a refinement (8.2). While it is argued that the international legal order has the potential to generate sufficient communitarian semantics for the sake of the ascertainment of international legal rules, it will nonetheless be explained that those actors participating in the emergence of such social practice may be lacking sufficient social consciousness (8.3). This section will then demonstrate how the model of formal law-ascertainment based on the social practice of law-applying authorities makes the question of the validity of international law moot from the vantage point of law-ascertainment (8.4). It will eventually shed light on some of the conciliatory virtues of the social thesis against the backdrop of the theoretical controversies riddling the general theory of international law (8.5).

8.1 The Foundations and Meaning of Law-Ascertainment Criteria: Communitarian Semantics

Formalism in law-ascertainment is, in itself, incapable of producing any meaningful criteria for the ascertainment of rules. The meaning of the formal standards of law-ascertainment ought to be sought elsewhere. As was explained in chapter 3, Hart himself recognized that law-ascertainment criteria—in his words: the 'rule of recognition'—are vague and open-textured.[3] This 'concession' by Hart is not, however, as ground-breaking as it is sometimes portrayed in general legal theory. Indeed, as was explained in chapter 3, the rejection of the idea of an intrinsic meaning of words was already found in Bentham's work. Bentham was loath to employ the expert language used by lawyers for he found that this was an intimidating tactic[4]—a feeling that was subsequently voiced by scholars affiliated to critical legal studies and structuralism.[5] Bemoaning the fact that such technical language has so often been used as an instrument of mystification and oppression to deceive men,[6] Bentham—probably

[3] H.L.A. Hart, *The Concept of Law* (2nd edn, OUP, Oxford, 1997) 144–50.

[4] H.L.A. Hart, *Essays on Bentham: Studies in Jurisprudence and Political Theory* (Clarendon, Oxford, 1982) 29–30.

[5] See M. Koskenniemi, 'Politics of International Law: 20 Years Later' (2009) 20 EJIL 7–19.

[6] J. Bentham, *An Introduction to the Principles of Morals and Legislation* (Kessinger, Whitefish, 2005, first published 1781, London) 332–3. On this particular point of Bentham's theory, see the remarks of

influenced by Hobbes[7]—dismissed the Aristotelian idea that words have meaning of their own. In doing so, he came to be one of the first thinkers to contend that sentences, not words, are the unit of meaning and that the meaning of sentences is thus informed by practice.[8] Bentham, although his accounts of legal statements remained reductive, thus opened the door for a conceptualization of the formal identification of rules based on social practice. In that sense, by breaking with the Aristotelian tradition, he prefigured the idea that the meaning of law-ascertainment criteria is based on communitarian semantics.

Such a concept was subsequently refined by the philosophers of language, and especially by Wittgenstein. According to that communitarian conceptualization of the meaning of rules which is found in the philosophy of language, the meaning of formal law-ascertainment criteria arises out of their *convergence in use*. That means that it is law-ascertainment 'at work' that informs the meaning of the formal criteria of law-identification. That also indicates that the meaning of law-ascertainment criteria originates in the convergences of the practice of law-applying authorities.[9] Short of any convergence, lawyers end up speaking different languages, thereby depriving law of any normativity.

It is this concept of the meaning of rules that influenced Hart and informed his social thesis described in chapter 3.[10] This correlatively proved instrumental in the development of his famous 'internal point' of view. The extent of Wittgenstein's actual influence on Hart has been subject to some controversy.[11] It has even been contended that Hart's foray into Wittgenstein's philosophy has been of little avail, because he actually failed to fully use his insights.[12] Yet, the communitarian semantics which he borrows from Wittgenstein have not been challenged by his

Hart: H.L.A. Hart, *Essays on Bentham: Studies in Jurisprudence and Political Theory* (Clarendon, Oxford, 1982) 9.

[7] T. Hobbes and E. Curley (ed), *Leviathan* (Hackett, Indianapolis, 1994) 175 and 242.

[8] H.L.A. Hart, *Essays on Bentham: Studies in Jurisprudence and Political Theory* (Clarendon, Oxford, 1982) 10.

[9] On the criticism of that part of Hart's argument by Dworkin, see *supra* 4.1.3. In his Postscripts, Hart has denied that he suffers from a semantic sting: H.L.A. Hart, *The Concept of Law* (2nd edn, OUP, Oxford, 1997) 246.

[10] H.L.A. Hart, *Essays on Bentham: Studies in Jurisprudence and Political Theory* (Clarendon, Oxford, 1982) 10. See also Hart's essay, 'Jhering's Heaven of Concepts and Modern Analytical Jurisprudence', reproduced in *Hart's Collected Essays in Jurisprudence and Philosophy* (Clarendon, Oxford, 1983) 265, 277. See the remarks by Stavropoulos, who argues that such a concept of meaning can only come from Wittgenstein: N. Stavropoulos, 'Hart's Semantics' in J. Coleman (ed), *Hart's Postscript: Essays on the Postscript to 'The Concept of Law'* (OUP, Oxford, 2001) 59, 86.

[11] T. Endicott, 'Herbert Hart and the Semantic Sting', in J. Coleman (ed), ibid, 39, 41. Lacey also argues that 'one can speculate with more confidence about the intellectual basis for Herbert's engagement with the linguistic philosophy school': N. Lacey, *A Life of H.L.A. Hart: The Nightmare and the Noble* Dream (OUP, Oxford, 2004) 142. She also submits that, at a later stage, Hart 'came to regard the illuminating power of linguistic philosophy as more limited than he had in the 1940s and 1950s': N. Lacey, ibid, 143. See also her comments, 218–19. See *contra* N. Stavropoulos, ibid, 59, 59.

[12] See J. Raz, 'The Nature and Theory of Law' in J. Coleman (ed), ibid, 1, 6; see also T. Endicott, 'Herbert Hart and the Semantic Sting' in J. Coleman (ed), ibid, 41.

followers.[13] This being said, neither Hart nor his followers have been very voluble as to the exact influence that Wittgenstein—whose written style was found by Hart to be scandalously obscure[14]—on their understanding of the social foundations of law-ascertainment criteria. This is why a brief inroad into Wittgenstein's philosophy is necessary here in order to supplement Hart's social thesis and allow it to be adapted to the specificities of international law. Moreover, as is widely assumed, especially by legal theorists, Wittgenstein's use of the concept of 'rules' in his work refers to all normative constraints which can guide the practice of individuals, and his insights are entirely relevant to the debate about the indeterminacy of law-ascertainment criteria.[15]

As is well-known, Wittgenstein denied the possibility of private language and thus participated in the demise of philosophical foundationalism.[16] Wittgenstein famously asserted the impossibility of private language in paragraph 201 of his *Philosophical Investigations.*[17] In this much-discussed text, Wittgenstein rejects the idea that language has a structure and a meaning that can be revealed through analysis. He argues that there is no such thing as a unified theory about any given linguistic concept. Wittgenstein's assertion on the impossibility of private language is considered to have brought general scepticism towards self-knowledge much further than Hume's scepticism about private causation.[18] However, contrary to other sceptics, Wittgenstein did not intend to leave that impossibility unresolved. This is the essence of the ensuing well-known paragraph 202 of his *Philosophical Investigations,* where he famously envisaged a communitarian foundation of the meaning of rules.[19] To Wittgenstein, clarification of the meaning of words—a task which he assigns to philosophy[20]—is all about how the participants in human activities

[13] See e.g. J. Coleman, *The Practice of Principle* (OUP, Oxford, 2001) 99. J. Coleman, 'Negative and Positive Positivism', in D. Patterson (ed), *Philosophy of Law and Legal Theory: An Anthology* (Blackwell, Oxford, 2003) 116, 121; See also D. Patterson, 'Wittgenstein and Constitutional Theory' (1993–1994) 72 Tex. L. Rev. 1837; D. Patterson, 'Wittgenstein on Understanding and Interpretation' (2006) 29 *Philosophical Investigations* 129–39; D. Patterson, 'Interpretation of Law' (2005) 42 San Diego L. Rev. 685.

[14] N. Lacey, *A Life of H.L.A. Hart: The Nightmare and the Noble Dream* (OUP, Oxford, 2004) 218–19.

[15] L. Wittgenstein, *Philosophical Investigations* (3rd edn, Blackwell, Oxford, 2001) para. 43. See the remarks of B. Bix, 'The Application (and Mis-Application) of Wittgenstein's Rule-Following Considerations to Legal Theory', in D.M. Patterson (ed), *Wittgenstein and Legal Theory* (Westview, Boulder, 1992) 209, 209.

[16] The abandonment of the varieties of philosophical foundationalism is described in R. Rorty's famous book, *Philosophy and the Mirror of Nature* (25th Anniversary Edition, Princeton UP, Princeton, 2009).

[17] L. Wittgenstein, *Philosophical Investigations* (3rd edn, Blackwell, Oxford, 2001) para. 201: 'This was our paradox: no course of action could be determined by a rule, because every course of action can be made out to accord with the rule. The answer was: If *any* action can be made out to accord with the rule, then it can also be made out to conflict with it. And so there would be neither accord nor conflict here'.

[18] On Hume's scepticism towards private causation, see D. Hume, *A Treatise of Human Nature* (Courier Dover, NY, 2003) 50. On the differences between Hume and Wittgenstein, see S.A. Kripke, *Wittgenstein on Rules and Private Language* (Harvard UP, Cambridge, 1982) 62.

[19] 'And hence also "obeying a rule" is a practice. And to *think* one is obeying a rule is not to obey a rule. Hence it is not possible to obey a rule "privately"; otherwise thinking one was obeying a rule would be the same thing as obeying it'.

[20] Wittgenstein, *Tractacus Logico-Philosophicus* (Dover, NY, 1999, first published 1922) 4.112.

conduct such a clarification.[21] It is how the word is used that will teach us the meaning of the word. The meaning of words thus stems from the agreement in action. This harmony in application is constitutive of our understanding of words.

It must be acknowledged that the interpretation of these two famous paragraphs has been the object of wide disagreement. Both the extent of his sceptical diagnosis[22] and that of the suggested antidote[23] have stirred enormous controversy and have taken their place among the most debated questions in the philosophy of language. Because these two paragraphs are so laconic and cryptic, they have been used by both supporters of the radical indeterminacy thesis and supporters of the relative indeterminacy thesis. For the sake of the argument made here, it is not necessary to grapple with the determination of the degree of Wittgenstein's scepticism, for it is not contested here that there is no inner meaning of words and that the language of law is fundamentally indeterminate. Rather, what is of greater relevance for the demonstration undertaken here is to zero in on the antidote. This being said, it is not the ambition of the following paragraphs to discuss or to solve the controversy pertaining to the tool which allows us to rein in the impossibility of meaning. Indeed, it is certainly not up to an international legal scholar barely versed in the philosophy of language to take up a position in a debate which is beyond his expertise. I thus want to avoid endorsing one particular reading of Wittgenstein that will itself lend support to criticism. Moreover, all that matters here is that our formal model of law-ascertainment is informed by this debate. It suffices here to sketch out the two main interpretations that have been made of Wittgenstein's conception of the meaning of rules, with a view to showing that they can provide some insight for the foundations of law-ascertainment criteria in general.

There are scholars who contend that Wittgenstein did not intend to convey that meaning is derived from the practice of rule-followers, but rather that only the rule itself can be the source of its meaning. They argue that Wittgenstein requires an 'internal relation' between a rule and a practice, and that the practice only shows that people are actually complying with the rule.[24] Departing from that first interpretation, there are other scholars who understand Wittgenstein as constructing the determination of meaning as an entirely social question. According to that interpretation, meaning is not found in the rule itself but lies in the temporary consensus of the society. It is grounded in a 'bedrock of practice'[25] by the community of

[21] See the famous example by L. Wittgenstein, *Philosophical Investigations* (3rd edn, Blackwell, Oxford, 2001) paras 1, 3e.

[22] See, for instance, the interpretation of Kripke, *Wittgenstein on Rules and Private Language* (Harvard UP, Cambridge, 1982) 7–54. See the rejection of that interpretation by B. Bix, 'The Application (and Mis-Application) of Wittgenstein's Rule-Following Considerations to Legal Theory', in D.M. Patterson (ed), *Wittgenstein and Legal Theory* (Westview, Boulder, 1992) 209, 209. See also the remarks by G.A. Smith, 'Wittgenstein and the Sceptical Fallacy', in D. Patterson (ed), ibid, 157–88 or B. Langille, 'Political World' in D. Patterson (ed), ibid, 233–47.

[23] This controversy is especially discussed by D. Patterson, 'Law's Pragmatism: Law as Practice and Narrative', in D.M. Patterson (ed), ibid, 85–121, 85.

[24] A classical example of that approach is that of G.P. Baker and P.M.S. Hacker, *Scepticism, Rules and Language* (Blackwell, Oxford, 1984).

[25] B. Langille, 'Revolution Without Foundations' (1988) 33 McGill L. J. 451, 498.

rule-followers. It is thus the conduct of the social group that determines the meaning of the rule—at least what constitutes acting in accordance with the rule.[26] This interpretation is the so-called 'community consensus'.[27] It corresponds with the 'private language argument' as was interpreted by Kripke.[28] Attempts have been made to bridge these two approaches by Dennis Patterson, who has advocated an antidote to the paradox of rule-following which not only rests on the community consensus but also requires a disclosure of the purpose of the rule in the legal system—what he calls 'the point of the rule'.[29] The concept of 'the point of the rule' constitutes the purpose of the rule or its ground of justification. According to Patterson, short of any perception of the purpose of the rule within the practice of law, one cannot identify the meaning of that rule.

It does not seem necessary to delve further into this discussion. It is uncontested that it is the second interpretation of Wittgenstein (i.e. community consensus) that Hart had in mind.[30] This is also the understanding of Wittgenstein which proves the most relevant to the conception of formal law-ascertainment presented here. Furthermore, it should be noted that Wittgenstein is not the only philosopher who could offer some theoretical support for a conceptualization of the social foundations of law-ascertainment. Similar insights can be inferred from other philosophers, as is illustrated by Quine—although his work is more restricted to behavioural evidence of the meaning of rules taken in isolation, for he tries to infer from the behaviour of the speaker the meaning of his words.[31] Ultimately, whether the idea of communitarian semantics comes from Wittgenstein or not is of little importance. The argument made here does not need to seek any sort of authority in the philosophy of language. The short detour into the philosophy of language made in this book is solely directed at gaining additional indications as to the social foundations of law-ascertainment at the basis of the social thesis. By the same token, whether the communitarian semantics must be supplemented by a sense of purpose of the norm—i.e. the 'point of the rule' according to Patterson—by the rule-follower does not seem to require much discussion here either.

[26] N. Malcom, *Nothing is Hidden* (Blackwell, Oxford, 1986).

[27] D. Patterson, 'Law's Pragmatism: Law as Practice and Narrative', in D.M. Patterson (ed), *Wittgenstein and Legal Theory* (Westview, Boulder, 1992) 85, 86.

[28] S.A. Kripke, *Wittgenstein on Rules and Private Language* (Harvard UP, Cambridge, 1982). Kripke's interpretation of Wittgenstein has been much discussed. For a criticism, see B. Bix, 'The Application (and Mis-Application) of Wittgenstein's Rule-Following Considerations to Legal Theory', in D.M. Patterson (ed), ibid, 209, 210.

[29] D. Patterson, 'Law's Pragmatism: Law as Practice and Narrative', in D.M. Patterson (ed), ibid, 85, 95.

[30] It is not necessarily the same interpretation as Fuller—who was also influenced by Wittgenstein—endorsed. See L. Fuller, *The Morality of Law* (revised edn, Yale UP, New Haven, 1969) 186.

[31] M.V. Quine, *Word and Object* (MIT, The Technology Press, Cambridge, 1960); on the differences between Quine and Wittgenstein, see S.A. Kripke, *Wittgenstein on Rules and Private Language* (Harvard UP, Cambridge, 1982) 56. Noam Chomsky's critique of B.F. Skinner's *Verbal Behavior* is usually considered as a simultaneous critique of Quine's work. See N. Chomsky 'A Review of B. F. Skinner's Verbal Behavior', in L.A. Jakobovits and M.S. Mirón (eds), *Readings in the Psychology of Language* (Prentice-Hall, Englewood Cliffs, 1967) 142.

According to the formal model of law-identification discussed here, the foundations and meaning of law-ascertainment criteria are thus found in the converging practice of law-applying authorities. My argument embraces an 'exclusive internal point of view'[32] as to the meaning of the formal yardsticks that are used to ascertain the rules of international law. Yet, the *degree of convergence* necessary for a practice to provide enough meaning to law-ascertainment still needs to be spelled out. This is of special importance in international law where there is limited practice in law-ascertainment, for there are few law-applying authorities and—as described in the previous section[33]—these authorities have not always yielded a consistent practice as to what are those formal yardsticks that determine what is law and what is not law.

It will not be contested that establishing an absolute convergence between all the law-applying authorities of a legal system as to what the criteria for identifying the law are is probably elusive. This is a point astutely raised by Dworkin.[34] According to this argument, there will never be total agreement among law-applying authorities. Moreover, even when the law-applying authorities may on the surface yield the impression that they are applying the same law-ascertainment criteria, their readings of the meaning of these criteria may not be the same.[35] Indeed, there is always a risk that law-applying authorities are not talking about the same thing.

Yet, concurring with Wittgenstein and, subsequently, Hart and rejecting Dworkin's semantic sting objection,[36] I argue that the social foundation of formalism in the ascertainment of international legal rules does not call for actual, total, and absolute agreement among law-applying authorities. It essentially requires a shared *feeling* of applying the same criteria. In that sense, formalism in law-ascertainment is no different from ordinary language. Two persons may well be using the same words and believe that they attribute to them the same meaning, but in actual fact are talking past each other. That, however, does not preclude that they are speaking the same language. Accordingly, moderate misunderstandings that can beset the use of words—and hence the use of law-ascertainment criteria—do not constitute an insurmountable obstacle to the emergence of communitarian semantics. What is simply needed is the *feeling* of using the same criteria.[37] Needless to say that such a feeling will necessarily hinge on their respective understandings of formal law-ascertainment criteria *dovetailing to a reasonable extent.* Short of any minimal correspondence in meaning, law-applying authorities will never come to share the

[32] For a similar espousal of an 'exclusive internal point of view', see G.P. Fletcher, 'Law as a Discourse' (1991–1992) 13 Cardozo L. Rev. 1631, 1634.

[33] Cfr *supra* 7.2.4 and 7.2.5.

[34] Cfr *supra* 4.1.3.

[35] See W. Gallie, *Essentially Contested Concepts, Proceedings of the Aristotelian Society*, vol. 56 (Harrison, London, 1955–5), cited by B. Bix, 'The Application (and Mis-Application) of Wittgenstein's Rule-Following Considerations to Legal Theory', in D.M. Patterson (ed), *Wittgenstein and Legal Theory* (Westview, Boulder, 1992) 209, 220.

[36] Cfr *supra* 4.1.3.

[37] See the remarks of Raz: J. Raz, 'The Nature and Theory of Law', in J. Coleman (ed), *Hart's Postscript: Essays on the Postscript to 'The Concept of Law'* (OUP, Oxford, 2001) 1, 19. *Contra* B. Tamanaha, *A General Jurisprudence of Law and Society* (OUP, Oxford, 2001) 153–4.

feeling that they speak the same language and, hence, their practice will not generate any communitarian semantics.

It is further submitted that the reasons underlying such a feeling of a common language are without relevance. What matters is simply that law-applying authorities do in fact share such a feeling. This is consistent with the point made by Wittgenstein—at least as it has been interpreted by Kripke[38]—that convergence is a brute fact that is self-sufficient to be generative of a practice relevant for the establishment of law-ascertainment criteria. This similarly corresponds with what Hart defended when he submitted that the reason why law-applying authorities abide by the rule of recognition does not need to be answered and that the meaning of the rule of recognition is independent from the motive behind such converging attitudes of law-applying authorities.[39]

It must still be added that the existence of such a shared feeling presupposes the ability for each law-applying authority to check whether other law-applying authorities use the law-ascertainment criterion at stake according to a similar perception.[40] It is argued here that the current circulation of decisions of authorities called upon to apply international law and their translation into a language spoken by most of them are sufficient to ensure such a mutual confirmation system. This certainly is the case regarding decisions of international courts and tribunals. Modern developments have also sweepingly expanded the information available about domestic decisions involving questions of international law.[41] Moreover, these law-applying authorities have been resorting to a certain type of language which, despite being contingent on the specific legal tradition in which it is rendered, is usually accessible to most other law-applying authorities. This type of language constitutes a type of formalism that has not been tackled here, that is the formalism in legal argumentation.[42] While formal legal argumentation is obviously guilty of the contradictions highlighted by the realist and postmodern critiques described in chapter 4, that form of formalism has at least the virtue of ensuring a better readability of most judicial decisions. Despite all its inconsistencies, this type of formalism partakes in the 'readableness' of the practice of law-applying authorities, thereby allowing each authority to gain the feeling that they all share the same law-ascertainment language. The practice of other types of law-applying authorities also seems to be sufficiently disseminated, including through yearbooks and law reviews.[43]

[38] S.A. Kripke, *Wittgenstein on Rules and Private Language* (Harvard UP, Cambridge, 1982) 96.

[39] H.L.A. Hart, *The Concept of Law* (2nd edn, OUP, Oxford, 1997) 115–16. This part of Hart's argument has not always been construed like this. For a different interpretation of Hart on this point, see G.J. Postema, 'Coordination and Convention at the Foundations of Law' (1982) 11 JLS 165–203.

[40] S.A. Kripke, *Wittgenstein on Rules and Private Language* (Harvard UP, Cambridge, 1982) 99–107.

[41] See e.g. the International Law in Domestic Court (ILDC) Database, available at <http://www.oxfordlawreports.com/>.

[42] See my comments *supra* 2.1.2.

[43] This aspect of law reviews surely does not fall within the scathing criticisms of F. Rodell, 'Goodbye to Law Reviews' (1936) 23 Va. L. Rev. 38 and 'Goodbye to Law Reviews—Revisited' (1962) 48 Va. L. Rev. 279.

It is hoped that the foregoing sufficiently shows that the social foundations of law-ascertainment criteria cannot be conflated with utter objectivism. There is no such thing as an objective agreement among law-applying authorities as to the criteria to which they resort to distinguish between law and non-law. There is only a shared feeling that they use the same criteria to ascertain international legal rules. The account of formal law-ascertainment made here thus remains a sceptical one which does not purport to convey objectivism in law-ascertainment. It seems that the Kelsenian objection that the social thesis necessarily presupposes the same type of absolute and external standard as natural law is not compelling.[44]

The idea that a mitigation of indeterminacy can be found in communitarian semantics and that the meaning of rules is derived from the social practice of the rule-followers—in the case of law-ascertainment criteria, the practice of law-applying authorities—must now be further substantiated in the specific context of international law. In particular, I must revisit the abovementioned concept of law-applying authorities in a way that allows it to accommodate the specificities of international law.

8.2 The Concept of Law-Applying Authority in International Law: Judges, Non-State Actors, and Legal Scholars

According to the argument made here, the social practice that is instrumental in gauging the communitarian semantics necessary to provide meaning to law-ascertainment criteria is that of the law-applying authorities.[45] In Hart's view as was described in chapter 3, the concept of 'law-applying authorities' has been narrowly construed, for Hart devised his social thesis exclusively in the context of domestic law. The restricted concept of law-applying authorities makes its transposition in international law highly problematic. For the sake of determining those who provide the social foundations to the formal ascertainment of international legal rules, the concept of law-applying authorities must be refreshed with a view to accommodating the specificities of the application of international law.

As was mentioned in chapter 3, a refinement of the concept of law-applying authorities has been offered by Brian Tamanaha. According to the modernization proposed by Tamanaha, a law-applying authority is 'whomever, as a matter of social practice, members of the group (including legal officials themselves) identify and treat as "legal" officials'.[46] The social practice on which the rule of recognition is based must accordingly not be restricted to strictly-defined law-applying officials but

[44] J. Kammerhofer, *Uncertainty in International Law. A Kelsenian Perspective* (Routledge, London, 2010) 226. It is true that the social thesis may end up including the study of 'Is'-proposition in the scope of the science of law, thereby including sociological enquiries in the scope of a science primarily centered on the study of 'Ought'-proposition. If this is true, it is argued here that this may well be the price to pay for any theory of formal law-ascertainment. On this discussion, see also A. Somek, 'The Spirit of Legal Positivism' (2011) 12 *German Law Journal* 729, cfr *infra* 8.4.

[45] Cfr *supra* 3.1.3.

[46] B. Tamanaha, *A General Jurisprudence of Law and Society* (OUP, Oxford, 2001) 142.

must include all social actors.[47] This expansion of the concept of law-applying authority is undoubtedly of great relevance in a legal order—like the international legal order—which lacks any vertical and institutional hierarchy. Tamanaha's definition, although proving somewhat all-embracing to a certain extent, can help provide a better grasp on those who actually engage in the ascertainment of international legal rules and generate social practice of law-ascertainment. It surely points to the insufficiency of a too narrow construction of the concept of law-applying authority as well as to the necessity not to restrict the production of communitarian semantics to the practice of formal judicial authorities only. In the reality of international law, it can hardly be contested that other 'social actors' participate in the practice of law-ascertainment and should be taken into account in the determination of the communitarian semantics constitutive of the meaning of law-ascertainment criteria. The following paragraphs accordingly mention those social actors whose practice must be deemed relevant for the sake of the theory of formal ascertainment of international legal rules put forward here.

It must, as a preliminary point, be made very clear that being a 'social actor' whose practice of law-ascertainment is instrumental in the meaning of the formal criteria of the identification of law does not necessarily amount to being a formal international law-maker. It is true that some of the actors mentioned here may well wield some undeniable law-creating powers—as is illustrated by judges whose role in the development of international law is almost uncontested[48]—or some influence on the making of international law—as exemplified by the influence of non-State actors.[49] However, the potential law-creating or law-making role of these actors as regards the (progressive) development of substantive international legal rules is of no relevance here. Indeed, although law-determination by international courts may sometimes come close to law-creation and even if law-identification and law-creation may be carried out simultaneously,[50] the practice relevant for the sake of law-

[47] B. Tamanaha, ibid, 159–66.

[48] H. Kelsen, 'La Théorie Pure dans la Pensée Juridique' in C. Leben and R. Kolb (eds), *Controverses sur la Théorie Pure du Droit* (LGDJ, Paris, 2005) 173; H.L.A. Hart, *The Concept of Law* (2nd edn, OUP, Oxford, 1997) 136; See also Hart and A.M. Honore, *Causation in the Law* (OUP, Oxford, 1985) 5 or N. Bobbio, *Essais de théorie du droit* (Bruylant/LGDJ, Paris, 1998) 10 and 38; J. Raz, *Authority of Law* (Clarendon, Oxford, 1983) especially 41–52. As regards international law more specifically, see R. Jennings, 'What is International Law and How Do We Tell it When We See it' (1981) 37 *Annuaire Suisse de Droit international* 77; H. Thirlway, 'The Sources of International Law' in M. Evans (ed), *International Law* (2nd edn, OUP, Oxford, 2006) 115, 129–30; H. Lauterpacht, *The Development of International Law by the International Court* (2nd edn, Praeger, NY, 1958); M. Lachs, 'Some Reflections on the Contribution of the International Court of Justice to the Development of International Law' (1983) 10 Syracuse J. Int'l L. & Com. 239; R. Higgins, *Problems and Process: International Law and How We Use It* (OUP, Oxford, 1995) 202. A. Boyle and C. Chinkin, *The Making of International Law* (OUP, Oxford, 2007) 266–9 and 310–11. See however the statement of the ICJ in its Advisory Opinion on the *Legality of the Threat or Use of Nuclear Weapons*, 1996-I, ICJ Rep. 237, para. 18 (according to which the Court 'states the existing law and does not legislate' and this is so 'even if, in stating and applying the law, the Court necessarily has to specify its scope and sometimes not its general trend'). Art. 38 of the ICJ Statute also seems to lend support to a strictly cognitivistic task of international courts.

[49] See generally J. d'Aspremont, *Participants in the International Legal System—Multiple Perspectives on Non-State Actors in International Law* (Routledge, London, 2011).

[50] See R. Jennings, 'General Course on Principles of International Law' (1967-II) 121 RCADI 341.

ascertainment is alien to any question of a law-making power properly so-called. The communitarian semantics that they generate by identifying international legal rules do not constitute a substantive law-making exercise. The actors mentioned below simply partake in the semantics of the formal criteria of law-ascertainment, which—although they are often captured through the Hartian concept of the rule of recognition—do not constitute legal rules in the same sense as the substantive rules of international law.

There is no doubt that the central law-applying authority whose behaviour is the most instrumental in defining the standard of law-ascertainment is the International Court of Justice (ICJ). This is why its case-law was the object of much attention in the previous sections.[51] Yet, the ICJ is not the only law-applying authority in the international legal order. Arbitral tribunals have also applied international legal rules and thus participated in the elaboration of the linguistic indicators of law-ascertainment.[52] Moreover, and despite the ICJ occasionally being still endowed with a natural monopoly to set the tone in the international judicial arena,[53] a growing number of international tribunals have been applying international law, thereby participating in the elaboration of the criteria for the ascertainment of international legal rules. Furthermore, all these various tribunals are engaged in an uncontested 'cross-fertilization' which further shores up the importance of the social practice which they generate.[54]

Even though the contribution of the ICJ in this respect has not always been consistent and fully satisfying—as is illustrated by the fluctuations in its case-law regarding the formal evidence of custom,[55] the law-ascertainment criteria of unilateral promises,[56] or the evidence of intent to make law for the sake of the

[51] Cfr *supra* 7.2.

[52] For a recent example see the final award in the Abyei Arbitration, *The Government of Sudan/The Sudan People's Liberation Movement/Army*, 22 July 2009, paras 425–35 available at <http://www.pca-cpa.org/showpage.asp?pag_id=1306>.

[53] See the famous rebuke of the ICTY by the ICJ in its decision on 26 February 2007 in the case of the *Application of the Convention on the Prevention and Punishment of the Crime of Genocide (Bosnia and Herzegovina v. Serbia and Montenegro)*, ICJ Rep. (2007) para. 402–7; See also *Report of Stephen M. Schwebel, President of the International Court of Justice*, UN GAOR, 54th Sess., Agenda, Item 13, UN Doc. A/54/PV.39 (26 October 1999) 3–4; *Report of Gilbert Guillaume, President of the International Court of Justice*, UN GAOR 55th Sess., Agenda Item 13, UN Doc. A/55/PV.42 (26 October 2000) 7; See also G. Guillaume, 'The Future of International Judicial Institutions' (1995) 44 ICLQ 848–62, 860–2; G. Guillaume, 'La Cour Internationale de Justice. Quelques propositions concrètes à l'occasion du cinquantenaire' (1996) 100 *Revue générale de droit international public* 323, 331; S. Oda, 'Dispute Settlement Prospects in the Law of the Sea' (1995) 44 ICLQ 863–72, 864.

[54] See e.g. F. Jacobs, 'Judicial Dialogue and the Cross-Fertilization of Legal System: The European Court of Human Rights' (2008) 38 Texas Int'l L. J. 547; C. Koh, 'Judicial Dialogue for Legal Multiculturalism' (2004) 25 Mich. J. Int'l L. 979; P. Tavernier, 'L'interaction des jurisprudences des tribunaux pénaux internationaux et des cours européennes et interaméricaines des droits de l'homme', in P. Tavernier (eds), *Actualité de la jurisprudence internationale: à l'heure de la mise en place de la Cour pénale internationale* (Bruylant, Bruxelles, 2004) 251–61.

[55] Cfr *supra* 7.1 and 7.2.1.

[56] Compare ICJ, *Nuclear Tests case (Australia v. France)*, 20 December 1974, para. 43 and ICJ, *Military and Paramilitary Activities in and against Nicaragua (Nicaragua v. United States of America)*, Merits, ICJ Rep. (1986) para. 40.

identification of international treaties[57]—the practice of the ICJ has nonetheless proved more indicative than that of other tribunals. Whatever the varying weight of each of these tribunals, it is uncontested that the adjudicatory and judicial practice of law-ascertainment in the international arena, now emerging from a greater variety of tribunals, is thus far the most generative of communitarian semantics for the sake of law-ascertainment criteria in international law.

International courts and tribunals are not the only judicial authorities which generate communitarian semantics of law-ascertainment. Indeed, international law has long become more regulatory of internal matters and issues affecting individuals. Compliance with international law has accordingly incrementally required the adoption of domestic rules, thereby increasing the application of international law by domestic courts.[58] Even rules regulating inter-State relations have required domestic implementation. This infiltration by international law into domestic systems is thus a natural consequence of the extension *ratione materiae* of its object.[59] That international law now regulates objects previously deemed of domestic relevance is insufficient, however, to explain the growing application of international law by domestic courts. Because international law only enters domestic legal orders if so allowed, the greater presence of international law in the domestic legal orders of States is also the direct consequence of the growing amenability of States towards international law.[60] In this respect, it is not disputed that States are becoming less reluctant to let international law pervade and enter their own legal order. Incorporation is not the only means by which international law has been applied by domestic courts. Indeed, most States in the world instruct their courts to construe domestic law in a manner that is consistent with the international obligations of that State. If international law is not the 'law of the land' because it has not been incorporated, it may still yield effects in the domestic legal order if domestic judges interpret national law in accordance with international law.[61] The growing effect of international law

[57] Cfr *supra* 7.2.3.

[58] For an analysis of some significant decisions of domestic courts applying international law, see A. Nollkaemper, *National Courts and the International Rule of Law* (OUP, Oxford, 2011).

[59] According to Provost and Conforti, 'The truly legal function of international law essentially is found in the internal legal system of States'. See Provost and Conforti, *International Law and the Role of Domestic Legal Systems* (Martinus Nijhoff, Dordrecht, 1993) 8; J.H.H. Weiler, 'The Geology of International Law: Governance, Democracy and Legitimacy' (2004) 64 ZaöRV 547, 559–661; See also A. von Bogdandy, 'Globalization and Europe: How to Square Democracy, Globalization and International Law' (2004) 15 EJIL 885, 889; M. Kumm, 'The Legitimacy of International Law: A Constitutionalist Framework of Analysis' (2004) 15(5) EJIL 907, 917; See *contra* Arangio-Ruiz, 'Le domaine reservé. L'organisation internationale et le rapport entre le droit international et le droit interne'. Cours général de droit international public' (1990-VI) 225 RCADI, 29–479, especially 435–79.

[60] See generally J. Nijman and A. Nollkaemper, 'Beyond the Divide', in J. Nijman and A. Nollkaemper (eds), *New Perspectives on the Divide between National and International Law* (OUP, Oxford, 2007) 341–60.

[61] This principle of *consistent interpretation* of domestic law is also known as the 'Charming Betsy' principle. See US Supreme Court, *Murray v. The Schooner Charming Betsy* 6 US (2 Cranch) 64 (1804); see also *Restatement (Third) of Foreign Relations Law*, § 114 (1987). On the 'Charming Betsy' principle, see generally R.G. Steinhardt, 'The Role of International Law as a Canon of Domestic Statutory Construction' (1990) 43 Vand. L. Rev. 1103 or J. Turley, 'Dualistic Values in an Age of International Legisprudence' (1993) 44 Hastings L. J. 185. A similar principle is found in regional legal orders, as is illustrated by

in the domestic legal order through incorporation and consistent interpretation has been accompanied by a general amenability of domestic judges towards international law as a whole, irrespective of whether it is incorporated into national law and is binding upon the State.[62] Whether the entry of international law into domestic legal orders takes the path of incorporation, consistent interpretation, or simple persuasiveness, and to whomever this entry can be traced back, it is uncontested that international law is becoming increasingly present in domestic legal orders and is relentlessly applied by domestic courts. In applying international law, these domestic courts are thus called upon to ascertain its rules, thereby participating in the general practice of international law-ascertainment. It has thus become undeniable that domestic courts count as actors participating in the generation of the communitarian semantics of law-ascertainment as well.[63]

Despite the multiplicity of international and domestic judicial authorities engaged in the ascertainment of international legal rules, their practice has remained too scarce to generate sufficient communitarian semantics. After all, these law-applying authorities are of a limited number and their case-law is proportionally modest, especially if compared to the practice of law-ascertainment of domestic legal rules generated by domestic courts. This is precisely why, in line with Tamanaha's proposition as described in chapter 3, the practice of other actors engaged in the application of international law should be included in the social practice necessary to establish the social practice at the heart of formal law-ascertainment in international law.

It cannot be denied that some non-State actors also provide interesting insights as to the meaning of law-ascertainment criteria. Although it is expected that other actors than those mentioned here will come to influence the social practice of international law-ascertainment, particular mention should be made here of the International Committee of the Red Cross (ICRC). It is true that the recent study produced by the ICRC on customary international law[64] provoked some severe reservations in terms of the consistency of its methodology in the establishment of

the European legal order where European law ought to be interpreted in conformity with international law. See Case 41/74 *Van Duyn v. Home Office* [1974] ECR 1337; see also *Poulsen and Diva Corp.* [1992] ECR-I 6019.

[62] See generally, Y. Shany, 'National Courts as International Actors: Jurisdictional Implications' *Hebrew University International Law Research Paper* No. 22–08 (October 2008). See also the remarks by E. Benvenisti and G.W. Downs, 'National Courts, Domestic Democracy, and the Evolution of International Law' (2009) 20 EJIL 59–72; Betlem and Nollkaemper, 'Giving effect to Public International Law' (2003) 14 EJIL 569; see also J. d'Aspremont, 'Systemic Integration of International Law by Domestic Courts: Domestic Judges as Architects of the Consistency of the International Legal Order', in A. Nollkaemper and O.K. Fauchald (eds), *Unity or Fragmentation of International Law: The Role of International and National Tribunals* (Hart, Oxford, 2011) (forthcoming).

[63] On the application of international law by domestic courts, see generally K. Knop, 'Here and There: International Law in Domestic Courts' (2000) 32 NYU JILP 501; A. von Bogdandy, 'Pluralism, direct effect, and the ultimate say: On the relationship between international and domestic constitutional law' (2008) 6 ICON 397–413.

[64] J.-M. Henckaerts, 'Study on Customary International Humanitarian Law: a Contribution to the Understanding and Respect for the Rule of law in Armed Conflict' (2005) 87 *International Review of the Red Cross* 175–212.

customary international law[65]—a large part of which can be traced back to the non-formal character of custom-ascertainment for which the ICRC cannot be blamed. Yet, it cannot be denied that the determination of what is law and what is non-law by the ICRC—as is illustrated by the extent to which States took pains to react to it—constitutes a practice of law-ascertainment that is to be reckoned with. A few other non-State actors are probably also instrumental in the consolidation of a practice of law-ascertainment.[66] It is not my intention to list them all here.[67] It must simply be recalled once again that recognizing that law-ascertainment by non-States actors like the ICRC constitutes relevant practice from the standpoint of the social thesis does not amount to saying that these bodies or entities are endowed with law-making authority.[68]

It could be tempting to include the International Law Commission (ILC) among those non-state bodies which engage in a practice of ascertainment of international legal rules. Certainly, the ILC ascertains international legal rules when it codifies international law. In this respect, its codification undertakings could potentially yield some relevant social practice for the sake of law-ascertainment. Yet, the ILC is also endowed with the responsibility of proposing progressive developments of international law. Whilst these two tasks ought to be clearly distinguished according to its Statute,[69] the practice shows that the ILC carries them out simultaneously and does not deem it necessary to make any distinction in this regard.[70] The final outcome of the ILC's work, whatever form it may take,

[65] See the critique of A. Boyle and C. Chinkin, *The Making of International Law* (OUP, Oxford, 2007) 36. See also the critique expressed by J.B. Bellinger and W.J. Haynes, 'A U.S. Government Response to the International Committee of the Red Cross's Customary International Humanitarian Law Study' (2007) 46 ILM 514, also available at <http://www.defense.gov/home/pdf/Customary_International_Humanitarian_Law.pdf>; See the reaction of J.-M. Henckaerts, 'Customary international humanitarian law—a response to US comments' (2007) *International Review of the Red Cross* 473.

[66] See e.g. the 2004 *Report of the UN Secretary General's High Level Panel*, available at <http://www.un.org/secureworld/>. See also the 2001 *Report of the Independent International Commission on Intervention and State Sovereignty* (established by the Government of Canada in September 2000), available at <http://www.iciss.ca/report-en.asp>.

[67] On the role of non-State actors in the international legal order, see generally J. d'Aspremont (ed), *Participants in the International Legal System—Multiple Perspectives on Non-State Actors in International Law* (Routledge, London, 2011).

[68] Such a perception often permeates the legal scholarship. See generally, C. Thomas, 'International Financial Institutions and social and economic rights: an exploration' in T. Evans (ed), *Human Rights Fifty Years On: A Reappraisal* (Manchester UP, Manchester,1998) 161–85, especially 163; for a mild approach, see I.R. Gunning, 'Modernizing Customary International Law: The Challenge of Human Rights' (1990–1991) 31 Va J. Int'l L. 211; A.-M. Slaughter is not far from recognizing such a law-making role to individuals: 'The Real New World Order' (1997) 76 *Foreign Affairs* 183. See also E. Beigzadeh, 'L'évolution du droit international public', in E. Jouannet, H. Ruiz-Fabri, and J.-M. Sorel (eds), *Regards d'une génération sur le droit international public* (Pedone, Paris, 2008) 75, 78. For a criticism of that perception, see J. d'Aspremont, 'The Doctrinal Illusion of Heterogenity of International Lawmaking Processes', in H. Ruiz-Fabri, R. Wolfrum, and J. Gogolin (eds), *Select Proceedings of the European Society of International Law*, vol. 2 (Hart, Oxford, 2010) 297–312.

[69] See e.g. arts 16–18 of the ILC Statute, UN General Assembly Resolution 174 (II), 21 November 1947. The Statute, as was subsequently amended, is available at <http://www.un.org/law/ilc/>.

[70] This is why the Commission suggested that such a distinction be abolished. See the *Report of the International Law Commission*, 48th session (1996), A/51/10, para. 147(a) and paras 156–9. On that

will generally fall short of making any distinction between those rules that have been codified and those that originate in a progressive development. It is usually the commentary that will indicate whether a rule must be considered the mere codification of an existing rule or whether it constitutes a progressive development of international law. But such indications do not always suffice, and rules meant by the ILC to be progressive development of international law are sometimes subsequently elevated to rules that have been the object of a codification by the judicial bodies applying them.[71] The almost impossibility of distinguishing between progressive development and codification explains why the ILC's contribution to the practice of law-ascertainment ought to be seen as very modest. The same is probably true with respect to the *Institut de Droit international*.[72]

Finally, mention must be made of the secondary role played by international legal scholars in the ascertainment of international legal rules. It is argued here that international legal scholars, although they are not at the origin of a practice of law-ascertainment generative of communitarian semantics, undoubtedly participate in the fine-tuning and streamlining of the formal criteria of law-ascertainment which, in turn, are picked up by the social actors involved in the application of international legal rules. In other words, it is submitted here that legal scholars come to play the role of grammarians of formal law-ascertainment who systematize the standards of distinction between law and non-law.

It is undeniable that scholars may occasionally be conducive to the progressive development of primary norms. Indeed, while they certainly are not law-makers,[73] international legal scholars often play a public role or participate in public affairs.[74]

aspect of the ILC Statute, see J. d'Aspremont, 'Les travaux de la Commission du droit international relatifs aux actes unilatéraux des Etats' (2005) 109 *Revue générale de droit international public* 163–89.

[71] See the famous contention of the ICJ that art. 16 of the 'Articles on the Responsibility of a State for its Internationally Wrongful Acts' corresponds with a rule of customary international law, a position contrasting with that of the Special Rapporteur of the International Law Commission. Compare ICJ, *Application of the Convention on the Prevention and Punishment of the Crime of Genocide (Bosnia and Herzegovina v. Serbia and Montenegro)*, 26 February 2007, ICJ Rep. (2007), para. 420 and J. Crawford, *The International Law Commission's Articles on State Responsibility, Introduction, Text and Commentaries* (CUP, Cambridge, 2005) 148.

[72] On the Institut de Droit international, see e.g. F. Rigaux, 'Non-State Actors from the Perspective of the Institut de Droit international', in J. d'Aspremont (ed), *Participants in the International Legal System—Multiple Perspectives on Non-State Actors in International Law* (Routledge, London, 2011) 179.

[73] J. d'Aspremont, 'Softness in International Law: A Self-serving Quest for New Legal Materials' (2008) 19(5) EJIL 1075–93; A. Bianchi, 'Une generation de "communautaristes"', in E. Jouannet, H. Ruiz-Fabri, and J-M. Sorel (eds), *Regards d'une génération sur le droit international* (Pedone, Paris, 2008) 95–105, 105; J. Kammerhofer, 'Law-Making by Scholarship? The Dark Side of 21st Century International Legal "Methodology"', in J. Crawford et al. (eds), *Selected Proceedings of the European Society of International Law*, tome 3 (Hart, Oxford, 2011) (forthcoming), available at <http://ssrn.com/abstract=1631510>.

[74] For an illustration of the public role that scholars may play according to the conception submitted here, see M. Craven, et al., 'We Are Teachers of International Law' (2004) 17 LJIL 363; See also the letter published in the Guardian, 'War Would be Illegal', 7 March 2003, available at <http://www.guardian.co.uk/politics/2003/mar/07/highereducation.iraq/print>; See also the 'appel de juristes de droit international concernant le recours à la force contre l'Irak' initiated by the Centre de droit international of the Free University of Brussels (ULB) in January 2003, reference available at <http://www.ridi.org/adi/special/

Although international legal scholars themselves may be tempted to see their offerings as more influential than they really are,[75] and even though their contribution is more modest today than it used to be a century ago—for States have grown weary of the influence that scholars can have[76]—their writings, their opinions, and their decisions also influence law-making and international legal adjudication.[77] Article 38 of the Statute of the International Court of Justice has long shrouded the influence of scholars and judges upon law-making in a formal veil by elevating them to a 'subsidiary means for the determination of rules of law'. Nothing could be more illusory than the formalization of their influence on law-making which—albeit recognized as secondary—is not tangible in the making of international law and can hardly be captured in formal terms. The role of legal scholars in the making of substantive rules of international law falls outside the ambit of our inquiry. All that matters is to shed light on their contribution to the practice of law-ascertainment and their corresponding contribution to the production of communitarian semantics.

Clearly legal scholars do not constitute law-applying authorities *sensu stricto.* Nor are they social actors as was understood by Tamanaha. Indeed, strictly speaking they do not apply the law but interpret and comment upon it. However, it cannot be denied that international legal scholars have always constituted grammarians of the language of international law.[78] By contrast with domestic

index.htm>. On the idea that international legal scholars are not immune from the political debates in which they have been claiming a say, see L. Mälksoo, 'The Science of International Law and the Concept of Politics. The Arguments and Lives of the International Law Professors at the University of Dorpat/Iurev/Tartu 1855–1985' (2005) 76 BYBIL 499–500.

[75] For a classical example of this belief, see O. Schachter, 'The Invisible College of International Lawyers' (1977–1978) 72 NYULR 217: 'We should be mindful, however, that international lawyers, both individually and as a group, play a role in the process of creative new law and in extending existing law to meet emerging needs. This legislative role is carried out principally through multilateral treaties, but it may also be accomplished through the evolution of customary international, the use of general principles.... In all of these processes, the professional community may perform a significant function'.

[76] M. Virally, 'A Propos de la "Lex Ferenda"', in D. Bardonnet (ed), *Mélanges Reuter: le droit international: unité et diversité* (Pedone, Paris, 1981) 521–33, 520.

[77] See the famous statement of Justice Gray in the case of *The Paquete Habana* and the *Lola* in 1920: '... where there is not treaty, and no controlling executive or legislative act or judicial decision, resort must be made to the customs and usages of civilized nations; and, as evidence of these, to the works of jurists and commentators, who by years of labor, research and experience, have made themselves peculiarly well acquainted with the subject of which they treat. Such works are resorted to by judicial tribunals, not for the speculations of their authors concerning what the law ought to be, but for trustworthy evidence of what the law really is' (cited by R. Jennings, 'International Reform and Progressive Development', in G. Hafner et al. (eds), *Liber Amicorum Professor Ignaz Seidle-Hohenveldern in honour of his 80th Birthday* (Kluwer Law International, The Hague, 1998) 333). See also L. Mälksoo, 'The Science of International Law and the Concept of Politics. The Arguments and Lives of the International Law Professors at the University of Dorpat/Iurev/Tartu 1855–1985' (2005) 76 BYBIL 383, 499–500.

[78] See Dupuy: 'un internationaliste ne devrait jamais prétendre à autre chose que d'être un bon grammarien du language normatif du droit international'. ('Cours général de droit international public' (2002) 297 RCADI 9, 205). P. Reuter, 'Principes de droit international public' (1961-II) 103 RCADI 425–655, 459: 'Le droit n'est pas seulement un produit de la vie sociale, il est également le fruit d'un effort de pensée, s'efforçant d'agencer les données ainsi recueillies dans un ensemble cohérent et aussi logique que possible. C'est l'aspect systématique du droit international, il est à la fois plus important et plus délicat que celui des droits nationaux. Il est plus important parce que les sociétés nationales, du fait qu'elles sont

law,[79] the systematization of international law has primarily been an achievement of legal scholarship rather than of legal practice.[80] International law would not have reached its current level of systemic development without the input of international legal scholarship. One of the paramount tasks undertaken as grammarians has been the systematization and the streamlining of the criteria for the distinction between law and non-law.[81] While their work in this respect does not constitute, strictly speaking, the practice of law-applying authorities, the law-ascertainment criteria carved out and polished by legal scholars have been very conducive to shaping the practice of law-applying authorities. That means that international legal scholars do not themselves yield social practice. Yet, they clearly impact on that practice by contributing to the elaboration of the communitarian semantics of law-ascertainment in international law.

This role played by international legal scholars in the streamlining of the communitarian semantics is inevitably accompanied by a need for a greater self-reflective consciousness. Indeed, international legal scholars should neither deny nor minimize their contribution to the social practice of law-ascertainment under the guise of purely cognitivistic responsibility, but should come to terms with the extent of their impact on the emergence of communitarian semantics and assume it. Whilst the motives behind the practice of law-ascertainment are irrelevant as to the existence of this social practice, unveiling the motives and the reasoning behind legal scholars' grammatical postures should thus be a prevalent attitude of the profession. The call for a 'culture of formalism'[82] construed as a communicative practice aimed at the universality of legal argumentation takes on even more relevance. Hence, the work of international legal scholars affiliated with critical legal studies and deconstructivism is particularly germane for those construing the role of international legal scholars as falling within the ambit of the social thesis.[83]

profondément centralisées par l'autorité étatique, engendrent un droit déjà systématisé par ses conditions d'élaboration. Au contraire, la "décentralisation du pouvoir politique" qui règne dans la société internationale rejette sur le juriste un fardeau plus lourd. Il est plus délicat parce que le désordre de la société internationale n'est pas tant désordre de la pensée que désordre du pouvoir; certes le juriste peut se laisser aller à la systématisation, mais s'agit-il de systématiser seulement ses pensées ou de systématiser aussi la réalité ? Certes, de par sa nature même, le droit est avide d'ordre mais à quoi servirait-il, par excès de rigueur dans la pensée, de poursuivre une systématisation en dehors du cadre des solutions admises'. See also G.J.H. Van Hoof, *Rethinking the Sources of International Law* (Kluwer, Deventer, 1983) 291 or J. Von Bernstorff and T. Dunlap, *The Public International Law Theory of Hans Kelsen—Believing in Universal Law* (CUP, Cambridge, 2010) 266.

[79] The Code Napoléon has been instrumental in the systematization of continental European domestic orders.

[80] For some general thoughts on the contribution of legal scholars to the systematization of law, see N. MacCormick, *Institutions of Law: An Essay in Legal Theory* (OUP, Oxford, 2008) 6.

[81] A. D'Amato, 'What 'Counts' as Law?' in N.G. Onuf (ed), *Law-Making in the Global Community* (Carolina Academic Press, Durham, 1982) 83, 106–7; See also M. Virally, 'A Propos de la "Lex Ferenda"', in D. Bardonnet (ed), *Mélanges Reuter: le droit international: unité et diversité* (Pedone, Paris, 1981) 521–33, 532.

[82] Cfr *supra* 2.1.2.

[83] For a concise account of this stream of scholarship, cfr *supra* 4.2.4.

The practice of law-ascertainment generating the communitarian semantics necessary to ensure the meaning of the formal criteria of law-ascertainment advocated above is thus made by a multi-fold practice by a diverse set of social actors, including international judges and a few non-State actors. International legal scholars, while they do not themselves directly yield a practice of law-ascertainment, undoubtedly partake in the shaping of the communitarian semantics necessary to ensure the meaningfulness of formal law-ascertainment criteria. The role played in this regard by domestic courts and non-State actors in generating social practice for the sake of the meaning of the law-ascertainment criteria of the international legal system, participates in the reinforcement of the possibility for the international legal system of producing a vocabulary enabling the ascertainment of the rules of which it is composed.

The plurality of the sources of the communitarian semantics necessary for the meaningfulness of law-ascertainment criteria nonetheless accentuates the risk of conflicting social practice. This is of particular import since, as has been explained above, a reasonable degree of convergence is necessary to ensure that formal law-ascertainment not be riddled with utter indeterminacy. For this social practice to remain sufficiently consistent, the argument could be made that the central role currently played by international courts and tribunals in this respect should be preserved. This inevitably accentuates the State-centricism of the current configuration of the production of communitarian semantics in the international legal order. Yet, the claim for the preservation of the role of international courts and tribunals does not constitute an all-out support for how the social practice necessary for formal ascertainment of international legal rules actually and currently emerges. Indeed, the abovementioned account of the main features of the contemporary practice constitutive of communitarian semantics of the formal standards of law-ascertainment does not seek to prejudge its *adequateness*. For instance, it cannot be denied that the social practice of law-ascertainment, as it currently stands, still suffers from the structural biases identified by the feminist approaches to international law.[84] The same is true with the prejudices identified by the Third World Approaches to International Law (TWAIL).[85] These cogent critiques may well call for an amendment to the composition of the various bodies participating in the production of the communitarian semantics for the sake of formal law-identification or the way it is disseminated. This book is nonetheless not the place to study this wide variety of biases and the way in which they should be addressed.[86] The foregoing simply shows that, as far as international law is concerned, there exists a heterogeneous community able to produce enough communitarian semantics to endow formal international law-ascertainment criteria with sufficient meaning. It also demonstrates that the law-ascertainment theory put forward here has the ability to renew itself from within and potentially take into account new practices—by new actors—more attentive to the

[84] See *supra* note 200 (chapter 4).

[85] See *supra* note 201 (chapter 4).

[86] On some of the biases behind the role of international judges, see generally L.V. Prott, *The Latent Power of Culture and the International Judge* (Professional Books, Abingdon, 1979).

biases and prejudices of the current social practice of law-ascertainment in the international society.

8.3 The Deficient Social Consciousness of Law-Applying Authorities in the International Legal Order

Whilst the account made here shows, in my view, that the international society, in spite of its limited institutionalization, is *in a position* to produce sufficient communitarian semantics for the sake of the social thesis, it seems more questionable whether the current configuration of the international legal society allows the emergence of a sustainable *feeling* of convergence of the practices of law-ascertainment. Indeed, as was explained above,[87] for communitarian semantics to be generated, the mere existence of a practice is insufficient. What is also needed is a sense by the abovementioned actors that they are using the same criteria and thus the sense that they belong to the same linguistic community.[88] Such a social consciousness may well be lacking in the current configuration of the international society, thereby hampering the emergence of a meaningful social practice. For instance, international judges, even though they seem to be generally heedful of the need to achieve the overall consistency of international legal rules,[89] do not manifest much sense of membership to the same linguistic community in terms of law-ascertainment. In general, questions of international law-ascertainment are tackled by national and international law-applying authorities in total isolation of each other's practice. International law-ascertainment is not conceived by the actors taking part in the emergence of a social practice as necessitating a common language. It could even be contended that issues of law-ascertainment have grown secondary, not only in the legal scholarship,[90] but also in the adjudicatory practice.[91] It is accordingly argued here that the problem is thus not really the fragmentation of the production of the social practice but rather the absence of social consciousness among the variety of actors contributing to the production of communitarian semantics. The problems of law-ascertainment in international law nowadays are thus not only the result of an illusory formalism—as was demonstrated above[92]—but also that of the limited social consciousness of law-applying authorities.

For a social consciousness to emerge among all the actors partaking in law-ascertainment practice at the international level, a greater—even informal—

[87] Cfr *supra* 8.2.

[88] See the remarks of Raz: J. Raz, 'The Nature and Theory of Law' in J. Coleman (ed), *Hart's Postscript: Essays on the Postscript to 'The Concept of Law'* (OUP, Oxford, 2001) 1, 19. *Contra* B. Tamanaha, *A General Jurisprudence of Law and Society* (OUP, Oxford, 2001) 153–4.

[89] See ICJ, *Ahmadou Sadio Diallo (Republic of Guinea v. Democratic Republic of the Congo)*, 30 November 2010, para. 66, available at <http://www.icj-cij.org/docket/index.php?p1=3&p2=3&code=gc&case=103&k=7a>.

[90] Cfr *supra* 1.

[91] Cfr *supra* 7.2.3.

[92] Cfr *supra* 7.1 and 7.2.

collaboration—and thus mutual respect—among the abovementioned law-applying authorities is needed. This finding inevitably brings the question of judicial dialogue into the limelight. The question of dialogue between international law-applying authorities is not new and does not need to be taken on here.[93] It is only necessary to emphasize now that, applied to international law, the social thesis reinforces the pertinence of the work of those liberal scholars who have examined the dynamics of the dialogues between law-applying authorities around the world.[94] In my view, such studies should now be pursued with a greater heed of law-ascertainment practice.

It must be acknowledged that the necessity of a greater social consciousness by actors participating in the emergence of communitarian semantics for the sake of meaningful ascertainment of rules may stir up fears of an exercise of 'power'—however secondary and diffuse it may be—by another 'invisible college'[95] or professional community. Such fears are certainly not ill-founded. They call for means to ensure better legitimacy of the process of production of communitarian semantics by these actors. The question of legitimacy in the making of communitarian semantics by the actors mentioned above is accordingly a serious concern that ought to be borne in mind, especially if those actors participating in the social practice of law-ascertainment were to grow more aware of their responsibilities in this regard and develop a stronger sense of community. However severe the need to ensure greater legitimacy of the production of the social practice necessary for meaningful law-ascertainment may someday be, it seems important to point out, at this stage, that the legitimacy of processes of production of communitarian semantics for the sake of law-ascertainment ought not be envisaged in the same terms as the legitimacy of the making of primary rules. First, it is not certain that, in producing communitarian semantics for law-ascertainment, these abovementioned actors exercise anything that resembles 'power'. Second, even if we were to consider that the production of communitarian semantics constitutes a sort of power in disguise, such a power could not be equated with the public authority that they may simultaneously be exercising when developing primary rules of international law.[96] I am of the opinion that the legitimacy of the former ought not to be conceived according to the patterns of legitimacy designed for the latter. This being said, the question of legitimacy of the production process of the social practice necessary for the ascertainment of international legal rules is too sweeping a debate to be further discussed here. It is a question which I consciously and purposely leave for future research. Yet, the foregoing was only meant to highlight that the application of the social thesis to the ascertainment of international legal rules inevitably necessitates that the question of the legitimacy

[93] See generally A.-M. Slaughter, 'A Global Community of Courts' (2003) 44 Harv. Int'l L. J. 191.

[94] See e.g. the famous work of those scholars affiliated with the liberal school of international law mentioned above. See e.g. A.-M. Slaughter, 'A Global Community of Courts' (2003) 44 Harv. Int'l L. J. 191.

[95] The expression was famously coined by O. Schachter 'The Invisible College of International Lawyers' (1977) 72 Northwest. U. L. Rev. 217–26.

[96] On the development of primary rules by courts and tribunal, see *supra* note 48. On the role of international legal scholars in the developments of primary rules, see *supra* note 73.

of the processes leading to the production of communitarian semantics for the sake of law-identification is not disregarded.

8.4 The Vainness of the Question of the Validity of International Law

The previous sections have spelled out the various components of the social thesis which support the model of formal ascertainment of international legal rules presented in this book. It has been argued that the practice of various social actors can generate communitarian semantics indispensable to reining in the indeterminacy of the language on which formal law-ascertainment is based while not falling back into pure objectivism. The move away from objectivism inherent in the model of formal law-ascertainment advocated here is further underpinned by the immediate consequences of its social foundations to the question of the validity of international law as a whole. Indeed, grounding the formal ascertainment of international legal rules in the practice of law-ascertainment allows us to circumvent, for the sake of law-ascertainment, some of the abiding theoretical difficulties inherent in the question of the overall validity of international law and which have been at the centre of some of the critiques described in chapter 4.[97]

Ensuring the overall validity of the international legal system has been one of the abiding riddles of the theory of international law.[98] It is well-known that Kelsen—who, on this point, was partly followed by some important international legal scholars like Anzilotti[99] or Guggenheim[100]—argued that the whole system necessarily rests on a Grundnorm which itself must be presupposed.[101] It surely is not the place to discuss this aspect of Kelsen's theory.[102] Kelsen's ambition to design a general theory of law may well have required such a construction.[103] It is argued here, however, that, *as far as the ascertainment of international legal rules is concerned*, the social thesis makes the question of the validity of the international legal order as a whole utterly vain. Ascertaining legal rules only necessitates a sufficiently clear and consistent social practice able to produce enough communitarian semantics. This

[97] I have further elaborated on that point in J. d'Aspremont, 'Hart et le positivisme postmoderne' (2009) 3 *Revue générale de droit international public* 635–54.

[98] On positivism in international law, see my remarks *supra* 2.1.2.

[99] Anzilotti adopted Kelsen's understanding of validity as resting on a hypothetical norm: D. Anzilotti, *Scritti di diritto internazionale pubblico* (Cedam, Padova, 1956–7) 57.

[100] G. Schwarzenberger, *International Law* (3rd edn, Stevens, London, 1957); P. Guggenheim, 'What is positive international law?', in G. Lipsky, *Law and Politics in the World Community, Essays on Hans Kelsen's Pure Theory and Related Problems of International Law* (University of California Press, Berkeley, 1953) 15–30.

[101] H. Kelsen, 'Théorie générale de droit international public: problèmes choisis' (1932–IV) 42 RCADI 117, 124–37.

[102] It is well-known that some scholars have construed that aspect of Kelsen's theory as a 'closure of convenience'. See e.g. N. Bobbio and D. Zolo, 'Hans Kelsen, the Theory of Law and the International Legal System: A Talk' (1998) 9 EJIL 355–67, 355. For an attempt to rebut that point, see J. Kammerhofer, *Uncertainty in International Law: A Kelsenian Perspective* (Routledge, London, 2010) 197 and 231.

[103] On Kelsen, cfr *supra* 3.1.3.

social practice does not need to unfold under the umbrella of a Grundnorm that guarantees the validity of the international legal system and ought not to be subject to a judgment of validity to produce the communitarian semantics necessary for law-ascertainment.[104] The social practice of law-ascertainment is not valid or invalid, for it simply is a fact. In other words, if the formal ascertainment of international legal rules is solely a question of social practice by law-applying authorities and a few non-state actors as has just been argued above,[105] it is not necessary to seek the validation of that practice. What matters is simply that law-applying authorities, sharing some sufficient social consciousness and making use of similar law-ascertainment language, do actually recognize some norms as constituting international legal rules.

It is true that the existence of the legal system is to some extent dependent on there being valid legal rules within that system. Indeed, if a legal system does not recognize any single rule as valid, it can hardly exist as a legal system. Yet, this does not mean that, from the standpoint of law-ascertainment, the existence of a legal system boils down to a question of validity similar to that of individual rules[106]—and this is the reason why validity is not necessarily tautological and circular as it has sometimes been contended.[107] If we can say of the system itself that it is valid, this is only in the sense that its rules are valid.[108] Seen through the lens of law-ascertainment, the existence of a legal system—and the same is true with respect to the international legal system—is not a question of validity.[109] While the validity of a given norm must be appraised in the light of the norm from which it is derived, it makes no sense, from the standpoint of law-ascertainment, to gauge the legal system as a whole in the same manner.[110] The existence of the (international) legal system boils down to a *mere question of fact.*

[104] As Kelsen himself would argue, there cannot be contradiction between an 'Ought' proposition and an 'Is' proposition, that is, between a rule and a fact. See H. Kelsen, *Introduction to The Problems of Legal Theory* (Clarendon, Oxford, 1992) 30.

[105] Cfr *supra* 8.2.

[106] It is commonly accepted that a rule which is not valid within that system is not a legal rule within that system. See J. Raz, *Authority of Law* (Clarendon, Oxford, 1983) 146; Kelsen, for his part, famously argued that validity is the specific form of existence of legal rules in a given system, such contention applying to all norms. See H. Kelsen, *General Theory of Law and State* (Harvard UP, Cambridge, 1945) 175–7; See, however, the critique by Scandinavian realists, who see a contradiction between the existence of the rule and its reality. See A. Ross, *Introduction à l'empirisme juridique* (LGDJ, Paris, 2004) 25–6.

[107] This argument has been made by M. Koskenniemi, '*Hierarchy in International Law: A Sketch*' (1997) 8(4) EJIL 566–82, 578.

[108] J. Raz, *Authority of Law* (Clarendon, Oxford, 1983) 148.

[109] See H.L.A. Hart, *The Concept of Law* (Clarendon, Oxford, 1997) 100. See in particular 108–9: 'We only need the word "validity" and commonly only use it to answer questions which arise within a system of rules where the status of a rule as a member of the system depends on its satisfying certain criteria provided by the rule of recognition. No such question can arise as to the validity of the very rule of recognition which provides the criteria; it can neither be valid nor invalid, but simply accepted as appropriate for use in this way'. In the same vein, see J. Raz, ibid, 69; See also M. Virally, *La pensée juridique* (LDGJ, Paris, 1960) 140.

[110] It would be misleading to conceal that such a 'retreat' in the direction of empirical sources has remained—although unconvincingly—immune from controversy. See S. Coyle, 'Hart, Raz and the Concept of Legal System' (2002) 21 *Law and Philosophy* 288–9.

Authors embracing a Kelsenian understanding of law will commonly argue that abandoning the question of the validity of the international legal system by grounding law-ascertainment in social practice demotes legal science to legal sociology.[111] Whether this is true or not, it is argued here that this objection does not really undermine the theory of ascertainment presented here, for it only pertains to a question of how one construes the mission(s) of the (international) legal scholarship and the scope of the science of law. This is a fundamentally different debate from that of law-ascertainment which is at the heart of this book. Ultimately, even if the social thesis, by bypassing the question of the validity of the international legal system as a whole and grounding law-ascertainment in facts, were to lead legal science to encapsulate sociological analysis, such an enlargement of scope of the science of law—far from being unprecedented[112]—would then be the necessary condition for a lasting and solid theory of ascertainment of international legal rules.

It is true that, if applied to international law, the contention that the existence of the international legal system is a question of fact is not utterly unheard. Some international legal scholars, albeit falling short of grounding their contention in a strong theory of law-ascertainment,[113] have occasionally claimed that the question of the validity of international law as a whole is pointless and that questions of validity ought to be restricted to problems of existence of individual rules.[114] It is hoped that the argument made in this section provides some theoretical underpinnings to their discerning intuitions.

8.5 The Conciliatory Virtues of the Social Thesis for the International Legal Scholarship

It must finally be highlighted that the social thesis discussed here—i.e. the idea that the foundations of formalism in the ascertainment of international legal rules is to be sought in the practice of law-applying authorities—has some doctrinal conciliatory virtues, for, in my view, it helps reconcile some allegedly antonymic trends in

[111] J. Kammerhofer, *Uncertainty in International Law. A Kelsenian Perspective* (Routledge, London, 2010) 227.

[112] It probably is a lesson learned from Legal Realism as well as the Policy-Oriented Jurisprudence. Cfr *supra* 4.1.2 and 4.2.3. For a contemporary attempt to ground the study of international law in its social context, see M. Hirsch, 'The Sociology of International Law: Invitation to Study International Rules and Their Social Context' (2005) 55 UTLJ. 891. On the possible roles for sociology in the study of international law, see also A. Carty, 'Sociological Theories of International Law', in *Max Planck Encyclopedia of Public International Law*, available at <http://www.mpepil.com> paras 42–6.

[113] On the anti-theoretical attitude of the international legal scholarship, cfr *supra* 3.2.2.

[114] See e.g. I. Brownlie, 'International law at the fiftieth anniversary of the United Nations: general course on public international law' (1995) 255 RCADI 9–228, 30–1. In the same sense, G. Fitzmaurice, 'The general principles of international law considered from the standpoint of the rule of law' (1957-III) 92 RCADI 1–227; L. Condorelli, 'Custom', in M. Bedjaoui (ed), *International Law: Achievements and Prospects* (Martinus Nijhoff, The Hague, 1991) 179–211, 180.

international legal scholarship and accommodate some of the arguments on which the critiques of formalism described in chapter 4 have been built.

First, it must be recalled that the social thesis is not meant to describe the whole phenomenon of law and in particular the flux of dynamics at the heart of the creation and operation of international law.[115] The social thesis, as has been presented here, only informs the meaning of the formal indicators which allows a distinction between law and non-law. In that sense, the social thesis is not necessarily incompatible with some of those theories of international law aimed at describing the whole phenomenon of law in the international society, even if they are inspired by modern natural law theories.[116] Likewise, the social thesis undoubtedly makes room for a decreased emphasis on words and an ever-increasing emphasis on behaviour as was advocated by the legal realists whose critiques of formalism were presented in chapter 4. Furthermore, the social thesis that is developed here helps alleviate some of the concerns having inspired the sociological approaches to international law, for which international law cannot be severed from the context of its making or that of its application.[117] I also hope that the foregoing has shown that the rejuvenation of formalism put forward here comes with some cosmopolitan virtues,[118] for it has been suggested here that the concept of law-applying authorities generating social practice ought to be revamped so as to include a wide variety of actors reflecting the current move away from a State-centrist to a more cosmopolitan international society.[119]

Attention is also drawn to the fact that the conceptualization presented here underpins the continuously mutually enriching character of the multiple strands of the contemporary international legal scholarship. For instance, it has been shown that the current configuration of the processes of production of communitarian semantics in the international legal order makes the call for 'a culture of formalism' developed by Martti Koskenniemi[120] even more relevant.[121] Likewise, the social thesis leaves intact some of the objections of the critique inspired by critical legal studies and deconstructivism. In particular, the social thesis, by *easing* the indeterminacy of the source thesis by grounding it in a social practice, only helps contain indeterminacy at the level of law-ascertainment but does not purport to allay the contradictions of international legal argumentation.[122] In the same vein, because the production of the communitarian semantics necessary to ensure an elementary meaning of the formal yardstick of law-ascertainment still suffers from gender, cultural, and geographical biases, the conceptualization of the foundations of

[115] Cfr *supra* 2.1.1 and 2.1.2.

[116] Cfr *supra* 4.2.1 and 5.1.

[117] Cfr *supra* 4.2.1.

[118] On the various conceptions of cosmopolitanism in international legal studies, see P. Glenn, 'Cosmopolitan Legal Orders', in A. Halpin and V. Roeben, *Theorising the Global Legal Order* (Hart, Oxford, 2009) 25–37; see also the various contributions found in R. Pierik and W. Werner (eds), *Cosmopolitanism in Context: Perspectives from International Law and Political Theory* (CUP, Cambridge, 2010).

[119] Cfr *supra* 8.2.

[120] Cfr *supra* 2.1.2.

[121] Cfr *supra* 8.3.

[122] Cfr *supra* 2.1.2 and 6.1.

formalism adopted in this book can still benefit from the insights of the feminist[123] and Third World.[124] approaches to international law and do not exclude them at all. In addition, the need to ensure a social consciousness among the actors contributing to the emergence of a social practice for the sake of the ascertainment of international legal rules bolsters the need to continue researching the channels of dialogue among law-applying authorities, as has been pursued by scholars affiliated with the so-called liberal school of international law.[125]

Despite the non-exclusive, non-confrontational, and conciliatory character of the formalism defended here, it is less certain that, like any model of formal law-ascertainment, the argument made here can be reconciled with legal pluralism.[126] Indeed, if legal pluralism is understood as eschewing legal unity and a common framework of identification,[127] the preservation of formal indicators for international law-ascertainment purposes may well come at the expense of legal pluralism.[128]

By the same token, I acknowledge that formalizing law-ascertainment criteria by social practice remains at odds with theories of the sources of international law based on substantive validity.[129] This being said, it cannot be excluded that the social practice generating communitarian semantics for the sake of law-ascertainment has itself been inspired by normative considerations.[130] In that sense, the theory of law-ascertainment presented here could be usefully complemented by research on the normative driving forces of the practice of law-ascertainment. However, the inspiration that law-applying authorities could draw from normative principles does not in itself elevate such principles into a law-ascertaining criterion, law-identification remaining as operated solely on the basis of the linguistic indicators generated by that practice.

A last remark is necessary given the possibility that a theory of international law-ascertainment based on social practice—as the one that was presented here—be perceived as 'apologetic' in the sense in which scholars affiliated with critical legal

[123] See *supra* note 200 (chapter 4).

[124] See *supra* note 201 (chapter 4).

[125] See generally A.-M. Slaughter, 'A Global Community of Courts' (2003) 44 Harv. Int'l L. J. 191.

[126] N. Krisch, *Beyond Constitutionalism—The Pluralist Structure of Postnational Law* (OUP, Oxford, 2010) 11–12 and 69–105.

[127] On the multiple meaning of legal pluralism, see N. Krisch, ibid, 71–8.

[128] See, however, on the possibility of withholding a rule of recognition and safeguarding pluralism, S. Besson, 'Theorizing the Sources of International Law', in S. Besson and J. Tasioulas (eds), *The Philosophy of International Law* (OUP, Oxford, 2010) 163, at 184; W. Twining, 'Implications of 'Globalisation' for Law as a Discipline'in A. Halpin and V. Roeben, *Theorising the Global Legal Order* (Hart, Oxford, 2009) 44–5. On the specific question of whether Hart's theory can sustain legal pluralism, see J. Waldron, 'Legal Pluralism and the Contrast Between Hart's Jurisprudence and Fuller's', in P. Cane (ed), *The Hart-Fuller Debate in the Twenty-First Century* (Hart, Oxford, 2010), 135–55 and M. Davies, 'The Politics of Defining Law', in P. Cane (ed), *The Hart-Fuller Debate in the Twenty-First Century* (Hart, Oxford, 2010) 157–67.

[129] Cfr *supra* 4.2.1 and 5.1.

[130] In the same vein, see B. Kingsbury and M. Donaldson, 'From Bilateralism to Publicness in International Law', in *From Bilateralism to Community Interest: Essays in Honour of Judge Bruno Simma* (OUP, Oxford, 2011) 79, at 89.

studies or deconstructivism understand this notion.[131] Even though the previous sections have shown that, in the context of international law, the concept of law-applying authorities should be more heterogeneous than it is in domestic law—and include the practice of a variety of non-state actors—it cannot be contested that the social thesis inevitably grants considerable importance to the positions of public authorities, be they organs of international organizations or organs of States. It is argued, however, that the possible 'apologetic' character of the social thesis does not automatically resuscitate the contradiction[132] of being simultaneously utopian. Indeed, despite the inevitable normativity inherent in the empirical methodology that accompanies the social thesis,[133] the theory of ascertainment based on social practice that is defended here, being entirely dependent on communitarian semantics,[134] estranged from the Kantian universality and Grotian eclecticism found in constitutionalist and liberal theories[135] and liberated from the quest for the validity of international law as a whole,[136] cannot, in my view, be equated with an utopian and naïve objectivism.[137]

[131] M. Koskenniemi, *From Apology to Utopia* (CUP, Cambridge, 2005) 326. Cfr also *supra* 4.2.4.

[132] This contradiction is described in M. Koskenniemi, ibid, 303.

[133] Cfr *supra* 6.3.

[134] Cfr *supra* 8.1.

[135] Cfr *supra* 2.2 and 3.2.3. I have even more clearly backed away from Kantian universality and Grotian eclecticism elsewhere. See J. d'Aspremont, 'The Foundations of the International Legal Order' (2007) 18 FYIL 219–55.

[136] Cfr *supra* 8.4.

[137] See *contra* the scholars espousing a Kelsenian understanding of law who argue that the social thesis presupposes the same type of absolute and external standard as natural law does. See e.g. J. Kammerhofer, *Uncertainty in International Law. A Kelsenian Perspective* (Routledge, London, 2010) 226. See also A. Somek, 'The Spirit of Legal Positivism' (2011) 12 *German Law Journal* 729. For a discussion of that point see *supra* 8.2 and 8.4.

9

Concluding Remarks: Ascertaining International Legal Rules in the Future

We undoubtedly live in an age of pluralized normativity. Indeed, as was explained above,[1] both the norm-making processes and the norms produced thereby at the international level have undergone a profound pluralization. Such a pluralized normativity is not a new phenomenon but it has grown to a degree never witnessed before. It is even fair to say that most of the international normative activity nowadays manifests itself in one these pluralized forms of exercise of public authority. There is no reason why this phenomenon will not continue unabated in the future. Accordingly, the conceptualization of the norms generated by these pluralized exercises of public authority will surely remain a chief area of inquiry of the international legal scholarship in the 21st century. This book has focused on traditional forms of international law-making and sought to lay bare the illusions of formalism in the mainstream theory of the sources of international law as well as the lack of social consciousness of those authorities applying international law. However, on the occasion of these final recapitulatory remarks, a few words must be said about the relevance of formal law-ascertainment for current and future scholarly debates about pluralized norm-making at the international level.

It has been explained here that, confronted with the growing normative activity outside the classical law-making framework, international legal scholars have been inclined to deformalize the ascertainment of international legal rules with a view to capturing these new manifestations of public authority in their conceptual 'net'.[2] Such a stretch of international legal scholars' nets—which has materialized in an growing use of non-formal law-ascertainment criteria—has most of the time[3] been driven by lofty purposes, primarily the domestication of these new exercises of

[1] Cfr *supra* chapter 1.

[2] 'We can catch nothing at all except that which allows itself to be caught in precisely our net': F. Nietzsche, *Daybreak. Thoughts on the Prejudices of Morality, Book II, Aphorism, para. 117* (CUP, Cambridge, 1982) 73. I owe this citation to Andrea Bianchi. For further insights on this idea, see A. Bianchi, 'Reflexive Butterfly Catching: Insights from a Situated Catcher', paper submitted for the Informal International Public Policy Making (IIPPM) Geneva Workshop, 24–25 June 2010 (on file with the author), to be published in J. Pauwelyn, R. Wessel, and J. Wouters (eds), *Informal International Law Making—Mapping the Action and Testing Concepts of Accountability and Effectiveness* (forthcoming 2011). See also *supra* 5.1 and 5.2.

[3] See however the occasional self-serving quest for new legal materials, *supra* 5.3.

public authority, their subjection to accountability mechanisms, and a better programmation of the emergence of new rules of international law.[4] Some very serious doubts have nonetheless been cast in the previous chapters as to whether deformalization of law-ascertainment actually contributes to the realization of any of these noble objectives.[5] It has also been argued in the previous chapters that, besides failing to meet the objectives assigned thereto, the deformalization at play in contemporary theory of the sources of international law comes with a disproportionately high price in terms of normativity and authority of international law, meaningfulness of scholarly debate, and the possibility of a critique of international legal rules.[6] Likewise, such a deformalization is not without impact on respect for the rule of law at the international level. Indeed, as has been explained above, deformalization may also serve the interest of those actors that are seeking to preserve some unfettered room for manoeuvre and evade their international obligations and which, for that reason, may find it particularly useful that rule-ascertainment remains non-formal.[7]

Against that backdrop, this book has made the argument that the pluralization of international norm-making—including the deformalization of norm-making processes themselves—ought not necessarily to be accompanied by a deformalization of law-ascertainment. Indeed, deformalization of the former does not automatically call for a deformalization of the latter. More specifically, it has been shown that the use of specific linguistic indicators for the sake of law-ascertainment is not at loggerheads with the use of non-formal norm-making procedures, for the practice of resorting to written linguistic indicators contemplated here does not require international legal acts to be devised in accordance with a formally-defined procedure. It has even been shown that elaborating formal indicators for the identification of international legal acts allows a greater and sustainable use of non-formal law-making procedures while simultaneously preserving the possibility of distinguishing law from non-law without which law's authority, the meaningfulness of scholarly debates, the possibility of a critique of international legal rules, as well as some elementary respect for the rule of law, would be gravely enfeebled.

The attempt of this book to provide a counter-point to the current deformalization of law-ascertainment in the theory of the sources of international law has clearly remained alien to any endeavour to rehabilitate or defend mainstream theory of the sources of international law. On the contrary, this book has sought to shed some light on the illusions of formalism which shroud the mainstream theory of the sources of international law.[8] Unearthing such mirages of formalism has been construed here as the prerequisite to initiating a rejuvenation of formal law-ascertainment in the age of pluralized normativity. Indeed, it is only once the theory of the sources of international law has been stripped of its fake formalist trappings that it can be more critically re-evaluated, especially in the context of the above-mentioned pluralized forms of exercise of public authority at the international level.

[4] Cfr *supra* 5.3. [5] Cfr *supra* 5.3. [6] Cfr *supra* 2.2.
[7] Cfr *supra* 2.2. [8] Cfr *supra* 7.1.

Arguing for the relevance of formal law-ascertainment grounded in social practice and the need to dismantle some of the illusions of formalism embedded in the mainstream theories of sources of international law has not been the sole ambition of this book. It has also sought to reveal some of the specificities of the theoretical foundations of formal ascertainment of international legal rules, especially when it comes to the social practice necessary to endow formal law-ascertainment indicators with sufficient meaning as to avoid utter indeterminacy. In this regard, the spotlight has been turned on the growing role of domestic courts and a growing number of non-state actors—next to international courts and tribunals—in the production of the communitarian semantics necessary for the use of relatively determinate formal law-indicators. This aspect—and the deficient social consciousness by law-applying authorities in the international legal order that has been noted on that occasion—constitute one of the particular characteristics of formal ascertainment of international legal rules. Needless to say, the exact same customization will be required in devising the formal ascertainment of the normative products of today and tomorrow's pluralized exercise of public authority if the source and social theses are to retain any relevance in this framework. As in the case of an application of the social thesis to the international legal order, the insights gained from the 'culture of formalism', TWAIL, and feminist critiques, as well as the liberal studies on the dialogue between law-applying authorities, will probably remain of utmost relevance.

While demonstrating that problems of ascertainment of international legal rules nowadays are the result of simultaneous and mutually reinforcing factors—amongst others, the move away from formal law-ascertainment, the illusions of formalism that permeate the mainstream theory of the sources of international law, or the limited social consciousness of law-applying authorities in generating communitarian semantics in the practice of international law-ascertainment—this book has not meant to clinch all the debates pertaining to the formal ascertainment of international legal rules. Regarding for instance the comprehensive determination of those actors that participate in the production of the communitarian semantics necessary to ensure the relative determinacy of formal law-ascertainment or the legitimacy and appropriateness of current social practice-making processes at the international level, this book has only done some very preliminary spadework, limiting itself to showing that the model of law-ascertainment based on the source and social theses is endowed with an—often underestimated—ability to renew itself from within and take into account changes in social practice as well as among the law-applying authorities conducive thereto. Far from resolving all the controversies riddling the ascertainment of rules, the argument made in this book rather calls for a continuous attention to the evolving social practice of law-applying authorities, broadly conceived.

Many of these conclusions hold for the new manifestations of the exercise of public authority at the international level. The insights that can be gained from the model of law-ascertainment presented here are irrespective of whether or not these new forms of exercise of public authority constitute international law, properly so-called.[9] However we construct and apply rule-ascertainment in respect of these new forms of exercise of public authority, and whether or not we include them in traditional international law, it is submitted here that the relevance of formalism—construed here as the use of formal law-ascertainment indicators based on a social practice—will not evaporate in a world of pluralized normativity and postnational law. In that sense, I contend that formal rule-ascertainment remains germane beyond the traditional forms of international law-making which have been examined here. It is true that formalism itself, as has been continuously argued here, does not provide any descriptive framework to capture these new forms of exercise of public authority.[10] It is also true that the mere transposition of the law-ascertainment theory elaborated here to new normative orders and processes cannot be mechanical. In the same way that the source and social theses cannot be converted from general legal theory to the theory of the sources of international law without sweeping adaptions, we must resist the temptation of simply filling the voids created by the new forms of exercise of public authority at the international level with what we already know.[11] However, in a world of pluralized normativity and postnational law, the necessity for legal boundaries[12] will remain unaffected and, with it, the necessity for formal rule-ascertainment criteria. There is thus little doubt, in the view of the author of these lines, that the configuration as well as the foundation of the ascertainment of the rules produced by these new forms of exercise of public authority can be usefully informed by the abovementioned theory of international law-ascertainment grounded in the social practice of—widely construed—law-applying authorities.

[9] In the framework of the current and future scholarly pursuits to cognize these pluralized normative activities at the international level, it is utterly conceivable, at least theoretically, that the mainstream model of ascertainment of international legal rules be reconstructed in a way that allows the normative products thereof to fall in the remit of international law. New formal international law-ascertainment criteria could indeed be devised as to elevate the norms originating in these pluralized exercises of public authority at the international level into rules of international law. It has not been the ambition of this book to prejudge the outcome of this scholarly reflection. Yet, it must be acknowledged that such attempts would inevitably stumble on a paradox. Indeed, it can hardly be contested that the products of such normative activities have been consciously and purposely used and designed by international actors to remain outside the traditional channels of international and domestic law-making. If encapsulated in international law by virtue of newly designed law-ascertainment criteria, any inclusive theory of the sources of international law would most likely prod international actors to reinvent again other forms of norm-making processes to escape such an ever-expanding international law. In that sense, any new expansion of international law towards a more inclusive conceptualization of the sources of international law could arouse a new move by international actors towards even more deformalized forms of norm-making. Such a paradox does certainly not mean that attempts to revamp the ascertainment of international legal rules with a view to embracing pluralized forms of exercise of public authority ought to be abandoned. This simply calls for a greater awareness of the risk that international legal scholars and international actors run of ending up in a perpetual circular move that can aggravate the disconnect between them.

[10] Cfr *supra* 2.1.1 and 2.1.2.

[11] See N. Krisch, *Beyond Constitutionalism—The Pluralist Structure of Postnational Law* (OUP, Oxford, 2010) 26: 'We tend to fill voids with what we know. When we are thrown into unfamiliar spaces, we try to chart them with maps we possess, construct them with the tools we already have'.

[12] On the relevance of legal boundaries for postnationalism, see H. Lindahl, 'A-Legality: Postnationalism and the Question of Legal Boundaries' (2010) 73 MLR 30–56.

APPENDIX 1

Debate on EJIL Talk! Blog

In December 2012, the EJIL Talk Blog (www.ejiltalk.com) hosted an online symposium on *Formalism and International Law*, to which the author and expert commentators contributed. The debate that ensued is reproduced here.

The exchange included comments by Carlos Espósito (Universidad Autónoma de Madrid), and Philip Allott (Trinity College, Cambridge). The author then responded to their critiques and submitted his concluding remarks.

Comment on d'Aspremont's *Formalism and the Sources of International Law*: We Don't Just Talk Past Each Other; We Disagree!

Carlos Espósito

Jean d'Aspremont is concerned with the effects of the Babel syndrome created by legal pluralism. He is bewildered that international scholars 'talk past each other': the impression that international legal scholarship has become "a cluster of different scholarly communities, each using different criteria for the ascertainment of international legal rules" (3). This is the justification for his impressive intellectual effort to present a 'theory of the ascertainment of legal rules' and engage in the politics of formalism (29).

His theory is rooted in Herbert Hart's famous source and social theses, which are reinterpreted by d'Aspremont to fit international law. In d'Aspremont's theory, "law-ascertainment in international law must be conceived independently of article 38 [of the ICJ Statute], which was not only conceived to serve another purpose, but also leaves too much room for non-formal law-ascertainment"(150). He favours the use of written linguistic indicators (formal law-ascertainment is only possible for rules enshrined in a written instrument) to guarantee formal law-ascertainment in international law and move away from intent-based systems to determine international legal rules.

D'Aspremont affirms that his proposal amounts to "a complete reversal of our theoretical perspectives which allows the ascertainment of treaties and other international legal acts to do away with the speculations inherent in the establishment of intent and makes it exclusively dependent on the use of linguistic indicators" (192). The source thesis, by which rules are ascertained through their pedigree, is completed by the social thesis, which provides the foundations for the formal law-ascertainment of rules in the social practice of law-applying authorities. That is, in a nutshell, D'Aspremont's recipe to secure true common legal language in "an age of pluralized normativity" (221), a goal that cannot be achieved by other techniques of law identification based on impact, compliance, process, or intent.

A blog post is, of course, not the ideal medium to review in detail the many interesting points raised by d'Aspremont in his encyclopedic, often complex, but absolutely remarkable piece of scholarship. I would rather advance three interconnected comments on some of the more controversial aspects of his book.

The first concerns the very practice of international law. I believe that the author does not take sufficiently seriously the fact that his scholarly drama is not a tragedy for practitioners—for most practitioners it is not even a drama (indeed, in his LCIL Friday Lunchtime Lecture he even said that practitioners are 'happy" with customary law as it is). In the book, d'Aspremont concedes that his arguments "may at times seem arcane to those who are actually engaged in the practice of international law," and that "[i]t is true that, by contrast to the determination of the content of the law, the ascertainment of international legal rules is not a continuous and recurring controversy in practice" (8).

D'Aspremont says that these contemporary debates are too important to be ignored by practitioners, who will eventually be affected by deformalization (9). But this is not enough to justify all the efforts and changes that adopting his thesis would demand from practitioners. I must admit that I am also perplexed by this fact, because as a scholar I do share with the author the sense of confusion about the law-ascertainment of non-written rules, such as customary international law and general principles of law. However, I must also acknowledge that d'Aspremont's arguments do not seem to be sufficiently persuasive to involve the practitioners in the politics of formalism, whatever the costs of the present practice.

The second concerns the nature of d'Aspremont's theoretical ambition. In other words, is the book an argument or a theory? The subtitle is "a theory of the ascertainment of legal rules." However, even when he struggles to differentiate himself from Koskenniemi's culture of formalism, which is clearly not a theory, d'Aspremont's book could be read as a sophisticated theoretical development of such programme. Indeed, d'Aspremont accepts that his is also a political endeavour, that legal scholars may get involved in the politics of formalism or just keep doing what they do based on varied agendas, such as the expansion of international law or its object, among others (130–134). For d'Aspremont, "formal law-ascertainment is, more modestly, nothing more than a political choice for the preservation of the normative character of international law, the meaningfulness of the international legal scholarship, the possibility of a critique of law, and the rule of law" (145).

This is not how I read the jurisprudential debates on the source and social theories between positivists, either exclusive or inclusive, and its critics—and it's just an example, as I am not in favour of bringing that kind of "parochial debate' to the field of international law. These theories have both a normative and descriptive ambition which may be excellent or poor, but not optional. To put it in Solum's words, they are playing 'King of the hill'. D'Aspremont's argument would be a theory if he defends his criteria of law as exhaustive. In other words, I would suggest that d'Aspremont defends the proposition that conventional written linguistic indicators are the only valid legal criteria to determine or ascertain international legal norms. That would be really provocative, and I like it.

Of course, and this is my third point, that would bring us back to the social practice, because it is far from clear that international law-applying authorities, whatever its definition, will come to share the kind of formalism defended by d'Aspremont, and so drastically limit the legal criteria to determine what is law and, by that token, also the content of law. In my view the author's efforts to radically separate formal law-ascertainment from the determination of the content of law is not convincing. Suffice to say that the discussion on the social thesis between positivists and Ronald Dworkin concerns the best explanation of how people argue about the content of law.

In concluding, and with another provocative statement that I know Jean d'Aspremont will enjoy, I would like to suggest that international law scholars don't talk past each other; we disagree!

Comments on Jean d'Aspremont, *Formalism and the Sources of International Law: A Theory of the Ascertainment of Legal Rules*

Philip Allot

Jean d'Aspremont's book evokes subliminally two recurring nightmares—one social, one intellectual. Socially, it reminds us of the failure of law to secure its proper place in international society. Intellectually, it reminds us of the part played by the modern university in the disempowering of the human mind.

The conventions of monograph-writing require that the author survey the territory in which he or she intends to plant something new—employed, as John Locke modestly said of himself, 'as an under-labourer in clearing the ground a little, and removing some of the rubbish that lies in the way of knowledge'. In fact, as d'Aspremont himself notes, most self-conscious intellectual innovators, before the advent of the modern university, did not devote much explicit effort to disposing of the writings of their predecessors. Locke himself certainly did not do so, either in the Essay or the Two Treatises.

In the present case, 'clearing the ground a little' produces a mountain of footnotes listing hundreds of writings expressing, and endlessly recycling, every conceivable view, and many inconceivable views, about the essence of International Law, or its lack of an essence. It requires the author to sift through the output of an industrial-scale intellectual effort, to sort out the countless academic sects (many of them blessed with brand-names ending in -ism), and to locate them in relation to each other. And it requires him to perform the impossible—but academically expected—task of making sober judgments about their relative merits.

And, all the while, the wicked world goes on its merry way to ruin. Why would anyone choose to write creatively and intelligently about the philosophy of International Law? They are unlikely to be heard by those who exercise international public power—politicians, diplomats, civil servants, intergovernmental officials, international judges and arbitrators, legal practitioners—the international ruling class, a self-satisfied and self-regarding conspiracy, many of whose members have the crudest ideas about the nature of law, and many of whose members relentlessly abuse public power, national and international.

It is important to understand two things. Holders of public power are the product of ideas, ideas that they did not invent. Holders of public power use other people's ideas as instruments of power. If a more or less abstract idea might be useful to them, they will appropriate it—ideas of religion or philosophy or morality or political theory or natural science or human psychology—not only to justify their possession of power but also to exercise that power more efficiently. Words are power. Words are weapons. The power of the powerful includes the power to incorporate ideas into the language of power.

I won't comment in detail on the intricacies of d'Aspremont's exposition. But I must say that I would differ from some of his accounts and judgments of legal philosophies and theoretical positions with which I am myself familiar. (I'm sorry that he devotes respectful attention to Herbert Hart and Ludwig Wittgenstein—both of them being of minimal continuing intellectual significance.) For me, the book is important at a more general level. The important question is—what general lessons can we learn from d'Aspremont's heroic work of synthesis and analysis?

The first lesson is that the intellectual closed garden of the modern university system means that more or less sophisticated ideas only escape haphazardly and fortuitously into the outside world where, if they are not appropriated by public power or mass culture, they wither and die. The Monographismus of the universities, like the Essayismus of public intellectuals (to invoke Robert Musil's perceptive nosology), immunises public power and the public mind from the threat of transformatory ideas.

The second general lesson is that the ideas that are appropriated by public power are chronically confused in their effects. Good and goodish ideas may become less good ideas, or actually evil ideas, after their political appropriation. (And now I'm going to imply some significant differences from d'Aspremont's generally benign accounts and judgments.)

Vitoria's theological universal law-thought reminded the new colonialists of the better side of their human nature; but they could read it as an implicit acceptance of the fact of mega-colonialism. Grotius used a wild Renaissance historiography (including the Bible, mythology, miscellaneous literature, Greek and Roman self-fantasising) to remind the Thirty-Years-Warmongers that barbarism is a choice not a fatality; but, for warmongers, then and thereafter, this meant that barbarism remained a possible choice. Hobbes intended to subject law to the highest purposes of society; but public power holders (including judges) could read it as the sacralising of 'the law', however immoral, not to say criminal, any particular 'law' might be (and, in England, that meant many of the—largely property-based—laws).

The US Constitution-makers and the Federalist Papers almost gave the game away about the ambiguous bargain of 'democracy'. The law protects the rich against the overwhelming natural power of the masses; and the masses may be permitted, by the powerful, to use the law to protect themselves against the inevitable abuse of power by the rich. Adam Smith imagined an equality of economic freedom in the socialising-through-law of self-interest (with its roots in greed); but, for most people, collective social wealth-making came to mean ultimate personal and legal subjection, in accordance with Smith's charming idea of the division of labour (that is to say, the ruthless integration of labour).

And the oh-so-elegant Vattel ('one of us', in the eyes of governments) used a modicum of Renaissance humanism to imagine an inherent and natural egalitarianism and voluntarism in international politics, which, paradoxically, allowed governments to believe that it must also be inherent and natural that the will of some of them is, in practice, very much more equal than the will of others. Vattel's system—the actual international constitutional system—is a system of limited and self-interested reciprocity among the most powerful, which may or may not happen to be in the interest of the less powerful, a system of international oligarchy. Perhaps this reflects the true nature of all government, whatever the ingenious stories we tell about it. That may be Aristotle's unspoken conclusion in the Politics. Tyranny and oligarchy and democracy are three unstable sides of a single coin—and revolution is a toss of that coin.

So, the third lesson of d'Aspremont's painstaking survey is that we must always ask, when faced with sets of ideas, not whether they are true or right or good or better (to which he devotes so much effort), but whether those ideas are capable of being appropriated by public power and, if so, whether public power could appropriate them in such a way that their potential good would be likely, when applied in practice, to outweigh their potential harm. That is how I must judge d'Aspremont's own ideas.

Strangely, despite the book's subtitle, he only puts forward an explicit theoretical proposal of his own in a modestly expressed section in the last part of the book. I was hoping that most of the book would be devoted to a revolutionary new theory of the sources of International Law—or even a revolutionary restoration of the true sources—customary law (in the ancient sense of that term—in which opinio iuris has nothing to do with opinion) and treaties (as a source of legal relations and an emerging form of legislation—compare: the development of the sources of law in national societies).

A constantly repeated theme of the book is that one should distinguish three things—the process for the ascertainment of a rule as a rule of law; the evidence suggesting that a particular rule is accordingly a rule of law; and ascertainment of the content of that rule. The word formalism is entangled in so many different theoretical disputes about law that it might have been better to avoid using it as a keyword in this book. Sources is a better word. The main bulk of the book is concerned with the first of the three topics. Can there be a rule of law determining, on formal grounds, what is to be regarded as a rule of law?

I agree strongly with a view expressed in the first chapters of the book that one might think that settled ideas about the nature of law are at least as necessary in international society as they are in national society. A legal system without an accepted and efficient idea of the law-making sources of law cannot be an effective legal system.

And I strongly support the idea (expressed here in my own words!) that the Rule of Law, a great achievement born of arduous social experience, is a farce if the essential and distinctive character of law is not an idea that dominates the minds of actual holders of public power. Incidentally, d'Aspremont evidently understands the idea correctly—as opposed to many who do not understand it or, for their own purposes, choose to misunderstand it. The idea of the Rule of Law means that all public power is subject to the law, as finally determined by the courts. And international public power is public power.

The book seems to me to be suffused with an undercurrent of longing to rise above the fearful cacophony (d'Aspremont's word) of the theoretical writing—and to bring rational order to the dreadful mess of practical international behaviour—with its crazy proliferation of forms of intergovernmental acts and instruments, the more or less worthless theoretical ruminations of international courts and tribunals, the sublime indifference of governments and legal practitioners to the theoretical anarchy of their behaviour.

Until I read this book, I hadn't realised the extent to which the conceptual structure of International Law has decayed (to borrow Tony Carty's word) over recent decades. Over the last sixty or seventy years, International Law has increased immensely in volume, density and complexity, approximating more and more to the substance of an advanced legal system. But it seems that a (the, even) prevailing view now is that law is what people think it is, a legal rule is what people think it is, a legal act is what people think it is. It is an appalling state of affairs.

The primary function of the constitution in national legal systems is to assign and control law-making power. And the reason for this is a lesson learned from many millennia of human social experience. Law determines the lives of people, using legally authorised physical force if necessary. It follows that the people must know the source of the law that determines their lives; and the holders of public power must know that they have no other legal power than the power that the law gives them. Law seen in this way is one of the greatest achievements of the self-ordering human species. (Even in the UK, with an unwritten constitution, we, the people, can know that we have three sources of law—in a descending hierarchy—EU law, statute law (made by or under an Act of Parliament), and the Common Law—the first having been added by a virtually revolutionary event in 1973.)

Jean d'Aspremont proposes that we should introduce some more rigour into the subjectivity of law ascertainment. He refers to the view (news to me) that Hart's system is a 'social thesis' of law (the source of the validity of law is a matter to be determined by society—a wonderful banality compared with Kelsen's Kantian analysis of the logically necessary self-contained structure of a legal system). And he mentions Wittgenstein's remarkable personal discovery (of the age-old philosophical position) that the meaning of language is socially constructed, so that law-language, even when law is speaking about itself, must also be socially constructed!

He passes in review the various 'social actors' who might be included 'in the determination of the communitarian semantics constitutive of the meaning of law-ascertainment' (page 204) [ghostly presence of American Pragmatism, Habermas, Rorty . . .]—international courts and tribunals, domestic courts, the International Law Commission (God forbid!), legal scholars (God forbid!), the better sort of international NGO, among others. For me, the most important 'social actors' are the people—the least likely to be heard.

Certainly governments would want to have their say. They have useful experience in the making of the international system. In the 19th century, they appropriated ideas of law and consent from post-revolutionary democracy in national societies, leaving behind the rest of the paraphernalia of democracy. In the 20th century, they appropriated the idea of a court, but without the essential characteristics that attendance at court is not voluntary and the law applied by the court is not made by the parties before the court. After 1918, they appropriated the dubious ideas of just war and self-determination, and incorporated them into international systems that remained under their control. After 1945, they appropriated the idea of human rights, reconceived in superficial remorse for horrors that they themselves had caused, legislating and institutionalising the idea into something unthreatening. And governments used their ILC to articulate a fantasy category of state responsibility, as opposed to the legal liability that attaches specifically and inherently to every legal relation, undermining the effectiveness of countless international legal relations.

And now governments are allowing their International Law Commission to apply its collective mind to a new topic—'the formation and evidence of customary international law'. Ultimate political appropriation of an ultimate idea. The Commission will, as always, seek the views of governments, and other holders of international public power, on this interesting problem of legal philosophy. And no doubt they will consult with 'social actors', possibly even 'legal scholars'.

And, if the worst comes to the worst, governments may finally succeed in establishing law in its proper place in international society—in accordance with their own understanding of the word 'proper'. And we, the people, will persist in our effort to make International Law into the true law of a true international society.

The Ruins of the Sources Theory and the Garden of Eden: A Rejoinder to Carlos Esposito and Philip Allott

Jean d'Aspremont

I feel indebted to Carlos Esposito and Philip Allott who have taken so much of their—precious—time to engage with the argument developed in my book Formalism and the Sources of International Law. In a professional community where constant solicitation and correlative overcommitment have become pathological, taking pains to engage with and constructively criticize peers' works amounts to a manifestation of respect which, coming from such highly esteemed figures, is greatly flattering. I simultaneously rejoice at the fact that their—deliciously phrased and doled out—criticisms touch on the very points which, in my view, have always deserved to be debated across the interpretative community of international law. In this brief rejoinder, I shall limit myself to mention a few of them and sketch out my thoughts on the matter.

The communicative protocols of modern academia

Philip Allott eloquently—and very cynically—repudiates the painstaking (and almost insane) exercise of writing a monograph on a subject like that of this book, and especially the accompanying necessity to indulge in gluttonously encyclopedic referencing. I share Allott's disdain for such practices. This is what I have expressed in the book in the paragraph he referred to (p. 38).

However, I have long come to terms with the absurdity of many of the communicative protocols of our interpretative community. I have come to believe that scorning and disregarding them may undermine the dissemination of one's ideas and, worse, its validation by one's peers—the latter being trained to (and formatted by) the same communicative conventions. In other words, and as I have explained here, I believe that the protocols bemoaned by Allott are the price to pay to be admitted in the argumentative arena of international law.

Probably the same holds with respect to the fully justified remark made by Carlos Esposito about the idea of a "theory". In today's thinking in social sciences, everything is presented as theory but hardly anything qualifies as theory. Admittedly, on these matters, it is often difficult to resist the spin-doctors of publishers for whom theories sell much better than mere arguments or theoretical frameworks. But there is certainly nothing to be lamented in such a concession. Communicative protocols and semantics (as well the techniques to secure semantic authority) inevitably and constantly evolve in any interpretative community. The semantic travesty flagged by Carlos Esposito is itself the expression of a contemporary practice which it is sometimes wiser to assume than to repudiate.

Idiosyncrasy and cross-current epistemological quest

Even if one uses the communicative protocol of one's profession, one can still be moving crosscurrent. In this regard, I believe it is not an overstatement to say that the argument made in the book under discussion does not belong to the shows currently heard on the Broadway of international legal scholarship. This is why it is not surprising to read Philip

Allott's elegantly writing that the book "seems . . . to be suffused with an undercurrent of longing to rise above the fearful cacophony (d'Aspremont's word) of the theoretical writing—and to bring rational order to the dreadful mess of practical international behaviour (. . .), the more or less worthless theoretical ruminations of international courts and tribunals, the sublime indifference of governments and legal practitioners to the theoretical anarchy of their behaviour."

This being said, idiosyncrasy should never be sought for the sake of provocation—although being provocative is often palatable and sometimes very efficient. If idiosyncrasy is of any relevance, it is because it can help all those engaged in the argumentative arena of international law take a step back from their—often mechanically and uncritically repeated—cognitive tools as well as social conventions inherited from their schoolmasters. In the following paragraphs, I accordingly would like to address some of the points where Esposito and Allott believe that the critical distance called upon by the book is either unnecessary or misplaced.

The empirical sting

Part of the idiosyncrasy of the argument is to be traced back to one of the three objections raised by Carlos Esposito. It pertains to what I would personally call the "empirical sting", that is the idea that the crisis of the theory of sources is a purely scholarly predicament. This objection means that the deformalization discussed by the book is not impinging on the practitioners for whom the system functions properly, as rules can be decently identified. According to this argument, the challenge for practitioners is to persuade adversaries as to the exact content of rules. It is not about identifying them.

This argument is certainly not without merit. Isn't the crisis of the theory of sources (provoked by the move towards deformalization) a pure product of one specific branch of the interpretative community of international law, namely legal scholars? Isn't this crisis a storm in the tiny cup of tea of the international legal scholarship? This is an objection which I heard at NYU during some exchanges with the students of Benedict Kingsbury and Joseph Weiler.

As I explained on that occasion, I appreciate that practices in judicial circles may seem less affected by the abovementioned move towards deformalization. Counsel and judges perpetuate their exchanges for securing semantic authority, fighting about content-determination rather than law-ascertainment. In that sense, content-determination is the crux of courtrooms argumentative practices, not law-ascertainment. Regarding the former, international lawyers are said to have devised the most ingenious—albeit the most deceitful—theory ever created in the modern thinking about international law: the theory of interpretation. And, still according to this view, it is the theory of interpretation, not the theory of sources, that is in crisis.

This objection calls for two remarks. First, the theory of interpretation is meant to be in a crisis. Being a vain—but necessary—attempt to convey the idea of immanent rationality of legal argumentation, it inevitably appears mistreated in practice. Not being able to produce one single legal truth, it necessarily looks subject to abuse in any case where law is applied. But this does not automatically mean, contrary to what Esposito claims, that law-ascertainment criteria are the object of a consensus among the actors involved in courtrooms.

And this leads me to my second point. I believe that the conceptual mayhem currently witnessed in the international legal scholarship already trickles in the practice of courts and tribunals. There probably is an easy explanation to this. Despite their existential and self-legitimizing need to claim the possibility of immanent rationality, those judges who have been to law schools and/or have had a stint in the legal academy are well aware of the conceptual havoc in which international law ascertainment has been left in the legal scholarship. When they do not turn such deficiencies to their advantage—for instance by making use of the comfort zone of customary international law—they try to obfuscate those deficiencies (a feat!) with a view to salvaging the pretense of existing law-ascertainment techniques.

In my view, it is not certain that such a performance can be reproduced in perpetuum. I actually believe that the end of this era of denial in international adjudicatory practice is in sight. This is probably what the current disinterest of international courts and tribunals for the criteria of law-ascertainment—e.g. with respect to treaty-identification—manifests. After several decades during which they attempted to develop sophisticated techniques in this respect, courts and tribunals are now growingly aware of the theoretical confusion shrouding the theory of sources—which they contributed to aggravate—and will soon be inevitably forced to acknowledge that the current deficient law-identification criteria undermine the production of authoritative decisions which is at the heart of their judicial business.

The ruins of the theory of sources

If we leave aside the practice of courts and tribunals—and that of other law-applying authorities—it seems to me that the confusion reigning in the thinking about the theory of sources is even more glaring. It is interesting to recall here that when Philip Allott and I met last spring in Cambridge on the occasion of a presentation of the book at the Lauterpacht Centre (which Philip was kind enough to introduce and chair), we found each other in total agreement as to the capacity of the theory of sources to transform political events as well as their "democratic" virtues. This is what led both of us to deplore the ruins in which legal scholars have left the theory of sources. He seems to have lately found such rubbles to be even more dreadful than he originally thought (he writes: "Until I read this book, I hadn't realised the extent to which the conceptual structure of International Law has decayed (to borrow Tony Carty's word) over recent decades").

Whilst agreeing on the symptoms and the antidote, Allott and I probably disagree on the routes for recovery and the astrologic signs that could guide such a journey. This discrepancy is certainly fundamental. In social science, the debate that matters the most is that about the route to follow, not about where the journey ends. Yet, I do not think that our difference of views about how to secure the antidote is what needs to be discussed in this blog—whose format remains paradoxically constraining for debates about such foundational questions. What matters more here is to realize both the illusions created through the current mainstream theory of sources and the illusions found behind the current moves towards deformalization. Both are equally pernicious. Both are equally fallacious and misleading. They maintain scholars in a dangerous and self-enslaving state of passivity. Both lead to cloistering scholars—as well as, for Allott, the society which they serve—into a Garden of Eden.

Debating the possibility for the antidote: the social practice of law-applying authorities

One particular antidote which the book suggests is the preservation of room for the emergence of social practice which will provide the communitarian semantics necessary for the coalescence of formal yardsticks to distinguish law from non-law. Carlos Esposito insightfully highlights the difficulty to find social practice which can be conducive to formal criteria to distinguish law from non-law.

Needless to say that I am aware that the identification of those participating (and contributing to) the social practice—and thus the way this social practice is cognized and constructed—constitute the most daunting intellectual challenge which the argument made in this book leaves us with. This challenge does not only point to the question of how to construct law in the legal scholarship. It also raises questions pertaining to the political choices about who is empowered to generate practice conducive to the emergence of social practice determinative of law-ascertainment criteria. In my view, this certainly is the most central question, for the way in which one understands the concept of 'law-applying authority'—and thus the corresponding social-practice generative processes—will be determinative of the criteria that allow to distinguish law and non-law. May the disagreement expressed by Carlos Esposito—and my own rejection of his contention that law-applying authorities cannot share some kind of formalism—suffice to demonstrate that we cannot afford ignoring this debate.

Leaving the Garden of Eden and reinventing the theory of sources?

I shall eventually return to the ambition of the book. Indeed, Philip Allott is not far from regretting the lack of ambition of the book which, in his eyes, only sets the stage for a revolutionary restoration of the true sources but fall short of carrying out such a revolution. It is crucial to highlight here that this has been a conscious decision from the very start of this project. Indeed, the book "only" aims at offering a theoretical framework for a greater awareness of (and self-reflection about) the responsibility of those potentially engaged in the (reflection about the) production of communitarian semantics that shape the theory of sources. The book was also meant to give observers—and especially legal scholars—a better grasp of the dynamics at play in the formation and evolutions of the cognitive languages of the interpretative community of international law. In that sense, this work has never been meant to carry out a revolution.

There are probably three reasons for this choice for modesty. First, because it is not certain that those currently engaged in the practices of the theory of sources—whether States, judges, activists, legal scholars to name only a few—are interested in leaving the Garden of Eden where customary international law, for instance, can accommodate any political project—reformist, restrictionist, programmatist, self-empowering, etc.

Second, and more importantly, because it is not certain that it is up to legal scholars to take the lead in this revolution by (re-)designing the rules of cognition of a new international legal system. While certainly endowed with responsibilities of grammarians, international legal scholars have neither the means nor the legitimacy to lead what would then be a rather aristocratic revolution. The argument made in this book thus comes with a feeling of humility about what legal scholars can ever hope to achieve: they are simply not sources of social practice for the sake of the theory of sources.

But there is a third and last reason for the book stopping short of reinventing a new Garden of Eden. This probably brings us back to the constraints inherent in the communicative protocols pertaining to how the production of knowledge in social science operates. Complex arguments need to be doled out carefully, as overwhelming one's peers carries the risk of undermining the reception and validation of one's argument as well as its crystallization. This is probably something which Wittgenstein underestimated.

Likewise, an argument—and eventually a vision about one of the multiple possible ways in which (international) law can be constructed—necessitate that reflection be gradually disclosed and unveiled. Persuasion and peer-validation constitute a progressive process. In that sense, it is not to please publishers that one splits, scatters or postpones the further depiction of (the consequences of) one's vision of the social science of law and that of its object. It is simply to make room for intermediate mutually enriching engagements and allow the continuation of one's reflection without premature self-generated and uncritical constraints of one's own thinking. A comprehensive presentation and discussion of all implications of the—already complex—theoretical framework set in this book are thus left for the next step in the long and intricate process of knowledge production—and, hence, the next piece of work devoted to this question.

APPENDIX 2

International Law as a Technical Discipline: Critical Perspectives on the Narrative Structure of a Theory

*Sahib Singh**

1. Introduction

It has gradually occurred to me that to engage with theory requires one to resign himself to an existence defined by epistemological crises. Moments of resolution permeate and stabilize this existence, but they are fleeting. In such moments, beliefs (those schemata we use to impose intelligence upon the world) are held with a resilience that belies their perpetual turmoil. But epistemic crises consistently emerge for the thorough theorist who confronts, and accepts, the potential invalidity, limits or various interpretations of his schemata. This may lead to ruptures within his thought or (more likely) its incremental evolution—both merely contingent and temporary determinations to any such crisis. In addition to this, the theorist also realizes that his beliefs, his schemata, are to a large extent constituted and defined by the continued contestation over their validity and interpretation. The theorist knows both that incoherence lies within his theory and that rival theories, positing different possibilities, make equally justifiable claims upon him. But epistemic crises continue to punctuate belief because the theorist is constantly confronted with the knowledge that there are, and will be, no independent or common criteria which may allow him to chose between theories.[1] Knowing this, the theorist ought to forge a path of (continuously) recasted narratives. This is both the plight and virtue of his endeavor.

This is not to valorize the theorist, his condition or even his endeavor in a legal world where thought and education are dominated by programmatic pragmatism and practicality. Rather, it is a prolegomena to how theory ought to be approached—a matter which will be returned to later. For now, it concerns the sensitivities an observer ought to afford a theorist. It guards against approaching theoretical work with the simplistic rigidity that readers so often ascribe to the written word and a single piece of work. The value of Professor d'Aspremont's monograph is found in understanding the intellectual context within which his argument emerges. Context, here, means both the place his

* PhD Candidate, University of Cambridge; Visiting Lecturer of International Law, University of Vienna [sahib.g.singh@gmail.com]. I would like to thank David Kennedy and Martti Koskenniemi for their thoughts and encouragement. This note, with variations, will be forthcoming in the *British Yearbook of International Law*. All numbers in parenthesis within the main text are page references to the book under review.

[1] See generally, A. MacIntyre, 'Epistemological crises, dramatic narrative, and the philosophy of science' (1977) 60 *The Monist* 453.

book takes in his broader work on theory—understanding it as a fleeting moment of resolution—one at odds with his other forays into theory and the place of his project—his resurrection of international legal positivism[2]—within the broader intellectual theatrics of theoretical thought in international law.

But I digress. Jean d'Aspremont's book is welcome for its intellectual rigour and more importantly, the timing of its intervention in jurisprudential thinking in international law. It is rare that a book remains so measured and accessible despite undertaking the Herculean task of synthesizing the scholarly output of a number of theoretical schools within international law. That this one does so is a testament to its author. It is precisely this rigour that lays the foundations, or more accurately opens up the conceptual space, for d'Aspremont's revival of analytical jurisprudence and the work of HLA Hart. He seeks to resurrect a school that has taken the proverbial battering from various intellectual camps, both American and European, and whose last remaining enclave may well be the shores of Britain.

But despite d'Aspremont's trails through the terrain of theory, his central thesis is quite simple: ascertaining the sources of international law needs to be formalized and this can only be achieved by grounding their cognition in the social practice of a wide range of law-applying authorities. This is a thesis, not a theory; let alone a general theory of international law (8). It is better understood as a mild intervention in international legal academic discourse; a gentle reminder that when one talks about and uses international law, one talks specifically of law (not economics, philosophy or international relations theory) as grounded in identifiable rules and social facts (even if it is so much more than this). The reminder is one of the intricacies of disciplinarity and of the particularities of international law. Interdisciplinarity, in certain forms (usually of a US variant), carries with it dubious politics. The timeliness of this reminder is the overbearing virtue of this book. This message must not get lost when examining, and/or disagreeing with, the finer details of *Formalism and the Sources of International Law*. But it is with the details that this reviewer has his quibbles.

This paper is purposefully structured by a critical narrative analytic methodology. This will highlight the book's strategies of persuasion and the aesthetic structure of d'Aspremont's argument; his supporting theses, his intellectual maneuvers and the contexts in which these are brought to bear on the reader. This type of methodology also allows a review to comment on (some of) the conventions of knowledge production in international legal theory. Given that narratives are works of cohesion, critical narrative analysis is aimed at highlighting the small but fundamental inconsistencies within the story presented. Used as an analytic tool, it provides the (false) image that the narrator of the narrative (here, the reviewer) provides a more cogent understanding of the strategies at play in a narrative than the original narrative itself. The reader should resist the urge to think of this review in such a manner, instead conceiving of identified inconsistencies as nothing more than plausible alternative viewpoints.

[2] See e.g. J. d'Aspremont and J. Kammerhofer, *International Legal Positivism in a Post-modern World* (Cambridge: CUP, *forthcoming* 2013); J. d'Aspremont, 'Reductionist Legal Positivism and International Law', (2012) 106 *Proceedings of the Annual Meeting of the American Society of International Law* (forthcoming); 'Wording in International Law' (2012) 25 *Leiden Journal of International Law* 575; 'Formalism and the Sources of International Law' (Lecture, University of Cambridge Lauterpacht Centre of International Law, 27 April 2012).

Using this methodology, this paper will be structured as follows. Section 2 will begin by highlighting two sub-narratives that emerge and dominate the book: order and intellectual specialization. Sections 3–6 will examine the book's structural aesthetics, namely its manoeuvres, concessions, circumventions and other strategies of persuasion. It is through these that the book's narrative and sub-narratives play out convincingly. Each of these sections (3–6) will explore the contours and internal frictions of the identified structural aesthetic—and they are generally organized in accordance with the book's layout. These include: the discourse of necessity as a prelude to constructive argument (section 3), conciliatory methodological techniques and the politics of theory (section 4), the virtues and failures of having an adversary (section 5) and finally the value of the book's main thesis (section 6). The paper will then offer its concluding remarks (section 7).

2. Dominant Sub-Narratives: Order and the Nature of Theory

Historically the enduring rhetorical allure of order, coherence and systemacity is remarkable. These concepts are never more prevalent than at times of intellectual specialization and uncertainty, characteristics apt to describe the current state of international legal theory.[3] Their contemporary intellectual charm, despite Foucault and Derrida's effect on legal theory, ensures they lie seductively in both the structural aesthetics of d'Aspremont's book and within the essence of his central thesis. The book's narrative is quite clear, as are its aesthetics and tenets as a project of renewal: not only may we *neatly* categorize vast areas of theory, its achievements, failings and loopholes, but we can find communitarian coherence (the new objectivity) in the practice of applying international law despite lacking a cohesive social consciousness. Method can be compartmentalized; a theory can function within a specialized and constructed corner; and social observation science works. Order, agreement and consensus are the only ways our discipline can move forward.

This narrative is not new. Rather, it bears all the hallmarks of the inter-war discourse within international law.[4] Then it was a narrative that rejected conceptualism and the trappings of legal formalism, its sociological roots centered social observation as the basis of knowledge and determinate sources were considered the key to a determinate law. Not much has changed. This historical circularity only illuminates the international legal theorist's pathological desire for determinacy, pitting order against disorder, scientific approaches against metaphysics and progress against stagnation. The 'disciplinary hamster wheel'[5] continues to spin unbounded. Rehabilitation was needed then; rediscovery and

[3] See P. Allott, 'Law and Social Evolution: Post-Evolutionary Human Involution', ASIL-ESIL Workshop University of Cambridge Speech, 20–21 September 2012; S. Singh, 'Two Potential Paths Forward from Fragmentation Discourse: Sociology and Ethics', (2011) 105 *Proceedings of the American Society of International Law* 130.

[4] See M. Koskenniemi, *The Gentle Civilizer of Nations. The Rise and Fall of International Law 1870–1960* (Cambridge: CUP, 2002), 266–352 S. Astorino, 'The Impact of Sociological Jurisprudence on International Law in the Interwar Period' (1996) 34 *Duquesne Law Review* 277. For an excellent examination of the narratives on sources in the inter-war period see, T. Skouteris, *The Notion of Progress in International Law Discourse* (PhD Thesis, Leiden University, 2008), Chapter 3.

[5] D. Kennedy, 'When Renewal Repeats: Thinking Against the Box', (2000) 32 *New York University Journal of International Law and Politics* 335, 407.

renewal are needed now. And then, as in now, it was greater determinacy in the sources of international law that could provide the answer. The structural aesthetics (the manoeuvres, concessions and circumventions) of d'Aspremont's narrative draws great inspiration from its periodic ancestor.

But it is accompanied by the narrative customs of theorising in contemporary intellectual society. Grand theory has certainly met its demise. But the contemporary approach I talk of here is akin to Kuhn's methodological incommensurability. Contemporary theory takes the approach that certain theoretical approaches are *a priori* incompatible with other theories. To chose one is to forego another (positivism/naturalism, idealism/realism etc.). It ought to be born in mind that this approach, whilst dominant, comes with its own dubious politics and approach to rationality. At its essence the Kuhnian *methodenstreit* induces a strong immunity against critique within theory. It allows a theorist to strike down as irrelevant precisely those whom it considers its greatest rivals. It is precisely this that structures d'Aspremont's approach to his thesis. His resurrection of Hart, contentious in itself, is tentative at best and highly guarded against its harshest critics at worst. And this Kuhnian strain of methodology becomes a dominant aspect of d'Aspremont's narrative.

The key question is how these central narratives and sub-narratives, of coherence and methodological incommensurability, manifest themselves in d'Aspremont's work. What are the structural aesthetics of *Formalism and the Sources of International Law* that ensure its goals, and those of its narratives, are achieved?

3. The First Structural Aesthetic: The Discourse of Necessity

At the forefront is the discourse of necessity. d'Aspremont's resurrection and renewal of source formalism is not merely posited as being desirable or preferable, but as imminently essential. This discourse presents itself in two argumentative moves.[6]

First, only the image of disorder (as a negative idea) can beget order as a persuasive ideal. The book's author has no problem with presenting us with his version of disorder within international law. Scholarly debates are 'cacophonic' (not far 'from becoming a henhouse or a Tower of Babel' (34)), occurring amongst 'a cluster of different scholarly communities' (3) that seemingly 'talk past each other' because each of them uses 'different criteria for the ascertainment of legal rules' (34). But the inability to determine what is law, we are told, is the most insidious form of disorder. The rigour of distinguishing law from non-law is getting lost in this complex legal world (1). Not only are there so many rules but the ways in which norms are made have 'undergone an intricate and multi-fold pluralization' (2). The formal sources we currently employ have 'grown inappropriate to capture contemporary international norms' (3). Disorder emerges amidst this normative and discursive complexity.

[6] There is a potential third move that emerges; d'Aspremont seeks to address a lacunae in international academic writing. Specifically, his work is necessary due to the 'disinterest in the ontology of formal law-ascertainment in the international legal scholarship of the 20th and 21st centuries' (74) and because 'international legal scholarship has remained largely averse to investigations of the theoretical foundations of formal law-ascertainment' (75), despite a few exceptions.

The second move, intrinsically associated with the first, links disorder (and the answer of order) with existential issues[7] within international law. The outlined disorder is not merely a trifling issue of reality, but is one that cuts to the core of our discipline. If we cannot separate law from non-law how can the normative character (namely, law's ability to generate and effect change in the behaviour of its addressees) of international law survive? (30) If legal rules have no normativity how can international law retain its authority? (31–33) If international law lacks authority and normativity, separately and interdependently, is the discipline itself being sidelined? If the identification of rules lies along some arbitrary normative '*continuum*' (1) how can international law retain its disciplinary and discursive individuality from the grasp of international politics? If the conceptualization of norms is based on examining their effects (namely, 'whether and how subjects . . . come to accept those norms, rules and standards'[8]) then are we not endearing a new natural law within the discipline? Is this not merely the guise under which political science (seen in the turn to legitimacy and public authority research) becomes the grounding for research into international law?

These are the ever-present, if sometimes subtle, questions which are pressed onto the reader with an imminence that does credit to their, and the book's, necessity. d'Aspremont forces the reader to confront these questions and, more importantly, makes this confrontation indispensible. Source formalism is the savior of international law's normativity (and thence its essence as a discipline). Deformalization is the enemy (119–130)—and it is pervasive in practice and theory.

And so the book's narratives and sub-narratives are painted as necessary through its imagery of disorder and the imminent dangers within the discipline's heart. But if the discourse of necessity is the first structural aesthetic of *Formalism and the Sources of International Law*, then one would think that an exposition of the project is the next logical step. This is not the case.

4. The Second Structural Aesthetic: A Marketable or Hegemonic Methodology?

Rather, what emerges is a concerted effort to delineate and demarcate, from competing theories, the conceptual space in which the book's thesis can function effectively. The 'rejuvenation' (5) of source formalism is attained as much by this process of demarcation, as by the virtues of its central thesis.

It is arguable that the first three substantive chapters of the book (Chapters 2–4) are concerned with precisely this. d'Aspremont begins by delineating his specific type of formalism as not one of legal argumentation, process-based law creation or State consent, but as one of the ascertainment of rules according to formal yardsticks (12–25). This

[7] d'Aspremont does at one stage seem to recognise that *one* of the key topics considered within his book, that of determinacy, indeterminacy and disambiguation, is an 'existential question' that 'will abidingly continue to fuel scholarly debates' (143). I suggest that this is only one existential question of many.

[8] J. Klabbers, 'Law-making and Constitutionalism' in J. Klabbers, A. Peters, G. Ulfstein (eds.), *The Constitutionalization of International Law* (Oxford: OUP, 2009), 98. Quoted at (122).

argumentative clarity would be welcome if it were not debatable that the most important of d'Aspremont's distinctions (between his formalism and that of legal argumentation) would eventually collapse (see section 6.2 below). We are then assured that there is good pedigree in the theoretical treatment of source formalism both in general legal theory and international legal theory. We are taken from Austin and Bentham, to Kelsen and Hart, before resting on Twining and Tamanaha in general legal theory (38–62). The book's narrative focus rests squarely on how the social observational understanding of the source thesis had been refined over time, not on the rupturing disagreements between these theorists. The sharp divide between Hart and Kelsen is all but sidelined as a coherent picture of the book's central thesis is painted.

I would go so far as to say that this is the book's defining aesthetic. The book's thesis and theoretical premises is demarcated from competing and fellow theories using a number of rhetorical styles. Conciliation with the tenets of competing theories (217–220) allows the author to downplay the force of their critiques. Where critiques are acknowledged, their significance is bracketed. We are thrown into Dworkin, but his devastating critique of Hart's social thesis is not fully considered nor answered (88–90). 'New Legal Realism cannot be construed as a proper critique of formalism' (105), even if its emphasis on socio-structural considerations would have a great deal to say about the limits of d'Aspremont's social thesis. The mainstay of the critique emanating from CLS has been directed towards the 'discipline' (114), the 'legal consciousness of the legal profession' (93) and the formalism of legal argumentation (112–3). The acknowledgement that these scholars have also 'delivered a fundamental critique of law-ascertainment models' (115), offered 'the most powerful [contemporary] critique' (110), and not 'spared the social thesis' (116)—are all emphatic statements deserving of a greater exposition.

But this structural aesthetic, that of defining and marketing the conceptual space in which the book's thesis seeks to function, is marked by an interminable tension.

On the one hand, d'Aspremont can defend his disinterest in the details of fundamental critiques, because the impact of these competing theories is heavily circumscribed by Kuhn's methodological incommensurability (as defined above). CLS and New Legal Realism 'see different things when they look from the same point in the same direction'; they exist in 'different worlds'[9] to the book's thesis. This methodological maneuver, as suggested above, introduces a limited but vital immunity from the full effects of critique. On the other hand, d'Aspremont presents his thesis as having 'doctrinal conciliatory virtues, for . . . it helps reconcile some allegedly antonymic trends in international legal scholarship' (217–8). This position assumes that discourse between theories is possible without understanding being inherently asymmetrical; that discourse can lead to conciliation; and that methodological incommensurability can be avoided.

Each position has suitable intellectual pedigree. But arguably, each is reliant on the existence of the other. A Kuhnian position is only conceivable if it is possible for there to be a position where one can understand each of the competing theories in order to glean their incommensurability. Such a position and understanding is not possible without the determinate functioning of rationality and discourse. The problem of d'Aspremont's structural aesthetic is not that he attempts to adopt both positions, but that he does not explore the full consequences and potential of adopting these competing methodologies

[9] T. Kuhn, *The Structure of Scientific Revolutions* (Chicago: Chicago University Press, 1970), 150.

together. His book's failing is that it privileges conciliatory discourse over the exposition of his thesis' greatest critiques, leaving one with a sense that Kuhn's *methodenstreit* is superficially and strategically employed.[10] The strategies of marketing an idea, it seems, are still so dominantly liberal.

However, this conclusion ought not to be solidified, for there remains another plausible interpretation of d'Aspremont's methodological maneuver. It is premised on intellectual specialization and hegemonic theory in the structure of international legal discourse. d'Aspremont's formalism is *only* concerned with the identification of rules: it is 'modest'.[11] This allows for and necessitates that other theories 'explain the whole phenomenon of law'.[12] It can 'underpin the continuously mutually enriching character of... multiple strands of contemporary international legal scholarship' (218) because it is 'non-exclusive, non-confrontational, and conciliatory' (219). It presumes that it can promote 'ecumenism'[13] or unity within international legal scholarship. There are two issues at the heart of this.

First is understanding that unity across international legal scholarship can only be achieved if the discourse is carved up into component parts governed by different theories. Neo-formalism can govern the identification of rules through governing the sources of international law. Constructivists and International Legal Realists can examine the international legal discipline as a social construct and the *application* of legal rules. And so on. This approach also enables d'Aspremont to so easily cast aside other theories. It is an approach that identifies intellectual movements as works of theoretical specialization. But it neither embraces unity, nor a measure of Kuhnian incommensurability (because you are not looking from the same point to start with, but at different points). The discourses of reality, and more importantly, reality itself *cannot* be carved up in this manner. Matters are not so neat. Theory cannot be 'non-confrontational' and it especially cannot be so when we are concerned with the sources of international law: the gateway to legality. If each of these factors and considerations are merged it is difficult to not conceive of d'Aspremont's neo-formalism as seeking a theoretical monopoly over international law's

[10] Later writings do little to assuage this concern. See d'Aspremont, 'Reductionist Legal Positivism', *supra* note 2, 5. 'I nonetheless appreciate that reducing ILP [International Legal Positivism] to a theory of ascertainment remains quite problematic to a number of people. To classical positivists, for instance, this is a betrayal of the quest for legal certainty toward which ILP should, in their view, be entirely geared. To Kelsenian scholars, such an approach is not different from naturalism and condemns international lawyers to be sociologists. To Dworkinians, Hart's idea that lawyers must share the same law ascertainment tests makes disagreement between law-applying authorities impossible, because an agreement about the law ascertainment tests involves agreement about their correct application (this is the so-called semantic sting argument). Eventually, to legal realists and critical legal scholars, Hartian reductionist positivism is naïve because even if grounded in social practice, the theory of sources it relies on is bound to fall into the trap of objectivism, as there is inevitably a need for a "value fact" to capture the practice of law-applying authorities. Some of these objections are surely weighty and must be assumed. Indeed, the reductionism advocated here makes ILP an extremely modest approach. It is also true that it presupposes some empiricism, which can never be seen as objective and necessarily relies on some "value fact". Such an empiricism is inherent in the social foundation of law and is precisely what allows the theory of sources to be made dynamic. If this condemns international lawyers to be sociologists, so be it.'—so much for conciliation.

[11] *Ibid.*, 6. [12] *Ibid.*

[13] *Ibid.*

key: its sources. The 'responsibility assigned to [my project] remains, in my view, of *primary* importance.'[14] It is a hegemonic maneuver garbed in conciliatory clothing.

5. The Third Structural Aesthetic: Saving Disciplinarity from The Spectre of the Absent Adversary

It has almost become a precondition after postmodernism for scholars and intellectuals to divulge the politics and biases of their theories. This is reflected in Chapter 6 of d'Aspremont's book. But equally, narratives that aim at persuasion (the ideal for most ideas) requires not merely the exposition of one's own politics, but the demonstration that these are more appealing than the politics and motives of one's adversary. The ideals of apparent transparency, theoretical and political pluralism in the best democratic ideal and the possibility of theory-independent (and therefore self-validating) choice, all flatter the reader.

The choices provided by d'Aspremont offer the first real glimpse into the core of his project. The initial choice presented is between the politics of deformalization (expanding international law's normative reach and stretching the frontiers of disciplinary discourse) (130–4) and those of formalism (preserving the normative character of international law and therefore its authority, legitimacy and efficacy) (145) in the ascertainment of rules. The second choice is between accepting indeterminacy or striving 'to disambiguate legal rules' (142). These are both political choices about what legal scholarship should be. But these choices only scratch the surface. A surface upon which deformalization in sources scholarship is cast as the adversary of formalism and where indeterminacy can be stemmed or tempered through social practice (141).

But deformalization itself is not the enemy and arguments over the level of indeterminacy are somewhat beside the point. The absent, but constantly looming, adversary in d'Aspremont's argument is the functioning of a destructive interdisciplinarity.[15] Let me clarify.

Disciplines are social constructs, subject to the direction and whimsy of its participants. A discipline's continuity and evolution depends, like all traditions, on the unwavering sustainability of a core set of beliefs and rules.[16] But it is also constituted by continuous conflict over interpretations of its identity and its limits. Epistemic disagreements are key to any discipline: its sustenance, renewal and its fortitude. But where such disagreements destabilize the core beliefs and rules of a discipline, it is only

[14] *Ibid.* (emphasis added)

[15] I think it is extremely important to distinguish between the interdisciplinarity that I target in this paper and other interdisciplinary approaches. The former is destructive of the international legal discipline, whereas movements towards the history of international law, its basis as a social construct or its nature as a discourse—as a series of linguistic maneuvers—attempt to work within the nuances of the discipline. There is much merit to this type of work.

[16] James Crawford has spoken of international law as a discipline and stated: 'the system is ordered such that entrenched ideas are unlikely to succumb, as distinct from being modified through practice or the accretion of new ideas and values'. The continuity of these 'entrenched ideas' is vital to a discipline. J. Crawford, 'Manley O. Hudson Medal Lecture: International Law as a Discipline and Profession', (2012) 106 *Proceedings of the American Society of International Law*, 6 (forthcoming).

then that it is at risk of descending into incoherence and thence rupture. The key to grasping this lies in understanding the exact *nature* of the conflict that ensues between speakers of a discipline.

d'Aspremont understands that international law is constituted by 'battle[s] within the profession' and 'battle[s] among professions' (133). He understands the significance of Foucault (fn. 98, 133). But there is a disconnect in identifying the *nature* of the conflict. d'Aspremont understands deformalization as the enemy. Not its users, not any particular variant of it—but it as a concept within law. But the adversary is not deformalization. It is those that speak its language and what they represent. It is the specific contemporary nature of deformalization discourse (both in and outside source theory) that is so corrosive.

d'Aspremont considers that to devise sources theory based on moral or ethical criteria (119), or on the effects and subject acceptability of norms (122), or resting the ascertainment of rule depends on the process of law (127), is to embrace deformalization. Each of these stands true. But there is a persistent focus on the middle and latter of these within the book (4, 29, 68, 105–110, 122–128). This is not without significance. d'Aspremont rightly takes issue with compliance with rules being used as a yardstick for ascertaining these rules (122). He rallies against the following effects-based understanding of law-ascertainment:

> Once it is recognised that law's existence is best measured by the influence it exerts, and not by formal tests of validity rooted in normative hierarchies, international lawyers can finally eschew the preoccupation with legal pedigree (sources) that has constrained creative thinking within the discipline for generations.[17]

There is a "good" pedigree of American scholars who have sought to reduce law to its effectiveness and compliance.[18] Law is reduced to economic functionality. 'In economic terms, law is relevant to the extent that it generates a marginal increase in compliance.'[19] The particularities of legality are displaced by rational choice assumptions. What is law and whether it is effective is collapsed as a central distinction-nullifying the relevance of European jurisprudential thought. Self-interest is not an analytical tool, but a determining directive: '[i]nternational law emerges from states' pursuit of self-interested policies on the international stage... It is not a check on self-interest, it is a product of self-interest.'[20] The grammar and language of compliance and effectiveness is that of the technocrat, of the political scientist. Its persistent link between rational analysis and claims to scientific methodology ensures that it hides its ideological biases in its claims to a certain, better, objectivity of how things work.

None of this would be problematic if it were concerned with providing merely another angle of observation. But this project is not so neutral. It is, rather, one of academic

[17] J. Brunnée and S. Troope, 'International Law and Constructivism, Elements of an International Theory of International Law', (2000–1) 39 *Columbia Journal of Transnational Law* 19, 65 (quoted at fn. 28, p. 122).

[18] Most recently see, E. Posner and A. Sykes, *Economic Foundations of International Law* (Cambridge, MA: Harvard University Press, 2013).

[19] A. Guzman, *How International Law Works. A Rational Choice Theory* (New York: OUP, 2008), 22–3.

[20] J. Goldsmith and E. Posner, *The Limits of International Law* (New York: OUP, 2005), 13.

conquest. The spectre behind d'Aspremont's exposition of deformalization is in fact the politics of interdisciplinarity.[21]

As I see it, the conquest of political science methodology and conceptualizations takes place with two argumentative moves. These are specific considerations that are to be distinguished from the broader movement within international legal research to consider and ground concepts of legitimacy, fairness, accountability, governance and public authority—a development troubling in and of itself. The two moves of note are as follows.

First, scholars have argued for the irrelevance of distinguishing between legal forms and in some cases, for the irrelevance of form *in toto*. Whether one is concerned with soft law, standards or rules in a formalist sense, they are deemed irrelevant to determining how the international legal system influences state behaviour.[22] The concern of whether a norm is a rule of the legal system is considered irrelevant and beside the point. So much for the specifically legal.

Second and most detrimentally, scholars—as d'Aspremont notes in regards to Brunnée and Troope above—allow the existence and ascertainment of a rule to be determined by whether it exerts influence. So the master signifier of the international legal language, its sources, is not merely irrelevant, but ought to be replaced by a political scientific determinant. Academic conquest cannot be more hegemonic and subversive than this. Symbolic contestations are not novel considerations, but given the relationship between poststructuralism and structuralism, we have been taught that the ultimate political battle within a discourse lies in controlling its master signifier. The actor that is able to define this is able to determine the direction of the discourse. Source doctrine and the determinant of legal rules should be economic considerations. Political science governs.

The point I have made thus far is that it is not deformalization as a concept that is the enemy, but a very specific disciplinary movement that espouses and benefits from it. The hegemonic politics of interdisciplinarity is the intra-disciplinary discourse that requires resistance and refutation. When we look at the politics of deformalization we in fact see the politics of interdisciplinarity. Foucault needs to be far more than a footnote: what types of knowledge and discourse are disqualified by a greater claim to objectivity made by law and economics? Which discursive subjects—which subjects of experience and knowledge—are diminished or sidelined by the claims made by law and economics on the discourse of international law?[23] The underlying motive of the identified strain of US thought is one of discursive dominance. But the politics of deformalization articulated by d'Aspremont (130–6) does not fully expose this. It is not deformalization that is the enemy, but the far more subversive politics of interdisciplinarity. Here deformalization is a tool—a means towards the end of destabilizing the international legal discipline.

This is not a trifling point of semantics, but one that goes to the heart of disciplinary continuity. As I explained earlier, disciplines are constituted by vigorous disagreement

[21] The spectre of interdisciplinarity not only lies over the specific type of deformalization identified by d'Aspremont, but also his critique of the role of intent in the ascertainment of rules (178–84). The turn towards intent is a key component of the law and economics movement, albeit not on the ascertainment of rules. Due to this difference I have chosen to highlight the possibility of the link and not to explore it. But it remains a key contribution for asking which actor and whose intention is elevated in the current institutional settings of international law.

[22] Guzman, *supra* note 19, 9 and 142–7.

[23] These questions are paraphrased from the oft-quoted section of Foucault's 'Two Lectures' in M. Foucault, *Power/Knowledge* (New York: Pantheon, 1980), 85.

over their identity. Disciplines are also susceptible to lapsing into incoherence and thus rupturing. The stakes of argumentative conflict or disagreement are dependent on the *nature* of this disagreement. The point I wish to make is that the stakes of a destructive interdisciplinarity place a novel form of disagreement, of conquest, within the core beliefs and rules of the international legal discipline. By comparison, the politics of formalism and deformalization, as general rhetorical tropes, are trifling and *normalized* disagreements within the discipline. Both have long been part of the drama of the governance of international law and it is difficult to see modern manifestations as anything but variations on a theme. In short, the discipline is not threatened with incoherence by ideas and rhetorical strategies it has long internalized and *normalized*.

By contrast, the destructive interdisciplinarity described here not only attempts to destabilize the core tenets of our discipline, but also seeks to colonize them. The renewed sophistication of these attempts has ensured their entrenchment within US academic and policy circles. This appropriation can only be a worrying development for the international legal discipline. And d'Aspremont's analysis is constantly submerged in the spectre of this absent adversary, with its dubious politics. The choice no longer lies between deformalizing and formalizing strategies (and their politics)—as Chapters 5 and 6 would have us believe. These are welcome and understandable maneuvers within international legal argument. The choice, now, lies between the politics of a colonizing interdisciplinarity and the known rhetorical tropes of our discipline.

So whilst d'Aspremont's narrative structure has and requires an adversary, I suggest it is the spectre of his absent adversary that plays a larger role in his politics and the politics of choice he presents to the reader.[24]

6. The Fourth & Final Structural Aesthetic: Ordering the 'Cacophonic Hen House' with Determinacy, Hart & Wittgenstein

The final oeuvre of d'Aspremont's narrative plot is the exposition of his thesis and the structuring aesthetic of this thesis: relative determinacy and order. The reader has been persuaded of its necessity (not merely its desirability), the aesthetic of its methodology and the liberal ideal possibility of free political choice.[25] Now we arrive at a thesis that progresses in two argumentative steps as the reader is urged to embrace Hartian source formalism and a significantly narrowed legal positivism. The first of these steps is a

[24] Or if the reader is of the opinion that this is just a question of semantics, in the alternative, I contend that he has insufficiently explored the consequences of the adversary he has chosen. If this path is taken, it is the specific type of deformalization (effect-based law ascertainment) that is the enemy and not deformalization as a concept.

[25] I state the choice outlined in section 5 is 'the liberal ideal possibility of free political choice' because I contend that the possibility that key political choices are solely centered within the individual exercise of personal freedom, is a liberal ideal-type. Various social theories have demonstrated that this type of agency is tempered by structural constraints and indeed defined by them. Individual choice is always historically and socially structured (but not determined). Transparencies of the politics involved in the posited choice can both highlight these structures and disguise them. The appearance of free choice should *always* be questioned.

'reductionist' approach to his neo-positivist and neo-formalist project.[26] The second is an exposition of a theory of language that enables his social source thesis. This second move finds difficulty in reconciling itself with his later work. It also helps d'Aspremont construct the potential for an essential *convergence* in social practice data—an indispensable prerequisite to his social source thesis. Each maneuver will be addressed (section 6.2) but a brief descriptive exposition of d'Aspremont thesis will be addressed first (section 6.1).

6.1 The Ascertainment of Legal Rules: Neo-Formalism and Hartian Positivism

Jean d'Aspremont's work over the last two years illustrates a strong relationship between the formalism he advocates in *Formalism and the Sources of International Law* and his project concerning international legal positivism. He had stated that his book 'falls short of supporting legal positivism as a whole' (26) and that his defence of source formalism could not be conflated with a plea for international legal positivism (8). But he has since advocated for and started to develop a contemporary school of international legal positivism (ILP) with Jörg Kammerhofer.[27] Whilst many can and should question the viability of such a school based on diametrically opposite approaches to positivism, there is also established inconsistencies between d'Aspremont's book and his later work within the ILP project.[28] His source formalism remains at the masthead in both projects. But what are the precise contours of this source formalism?

A succinct neo-positivist position within contemporary literature states that the validity of a norm, its legal existence, is determined solely by its pedigree—its conformity with a system's sources (the source thesis). This position is common to Kelsenian and Hartian variants of positivism. But d'Aspremont requires two further steps: (a) that the source thesis ensures that pedigree is *formal* (148); and (b) that the source thesis be complimented by a variant of Hart's social thesis. Each will be briefly explored in turn.

d'Aspremont's Formal Source Thesis

'[I]t is only possible for a social practice of law-ascertainment by law-applying authorities to provide relative determinacy to formal categories on which any formal model of law-identification is based if standards of pedigree of international rules are fashioned in a manner that lends limited room to indeterminacy.' (148) This thesis requires that he reject the mainstream theory of sources enshrined in Article 38 of the ICJ Statute (149–50) and turn to a critique of those sources that are not based on the written word—for it is these that do not possess the right degree of formality (174). This includes

[26] d'Aspremont, 'Reductionist Legal Positivism', *supra* note 2; see also d'Aspremont & Kammerhofer, *supra* note 2.

[27] See d'Aspremont & Kammerhofer, *supra* note 2; J. Kammerhofer, *Uncertainty in International Law. A Kelsenian Perspective* (London: Routledge, 2010); J. Kammerhofer, 'A Pure Theory of Law and its "Modern" Positivism: International Legal Uses for Scholarship' (2012) 106 *Proceedings of the American Society of International Law* (forthcoming).

[28] However, broader tenets of the international legal positivist project are adopted. These include (a) separate of what the law is from what it should be; (b) formalism in the sources of international law; (c) cognition of law as the function of international legal scholarship; (d) embracing value-relativism in methodology. See, 'Introduction' in d'Aspremont & Kammerhofer, *ibid.*, 7–8.

customary international law, general principles of law and oral promises made by States. These sources have been shrouded in appearances of formality by collapsing important distinctions, 'the *making*, the *evidence*, ... the *determination of the content*' (151) from the ascertainment of legal rules. Each of the former determinations have been 'relentlessly cloaked ... with a veil of formalism' (15) and these 'mirages of formalism that shroud the traditional theory of sources and which have allowed legal scholarship to live in an illusion of relative certainty regarding the identification of international legal rules' (150) ought to be exposed and discarded. Even if this is exposed, and we are left with only formality in the ascertainment of legal rules through sources expressed in the written word (178), then such sources cannot be dependent on the 'intent of the authors of these acts' (179), unless said intent is translated in graspable material and linguistic indicators (182).

So, d'Aspremont's neo-formalist project in *Formalism and the Sources of International Law* is a normative one. It makes claims as to how the law of sources should be. Customary international law and other non-written sources only proliferate indeterminacy and therefore non-normativity in international law.[29] We are told that it is 'argued here that only the systemic use of written linguistic indicators can ensure formal law-ascertainment in international law' (186). We are told that we are concerned solely with the *formal ascertainment* of norms (not their creation, content etc.) and that '*both the content* [of the norm] *and the container* [written instrument, treaty etc.] *can potentially serve as formal a formal signpost that indicates whether the norm in question is an international legal rule.*' (175). But for d'Aspremont the formal ascertainment of rules lies with 'the container (*instrumentum*) of the rule' and that it is here that 'a distinction between law and non-law must be sought' (178). It is solely a norms *form* that determines its formal pedigree and not the norm itself (its *content*).

So the book first exposes the indeterminacy (which is equated with peering behind the veil of formalization), within law-applying practice and scholarly discourse, which runs through both written and non-written sources. d'Aspremont then seeks to stem this indeterminacy by making normative claims through his formalism. These include that neo-formalism: (a) should only be concerned with the ascertainment of norms; (b) sources are only really formally adequate if they are enshrined in written instruments; and (c) it is the container of a norm that determines its legal validity, not the norm itself.

A Variant of Hart's Social Thesis

d'Aspremont considers his source formalism as insufficient to limit indeterminacy in the sources of international law (193). The social thesis compliments the book's formalism, since it seeks to domesticate the indeterminacy of language by grounding the meaning of said language in the social practice of law-applying authorities. At its essence the social thesis in the context of d'Aspremont's formalism states: the meaning of sources, or specifically those that meet the aforementioned formal criteria, and their determinant—the ultimate rule of recognition, are derived from the social practice of law-applying authorities (51–3). The functionality of this thesis requires a cogent theory of language, a method to identify the relevant law-applying authorities and the

[29] See also J. d'Aspremont, 'International Customary Investment Law: Story of a Paradox' in E. Brabandere and T. Gazzini (eds.), *Sources of Transnational Investment Law* (The Hague: Martinus Nijhoff, 2012).

ascertainability of an internal point of view (itself a social fact)[30] of these law-applying authorities within the international legal system. It would seem that in answer to these requirements we are thrown into Wittgenstein, Hart and Tamanaha and finally an unfulfilled (and arguably unfulfillable) psychoanalytics. And so the tenets of d'Aspremont's conservative theoretical grounding is set.

Wittgenstein is invoked for the proposition that 'it is how the word is used that will teach us the meaning of the word' (199). Clarification of the meaning of words is premised in the communitarian approach to these words; consensus and convergence in the practice of language offers and *determines* meaning (196–200). This is how we may determine the meaning of formal law-ascertainment criteria. But to clarify, this does not mean that absolute agreement in the practical use of the word by an identified social group is necessary; it is 'probably elusive' (201). All d'Aspremont requires for 'the social foundation of formalism in the ascertainment of international legal rules' is that law-applying authorities have 'a shared *feeling* of applying the same criteria' (201–2).

But who are the relevant law-applying authorities? Whose social practice needs to be examined and determines the meaning of our formal sources? Tamanaha is used to remedy Hart's methodological insufficiency at this juncture (17, 203–4). d'Aspremont invokes Tamanaha's method for identifying relevant law-applying authorities in international law, namely: 'whomever, as a matter of social practice, members of the group (including legal officials themselves) identify and treat as "legal" officials'.[31] So, the social practice of law-applying authorities will determine who those law-applying authorities are. And these self-defined law-applying authorities' social practice will determine the legal rules (the ultimate rule of recognition and secondary rules) that determine who are lawful law-applying authorities as well as the meanings of our formal sources. The trappings of an endlessly circular logic abound. And we are left with only tentative notions of who the relevant law-applying authorities are (judicial authorities (international and domestic), ICRC, ILC).

Finally, we are left with the psychoanalytic understanding of the international legal professionals. After being assured of the determinacy-limiting tenets of d'Aspremont's social source thesis, we are told that 'international society... is *in a position* to produce sufficient communitarian semantics... [but] it seems more questionable whether the current configuration of the international legal society allows the emergence of a sustainable *feeling* of convergence of the practices of law-ascertainment.' (213). There is a communitarian deficiency in the social consciousness of international legal professionals—but one that can be remedied only through rallying around *this*, d'Aspremont's, common project.

6.2 Ideological Consolidation & A Pathological Desire for Determinacy: Its Guises and Its Politics

The pathological desire to bring closure to the determinacy/indeterminacy debate within law is excessive in its hubris, but more so, entirely unnecessary. Academic musings feel the ethical imperative to either cultivate indeterminacy or impose determinacy. Doing so

[30] HLA Hart, *The Concept of Law* (Oxford: OUP, 1997, 2nd edn), 116–7.

[31] B. Tamanaha, *A General Jurisprudence of Law and Society* (Oxford: OUP, 2001), 142 quoted by d'Aspremont at (203).

will, of course, bring new possibilities for law or a normative power and legitimacy that it has not before experienced. These debates and assertions are marked by one having to make a choice between an arbitrary dichotomy: relative determinacy or absolute indeterminacy (e.g. 142).

Formalism and the Sources of International Law offers little that is new to this narrative. It is a project of 'disambiguation' (143): the source and social thesis are each aimed at making international law more determinate (148, 193). The indeterminacy of formal law-ascertainment criteria 'is more restricted than what is often asserted' (141). The 'international legal order provides at the least the possibility of a significant social practice which helps stem the indeterminacy of law-ascertainment mechanisms that is perpetuated by formalism itself.' (141). But before examining the implausibility of these assertions, the nature of indeterminacy and determinacy as concepts within international legal discourse need to be briefly explored.

Clarifying Concepts of Indeterminacy & Foundations of Determinacy

Given the contemporary preoccupation with indeterminacy it is surprising that there is so little work done on clarifying different types of indeterminacy that arise in jurisprudential discourse. What is the object of indeterminacy—concepts, rules, discourses, words, etc.? And what type of indeterminacy do theories concern themselves with—linguistic or semantic ambivalence, radical, argumentative, discourse-based? These are important questions that cannot be fully addressed here. I will simply differentiate between the different types of indeterminacy advanced in d'Aspremont's book and those espoused by CLS scholars. I will then look at some of the conceptual foundations ascribed to determinacy and indeterminacy in legal practice and discourse.

Clarifying the Nature of d'Aspremont's Indeterminacy

The need for clarification arises from my reading of Chapters 4, 6 and 8 of *Formalism and the Sources of International Law.*[32] It also arises from an introductory reading of d'Aspremont's latest project: an edited book entitled *International Legal Positivism in a Post-Modern World.* One can be forgiven for thinking, subsequent to a reading of both works,

[32] There are two exacerbating factors. First, in several key passages on indeterminacy and his thesis to temper it, d'Aspremont does not state that he is focusing on linguistic or sematic indeterminacy (140–1). The term 'indeterminacy' is used as if self-explanatory (141). This is curious given that the term has been given specific and varied meanings within the works of Koskenniemi and his critics. Second, d'Aspremont goes on to assert that he 'leaves intact *some* of the objections of the critique inspired by critical legal studies and deconstructivism. In particular, the social thesis, by *easing* the indeterminacy of sources by grounding it in social practice, only helps contain indeterminacy at the level of law-ascertainment but does not purport to allay the contradictions of international legal argumentation.' (218) Does this mean that CLS' argumentative indeterminacy only attaches to the application of rules and not their ascertainment and so argumentative indeterminacy is irrelevant to d'Aspremont's project? (This reading also emerges from an introductory reading to d'Aspremont's edited volume). Or does it mean that argumentative indeterminacy is assumed as a critique by the book for the purpose of its thesis? These are neglected and important questions. It is presumed in this review, due to other passages in the book (139), that d'Aspremont's focus is only on tempering semantic or linguistic indeterminacy. The latter reading (of the book not arguing against argumentative indeterminacy) is assumed (and critiqued) in this review. For the critique of the former reading and argument see my chapter in d'Aspremont & Kammerhofer, *supra* note 2.

that the indeterminacy confronted by d'Aspremont is precisely the same as that advanced by various strands of CLS and that consequently his approach to determinacy is in fact postmodern. This is not the case.

d'Aspremont's thesis is concerned with linguistic indeterminacy: the relative open-endedness of language (139). It is a distinctly Hartian variant of indeterminacy.[33] Words and expressions that comprise rules may be considered as having a 'core' meaning and therefore relatively determinate, or they may be considered relatively indeterminate and their meaning will operate in the 'penumbra of uncertainty'.[34] I do not think scholars such as Koskenniemi would wholly disagree with this qualification of linguistic or semantic indeterminacy—even if this is not their charge.[35] But I do think a general clarification is necessary: d'Aspremont does *not* deal with linguistic indeterminacy as a complete concept, but only one variant of it.

Despite their common label, d'Aspremont's understanding of linguistic indeterminacy is substantially different to its corollary in CLS scholarship. Both schools understand linguistic indeterminacy to be concerned with the meaning of words. But each posits different theories of language in the construction of this meaning. The semantic indeterminacy critique often found in CLS takes its roots in Saussurean structural linguistics.[36] It asserts that (legal) words have no core meaning—nothing is intrinsic to the word itself. The meaning of a word is dependent on its relationship with other words: specifically on the '*formal* differences'[37] between them. Meaning emerges from understanding what an object or spoken word is not, rather than any ontological understanding of what it is. Common use of a word may permit communication, but use cannot establish the core of a word (*contra* Hart). Different theories including deconstruction and poststructuralism have built on Saussure's theory and influenced certain strands of CLS. Broadly speaking under the former theories, words and texts are self-generating devices in a continuous process of textual production, an 'infinite relay of meaning from signifier to signified'.[38] Structural linguistics is not about maintaining, or even obtaining, a conceptual space for determinacy, because relative indeterminacy permeates both the core and periphery of a word. In the parlance of, but fundamentally *contra*, Hart, the meaning of a word always functions in the 'penumbra' and is constantly shifting. Meaning is utterly impermanent and completely temporary.

So what d'Aspremont's analysis of his linguistic indeterminacy thesis excludes is the immediate importance of one's theory of language. His theoretical claim that linguistic indeterminacy can be stemmed or tempered through his social source thesis depends on one accepting his (under-exposed) theory of language. But the choice between conceiving language as being concretized through unified social practice and thinking of it as a constantly slipping structure based on irreconcilable but mutually dependent contradictions, seems somewhat arbitrary. It is arbitrary. There are no independent or common

33 Hart, *supra* note 30, 124–36. 34 *Ibid.*, 134.

35 See his notions of semantic indeterminacy in M. Koskenniemi, *From Apology to Utopia: The Structure of International Legal Argument (Reissue with a New Epilogue)* (Cambridge: CUP, 2005), 590–3.

36 F. Saussure, *General Course in Linguistics* (Chicago: Open Court, trans. Roy Harris, 1983), 65 *et seq.*

37 Koskenniemi, *supra* note 35, 9.

38 F. Jameson, *The Prison-House of Language* (Princeton, NJ: Princeton University Press, 1972), 182.

criteria offered to choose between these two competing theories. But a choice between theories remains completely necessary for it determines not whether we look at social practice, but what types of social practice we look at and their significance. Theory, within d'Aspremont's project, structures his empiricism: a consideration that is neither acknowledged nor explored within the book. And equally his empiricism (the turn to specific types of social practice data) structures his concepts or ideas (of indeterminacy).

This leaves us in the curious position of knowing that a greater indeterminacy critique, discourse indeterminacy, structures d'Aspremont's search for linguistic or semantic determinacy. Let me explain. In seeking determinacy of formal legal rules of law-ascertainment, international legal discourse is displaced by another discourse: that of semiotics. Yet semiotics suffers from its own discourse-based indeterminacy: conflicts and contradictions over what the discourse is and how it is constituted, abound. It is an indeterminacy best expressed by the fact that we may choose between several competing and conflicting theories of language over the construction of meaning. A choice between theories is required before we can conceive of the indeterminacy advanced by d'Aspremont in the formal sources of international law. The first striking point is that working towards determinacy in one discourse (international law) only throws us into the very real indeterminacy of another discourse (semiotics). The second point is that the first step is denied. The image of determinacy (or working towards it) within international law is solidified only through the appearance of solid epistemological foundations: an external and objective (in the sense of Rorty) guarantee of process and method is found in the social practice of law, in empiricism. What could be more valued than images of what actually happens. But this simply relocates politics within doctrine rather than terminate it. This leads me to a third and final point: indeterminacy is interminable in the abstract. Determinations, in practice, do not end indeterminacy but highlight the contingencies and politics of choice. Linguistic indeterminacy opens the door to discourse-based indeterminacy and one will always slide from one discourse into another, one being no less determinate than the last. Any and all claims to a greater determinacy are structured by the interminability of this process. Given this it is difficult to see how d'Aspremont can then bracket argumentative and discourse-determinacy (218) and only focus on linguistic indeterminacy.

The Foundations Given to Concepts: (In)Determinacy & Normativity

This brings me to a few remarks on the political claims we attach to determinacy and indeterminacy discourses in international law. It cannot be doubted that they are conceptual categories that are used to structure our experience of the international legal world. But they are also categories that are manipulated and constantly constructed. When invoked in debates over the nature of and prospects for law, presumptive claims are made upon the foundations of both determinacy and indeterminacy.

Perhaps the greatest enabler of the pathological resort to determinacy in jurisprudence is the link made between it and law's normativity and authority.[39] The idea is that clearer, more determinate and predictable rules (as opposed to being merely intelligible) increase law's authority, normativity, legitimacy and ultimately its efficacy. This lies at the heart of

[39] The relationship between law's normativity and its authority, is also a complex one which has been reduced in this paper in the same manner that d'Aspremont draws the correlation in his monograph.

d'Aspremont's thesis (29–32): greater determinacy and less ambiguity in the formal sources of international law leads to its enhanced authority, normativity, legitimacy and efficacy (140–5). Determinacy is valorized on the foundations of this claim and it is one that is too bold, if not incorrect. Before explaining this remark, it should be made clear that the claim is concerned with both linguistic and argumentative (in)determinacy (as argued by Koskenniemi). I think the strength of the link between determinacy and the authority and efficacy of international law, is both an overstated and dangerous one. And one that besets scholarship regarding international law's sources doctrine.

It cannot be forgotten that international law's normativity and its efficacy are multi-faceted concepts that are, here, being simplified in their connection to determinacy and law-ascertainment in sources doctrine. The doctrine has a number of roles apart from law-ascertainment in international law, each with different claims of influence on the normativity of international law.[40] The first such role is to govern the creation of norms.[41] A second such role is its ability to generate ascertainment criteria that can incorporate continuously contemporary law-making practices (i.e. claims to new sources). By incorporating both of these roles, the source doctrine makes a variety of different claims upon international law's normativity. Both are equally necessary to the discipline's legitimacy, efficacy and indeed, continuity. But each requires a deformalized approach (despite 'fruitless' attempts to formalize evidence-based examinations of law-creation (153)) marked by respect for abstract categories and loose analysis in order for their roles to be continuously filled. Whilst d'Aspremont seeks to enhance determinacy in the sources of international law (and therefore the law's normativity), I think he under-estimates the importance of countervailing reasons for the same doctrine that require indeterminacy (both linguistic and argumentative) and deformalization in order to buttress the normativity and efficacy of international law.

A doctrine whose very function is to open up the international legal field to a proliferation of legal rules and legal argumentation can only do so by embracing and manipulating the categories of formalism/deformalization and determinacy/indeterminacy as rhetorical strategies that function differently in their various discursive roles. But harnessing these strategies requires displacing the preconceived notion that determinacy (achieved through formalism or otherwise) has a superior claim to international law's normativity, authority and efficacy.

From the foregoing it should be clear that both the concepts of determinacy and indeterminacy and their foundations have a dubious but central footing in the book's narrative.

[40] Koskenniemi's definition of his indeterminacy ought to be born in mind when considering the various reasons and roles of the sources doctrine in this paragraph: 'And because no rules is more important than the reason for which it is enacted, even the most unambiguous rules is infected by the disagreements that concern how that reason is to be understood and how it ranks with competing ones' Koskenniemi, *supra* note 35, 591.

[41] 'It should be remembered at the outset that in considering the sources of international law, we are looking not only at the test of validity of law—the touchstone of what is law and what it is not—but also at the ways in which law is made and changed.' R. Jennings, 'What is International Law and How do we Tell it when we See it' (1980) 37 *Annuaire Suisse de Droit International* 59, 60.

The Contingent & Ideological Nature of Social Factual Observation as Method

The crux of d'Aspremont's *Formalism and the Sources of International Law* is found in the tenets of his social thesis (see section 6.1 above). It is a method that ensures we do not speak of international law's sources as rules or concepts, but as simply that which emerges from social facts (194). More so, it is a method that courts commonsense and plausibility, lays claim to the possibility of coherence in international legal practice and therefore also to stability (and linguistic determinacy) in the forms of international law. It is, above all, a method that has two entrenched and highly specific narrative maneuvers. These may, for now, be loosely stated as: (a) the exclusion of philosophical theory; (b) a reductive approach to the manner in which meaning is constructed and understandable; both of which leads to the ideological consolidation of the status quo. Each is considered in turn.

But each of these narrative particularities are only possible due to the specific rationality attached to circular reasoning. It is this that lies at the heart of d'Aspremont's social thesis and its attendant empiricism. We are told that: the criteria for determining what constitutes an international legal rule may be ascertained from the social practice of law-applying authorities; the rule of recognition is also an observable social fact; and it is legal social practice that also determines which institutional and non-institutional organs comprise law-applying authorities. Legal reality is reconstructed *only* through legal social facts. Legal reality may *only* be reconstructed through observable reality. And above all, what constitutes legal social fact is determined solely by legal social facts.

Excluding Theory from Reconstructing Reality

There are no preconceptual or even pretheoretical data...[42]

Social scientific observation functions by virtue of a consistently self-referential logic. This rationality ensures that it can be perceived to demarcate itself from the rationalities of external method. Legal social facts may determine themselves within the social context of a specific legal system. Ideas need not structure facts, and *vice versa*. But social scientific observation as an empirical methodology can only succeed in underlining precisely that which it seeks to evade and exclude. Can the social thesis and analytical jurisprudence sever the link between theory and fact and exclude metaphysical or historical enquiry, without assuming (and disguising) an *a priori* theory at its own foundations?

It is here that we find the Achilles heel of d'Aspremont's project. Perhaps most marked in d'Aspremont's book (and his neo-positivist project) is the lack of sensitivity shown to a conceptual analysis of law. As noted earlier, he outlines but leaves wholly unexplored the CLS critique of the social thesis. '[CLS] scholars have usually endorsed the idea that practice cannot be cognized without predefined categories, and hence, there cannot be a non-normative empirical study of international law' (116). It is perhaps too simplistic to consider his lack of engagement with conceptual analysis as a political gambit of theory advanced by Kuhnian methodology. The critique, here, of d'Aspremont is that his approach is arguably less ambiguous than Hart's and that the underexplored CLS critique highlights the contingency of his method.

[42] A. MacIntyre, *Whose Justice? Which Rationality?* (London: Duckworth, 1988), 333.

The notion that concepts, ideas and theories could be central to reconstructing and ordering reality was something Hart was acutely aware of, but seemingly hesitant to explore. In *Positivism and the Separation of Law and Morals*, Hart noted that it was an 'important truth that a pure analytical study of legal concepts, a study of meaning of the distinctive vocabulary of law, [is] as vital to our understanding of the nature of law as a historical or sociological studies, though of course it could not supplant them.'[43] Conceptual analysis is clearly not sufficient for reconstructing legal reality, but is his sociological observation? At this stage of his thinking Hart does not clarify the role that conceptual analysis plays alongside his sociological jurisprudence. He was however highly sceptical of conceptual analysis because of the problematic indeterminacy of the meaning of a concepts and various conceptions of concepts. In his retort to Dworkin he also explicitly rejects that a conceptual analysis can structure his sociological jurisprudence because for him the meaning of the concept of law (the conceptual analysis) is entirely distinct from the criteria of its application (his sociological or empirical analysis).[44] Apparently Salmond was right. The concept of law (and conceptions of the concept) cannot structure what we cognise as the law. Hart's ambiguity highlights the complexity of the issue for a theorist. But for d'Aspremont we find no such continuous resort to the boundaries of his theoretical analysis.[45] What is the role of concepts for d'Aspremont's empirical theorising? It is not enough to state that we are working in different theoretical Kuhnian paradigms.

d'Aspremont does restate the CLS critique that an empirical study of law cannot be conducted without predefined categories; it cannot be atheoretical or non-normative (116). But does he accept it? It would seem that his later work would suggest that conceptual and empirical analyses are two different ways to approach jurisprudence.[46] He rejects Dworkin, Finnis and Kelsen, as eclectic a mix as that is. His posited political choices, between determinacy/indeterminacy and greater/less authority of law, bring us no closer to understanding which theory and concepts structure the contours of his social thesis and how they do so.

The Achilles heel of d'Aspremont's project is not merely the lack of engagement with the relevance of conceptual analysis in imposing intelligence upon empirical data. It is also a slight misstatement of the CLS critique.[47] This critique states that both empirical and conceptual analyses of international law are mutually reliant. Both are dependent on each other. Different descriptive projects highlight different social facts by claiming greater plausibility and a thorough empirical methodology. The American school of thought on law and economics does precisely this (see section 5 above). A choice between different empirical theories cannot be determined by the criteria they themselves set. We must reach outside their views of social practice data to what led to the choice of this data; to the theories underlying this choice, to the conceptual matrices that define and structure this data. Conceptual analysis on its own standing is equally problematic. One sees the slow slide into various conceptualizations of a concept. This does not necessarily mean absolute relativism, but that concepts are assimilated in specific social backgrounds. Yet it

[43] H.L.A. Hart, 'Positivism and the Separation of Law and Morals' in H.L.A. Hart, *Essays on Jurisprudence and Philosophy* (Oxford: Oxford University Press, 1983) 49, 57.

[44] Hart, *Concept*, *supra* note 30, 246.

[45] See d'Aspremont's reference to Salmond in 'Wording', *supra* note 2, 600 and fn. 75.

[46] *Ibid.* [47] See generally, Koskenniemi, *supra* note 35, 219–23, 516–21.

is facts (historical and social) that ground concepts. The point made by CLS is that despite being separately indeterminate and reductionist, both conceptual and empirical analyses must reach beyond their theoretical premises and rationalities towards each other. A non-reductive social theory of law requires that a particular method recognise its constant reach beyond its own parameters.

The reconstruction of the sources doctrine envisaged by d'Aspremont's social thesis is that of a decisive discourse. As a method, its reconstruction of legal reality is self-regulated and dominated by a naturalized circular logic. What is hidden in this circular logic is the method's continuous need to resort beyond itself to be persuasive. What is hidden is the theory, and the *nature* of the theory, that structures the relevance and significance of social practice data across international law. This is not simply to say that we must resort to conceptual analysis. It does not. It is to say that if we are to avoid a reductive methodology of the criteria that determines legal from non-legal, we must resort to: highlighting what theory and definitions of concepts structures d'Aspremont's social thesis; understanding the specific social and historical background and setting in which these concepts are constructed and assimilated; and recognising that method must have continuous mutual reliance between theory and fact.

Theory is not external to legal reality any more than observable facts are determinative of it.

Constructing Coherence: Meaning, Symbolic Conflict and the Social Thesis

The self-referential logic of the social thesis[48] is not merely dependent on the consistent exclusion of foundational theory, but more so a reductive approach to the constitution of meaning. It reassures us that the meaning of words can be gleaned merely from their use and that any specific legal system provides 'convergence in use' (197), a coherence which would indicate intersubjective agreement. But coherence is always a construct—one dependent on abstract organizing categories. This paper now turn to examine the nature and process of this construction through three questions: (a) how is meaning constituted in the social thesis?; (b) how is the social thesis made possible and what role do abstract and indefinable requirements play?; and (c) what does one find in the legal social practice of international law? Each is considered in turn.

Any theory that is dependent on finding a controlling degree of intersubjectivity in its object of observation must rely on a method that requires a degree of reductionism. The question is whether this degree of reductionism remains appropriate, so as not to overly reduce the complexity of its object of observation. The first point to be made is that the social thesis overly reduces (and outright ignores) the intricacies by which meaning is

[48] It should be noted here that d'Aspremont's social thesis plays two distinct functions within his projects; normative and descriptive. A separate critique to be made, but not fully explored here, is that the normative bent of his social source thesis outlined in *Formalism and the Sources of International Law* undermines the descriptive functioning of the source thesis in his neo-positivist project in *International Legal Positivism in a Post-Modern World*. In the former, the social thesis is distinctly normative: it used solely as a method to make the more formal sources more determinate (192–4, 197, 213). In contrast, in the latter—d'Aspremont's neo-positivist project, the social thesis is purely descriptive. It is the methodology used to determine what the law is, buttressing the central positivist proposition that what the law is is in no way dependent upon what the law should be. Determinacy is not imposed, but rather uncovered. The normative social source thesis found in this book runs contrary to the tenets of the later neo-positivist argument. This critique is further explored in Singh, *supra* note 32.

constituted. For d'Aspremont, the 'meaning of formal law-ascertainment criteria arises out of their *convergence in use*' (197) and following Wittgenstein, 'the meaning of words . . . is all about how the participants in human activities conduction such a clarification . . . [i]t is how the word is used that will teach us the meaning of a word.' (198–9). Meaning is reduced to use and a community consensus of use. But meaning is *not* a stable property attachable to language. It is, as John Thompson noted, 'a fluctuating phenomenon which is constituted as much by the conditions of production as by the conditions of reception.'[49] Meaning is as much about understanding the specific historico-social conditions in which words and expressions are used (by law-applying authorities), as it is about interpretation in the reconstruction of these conditions (by the sociological legal theorist). Both Hart and d'Aspremont deflect the conditioning relevance (on meaning) of historical situationality and study. And certainly both ignore the constitutive and hermeneutic element of reconstructing language's structuring features. Their method ignores, as Foucault once stated, the unfailing question of 'what was being said in what was said?'[50] The construction of meaning requires more than d'Aspremont offers: we must also be thrown into hermeneutics and critical theory (as distinct from CLS).

The second point to be made is that the social thesis may only work as a method that introduces determinacy, if it adopts abstract and effectively immeasurable requirements. If the meaning of formal sources only emerges through 'convergence in use' (197) and 'community consensus' (200), one must examine what is precisely meant by convergence. How is intersubjectivity to be found (or rather, constructed)? For d'Aspremont there cannot be 'actual, total and absolute agreement among law-applying authorities' (201). All that is required to satisfy the requirement of intersubjectivity is 'a shared *feeling* of applying the same [formal law-ascertainment] criteria' (201). We are thrown from the promise of empiricism and measurable requirements into the immeasurable and absolutely abstract. What emerges is a social thesis that is held together and whose functionality is dependent on ungroundable psychoanalytics. How can one grasp this shared feeling that defines the internal point of view? It is impossible to tell whether law-applying authorities share said feeling unless it is expressed in one form or another. It seems difficult to argue that this logic, if followed, does not lead us into the trappings of the imminent intelligibility of formal language so regularly used by law-applying authorities—precisely what d'Aspremont states his formalism cannot be conflated with and which he rails against (18–21, 202). The social thesis' ability to cognise and construct coherence in international legal social practice is enabled by an abstract requirement that compels one to cast aside the empiricism (the foundations of the method) and eventually return to an objectionable formalism.

Finally, we turn to what is found when we look at the practice of law-applying authorities across international law. d'Aspremont does not see a shared feeling amongst law-appliers that they 'are using the same criteria' (213). He notes the 'absence of social consciousness' (213) amongst these actors. The social thesis cannot function to bring determinacy to international law's formal sources and their criteria. But its failure is *not* determined by the material reality of international law, but rather the absence of a social consciousness, a social identity:

[49] J. Thompson, 'Language and Ideology: a Framework for Analysis' (1987) 35 *The Sociological Review* 516, 520.

[50] M. Foucault, *The Archaeology of Knowledge* (Abingdon: Routledge, 2002), 30.

It is accordingly argued there that the problem is thus not really the fragmentation of the production of social practice but rather the absence of social consciousness among the variety of actors contributing to the production of communitarian semantics. (213)

In *Formalism and the Sources of International Law*, the material realities of international law do not defeat the social thesis. But they should and do. The point to be made, and that omitted by d'Aspremont, is that the material realities of international law *do* shape (but are not determinative of) social consciousness, the social identity of its actors and the functioning of language. Karl Marx was, in this regard, right:

[L]egal relations . . . are to be grasped neither from themselves nor from the so-called general development of the human mind, but have their roots in the material conditions of life . . . It is not the consciousness of men that determines their being, but, on the contrary, their social being that determines their consciousness.[51]

But what can be said of the material realities of international law? It is in answering this question that we come to a shift in d'Aspremont's works on theory. Subsequent to the publication of his monograph, he published an editorial piece entitled *Wording in International Law.* In this latter piece we see the emergence of a disguised rupture in d'Aspremont's thinking. I use the word disguised for two reasons. First the piece states its concern as international legal scholarship and not the practice of law-appliers[52] and secondly, because d'Aspremont goes out of his way to establish a congruency and consistency with his earlier monograph. He maintains and persists with his unattainable ideal horizon of a coherent linguistic community within international law that shares a common vocabulary.[53] The 'search for a common vocabulary—which boils down to a quest for social identity—allows the existence of a communicative platform where the interpretive community can develop itself.'[54] It is a quest; an unattainable possibility.

But this idealistic liberalism is shackled by the realistic tenor of the rest of the editorial. It paints a picture of irrepressible and irreversible symbolic conflict. d'Aspremont introduces international legal scholarship as the site of a number of different epistemic communities who are thrown into conflict by their substantive (rather than methodological) Kuhnian incommensurability and their engagement in a competition for authority, symbolic power ('naming')[55] and ultimately 'for the production of knowledge'[56] through symbolic control. And despite d'Aspremont's qualifications,[57] much of this resonates within the practice of courts and other law-applying actors across international law.

When one looks at their social practice, you do not find coherence *across* international law. But what you may find is that in the elaboration of norms and their application (the methodological domain for the social thesis) there are small pockets of intersubjectivity delineated along institutional lines or even more concretely, in various interpretive or epistemic communities. But such communities and institutions also compete for

[51] K. Marx, 'Preface to a Critique of Political Economy' in D. McLellan (ed.) *Karl Marx: Selected Writings* (Oxford: OUP, 2000, 2nd edn.) 424, 425.

[52] Wording, *supra* note 2, 577–8, 583. See also 213–4 of monograph under review.

[53] *Ibid.*, 599–601.

[54] *Ibid.*, 599.

[55] *Ibid.*, 576.

[56] *Ibid.*, 582.

[57] *Ibid.*, 578: 'the observations formulated here cannot always be mechanically transposed to the wording by courts or NGOs that are part of the interpretive community of international law.'

symbolic power with each other. The quest is for control over the meaning of norms and how those norms are constituted. Different regimes, different communities and different institutions seek to (and inevitably do, even when they do not seek to) interpret and portray the international legal world in a way most favorable to their own perspective. This, moreover, is done through a process of naturalization. An epistemic community or institutional regimes may sometimes reject outright the applicability of other normative vocabularies, but more regularly than not it is discourse and engagement which defines the relationship. But discourse, here, is a precursor to colonization. A particular vocabulary will engage, seemingly naturally, with other external vocabularies but define them on their own terms. The classification of an issue as one of human rights, trade law, investment law etc. is not an innocent one. Such relatively empty, but powerful and classifying, terms are manipulated by various participants as social constructs and used to colonize particular situations—thereby highlighting some preferences above others.[58]

The international legal system is an atomized one, where social centers are dispersed and where conflict is rife. What emerges is a series of language-games where intersubjective centers seek to outmaneuver communicational adversaries. It is a relationship of conflict that should be limited by international law's structural constraints. One such structural constraint is arguably the sources of international law: they determine what rules are acceptable and in accordance to settled criteria. But limits, constraints are consistently implemented in a manner that allows for and encourages the greatest possibly flexibility. This is precisely because they are not merely regulators of international law's language games, but stakes within these games. But limits and constraints on language games are not always strategically employed stakes within communicative and symbolic conflict. International law, like all other structures, has certain embedded limits: we know more concretely and with greater certainty about what constitutes a treaty and the criteria for determining said source. But as long as the meaning of treaties as a source and its criteria are contested and continue to be stakes within language games and between communicative adversaries, the limits of this structural limit will never be fully or permanently established.

Certainly for now, the meaning of norms alongside sources and the criteria for determining them are all fodder for hegemonic language strategies. This is the nature of symbolic conflict across international law.

I do not, however, seek to persuade the reader that my briefly stated view of international law's material reality is determinative of the matter. It is irrelevant whether one agrees with my characterizations or not. I seek to make two points. First, it is not a deficiency of social consciousness that renders the social thesis unworkable—but rather the material conditions (institutional and linguistic) of international law that have established this deficiency. The second point to made is that d'Aspremont's own shift in theoretical approach towards the presence of symbolic conflict—when extrapolated to the practice of law—applying authorities—undermines the very possibility of his initially stated social thesis. The latter requires coherence and convergence in social practice data across international law. The former (symbolic conflict) demonstrates it as an impossibility. An impossibility not only due to the atomization of the social within international

[58] M. Koskenniemi, 'The Politics of International Law—20 Years On' (2009) 20 *European Journal of International Law* 7, 11–12.

law, but because d'Aspremont's new theory (understanding) of reality is one constituted by conflict and competition. Because his normative social thesis cannot account for this conflict it is left bereft of its claim to be able to determine what the law is, or more specifically, its ability to determine what international law's formal law-ascertainment criteria are—even despite its considerable attempts to construct coherence through remarkably abstract categories. Being able to reconstruct what the law is requires a gentle and nuanced move towards dialectics.

Given the analysis of this section (6.2), it would seem that d'Aspremont's social thesis as a method, is suspect to a number of not inconsiderable problems. The two core problems of the method and its use in *Formalism and the Sources of International Law* were its deployment of a circular logic and its subversion by the rupture in d'Aspremont's theoretical thoughts. The first of these leads to the following problem—as worded by Herbert Marcuse:

> [T]he criteria for judging a given state of affairs are those offered by ... the given state of affairs. The analysis is 'locked' the range of judgment is confined within a context of facts which excludes judging the context in which the facts are made ... and in which their function, and development are determined.[59]

The self-referential logic of the social thesis ushers both its exclusion of precisely on what it depends: high theory and conceptualism. It also advances a reductive approach to construction of reality. But the nature of d'Aspremont's change of direction in theory ensured the unworkability of the social thesis both for law in general and the formal sources in particular. But it has the capability to refute the possibility of the social thesis on empirical grounds and not as a result of an immeasurable psychoanalytic concept—social consciousness.

7. Conclusion

At its heart, above the drama and intricacies of its detail, this review has been about three things. First it has been about how narratives of theory are constructed in today's academy; a commentary on the necessary structure of ideas in today's bustling market-place. But more than merely being a narrative on a narrative, its purpose has been to highlight the fragility of narratives. Theories, like stories, are constructed through subtle and not-so-subtle maneuvers. Much is to be said about the way subtler characteristics of a story continuously unfold and structure the larger plot or thesis. My purpose has been to bring this to light through critical narrative analysis. The second matter at the heart of this review is that of the nature of theorising. It has been about how ruptures in our approaches constitute not only the development of a theorist but also the potential gravity of an adopted theoretical position. Much is to be said about exploring the points of rupture, rather than the points of continuity in the work of contemporary theorists.[60] For it in the former that one sees the exciting potential for new avenues of enquiry. The

[59] H. Marcuse, *One-Dimensional Man: Studies in the Ideologies of Advanced Industrial Society* (Boston: Beacon Press, 1991, 2nd edn) 115–6.

[60] See for example my engagement with Martti Koskenniemi's work: S. Singh, 'The Potential of International Law: Fragmentation and Ethics' (2011) 24 *Leiden Journal of International Law* 23.

final matter of concern is that of the politics of method or theory. A large portion of this paper has been about demonstrating that methods immunize themselves from critique using crafted techniques and that these same theories deny their need to rely on reference points external to their self-referential logic.

Each one of these matters bears closer scrutiny that I am able to afford here—but each of these matters have structured and dominated my enquiry. For now, it suffices, nay it is indispensible, to note that Jean d'Aspremont's *Formalism and the Sources of International Law* ought to be read widely by legal theorists and international legal scholars. It represents the work of a fine, if evolving, theorist.

APPENDIX 3

Review Essay
Towards A Communicative Theory of International Law *

*Timothy Meyer***

> 'The Lord came down to see the city and the tower the people were building. The Lord said, "If as one people speaking the same language they have begun to do this, then nothing they plan to do will be impossible for them."'
>
> —Genesis 11: 5–6

1. Introduction

Article 38 of the *Statute of the International Court of Justice* proclaims that the Court shall apply 'international conventions', 'international custom', 'the general principles of law recognized by civilized nations', and as a subsidiary means for the determination of the rules of law, 'judicial decisions and the teachings of the most highly qualified publicists'. Although expressly framed as a list of applicable law in disputes before the International Court of Justice ('ICJ') and not as an exhaustive list of the sources of international law, generations of law students have been taught that the sources of international law can be found simply by reading art 38. Armed with this succinct menu, graduates sally forth into international legal practice where they find that the neat world of art 38 is a fiction.

For upon entering international legal practice in almost any field it is readily apparent that art 38 misses entire categories of norms that international lawyers and states appear to treat as if they have some legal consequence. In some cases, international lawyers try to resolve this tension by describing putative legal norms as customary international law, despite implausible evidence as to the state practice and *opinio juris* that accompany them.[1] In other instances, instruments are described as 'soft law', suggesting that they have some legal qualities while lacking others.[2] Some of these soft law norms are created by non-governmental organisations, meaning that under traditional state-centric theories of international law they cannot be binding law.[3] Yet many, if not most, lawyers have the intuition that, despite the traditional

* This review essay first appeared in the *Melbourne Journal of International Law*, Vol. 13, p. 921, 2012.

** Assistant Professor of Law, University of Georgia School of Law.

[1] See Daniel Bodansky, 'Prologue to a Theory of Non-Treaty Norms' in Mahnoush H Arsanjani et al (eds), *Looking to the Future: Essays on International Law in Honor of W Michael Reisman* (Martinus Nijhoff, 2010) ; Hiram E Chodosh, 'Neither Treaty nor Custom: The Emergence of Declarative International Law' (1991) 26 *Texas International Law Journal* 87.

[2] See, eg, Kenneth W Abbott and Duncan Snidal, 'Hard and Soft Law in International Governance' (2000) 54 *International Organization* 421.

[3] See, eg, Alan Boyle and Christine Chinkin, *The Making of International Law* (Oxford University Press, 2007) 89 (listing examples of soft law instruments promulgated by non-state actors, including:

doctrine of sources, juris-generation is no longer the sole province of the state.[4] Some scholars have thus produced theories to explain the normative force of new kinds of quasi-legal rules,[5] while others have emphatically pushed back and argued for the preservation of traditional and strict notions of what constitutes 'law'.[6]

Into this cacophony enters Jean d'Aspremont, an associate professor of international law at the Centre for International Law at the University of Amsterdam. His book, *Formalism and the Sources of International Law,*[7] builds on his earlier work published in the *European Journal of International Law*[8] and the *Finnish Yearbook of International Law,*[9] among other places.[10]

The book is a greatly welcome addition to the literature on the sources of international law. Drawing on both general and international legal theory, d'Aspremont develops a formalist theory of how linguistic indicators can and should be used to identify legal norms and distinguish them from non-legal norms. The book is divided into eight chapters. The early chapters introduce the study and defend a formalist approach to identifying legal norms, while the middle chapters explore the intellectual history of formalism in legal thought and international legal thought in particular. Later chapters examine critiques of formalism and the deformalisation of sources of international law. The final two chapters present d'Aspremont's theory of formal 'law-ascertainment' (or as I shall sometimes refer to it, identification)—an approach to determining whether a particular instrument or norm gives rise to legal obligations.

D'Aspremont's book is ambitious in scope; part intellectual history and part legal theory. In this essay, I shall focus on a few key points. My main objective is to connect d'Aspremont's application of general legal theory, based on H L A Hart's social thesis and Ludwig Wittgenstein's theory of communitarian semantics, to institutionalist thinking in international law. Although perhaps not obviously connected at first blush,

International Law Association, *Helsinki Rules on the Uses of the Waters of International Rivers and Comments* (Paper presented at the 52nd Conference, Helsinki, Finland 1966), *The Limburg Principles on the Implementation of the International Covenant on Economic, Social and Cultural Rights,* UN ESCOR, 43rd sess, Annex, UN Doc E/CN.4/1987/17, 'The *Maastricht Guidelines* on Violations of Economic, Social and Cultural Rights' (1998) 20 *Human Rights Quarterly* 691, 693–4. and Stephen Macedo (ed) *The Princeton Principles on Universal Jurisdiction* (Princeton, 2001).

[4] See, eg, Boyle and Chinkin, above n 3, 41–5 (discussing the increasing role of non-state actors in international lawmaking and the literature thereon).

[5] See, eg, David M Trubek et al, '"Soft Law", "Hard Law" and EU Integration' in Gráinne de Búrca and Joanne Scott (eds), *Law and New Governance in the EU and the US* (Hart Publishing, 2006) 65, 66–7. See also Orly Lobel, 'The Renew Deal: The Fall of Regulation and the Rise of Governance in Contemporary Legal Thought' (2004) 89 *Minnesota Law Review* 342, 394–5, discussing the use of soft law in international law to accomplish what cannot be accomplished through traditional legal pathways.

[6] See, eg, Prosper Weil, 'Towards Relative Normativity in International Law?' (1983) 77 *American Journal of International Law* 413, 415 n 7: 'sublegal obligations are neither "soft law" nor "hard law": they are simply not law at all'.

[7] Jean d'Aspremont, *Formalism and the Sources of International Law* (Oxford University Press, 2011).

[8] Jean d'Aspremont, 'Softness in International Law: A Self-Serving Quest for New Legal Materials: A Rejoinder to Tony D'Amato' (2009) 20 *European Journal of International Law* 911; Jean d'Aspremont, 'Softness in International Law: A Self-Serving Quest for New Legal Materials' (2008) 19 *European Journal of International Law* 1075.

[9] Jean d'Aspremont, 'The Foundations of the International Legal Order' (2007) 18 *Finnish Yearbook of International Law* 219.

[10] See, eg, Jean d'Aspremont, 'The Doctrinal Illusion of Heterogeneity of International Lawmaking Processes' in Hélène Ruiz-Fabri, Rüdiger Wolfrum and Jana Gogolin (eds), *Select Proceedings of the European Society of International Law: Volume 2, 2008* (Hart Publishing, 2010).

d'Aspremont's theory of law-identification—if extended beyond the formal dichotomy between law and non-law on which he places his emphasis to encompass broader notions of how states signal their commitments to each other—opens the door to what I refer to as a communicative theory of international law. In short, d'Aspremont's theory of law-identification explains how states shape each other's expectations about how they will behave in the future. In institutionalist theories of international law, as in d'Aspremont's theory, these expectations—rather than the intent of the parties that is the cornerstone of jurisprudential approaches to international law—are critical. States apply sanctions to each other when their legal expectations are disappointed rather than when a state fails to honour its intentions. How states communicate with each other is thus a critical aspect of institutionalist theory, because it explains how states translate their intentions—the traditional focus of jurisprudence—into expectations; the critical aspect of an institutionalist theory of international law. D'Aspremont's descriptive account of how legal language is formed and used to indicate commitment suggests a research agenda focused on the use of language in legal instruments as a means of testing broader ideas about how states design international instruments and the role of reputation in international law.

In Part II, I shall briefly review the book's key arguments, focusing on the defence of formalism in law-identification, the putative need to have a sharp distinction between law and non-law and the workings of d'Aspremont's theory of formal law-ascertainment. In Part III(A), I shall consider whether the defence of formalism and the alleged need for a sharp distinction between law and non-law is compelling in light of research from behaviouralist and institutionalist perspectives on how ambiguity can increase the effectiveness of the law. In Part III(B), I shall argue that d'Aspremont's theory of law-identification, when expanded beyond the narrow context in which d'Aspremont applies it, helps fill a significant gap in institutionalist thinking about how international law structures incentives to comply with the law. Specifically, the theory of law-identification laid out in *Formalism and the Sources of International Law* offers an explanation of how states communicate, or fail to communicate, expectations to each other. This account of communication between states fills an important gap in institutionalist theories of international law.

2. The Role of Formalism in Finding International Law

In 1955, Sir Hersch Lauterpacht wrote that 'the absence of agreed rules partaking of a reasonable degree of certainty is a serious challenge to the legal nature of what goes by the name of international law'.[11] This quotation captures an intuition felt by many international lawyers—that an essential task of international lawyers is to say what the law is. The goal of clarifying the law is often associated with international lawmaking processes and institutions, from dispute resolution to the codification of customary international law.[12]

[11] Hersch Lauterpacht, 'Codification and Development of International Law' (1955) 49 *American Journal of International Law* 16, 19.

[12] See, eg, Lassa Oppenheim, *International Law: A Treatise* (Longmans, Green and Co 1905) vol 1 39–43; Timothy Meyer, 'Codifying Custom' (2012) 160 *University of Pennsylvania Law Review* 995. For an argument that non-compliance with legal rules may stem from ambiguity and imprecision, see Abram

By defending his call for a renewed formalism in identifying international legal norms on the grounds that formalism reduces ambiguity and indeterminacy in the law, d'Aspremont is thus in good company. He argues that

> some elementary formal law-ascertainment in international law [is] a necessary condition to preserve the normative character of international law, in that uncertainty regarding the existence of international legal rules prevents them from providing for meaningful commands.[13]

He goes on to argue that, in the absence of formal identification criteria, actors cannot anticipate the effects of rules and thus legal rules 'fall short of generating any change in the behaviour of its addressees'.[14] D'Aspremont thus calls for 'the preservation of the distinction between law and non-law' and the use of formal indicators to mark the boundary between the two[15] in order to further the effectiveness of international law, which is to say its ability to change state behaviour by inducing states to try to comply with legal rules.[16] In short, he believes that clarity promotes effectiveness.

Formalism itself is hardly a self-defining term. The early chapters of the book are devoted to reviewing the history of formalism, its different conceptions and its critics (in both general and international legal theory). In the interest of space, I will not discuss at length the very comprehensive and illuminating review of the intellectual and philosophical history of formalism that d'Aspremont offers. Suffice it to say that these chapters should be required reading for anyone interested in the origins of contemporary debates about the sources of international legal rules. Particularly noteworthy is Chapter 5, which discusses some possible agendas behind efforts to deformalise international law, including: efforts to expand international law's reach; to solve accountability problems thought to arise from the pluralism of international norm-creation; a 'self-serving quest for new legal materials';[17] and, of course, advocacy by counsel in international judicial proceedings who use the deformalisation of law-ascertainment as a way to expand the set of possible rules at the service of their clients.[18] Although one might wish that d'Aspremont had developed the nuances of these motivations a bit more,[19] this discussion challenges the reader, particularly the reader interested in soft

Chayes and Antonia Handler Chayes, *The New Sovereignty: Compliance with International Regulatory Agreements* (Harvard University Press, 1995).

[13] D'Aspremont, *Formalism and the Sources of International Law*, above n 7, 29–30 (emphasis altered).

[14] Ibid 30. D'Aspremont also grounds his call for formalism on a need for lawyers to maintain their authority within the norm-making and political processes, to promote coherent scholarly debates about international rules and indeed to make a critique of international law possible, and to promote rule of law values: at 31–6.

[15] Ibid 5.

[16] Ibid 30–1.

[17] Ibid 133.

[18] Ibid 130–4.

[19] In particular, d'Aspremont's discussion of a 'self-serving quest for new legal materials' suggests that competition among international legal scholars to distinguish themselves has driven legal scholars to expand the bounds of what is considered law for reasons of professional advancement, rather than out of an intellectual conviction that new forms of international ordering should be studied alongside law. While there is no doubt some truth in what d'Aspremont says, there is a less cynical view of this phenomenon. Much of non-legal or quasi-legal ordering could easily be structured as 'law' if the parties generating the norms so wished. For example, social norms could be embedded in enforceable contracts or enacted as statutes, while non-binding international agreements could be made binding. Thus, for those scholars

law or customary international law, to think about how and why she deploys the theory of the sources of international law.

D'Aspremont himself adopts a definition of formalism based on the so-called 'source thesis', which 'provides that law is ascertained by its pedigree defined in formal terms and that, as a result, identifying a norm as a legal norm boils down to a formal pedigree test'.[20] He modifies the 'source thesis' with reference to H L A Hart's social thesis, under which the formal indicators—the pedigree a rule must have to be deemed legal—are determined by 'the converging practice of law-applying authorities'.[21] Following Brian Tamanaha's work,[22] d'Aspremont adopts an expansive notion of what constitutes a law-applying authority, including judges, non-state actors and legal scholars.[23] D'Aspremont therefore argues that the indicators that should be used to identify legal norms are not determined independently of legal practice, but rather emerge (and in his view, hopefully converge) organically from the practice of international legal actors.[24]

Although one can imagine different kinds of indicators emerging from social practice, d'Aspremont focuses on the role of linguistic indicators.[25] His theory is, in essence, a theory of how international legal actors can and should communicate with each other and of the benefits of developing a common legal language to signal legal commitment. Determining what constitutes the 'convergences of the practice of law-applying authorities'[26] is an exercise in communitarian semantics, derived from the philosophy of language and particularly Wittgenstein's work. On this account, rules (including rules of recognition) are specific to the social contexts in which they emerge.[27] The meaning of a rule is determined by 'the conduct of the social group'.[28]

D'Aspremont's theory is thus both a descriptive account of how international legal actors to develop a set of shared linguistic tools that they understand are used to mark the creation of a legal obligation, as well as a normative call for such development. Critically, d'Aspremont's emphasis is on language's power to mark legal obligation, rather than other possible markers such as compliance with formal procedures. As an example of a

interested in the design of legal systems, studying traditional international law alongside new forms of 'non-law', to use d'Aspremont's term, is necessary because the attribute of interest—formal legality—is endogenous. Put differently, to understand why a norm is a formal legal norm requires studying the comparative considerations that went into structuring the norm as such.

[20] D'Aspremont, *Formalism and the Sources of International Law*, above n 7, 13.

[21] Ibid 201. See also H L A Hart, *Essays on Bentham: Studies in Jurisprudence and Political Theory* (Clarendon Press, 1982).

[22] Brian Z Tamanaha, *A General Jurisprudence of Law and Society* (Oxford University Press, 2001).

[23] D'Aspremont, *Formalism and the Sources of International Law*, above n 7, 203.

[24] Ibid 13–15. He carefully distinguishes formalism in law-ascertainment from the evidentiary process that may be associated with proving a rule exists and the process of interpreting a rule. Evidentiary procedures involve proving, for example, the existence of a document alleged to contain a legal rule or a conversation alleged to have created a contract. Whether a legal rule actually arises from the document or conversation is the subject of law-ascertainment. Only after a rule has been ascertained can its content be interpreted.

[25] Ibid 12: 'this book...seeks to demonstrate that written linguistic indicators should play the predominant role in the ascertainment of international legal rules...'.

[26] Ibid 197.

[27] Ibid 200. See generally, Norman Malcolm, *Nothing is Hidden: Wittgenstein's Criticism of His Early Thought* (Blackwell, 1986); Dennis Patterson, Law's Pragmatism: Law as Practice and Narrative in Dennis Patterson (ed), *Wittgenstein and Legal Theory* (Westview, 1992) 85, 86.

[28] D'Aspremont, *Formalism and the Sources of International Law*, above n 7, 200.

formal linguistic indicator, d'Aspremont offers the ritualistic language used in Security Council resolutions that create binding obligations under Chapter VII of the *Charter of the United Nations*. There, the Security Council intones that there has been a breach of or threat to international peace and security, invokes Chapter VII, and then 'decides' upon the obligations imposed on members.[29] These kinds of ritualistic linguistic indicators, understood by the legal community to connote the creation of a legal obligation, provide a pedigree that can be evaluated objectively to determine whether an instrument in fact creates binding legal obligations.

D'Aspremont acknowledges that states already pay a great deal of attention to linguistic indicators of their intent to be legally bound by an agreement, citing in particular the *Copenhagen Accord*[30] as an example of an instrument in which states clearly signaled the political nature of the instrument.[31] The list of examples of international instruments that are clearly not intended to be legally binding could easily be expanded to include, to name but a very few: the *Basel Accords on Capital Adequacy* ('*Basel Accords*');[32] the *Nuclear Suppliers Group Guidelines*;[33] the *Rio+20 Declaration*;[34] and various memoranda of understanding on cooperation between, for example, national antitrust authorities.[35]

Yet d'Aspremont is correct to note that ambiguity plagues a variety of contemporary instruments. Perhaps the clearest example are the decisions of Conferences of the Parties ('COP') to various treaties that appear to extend beyond the lawmaking authority granted to the COP. For example, the *Kyoto Protocol to the United Nations Framework Convention on Climate Change*[36] specifies that any compliance mechanism resulting in binding legal consequences must be adopted by means of a formal amendment to the *Protocol*. Yet the *Kyoto Compliance Mechanism*,[37] which contemplates imposing

[29] Ibid 190.

[30] Conference of the Parties, United Nations Framework Convention on Climate Change, *Report of the Parties on its Fifteenth Session, Held in Copenhagen from 7 to 19 December 2009—Addendum—Part Two: Action Taken by the Conference of the Parties at Its Fifteenth Session*, UN Doc FCCC/CP/2009/11/Add.1 (30 March 2010).

[31] D'Aspremont, Formalism and the Sources of International Law, above n 7, 183 n 190.

[32] Basel Committee on Banking Supervision, *Basel III: International Framework for Liquidity Risk Management, Standards and Monitoring* (Bank for International Settlements, 2010); Basel Committee on Banking Supervision, *Basel III: A Global Regulatory Framework for More Resilient Banks and Banking Systems* (Bank for International Settlements, 2011).

[33] Nuclear Suppliers Group, *Guidelines for Nuclear Transfers* IAEA Doc INFCIRC/254/Rev.10/Part1, Nuclear Suppliers Group, (July 2011); Nuclear Suppliers Group, *Guidelines for Transfers of Nuclear-Related Dual-Use Equipment, Materials, Software and Related Technology* IAEA Doc INFCIRC/254/Rev.10/Part1, (June 2010).

[34] *The Future We Want*, GA Res 66/288, UN GAOR 66th sess, 123rd plen mtg, Agenda Item 19, UN Doc A/RES/66/288 (11 September 2012) annex.

[35] See, eg, *Memorandum of Understanding on Antitrust Cooperation between the United States Department of Justice and the United States Federal Trade Commission, and the Ministry of Corporate Affairs (Government of India) and the Competition Committee of India* <http://www.ftc.gov/oia/agreements/1209indiamou.pdf.>.

[36] Opened for signature 16 March 1998, 2303 UNTS 148 (entered into force 16 February 2005).

[37] Compliance with the Kyoto Protocol is handled by the Compliance Committee. See Conference of the Parties, United Nations Framework Convention on Climate Change, *Report of the Conference of the Parties to the Kyoto Protocol on Its First Session, Held in Montreal from 28 November to 10 December 2005—Addendum—Part Two: Action Taken by the Conference of the Parties to the Kyoto Protocol at Its First Session*, UN Doc FCCC/KP/CMP/2005/8/Add.3 (30 March 2006) 92 Decision 27/CMP.1.

penalties such as reduced emissions limits in future emissions reductions agreements, was adopted by a simple decision of the parties. Similarly, the *Convention on International Trade in Endangered Species of Wild Fauna and Flora* ('*CITES*') endows the COP with the ability, among other things, to 'make recommendations for improving the effectiveness of *CITES*'.[38] Since 'recommendations' are not legally binding, this authority would appear to authorise the COP to do little more of a legally binding nature than subject species to the strict trade controls spelled out in *CITES* for species listed in Appendix I,[39] or the slightly less strict controls that apply to Appendix II species.[40] Despite this paucity of legal mandate, the *CITES* COP has erected a complicated compliance mechanism in which roles are assigned to the COP itself and a body created by the COP, referred to as the Standing Committee.[41] The compliance mechanism can result in 'recommendations' from the Standing Committee to the Parties to suspend trade with a particular party if they are in the view of the Standing Committee violating *CITES* either in the way it administers the Convention's trade controls or by failing to file reports *CITES* mandates.[42] These compliance procedures appear not to be legally binding due to the absence of treaty authorisation for the COP to impose binding consequences. They are, however, adopted by the COP in accordance with a legislative process and result in real-world consequences that prompt changes in state behaviour, facts that muddy the legal status of the *CITES* compliance mechanism.[43]

Ambiguity as to whether an instrument is legally binding is, in d'Aspremont's view, a product of international law's traditional reliance on parties' intent, an insufficiently formal criterion that gives rise to indeterminacy about whether an instrument is in fact legally binding.[44] Intent is 'a fickle and indiscernible psychological element'.[45] Resort to intent as the ultimate indicium of bindingness in international law thus introduces into treaties one of the main problems with customary law—the difficulty of ascertaining the psychological state of complex organisations. The problems of indeterminacy are compounded when one moves beyond written international instruments. D'Aspremont claims that unwritten legal rules are currently not subject to formal law-ascertainment.[46] In his view, the indeterminacy that has plagued debates about customary international

[38] *Convention on the International Trade in Endangered Species of Wild Fauna and Flora*, opened for signature 3 March 1973, 993 UNTS 244 (entered into force 1 July 1975) art XI ('*CITES*'). The Conference of the Parties' other powers are primarily administrative in nature, such as making provisions for the Secretariat's operation.

[39] Ibid art III.

[40] Ibid art IV.

[41] Conference of the Parties, Convention on the International Trade in Endangered Species of Wild Fauna and Flora, *Decisions of the Conference of the Parties to* CITES *in Effect after the Twelfth Meeting, Held in Santiago from 3 to 15 November 2002*, UN Doc CITES/CP/2002/12.84 Decision 84.; Conference of the Parties, Convention on the International Trade in Endangered Species of Wild Fauna and Flora, *Decisions of the Conference of the Parties to* CITES *in Effect after the Fourteenth Meeting, Held in The Hague from 3 to 15 June 2007*, UN Doc CITES/CP/2007/14.3 Decision 3.

[42] See David Hunter, James Salzman and Durwood Zaelke, *International Environmental Law and Policy* (Foundation Press, 4th ed, 2011) 1079 (discussing the *CITES* compliance mechanism).

[43] Ibid 1079 (describing how the possibility of trade sanctions imposed through the *CITES* compliance process prompted Dominica, Rwanda and Vanuatu to come into compliance with their reporting obligations).

[44] D'Aspremont, *Formalism and the Sources of International Law*, above n 7, 178–82.

[45] Ibid 180.

[46] See ibid ch 7.

law can be traced to the informal criteria that are used to identify custom.[47] Moreover, while oral treaties and promises could in principle be identified using formal linguistic indicators, in practice they have tended to turn on the non-formal criterion of the intent of the parties, making distinction between binding oral promises and mere political statements difficult.[48]

D'Aspremont argues that substituting written indicators for intent goes a long way towards providing a solution to the indeterminacy that exists in identifying legal rules.[49] Although he suggests that the creation of a legal obligation through formal procedures could also play a role in formal law-identification, the resort to written indicators does not require formal procedures.[50] As the discussion regarding legislative decision-making by COPs indicates, there is wisdom in d'Aspremont's view on the limits of procedures to mark formal lawmaking. Procedures, such as bicameralism and presentment to create a statute or notice-and-comment rulemaking by agencies in the United States, are commonly used as a formal marker of the creation of a legal obligation in domestic contexts.[51] But the creative use of legislative bodies in international law to effectively amend treaties without formal amendment calls into question whether procedures can play the same role in international law. The institutions states create to engage in norm-production do not feel compelled to adhere tightly to the procedures of rulemaking spelled out in their constitutive treaties and yet, in the case of the compliance systems of the *Kyoto Protocol* and *CITES*, states appear to treat certain of these instruments as if they are legally binding.

D'Aspremont also recognises that the use of written linguistic indicators cannot totally eliminate indeterminacy in law-identification.[52] Indeed, its success in introducing determinacy is contingent on the convergence of social practices among law-applying authorities, an empirical fact that it is by no means clear exists.[53] Indeed, Harlan Cohen has argued that the fragmentation of international law is not the product of conflicting legal rules, but rather the product of disagreement about the sources of law itself,[54] a point that d'Aspremont acknowledges.[55] If Cohen is correct, it is not clear that formalism offers any greater respite from the indeterminacy of international law-identification than deformalised criteria. D'Aspremont attempts to elude this difficulty by making two moves. First, he argues that perfect convergence in social practices is not necessary, but rather only a 'feeling' that law-applying authorities are speaking the same language.[56]

[47] Ibid 162–70. [48] Ibid 171–3.

[49] Ibid 185–6. See also at 182–3: d'Aspremont acknowledges that the process of identifying intent has itself been subjected to formal identification through the use of procedural devices but, as discussed above, does not believe that these procedural indicators have gone far enough in resolving ambiguity about whether an obligation is binding.

[50] Ibid 189.

[51] *United States Constitution* art I § 7.

[52] D'Aspremont, *Formalism and the Sources of International Law*, above n 7, 189.

[53] Ibid 197: 'Short of any convergence, lawyers end up speaking different languages, thereby depriving law of any normativity'.

[54] Harlan Grant Cohen, 'Finding International Law Part II: Our Fragmenting Legal Community' (2012) 44 *New York University Journal of International Law and Politics* 1050.

[55] D'Aspremont, *Formalism and the Sources of International Law*, above n 7, 34: 'It is as if the international legal scholarship had turned into a cluster of different scholarly communities, each of them using different criteria for the ascertainment of international legal rules'.

[56] Ibid 201.

While one can sympathise with d'Aspremont's intuition that perfect convergence is not necessary, the notion of a 'feeling' of commonality seems somewhat underspecified.

Secondly, acknowledging the questionable empirical basis for a convergence of social practice among international lawyers, d'Aspremont calls for a greater 'social consciousness' among law-applying authorities.[57] He places particular emphasis on the role of informal cooperation and networks among international judges and tribunals.[58] Judicial dialogue can promote the social consciousness required to sustain the book's approach to formalism, and so d'Aspremont urges greater attention to the interaction between international tribunals and judges.[59]

D'Aspremont's theory of formal law-ascertainment can thus be divided into its descriptive and its normative components. Descriptively, he offers a revitalised version of formalism, based on Hart's social thesis, in which the convergence of practice among international legal actors leads to linguistic indicators that become focal points for states in identifying the legal significance of international instruments.[60] Normatively, d'Aspremont calls for greater convergence in the use of linguistic indicators, for the primacy of linguistic indicators over other possible law-identifying criteria, for the use of linguistic indicators to police the boundaries between law and non-law and ultimately for the conscious development of a common legal language of commitment.

3. A Communicative Theory of International Law

In this Part, I discuss the implications of institutionalist theories of international law for d'Aspremont's theory, and in turn the contribution of his theory of law-ascertainment to institutionalist theories. Institutionalism is a school of thought originating in international relations that studies the ways in which states use international institutions to facilitate cooperation. At its base, institutionalism is a behavioural school of thought, asking how international institutions change patterns of state conduct.[61] Although law is only one institution of interest to international relations scholars, legal scholars have in recent years borrowed the insights from institutionalist theory to explain why international legal institutions look as they do and when we can expect international law to generate compliance and change state behaviour.[62]

[57] Ibid 213.

[58] Ibid 213–14.

[59] Ibid 214.

[60] See, eg, ibid 16.

[61] See, eg, Barbara Koremenos, 'Institutionalism and International Law' in Jeffrey L Dunoff and Mark A Pollack (eds), *International Law and International Relations: Synthesizing Insights from Interdisciplinary Scholarship* (Cambridge University Press, 2012) Starting Page. Not Real Title, Not Yet Published

[62] To name but a very few, see Andrew Guzman, *How International Law Works: A Rational Choice Theory* (Oxford University Press, 2012); Kal Raustiala, 'Form and Substance in International Agreements' (2005) 99 *American Journal of International Law* 581; Jeffrey L Dunoff and Mark A Pollack (eds), *International Law and International Relations: Synthesizing Insights from Interdisciplinary Scholarship* (Cambridge University Press, 2012); Laurence R Helfer, 'Exiting Treaties' (2005) 91 *Virginia Law Review* 1579; Timothy Meyer, 'Power, Exit Costs, and Renegotiation in International Law' (2010) 51 *Harvard International Law Journal* 379; Gregory C Shaffer and Mark A Pollack, 'Hard Law vs Soft Law: Alternatives, Complements and Antagonists in International Governance' (2010) 94 *Minnesota Law Review*

It might seem that institutionalist theories of international law are far afield from a study of the formal ascertainment of legal rules. However d'Aspremont's defence of formalism is based on an argument that formalism in law-identification and a sharp bifurcation between law and non-law is necessary to maintain law's ability to change behaviour. His defence thus invites dialogue with other behavioural theories of international law. As I shall argue below, I believe the dialogue to be very fruitful for both institutionalist theories of international law and for d'Aspremont's own theory.

A. A Need for Formalism?

Institutionalist theories of international law hold that international law can generate changes by reducing transaction costs to negotiation, facilitating informational exchange and reducing uncertainty, and providing monitoring and enforcement procedures and tools that increase sanctions for violations of legal rules.[63] Sanctions are critical for such theories because they provide incentives to change state behaviour. Institutions allow states to commit to abiding by rules by making sanctions for violation more likely. There are roughly speaking three different kinds of sanctions: retaliatory, reciprocal and reputational.[64] Retaliatory sanctions are imposed in response to a breach of an obligation but the sanction need not be related to the obligation breached. Classic examples include military or economic sanctions. Reciprocal sanctions are imposed when a state ceases to comply with its own obligations under a legal rule because another state has breached an obligation. Finally, reputational sanctions are imposed when a state changes its view of how likely another state is to honour its obligations in the future. Such changes in reputation are costly because states with poor reputations may be excluded from international agreements or may have to offer greater concessions in order to induce other states to risk an agreement with them.[65] Of course, states can impose sanctions simply to try to change another state's behaviour. The key for institutionalist theories of law is that the existence of a legal obligation makes sanctions more likely by, for example, lowering the cost of a sanctioning state imposing retaliatory sanctions or by authorising reciprocal withdrawal from a treaty that has been breached by the other party. This marginal increase in the incentive to comply with a legal rule, owing to the increased possibility of being sanctioned, provides international law's 'compliance pull'. Reputational sanctions are especially important for institutionalist theories of international law because, unlike other kinds of sanctions, they are costless to impose and are thus the most frequently applied kind of sanction.[66]

Institutionalist theories of international law call into question d'Aspremont's assertion that making international law effective requires a sharp distinction between law and non-law that is policed with formal indicators.[67] Institutionalist theories, particularly

706; Rachel Brewster, 'The Remedy Gap: Institutional Design, Retaliation, and Trade Law Enforcement' (2011) 80 *George Washington Law Review* 102.

[63] See, eg, Koremenos, above n 61.

[64] See, eg, Guzman, *How International Law Works: A Rational Choice Theory*, above n 62, ch. 2.

[65] Ibid ch 3.

[66] See, eg, Ibid.

[67] D'Aspremont, *Formalism and the Sources of International Law*, above n 7, 122. D'Aspremont discusses what he terms effect- or impact-based conceptions of international law-ascertainment, whereby

reputational accounts, explain how much of the variation in formality and bindingness we observe in international legal ordering enhances the ability of states to cooperate. In particular, reputational theories explain how soft law—norms that are neither binding law nor purely political agreement, but have some lesser legal consequences—can improve the effectiveness of law. There are at least two ways in which soft law increases the effectiveness of international law.

First, soft law expands the range of instruments available to states and therefore makes regulation of certain topics more likely and may indeed make stricter regulation of certain areas possible. Variation in degrees of legality allows states to signal to each other the likelihood they will comply with an obligation. It allows them, in other words, to control the expectations of other states that determine the kinds of sanctions they face for violating a legal obligation. When a state makes a legal commitment, it pledges its reputation for complying with legal rules. If it makes a promise and fails to abide by that promise, the state suffers reputational harm that may hurt its ability to cooperate in the future. States thus have an incentive to be truthful about the likelihood they will comply with an obligation.

States develop levels of commitment in order to calibrate the expectations of their partners. Commitments that do not rise to the level of a binding obligation entail less of a pledge of reputational capital, and therefore less of a sanction in the event of a violation. In a sense, the difference between legally binding commitments in treaties and informal or soft law pledges is the difference between saying 'I shall arrive for dinner at six' as opposed to 'I hope to arrive at dinner by six'. The former connotes certainty on the part of the speaker and therefore creates firmer expectations in the mind of the hearer than does the latter statement. In the case of the former statement, if the declarant fails to arrive at six the hearer is more likely to reassess the credibility of the declarant's statements. In short, the hearer is more likely to be disappointed (and perhaps to rethink the guest list for future dinners) because the declarant raised his expectations.

Having a menu of commitment levels is valuable to states because it allows them to reduce the costs of violations that are unavoidable,[68] may facilitate renegotiation in areas of the law that are rapidly changing,[69] may allow states to broaden the reach of norms beyond those states who have formally consented to the norm[70] and creates an opportunity for states to engage in dynamic contestation of legal norms.[71] These benefits, in turn, increase the ability of states to cooperate, a crucial goal of legal ordering. Faced with a binary decision between law and non-law, states might well choose to forego legal commitments entirely to save, for example, renegotiation costs incurred in a fast-changing area like international financial law. In so doing, of course, these states would also

international legal rules are identified in terms of their ability to effect state behaviour. Institutionalism, properly understood, does not define legal rules in terms of their effects, as doing so conflates effects with causes. See Raustiala, above n 62, 582.

[68] Andrew Guzman, 'The Design of International Agreements' (2005) 16 *European Journal of International Law* 579; see also Chris Brummer, *Soft Law and the Global Financial System* (Cambridge University Press, 2011).

[69] See Timothy Meyer, 'Soft Law as Delegation' (2009) 32 *Fordham International Law Journal* 888.

[70] See Andrew Guzman and Timothy Meyer, 'International Soft Law' (2010) 2 *Journal of Legal Analysis* 171.

[71] See Shaffer and Pollack, above n 62.

forego the benefits of cooperation that arise from negotiating soft law instruments such as the *Basel Accords*. Moreover, states may be willing to make stricter soft law commitments rather than hard law commitments because the costs of violation are lower if they fail to live up to the stricter standards.[72] Whatever problems it may create for courts trying to apply the law, this variety lubricates international bargaining by giving states more choices when designing international agreements.

Second, d'Aspremont assumes that clarity about the legal effect of a rule is a virtue from the standpoint of effectiveness. This assumption is common in international legal scholarship. The managerialist school, for example, has, at its base, assumed that states have a predisposition to comply with international law.[73] On this account, most non-compliance with international law can be traced to ambiguity and indeterminacy, as well as informational problems and resource constraints.[74] Clarification of legal rules and increased transparency in legal process are cures for these compliance ills.

But ambiguity and indeterminacy have a number of benefits that are frequently overlooked, making the claim that clarification of a norm's legal status (and therefore a formalist approach aimed at such clarification) is a desirable one that might deserve a more robust defence than that given it by d'Aspremont. The benefits of ambiguity and indeterminacy of legal rules flow from the effects on behaviour of uncertainty about what will be considered compliance. Behavioural studies have shown that under certain conditions, such as where individuals are risk averse or have a predisposition to comply with the law, a lack of clarity as to what the law requires can enhance efforts to comply with the law.[75] The logic behind this counterintuitive finding is that individuals will make extra efforts to ensure they are compliant when what counts as compliance is unclear. They will leave themselves a margin of error. Providing clarity in what the law requires removes the need for this margin. Even individuals predisposed to comply with the law need only make the minimum effort necessary to comply. Extending this logic to states suggests that the managerialist account of the need for clarity in the law is backwards. If states truly have a predisposition to comply with the law (one that is independent of the sanctions they face for violation), then clarity may reduce their efforts to comply, thereby reducing the effectiveness of the law in changing state behaviour.

Beyond the benefits of ambiguity, dynamism in the law (with the associated lack of clarity) and in legal language also has benefits that are lost in a formalist approach to law-identification. As d'Aspremont notes, international law has seen an explosion in the numbers of actors claiming authority in the international legal system.[76] Moreover, international law has changed its approach to the relationship between states and individuals. Investment law (under investment treaties) now accords corporations the

[72] Raustiala, above n 62, 610.

[73] See, eg, Chayes and Handler Chayes, above n 12.

[74] Ibid 9–28.

[75] See, eg, John E Calfee and Richard Craswell, 'Some Effects of Uncertainty on Compliance with Legal Standards' (1984) 70 *Virginia Law Review* 965. For a review on the literature relating to the effect of uncertainty on compliance decisions, see James Alm, Betty Jackson and Michael McKee, 'Institutional Uncertainty and Taxpayer Compliance' (1992) 82 *American Economic Review* 1018.

[76] D'Aspremont, *Formalism and the Sources in International Law*, above n 7, 2.

right to bring direct causes of action against states,[77] and human rights law has evolved to regulate the purely internal conduct by a state towards its own citizens,[78] something largely unthinkable a hundred years ago. Many scholars, including d'Aspremont, have noted that this shift has been accompanied by greater variation in the kinds of criteria that legal actors apply in determining whether an instrument creates legal obligations.[79] D'Aspremont's theory is, of course, a reaction to this underlying fragmentation of sources doctrine.[80] D'Aspremont recognises that international law, and particularly the lawmaking process, is much more dynamic that the formal approach he advocates would suggest.[81] Formalism is useful, he argues, chiefly for the exercise of law-identification.

But I doubt that d'Aspremont's theory can be so neatly cabined. The identification of formal indicators through resort to community consensus about legal language implies a dynamism to d'Aspremont's approach to formalism that belies his call for a greater convergence in legal language among law-applying authorities. Languages, after all, are constantly evolving to express new ideas and sentiments. It should hardly be surprising, given the radical changes in how international law regulates states and in particular the relationship between states and non-state actors discussed above, that legal language would also change and perhaps fragment. Put differently, d'Aspremont's normative call for convergence on the use of legal language in the process of law-identification is somewhat at odds with the descriptive aspects of his theory. Consensus about the meaning of legal terminology can form and dissolve over time. This dynamism and the ambiguity it produces at times, even just at the level of law-identification, seems valuable insofar as it allows the doctrine of sources to evolve to take into account international law's contemporary challenges.

Finally, although assessing compliance in order to apply sanctions is critical to an institutionalist theory of international law, there is really only one kind of actor in the international system that is required to resolve with clarity the question of whether a law has been complied with (and thus whether an instrument creates legal obligations): international tribunals. States and negotiators can proceed to bargain over the resolution of a dispute without ever resolving some underlying uncertainty about whether a legal obligation exists. But in the process of resolving disputes, courts are tasked with making binary determinations as to who is right and wrong in a dispute and in what ways. A theory of the law that caters to or privileges this need of tribunals might be termed an adjudicative theory of law.[82] D'Aspremont's theory is based on such an adjudicative understanding of international law. In his view, 'there is no doubt that the central law-

[77] See Cohen, Finding International Law Part II: Our Fragmenting Legal Community, above n 54, 1083–4.

[78] Ibid 1074–5.

[79] D'Aspremont, *Formalism and the Sources of International Law*, above n 7, 34. See also Cohen, Finding International Law Part II: Our Fragmenting Legal Community, above n 54; Bodansky, above n 1.

[80] See also Cohen, Finding International Law Part II: Our Fragmenting Legal Community, above n 54.

[81] D'Aspremont, *Formalism and the Sources of International Law*, above n 7, 5: 'While not being construed as a tool to delineate the whole phenomenon of law—especially the flux of dynamics at the origin of the creation of legal rules, the content thereof, or the sense of obligation therein' (emphasis altered).

[82] See Harland Grant Cohen, 'International Law's Erie Moment' (2013) 34 *Michigan Journal of International Law* (forthcoming)

applying authority whose behaviour is the most instrumental in defining the standard of law-ascertainment is the International Court of Justice'.[83]

Yet this pride of place accorded the ICJ (and after the ICJ, other tribunals) overlooks the fact that much of international practice still occurs outside of the shadow of international tribunals. International disputes are still regularly resolved, not by resort to formal courts, but through negotiated resolutions that provide the basis for future legal claims.[84] In short, much of international law remains directly under the control of states. States keep track of and publicise their own practices in order to communicate to each other their beliefs about what the law requires, beliefs that are played out in a variety of interactions far away from The Hague. The United States Department of State, for example, annually publishes the *Digest of the US Practice in International Law.*[85] Moreover, much of the contestation over international legal process is about defining what those obligations are in the first place. States are simultaneously the subjects and creators of international law. In the latter role, they are constantly renegotiating the terms of their commitments to each other. In doing so, they apply the law because the law shapes their bargaining positions. But formal law-ascertainment criteria are less important where this latter task is concerned.[86] Instead of being concerned with the mechanical task of categorising the kinds of commitments states have made to each other in the past, states are concerned with defining their obligations going forward. Such a task can accommodate some uncertainty as to the legal status of the obligations being debated. Certainty is but a means, and far from the only one, to the end of a negotiated resolution. Indeed, many international disputes recognise this reality explicitly, setting parameters for state negotiations rather than declaring firmly a resolution to a particular dispute.[87]

B. Communication and Expectations

Institutionalist theories of law thus offer an explanation for why the existence of quasi-legal norms and, similarly, ambiguity about the legality of a norm, may be desirable from a behavioural perspective. The existence of quasi-legal norms may allow states to regulate some areas that would be unregulated in a world in which states could only choose between binding and non-binding agreements. Moreover, ambiguity may in certain instances increase compliance efforts.

Yet institutionalist theories do not specify precisely how states go about signalling their desired level of commitment in an instrument. They assume that there are binding commitments, soft law commitments, and purely political commitments, but offer at best a thin description of how states distinguish between these different categories. These theories, in other words, tend to assume flawless communication between states, rather

[83] D'Aspremont, *Formalism and the Sources of International Law*, above n 7, 205.

[84] For a theory of international law's evolution in response to negotiated resolutions of claims, see Anthony D'Amato, *The Concept of Custom in International Law* (Cornell University Press, 1971) 92–8.

[85] CarrieLyn D Guymon (ed), 'Digest of United States Practice in International Law 2011' (United States Department of State). Available at <http://www.state.gov/s/l/2011/index.htm.>.

[86] This is not to say that having a theory of what constitutes a legally binding obligation—that is, a theory of the pure type—is not important. Such a theory provides a measuring stick by which to judge the legality of different kinds of instruments. I mean only to say that the approach to determining what constitutes a legally binding obligation need not be devoid of uncertainty.

[87] *Gabcíkovo–Nagymaros Project (Hungary v Slovakia) (Judgment)* [1997] ICJ Rep 7, 78–9 [141]–[142].

than exploring how states in fact communicate their desired level of commitment.[88] States do not communicate with each other without error, however. What one state believes it is signaling is not necessarily what another states hears. Institutionalist theories thus require an account of how states indicate the level of commitment associated with a particular legal instrument.

Enter d'Aspremont's theory of law-identification. One of the key contributions of d'Aspremont's theory is the recognition that treaty law has remained beholden to the psychological notion of 'the intent of the parties'.[89] The reasons for this allegiance stem from the contractual nature of international agreements, as well as a more general concern about sovereignty that permeates certain quarters in international law. A fidelity to the intent of the parties vindicates a respect for sovereignty because it ultimately leaves the control of what obligations bind a state in that state's own hands.

But the intent of the parties is at best secondarily relevant once we consider a theory of international law based on incentives to comply. An institutionalist account of international law—one that emphasises how international legal institutions change the incentives for state behaviour by creating sanctions for deviating from legal rules—cares not about the intent of a party when it gives its consent to be bound to an obligation. Rather, it cares about the expectations that are created in the parties that will apply future sanctions. When those expectations are disappointed, sanctions (reputational or otherwise) are applied. Once a legal obligation is created, a state bases its future behaviour on the expectations of other states because those expectations—and not the state's intent when it entered into the legal commitment—determine the kinds of penalties the state will face. Intent, of course, remains relevant insofar as a state has an incentive to set the expectations of other states in line with its own intentions. But on this account what matters it not intent per se. Rather, it is how intent is communicated and perceived by other states.

This insight is critical. Theories of international law, particularly theories of customary international law, have focused on *opinio juris*, the psychological component of the law.[90] Yet institutionalism's focus on expectations as the basis for sanctions makes clear that international law is most likely to be effective in generating behavioural change, not when states act out of a sense of legal obligation, but rather when there are shared expectations about the kinds of obligations created by an instrument and what the instrument requires of states. D'Aspremont's theory thus very helpfully provides a jurisprudential underpinning for institutionalism's focus on expectations

[88] For an argument that international law proceeds through justificatory discourse and that international law is enfeebled when that discourse breaks down see Monica Hakimi, 'A Functional Approach to Targeting and Detention' (2012) 110 *Michigan Law Review* 1365, 1367–8: 'international law operates largely through a process of justificatory discourse'; see also Ian Johnstone, *The Power of Deliberation* (Oxford University Press, 2011) 22–7: 'lawmaking... is a process of communication'; W Michael Reisman, 'International Lawmaking: A Process of Communication' (Speech delivered at the Harold D Lasswell Memorial Lecture before the American Society of International Law, 24 April 1981) in (1981) 75 *American Society of International Law Proceedings* 101, 105.

[89] See d'Aspremont, *Formalism and the Sources of International Law*, above n 7, 178–82.

[90] For an argument that state practice is declining in importance and can be dispensed with for certain kinds of customary norms, see, eg, Niels Petersen, 'Customary International Law without Custom? Rules, Principles, and the Role of State Practice in International Norm Creation' (2008) 23 *American University International Law Review* 275.

rather than intent. At the same time, it provides institutionalist scholars with an empirical field of study: the comparative use of language in written instruments across time and fields. A communicative theory of international law would seek to explain the development and use of legal language across regions, substantive legal fields and in different kinds of legal instruments.

Effective communication requires a common legal language, the development of which d'Aspremont's version of the social thesis can explain. A common legal language allows the intentions of one party to be translated into the expectations of other parties. As d'Aspremont points out and as discussed above, the indicators currently in existence do not rid us of indeterminacy entirely. Nor, as I have argued, is it clear that zero is the optimal amount of indeterminacy about what constitutes a legal obligation. Nevertheless, a communicative theory of international law grounded in the institutionalist logic of sanctions does require some minimum level of ability to communicate to translate the intentions of one party into the expectations of others.

Of course, many of these formal indicators in fact exist. For example, denoting an instrument as an 'agreement' suggests the instrument is binding; denoting an instrument as a 'memorandum of understanding' suggests it is not. Referring to the signatories to an instrument as 'parties' suggests the instrument is binding; referring to them as 'participants' suggests it is not. At the level of individual obligations, 'shall' connotes a binding obligation, while 'should' indicates a non-binding obligation.

But we would not expect the development of this common language to stop at linguistic indicators marking the distinction between law and non-law, d'Aspremont's focus. Instead, based on the need to signal variation in commitment levels, one might predict that states would develop a robust set of linguistic indicators that allow them to calibrate the level of commitment associated with a particular obligation. For example, one of the key attributes of soft law obligations is that they are not purely political commitments. Rather, they have some quasi-legal attribute: they implicate in some way a state's reputation for complying with its legal obligations. But what sort of linguistic indicators mark these kinds of obligations and distinguish them both from binding obligations and from purely political commitments? Can evidence for the existence and importance of soft law be found in the use of language in international instruments?

One possible indicator is a textual reference to a binding legal obligation, indicating that states view the soft law obligations as related to binding legal obligations. This relationship distinguishes the soft law obligation from the purely political one. By including a reference to a binding legal obligation in an otherwise non-binding instrument, states signal to each other that they view the obligations therein as more than purely political commitments. Moreover, tracing the textual references between different kinds of instruments might allow scholars to develop a typology of different kinds of instruments based on linguistic usage. Instruments that are more closely associated with clearly binding legal instruments might be more frequently invoked by states both in judicial proceedings as well as in diplomatic correspondence.

More generally, a communicative theory of international law opens a potentially fruitful line of research into how language is used in different legal communities. If, as I have suggested above, the legal language states use to mark different levels of legal agreement is dynamic, then the use of legal language in instruments across time, regions and substantive fields may shed light on underlying patterns of international lawmaking. Variation between, for example, the way in which linguistic indicators are used in human rights law versus trade law may indicate that specialisation in international law has in fact produced distinct legal communities. Such a finding would have significant implications for how we think about the fragmentation of international law,[91] as well for reputational accounts of international law, where one of the central questions is whether states have a single reputation for compliance or have multiple reputations based on issue area.[92] In conjunction with a more nuanced typology of different levels of commitment based on linguistic indicators and cross-references to other instruments, scholars might be able to map the relative legalisation of international relations across time, issue area and geography.

4. Conclusion

In the tale of the Tower of Babel, the people of the earth are said to have spoken a common language. Because of their ability to communicate with each other, there were no limits to their potential and they settled in a plain to build a city and tower that would reach to the heavens. Displeased, God shattered their unified language and scattered them across the earth. In many ways, the story of Babel captures the hopes and fears of international lawyers. If international law speaks with a common voice, it offers the possibility of cooperative solutions to some of the world's most vexing problems. But if lawyers fail to speak in one tongue, international law loses its force and nations may be scattered.[93]

In *Formalism and the Sources of International Law*, d'Aspremont has offered one of the most insightful defences of this view in many years. He skilfully shows how a common legal language can emerge to delineate the multitude of international instruments those which give rise to legal obligations from those which do not. Moreover, he has offered a thoughtful defence of the virtue of developing this common legal language for the purpose of marking the boundary between the legal and the non-legal, between law and politics.

Languages are constantly changing, however, and pushing for unity of language has costs. Changes in languages happen for important reasons. Underlying ideas change and the speakers—the participants in the legal system—also change over time. Moreover, more varied language and more varied law increases the ability of international legal actors, most importantly states, to tailor the level of commitment in their rules to the specific nature of the problem in question. There is no doubt that pluralism in international legal sources comes with costs and creates confusion. At the same time, however, this increase in language also creates the possibility of order where there would only be anarchy, of cooperation where a bifurcated world of law and non-law would relegate certain matters to pure politics.

At the same time, d'Aspremont's theory of linguistic indicators in international law has opened a potentially fruitful avenue of research for international lawyers. His descriptive

[91] See Cohen, Finding International Law Part II: Our Fragmenting Legal Community. above n 54.

[92] See Guzman, *How International Law Works: A Rational Choice Theory*, above n 62, ch. 3; Rachel Brewster, 'Unpacking the State's Reputation' (2009) 50 *Harvard International Law Journal* 231.

[93] Cf Anthony Carty, 'The Yearning for Unity and the Eternal Return of the Tower of Babel' (2007) 1 *European Journal of Legal Studies* 4.

account of how linguistic indicators can provide a common set of expectations offers jurisprudential micro-foundations for institutionalist theories of international law that rely on expectations—rather than the well-worn concept of intent—to impose the sanctions that make international law effective. A robust study of the language of international law and, in particular, how uses in language converge and diverge across time and issue areas might well help explain much of the dynamism in international law that has characterised the last century.

Bibliography

Abbott, K.W., 'Modern International Relations Theory: A Prospectus for International Lawyers' (1989) 14 *Yale Journal of International Law* 335.

——and Snidal, D., 'Hard and Soft Law in International Governance' (2000) 54 *International Organization* 421.

Abi-Saab, G., 'A "New World Order"? Some Preliminary Reflections' (1994) 7 *Hague Yearbook of International Law* 87.

——'Cours général de droit international public' (1987) 207 *Recueil des Cours de l'Académie de Droit International* 9.

——'Eloge du "droit assourdi"—Quelques réflexions sur le rôle de la soft law en droit international contemporain', in *Nouveaux itinéraires en droit: Hommage à François Rigaux* (Bruylant, Brussels, 1993).

——'International Law and the International Community: The Long Road to Universality', in R.St.J. Macdonald (ed), *Essays in Honour of Wang Tieya* (Martinus Nijhoff, The Hague, 1994).

——'La coutume dans tous ses états ou le dilemme du développement du droit international général dans un monde éclaté', in *Essays in Honor of Roberto Ago* (Giuffrè, Milan, 1987).

——'Les sources du droit international: Essai de déconstruction', in E. Jiménez de Aréchaga and M. Rama-Montaldo, *Le droit international dans un monde en mutation, liber Amicorum en hommage au professeur Eduardo Jiménez de Aréchaga* (Fundacion de Cultura Universitaria, Montevideo, 1994).

Achour, Y.B., *Le rôle des civilisations dans le système: droit et relations internationales* (Bruylant, Brussels, 2003).

Ago, R., 'Diritto positivo e diritto internazionale', in *Comunicazioni e Studi* VII (Università di Milano, Milano, 1955).

——'Droit des traités à la lumière de la Convention de Vienne' (1971) 134 *Recueil des Cours de l'Académie de Droit International* 297.

——'Le délit international' (1939) 68 *Recueil des Cours de l'Académie de Droit International* 415.

——'Positive Law and International Law' (1957) 51 *American Journal of International Law* 691.

——'Science juridique et droit international' (1956) 90 *Recueil des Cours de l'Académie de Droit International* 851.

Akande, D., 'Nuclear Weapons, Unclear Law? Deciphering the Nuclear Weapons Advisory Opinion of the International Court' (1997) 68 *British Yearbook of International Law* 165.

Akehurst, A., 'Custom as a Source of International Law' (1974–75) 47 *British Yearbook of International Law* 1.

Allott, P., *Eunomia* (Oxford University Press, Oxford, 2001).

——'Language, Method and the Nature of International Law' (1971) 45 *British Yearbook of International Law* 79.

——'The Concept of International Law' (1999) 10 *European Journal of International Law* 31.

Alvarez, J.E., *International Organizations as Law-makers* (Oxford University Press, Oxford, 2005).

Angelet, N., and Suy, E., 'Article 25', in J.P. Cot and M. Forteau, *La Charte des Nations Unies: Commentaire article par article* (3rd edn, Economica, Paris, 2005).

Anghie, A., *Imperialism, Sovereignty and the Making of International Law* (Cambridge University Press, Cambridge, 2004).

——and Chimni, B.S., 'Third World Approaches to International Law and Individual Responsibility in Internal Conflicts' (2003) 2 *Chinese Journal of International Law* 77.

Anzilotti, D., *Corso di diritto internazionale: lezioni tenute dell'università di Roma nell'anno scolastico 1922–23* (Athenaeum, Roma, 1923).

——*Cours de droit international, premier volume: introduction—theories générales* (Sirey, Paris, 1929).

——*Scritti di diritto internazionale pubblico* (Cedam, Padova, 1956–7).

Arangio-Ruiz, G., 'Le domaine réservé: L'organisation internationale et le rapport entre le droit international et le droit interne-Cours général de droit international public' (1990) 225 *Recueil des Cours de l'Académie de Droit International* 9.

Arato, A., and Piccone, S. (eds), *The Essential Frankfurt School Reader* (Urizen Books, New York, 1978).

Aron, R., *Paix et guerre entre des nations* (Calmann-Lévy, Paris, 1984).

Asser Instituut, *International Law and the Grotian Heritage* (T.M.C. Asser Instituut, The Hague, 1985).

Aust, A., *Handbook of International Law* (Cambridge University Press, Cambridge, 2005).

——*Modern Treaty Law and Practice* (2nd edn, Cambridge University Press, Cambridge, 2007).

——'The Theory and Practice of Informal International Instruments' (1986) 35 *International and Comparative Law Quarterly* 787.

Austin, J., *The Province of Jurisprudence Determined and the Uses of the Study of Jurisprudence* (Hackett Publishing, Indianapolis, first published 1832, reprinted 1998).

Bachand, R., 'La critique en droit international: Réflexions autour des livres de Koskenniemi, Anghie et Miéville' (2006) 19 *Revue Québecoise de Droit International* 1.

Baker, G.P., and Hacker, P.M.S., *Scepticism, Rules and Language* (Blackwell, Oxford, 1984).

Baker, R.B., 'Customary International Law in the 21st Century' (2010) 21 *European Journal of International Law* 173–204.

Balkin, J.M., 'Deconstruction', in D. Patterson (ed), *A Companion to Philosophy of Law and Legal Theory* (Blackwell, Oxford, 1999).

——'Deconstructive Practice and Legal Theory' (1987) 96 *Yale Law Journal* 743.

Barnidge, R., 'Questioning the Legitimacy of Jus Cogens in the Global Legal Order' (2008) 38 *Israel Yearbook on Human Rights* 199.

Barsalou, J., 'La doctrine de l'objecteur persistant en droit international' (2006) 19 *Revue Québecoise de Droit International* 1–18.

Basdevant, J., 'Règles générales du droit de la paix' (1936) 58 *Recueil des Cours de l'Académie de Droit International* 471.

Baxi, U., 'What may the Third World expect from International Law?' (2006) 27 *Third World Quarterly* 713.

Baxter, R., 'International Law in "Her Infinite Variety"' (1980) 29 *International and Comparative Law Quarterly* 549.

Beckett, J., 'Behind Relative Normativity: Rules and Process as Prerequisite of Law' (2001) 12 *European Journal of International Law* 627.

——'Countering Uncertainty and Ending Up/Down Arguments: Prolegomena to a Response to NAIL' (2005) 16 *European Journal of International Law* 213.

——'Rebel Without a Cause? Martti Koskenniemi and the Critical Legal Project' (2006) 7 *German Law Review* 1045.

Bederman, D.J., *Custom as a Source of Law* (Cambridge University Press, Cambridge, 2010).

——*International Law in Antiquity* (Cambridge University Press, Cambridge, 2001).

——'International Law in the Ancient World', in D. Armstrong (ed), *Routledge Handbook of International Law* (Routledge, London, 2009).

——'The Souls of International Organizations: Legal Personality and the Lighthouse at Cape Spartel' (1996) 36 *Virginia Journal of International Law* 275.

Bedjaoui, M., *Pour un nouvel ordre économique international* (UNESCO, Paris, 1979).

——(English translation), *Towards a new international economic order* (Holmes & Meier, Paris, 1979).

Beigzadeh, E., 'L'évolution du droit international public', in E. Jouannet, H. Ruiz-Fabri, and J.M. Sorel (eds), *Regards d'une génération de juristes sur le droit international* (Pedone, Paris, 2008).

Bellinger, J.B., and Haynes, W.J., 'A U.S. Government Response to the International Committee of the Red Cross Study "Customary International Humanitarian Law"' (2007) 86 *International Review of the Red Cross* 443.

Bentham, J., *A Fragment on Government* (Cambridge Texts on the History of Political Thought, Cambridge University Press, Cambridge, 1988).

——*An Introduction to the Principles of Morals and Legislation* (Kessinger Publishing, Whitefish, Mt., 2005, first published 1781, London).

Benvenisti, E., and Downs, G.W., 'National Courts, Domestic Democracy, and the Evolution of International Law' (2009) 20 *European Journal of International Law* 59.

Berman, P.S., 'A Pluralist Approach to International Law' (2007) 32 *Yale Journal of International Law* 301.

Besson, S. 'Theorizing the Sources of International Law', in S. Besson, and J. Tasioulas (eds), *The Philosophy of International Law* (Oxford University Press, Oxford, 2010).

Betlem, G., and Nollkaemper, A., 'Giving effect to Public International Law and European Community Law before Domestic Courts: A Comparative Analysis of the Practice of Consistent Interpretation' (2003) 14 *European Journal of International Law* 569.

Bianchi, A., 'Une generation de "communautaristes"', in E. Jouannet, H. Ruiz-Fabri, and J.-M. Sorel (eds), *Regards d'une génération sur le droit international* (Pedone, Paris, 2008).

Bierly, J.-L., 'The "Lotus" Case' (1928) 44 *Law Quarterly Review* 154.

Bingham, T., 'The Alabama Claims Arbitration' (2005) 54 *International and Comparative Law Quarterly* 1.

Bix, B., 'Natural Law', in D. Patterson (ed), *A Companion to Philosophy of Law and Legal Theory* (Blackwell, Oxford, 1999).

——'The Application (and Mis-Application) of Wittgenstein's Rule-Following Considerations to Legal Theory', in D. Patterson (ed), *Wittgenstein and Legal Theory* (Westview Press, Boulder, Co., 1992).

Blutman, L., 'In the Trap of a Legal Metaphor: International Soft Law' (2010) 59 *International and Comparative Law Quarterly* 605.

Bobbio, N., 'Kelsen et les sources du droit' in *Essais de théorie du droit* (translated by M. Guéret) (Bruylant/LGDJ, Paris, 1998).

——and Zolo, D., 'Hans Kelsen, the Theory of Law and the International Legal System: A Talk' (1998) 9 *European Journal of International Law* 355.

——Guéret, M., and Agostini, C., *Essais de théorie du droit* (Bruylant/LGDJ, Paris, 1998).

Bodansky, D., 'Prologue to a Theory of Non-Treaty Norms', in M. Arsanjani, J.K. Cogan, R.D. Sloane, and S. Wiessner (eds), *Looking to the Future: Essays on International Law in Honor of W. Michael Reisman* (Brill, Leiden, 2011) 119–34.

——'The Legitimacy of International Governance: A Coming Challenge for International Environmental Law?' (1999) 93 *American Journal of International Law* 596.

Bos, M., *A Methodology of International Law* (T.M.C. Asser Instituut, Amsterdam/New York/ Oxford, 1984).

——'The Recognized Manifestations of International Law, A New Theory of "Sources"' (1977) 20 *German Yearbook of International Law* 9.

Bouthillier, Y., and Bonin, J.-F., 'Article 3', in P. Klein and O. Corten (eds), *Les Conventions de Vienne sur le Droit des Traités: Commentaire article par article* (Bruylant, Bruxelles, 2006).

Boyle, A., 'Some Reflections on the Relationship of Treaties and Soft Law' (1999) 48 *International and Comparative Law Quarterly* 901.

——and Chinkin, C., *The Making of International Law* (Oxford University Press, Oxford, 2007).

Boyle, J., 'Ideals and Things: International Legal Scholarship and the Prison-House of Language' (1985) 26 *Harvard Journal of International Law* 327.

——'Positivism, Natural Law and Disestablishment: Some Questions Raised by MacCormick's Moralistic Amoralism' (1985–86) 20 *Valparaiso University Law Review* 55.

Bradley, C.A., and Gulati, M., 'Withdrawing from International Custom' (2010) 120 *Yale Law Journal* 202.

Brierly, J.L., and Waldock, C.H.M. (ed), *The Law of Nations: An Introduction to the International Law of Peace* (6th edn, Clarendon Press, Oxford, 1963).

Brölmann, C., 'A Flat Earth? International Organizations in the System of International Law', in J. Klabbers (ed), *International Organizations, Series: Library of Essays in International Law* (Ashgate, Farnham, 2006) 183–206.

——*The Institutional Veil in Public International Law—International Organisations and the Law of Treaties* (Hart Publishing, Oxford, 2007).

Brownlie, I., 'International Law at the Fiftieth Anniversary of the United Nations: General Course on Public International Law' (1999) 255 *Recueil des Cours de l'Académie de Droit International* 9.

——*Principles of Public International Law* (6th edn, Oxford University Press, Oxford, 2003).

——*Principles of Public International Law* (7th edn, Oxford University Press, Oxford, 2008).

——*The Rule of Law in International Affairs: International Law at the Fiftieth Anniversary of the United Nations* (Martinus Nijhoff, The Hague, 1998).

Brunnée, J., and Toope, S.J., 'An Interactional Theory of International Legal Obligation', in J. Brunnée and S.J. Toope, *Legitimacy and Persuasion in International Law* (University of Toronto Legal Studies Research Paper/Cambridge University Press, Cambridge, 2008) available at <http://ssrn.com/abstract=1162882>.

————'International Law and Constructivism: Elements of an International Theory of International Law' (2000) 39 *Columbia Journal of Transnational Law* 19.

————*Legitimacy and Legality in International Law. An Interactional Account* (Cambridge University Press, Cambridge, 2010).

Buchanan, A., *Justice, Legitimacy and Self-Determination: Moral Foundations for International Law* (Oxford University Press, Oxford, 2007).

Bull, H., *The Anarchical Society: A Study of Order in World Politics* (Macmillan Publishers, London, 1977).

Bustamante, T., 'Comment on Petroski—On MacCormick's Post-Positivism' (2011) 12 *German Law Journal* 693.

Buzzini, G., 'La Théorie des sources face au droit international général' (2002) 106 *Revue Générale de Droit International Public* 581.

Byers, M., *Custom, Powers and the Power of Rules: International Relations and Customary International Law* (Cambridge University Press, Cambridge, 1999).

Campbell, T., *The Legal Theory of Ethical Positivism* (Dartmouth Publishing, Aldershot, 1996).

Cane, P., (ed), *The Hart-Fuller Debate in the Twenty-First Century* (Hart Publishing, Oxford, 2010).

Capotorti, F., 'Cours général de droit international public' (1994) 248 *Recueil des Cours de l'Académie de Droit International* 9.

Capps, P., 'The Kantian Project in Modern International Legal Theory' (2001) 12 *European Journal of International Law* 1003.

——and Rivers, J., 'Kant's Concept of International Law' (2010) 16 *Legal Theory* 229.

Carreau, D., *Droit International* (8th edn, Pedone, Paris, 2004).

Carty, A., 'Conservative and Progressive Visions in French International Legal Doctrine' (2005) 16 *European Journal of International Law* 525.

——'Sociological Theories of International Law', *Max Planck Encyclopedia of Public International Law*, available at <http://www.mpepil.com>.

Cass, D.Z., 'Navigating the Newstream: Recent Critical Scholarship in International Law' (1996) 65 *Nordic Journal of International Law* 341.

Cassese, A., *International Law* (2nd edn, Oxford University Press, Oxford, 2005).

Catlin, G.E.G., 'Thomas Hobbes and Contemporary Political Theory' (1976) 82 *Political Science Quarterly* 1.

Cazala, J., 'Jeremy Bentham et le droit international' (2005) 109 *Revue Générale de Droit International Public* 365.

Charlesworth, H., 'Customary International Law and the Nicaragua Case' (1984–1987) 11 *Australian Yearbook of International Law* 1.

——'Feminist Ambivalence about International Law' (2005) 11 *International Legal Theory* 1.

——'Human Rights and the Rule of Law after Conflict', in P. Cane (ed), *The Hart-Fuller Debate in the Twenty-First Century* (Hart Publishing, Oxford, 2010).

Charney, J.I., 'International Lawmaking: Article 38 of the ICJ State Reconsidered', in J. Delbrück and E. Heinz (eds), *New Trends in International Lawmaking, International 'Legislation' in the Public Interest* (Duncker & Humblot, Berlin, 1997).

——'The Persistent Objector Rule and the Development of Customary International Law' (1986) 56 *British Yearbook of International Law* 1.

——'Universal International Law' (1993) 87 *American Journal of International Law* 529.

Charpentier, J., *La Reconnaissance internationale et l'évolution du droit des gens* (Pedone, Paris, 1956).

Chaumont, C., 'Cours général de droit international public' (1970) 129 *Recueil des Cours de l'Académie de Droit International* 333.

Chayes, A., Ehrlich, T., and Lowenfeld, A.F., *International Legal Process: Materials for an Introductory Course* (Little, Brown & Co., Boston, 1968).

Chayet, C., 'Les accords en forme simplifiée' (1957) 3 *Annuaire Francois de Droit International* 205.

Chen, L., 'Perspectives from the New Haven School' (1993) 87 *American Society of International Law Proceedings* 407.

Cheng, B., 'Epilogue: On the Nature and Sources of International Law', in B. Cheng (ed), *International Law: Teaching and Practice* (Stevens & Sons, London, 1982).

Cheng, B., 'United Nations Resolution on Outer Space: "Instant" International Customary Law?' (1965) 5 *Indian Journal of International Law* 23.

Chesterman, S., 'Global Administrative Law', Working Paper for the S.T. Lee Project on Global Governance (2009), New York University Public Law and Legal Theory Working Papers, Paper 152, available at <http://lsr.nellco.org/nyu_plltwp/152>.

Chevrette, F., and Cyr, H., 'De Quel Positivisme Parlez-vous?', in L. Rolland and P. Noreau (eds), *Mélanges Andrée Lajoie: Le droit, une variable dépendante* (Themis, Montreal, 2008).

Chimni, B.S., *International Law and World Order: A Critique of Contemporary Approaches* (Sage, New Delhi, 1993).

Chinkin, C., 'A Mirage in the Sand? Distinguishing Binding and Non-Binding Relations Between States' (1997) 10 *Leiden Journal of International Law* 223.

——'The Challenge of Soft Law: Development and Change in International Law' (1989) 38 *International and Comparative Law Quarterly* 850.

——Wright, S., and Charlesworth, H., 'Feminist Approaches to International Law' (1991) 85 *American Journal of International Law* 613.

Chomsky, N., 'A Review of B. F. Skinner's Verbal Behavior', in L.A. Jakobovits and M.S. Mirón (eds), *Readings in the Psychology of Language* (Prentice-Hall, Englewood Cliffs, NJ, 1967).

Cohen, H.G., 'Finding International Law: Rethinking the Doctrine of Sources' (2005) 93 *Iowa Law Review* 65.

Coleman, J., 'Authority and Reason', in R.P. George (ed), *The Autonomy of Law: Essays of Legal Positivism* (Oxford University Press, Oxford, 1996).

——(ed), *Hart's Postscript: Essays on the Postscript to The Concept of Law* (Oxford University Press, Oxford, 2001).

——'Incorporationism, Conventionality and the Practical Difference Thesis', in J. Coleman (ed), *Hart's Postscript: Essays on the Postscript to the Concept of Law* (Oxford University Press, Oxford, 2001).

——'Negative and Positive Positivism', in D. Patterson (ed), *Philosophy of Law and Legal Theory: An Anthology* (Blackwell Publishing, Oxford, 2003).

——*The Practice of Principle* (Oxford University Press, Oxford, 2001).

——and Leiter, B., 'Legal Positivism', in D. Patterson (ed), *A Companion to Philosophy of Law and Legal Theory* (Blackwell, Oxford, 1996).

Collins, R., 'Constitutionalism as Liberal-Juridical Consciousness: Echoes from International Law's Past' (2009) 22 *Leiden Journal of International Law* 251.

Combacau, J., 'Le droit international: bric-à-brac ou système' (1986) 31 *Archives du Philosophie du Droit* 85.

——and Alland, D., 'Primary and Secondary Rules in the Law of State Responsibility: Categorizing International Obligations' (1985) 16 *Netherlands Yearbook of International Law* 81.

Comte, A., *Discours sur l'esprit positif* (Vrin, Paris, 2003).

Condorelli, L., 'Custom', in M. Bedjaoui (ed), *International Law: Achievements and Prospects* (Martinus Nijhoff, The Hague, 1991).

Conforti, B., *The Law and Practice of the United Nations* (3rd edn, Martinus Nijhoff, Leiden, 2005).

——'The Theory of Competence in Verdross' (1995) 6 *European Journal of International Law* 70.

——and Provost, R., *International Law and the Role of Domestic Legal Systems* (Martinus Nijhoff, Dordrecht, 1993).

Corbett, P.E., 'The Consent of States and the Sources of the Law of Nations' (1925) 6 *British Yearbook of International Law* 20.

Corten, O., *Le discours du droit international: Pour un positivisme critique.* (Pedone, Paris, 2009).

——*Méthodologie du droit international public* (Editions de l'Université de Bruxelles, Brussels, 2009).

Cot, J.-P., 'Appearing "for" or "on behalf of" a State: the Role of Private Counsel before International Tribunals', in N. Ando, E. McWhinney, R. Wolfrum et al. (eds), *Liber Amicorum Judge Shigeru Oda,* vol 2 (Kluwer, The Hague, 2002), 835–47.

Coyle, S., 'Hart, Raz and the Concept of a Legal System' (2002) 21 *Law and Philosophy* 275.

——'Thomas Hobbes and the Intellectual Origins of Legal Positivism' (2003) 15 *Canadian Journal of Law and Jurisprudence* 21.

Craven, M., *The Decolonization of International Law* (Oxford University Press, Oxford, 2007).

——et al., 'We Are Teachers of International Law' (2004) 17 *Leiden Journal of International Law* 363.

Crawford, J., *The International Law Commission's Articles on State Responsibility, Introduction, Text and Commentaries* (Cambridge University Press, Cambridge, 2005).

Crema, L., 'Disappearance and New Sightings of Restrictive Interpretation(s)' (2010) 21 *European Journal of International Law* 681–700.

Criddle, E.J., and Fox-Decent, E., 'A Fiduciary Theory of Jus Cogens' (2009) 34 *Yale Journal of International Law* 331.

Cullison, A.D., 'Morality and the Foundations of Legal Positivism' (1985) 20 *Valparaiso University Law Review* 62.

Curley, E., (ed), *Hobbes, Leviathan: With Selected Variants from the Latin Edition of 1668* (Hackett, Indianapolis, 1994).

D'Amato, A., 'Book Review of R. Cook (ed), *Human Rights of Women: National and International Perspectives*' (1994) 89 AJIL 840.

——'International Law and Rawls' Theory of Justice' (1975) 5 *Denver Journal of International Law and Policy* 525.

——'International Law as an Autopoietic System', in R. Wolfrum and V. Röben (eds), *Developments of International Law in Treaty Making* (Springer, Berlin, 2005).

——'Is International Law Really "Law"?' (1984–85) 79 *Northwestern University Law Review* 1293.

——'It's a Bird, It's a Plane, It's Jus Cogens' (1990–91) 6 *Connecticut Journal of International Law* 1.

——'Pragmatic Indeterminacy' (1990) 85 *Northwestern University Law Review* 148.

——*The Concept of Custom in International Law* (Cornell University Press, New York, 1971).

——'The Need for a Theory of International Law' (Northwestern University School of Law, Public Law and Legal Theory Research Paper Series, 2007).

——'Trashing Customary International Law' (1987) 81 *American Journal of International Law* 101.

——'What "Counts" as Law?', in N.G. Onuf (ed), *Law-Making in the Global Community* (Carolina Academic Press, Durham, 1982).

d'Argent, P., 'De la fragmentation à la cohésion systémique: la sentence arbitrale du 24 mai 2005 relative au "Rhin de fer" (Ijzeren Rijn)', in *Droit du pouvoir, pouvoir du droit: mélanges offerts à Jean Salmon* (Bruylant, Brussels, 2007).

——'Du commerce à l'emploi de la force: l'affaire des plates-formes pétrolières (arrêt sur le fond)' (2003) 49 *Annuaire français de droit international* 266.

d'Aspremont, J., 'Hart et le Positivisme Postmoderne' (2009) 113 *Revue Générale de Droit International Public* 5.

——'International Law in Asia: the Limits to the Constitutionalist and Liberal Doctrines' (2008) 13 *Asian Yearbook of International Law* 89.

——'La création internationale d'Etats democratiques' (2005) 109 *Revue Générale de Droit International Public* 889.

——'La Doctrine du Droit international et la tentation d'une juridicisation sans limite' (2008) 112 *Revue Générale de Droit International Public* 849.

——'Les dispositions non-normatives des actes juridiques conventionnels' (2003) 36 *Revue Belge de Droit International* 492.

——'Les réserves aux traités. Observations à la lumière de la Convention-cadre du Conseil de l'Europe pour la protection des minorités nationales', in *Les Minorités, Recueil des travaux de l'Association Henri Capitant*, tome LII/2002 (National Autonomous University of Mexico (UNAM), Mexico City, 2002) 487–514.

——'Les travaux de la Commission du droit international relatifs aux actes unilatéraux des Etats' (2005) 109 *Revue Générale de Droit International Public* 163.

——*L'Etat non démocratique en droit international: Etude critique du droit positif et de la pratique contemporaine* (Pedone, Paris, 2008).

——'Non-State Actors from the Perspective of Legal Positivism', in J. d'Aspremont (ed), *Participants in the International Legal System—Multiple Perspectives on Non-State Actors in International Law* (Routledge, London, 2011) 23.

——'Non-State Actors in International Law: Oscillating Between Concepts and Dynamics', in J. d'Aspremont (ed), *Participants in the International Legal System, Multiple Perspectives on Non-State Actors in International Law* (London, Routledge, 2011) 1.

——'Note de Lecture: O. Corten, Le discours du droit international, Paris Pedone, 2009' (2009) 4 *Revue Générale de Droit International Public* 964.

——(ed), *Participants in the International Legal System—Multiple Perspectives on Non-State Actors in International Law* (Routledge, London, 2011).

——'Post-Conflict Administrations as Democracy-Building Instruments' (2008) 9 *Chicago Journal of International Law* 1.

——'Regulating Statehood: The Kosovo Status Settlement' (2007) 20 *Leiden Journal of International Law* 649.

——'Softness in International Law: A Rejoinder to Tony d'Amato' (2009) 20 *European Journal of International Law* 911.

——'Softness in International Law: A Self-Serving Quest for New Legal Materials' (2008) 19 *European Journal of International Law* 1075.

——'The Doctrinal Illusion of Heterogenity of International Lawmaking Processes', in H. Ruiz-Fabri, R. Wolfrum, and J. Gogolin (eds), *Select Proceedings of the European Society of International Law* (Hart Publishing, Oxford, 2010).

——'The Foundations of the International Legal Order' (2007) 18 *Finnish Yearbook of International Law* 219.

——'The Recommendations Made by the International Court of Justice' (2007) 56 *International and Comparative Law Quarterly* 185.

——'The Systemic Integration of International Law by Domestic Courts: Domestic Judges as Architects of the Consistency of the International Legal Order', in A. Nollkaemper and O.K. Fauchald (eds), *Unity or Fragmentation of International Law: The Role of International and National Tribunals* (Hart Publishing, Oxford, 2011) (forthcoming).

——'Unilateral v. Multilateral Exercises of Universal Criminal Jurisdiction' (2010) 43 *Israel Law Review* 301.

——'Uniting Pragmatism and Theory in International Legal Scholarship: Koskenniemi's From Apology to Utopia Revisited' (2006) 19 *Revue Québecoise de Droit International* 353.

——and Dopagne, Fr., 'Two Constitutionalisms in Europe: Pursuing an Articulation of the European and International Legal Orders' (2009) 68 *Heidelberg Journal of International Law (ZaöRV)* 939.

——and Kammerhofer, J., (eds), *International Legal Positivism in a Postmodern World* (Cambridge University Press, Cambridge, 2012) (forthcoming).

Daillier, P., and Pellet, A., *Droit international public* (6th edn, LGDJ, Paris, 1999).

Daillier, P., Forteau, M., and Pellet, A., *Droit international public* (8th edn, LGDJ, Paris, 2009).

Danilenko, G.M., *Law-Making in the International Community* (Martinus Nijhoff, Dordrecht, 1993).

——'The Theory of International Customary International Law' (1998) 31 *German Yearbook of International Law* 9–47.

Darcy, S., and Powderly, J., (eds), *Judicial Creativity at the International Criminal Tribunals* (Oxford University Press, Oxford, 2011).

Davies, C., 'The Politics of Defining Law', in P. Cane (ed), *The Hart-Fuller Debate in the Twenty-First Century* (Hart Publishing, Oxford, 2010), 157–67.

De Jong, H.M., and Werner, W.W., 'Continuity and Change in Legal Positivism' (1998) 17 *Law & Philosophy* 233.

de la Rasilla del Moral, I., 'At King Agramant's Camp—Old Debates, New Constitutional Times' (2010) 8 *International Journal of Constitutional Law* 3.

——'Martti Koskenniemi and The Spirit of the Beehive in International Law' (2010) 10 *Global Jurist* article 4.

De Martens, F., *Droit des gens* (Aillaud, Paris, 1831).

De Martens, G.F., *Primae lineae iuris gentium Europaearum practici in usum auditorum adumbratae* (Johann Christian Dieterich, Göttingen, 1785).

de Saussure, F., and Baskin, W. (translator), *Course in General Linguistics* (The Philosophical Library, New York, 1959).

de Vattel, E., and Fenwick, C.G. (translator), *The Law of Nations* (Carnegie Institution of Washington, Washington DC, 1916).

de Visscher, C., 'Justice et médiation internationales' (1928) 9 *Revue de droit international et de leígislation compareíe* 33.

——'La codification du droit international' (1925) 6 *Recueil des Cours de l'Académie de Droit International* 325.

——*Théories et réalités en droit international public* (4th edn, Pedone, Paris, 1970).

de Vitoria, F., Pagden, A., and Lawrance, J. (eds), *Political Writings* (Cambridge University Press, Cambridge, 1991).

de Wet, E., 'The Emergence of International and Regional Value Systems as a Manifestation of the Emerging International Constitutional Order' (2006) 19 *Leiden Journal of International Law* 611.

——'The International Constitutional Order' (2005) 55 *International and Comparative Law Quarterly* 51.

Degan, V., *Sources of International Law* (Kluwer Law International, The Hague, 1997).

Delbrück, J., 'Prospects for a "World (Internal) Law?": Legal Developments in a Changing International System' (2002) 10 *Indiana Journal of Global Studies* 401.

——and Heinz, U.E., (eds), *New Trends in International Lawmaking: International 'Legislation' in the Public Interest* (Duncker & Humblot, Berlin, 1997).

Detmer, D., 'Heidegger and Nietzsche on "Thinking in Values"' (1989) 23 *Journal of Value Inquiry* 275.

Diez de Velasco Vallejo, M., 'Législation et codification dans le droit international actuel', in *Essays in honor of Roberto Ago* (Giuffrè, Milano, 1987).

Divac Öberg, M., 'The Legal Effects of Resolutions of the UN Security Council and General Assembly in the Jurisprudence of the ICJ' (2005) 16 *European Journal of International Law* 879.

Dixon, M., *Textbook on International Law* (6th edn, Oxford University Press, Oxford, 2007).

Donaghue, S., 'Normative Habits, Genuine Beliefs and Evolving Law: Nicaragua and the Theory of Customary International Law' (1995) 16 *Australian Yearbook of International Law* 327.

Draetta, U., 'The Role of In-House Counsel in International Arbitration' (2009) 75 *Arbitration* 470–80.

Dumberry, P., 'Incoherent and Ineffective: The Concept of Persistent Objector Revisited' (2010) 59 *International and Comparative Law Quarterly* 779.

Dunbar, N.C.H., 'The Myth of Customary International Law' (1983) 8 *Australian Yearbook of International Law* 1.

Dunoff, J.L., and Trachtman, J.P., (eds), *Ruling the World? Constitutionalism, International Law, and Global Governance* (Cambridge University Press, Cambridge, 2009).

Dupuy, P.-M., 'A propos de l'opposabilité de la coutume générale: enquête brève sur l' "objecteur persistant"', in *Le droit international au service de la paix, de la justice et du développement. Mélanges offerts à Michel Virally* (Pedone, Paris, 1991).

——'Cours général de droit international public' (2002) 297 *Recueil des Cours de l'Académie de Droit International* 9–490.

——'L'unité de l'ordre juridique international: Cours général de droit international public' (2002) 297 *Recueil des Cours de l'Académie de Droit International* 9.

——'Soft Law and the International Law of the Environment' (1991) 12 *Michigan Journal of International Law* 420.

——'Some Reflections on Contemporary International Law and the Appeal to the Universal Values: A Response to Martti Koskenniemi' (2005) 16 *European Journal of International Law* 131.

——'The European Tradition of International Law: Charles de Visscher' (2000) 11 *European Journal of International Law* 871.

——'Théorie des sources et coutume en droit international contemporain', in *Le droit international dans un monde en mutation: liber amicorum en hommage au Professeur Eduardo Jimenez de Arechaga* (Fundación de Cultura Universitaria, Montevideo, 1994).

Dupuy, R-J., 'Declaratory Law and Programmatory Law: From Revolutionary Custom to "Soft Law"', in R.J. Akkerman et al., *Declarations on Principles: A Quest for Universal Peace* (Academic Book Services Holland, Groningen, 1977).

——'Droit déclaratoire et droit programmatoire de la coutume sauvage a la "soft law"', in Société française pour le droit international, *L'élaboration du droit international public—Colloque de Toulouse* (Pedone, Paris, 1975).

Duxbury, N., 'Post-Realism and Legal Process', in D. Patterson (ed), *A Companion to Philosophy of Law and Legal Theory* (Blackwell, Oxford, 1999).

Dworkin, R., *Law's Empire* (Fontana Press, London, 1986).

——'The Model of Rules', in D. Patterson (ed), *Philosophy of Law and Legal Theory: An Anthology* (Blackwell Publishers Ltd, Oxford, 2003).

—— *Taking Rights Seriously* (Harvard University Press, Cambridge, 1977).

Dyzenhaus, D., 'Hobbes and the Legitimacy of Law' (2001) 20 *Law and Philosophy* 461.

——*Legality and Legitimacy: Carl Schmitt, Hans Kelsen and Hermann Heller in Weimar* (Clarendon Press, Oxford, 1997).

——'The Grudge Informer Case Revisited' (2008) 89 *New York University Law Review* 1000.

Eisemann, P.-M., 'Le gentlemen's agreement comme source du droit international' (1979) 106 *Journal du Droit International* 326.

El-Shakankiri, A., *La philosophie juridique de Jeremy Bentham* (LGDJ, Paris 1970).

Elias, O., and Lim, C., '"General principles of Law", "Soft Law" and the Identification of International Law' (1997) 28 *Netherlands Yearbook of International Law* 3.

———— *The Paradox of Consensualism in International Law* (Kluwer Law International, The Hague, 1998).

Elias, T. O., 'Problems Concerning the Validity of Treaties' (1971) 134 *Recueil des Cours de l'Académie de Droit International* 333.

Endicott T., 'Herbert Hart and the Semantic Sting', in J. Coleman (ed), *Hart's Postscript: Essays on the Postscript to 'The Concept of Law'* (Oxford University Press, Oxford, 2001).

Erlanger, H., Garth, B., Larson, J., Mertz, E., Nourse, V., and Wilkins, D., 'New Legal Realism Symposium: Is it Time for a New Legal Realism?' (2005) 2 *Wisconsin Law Review* 335.

Fabri, H., and Sorel, J.M., (eds), *Regards d'une géneration de juristes sur le Droit International* (Pedone, Paris, 2008).

Falk, R.A., 'Casting the Spell: The New Haven School of International Law' (1995) 104 *Yale Law Journal* 1991.

—— *The Role of Domestic Courts in the International Legal Order* (Syracuse University Press, Syracuse, 1964).

——'To What Extent are International Law and International Lawyers Ideologically Neutral?, in A. Cassese and J.H.H. Weiler (eds), *Change and Stability in International Law-Making* (Berlin, De Gruyter, 1988).

Fassbender, B., 'The Meaning of International Constitutional Law', in N. Tsagourias (ed), *Transnational Constitutionalism: International and European models* (Cambridge University Press, Cambridge, 2007).

Fastenrath, U., 'Relative Normativity in International Law', 4 *European Journal of International Law* (1993) 305.

Fidler, D.P., 'Revolt Against or From Within the West? TWAIL, the Developing World, and the Future Direction of International Law' (2003) 2 *Chinese Journal of International Law* 29.

Finnis, J., 'On Hart's Ways: Law as Reason and as Fact', in M. Kramer et al. (eds), *The Legacy of H.L.A. Hart: Legal, Political and Moral Philosophy* (Oxford University Press, Oxford, 2008).

——'On the Incoherence of Legal Positivism', in M. Patterson (ed), *Philosophy of Law and Legal Theory: An Anthology* (Blackwell Publishing Ltd, Oxford, 2004).

——'The Truth in Legal Positivism', in R.P. George (ed), *The Autonomy of Law: Essays of Legal Positivism* (Oxford University Press, Oxford, 1996).

Fitzmaurice, G., 'Judicial Innovation—Its Uses and Its Perils', in R.Y. Jennings (ed), *Essays in Honour of Lord McNair* (Stevens & Sons, London, 1965).

Fitzmaurice, G., 'Some Problems Regarding the Formal Sources of International Law', in F.M. Van Asbeck et al. (eds), *Symbolae Verzijl: présentées au professeur J.H.W. Verzijl à l'occasion de son LXX-ième anniversaire* (Martinus Nijhoff, The Hague, 1958).

——'The General Principles of International Law Considered from the Standpoint of the Rules of Law' (1957) 92 *Recueil des Cours de l'Académie de Droit International* 1.

——'*Vae Victis* or Woe to the Negotiator: Your Treaty or our "Interpretation" of it' (1971) 65 *American Journal of International Law* 372.

Fitzmaurice, M., 'The Identification and Character of Treaties and Treaty Obligations Between States in International Law' (2003) 73 *British Yearbook of International Law* 141.

Fletcher, G., 'Comparative Law as a Subversive Discipline' (1998) 46 *American Journal of Comparative Law* 683.

——'Why Kant' (1987) 87 *Columbia Law Review* 421.

Fletcher, G.P., *Basic Concepts of Legal Thought* (Oxford University Press, Oxford, 1996), 32–3.

——'Law as a Discourse' (1992) 13 *Cardozo Law Review* 1631.

Focsaneanu, L., 'Le droit interne de l'Organisation des Nations Unies' (1957) 3 *Annuaire Français de Droit International* 315–49.

Foucault, M., *L'archéologie du savoir* (Gallimard, Paris, 1969).

——'Nietzsche, Genealogy, History', in D. Bouchard and S. Simon (eds), *Language, Counter-Memory, Practice: Selected Essays and Interviews by Michel Foucault* (Cornell University Press, New York, 1977).

——'The Order of Discourse', in R. Young (ed), *Untying the Text: a Poststructuralist Reader* (Routledge, London, 1981).

Franck, T., *Fairness in International Law and Institutions* (Oxford University Press, Oxford, 1995).

——'Fairness in the International Legal and Institutional System: General Course on Public International Law' (1993) 240 *Recueil des Cours de l'Académie de Droit International* 9.

——'Legitimacy of the International Legal System' (1988) 82 *American Journal of International Law* 705.

——'Some Observations on the ICJ's Procedural and Substantive Innovations' (1987) 81 *American Journal of International Law* 119.

——*The Power of Legitimacy Among Nations* (Oxford University Press, Oxford, 1990).

Frankenberg, G., 'Critical Theory', *Max Planck Encyclopedia of Public International Law*, available at <http://www.mpepil.com>.

Friedmann, W., *The Changing Structure of International Law* (Stevens & Sons, London, 1964).

Fuller, L., 'Positivism and Fidelity to Law: A Reply to Professor Hart' (1958) 71 *Harvard Law Review* 631.

——*The Morality of Law* (Revised edn, Yale University Press, New Haven, 1969).

Gaja, G., 'Positivism and Dualism in Dionisio Anzilotti' (1992) 3 *European Journal of International Law* 123.

Gallié, M., 'Les théories tiers-mondistes du droit international (TWAIL): un renouvellement?' (2008) 39 *Etudes Internationales* 17.

Gautier, P., 'Article 2', in P. Klein and O. Corten, *Les Conventions de Vienne sur le Droit des Traités: commentaire article par article* (Bruylant, Bruxelles, 2006).

——*Essai sur la définition des traités entre états: la pratique que la Belgique aux confins du droit des traités* (Bruylant, Brussels, 1993).

——'Les accords informels et la Convention de Vienne sur le droit des traités entre Etats', in *Droit du pouvoir, pouvoir du droit: mélanges offerts à Jean Salmon* (Bruylant, Bruxelles, 2007).

Gentili, A., and Rolfe, J.C. (translator), *On the Law of War* (Clarendon Press, Oxford, 1933).

Gersen, J.E., and Posner, E., 'Soft Law' (2008) 61 *Standford Law Review* 573.

Ginsburg, T., and Shaffer, G., 'Empirical Work in International Law', University of Minnesota Law School, Legal Studies Research Paper Series, Research Paper No. 09–32, available at <http://papers.ssrn.com/sol3/papers.cfm?abstract_id=1444448>.

Glenn, P., 'Cosmopolitan Legal Orders', in A. Halpin and V. Roeben, *Theorising the Global Legal Order* (Hart Publishing, Oxford, 2009) 25–37.

Glennon, M.J., 'How International Rules Die' (2005) 93 *Georgetown Law Journal* 939.

Goetsch, C.C., 'The Future of Legal Formalism' (1980) 24 *American Journal of Legal History* 221.

Goldmann, M., 'Inside Relative Normativity: From Sources to Standard Instruments for the Exercise of International Public Authority' (2009) 9 *German Law Journal* 1865.

Goldsmith, J., and Posner, E., *The Limits of International Law* (Oxford University Press, Oxford, 2005).

Goodman, C., 'Acta Sunt Servanda?: A Regime for Regulating the Unilateral Acts of States at International Law' (2004) 25 *Australian Yearbook of International Law* 43.

Gowlland-Debbas, V., 'Judicial Insights into Fundamental Values and Interests of the International Community', in A.S. Muller, D. Rai, and J.M. Thuránszky (eds), *The International Court of Justice: Its Future Role After Fifty Years* (Martinus Nijhoff, The Hague, 1997).

Greenawalt, K., 'Too Thin and Too Rich', in R.P. George (ed), *The Autonomy of Law: Essays of Legal Positivism* (Oxford University Press, Oxford, 1996).

Greig, D.W., 'Oppenheim Revisited: An Australian Perspective' (1992) 14 *Australian Yearbook of International Law* 227.

Grewe, W., and Byers, M. (translator), *The Epochs of International Law* (De Gruyter, Berlin, 2000).

Gruchalla-Wesierski, T., 'A Framework for Understanding "Soft Law"' (1984–85) 30 *McGill Law Journal* 37.

Guggenheim, P., 'Contribution à l'histoire des sources du droit des gens' (1958) 94 *Recueil des Cours de l'Académie de Droit International* 1.

——'Les origines de la notion autonome du droit des gens', in F.M. van Asbect et al. (eds), *Symbolae Verzijl: présentées au professeur J.H.W. Verzijl à l'occasion de son LXX-ième anniversaire* (Martinus Nijhoff, The Hague, 1958).

——*Traité de droit international public, vol I* (Georg & Cie, Genève, 1953).

——'What is Positive International Law?', in G. Lipsky (ed), *Law and Politics in the World Community: Essays on Hans Kelsen's Pure Theory and Related Problems of International Law* (University of California Press, Los Angeles, 1953).

Guillaume, G., 'La Cour Internationale de Justice. Quelques propositions concrètes à l'occasion du cinquantenaire' (1996) 100 *Revue Générale de Droit International Public* 321.

——'The Future of International Judicial Institutions' (1995) 44 *International and Comparative Law Quarterly* 848.

Gunning, I.R., 'Modernizing Customary International Law: The Challenge of Human Rights' (1991) 31 *Virginia Journal of International Law* 211.

Guzman, A.T., 'A Compliance-Based Theory of International Law' (2002) 90 *California Law Review* 1823.

Guzman, A.T., *How International Law Works: A Rationale Choice Theory* (Oxford University Press, Oxford, 2008).

——'Saving Customary International Law' (2005) 27 *Michigan Journal of International Law* 115.

——'The Design of International Agreements' (2005) 16 *European Journal of International Law* 579.

Haggenmacher, P., 'La doctrine des deux éléments du droit coutumier dans la pratique de la Cour internationale' (1986) 90 *Revue Générale de Droit International Public* 5.

Haldemann, F., 'Gustav Radbruch vs. Hans Kelsen: A Debate on Nazi Law' (2005) 18 *Ratio Juris* 162.

Halpin, A., and Roeben, V., *Theorising the Global Legal Order* (Hart Publishing, Oxford, 2009).

Hamzeh, F.S., 'Agreements in Simplified Form—Modern Perspective' (1968–69) 43 *British Yearbook of International Law* 179.

Hanson, D.W., 'Thomas Hobbes' "Highway to Peace"' (1984) 38 *International Organization* 329.

Harlow, C., 'Global Administrative Law: The Quest for Principles and Values' (2006) 17 *European Journal of International Law* 187.

Hart, H.L.A., 'American Jurisprudence through English Eyes: The Nightmare and the Noble Dream' (1976–1977) 11 *Georgia Law Review* 969.

——*Essays on Bentham: Studies in Jurisprudence and Political Theory* (Clarendon Press/Oxford University Press, Oxford, 1982).

——'Jhering's Heaven of Concepts and Modern Analytical Jurisprudence', in H.L.A. Hart, *Essays in Jurisprudence and Philosophy* (Clarendon Press/Oxford University Press, Oxford, 1983).

——'Positivism and the Separation of Law and Morals' (1958) 71 *Harvard Law Review* 593.

——*The Concept of Law* (2nd edn, Oxford University Press, Oxford, 1997).

——and Honoré, A.M., *Causation in the Law* (Clarendon Press, Oxford, 1959).

Hathaway, J., 'America, Defender of Democratic Legitimacy' (2000) 11 *European Journal of International Law* 121.

——*Rights of Refugees under International Law* (Cambridge University Press, Cambridge, 2005).

Henckaerts, J.-M., 'Customary International Humanitarian Law: A Response to US Comments' (2007) 89 *International Review of the Red Cross* 473.

——'Study on Customary International Humanitarian Law: a Contribution to the Understanding and Respect for the Rule of Law in Armed Conflict' (2005) 87 *International Review of the Red Cross* 175.

Henkin, L., *How Nations Behave: Law and Foreign Policy* (2nd edn, Columbia University Press, New York, 1979).

——'Human Rights and State "Sovereignty"' (1996) 25 *Georgia Journal of International and Comparative Law* 31.

——*International Law: Politics and Values* (Martinus Nijhoff, Dordrecht, 1995).

——'International Law: Politics, Values and Functions: General Course on Public International Law' (1989) 216 *Recueil des Cours de l'Académie de Droit International* 9.

Higgins, R., 'Policy Considerations and the International Judicial Process' (1968) 17 *International and Comparative Law Quarterly* 58.

——*Problems and Process: International Law and How We Use It* (Oxford University Press, Oxford, 1995).

——'The Advisory Opinion on Namibia: Which UN Resolutions are Binding under Article 25 of the Charter' (1972) 21 *International and Comparative Law Quarterly* 270.

——'The Identity of International Law', in B. Cheng (ed), *International Law: Teaching and Practice* (Stevens & Sons, London, 1982).

Hillgenberg, H., 'A Fresh look at Soft Law' (1999) 10 *European Journal of International Law* 499.

Himma, K.E., 'Bringing Hart and Raz to the Table: Coleman's Compatibility Thesis' (2001) 21 *Oxford Journal of Legal Studies* 609.

——'Hart and Austin Together Again for the First Time: Coercive Enforcement and Theory of Legal Obligation' (Working Draft, 2006) available at <http://papers.ssrn.com/sol3/papers.cfm?abstract_id=727465>.

——'The Instantiation Thesis and Raz's Critique of Inclusive Positivism' (2001) 20 *Law and Philosophy* 61.

Hirsch, M., 'The Sociology of International Law: Invitation to Study International Rules and Their Social Context' (2005) 55 *University of Toronto Law Journal* 891.

Hobbes, T., and Cropsey, J. (eds), *A Dialogue Between a Philosopher and a Student of the Common Laws of England* (University of Chicago Press, Chicago, 1997).

——and Curley, E. (eds), *Leviathan* (Hackett, Indianapolis, 1994).

Homes, O.W., 'The Path to Law' (1897) 10 *Harvard Law Review* 457.

Horwitz, M.J., 'The Rise of Legal Formalism' (1975) 19 *American Journal of Legal History* 251.

Hume, D., *A Treatise of Human Nature* (Courier Dover Publications, New York, 2003).

Hutchinson, D.N., 'The Significance of the Registration and Non-Registration of an International Agreement in Determining Whether or Not it is a Treaty' (1993) 46(2) *Current Legal Problems* 257.

Ida, R., 'Formation des normes internationales dans un monde en mutation. Critique de la notion de Soft Law', in D. Bardonnet et al. (eds), *Le droit international au service de la paix, de la justice et du développement: Mélanges en hommage à Michel Virally* (Pedone, Paris, 1991).

Jacobs, F., 'Judicial Dialogue and the Cross-Fertilization of Legal Systems: The European Court of Justice' (2003) 38 *Texas International Law Journal* 547.

Jacqué, J.-P., 'A propos de la promesse unilatérale', in D. Bardonnet et al. (eds), *Le Droit International: unité et diversité. Mélanges offerts à Paul Reuter* (Paris, Pedone, 1981).

——'Acte et norme en droit international' (1991) 227 *Recueil des Cours de l'Académie de Droit International* 357.

——*Eléments pour une théorie de l'acte juridique en droit international public vol 69* (LDGJ, Paris, 1972).

Janis, M.W., *An Introduction to International Law* (2nd ed, Little, Brown & Co, Boston, 1993).

——'Sovereignty and International Law: Hobbes and Grotius', in R.St.J. Macdonald (ed), *Essays in Honour of Wang Tieya* (Martinus Nijhoff, The Hague, 1994).

Jenks, C.W., *The Common Law of Mankind* (Stevens & Sons, London, 1955).

Jennings, R., 'General Course on Principles of International Law' (1967) 121 *Recueil des Cours de l'Académie de Droit International* 323.

——'International Reform and Progressive Development', in G. Hafner et al. (eds), *Liber Amicorum Professor Ignaz Seidle-Hohenveldern in honour of his 80th Birthday* (Kluwer Law International, The Hague, 1998).

——'Law-Making and Package Deal', in D. Bardonnet et al. (eds), *Le Droit International: unité et diversité. Mélanges offerts à Paul Reuter* (Pedone, Paris, 1981).

Jennings, R., 'The Identification of International Law', in B. Cheng (ed), *International Law: Teaching and Practice* (Stevens & Sons, London, 1982).

——and Watts, A., *Oppenheim's International Law* (9th edn, Longman, London, 1992).

Jennings, R.Y., 'Nullity and Effectiveness in International Law', in Bowett, D.W. et al. (eds), *Cambridge Essays in International Laws: Essays in Honour of Lord McNair* (Stevens & Sons, London, 1965).

——'What is International Law and How Do We Tell it When We See it?' (1981) 37 *Annuaire Suisse de Droit international* 59.

Jessup, P., *Transnational Law* (Yale University Press, Connecticut, 1956).

Johnston, D., 'Theory, Consent and the Law of Treaties' (1992) 12 *Australian Yearbook of International Law* 109.

Johnston, D.M., 'Functionalism in the Theory of International Law' (1988) 26 *Canadian Yearbook of International Law* 3.

Jouannet, E., *Emer de Vattel et l'émergence doctrinale du droit international classique* (Pedone, Paris, 1998).

——'French and American Perspectives on International Law: Legal Cultures and International Law' (2006) 58 *Maine Law Review* 291.

——'Présentation', in O. Corten, *Le discours du droit international: pour un positivisme critique* (Pedone, Paris, 2009).

——'Présentation critique', in M. Koskenniemi and E. Jouannet, *La politique du droit international* (Pedone, Paris, 2007).

——'Regards sur un siècle de doctrine française du droit international' (2000) 46 *Annuaire Français de Droit International* 1.

Kammerhofer, J., 'Introduction', in *Permanent Court of International Justice, Advisory Committee of Jurists, Procès-verbaux of the Proceedings of the Committee, June 16th–July 24th 1920, with Annexes* (Lawbook Exchange Ltd, Clark, NJ, 2006).

——'Kelsen—Which Kelsen?' (2009) 22 *Leiden Journal of International Law* 225.

——'Law-Making by Scholarship? The Dark Side of 21st Century International Legal "Methodology"', in J. Crawford et al. (eds), *Select Proceedings of the European Society of International Law vol 3* (Hart Publishing, Oxford, 2010) available at <http://papers.ssrn.com/sol3/papers.cfm?abstract_id=1631510>.

——'The Benefits of the Pure Theory of Law for International Lawyers, or: What Use is Kelsenian Theory?' (2007) 12 *International Legal Theory* 5.

——*Uncertainty in International Law: A Kelsenian Perspective* (Routledge, London, 2010).

——'Uncertainty in the Formal Sources of International Law: Customary International Law and Some of its Problems' (2004) 15 *European Journal of International Law* 523.

Kar, R.B., 'Hart's Response to Exclusive Legal Positivism' (2007) 95 *Georgetown Law Journal* 393.

Keene, E., 'The Age of Grotius', in D. Armstrong (ed), *Routledge Handbook of International Law* (Routledge, London, 2009).

Kelly, P.P., 'The Twilight of Customary International Law' (2000) 40 *Virginia Journal of International Law* 449.

Kelman, M., *A Guide to Critical Legal Studies* (Harvard University Press, Cambridge, 1987).

Kelsen, H., *General Theory of Law and State* (Harvard University Press, Cambridge, 1945).

——*Introduction to the Problems of Legal Theory* (Clarendon, Oxford, 1992).

——'Law, State and Justice in the Pure Theory of Law' (1948) 57 *Yale Law Journal* 377.

——'Les rapports de système entre le droit interne et le droit international public' (1926) 4 *Recueil des Cours de l'Académie de Droit International* 227.

——'Théorie du droit international coutumier' (1939) 1 *Revue Générale de Droit International Public* 253.

——'Theorie du droit international public' (1953) 84 *Recueil des Cours de l'Académie de Droit International* 1.

——'Théorie générale du droit international public: problèmes choisis' (1932) 42 *Recueil des Cours de l'Académie de Droit International* 117.

Kennan, G., *American Diplomacy 1900–1950* (University of Chicago Press, Chicago, 1951).

Kennedy, D., 'A New Stream of International Legal Scholarship' (1988) 7 *Wisconsin International Law Journal* 1.

——'A New World Order: Yesterday, Today and Tomorrow' (1994) 4 *Transnational Law and Comparative Problems* 329.

——'A Rotation in Contemporary Legal Scholarship' (2011) 12 *German Law Journal* 338.

——'Critical Theory, Structuralism and Contemporary Legal Scholarship' (1986) 21 *New England Law Review* 209.

——'International Law and Nineteenth Century: History of an Illusion' (1996) 65 *Nordic Journal International Law* 385.

——'The Disciplines of International Law and Policy' (1999) 12 *Leiden Journal of International Law* 9.

——'The International Style in Postwar Law and Policy' (1994) 1 *Utah Law Review* 7.

——'The Sources of International Law' (1987) 2 *American University Journal of International Law and Policy* 1.

——'Theses about International Law Discourse' (1980) 23 *German Yearbook of International Law* 353.

——'When Renewal Repeats: Thinking Against the Box' (2000) 32 *New York University Journal of International Law and Politics* 335.

Kennedy, D., 'A Semiotics of Legal Argument' (1991) 42 *Syracuse Law Review* 75.

—— *The Rise and Fall of Classical Legal Thoughts* (Beard Books, Washington DC, 2006).

Keohane, R., 'International Relations and International Law: Two Optics' (1997) 38 *Harvard International Law Journal* 487.

Khosla, M., 'The TWAIL Discourse: The Emergence of a New Phase' (2007) 9 *International Community Law Review* 291.

Kingsbury, B., 'A Grotian Tradition of Theory and Practice? Grotius, Law and Moral Skepticism in the Thought of Hedley Bull' (1997) 17 *Quinnipiac Law Review* 3.

——'Legal Positivism as Normative Politics: International Society, Balance of Power and Lassa Oppenheim's Positive International Law' (2002) 13 *European Journal of International Law* 401.

——'The Concept of "Law" in Global Administrative Law' (2009) 20 *European Journal of International Law* 23.

——'The International Legal Order', in P. Cane and M. Tushnet (eds), *The Oxford Handbook of Legal Studies* (Oxford University Press, Oxford, 2003).

——'The International Legal Order', NYU Law School Public Law & Legal Theory Research Paper No. 01–04 (2003); Institute for International Law and Justice (IILJ) History and Theory of International Law Series, Working Paper No. 2003/1.

——and Casini, L., 'Global Administrative Law Dimensions of International Organizations Law' (2009) 6 *International Organizations Law Review* 319–358, available at <http://papers.ssrn.com/sol3/papers.cfm?abstract_id=1539564>.

——and Donaldson, M., 'From Bilateralism to Publicness in International Law', *From Bilateralism to Community Interest: Essays in Honour of Judge Bruno Simma* (Oxford University Press, Oxford, 2011) (forthcoming).

Kingsbury, B., and Straumann, B., (eds), *The Roman Foundations of the Law of Nations* (Oxford, Oxford University Press, 2011).

——Krisch, N., and Steward, R., 'The Emergence of Global Administrative Law' (2005) 68 *Law and Contemporary Problems* 15.

Kinsch, P., 'On the Uncertainties surrounding the Standard of Proof in Proceedings before International Courts and Tribunals', in G. Venturini and S. Bariatti (eds), *Individual rights and international justice—Liber Fausto Pocar* (Giuffrè, Milan, 2009).

Kirgis, F.L., 'Custom on a Sliding Scale' (1987) 81 *American Journal of International Law* 146.

Kiss, A.C., 'Les traités-cadres: une technique juridique caractéristique du droit international de l'environnement' (1993) 39 *Annuaire français de droit international* 792.

Klabbers, J., 'Constitutionalism and the Making of International Law: Fuller's Procedural Natural Law' (2008) 5 *Foundations: Journal of Extreme Legal Positivism* 84.

——'Constitutionalism Lite' (2004) 1 *International Organizations Law Review* 31.

——'Institutional Ambivalence by Design: Soft Organizations in International Law' (2001) 70 *Nordic Journal of International Law* 403.

——'Law-making and Constitutionalism', in J. Klabbers, A. Peters, and G. Ulfstein (eds), *The Constitutionalization of International Law* (Oxford University Press, Oxford, 2009) 81.

——'Not Re-Visiting the Concept of Treaty', in A. Orakhelashvili and S. Williams (eds), *40 Years of the Vienna Convention on the Law of Treaties* (BIICL, London, 2010).

——'Qatar v. Bahrain: the Concept of "Treaty" in international law' (1995) 33 *Archiv des Völkerrechts* 361

——'Setting the Scene', in J. Klabbers, A. Peters, and G. Ulfstein (eds), *The Constitutionalization of International Law* (Oxford University Press, Oxford, 2009).

——*The Commodification of International Law: Select Proceedings of the European Society of International Law, vol 1* (Hart Publishing, Oxford, 2008) 341–58.

——*The Concept of Treaty in International Law* (Kluwer Law International, The Hague, 1996).

——'The Paradox of International Institutional Law' (2008) 5 *International Organizations Law Review* 1.

——'The Redundancy of Soft Law' (1996) 65 *Nordic Journal of International Law* 167.

——'The Undesirability of Soft Law' (1998) 67 *Nordic Journal of International Law* 381.

Klein, P., and Corten, O., (eds), *Les conventions de Vienne sur le droit des traités: commentaire article par article* (Bruylant, Brussels, 2006).

Knop, K., 'Here and There: International Law in Domestic Courts' (2000) 32 *New York University Journal of International Law and Politics* 501.

Koch, C., 'Judicial Dialogue for Legal Multiculturalism' (2004) 25 *Michigan Journal of International Law* 879.

Koh, H.H., 'The 1998 Frankel Lecture: Bringing International Law Home' (1998) 35 *Houston Law Review* 623.

——'Why Do Nations Obey International Law?' (1997) 106 *Yale Law Journal* 2599.

Kohen, M., 'Introduction', in M.G. Kohen (ed), *Secession: International Law Perspectives* (Cambridge University Press, Cambridge, 2006).

Kolb, R., 'Du domaine réservé: Réflexion sur la théorie de la compétence nationale' (2006) 110 *Revue Générale de Droit International Public* 597.

——'Principles as Sources of International Law (with Special Reference to Good Faith)' (2006) 53 *Netherlands International Law Review* 1.

——*Réflexions de philosophie du droit international. Problèmes fondamentaux du droit international public: Théorie et Philosophie du droit international Law* (Brussels, Bruylant, 2003).

——'Selected Problems in the Theory of Customary International Law' (2003) 50 *Netherlands International Law Review* 119.
—— *Théorie du ius cogens international: essai de relecture du concept* (Presses Universitaires de France, Paris, 2001).
Korhonen, O., 'New International Law: Silence, Defense or Deliverance?' (1996) 7 *European Journal of International Law* 1.
Koskenniemi, M., 'Carl Schmitt, Hans Morgenthau and the Image of Law in International Relations', in M. Byers (ed), *The Role of Law in International Politics: Essays in International Relations and International Law* (Oxford University Press, Oxford, 2000).
——'Constitutionalism as Mindset: Reflection on Kantian Themes about International Law and Globalization' (2007) 8 *Theoretical Inquiries in Law* 22.
——'Formalism, Fragmentation, Freedom' (2007) 4 *No Foundations: Journal of Extreme Legal Positivism* 1.
——*From Apology to Utopia: The Structure of International Legal Argument* (Cambridge University Press, Cambridge, 2005).
——'International Law in a Post-Realist Era' (1995) 16 *Australian Yearbook of International Law* 1.
——'International Legal Theory and Doctrine', *Max Planck Encyclopedia of Public International Law*, available at <http://www.mpepil.com>.
——'Into Positivism: Georg Friedrich von Martens (1756–1821)' (2008) 15 *Constellations* 189–207.
——'Lauterpacht: The Victorian Tradition in International Law' (1997) 8 *European Journal of International Law* 215.
——'Letter to the Editors of the Symposium' (1999) 93 *American Journal of International Law* 351.
——'Repetition as Reform' (1998) 9 *European Journal of International Law* 405.
——'The Fate of Public International Law: Between Technique and Politics' (2007) 70 *Modern Law Review* 1.
—— *The Gentle Civilizer of Nations: The Rise and Fall of International Law* 1870–1960 (Cambridge University Press, Cambridge, 2001).
——'The Legacy of the Nineteenth Century', in D. Armstrong et al. (eds), *Routledge Handbook of International Law* (Routledge, London, 2009).
——'The Normative Force of Habit: International Custom and Social Theory' (1990) 1 *Finnish Yearbook of International Law* 77.
——'The Politics of International Law' (1990) 1 *European Journal of International Law* 4.
——'The Politics of International Law: 20 Years Later' (2009) 20 *European Journal of International Law* 7.
——'The Pull of the Mainstream' (1990) 88 *Michigan Law Review* 1946.
——'What is International Law For?', in M. Evans (ed), *International Law* (2nd edn, Oxford University Press, Oxford, 2006).
Kramer, M., *In Defense of Legal Positivism: Law Without Trimmings* (Oxford University Press, Oxford, 1999).
——Grant, C., and Colburn, B., and Hatzistavrou, A., (eds), *The Legacy of H.L.A. Hart: Legal, Political and Moral Philosophy* (Oxford University Press, Oxford, 2008).
Kratochwil, F., 'Legal Theory and International Law', in D. Armstrong (ed), *Routledge Handbook of International Law* (Routledge, New York, 2009).
——*Rules Norms and Decisions: On the Conditions of Practical and Legal Reasoning in International Relations and Domestic Affairs* (Cambridge University Press, Cambridge, 1989).

Kress, K., 'Legal Indeterminacy', in D. Patterson (ed), *Philosophy of Law and Legal Theory: An Anthology* (Blackwell, Oxford, 2003).

Kripke, S.A., *Wittgenstein on Rules and Private Language* (Harvard University Press, Cambridge, 1982).

Krisch, N., *Beyond Constitutionalism—The Pluralist Structure of Postnational Law* (Oxford University Press, Oxford, 2010).

Kritsiotis, D., 'The Power of International Law as a Language' (1998) 34 *California Western Law Review* 397.

Krygier, M., 'The Concept of Law and Social Theory' (1982) 2 *Oxford Journal of Legal Studies* 2.

Kumm, M., 'The Legitimacy of International Law: A Constitutionalist Framework of Analysis' (2004) 15 *European Journal of International Law* 907.

Kuo, M-S., 'The Concept of "Law" in Global Administrative Law: A Reply to Benedict Kingsbury' (2009) 20 *European Journal of International Law* 997.

Lacey, N., *A Life of H.L.A. Hart: The Nightmare and the Noble Dream* (Oxford University Press, Oxford, 2004).

——'Philosophy, Political Morality, and History: Explaining the Enduring Resonance of the Hart-Fuller Debate' (2008) 83 *New York University Law Review* 1059.

Lachs, M., 'Some Reflections on Substance and Form of International Law', in W. Friedmann, L. Henkin, and O. Lissitzyn (eds), *Transnational Law in a Changing Society, Essays in Honor of P. Jessup* (Columbia University Press, New York, 1972).

——'Some Reflections on the Contribution of the International Court of Justice to the Development of International Law' (1983) 10 *Syracuse Journal of International Law and Commerce* 239.

Ladreit de Lacharrière, G., 'Aspects du relativisme du droit international', in A. Bos and H. Siblesz (eds), *Realism in Law-Making: Essays on International Law in Honour of Willem Riphagen* (Martinus Nijhoff, Dordrecht, 1986).

Lagrange, E., 'Retour sur un classique: A. Verdross, Die Verfassung der Völkerrechtsgemeinschaft' (2008) 4 *Revue Générale de Droit International Public* 984.

Langille, B., 'Political World', in D. Patterson, *Wittgenstein and Legal Theory* (Westview Press, Boulder, Co., 1992).

——'Revolution Without Foundations' (1988) 33 *McGill Law Journal* 451.

Lasswell, H., and McDougal M.S., *Jurisprudence for a Free Society: Studies in Law, Science, and Policy* (New Haven Studies in International Law, Martinus Nijhoff Publishers, Leiden, 1992).

———— 'Legal Education and Public Policy: Professional Training in the Public Interest' (1943) 52 *Yale Law Journal* 203.

Lauterpacht, E., '"Partial" Judgments and the Inherent Jurisdiction of the International Court of Justice', in V. Lowe and M. Fitzmaurice (eds), *Fifty Years of the International Court of Justice: Essays in Honour of Sir Robert Jennings* (Cambridge University Press, Cambridge, 1996).

Lauterpacht, H., *Recognition in International Law* (Cambridge University Press, Cambridge, 1947).

——'Restrictive Interpretation and the Principle of Effectiveness in the Interpretation of Treaties' (1949) 26 *British Yearbook of International Law* 48.

—— *The Development of International Law by the International Court* (2nd edn, Praeger, New York, 1958).

—— *The Function of Law in the International Community* (Clarendon Press, Oxford, 1933).

——'The Legal Effects of International Organisations', in D.W. Bowett (ed), *Essays in honour of Lord McNair* (Stevens & Sons, London, 1965).

Lawrence, T.J., *The Principles of International Law* (7th edn, MacMillan, London, 1923).

Le Fur, L., 'La théorie du droit naturel depuis le XVIIème siècle et la doctrine moderne' (1927) 18 *Recueil des Cours de l'Académie de Droit International* 259.

——'Philosophie du droit international' (1921) 29 *Revue Générale de Droit International Public* 565.

Leben, C (ed), *Hans Kelsen: Ecrits français de droit international* (Presses Universitaires de France, Paris, 2001).

——and Kolb, R., (eds), *Controverses sur la Théorie Pure du Droit* (Panthéon-Assas, Paris, 2005).

Lefkowitz, D., 'The Sources of International Law: Some Philosophical Reflections', in S. Besson and J. Tasioulas (eds), *The Philosophy of International Law* (Oxford University Press, Oxford, 2010).

Leiter, B., 'Legal Realism', in D. Patterson (eds), *A Companion to Philosophy of Law and Legal Theory* (Blackwell, Oxford, 1999).

Lepard, B.D., *Customary International Law, A New Theory with Practical Applications* (Cambridge University Press, Cambridge, 2010).

Lewellyn, K., 'A Realistic Jurisprudence: the Next Step', in D. Patterson (ed), *Philosophy of Law and Legal Theory: An Anthropology* (Blackwell, Oxford, 2003).

Lieberman, D., 'From Bentham to Benthamism' (1985) 28 *The Historical Journal* 199.

Lillich, R.B., 'The Growing Importance of Customary International Human Rights Law' (1996) 25 *Georgia Journal International and Comparative Law* 1.

Lindahl, H., 'A-Legality: Postnationalism and the Question of Legal Boundaries' (2010) 73 *Modern Law Review* 30–56.

Lipson, C., 'Why are some international agreements informal' (1991) 45 *International Organization* 495.

Lixinski, L., 'Treaty Interpretation by the Inter-American Court of Human Rights: Expansionism at the Service of the Unity of International Law' (2010) 21 *European Journal of International Law* 585–604.

Lorimer J., *Principes de Droit International* (translated by E. Nys) (C. Muquardt, Brussels, 1884).

Lowe, V., *International Law* (Oxford University Press, Oxford, 2007).

Lukes, S., *Emile Durkheim: His Life and Work, a Historical and Critical Study* (Stanford University Press, Palo Alto, Ca., 1985).

Macaulay, S., 'The New Versus the Old Legal Realism: Things Ain't What They Used to Be' (2005) 2 *Wisconsin Law Review* 365.

MacCormick, N., *Institutions of Law: An Essay in Legal Theory* (Oxford University Press, Oxford, 2008).

——'The Concept of Law and the Concept of Law', in R.P. George (ed), *The Autonomy of Law: Essays of Legal Positivism* (Oxford University Press, Oxford, 1996).

Malcom, N., *Nothing is Hidden* (Blackwell, Oxford, 1986).

Mälksoo, L., 'The Science of International Law and the Concept of Politics' (2005) 76 *British Yearbook of International Law* 245.

Marks, S., *The Riddle of All Constitutions: International Law, Democracy and the Critique of Ideology* (Oxford University Press, Oxford, 2000).

Marmor, A., 'Legal Conventionalism', in J. Coleman (ed), *Hart's Postscript: Essays on the Postscript to The Concept of Law* (Oxford University Press, Oxford, 2001).

Martineau, A.-C., 'The Rhetoric of Fragmentation: Fear and Faith in International Law' (2009) 22 *Leiden Journal of International Law* 1.

May, L., *Crimes against Humanity: A Normative Account* (Oxford University Press, Oxford, 2005).

——'Habeas Corpus and the Normative Jurisprudence of International Law' (2010) 23 *Leiden Journal of International Law* 291.

May, T., 'On Raz and the Obligations to Obey Law' (1997) 16 *Law and Philosophy* 19.

McCorquodale, R., 'An Inclusive International Legal System' (2004) 17 *Leiden Journal of International Law* 477.

McDougal, M.S., 'A Footnote' (1963) 57 *American Journal of International Law* 393.

——'International Law and the Future' (1979) 50 *Mississippi Law Journal* 259.

——'International Law, Power and Policy' (1952) 83 *Recueil des Cours de l'Académie de Droit International* 133.

——'International Law, Power, and Policy: A Contemporary Conception' (1953) 82 *Recueil des Cours de l'Académie de Droit International* 133.

——'Law as a Process of Decision: A Policy-oriented Approach to Legal Study' (1956) 1 *Natural Law Forum* 53.

——'Some Basic Theoretical Concepts about International Law: A Policy-Oriented Framework of Inquiry' (1960) 4 *Journal of Conflict Resolution* 337.

——'The International Law Commission's Draft Articles upon Interpretation: Textuality Redivivus' (1967) 61 *American Journal of International Law* 992.

——and Reisman, W.M., *International Law in Contemporary Perspective* (Foundation Press, New Haven, 1981).

——Lasswell, H., and Reisman, W.M., 'Theories about International Law: Prologue to a Configurative Jurisprudence' (1968) 8 *Virginia Journal of International Law* 188.

McLachlan, C., 'The Principle of Systemic Integration and Article 31(3)(c) of the Vienna Convention' (2005) 54 *International and Comparative Law Quarterly* 279.

McNair, A.D., *The Law of Treaties* (Clarendon Press, Oxford, 1961).

Megret, F., 'International Law as Law', in J. Crawford and M. Koskenniemi (eds), *Cambridge Companion to International Law* (Cambridge University Press, Cambridge, 2011) (forthcoming), available at <http://papers.ssrn.com/sol3/papers.cfm?abstract_id=1672824>.

Meijers, H., 'How is International Law Made?—The Stage of Growth of International Law and the Use of Its Customary Rules' (1979) 9 *Netherlands Yearbook of International Law* 3.

Mendelson, M.H., 'The Formation of Customary International Law' (1998) 272 *Recueil des Cours de l'Académie de Droit International* 159.

Meron, T., *Human Rights and Humanitarian Norms as Customary International Law* (Oxford University Press, Oxford, 1989).

Mickelson, K., 'Rhetoric and Rage: Third World Voices in International Legal Discourse' (1998) 16 *Wisconsin International Law Journal* 353.

——'Taking Stock of TWAIL Histories' (2008) 10 *International Community Law Review* 355.

Mill, J.S., *Auguste Comte and Positivism* (Trübner, London, 1865) (first published in the Westminster Review in 1865).

Morelli, G., 'Cours général de droit international public' (1956) 89 *Recueil des Cours de l'Académie de Droit International* 437.

Morgenthau, H., *Politics Among Nations* (2nd edn, Alfred A. Knopf, New York, 1954).

——*Politics Among Nations* (4th edn, Alfred A. Knopf, New York, 1967).

——'Positivism, Functionalism and International Law' (1940) 34 *American Journal of International Law* 264.

——*Scientific Man v. Power Politics* (Latimer, London, 1947).

Mosler, H., *The International Society as a Legal Community* (Sijthoff & Noordhoff, Alphen aan den Rijn, 1980).
Münch, F., 'A propos du droit spontané', in *Studi in onore di Giuseppe Sperduti* (Giuffrè, Milan, 1984).
Murphy, J.B., *Philosophy of Positive Law: Foundations of Jurisprudence* (Yale University Press, Yale, 2005).
Murphy, L., 'Better to See Law This Way' (2008) 83 *New York University Law Review* 1088.
——'Concepts of Law' (2005) 30 *Australian Journal of Legal Philosophy* 1.
——'The Political Question of the Comcept of Law', in J. Coleman (ed), *Hart's Postscript: Essays on the Postscript to 'The Concept of Law'* (Oxford University Press, Oxford, 2001).
Mutua, M., 'What is TWAIL?' (2000) 94 *American Society of International Law Proceedings* 31.
Naffine, N., 'The Common Discourse of Hart and Fuller', in P. Cane (ed), *The Hart-Fuller Debate in the Twenty-First Century* (Hart Publishing, Oxford, 2010) 217–25.
Nagel, T., 'Hobbes's Concept of Obligation' (1959) 68 *The Philosophical Review* 68.
Niebuhr, R., *Moral Man and Immoral Society: A Study in Ethics and Politics* (Charles Scribner's Sons, New York, 1932).
Nietzsche, F., and Hollingdale, R.J. (translator), *Daybreak. Thoughts on the Prejudices of Morality* (Cambridge University Press, Cambridge, 1982).
Nijman, J., *The Concept of International Legal Personality: An Enquiry Into the History and Theory of International Law* (TMC Asser Press, The Hague, 2004).
——and Nollkaemper, A., 'Beyond the Divide', in J. Nijman and A. Nollkaemper (eds), *New Perspectives on the Divide between National and International Law* (Oxford University Press, Oxford, 2007) 341–60.
Nollkaemper, A., *National Courts and the International Rule of Law* (Oxford University Press, Oxford, 2011).
——'The Internationalized Rule of Law' (2009) 1 *Hague Journal on the Rule of Law* 74.
Nourse, V., and Shaffer, G., 'Varieties of New Legal Realism: Can A New World Order Prompt A New Legal Theory' (2009) 95 *Cornell Law Review* 61.
Nussbaum, A., *A Concise History of the Law of Nations* (Revised edn, The MacMillan Company, New York, 1954).
Nys, E., 'The Codification of International Law' (1911) 5 *American Journal of International Law* 871.
O'Connell, D.P., *International Law*, vol 1 (2nd edn, Stevens & Sons, London, 1970).
O'Connell, M.E., 'Legal Process School', *Max Planck Encyclopedia of Public International Law*, available at <http://www.mpepil.com>.
——'New International Legal Process' (1999) 93 *American Journal of International Law* 334.
Oda, S., 'Dispute Settlement Prospects in the Law of the Sea' (1995) 44 *International and Comparative Law Quarterly* 863.
Oeter, S., 'The German Influence on Public International Law', in Société française pour le droit international, *Droit International et diversité juridique, Journée franco-allemande* (Pedone, Paris, 2008).
Okafor, O.C., 'Newness, Imperialism, and International Legal Reform in Our Time: A TWAIL Perspective' (2005) 43 *Osgoode Hall Law Journal* 17.
Onuf, N., 'Civitas Maxima: Wolff, Vattel and the Fate of Republicanism' (1994) 88 *American Journal of International Law* 280.
——'Do Rules Say What They Do? From Ordinary Language to International Law' (1985) 26 *Harvard Journal of International Law* 385.

Onuf, N., 'Global Law-Making and Legal Thought', in N. Onuf (ed), *Law-Making in the Global Community* (Carolina Academic Press, Durham, 1982).

——'The Constitution of International Society' (1994) 5 *European Journal of International Law* 1.

——*World of Our Making: Rules and Rules in Social Theory and International Relations* (University of South Carolina Press, South Carolina, 1989).

Oppenheim, L., *International Law*, vol. 1 (8th edn, Longmans, London, 1955).

——*International Law* (3rd edn, Longmans, London, 1920 & 1921).

——*International Law* (5th edn, Longmans, London, 1935).

——*International Law: A Treatise* (1st edn, Longmans, Green & Co, New York, 1905).

——'The Science of International Law: Its Task and Method' (1908) 2 *American Journal of International Law* 313.

Orakhelashvili, A., 'Natural Law and Justice', *Max Planck Encyclopedia of Public International Law*, available at <http://www.mpepil.com>.

——*The Interpretation of Acts and Rules in Public International Law* (Oxford University Press, Oxford, 2008).

Orford, A., 'Embodying Internationalism: the Making of International Lawyers' (1998) 19 *Australian Yearbook of International Law* 1.

——'The Destiny of International Law' (2004) 17 *Leiden Journal of International Law* 442.

——'The Gift of Formalism' (2004) 15 *European Journal of International Law* 179.

Patterson, D., 'Interpretation of Law' (2005) 42 *San Diego Law Review* 685.

——'Law's Pragmatism: Law as Practice and Narrative', in D.M. Patterson, *Wittgenstein and Legal Theory* (Westview Press, Boulder, Co., 1992).

——'Normativity and Objectivity in Law' (2001) 43 *William and Mary Law Review* 325.

——(ed), *Philosophy of Law and Legal Theory: An Anthology* (Blackwell, Oxford, 2003).

——'Postmodernism', in D. Patterson (ed), *A Companion to Philosophy of Law and Legal Theory* (Blackwell Publishers Ltd, Oxford, 1999).

——'Wittgenstein and Constitutional Theory' (1993–1994) 72 *Texas Law Review* 1837.

——'Wittgenstein on Understanding and Interpretation' (2006) 29 *Philosophical Investigations* 129.

Paulson, S., 'The Neo-Kantian Dimension of Kelsen's Pure Theory of Law' (1992) 12 *Oxford Journal of Legal Studies* 311.

——'Toward Periodization of the Pure Theory of Law', in L. Gianformaggio (ed), *Hans Kelsen's Legal Theory: A Diachronic Point of View* (Giappichelli, Turin, 1990).

Paulus, A.L., 'International Law After Postmodernism' (2001) 14 *Leiden Journal of International Law* 737.

Payandeh, M., 'The Concept of International Law in the Jurisprudence of H.L.A. Hart' (2010) 21 *European Journal of International Law* 967.

Pellet, A., 'Article 38', in A. Zimmermann, C. Tomuschat, and K. Oellers-Frahm (eds), *The Statute of the International Court of Justice* (Oxford University Press, Oxford, 2002).

——'Complementarity of International Treaty Law, Customary Law and Non-Contractual Law-Making', in R. Wolfrum and V. Röben (eds), *Developments of International Law in Treaty Making* (Springer, Berlin, 2005).

——'Cours Général: Le droit international entre souveraineté et communauté internationale—La formation du droit international' (2007) 2 *Anuário Brasileiro de Direito Internacional* 14.

——'Le "bon droit" et l'ivraie—plaidoyer pour l'ivraie', in *Mélanges offerts à Charles Chaumont, Le droit des peuples à disposer d'eux-mêmes. Méthodes d'analyse du droit international* (Pedone, Paris, 1984).

——'Lotus que de sottises on profère en ton nom!: remarques sur le concept de souveraineté dans la jurisprudence de la Cour mondiale', *Mélanges en l'honneur de Jean-Pierre Puissochet: l'État souverain dans le monde d'aujourd'hui* (Paris, Pedone, 2008).

——'The Normative Dilemma: Will and Consent in International Law-Making' (1988–1989) 12 *Australian Yearbook of International Law* 22.

Perreau-Saussine, A., 'Immanuel Kant on International Law', in S. Besson and J. Tasioulas (eds), *The Philosophy of International Law* (Oxford University Press, Oxford, 2010).

Peters, A., 'Compensatory Constitutionalism: The Function of Potential of Fundamental International Norms and Structure' (2006) 19 *Leiden Journal of International Law* 579.

——'Global Constitutionalism Revisited' (2005) 11 *International Legal Theory* 39.

——Koechlin, L., Förster, T., and Fenner Zinkernagel, G., 'Non-State Actors as Standard Setters: Framing the Issue in an Interdisciplinary Fashion', in A. Peters, L. Koechlin, T. Förster, and G. Fenner Zinkernagel (eds), *Non-State Actors as Standard Setters* (Cambridge University Press, Cambridge, 2009).

Petersen, N., 'How Rational is International Law' (2010) 20 *European Journal of International Law* 1247.

——'The Role of Consent and Uncertainty in the Formation of Customary International Law', *Working paper of the Max Planck Institute for Research on Collective Goods of Bonn* 2011/4 (2011) available at <http://papers.ssrn.com/sol3/papers.cfm?abstract_id=1761142>.

Petersmann, E.-U., 'Constitutionalism and International Adjudication: How to Constitutionalize the U.N. Dispute Settlement System' (1999) 31 *New York University Journal of International Law and Politics* 753.

Phillimore, R., *Commentaries upon International Law*, 4 vols (AG Benning, London, 1854–1861).

Pierik, R., and Werner, W., (eds), *Cosmopolitanism in Context: Perspectives from International Law and Political Theory* (Cambridge University Press, Cambridge, 2010).

Pildes, R.H., 'Conflicts Between American and European Views: The Dark Side of Legalism' (2003–2004) 44 *Virginia Journal of International Law* 145.

Pino, G., 'The Place of Legal Positivism in Contemporary Constitutional States' (1999) 18 *Law and Philosophy* 513.

Posner, E., *The Perils of Global Legalism* (University of Chicago Press, Chicago, 2009).

Postema, G.J., 'Coordination and Convention at the Foundations of Law' (1982) 11 *Journal of Legal Studies* 165.

——'Law's Autonomy and Public Practical Reason', in R.P. George (ed), *The Autonomy of Law: Essays of Legal Positivism* (Oxford University Press, Oxford, 1996).

——'Rethinking the Efficacy of Law', in M. Kramer, C. Grant, B. Colburn, and A. Hatzistavrou (eds), *The Legacy of H.L.A. Hart: Legal, Political and Moral Philosophy* (Oxford University Press, Oxford, 2008).

Pound, R., 'Common law and Legislation' (1908) 21 *Harvard Law Review* 383.

——'Do We Need a Philosophy of Law' (1905) 5 *College Law Review* 339.

——'Mechanical Jurisprudence' (1908) 8 *Columbia Law Review* 605.

——'The Theory of Judicial Decisions' (1923) 36 *Harvard Law Review* 802.

Pretroski, K., 'Is Post-Positivism Possible' (2011) 12 *German Law Journal* 663.

Prost, M., 'All Shouting the Same Slogans: International Law's Unities and the Politics of Fragmentation' (2006) 17 *Finnish Yearbook of International Law* 131.

——*The Concept of Unity in Public International Law* (Hart Publishing, Oxford, 2011) (forthcoming).

——*Unitas multiplex—Les unités du droit international et la politique de la fragmentation* (McGill University, Montreal, 2008) available at <http://digitool.library.mcgill.ca/>.

Prott, L.V., *The Latent Power of Culture and the International Judge* (Abingdon, Professional Books, 1979).

Pufendorf, S., Oldfather C.H., and Oldfather W.A., (translators), *On the Law of Nature and of Nations* (Clarendon Press, Oxford, 1934).

Purvis, N., 'Critical Legal Studies in Public International Law' (1991) 32 *Harvard Journal of International Law* 81.

Quadri, R., *Diritto internazionale pubblico* (Liguori, Naples, 1968).

Quine, M.V., *Word and Object* (MIT, The Technology Press, Cambridge Mass., 1960).

Quinton, A., 'Hume', in R. Monk and F. Raphael (eds), *The Great Philosophers* (Phoenix Publishing, London, 2001).

Raimondo, F., 'General Principles of Law, Judicial Creativity and the Development of International Criminal Law', in S. Darcy and J. Powderly (eds), *Judicial Creativity at the International Criminal Tribunals* (Oxford University Press, Oxford, 2011) 45–59.

Ratner, S., and Slaughter, A.-M., 'Appraising the Methods of International Law: A Prospectus for Readers' (1999) 93 *American Journal of International Law* 292.

Ratner, S.R., 'From Enlightened Positivism to Cosmopolitan Justice: Obstacles and Opportunities', *From Bilateralism to Community Interest: Essays in Honour of Judge Bruno Simma* (Oxford University Press, Oxford, 2011) (forthcoming).

Raustiala, K., 'Form and Substance in International Agreements' (2005) 99 *American Journal of International Law* 581.

——and Slaughter, A.-M., 'International Law, International Relations and Compliance', in W. Carlnaes, T. Risse, and B. Simmons, B. (eds), *The Handbook of International Relations* (Sage Publications, London, 2002).

Rawls, J., *A Theory of Justice* (Revised edn, Harvard University Press, USA, 1999).

Raz, J., 'Legal Validity', in J. Raz, *The Authority of Law: Essays on Law and Morality* (Clarendon Press, Oxford, 1983).

——*Practical Reason and Norms* (Oxford University Press, Oxford, 1975).

——*The Authority of Law: Essays on Law and Morality* (Clarendon Press, Oxford, 1983).

——*The Concept of a Legal System* (2nd edn, Oxford University Press, Oxford, 1980).

——'The Nature and Theory of Law', in J. Coleman (ed), *Hart's Postscript: Essays on the Postscript to 'The Concept of Law'* (Oxford University Press, Oxford, 2001).

——'The Rule of Law and its Virtue', in J. Raz (ed), *The Authority of Law—Essays on Law and Morality* (Clarendon Press, Oxford, 1979).

——'Two Views of the Nature of the Theory of Law: A Partial Comparison', in J. Coleman (ed), *Hart's Postscript: Essays on the Postscript to 'The Concept of Law'* (Oxford University Press, Oxford, 2001).

Reisman, W.M., 'Lassa Oppenheim's Nine Lives' (1994) 19 *Yale Journal of International Law* 255.

——'Soft Law and Law Jobs' (2011) 2 *Journal of International Dispute Settlement* 25.

——'The Cult of Custom in the Late 20th Century' (1987) 17 *California Western International Law Journal* 133.

——'The View from the New Haven School of International Law' (1992) 86 *American Society of International Law Proceedings* 118.

Reuter, P., *Introduction au droit des Traités* (Armand Colin, Paris, 1972).

——*Introduction au droit des Traités* (3rd edn, Presses Universitaires de France, Paris, 1995).

——'Principes de droit international public' (1961) 103 *Recueil des Cours de l'Académie de Droit International* 425.

——'Traités et transactions. Réflexions sur l'identification de certains engagements conventionnels', in *Essays in Honor of Roberto Ago* (Giuffrè, Milan, 1987).

Riddell, A., and Plant, B., *Evidence before the International Court of Justice* (British Institute of International and Comparative Law, London, 1999).

Rigaux, F., 'Hans Kelsen on International Law' (1998) 9 *European Journal of International Law* 326.

——'Non-State Actors from the Perspective of the Institut de Droit international', in J. d'Aspremont (ed.), *Participants in the International Legal System—Multiple Perspectives on Non-State Actors in International Law* (Routledge, Oxford, 2011) 179.

Roberts, A.E., 'Traditional and Modern Approaches to Customary International Law: A Reconciliation' (2001) 95 *American Journal of International Law* 757.

——'Who Killed Article 38(1)(b)? A Reply to Bradley and Gulati' (2010) 21 *Duke Journal of Comparative & International Law* 173.

Rodell, F., 'Goodbye to Law Reviews' (1936) 23 *Virginia Law Review* 38.

——'Goodbye to Law Reviews—Revisited' (1962) 48 *Virginia Law Review* 279.

Rodriguez Cedeño, V., and Torres Cazorla, M.I., 'Unilateral acts of States', in *Max Planck Encyclopedia of International Law* (Oxford University Press, Oxford, 2008).

Rorty, R., *Philosophy and the Mirror of Nature* (25th Anniversary edn, Princeton University Press, Princeton, 2009).

Rosenne, S., 'International Court of Justice: Practice Direction on Agents, Counsel and Advocates', in Shabtai Rosenne (ed), *Essays on International Law and Practice* (Nijhoff, Leiden, 2007) 97.

Ross, A., *Introduction à l'empirisme juridique* (Bruylant/LGDJ, Brussels, 2004).

——'Le Concept de Droit selon Hart', in A. Ross, *Introduction à l'empirisme juridique* (Bruylant/LGDJ, Brussels, 2004).

Rossel, F., 'Goodbye Law Reviews' (1936–1937) 23 *Virginia Law Review* 38.

Rottleuthner, H., 'The Contribution of the Critical Theory of the Frankfurt School to the Sociology of Law', in A. Podgorecki and C. Whelan (eds), *Sociological Approaches to Law* (Taylor & Francis, London, 1981).

Rousseau, C., *Principes généraux du droit international public* (Pedone, Paris, 1944).

Sahovic, M., 'Le rôle et les méthodes de la codification et du développement progressif du droit international', in *Le Droit international 2* (IHEI Pedone, Paris, 1982).

Salmon, J., (ed), *Dictionnaire de droit international public* (Bruylant, Brussels, 2001).

——'Les Accords non formalisés ou "solo consensu"' (1999) 45 *Annuaire Francois de Droit International* 1.

Scarpelli, U., *Qu'est-ce que le positivisme juridique* (Bruylant/LGDJ, Paris, 1996).

Scelle, G., 'Essai sur les sources formelles du droit international', in *Recueil sur les sources en l'honneur de François Gény* (Sirey, Paris, 1935).

——*Précis de droit des gens, principes et systématique*, vol I (Paris, Dalloz, 2008).

——*Précis de droit des gens, principes et systématique*, vol II (Sirey, Paris, 1934).

Schachter, O., 'International Law in Theory and Practice: General Course in Public International Law' (1982) 178 *Recueil des Cours de l'Académie de Droit International* 1.

——'Non Conventional Concerted Acts', in M. Bedjaoui (ed), *International Law: Achievements and Prospects* (Martinus Nijhoff, The Hague, 1991).

——'The Invisible College of International Lawyers' (1977) 72 *Northwestern University Law Review* 217.

——'The Twilight Existence of Non-Binding International Agreements' (1977) 71 *American Journal of International Law* 296.

——'Towards a Theory of International Obligation' (1967–1968) 8 *Virginia Journal of International Law* 300.

Scharf, M., 'International Law in Crisis: A Qualitative Empirical Contribution to the Compliance Debate' (2009) 31 *Cardozo Law Review* 45.
Schauer, F., 'Formalism' (1998) 97 *Yale Law Journal* 509.
——'Postivism as Pariah', in R.P. George (ed), *The Autonomy of Law: Essays of Legal Positivism* (Oxford University Press, Oxford, 1996).
——'Rules and the Rule-Following Argument', in D.M. Patterson, *Wittgenstein and Legal Theory* (Westview Press, Boulder, Co., 1992).
Schlag, P., '"Le Hors de Texte, C'est Moi"—The Politics of Form and the Domestication of Deconstruction' (1990) 11 *Cardozo Law Review* 1631.
Schrijver, N., 'Les valeurs génerales et le droit des Nations Unies', in R. Chemain and A. Pellet (eds), *La Charte des Nations Unies, Constitution Mondiale?* (Pedone, Paris, 2006).
——'The Future of the United Nations' (2006) 10 *Max Planck Yearbook of United Nations Law* 1.
Schwarzenberger, G., *International Law,* vol 1 (3rd edn, Stevens & Sons, London, 1957).
——'Myths and Realities in Treaty Interpretation' (1968) 9 *Virginia Journal of International Law* 1.
——*Power and Politics* (3rd edn, Stevens & Sons, London, 1964).
——*The Inductive Approach to International Law* (Stevens & Sons, London, 1965).
Schwebel, S., 'The Effects of Resolutions of the UN General Assembly on Customary International Law' (1979) 73 *American Society of International Law Proceedings* 301.
Schwöbel, C., 'The Appeal of the Project of Global Constitutionalism to Public International Lawyers', available at <http://papers.ssrn.com/sol3/papers.cfm?abstract_id=1713201>.
Scobbie, I., 'The Theorist as Judge: Hersch Lauterpacht's Concept of the International Judicial Function' (1997) 8 *European Journal of International Law* 264.
——'Towards the Elimination of International Law: Some Radical Scepticism about Sceptical Radicalism' (1990) 61 *British Yearbook of International Law* 339.
——'Wicked Heresies or Legitimate Perspectives?', in M. Evans, *International Law* (2nd edn, Oxford University Press, Oxford, 2006).
Scott, C., '"Transnational Law" as Proto-Concept: Three Conceptions' (2009) 10 *German Law Journal* 877.
Scott, S.V., 'International Law as Ideology: Theorizing the Relationship between International Law and International Politics' (1994) 5 *European Journal of International Law* 313.
Searle, J., *Expression and Meaning* (Cambridge University Press, Cambridge, 1979).
——*Speech Acts* (Cambridge University Press, Cambridge, 1969).
Sebok, A.J., 'Misunderstanding Positivism' (1995) 93 *Michigan Law Review* 2054.
Seidl-Hohenveldern, I., 'Hierarchy of Treaties', in J. Klabbers and R. Lefeber (eds), *Essays on the Law of Treaties. A Collection of Essays in Honour of Bert Vierdag* (Martinus Nijhoff, The Hague, 1998).
Sette-Camara, J., 'The ILC Discourse and Method', *Essays in honor of Roberto Ago* (Giuffrè, Milan, 1987).
Shaffer, G., 'A Call for a New Legal Realism in International Law: The Need for Method', University of Minnesota Law School, Legal Studies Research Paper Series Research Paper No. 09–02, available at <http://papers.ssrn.com/sol3/papers.cfm?abstract_id=1323912>.
——'A New Legal Realism: Method in International Economic Law Scholarship', in C.B. Picker, I. Bunn, and D. Arner (eds), *International Economic Law—The State and Future of the Discipline* (Hart Publishing, Oxford, 2008) 29–42.
——and Pollack, M., 'Hard vs. Soft Law: Alternatives, Complements and Antagonists in International Governance' (2010) 94 *Minnesota Law Review* 706.

Shany, Y., 'National Courts as International Actors: Jurisdictional Implications', in *Hebrew University International Law Research Paper* No. 22–08 (October 2008).
Shapiro, S., 'On Hart's Way Out', in J. Coleman (ed), *Hart's Postscript: Essays on the Postscript to 'The Concept of Law'* (Oxford University Press, Oxford, 2001).
Shaw, M., *International Law* (5th edn, Cambridge University Press, Cambridge, 2003).
Shelton, D., *Commitment and Compliance, The Role of Non-Binding Norms in the International Legal System* (Oxford University Press, Oxford, 2000).
——'International Law and "Relative Normativity"', in M.D. Evans (ed), *International Law* (Oxford University Press, Oxford, 2006) 159–85.
——'Soft Law', in D. Armstrong (ed), *Handbook of International Law* (Routledge, New York, 2009).
Shimko, K. L., 'Realism, Neorealism and American Liberalism' (1992) 54 *The Review of Politics* 281.
Simma, B., 'From Bilateralism to Community Interest' (1994-VI) 250 *Recueil des Cours de l'Académie de Droit International* 217.
——'The Contribution of Alfred Verdross to the Theory of International Law' (1995) 6 *European Journal of International Law* 1.
——'Universality of International Law from the Perspective of a Practitioner' (2009) 20 *European Journal of International Law* 265.
——and Alston, P., 'The Sources of Human Rights Law: Custom, Jus Cogens and General Principles' (1988–1989) 12 *Australian Yearbook of International Law* 82.
——and Paulus, A., 'The Responsibility of Individuals for Human Rights Abuses in Internal Conflicts: A Positivist View' (1999) 93 *American Journal of International Law* 302.
Simpson, G., 'The Situation on the International Legal Theory Front: The Power of Rules and the Rule of Power' (2000) 11 *European Journal of International Law* 439.
——'Two Liberalisms' (2001) 12(3) *European Journal of International Law* 537.
Simpson, G. J., 'Imagined Consent: Democratic Liberalism in International Legal Theory' (1994) 15 *Australian Yearbook of International Law* 103.
Sindico, F., 'Soft Law and the Elusive Quest for Sustainable Global Governance' (2006) 19 *Leiden Journal of International Law* 829.
Siorat, L., *Le Problème des lacunes en droit international. Contribution à l'étude des sources du droit et de la fonction judiciaire* (LGDJ, Paris, 1958).
Skouteris, T., 'Fin de NAIL: New Approaches to International Law and its Impact on Contemporary International Legal Scholarship' (1997) 10 *Leiden Journal of International Law* 415.
——*The Notion of Progress in International Law Discourse* (LEI Universiteit, Leiden, 2008), chapter 3, later published as *The Notion of Progress in International Law Discourse* (T.M.C. Asser Press, The Hague, 2010).
Skubiszewski, K., 'Resolutions of the UN General Assembly and Evidence of Custom', in *Essays in Honor of Roberto Ago* (Giuffrè, Milan, 1987).
——'Unilateral Acts of States', in M. Bedjaoui (ed), *International Law: Achievements and Prospects* (UNESCO, Paris, 1991).
Slaughter, A.-M., 'A Global Community of Courts' (2003) 44 *Harvard International Law Journal* 191.
——'A Liberal Theory of International Law' (2000) 94 *Proceedings of the American Society of International Law* 240.
——*A New World Order* (Princeton University Press, Princeton, 2004).
——'Global Government Networks, Global Information Agencies, and Disaggregated Democracy' (2003) 24 *Michigan Journal of International Law* 1041.

Slaughter, A.-M., 'International Law in a World of Liberal States' (1995) 6 *European Journal of International Law* 503.

——'The Liberal Agenda for Peace: International Relations Theory and the Future of the United Nations' (1994) 4 *Transnational Law and Contemporary Problems* 377.

Sloan, F.B., 'General Assembly Resolutions Revisited (Forty Years Later)' (1987) 58 *British Yearbook of International Law* 124.

Smith, G.B., *Nietzsche, Heidegger, and the Transition to Postmodernity* (University of Chicago Press, Chicago, 1996).

Société Française pour le Droit International, *L'Etat de droit en droit international: Colloque de Bruxelles* (Paris, Pedone, 2007).

Somek, A., 'Defective Law', University of Iowa Legal Studies Research Paper No. 10–33 (2010).

——'Kelsen Lives' (2007) 18 *European Journal of International Law* 409.

——'The Concept of "Law" in Global Administrative Law' (2009) 20 *European Journal of International Law* 984.

——'The Spirit of Legal Positivism' (2011) 12 *German Law Journal* 729.

Soper, P., 'Law's Normative Claims', in R.P. George (ed), *The Autonomy of Law: Essays of Legal Positivism* (Oxford University Press, Oxford, 1996).

Sorel, J.-M., 'Article 31', in P. Klein and O. Corten (eds), *Les Conventions de Vienne sur le Droit des Traités. Commentaire article par article* (Bruylant, Bruxelles, 2006).

Sørensen, M., 'Principes de droit international public: cours général' (1960) 101 *Recueil des Cours de l'Académie de Droit International* 1.

Spiermann, O., 'A Permanent Court of International Justice' (2003) 72 *Nordic Journal of International Law* 399.

——*International Legal Argument in the Permanent Court of International Justice, The Rise of the International Judiciary* (Cambridge University Press, Cambridge 2005).

Stavropoulos, N., 'Hart's Semantics', in J. Coleman (ed), *Hart's Postscript: Essays on the Postscript to 'The Concept of Law'* (Oxford University Press, Oxford, 2001).

Steer, C., 'Non-State Actors in International Criminal Law', in J. d'Aspremont (ed), *Participants in the International Legal System—Multiple Perspectives on Non-State Actors in International Law* (Routledge, London, 2011) 295.

Stein, T.L., 'The Approach of the Different Drummer: The Principle of the Persistent Objector in International Law' (1985) 26 *Harvard International Law Journal* 457.

Steinhardt, R.G., 'The Role of International Law as a Canon of Domestic Statutory Construction' (1990) 43 *Vanderbilt Law Review* 1103.

Stern, B., 'La Coutume au coeur du droit international, quelques réflexions', in *Mélanges Reuter* (Pedone, Paris, 1981).

Strupp, K., 'Les règles générales du droit de la paix' (1934) 47 *Recueil des Cours de l'Académie de Droit International* 259.

Sur, S., 'La Coutume internationale' (1989) 3 *Juris-Classeur de Droit International* Fascicule 13.

——*L'interprétation en droit international public* (LGDJ, Paris, 1974).

Suy, E., 'Le Préambule', in *Liber Amicorum M. Bedjaoui* (Kluwer Law International, The Hague, 1999).

——*Les actes juridiques unilatéraux en droit international public* (LGDJ, Paris, 1962).

——'Unilateral Acts of States as a Source of International Law: Some New Thoughts and Frustrations', in *Droit du pouvoir, pouvoir du droit: mélanges offerts à Jean Salmon* (Bruylant, Brussels, 2007).

Tamahana, B., *A General Jurisprudence of Law and Society* (Oxford University Press, Oxford, 2001).

——'The Contemporary Relevance of Legal Positivism', St John's University School of Law, New York, Legal Studies Research Paper Series, Paper #07–0065 (January 2007).

Tasioulas, J., 'Customary International Law and the Quest for Global Justice', in A. Perreau-Saussine and J.B. Murphy (eds), *The Nature of Customary Law* (Cambridge University Press, Cambridge, 2007).

——'In Defence of Relative Normativity: Communitarian Values and the Nicaragua Case' (1996) 16 *Oxford Journal of Legal Studies* 85.

——'Opinio Juris and the Genesis of Custom: A Solution to the 'Paradox'' (2007) 26 *Australian Yearbook of International Law* 199.

Tavernier, P., 'L'interaction des jurisprudences des tribunaux pénaux internationaux et des cours européennes et interaméricaines des droits de l'homme', in P. Tavernier (ed), *Actualité de la jurisprudence internationale: à l'heure de la mise en place de la Cour pénale internationale* (Bruylant, Bruxelles, 2004).

Temminck Tuinstra, J.P.W., *Defence Counsel in International Criminal Law* (T.M.C. Asser Press, The Hague, 2009).

Tesón, F.R., *A Philosophy of International Law* (Westview Press, Boulder Co., 1998).

——'Feminism and International Law: A Reply' (1994) 33 *Virginia Journal of International Law* 647.

——'The Kantian Theory of International Law' (1992) 92 *Columbia Law Review* 53.

Thierry, H., 'Cours général de droit international public' (1990) 222 *Recueil des Cours de l'Académie de Droit International* 385.

——'The European Tradition in International Law: Georges Scelle' (1990) 1 *European Journal of International Law* 193.

Thirlway, H., *International Customary Law and Codification* (Sijthoff, Leiden, 1972).

——'The Recommendation made by the International Court of Justice: A Sceptical View' (2009) 58 *International and Comparative Law Quarterly* 151.

——'The Sources of International Law', in M. Evans (ed), *International Law* (2nd edn, Oxford University Press, Oxford, 2006).

Thomas, C., 'International Financial Institutions and Social and Economic Rights: An Exploration', in T. Evans (ed), *Human Rights Fifty Years On: A Reappraisal* (Manchester University Press, Manchester, 1998).

Tomuschat, C., 'International Law: Ensuring the Survival of Mankind on the Eve of a New Century: General Course on Public International Law' (1999) 281 *Recueil des Cours de l'Académie de Droit International* 9.

——'Obligations Arising for States Without or Against Their Will' (1993) 241 *Recueil des Cours de l'Académie de Droit International* 195.

Toope, S.J., 'Confronting Indeterminacy: Challenges to International Legal Theory' (1990) 19 *Proceedings of the Canadian Council of International Law* 209.

Triepel, H., *Völkerrecht und Landesrecht* (Scientia Verlag, Aalen, 1899).

Trimble, P.R., 'International Law, World Order and Critical Legal Studies' (1990) 42 *Stanford Law Review* 811.

Truyol y Serra, A., 'John Austin et la philosophie du droit', in *Archives de philosophie du droit* (Dalloz, Paris, 1970).

——'Théorie du droit international public—Cours général' (1981) 173 *Recueil des Cours de l'Académie de Droit International* 13.

Tsagourias, N., 'Book Review of M. Koskenniemi, "The Gentle Civilizer of Nations: The Rise and Fall of International Law 1870–1960"', 16 *Leiden Journal of International Law* (2003) 398.

——'Introduction', in N. Tsagourias (ed), *Transnational Constitutionalism: International and European Perspectives* (Cambridge University Press, Cambridge, 2007).

——(ed), *Transnational Constitutionalism: International and European Perspectives* (Cambridge University Press, Cambridge, 2007).

Tunkin, G.I., *Droit international public: problèmes théoriques* (Pedone, Paris, 1965).

—— *The Theory of International Law* (Harvard University Press, Cambridge, 1974).

Tuori, K., *Critical Legal Positivism* (Aldershot, Ashgate, 2002).

Turley, J., 'Dualistic Values in an Age of International Legisprudence' (1993) 44 *Hastings Law Journal* 185.

Tushnet, M., 'Critical Legal Studies: A Political History' (1991) 100 *Yale Law Journal* 1515.

——'Introduction to the Symposium 'Perspectives on Critical Legal Studies" (1984) 52 *George Washington Law Review* 239.

Twining, W., *General Jurisprudence: Understanding Law from a Global Perspective* (Cambridge University Press, Cambridge, 2009).

——'Implications of "Globalisation" for Law as a Discipline', in A. Halpin and V. Roeben, *Theorising the Global Legal Order* (Hart Publishing, Oxford, 2009), 39–59.

Unger, R.M., 'The Critical Legal Studies Movement' (1983) 96 *Harvard Law Review* 561.

—— *What Should Legal Analysis Become?* (Verso, London, 1996).

van der Molen, G., 'The Present Crisis in the Law of Nations', in *Symbolae Verzijl* (Martinus Nijhoff, The Hague, 1958).

Van Hoof, G.H.J., *Rethinking the Sources of International Law* (Kluwer Law International, The Hague, 1983).

Verdier, P.-H., 'Transnational Regulatory Networks and Their Limits' (2009) 34 *Yale Journal of International Law* 113.

Verdross, A., *Die Verfassung, der Volkerrechtsgemeinschaft* (Springer, Berlin, 1926).

——and Simma, B., *Universelles Volkerrecht* (3rd edn, Duncker & Humblot, Berlin, 1984).

Verhoeven, J., 'Considérations sur ce qui est commun: Cours général de droit international public' (2008) 332 *Recueil des Cours de l'Académie de Droit International* 9.

——*La Reconnaissance internationale dans la pratique contemporaine* (Pedone, Paris, 1975).

——'Le droit, le juge et la violence. Les arrêts Nicaragua c. Etats-Unis' (1987) 91 *Revue Générale de Droit International Public* 1161.

——'Les nullités du droit des gens', in *Droit International* 1 (Pedone, Paris, 1981).

——'Non-intervention: affaires intérieures ou 'vie privée'?', in *Mélanges en hommage à Michel Virally* (Pedone, Paris, 1991).

Verzijl, J.H.W., 'L'affaire du "Lotus" devant la Cour permanente de Justice internationale' (1928) 9 *Revue de droit international et de législation comparée* 1.

——'Western European Influence on the foundations of International Law' (1955) 1 *International Relations* 137.

Vignes, D., 'La Coutume surgie de 1973 à 1982 n'aurait-elle pas écartée la codification comme source principale du droit de la mer?', in *Liber Amicorum honouring Ignaz Seidl-Hohenveldern, Law of Nations Law of International Organizations World's Economic Law* (Carl Heymanns Verlag KG, Cologne, 1988).

Villey, M., *La formation de la pensée juridique moderne* (Quadridge/PUF, Paris, 2003).

Villiger, M.E., *Customary International Law and Treaties: A Study of their Interactions and Interrelations with Special Consideration of the 1969 Vienna Convention on the Law of Treaties* (Martinus Nijhoff, Dordrecht, 1985) 334–43.

Virally, M., 'A Propos de la "Lex Ferenda"', in *Mélanges Reuter* (Pedone, Paris, 1981).
——*La pensée juridique* (LDGJ, Paris, 1960).
Vitanyi, B., 'Les positions doctrinales concernant le sens de la notion de "principes généraux reconnus par les nations civilisées' (1982) 86 *Revue Générale de Droit International Public* 46.
von Bernstorff, J., 'Sisyphus was an international lawyer. On Martti Koskenniemi's "From Apologia to Utopia" and the place of law in international politics' (2006) 7 *German Law Journal* 1015.
——'The Changing Fortunes of the Universal Declaration of Human Rights: Genesis and Symbolic Dimensions of the Turn to the Rights in International Law' (2008) 19 *European Journal of International Law* 903–924.
——and Dunlap, T., *The Public International Law Theory of Hans Kelsen—Believing in Universal Law* (Cambridge University Press, Cambridge, 2010).
von Bogdandy, A., 'Globalization and Europe: How to Square Democracy, Globalization and International Law' (2004) 15 *European Journal of International Law* 885.
——'Pluralism, direct effect, and the ultimate say: On the relationship between international and domestic constitutional law' (2008) 6 *International Journal of Constitutional Law* 1.
——Dann, P., and Goldmann, M., 'Developing the Publicness of Public International Law: Towards a Legal Framework for Global Governance Activities' (2008) 9 *German Law Journal* 1375.
von Liszt, F., and Gidel, G., *Le Droit international: exposé systématique* (Pedone, Paris, 1928).
Walden, R.M., 'Customary International Law: A Jurisprudential Analysis, 13 *Israel Law Review* (1978) 86–102.
Waldron, J., 'Are Sovereigns Entitled to the Benefit of the International Rule of Law?', NYU Public Law and Legal Theory Research Paper Series, 09–01 (2009).
——*Law and Disagreement* (Oxford University Press, Oxford, 1999).
——'Legal Pluralism and the Contrast Between Hart's Jurisprudence and Fuller's', in P. Cane (ed), *The Hart-Fuller Debate in the Twenty-First Century* (Hart Publishing, Oxford, 2010) 135–55.
——'Normative (or Ethical) Positivism', in J. Coleman (ed), *Hart's Postscript: Essays on the Postscript to the Concept of Law* (Oxford University Press, Oxford, 2001).
Waline, V. M., 'Positivisme philosophique, juridique et sociologique', in *Mélanges Carré de Malberg* (Sirey, Paris, 1933).
Walter, C., 'International Law in a Process of Constitutionalization', in P.A. Nollkaemper and J.E. Nijman, *New Perspectives on the Divide Between National and International Law* (Oxford University Press, Oxford, 2007).
Waluchow, W.J., *Inclusive Legal Positivism* (Clarendon Press, Oxford, 1994).
Ward, I., *An Introduction to Critical Legal Theory* (Routledge, New York, 1998).
Weil, P., 'Le droit international en quête de son identité: cours général de droit international public' (1992) 237 *Recueil des Cours de l'Académie de Droit International* 9.
——'Towards Relative Normativity in International Law' (1983) 77 *American Journal of International Law* 413.
——'Vers une normativité relative en droit international' (1982) 87 *Revue Générale de Droit International Public* 1.
Weiler, J.H.H., 'The Geology of International Law—Governance, Democracy and Legitimacy' (2004) 64 *Heidelberg Journal of International Law (ZaöRV)* 547.
——'The Interpretation of Treaties—A Re-examination. Preface' (2010) 21 *European Journal of International Law* 507.

Weinrib, E.J., 'Legal Formalism', in D. Patterson (ed), *A Companion to Philosophy of Law and Legal Theory* (Blackwell Publishers Ltd, Oxford, 1999).

——'Legal Formalism: On the Immanent Rationality of Law' (1988) 97 *Yale Law Journal* 949.

Wellman, V.A., 'Authority of Law', in D. Patterson (ed), *A Companion to Philosophy of Law and Legal Theory* (Blackwell Publishers Ltd, Oxford, 1999).

Werner, W., 'The never-ending closure: constitutionalism and international law', in N. Tsagourias (ed), *Transnational Constitutionalism: International and European Perspectives* (Cambridge University Press, Cambridge, 2007).

Wheaton, H., *Elements of International Law* (Fellowes, London, 1836).

White, N., 'Separate but Connected: Inter-Governmental Organizations and International Law' (2008) 5 *International Organizations Law Review* 175.

Whiteman, M., 'Jus Cogens in International Law with a Projected List' (1977) 7 *Georgia Journal of International and Comparative Law* 609.

Widdows, K., 'On the Form and Distinctive Nature of International Agreements' (1976–1977) 7 *Australian Yearbook of International Law* 114.

Williams, B., *Utilitarianism: For and Against* (Cambridge University Press, Cambridge, 1973).

Williams, M.C., 'Hobbes and International Relations: A Reconsideration' (1996) 50 *International Organization* 213.

Willing Balch, T., *The Alabama Arbitration* (Allen, Lane & Scott, Philadelphia, 1900).

Wittgenstein, L., *Tractacus Logico-Philosophicus* (Dover Publications, New York, 1999).

——and Anscombe, G.E.M. (translator), *Philosophical Investigations* (3rd edn, Blackwell Publishing, Oxford, 2001).

Wolff, C., and Drake, J.H. (translator), *Law of Nations Treated According to A Scientific Method* (Clarendon Press, Oxford, 1934).

Woolsey, T.D., *Introduction to the Study of International Law* (4th edn, Scribner Armstrong & Co, New York, 1877).

Wrange, P., 'An Open Letter to My Students' (1996) 56 *Nordic Journal of International Law* 569.

Wright, R., 'Does Positivism Matter?', in R.P. George (ed), *The Autonomy of Law: Essays of Legal Positivism* (Oxford University Press, Oxford, 1996).

Yoshida, O., 'Soft Enforcement of Treaties: The Montreal Protocol's Noncompliance Procedure and the Functions of Internal International Institutions' (1999) 95 *Colorado Journal of Environmental Law & Policy* 95.

Zamora, S., 'Is There Customary International Economic Law?' 32 (1989) *German Yearbook of International Law* 9.

Zemanek, K., 'The Legal Foundations of the International System: General Course on Public International Law' (1997) 266 *Recueil des Cours de l'Académie de Droit International* 9.

Zolo, D., 'Hans Kelsen: International Peace through International Law' (1998) 9 *European Journal of International Law* 306.

Index